LANGUAGE

ISOLATES

Language Isolates explores this fascinating group of languages that surprisingly comprise a third of the language families (linguistic lineages) of the world.

Individual chapters written by experts on these languages examine the world's major language isolates by geographic regions, with up-to-date descriptions of many, including previously unrecognized language isolates. Each language isolate represents a unique lineage and a unique window on what is possible in human language, making this an essential volume for anyone interested in understanding the diversity of languages and the very nature of human language.

Language Isolates is key reading for professionals and students in linguistics and anthropology.

Lyle Campbell is a linguist, Professor Emeritus at the University of Hawai'i Mānoa. He has held joint appointments in Anthropology, Latin American Studies, Linguistics, and Spanish.

ROUTLEDGE LANGUAGE FAMILY SERIES

Each volume in this series contains an in-depth account of the members of some of the world's most important language families. Written by experts in each language, these accessible accounts provide detailed linguistic analysis and description. The contents are carefully structured to cover the natural system of classification: phonology, morphology, syntax, lexis, semantics, dialectology, and sociolinguistics.

Every volume contains extensive bibliographies for each language, a detailed index and tables, and maps and examples from the languages to demonstrate the linguistic features being described. The consistent format allows comparative study, not only between the languages in each volume, but also across all the volumes in the series.

The Bantu Languages
*Edited by Derek Nurse &
Gérard Philippson*

The Celtic Languages,
2nd Edition
Edited by Martin J. Ball & Nicole Müller

The Dravidian Languages, 2nd Edition
Edited by Sanford B. Steever

The Germanic Languages
*Edited by Ekkehard König &
Johan van der Auwera*

The Indo-Aryan Languages
*Edited by George Cardona &
Dhanesh K. Jain*

The Indo-European Languages,
2nd Edition
Edited by Mate Kapović

The Iranian Languages
Edited by Gernot Windfuhr

The Languages of Japan and Korea
Edited by Nicolas Tranter

The Khoesan Languages
Edited by Rainer Vossen

The Mongolic Languages
Edited by Juha Janhunan

The Munda Languages
Edited by Gregory D.S. Anderson

The Oceanic Languages
*Edited by John Lynch,
Malcolm Ross & Terry Crowley*

The Romance Languages
*Edited by Martin Harris &
Nigel Vincent*

The Semitic Languages
Edited by Robert Hetzron

The Sino-Tibetan Languages,
2nd Edition
*Edited by Graham Thurgood &
Randy J. Lapolla*

The Slavonic Languages
*Edited by Bernard Comrie &
Greville G. Corbett*

The Tai-Kadai Languages
Edited by Anthony Diller

The Turkic Languages
Edited by Éva Csató & Lars Johanson

The Uralic Languages
Edited by Daniel Abondolo

Language Isolates
Edited by Lyle Campbell

Other titles in the series can be found at www.routledge.com/languages/series/SE0091

LANGUAGE

ISOLATES

Edited by Lyle Campbell

Routledge
Taylor & Francis Group

LONDON AND NEW YORK

First published 2018
by Routledge
2 Park Square, Milton Park, Abingdon, Oxon OX14 4RN

and by Routledge
711 Third Avenue, New York, NY 10017

Routledge is an imprint of the Taylor & Francis Group, an informa business

British Library Cataloguing-in-Publication Data
A catalogue record for this book is available from the British Library

Library of Congress Cataloging-in-Publication Data
Names: Campbell, Lyle, editor.
Title: Language isolates / edited by Lyle Campbell.
Description: First edition. | Abingdon, Oxon ; New York : Routledge, 2017. |
    Series: Routledge language family series | Includes bibliographical references
    and index.
Identifiers: LCCN 2017016066 (print) | LCCN 2017038495 (ebook) | ISBN
    9781315750026 (E-book) | ISBN 9781138821057 (hardcover : acid-free paper)
Subjects: LCSH: Language isolates.
Classification: LCC P371 (ebook) | LCC P371 .L34 2017 (print) | DDC 407.2—dc23
LC record available at https://lccn.loc.gov/2017016066

ISBN: 978-1-138-82105-7 (hbk)
ISBN: 978-1-315-75002-6 (ebk)

Typeset in Times New Roman
by Apex CoVantage, LLC

CONTENTS

FIGURES

MAPS

TABLES

CONTRIBUTORS

Blench, Roger
University of Cambridge

Bowern, Claire
Yale University

Campbell, Lyle
University of Hawai'i at Mānoa

Dougherty, Thomas
University of Hawai'i at Mānoa

Georg, Stefan
University of Bonn, Germany

Hammarström, Harald
Max Planck Institute for the Science of Human History

Heaton, Raina
University of Oklahoma

Lakarra, Joseba A.
University of the Basque Country (La Universidad del País Vasco/Euskal Herriko Unibertsitatea)

Michalowski, Piotr
University of Michigan

Mithun, Marianne
University of California Santa Barbara

Okura, Eve
University of Hawai'i at Mānoa

Seifart, Frank
University of Amsterdam, University of Cologne

Smith, Alexander D.
University of Hawai'i at Mānoa

INTRODUCTION

Lyle Campbell

It may strike many of us as ironic for a volume on language isolates to appear in Routledge's *Language Family* series. However, as this book makes clear, language isolates are also language families – they just happen to be language families that have only a single member language, a language with no known relatives. And, to be extra clear, it could be added that by "relatives" we mean other languages related genetically, i.e. phylogenetically via descent from a common ancestor: a language isolate is a language which has not been shown to be the descendant of any ancestral language which has other descendants (daughters) in addition to the language isolate in question. The chapters of this volume show, moreover, that language isolates have more in common with other language families than has usually been realized.

The chapters presented here survey several of the world's most famous language isolates and the language isolates of various regions of the world. There are vastly more language isolates than most people, including most linguists, are aware of – c.159. That is 39% of the world's c.407 independent language families!

The absolute number of language isolates, is, however, uncertain and in fact will never be known, for several reasons. There are many unclassified, or unclassifiable, languages, where the documentation is so poor or non-existent that it is not possible to compare the language meaningfully to others to determine whether it may be related to any other language or not (see Campbell, this volume, for discussion). Moreover, in the case of some languages with some but limited attestation, opinion among scholars has differed with respect to whether the documentation is sufficient to determine that the language in question is an isolate because it cannot be shown to be related to any other or whether the available corpus is simply too scant to make such a determination, leaving the language unclassified. This raises an interesting but mostly unaddressed research question for language isolates: how much documentation, and of what sort, is necessary in order to determine whether a language is best considered unclassified or a language isolate? That is, when is sufficient information available so that when compared, no discernible relatives can be found for that language, leaving it a language isolate?

Another reason that the total number of language isolates is uncertain has to do with the vexed question of separate languages versus dialects. A language with dialects (variants of a single language) can be a language isolate if it has no known relatives. However, if there is sufficient diversification that the variants are not mutually intelligible and hence are considered distinct languages, then it is a matter of a family of related languages rather than a language with multiple dialects – and a family of multiple languages cannot by definition be considered a language isolate. Since the boundary between relatively divergent dialects of a single language and closely related language is sometimes difficult to determine, there are instances of disagreement among specialists where some see a language isolate, a single language with dialects, but others see a family of related languages and hence no language isolate. The language-versus-dialect issue poses another important research question, how to distinguish dialects from languages in such circumstances, one much addressed but so far without results that make the determination in uncertain or borderline cases any clearer.

Another reason that we do not know the exact number of language isolates involves "uncontacted" languages. In Brazil alone there are officially at least 40 "uncontacted" isolated indigenous groups, some count nearly 70, with around 90 for South America as a whole (see, for example, https://en.wikipedia.org/wiki/Uncontacted_peoples#South_America, accessed 9–6–2016). For many of these cases, it is not known whether the people speak a variety of an already identified language, a language currently unknown but which belongs to a known language family, a language that represents an as yet unknown language family, or a language with no other relatives in the world, an isolate.

With regard to linguistic theory and language typology, language isolates are of monumental importance. As languages unrelated to other languages, each language isolate represents an independent lineage among the world's languages, a unique development. Given the goal of linguistics to comprehend the full range of what is possible and impossible in human languages, the investigation of language isolates should hold a privileged position in linguistic research. Each language isolate constitutes an independent window on what can be found in the languages of the world, on what is possible in human language, and, through the study of languages on the potentials and limitations of the human cognition. Collectively, the language isolates of the world constitute an extremely rich and important laboratory for striving to achieve this goal to discover the full scope of what is possible in the human language.

Given this importance, endangered language isolates deserve extremely high priority in decisions about which languages to document and how to deploy resources and research efforts. (See Okura, this volume.) Already 59 of the 159 language isolates of the world are extinct (37%). Put in a larger perspective, all the languages belonging to c.96 of the world's c.407 independent language families (including language isolates) are extinct – 24% of the linguistic diversity of the world, calculated in terms of language families, is gone forever. However, nearly two-thirds of all extinct languages families are language isolates, 59 of those 96 (61%). Most of the remaining language isolates are endangered, many severely so. Truly, the loss of language isolates is taking an alarming toll on the linguistic diversity of the world. The loss of a language isolate represents the loss of an entire linguistic lineage. The loss of any language that has relatives constitutes a monumental loss of scientific information and cultural knowledge, comparable in gravity to the loss of a species, say, the Bengal tiger or the right whale. However, the extinction of a language isolate or of other whole families of languages is a tragedy comparable in magnitude to the loss of whole branches of the animal kingdom, similar to the loss of all felines or all cetaceans – a catastrophic loss of information and knowledge unparalleled and unimagined in biology. Yet this is what confronts us.

Because languages reflect the world's knowledge and wisdom, the loss of a language isolate means loss to our understanding of the range of potential ways of experiencing and understanding the world. Great reservoirs of historical information are recovered from the study of languages. Historical linguistic investigation gives us history of human groups, information about their contacts and migrations, their homeland, and past culture. All of this information and these insights into human experiences are irretrievably lost when a language is lost without adequate documentation.

Another research question is how can we find out about history of language isolates? Campbell (this volume) discusses a number of techniques for getting at the history of language isolates, showing that claims that these languages have no history are misguided. Not only can research on language isolates help us to comprehend what is possible in human languages and to understand the history of individual language isolates, it contributes to understanding of the history of humankind.

An important part of the history of many language isolates involves language contact. The identification of loanwords and of structural influences from other languages contributes to understanding the history of the speakers of these languages, but it also helps us eliminate similarities due to borrowing from considerations of possible genetic relationships with other languages. The methodological issue expressed in Swadesh's (1951) title "Diffusional Cumulation and Archaic Residue as Historical Explanation" is of crucial importance in attempts to find distant relatives of language isolates (and of larger language families, as well). We need to distinguish between the inherited and the diffused/borrowed, eliminating the latter from considerations of potential kinship.

Language contact must be dealt with effectively in the methodology for evaluating proposals of distant genetic relationship. Efforts no doubt will continue to attempt to show that various language isolates are not really isolates but are related to other languages as members of broader language families. This is to be encouraged and positive results to be hoped for. Nevertheless, proposals of such relatedness will gain little sympathy unless careful methods are followed. Most proposals attempting to show language isolates are related to other languages have not been accepted. We should not say, however, that we have learned nothing from the attempts. Indeed, we found in several cases that the evidence that certain languages are isolates is very strong, precisely because of the failure of many attempts to find relatives for them. In particular, the methodology for investigating distant genetic relationship has become much clearer, and we understand better why certain proposals fail and we know what considerations are important if a plausible, defensible hypothesis of a family relationship is to be found to have merit. (See Campbell and Poser 2008.) In assessing the evidence brought forward for these hypotheses, in several cases we have discovered numerous loanwords and have come to understand influences from language contact much better.

What does the future hold? We expect documentation of language isolates to be given priority, especially documentation of endangered language isolates, for the contributions they can make to linguistic theory and to understanding the history of human beings on the planet. We can anticipate that attempts to seek possible relatives of various language isolates will continue, occasionally with some success. However, it should not be expected that the total number of language isolates is going to shrink markedly. Possibly, though less likely, additional language isolates will be discovered. Where appropriate and possible, it is to be hoped and encouraged that effective language revitalization efforts will be undertaken to conserve these language isolates. It is hoped that the language isolates of the world will become better understood and their potential contributions better appreciated. Hopefully they will be analyzed carefully for the contributions they will make to linguistic theory and language typology and to the overall history of human language. The chapters of this book contribute towards those ends.

This volume, then – with 159 of the world's c.407 language families, albeit families with but a single member language – takes a rightful place in the Routledge's *Language Family* series. It involves 39% of all the language families of the world.

REFERENCES

Campbell, Lyle and William J. Poser. 2008. *Language Classification: History and Method.* Cambridge: Cambridge University Press.

Swadesh, Morris. 1951. Diffusional cumulation and archaic residue as historical explanation. *Southwestern Journal of Anthropology* 7: 1–21.

CHAPTER 1

LANGUAGE ISOLATES AND THEIR HISTORY

Lyle Campbell

1 INTRODUCTION

How many language isolates are there in the world? (And, how many language families are there?) Most linguists do not know, and opinions vary greatly. To answer these questions is complicated because of differing views about fundamental issues in historical linguistics and because of the limited amount of information that is available to us on a good number of these languages. This chapter attempts to answer the questions: how many language isolates are there? How can we advance knowledge of the history of language isolates? What lessons does the study of specific isolates offer for understanding better the history of language isolates in general and of other specific isolates? What are the prospects for finding relatives for some language isolates, for showing that they belong together with other languages in a family of related languages?[1]

So, what is a language isolate? The standard definition is that a language isolate is a language that has no known relatives, that is, that has no demonstrable phylogenetic relationship with any other language. It is a language which has not been shown to be the descendent of any ancestral language which has other descendants (other daughter languages). Thus, language isolates are in effect language families that have only one member. The best-known and most cited language isolates are Basque, Burushaski, and Ainu, though there are many others not so well known represented in this book.

Since language isolates are often contrasted with families made up of related languages, we also need to ask, what is a language family? A language family is a set of languages for which there is sufficient evidence to show that they descend from a single common ancestral language and are therefore phylogenetically related to one another. The total number of language families in the world is the set of independent families for which no genealogical relationship can be demonstrated with any other language family. A "family" can be composed of but a single language in the case of language isolates, languages with no known relatives.

The number of the world's language isolates, as we shall see, comes to c.159, but this is far from a secure answer to the question of how many there are. And, how many independent language families (including isolates) are there in the world? There are approximately 407 (cf. Campbell 2013:159). This number is relevant in considerations to come later in this chapter.

2 WHY LANGUAGE ISOLATES AND LANGUAGE FAMILIES ARE NOT SO VERY DIFFERENT

There are two senses in which language isolates are not very different from language families composed of multiple members. First, some language isolates may have had relatives in the past that have disappeared without coming to be known, leaving these languages isolated.

For example, Ket in Siberia is the only surviving language of the Yeniseian family (see Georg, this volume). Nevertheless, there were other Yeniseian languages, now extinct: Arin, Asan, Kott, Pumpokol, and Yugh (Vajda 2001). If these languages had disappeared without a trace, Ket would now be considered an isolate. However, since data from these extinct languages was registered before they disappeared, Ket was not left an isolate, rather a member of a family of languages, albeit the only surviving member. Examples such as Ket show that language isolates could well have once been members of languages families whose other relatives disappeared before they could come to be known. This shows one way in which language isolates are not so very different from languages families.

2.1 Did Basque have relatives?

This discussion, with Ket as an example, raises an interesting question: is it possible that Basque, the most famous of language isolates, once had relatives and is thus not really a language isolate? This brings up questions about (1) the relationship between Basque and Aquitanian and (2) the relationship of Basque "dialects" to one another. This discussion of possible relatives for Basque serves the purpose of further illustrating the point that language isolates are not so different from other language families.

Trask (1997:411) affirmed that "probably all Basque scholars now accept that Basque descended more or less directly from Aquitanian" (see also Trask 1995:87, 1997:35). However, is it possible that Aquitanian and Basque are related languages, two members of a language family, rather than Aquitanian being a direct ancestor of Basque?

It is possible that Basque is not a direct descendant of Aquitanian. The attestations of Aquitanian are from c. 2000 years ago (see below); however, most languages known from 2000 years ago have diversified into families of related languages: Romance, Finnic, Slavic, Germanic, Turkic, Mongolian, Polynesian, etc. It can be surmised that Aquitanian from so long ago may also have diversified into multiple languages. One possibility, if no other except Basque survived, is that Aquitanian could indeed be the direct ancestor of Basque. Another possibility, however, is that Aquitanian had a sister, or sisters, of its own, diversified from an earlier common ancestor, and that Basque descends from a sister of Aquitanian rather than directly from Aquitanian itself.

Although the attestations of Aquitanian are sufficient to confirm that modern Basque and Aquitanian are connected in some way, they also show differences from Basque sufficient to suggest the possibility that Aquitanian is not Basque's direct ancestor, but is a relative of Basque, that is, that possibly Aquitanian and Basque are sister languages representing two branches of an original proto-language. The corpus of Aquitanian data is limited to about 400 personal names and 70 names of deities, found in texts written in Latin. There are no Aquitanian texts larger than these names. (See Michelena 1988, Gorrochategui 1984, 1995, Trask 1997:398–403; see also Lakarra, this volume.) Compare in Table 1.1 the Aquitanian words (from c.100 CE) with those of Basque, on the one hand, and the Gothic words (from 382 CE) with those of English, on the other.

It is easy to see that, in spite of clear similarities between Aquitanian and Basque, there are also marked differences. It is also clear that the similarities and differences between the Gothic-English cognates are quite similar to those between Aquitanian and Basque. However, Gothic is not a direct ancestor of English – the two belong to distinct branches

TABLE 1.1 COMPARISON OF THE RELATION BETWEEN AQUITANIAN AND BASQUE WITH THAT BETWEEN GOTHIC AND ENGLISH

Aquitanian	Basque	Gothic	English
atta	aita	fadar	father
belex	beltz	swarts	black
bon-	on	goþs	good
sembe-	seme	sunus	son
hanna	anaia	broþar	brother
seni-	sehi/seiñ	magus	boy
oxson	otso	wulfs	wolf
siri(co)	suri	hweits	white

of Germanic. Their differences and similarities, when compared with those between Aquitanian and Basque, turn out to be quite similar. Therefore, it should be asked, could the relationship between Basque and Aquitanian be that of related languages as exists between Gothic and English (sister languages), and not like that between Latin and Spanish, where an ancestral language and one of its descendants are involved?

2.2 Could Basque have modern relatives?

Some languages which were once thought to be isolates have proven to be members of small families of related languages. This illustrates a second way in which language isolates and language families are not so different from one another. For example, Japanese would be a language isolate if the Ryukyuan languages (of Okinawa) had not been shown to be a separate languages independent of Japanese, so sisters of Japanese. Thus Japanese belongs to a family of languages (often called Japonic) and is no longer an isolate. Similarly, Etruscan, long considered an isolate, was shown to be related to Lemnian (in a language family now called Tyrsenian) (Steinbauer 1999:357–366; see Michalowski, this volume, for details). Korean, too was considered a language isolate, but Jejueo has been shown to be a distinct language, a sister of Korean, both now members of the Koreanic family and Korean is no longer a language isolate.

Such cases raise the question, is it possible that Basque constitutes a small family of languages? Basque would not be considered an isolate if Aquitanian should prove to be a separate language, not an ancestor of Basque but phylogenetically related to it. Also, when two or more 'dialects' are not mutually intelligible, by standard criteria they are considered separate languages. Basque would become a small family if its dialects have diversified so much that some are no longer mutually intelligible. This appears to be the case. It has been so long since Proto-Basque times (second century BCE[2]) that Basque well could have diversified into multiple languages. As Trask (1997:5) affirms, "the differentiation [between the dialects] is sufficiently distant that speakers of different areas can have significant difficulty understanding one another when using the vernacular form of Basque."

The classification of Basque dialects varies, with disagreements about how many dialects there are and how to classify them; however, it is often claimed that at least Zuberoa (Suletino, Souletin) is not mutually intelligible with the others (see, for example, Trask 1997:5). Given this, some have considered Basque not an isolate, but a small language family. The 2005 edition of *Ethnologue* (Ethnologue.com) listed three Basque languages, though later editions have only one, yet noting still "some inherent intelligibility among regional varieties except Souletin" (Lewis et al. 2016 [accessed 5–14–2016]).[3]

The main point here is not to insist that Basque once had relatives (questioning the nature of its relationship with Aquitanian) or that Basque has relatives now (if some varieties are mutual unintelligible); rather what is important in this discussion is to show that Basque easily could cease to be considered a language isolate and, therefore, that language families and language isolates are not so different.

3   'LANGUAGE ISOLATE' FURTHER CLARIFIED

It is necessary to distinguish language isolates from unclassified languages, languages so poorly known that they cannot be classified, though sometimes they are listed as isolates. An unclassified language is one for which there is not enough data (attestation/documentation) to determine whether it has relatives – for these languages, there is insufficient data to compare them meaningfully with other languages, and therefore any possible kinship they may have remains unknown. In contrast, for language isolates, there do exist data, and comparisons of these data with other languages do not reveal any linguistic kinship – the comparisons do not allow them to be grouped with other languages in any language family.

There are two sorts of unclassified languages. The first are extinct languages which are too poorly attested to be grouped with any other language or language family. Some examples include:

Aranama-Tamique, Texas
Baenan, Brazil
Camunico, Northeast Italy (survived to 2nd half of 1st millennium BCE)
Eteocretan, Crete, 7th–3rd centuries BCE (see Michalowski, this volume)
Gamela, Brazil
Iberian, spoken on the Iberian Peninsula (5th–1st centuries BCE or a bit later) (see Michalowski, this volume)
Kara, possible language of Korea, only from 13 toponyms
Kaskean, Northeast Anatolia 2nd millennium BCE
Koguryo possible language, NE China, Manchuria, Korea, 1st–8th centuries CE, known only from toponyms and a few words
Ligurian, Northeast Italy, few words, 300 BCE–100 CE
Maratino, Northeast Mexico
Minoan Linear A, undeciphered, 1800–1450 BCE
Mysian, Western Anatolia, before the 1st century BCE
Naolan, Tamaulipas, Mexico
Northern Picene, Adriatic coast of Italy, 1st millennium BCE
Pictish, Scotland 7th–10th centuries CE, few inscriptions
Puyo, Manchuria (with Koguryo?), few attested words
Quinigua, Northeast Mexico
Raetic, Northern Italy, Switzerland, Austria, 1st millennium BCE
Sicanian, Central Sicily, pre-Roman epoch
Solano, Texas, Northeast Mexico
Sorothaptic, Iberian Peninsula, pre-Celtic, Bronze Age
Tarairiú, Brazil
Wamoe (Huamoé), Brazil

Tartessian (Spain, 1st millennium BCE) is an interesting case, a language that until recently was considered unclassified, but for which Kaufman (2015) presents strong evidence that it was in fact a Celtic language.

Indus Valley (Harappan) (India and Pakistan, 2600–1900 BCE) is another interesting case, often listed as an unclassified language, based on undeciphered inscriptions. However, its status as a real writing system is disputed (cf. Farmer et al. 2004; Michalowski, this volume). (For several other unclassified languages of Asia and Europe, see Michalowski, this volume.)

The second kind of unclassified languages are the extant languages which cannot be classified for lack of data, languages not yet described sufficiently to compare them meaningfully with other languages in order to determine whether they may have relatives. Examples include:

- In Africa: Bung, Lufu, Kujargé, perhaps Mpre (Mpra) (Blench, this volume), and Rer Bare. Oropom is sometimes listed among unclassified African languages, though Blench (this volume) reports that it is probably a spurious language. Weyto is another "speculative" language sometimes listed among unclassified languages of Africa.
- In Asia and the Pacific: Sentinelese (Andaman Islands), Bhatola (India), Waxianghua (China), Doso (Papua New Guinea), Kembra (Indonesia Papua), and Lepki (Indonesia Papua).
- In South America there are many, for example: Ewarhuyana, Himarimã (perhaps Arawan?), Iapama (uncontacted, possibly speakers of a known neighboring language), Kaimbé, Kambiwá, Kapinawá, Korubo (maybe Panoan?), Pankararé, Truká, Tremembé, Wakoná, Wasu, etc. (See Campbell 2012, Zamponi in press; cf. Seifart and Hammarström, this volume.)

It should be noted that some of these unclassified languages could also be language isolates, but without evidence, we cannot know.

4 HOW MANY LANGUAGE ISOLATES ARE THERE, REALLY?

With the clarification that the unclassified languages do not count as language isolates, we return to the question, how many isolates are there in the world? The list, compiled from consensus reports from specialists in each region and in particular from the chapters in this book, follows. It is important, however, to point out that this list is not definitive, nor can it be, for several reasons. As mentioned in the introduction to this volume, scholars' opinions about whether something is considered a language isolate or not can and often do vary. In some situations where the amount of documentation available on a particular language is limited, there may be enough that some scholars believe it sufficient to show that the language has no relatives (and is hence an isolate) where other scholars consider the amount of documentation so limited that the language must be considered unclassified. In other cases, some scholars see only a single language with dialects – a language isolate – while others see a language family composed of closely related languages, sufficiently different from one another no longer to qualify as merely dialects of a single language. In several other cases, closer examination has shown that some entities thought to be language isolates are not in fact single languages but have relatives. Also, a number of languages commonly reported as isolates, upon careful inspection, turned out to have extremely scant attestation and thus must be considered unclassified instead. Finally, accounts of language isolates differ in another way, namely in terms of the names by which certain languages are known. In South America, for example, most languages are known by more than one name, and often a single name has been applied to more than one language (see Campbell 2012). When comparing different accounts, it is important to be careful with the problem of multiple names for single languages, so as not to extend lists of isolates falsely by the inclusion of the same thing under different names. For all these reasons, the number of language isolates reported in recent publications varies and is uncertain.

In the list here, extinct languages are indicated by an asterisk (*) after the name of the language.

Africa: [4] (see Blench, this volume)

Bangi Me	Hadza
Jalaa	Laal

Blench (this volume) list 12 other languages that have been reported/suggested as isolates, but which are controversial: **Bēosi** (Madagascar), **Dompo, Guanche** (Canary Islands), **Gumuz, Kujargé** (unclassified), **Kwadi** (unclassified),[4] **Meroitic** (now generally seen as a relative of Nubian), **Mpra** (perhaps unclassified), **Ongota, Oropom** (unclassified), **Sandawe**, and **Shabo**.

Asia: [9] (see Georg, and Michalowski, this volume)

Ainu	Burushaski
Elamite*	Kassite* (unclassified? Michalowski, this volume)
Hattian* (Hattic)	Kusunda
Nihali	Nivkh (Gilyak)[5]
Sumerian*	

Greater Andamanese (if it is a single language) may be another isolate, but this is uncertain (see Georg, this volume).

Hurrian (Hurro-Urartean) (in Northeast Anatolia) is now known to be a family of two separate languages, though earlier Urartean was thought to be a late form of Hurrian (see Michalowski, this volume).

Koreanic is a small family, with at least two members, Korean and Jejueo; Korean is often listed as a language isolate, but this is not accurate.

Sentinelese, on *North Sentinel* Island, one of the Andaman Islands, is sometimes listed as an isolate, but its status is unknown. As Georg (this volume) reports, "it may, thus, be just another Andamanese language, it may be exclusively related to Great Andamanese, it may be related to some other language of the greater region, or, then, to none at all."

Itel'men (Kamchadal), in southwest Kamchatka has sometimes been treated as a language isolate, but the evidence shows that it is related to Chukchi-Koryak (Chukchi, Koryak, Kerek, Alyutor) in the Chukotko-Kamchatkan language family (Georg, this volume).

Australia [5] (see Bowern, this volume).

Bachamal	Gaagudju*
Kungarakany*	Mangarrayi*
Tiwi	

Anindilyakwa (Enindhilyakwa), sometimes listed as an isolate, appears to belong with the Gunwinyguan family (itself a controversial grouping) (see Bowern, this volume). Bowern (this volume) also discusses additional possible language isolates in Australia and other interpretations of some of these.

Europe: [1]
> Basque

Some would include also **Iberian**, an extinct language of Spain, but it is better considered unclassified due to insufficient information.

As mentioned above, **Etruscan**, long considered an isolate, is related to **Lemnian** (Tyrsenian family) and so is not a true language isolate.

Pacific [c.55] (see Hammarström, this volume)

Abinomn	Abun
Afra (Usku)	Anêm
Ap Ma (Botin, Kambot, Kambrambo)	Asaba (Suarmin)
Baiyamo	Banaro
Bilua	Bogaya
Burmeso	Busa (Odiai)
Damal (Uhunduni, Amung Me)	Dibiyaso
Elseng (Morwap)	Dem
Duna	Fasu
Guriaso	Kaki Ae
Kapauri	Kamula
Kehu	Karami
Kibiri-Porome	Kimki
Kol	Kosare
Kuot	Lavukaleve
Marori (Moraori)	Masep
Mawes	Maybrat
Mor	Mpur
Pawaia	Pele-Ata
Powle-Ma ("Molof")	Purari (formerly "Namau")
Pyu	Sause
Savosavo	Sulka
Tabo (Waia)	Taiap
Tambora*	Tanahmerah
Touo	Wiru
Yale (Yalë, Nagatman)	Yele (Yélî Dnye)
Yerakai	Yetfa-Biksi

Some of these may eventually turn out to have relatives (Hammarström, this volume).

North America: [22] (cf. Mithun, this volume, Campbell et al. in press)

Adai*(?)	Beothuk*
Calusa*(?)	Cayuse*

Chimariko*	Chitimacha*
Coahuilteco*	Cotoname*
Esselen*	Haida (?)
Karankawa*	Karuk
Kootenai	Natchez*
Siuslaw*	Takelma*
Tonkawa*	Tunica*
Washo	Yuchi (Euchee)
Yana*	Zuni

The number of languages listed as isolates in North America varies considerably in different publications, and the differences illustrate some of the difficulties in determining whether something is or is not a language isolate and, consequently, what the total number of language isolates in the world is.

For example, **Alsean** is most commonly considered a small family of two closely related languages, **Alsea** and **Yaquina**. However, some consider these to be dialects of a single language and treat this "Alsea" as a language isolate.

Aranama is often listed as an 'isolate,' but the documentation is so poor it should probably better be considered unclassified/unclassifiable. As Mithun (this volume) says:

> Our entire documentation of the language consists of one single-word and one two-word phrase: *himiyána* 'water' and *Himiána tsýi!* 'Give me water!' These were recorded by Albert Gatschet in 1884 from a Tonkawa man known as Old Simon, who also provided a short vocabulary of Karankawa, another Texas language. Old Simon himself identified the language as Hanáma or Háname (Gatschet 1884). The only people indigenous to that area with a similar name were those known as the Aranama, Saranames, or Jaranames.

Calusa is usually listed as an isolate, although, as Mithun (this volume) explains, the language is known from only about a dozen words from 1575 from a Spanish captive among the Calusa and from 50–60 place names. Early accounts report that Calusa was distinct from other languages of the area. But as Mithun says, "with such a small record, however, its [Calusa's] status cannot be confirmed."

Solano is also usually listed as an isolate. Mithun (this volume) also explains the Solano corpus: "a sheet with 21 words. . . the page bore the following description: 'Near the end of the original book of baptisms of the San Francisco Solano Mission, 1703–1708, is a brief vocabulary, presumably of the Indians of that mission'." This documentation probably is not sufficient to permit the language to be classified.

In the case of **Keres(an)**, there is uncertainty about the Keresan dialect continuum. Most think it has enough diversity that at least two separate languages must be distinguished: Acoma-Laguna and Rio Grande Keresan. Some, however, believe Keres is a single language, an isolate, with several dialects.

Some consider **Atakapa** a single language which is an isolate; others see it as a small family, **Atakapan**, that includes Atakapa and **Akokisa**, and perhaps **Eastern Atakapa**, though it is uncertain from the documentation whether these are two or three separate languages or are all variants of a single one (see Mithun, this volume).

Adai has sometimes been considered 'unclassified' because of the limited documentation, 275 words recorded, c.1802, though usually it is listed as a language isolate.

Molala and **Klamath-Modoc**, formerly considered language isolates, together with the Sahaptian languages, belong to the Plateau (Plateau Penutian) language family (Campbell et al. in press).

Salinan, often listed as a language isolate, is a small family, composed of the two languages, Antoniano and Migueleño (see Campbell et al. in press).

Timucua may be a language isolate and is often considered one, but this is unclear. Some assign Timucua and **Tawasa** together as members of a **Timucuan** language family. However, the status of Tawasa is disputed (based on a list of 60 words from 1707). As Mithun (this volume) explains, a number of the Tawasa forms are so similar to Timucua that they may represent the same language. She says, "if Tawasa was actually Timucua itself or a dialect of that language, Timucua would remain an isolate." Also, if Tawasa was a separate but unrelated language, Timucua would be an isolate; however, if Timucua and Tawasa were separate but related languages, then Timucuan would be a language family. The status is just unclear.

Mexico and Central America [4] (see Heaton, this volume)

Cuitlatec*	Huave
Purhépecha (Tarascan)	Seri

There are three small language families in Central America that are sometimes listed as language isolates:

Jicaquean (Tol) (two languages in Honduras: **Tol** and **Jicaque of El Palmar**)
Lencan (two languages in El Salvador and Honduras: **Chilanga** [Salvadoran Lenca] and **Honduran Lenca**)
Xinkan (four languages in Guatemala: **Chiquimulilla**, **Guazacapán**, **Jumaytepeque**, and **Yupiltepeque**) (see Rogers 2016 for details.)

(Languages that had speakers in both southeastern Texas and northeastern Mexico are treated with North American languages; see the isolate Coahuilteco and several unclassified languages.)

South America [53] (see Seifart and Hammarström, this volume, and Zamponi in press)

Aikanã (Brazil)	Andaquí* (Colombia)
Andoque (Brazil, Peru)	Arutani (Awaké, Uruak) (Venezuela, Brazil)
Atacameño* (Cunza) (Chile)	Betoi* (Betoi-Jirara) (Colombia)
Camsá (Sibundoy) (Colombia)	Candoshi (Candoshi-Shapra) (Peru)
Canichana* (Bolivia)	Cayubaba (Cayuvava)* (Bolivia)
Chiquitano (Bolivia)	Chono* (Chile)
Cofán (A'ingaé) (Colombia, Ecuador)	Culli (Culle)* (Peru; unclassified?)
Esmeralda (Atacame) (Ecuador)	Fulniô (Yaté) (Brazil)
Guachí* (Brazil)	Guamó* (Venezuela)
Guató (Brazil)	Irantxe (Iranche, Mynky) (Brazil)
Itonama* (Bolivia)	Jeikó (Brazil)
Jotí (Yuwana) (Venezuela)	Kanoé (Kapixaná) (Brazil)

Kwaza (Koayá, Koaiá) (Brazil)
Máku* (Máko) (Brazil)
Mato Grosso Arara (Arara de Beiradão)
Mosetén-Chimané
Munichi* (Otanabe) (Peru)
Omurano* (Peru)
Payaguá* (Paraguay)
Puquina* (Bolivia)
Rikbaktsá (Brazil)
Taruma* (Brazil, Guyana?)
Tequiraca* (Aewa, Auishiri) (Peru)
Urarina (Peru)
Warao (Guyana, Surinam, Venezuela)
Yaruro (Pumé) (Venezuela)
Yurumanguí* (Colombia)

Leco* (Bolivia, extinct?)
Matanawí (Brazil)
Mochica* (Yunga, Chim) (Peru)
Movima (Bolivia)
Ofayé (Opayé) (Brazil)
Paez (Colombia)
Puinave
Purí-Coroado
Sapé (Kaliana)(*?) (Venezuela)
Taushiro (Pinche) (Peru)
Trumai (Trumaí) (Brazil)
Waorani (Auca, Sabela) (Ecuador)
Yánama* (Yagan) (Chile)
Yuracaré (Bolivia)

Seifart and Hammarström (this volume) and others list several additional South American languages as isolates, though several of these have relatives, making them members of language families, and others are better considered unclassified.

- **Gününa-Küne** (Puelche) belongs to the **Chonan** family (see Viegas Barros 2005).
- **Jirajaran** is a small family in Venezuela composed of **Jirajara**, **Ayomán** (Ayamán), and **Gayón** (Coyón) (all extinct).
- **Mosetén-Chinamé** is sometimes considered a small family (Mosetenan) of two very closely related languages, Mosetén and Chimané.
- **Otomacoan** is a small family in Venezuela, with **Otomaco** and **Taparita**.
- **Pirahã** is considered a language isolate by some and by others as a member of the **Muran** family, together with **Mura**, **Bohurá** (Buxwaray), and **Yahahí** (in Brazil). At issue is whether these are all varieties of a single language or are distinct but related languages.
- **Purí-Coroado** (Brazil) is a language isolate, though traditionally **Purí** and **Coroada**, together with Koropó, were considered members of a Purían language family; however, recent work reveals that Purí and Coroado are variants of the same language and that Koropó is not related to it, but seems to be related instead to the Maxakalían languages (see Zamponi in press).
- **Sechura** is often listed as a language isolate, but there is evidence for a **Sechuran-Catacoan** language family, with Sechura (Atalán, Sec) related to the Catacaoan languages (**Catacao** and **Colán**) (all in Peru). While these languages are extinct and poorly attested, Adelaar and Muysken (2004:400) find the data sufficient to support this family classification, while Seifart and Hammarström (this volume) consider Sechura a language isolate, not finding Adelaar and Muysken's evidence convincing.
- **Timote-Cuica**, often considered a language isolate, is probably a small family of languages (**Timotean**) in Venezuela, all extinct, composed of Timote-Cuica (Miguri, Cuica) and **Mucuchí-Maripú** (Mocochí, Mirripú). It is not clear whether **Timote** and **Cuica** were separate languages or were dialects of a single language. Timote may survive as **Mutú** (Loco, Mutús), an unstudied language (cf. Adelaar and Muysken 2004:125).

- **Tinigua**, sometimes considered an isolate, is a member of the **Tiniguan** family (in Colombia), together with extinct **Panigua**. Adelaar and Muysken (2004:620) also put extinct **Majigua** in Tiniguan, though it is essentially unattested.
- **Xukurú** is often considered a language isolate though, because it is poorly attested, it is also often considered unclassified. It is grouped with **Paratío**, also poorly documented, in the **Xukurúan** family, although the evidence for this is not conclusive (see Zamponi in press).

Though clearly related, members of the **Lule-Vilelan** family, **Vilela** and **Lule** (of Argentina) are often listed as isolates (see Viegas Barros 2001; cf. Campbell 2012 and Zamponi in press, for additional discussion of these).

Thus, the total number of isolates in the world comes to c.159 (as precise a figure as current circumstance permit). There are c.407 independent language families (including isolates), for which it is not possible to demonstrate a genetic relationship with any other language family. Isolates thus make up 39% of all 'language families', of the world's linguistic diversity, calculated in terms of language families. Seen from this perspective, isolates are not at all weird; they have as their 'cohorts' well over one-third of the 'language families' of the world.

So, to what do we owe the general attitude that language isolates are weird and suspicious, that languages with no relatives should not be tolerated? I believe this is due to scholars generally not knowing that there are many language isolates and not knowing that isolates really differ little from other languages families, as seen above, so there should be no particular motive to feel driven to try to get rid of them by assigning them as members to some higher-order language family.

5 HOW CAN WE ADVANCE OUR KNOWLEDGE OF THE HISTORY OF LANGUAGE ISOLATES?

How can we learn about the history of a language without relatives? De Saussure (1916:298) said that "we cannot derive anything from Basque because, being an isolate, it does not allow any comparison." Meillet (1925:11–12) said that "if a language is an isolate, it lacks history . . . so if we cannot find a way to demonstrate a relationship between Basque and some other language, there will never be any hope of finding out anything about its history" (see also Michelena 1995:101).[6] These claims raise the question, can we learn about the history of languages without relatives, and if so then how? Is an isolate indeed is a language without history? What lessons does the study of Basque and other language isolates offer for understanding better how to investigate the history of language isolates? These studies show that this claim is mistaken – isolates indeed have history and there are means of studying it. The means that can be employed to learn about the history of language isolates include:

Internal reconstruction
Evidence from loanwords
Comparative reconstruction based on dialects
Toponyms and other proper names
Philological study of attestations and historical reports
Language contact and areal linguistics
Wörter und Sachen

We turn to these topics now.

5.1 Internal reconstruction

Internal reconstruction is the best-known and most widely used tool to investigate the history of isolates. Excellent examples include Michelena (1988, 1995); Lakarra (1995, 2006; cf. this volume); and Trask (1997). For example, Lakarra (1995) applied internal reconstruction very effectively to reconstruct the roots of Pre-Proto-Basque, obtaining significant historical understanding of that language isolate. I present a single example to show the sort of historical information that can be learned. 'Wine' is commonly reconstructed in Proto-Basque as *ardano based on dialect variants *ardo, ardao, arno*, and *ardu*.[7] However even without this comparative information, based just on standard Basque *ardo* in isolation and *ardan-* in compounds, internal reconstruction takes us close to the *ardano reconstruction – other evidence internal to Basque reveals the change in which intervocalic *n* was lost, see below.

5.2 Philological investigation of attestations

Michelena (1988) and Gorrochategui (1984, 1993, 1995) have made very valuable studies of the older attestations of Basque (see also Lakarra, this volume). These include older citations of Basque forms, toponyms, personal names, deity names, and historical reports.

5.3 Comparative reconstruction

A less well-known but extremely valuable tool is the comparative method applied not to separate related languages, but to regional dialects. Instructive cases include: Basque (Gorrochategui and Lakarra 1996, 2001, Lakarra 1995, 1996, 2006, Michelena 1988, 1995, Trask 1997; see Lakarra, this volume); Ainu (Vovin 1993); Huave (Suárez 1975); and Tarascan (Friedrich 1971). These studies show that obviously Meillet, de Saussure, and others were mistaken in claiming that isolated languages do not lend themselves to any comparison and wrong in concluding that nothing can be known of the history of a language isolate if it has no relatives.

5.4 Loanwords

Loanwords are another source of evidence on the history of language isolates. For example, from the semantic content of the more than 300 ancient loanwords from Latin into Basque, it is clear that the Romans had much influence in the areas of laws, administration, technology, religion, and refined culture. Moreover, the relative age of many of these loanwords in Basque is known from phonological considerations. Many were borrowed before the changes in Romance that transformed the ten vowels, five long and five short, to a system of just seven vowels, and were borrowed before the palatalization of velar consonants before front vowels. These older loans in Basque reflect the pronunciations before these changes in Romance had taken place (Michelena 1988, 1995, Trask 1997).

In another case, from Mesoamerica, we know something of the history of Huave (isolate) and its speakers from words borrowed from Mixe-Zoquean (MZ). Some examples are:

Huave *pom* 'copal (incense)' < PMZ (Proto-Mixe-Zoquean) *poma* [obligatory in Mesoamerican ritual]
Huave *koy* 'rabbit' < PMZ *koya* [calendric name]
Huave *patsi* 'lizard' < PMZ *patsi* [calendric name]

Huave *pikI* 'feather' < PMZ **pik* [important in pre-Columbian trade]
Huave *kawak* 'chicozapote, mamey' < PMZ **kaʔwak* 'chicozapote fruit'
Huave *yati* 'anona, chirimoya [soursop]' < Zoque *yati, ati.*

Several of these loans show early cultural influence from Mixe-Zoquean on Huave, reflecting cultural concepts in ancient Mesoamerica. They support the hypothesis that the ancient Olmecs – the first highly successful agricultural civilization in Mesoamerica – spoke a Mixe-Zoquean language, as seen also in the Mixe-Zoquean influence on many other languages in the area (Campbell and Kaufman 1976).

5.5 Areal linguistic traits

Another source of information about the history of isolates is areal linguistics. A linguistic area (*Sprachbund*) is a geographical region in which, due to language contact, languages of the area share structural traits, not through inheritance, but due to borrowing/diffusion. Areal linguistic traits reveal historical contacts and help to explain certain changes in the languages involved, including language isolates, as exemplified by the following areal traits in Basque owed to contact with neighboring languages:

1   *s* is apico-alveolar in most Basque varieties but is apico-post-alveolar for most Basque speakers in France (Trask 1997:84), due to influence from French or Gascon-Bearnese.
2   Loss of intervocalic (lenis) *-n-* and *-l-* is a trait, shared also with Portuguese, Galician, and Asturian. (Trask 1997), originally probably from Gascón influence.
3   Basque initial *h-* is lost in most dialects (not in Zuberoa). This loss is probably due to influence first from Navarro-Aragonese and then from Spanish and French. (Trask 1997.)
4   Basque epenthesized a vowel before initial *r*, e.g. *errege* 'king' (borrowed from Latin *rege* [cf. earlier nominative *rex* [reks] < *reg-s*]) and *erloju* 'clock' (borrowed from Spanish *reloj*). This feature is shared also with Aragonese and Gascon. (Lakarra 1995:198.)
5   Older Basque, Aquitanian, and Iberian all basically lack *p*. (Michelana 1995:112, Trask 1995:78, 87.)

These areal facts also provide information about the history of Basque, of Basque contacts.

5.6 Wörter und Sachen

Wörter und Sachen strategies, for detecting past language-and-culture relations, can also provide information on the history of language isolates.

One *Wörter und Sachen* technique involves the analyzability of words (their morphological complexity) – words that can be analyzed into component parts are believed to be more recent than words which have no internal analysis. It is believed that words which can be analyzed into parts were created more recently than words which have no such internal composition, which are held to be potentially older forms (Campbell 2013:415–436). For example, Basque *garagardo* 'beer' is analyzable morphologically: *garagar* 'barley' + *ardo* 'wine'; therefore, it is inferred that the word for 'wine' is probably older in Basque than the word for 'beer', since 'beer' contains the word for 'wine' in it. Similarly, Basque *gari* 'wheat' is inferred to be older than *garagar* 'barley', since *garagar* involves a reduplicated from of the word for 'wheat' and thus is morphologically analyzable. And, the word for 'wheat' must also be older than that for 'beer', since the 'barley' component of 'beer' is morphologically complex, with 'wheat' in it. Basque *janarbi* 'radish' is analyzable as *jan* 'eat + *arbi* 'turnip'; it is thus inferred that the 'turnip' word is older than the 'radish' word.

Another *Wörter und Sachen* strategy involves the **analyzability of toponyms**. It is held that place names that can be analyzed into component parts probably are more recent in a language than those which have no such internal analysis. For example, it is inferred that *York* is older in English than *New York*, since the latter is composed of identifiable pieces, but not the former. In Basque, since the names of several rivers in the French Basque area have no clear etymology (not analyzable into parts), it is inferred that they are old names. However, the names of several rivers of Biscaya are analyzable, for example *Ibaizabal* from *ibai* 'river' + *zabal* 'wide', and *Artibai* from *arte* 'between(?)' + *ibai* 'river'. It is thus inferred that these latter, analyzable names are not as old in the language as the former.

A third *Wörter und Sachen* strategy involves words that bear non-productive (irregular) morphemes; these words are assumed to be possibly older than words composed only of productive (regular) morphemes. For example, the Basque morph -*di* is frozen, not productive; its presence in the animal names *ardi* 'sheep', *zaldi* 'horse', *idi* 'ox', and *ahardi* 'sow' suggests that these animals have been known for a long time.[8] However, it is possible to conclude only that words containing the non-productive morphology are old, but nothing can be inferred about the age of words lacking such forms. For example, for *otso* 'wolf' and *ahuntz* 'goat', lacking the non-productive morpheme, it is not possible to conclude anything about their age in the language based on this criterion.

In sum, based on the resources just seen, much is known of the history of Basque. This demonstrates, in turn, that we can learn about the history of isolates using these techniques.

6 DISCOVERY OF GENEALOGICAL RELATIONSHIPS FOR SOME LANGUAGE ISOLATES?

What prospects are there for coming to reliable classifications that would include some of the language isolates in larger family groupings than those currently known? It is possible to cite some relatively recent, successful cases that demonstrate a phylogenetic relationship for some languages previously considered isolates; some examples are:

Harakbmut-Katukinan (Adelaar 2000)
Korean and Jejueo
Lule-Vilelan (Lule and Vilela) (Viegas Barros 2001)
Tikuna-Yurí (see Seifart and Hammarström, this volume)
Tartessian, shown to be Celtic (Kaufman 2015)
Tyrsenian (Etruscan and Lemnian) (Steinbauer 1999:357–366; see Michalowski, this
    volume)
Western Torres Strait language and Pama-Nyungan (see Bowern 2007, this volume).

Judging from these successful instances, it can be expected that with more data and following adequate methods (see Campbell and Poser 2008), more cases of family relationship involving some language isolates will be discovered. Nevertheless, it is not to be expected that there will be a significant number of these.

7 CONCLUSIONS

The conclusions that follow from the discussion here include:

1   There is nothing unusual about isolates; there are c. 159 language isolates in the world.
2   Language isolates make up over one-third (39%) of the world's c. 407 independent families (including isolates).
3   Language isolates are not very different from language families that have languages with relatives. Isolates could easily have had relatives that are now lost and unknown, or an isolate's dialects can diversify further into related languages, members of a language family of multiple languages.
4   Language isolates have descriptive data; they are not to be confused with unclassified languages, which are not classified for lack of adequate data.
5   Progress has been made in a sense in the search for relatives of Basque and some other language isolates in that it has been demonstrated that many hypotheses of distant genetic relationship involving them are not supported by the evidence, and much more is known now of the methods necessary to demonstrate a phylogenetic relationship among languages (see Campbell and Poser 2008).
6   In spite of claims that nothing can be discovered about the history of language isolates, there are several tools (techniques) that can help to recover considerable historical information about these languages. These tools include: internal reconstruction, philological investigation of earlier attestations, comparative reconstruction based on the dialects, evidence from loanwords, language contact and areal linguistics, and *Wörter und Sachen* strategies.
7   It can be expected that with more data and dedication, and by employing adequate methods, new phylogenetic relationships may be discovered for some language isolates. However, it is not to be expected that there will be many such cases, and this is highly improbable in the case of Basque.

NOTES

1 Portions of this chapter are based on Campbell (2011), and parts of it appeared in Campbell (2016, a paper presented in 2010). I thank Joseba Lakarra for valuable feedback on an earlier version of this chapter.
2 Mitxelena (in various publications) dated Old Common Basque (the origin of all the moden dialects) to the fifth-sixth centuries CE, and this date is often cited. However, Proto-Basque dates to before contact with Romans (second century BCE). (Joseba Lakarra, personal communication.)
3 Joseba Lakarra (personal communication) points out that no investigation has been undertaken and no evidence presented to demonstrate the assumed non-intelligibity of Zuberoa (Suletino) with other Basque dialects, but that the now-extinct Roncalés dialect (closely linked with Suletino) was even more difficult to understand for almost all.
4 Kwadi is extinct and "its affiliation cannot be resolved" (Blench, this volume), although it is treated by some as Khoe.
5 Nivkh (Gilyak) has two fairly divergent varieties, and opinion has varied concerning whether they should viewed as separate languages or dialects of a single language.

Under the view that multiple languages are involved, the putative small family has been called *Amuric* (Georg, this volume).

6 For understanding the history of a single language, Meillet also accepted the evidence of changes in the history of that language (as seen in his historical treatments of Greek and Latin). In the case of Basque, however, he was uncertain or misinformed about the quantity and relevance of the changes Basque had undergone. (I thank Joseba Lakarra for pointing this out to me.)

7 This etymology of *ardano* is an old, popular one. Lakarra (this volume) goes beyond this, with *ardano* < *e-da-ra-dan-o*, with the prefixes *da-* 'locative/dative' and *ra-* 'causative' before a root *dan* 'to drink' plus the suffix *-o* 'completive', from something like 'that which is made to drink for' or 'that with which toasting is made'.

8 Joseba Lakarra (personal communication) indicates that the *-di* of these words is an allomorph of the archaic suffix *-ti* from the root *din* 'to come, be converted into'; this suffix served to derive ablative-prospectives, adjectives, and future-potentials, a case of the grammaticalization of a word meaning 'to come' in these functions.

REFERENCES

Adelaar, Willem F.H. 2000. Propuesta de un Nuevo Vínculo Genético entre dos Grupos Lingüísticos Indígenas de la Amazonia Occidental: Harakmbut y Katukina. *Actas I Congreso de Lenguas Indígenas de Sudamérica*, ed. by Luis Miranda, Lima, 2:219–236.

Adelaar, Willem F.H. and Pieter C. Muysken. 2004. *The Languages of the Andes*. Cambridge: Cambridge University Press.

Bowern, Claire. 2007. *Australian Models of Language Spread*. Paper presented at the International Conference on Historical Linguistics, 6–12 August 2007, University of Quebec, Montreal.

Campbell, Lyle. 2011. La Investigación Histórica de las Lenguas Aisladas, o ?es Raro el Vasco? *II. Congreso de la Cátedra Luis Michelana*, ed. by Joseba A. Lakarra, Joaquín Gorrochategui, and Blanca Urgell, 23–40. Vitoria Gasteiz: Editorial de la Universidad del País Vasco.

Campbell, Lyle. 2012. The Classification of South American Indigenous Languages. *The Indigenous Languages of South America: A Comprehensive Guide*, ed. by Lyle Campbell and Verónica Grondona, 59–166. Berlin: Mouton de Gruyter.

Campbell, Lyle. 2013. *Historical Linguistics: An Introduction* (3rd edition). Edinburgh: Edinburgh University Press, and Cambridge, MA: MIT Press.

Campbell, Lyle. 2016. Language Isolates and Their History, or, What's Weird, Anyway? *Berkeley Linguistics Society* 36: 16–31.

Campbell, Lyle, Victor Golla, Ives Goddard, and Marianne Mithun. In press. Languages of North America. *Atlas of the World's Languages*, ed. by J. Moseley and Ronald E. Asher. London: Routledge.

Campbell, Lyle and Terrence Kaufman. 1976. A Linguistic Look at the Olmecs. *American Antiquity* 41:80–89.

Campbell, Lyle and William J. Poser. 2008. *Language Classification: History and Method*. Cambridge: Cambridge University Press.

Farmer, Steve, Richard Sproat, and Michael Witzel. 2004. The Collapse of the Indus-Script Thesis: The Myth of a Literate Harappan Civilization. *Electronic Journal of Vedic Studies* 11:19–57.

Friedrich, Paul. 1971. Dialectal Variation in Tarascan Phonology. *International Journal of American Linguistics* 37:164–187.

Gorrochategui, Joaquín. 1984. *Onomástica Indígena de Aquitania*. Bilbao: Universidad del País Vasco.

Gorrochategui, Joaquín. 1993. Onomástica Indígena de Aquitania: Adiciones y Correcciones I. *Sprachen und Schriften des antiken Mittelmeerraums: Festschrift für Jürgen Untermann*, ed. by Frank Heidermanns, Helmut Rix, and Elmar Seebold, 145–155. Innsbruck: Innsbrucker Beiträge zur Sprachwissenschaft.

Gorrochategui, Joaquín. 1995. The Basque Language and Its Neighbors in Antiquity. *Towards a History of the Basque Language*, ed. by José Ignacio Hualde, Joseba A. Lakarra, and R.L. Trask, 31–63. Amsterdam: Benjamins.

Gorrochategui, Joaquín and Joseba Lakarra. 1996. Nuevas Aportaciones a la Reconstrucción del Protovasco. La Hispania Prerromana: Actas del VI Coloquio sobre Lenguas y Culturas de la Península Ibérica, ed. by Por F. Villar y J. d'Encarnação, 101–145. Salamanca: Ediciones Universidad de Salamaca.

Gorrochategui, Joaquín and Joseba Lakarra. 2001. Comparación Lingüística, Filología y Reconstrucción del Protovasco. *Religión, Lengua y Cultura Prerromanas de Hispania: Actas del VIII Coloquio sobre Lenguas y Culturas de la Península Ibérica*, ed. by Por F. Villar y J. d'Encarnação, 407–438. Salamanca: Ediciones Universidad de Salamaca.

Kaufman, Terrence. 2015. *Notes on the Decipherment of Tartessian as Celtic*. (Journal of Indo-European Studies Monograph Series, 62.). Washington, DC: Institute for the Study of Man.

Lakarra, Joseba A. 1995. Reconstructing the Pre-Proto-Basque Root. *Towards a History of the Basque Language*, ed. by José Ignacio Hualde, Joseba A. Lakarra, and R.L. Trask, 189–206. Amsterdam: Benjamins.

Lakarra, Joseba A. 1996. Sobre el Europeo Antiguo y la Reconstrucción del Protovasco. *Anuario del Seminario de Filología Vasca "Julio de Urquijo"* 30: 1–70.

Lakarra, Joseba A. 2006. Protovasco, Munda y Otros: Reconstrucción Interna y Tipología Holística Diacrónica. *Oihenart: Cuadernos de Lengua y Literatura* 21: 229–322.

Lewis, M. Paul, Gary F. Simons, and Charles D. Fennig (eds.). 2016. *Ethnologue: Languages of the World* (19th ed.). Dallas, TX: SIL International. www.ethnologue.com. [accessed 5–14–2016.]

Manterola, Julen. 2015. *Euskararen Morfología Historikorako. Artikuluak eta Erakusleak. (Towards a history of Basque Morphology: Articles and Demonstratives.)* Ph.D. dissertation, Universidad del País Vasco.

Meillet, André. 1925. *La Méthode Comparative en Linguistique Historique*. Oslo: H. Aschehoug & Co.

Michelena [Mitxelena], Luis [Koldo]. 1988. *Sobre Historia de la Lengua Vasca*, ed. by Joseba A. Lakarra. (*Suplementos del Anuario de Filología Vasca 'Julio de Urquijo'*, 10.) Donastia/San Sebastian: Diputación Foral de Guipúzcoa.

Michelena [Mitxelena], Luis [Koldo]. 1995. The Ancient Basque Consonants. *Towards a History of the Basque Language*, ed. by José Ignacio Hualde, Joseba A. Lakarra, and R.L. Trask, 101–135. Amsterdam: Benjamins.

Rogers, Chris. 2016. *The Use and Development of the Xinkan Languages*. Austin: University of Texas Press.

Saussure, Ferdinand de. 1916. *Cours de Linguistique Générale*. Paris: Payot.

Steinbauer, Dieter H. 1999. *Neues Handbuch des Etruskischen*. St. Katharinen: Scripta Mercaturae.

Suárez, Jorge. 1975. *Estudios Huaves*. (Colección Científica, Lingüística, 22.) México: Departamento de Lingüística, INAH.

Trask, Robert Lawrence. 1995. Origin and Relatives of the Basque Language: Review of the Evidence. *Towards a History of the Basque Language*, ed. by José Ignacio Hualde, Joseba A. Lakarra, and Robert Lawrence Trask, 65–99. Amsterdam: Benjamins.

Trask, Robert Lawrence. 1997. *History of Basque*. London: Routledge.

Vajda, Edward. 2001. *Yeniseian Peoples and Languages: A History of Yeniseian Studies*. London: Curzon.

Viegas Barros, J. Pedro. 2001. *Evidencias del Parentesco de las Lenguas Lule y Vilela*. (Colección Folklore y Antropología 4.) Santa Fe: Subsecretaría de la Provincia de Santa Fe.

Viegas Barros, J. Pedro. 2005. *Voces en el Viento. Raíces Lingüísticas de la Patagonia*. Buenos Aires: Mondragón Ediciones.

Vovin, Alexander. 1993. *A Reconstruction of Proto-Ainu*. Leiden: Brill.

Zamponi, Raoul. In press. Extinct Isolates, Unclassified Languages, and Families. *Amazonian Languages*, ed. by Patience Epps and Lev Michael. Berlin: Mouton de Gruyter.

CHAPTER 2

ANCIENT NEAR EASTERN AND EUROPEAN ISOLATES

Piotr Michalowski

1 ANCIENT NEAR EASTERN ISOLATES AND UNCLASSIFIABLE LANGUAGES

1.1 Introduction

Information on many ancient languages has been preserved in hundreds of thousands of cuneiform documents recovered from the remains of Near Eastern habitations, spanning a time frame from ca. 3300 BCE to at least the first century CE. The quantity and quality of this information varies: some languages are documented by vast amounts of literary, scholarly and administrative texts, some are known only from personal names, and still others merely by name. Because scribes often wrote in foreign languages, traces of interference from their native vernaculars can sometimes be detected. One such instance is documented in the fourteenth century BCE Akkadian language correspondence between the Egyptian Crown and its vassals in the Levant, in places such as Megiddo and Jerusalem, containing occasional glosses that reveal small glimpses of the correspondent's native Semitic Canaanite dialects that are otherwise undocumented. Slightly later, personal names and glosses texts from the Syrian city of Emar, not far from Aleppo, also written in imported scribal Akkadian, show traces of a local Semitic tongue that may have affinities with Ugaritic and ancient South Arabic (Arnaud 1995, del Olmo Lete 2012). Multilingualism was often the norm. This is well illustrated by a quote from an inscription written in Indo-European Luwian in the name of Yararis, a ninth/eighth century regent who ruled the city of Karkemish in what is now southeastern Turkey (Payne 2012: 87): "in the city's writing (=hieroglyphic Luwian), in Surean (=Phoenician) writing, in Assyrian writing (=Mesopotamian cuneiform), in Taimani (=South Arabic) writing. And I knew twelve languages." During the eighth and seventh centuries BCE, the Assyrians deported tens of thousands of people throughout their empire, and their wars resulted in population movements that created novel sociolinguistic situations. In one mid-seventh century letter, the writer reports that "there are many languages (being spoken) in the (Babylonian) city of Nippur under the protection of the king, my master" (Frame 2013: 88). These examples illustrate the complexities of language use, geography and identity of those times.

Scholars working with ancient written languages face particular challenges. The texts they work with were encoded in writing systems that underrepresented phonological detail to various degrees, but one also has to accept the fact that written language has its own norms and is often limited by rhetorical restrictions. Most important, many of the surviving texts were written in foreign male languages or dialects that were taught – mainly to young boys – by adults for whom these were not mother tongues.

Native sources also bear witness to the diversity of languages in early Western Asia and surrounding areas. Thus, the annals of Assurbanipal (668–627 BCE), the last great king of Assyria, include mention of a unique situation: a messenger had arrived at court, but "of all the languages of East and of West, over which the god Ashur has given me control, there was no interpreter of his tongue. His language was foreign, so that his words were not understood" (Cogan and Tadmor 1977: 68; the language was probably Indo-European Lydian). A late first-millennium BCE cuneiform tablet, likely from Babylon, contains 22 words in an unidentified language with their Babylonian equivalents (Lambert 1987). Recent excavations at an Assyrian provincial capital in present-day southwestern Turkey revealed a document from ca. 800 BCE that includes the names of 59 women; only 15 of these names can be classified as Akkadian, Hurrian or possibly Luwian, leaving us with 44 names in still another unidentified language or languages (MacGinnis 2012).

In historical times, much of Western Asia was dominated by speakers and writers of languages that belonged to the Afroasiatic (Ancient Egyptian, Akkadian [Babylonian/Assyrian], Eblaite, Aramaic Canaanite, Phoenician, Hebrew etc.); Indo-European (Hittite, Luwian, etc.); and Hurrian-Urartean families. In addition, there is evidence for unclassified languages and isolates. There is some measure of disagreement among scholars concerning the isolate status of specific languages, and many attempts have been made to link all of them to larger families or phyla. For many years, Urartean was considered a late form of Hurrian, but it is now recognized that the two were separate languages that belonged to a larger family used in Western Asia beginning with the middle of the third millennium (Benedict 1960). The fact that we can classify so many ancient languages as isolate or unclassifiable is obviously a consequence of two factors: modern vagaries of chance discovery and ancient sociopolitical choices that privileged specific registers of certain tongues for writing, ignoring their relatives whose preservation might have struck them off this specific list. It is equally obvious that numerous ancient languages and language families thrived in the oral sphere but disappeared into the mists of time.

1.2 Sumerian

Sumerian was the first written language in Western Asia, with the longest written history in the area. Beginning with the late fourth or early third millennium BCE, Sumerian was used for administrative records, school materials, eventually for literary, historical and scientific texts (see Section 2.1 on proto-cuneiform). The language died out some time before ca. 1900 BCE, but the date and processes that led to its extinction as a spoken vernacular are difficult to determine. Although in everyday records, inscriptions and eventually in literature it was replaced by Akkadian (a member of the Semitic family), the old language, Sumerian, continued to be used as a literary tongue to the very end of cuneiform literacy in the first century of the Common Era. The classic early grammar is Poebel (1923); more recent are Thompsen (1984), Attinger (1993), Edzard (2003), Zólyomi (2006), Kaneva (2006), Rubio (2007a), Michalowski (2008, in press) and Jagersma (2010); for a bibliography of studies of Sumerian grammar, see Peust (2011).

The basic word order of Sumerian was strongly SOV (AOV/SV); the morphology was agglutinative with marking of both heads and dependents. Except for one or two prefixed derivational morphemes, nouns bore only suffixes while verbs had both prefixes and suffixes, although more of the former than the latter. As a rule adjectives and numerals followed nouns, and main clauses followed subordinate clauses, although such order could be manipulated for semantic and stylistic purposes. Possessors were marked and followed the unmarked head in possessive (genitive) constructions. There was no overt marking of definite/indefinite properties. Sumerian was a pronoun-drop language: free pronouns were used only for focus or special accentuation. Alignment of nouns was ergative regardless of aspect while independent pronouns made no distinction between transitive and intransitive subject. The indexing patterns in verbs, however, reveal an aspectual split: ergative marking in the perfective and nominative/accusative in the imperfective.

1.2.1 Phonology

In view of the way in which the cuneiform writing system underdetermined the phonological inventory of the language and the very long history of Sumerian, much of it written by speakers of very different languages, it is virtually impossible to provide a credible description of its phonology. From the second millennium onward, the vowel inventory very much seems to resemble that of Akkadian (there are disagreements concerning the existence of /o/), as shown in Table 2.1.

For a variety of reasons, including the evidence of limited vowel harmony in verbal prefixes in one part of Babylonia during a relatively short time in the third millennium, scholars have proposed various larger vocalic inventories, e.g., Poebel (1923, six vowels); Keetman (2005, seven vowels); and Smith (2007, seven vowels). Smith proposed that early Sumerian included an ATR (advanced tongue root) feature, and his reconstruction is reproduced in Table 2.2. In recent years certain scholars have proposed that Sumerian vowels could be long or short, but the evidence for phonemic long vowels is highly dubious.

The consonantal inventory of Sumerian is equally contested. Once again, from the eighteenth century BCE on the consonants very much resemble what one finds in Akkadian, as shown in Table 2.3.

TABLE 2.1 SUMERIAN FOUR/FIVE VOWEL RECONSTRUCTION

i		u
	e	(o)
		a

TABLE 2.2 SUMERIAN SEVEN VOWEL RECONSTRUCTION

i			u
	e		
	ɛ	ə	
		a	

TABLE 2.3 STANDARD VIEW OF SUMERIAN CONSONANTS

p	t		k	
b	d		g	
	s	š		h(?)
	z			
		r	l	
	m	n	ŋ(?)	

TABLE 2.4 POSSIBLE LATE THIRD MILLENNIUM SUMERIAN CONSONANTS

p[b]	t[d]		k[g]	ʔ
pʰ[p]	tʰ[t]		kʰ[k]	
	s[s]	ʃ[š]	x(ḫ)	h
	ts[z]			
	tsʰ[r̃]			
	r	l		
m	n		ŋ	
	j			

The reconstruction of consonants in earlier phases of the language is highly uncertain. One speculative proposal concerning the late third millennium by Parpola (1975: 250), mostly repeated by Jagersma (2010: 33), has been influential. The latter is reproduced here, in that author's IPA notation, with the traditional notations in square brackets and with phonemes not recognized in Table 2.4 in parentheses.

Some scholars have reconstructed a glide /j/ and one or more glottal stops in early Sumerian. More realistically, one may claim that in most attested phases of the language glides were not phonemic but derived. Moreover, while certain words beginning with vowels may have been at some time pronounced with an initial glottal or creaky voice, such consonants were also not phonemic (Michalowski, in press). The precise nature of the nasal provisionally listed as /ŋ/ is uncertain.

1.2.2 Morphology

Sumerian nouns were divided between animate and inanimate gender and two numbers, singular and plural. Number was marked on pronouns and verbal indexes but only on animate nouns.

Nouns could be followed by other nouns in possessive relationship and by adjectives and/or numerals. Marking of number and case came at the end so that a Sumerian nominal phrase could contain several morphemes in a specific order: NOUN ADJECTIVE NUMERAL NOUN-Genitive-Number-Case, as in for example:

> *lugal gal kalam-ak-ene-ra*
> king great homeland-GEN-PL-DAT
> "For the great kings of the homeland."

As seen in this example, in nominal possession an unmarked possessor (head) noun was followed by the possessed noun marked with the genitive morpheme *-ak*, but the dative case occupied a different slot. This is usually described as case displacement, as Suffix-aufnahme, or as dependent-noun case preemption (Aristar 1995: 432). In pronominal possession, the possessed noun was followed by a pronominal suffix, according to the rules shown in Table 2.5, marking the possessor *lugal-ŋu*, "my king."

The same stems were used to form independent pronouns that could be marked by nominative, dative, comitative or similative case markers. Sumerian also had interrogative and demonstrative pronouns.

Sumerian nouns were marked by suffixed case markers that were sensitive to gender: as a rule, the spatial cases were restricted to inanimates, as evidenced by the following paradigm (with *lugal*, "king," *uru* (*iri*), "city," *tukul*, "weapon"), as shown in Table 2.6.

TABLE 2.5 POSSESSIVE SUFFIXES IN SUMERIAN

		Singular	Plural
1		-ŋu	-me
2		-zu	-zu(e)ne(ne)
3	animate	-ani	-anene
	inanimate	-bi	-bi(ene)

TABLE 2.6 SUMERIAN NOUN CASE SUFFIXES

Ergative	lugal-e	"king" (agent)
Absolute	lugal-O/uru-O	"king" (patient), "city" ("patient")
Dative	lugal-ra	"for/to the king"
Comitative	lugal-da	"with the king"
Equative	lugal/uru-gin	"like a/the king/city"
Ablative/Instrumental	uru-ta, tukul-ta	"from the city," "by means of a/ the weapon"
Allative	uru-še	"to/towards the city"
Inessive	uru-a	"in the city" ("for the city")
Terminative	uru-e	"next to the city"

The sole dedicated nominal plural marker (-ene) was restricted to animates. Plurality of both animate and inanimate nouns could be signaled by reduplication of a following adjective; even more restricted was the reduplication of the noun itself to mark plurality:

lugal-ene, "kings"
lugal gal-gal-e, "great kings (erg.)"
uru gal-gal, "great cities"
lugal-lugal, "(all?) kings"

Sumerian had a relatively rich inventory of adjectives but no regular morphological means for signaling comparative and superlative degrees. These regularly followed nouns (for example, *uru kug* "sacred/sanctified city"), but a small number of them could be preposed in poetic contexts (*kug inana* "sacred goddess Inana").

Few Sumerian adverbs are attested. These could be formed from nominal, adjectival, pronominal or verbal bases, most commonly with a suffix -*bi*, originally probably an inanimate deictic, added to adjectival roots, e.g. *gal-bi* "greatly." Another derivational morpheme -*eš* formed adverbs out of nouns and adverbs, e.g. *ud-eš* "daily," *gal-eš* "greatly"; sometimes, mostly in later texts, the two could be combined, e.g., *gal-bi-eš*, "greatly."

Verbs were either simple or complex, consisting of a noun that was most often marked as absolutive (often a body part) and an inflected verb. Sumerian had a complex agglutinative verbal morphology with five prefix and four suffix slots (the parsing of these morphemes differs from author to author). The prefixes marked mood, conjunction, inner aspect or voice (the matter is debated), multiple applicatives and main argument indexing. The applicatives included benefactive, comitative and locational/instrumental, and these could be utilized for several purposes (e.g. comitative and locative prefixes could be used to mark causatives). The suffixes marked aspect, main argument affixing and future tense for imperfectives. The verb (and the whole clause) could be followed by a nominalizer/subordinator/complementizer that turned a verb (phrase) into a noun (phrase). There were two aspects, perfective and imperfective. Most verbs marked the imperfective with a suffix on the root; a smaller class by means of stem reduplication; and a handful utilized supplicative stems sensitive to aspect, number and sometimes gender.

1.2.3 External affiliations

As observed by Parpola (2010: 181), soon after Sumerian was first identified as a language in 1853, attempts were made to link it with known languages, including Turkish, Finnish, Hungarian, Basque, Chinese, Tibetan and many more. Since then, efforts have been made to connect Sumerian with every major Eurasian language family with no apparent success. Most of these were written by people who have not studied Sumerian in depth, who have used out of date sources for their data and who have often taken conventionalized modern transcriptions of Sumerian words as phonologically precise. What follows is a selective listing of more recent attempts at linking Sumerian with other languages and language families.

In the middle of the last century, scholars proposed that Sumerian speakers were preceded in southern Mesopotamian by a population that spoke another language or languages, named by some as Euphratic, but as Rubio (1999) has shown, most of their examples can be explained as borrowings from Semitic and other languages. This conforms well to the idea that during the fourth millennium BCE Sumerian was one of a number of languages spoken in southern Mesopotamia (Komoróczy 1978). Høyrup (1992) took a different tack, attempting to explain Sumerian as a creole spoken by the early bureaucrats and scribes. Still different is Whittaker's proposal, explained in a number of studies, that early Sumerian was subject to interference from an early Indo-European "Euphratic" superstrate (e.g. Whittaker 2008, 2012, with earlier references).

Proponents of the Nostratic hypothesis have been uncertain about the relationship between Sumerian and this putative macrofamily. For example, Bomhard and Kerns (1994) loosely connected Sumerian with what they called Elamo-Dravidian and included them in Nostratic, albeit with reservations, but Bomhard (1997, 2008: 264, 2015: 316) now views Sumerian as only distantly related to this larger grouping. Quite differently, Sathasivam (1965, 1969) and Fane (1980) have argued that Sumerian was a Dravidian language, while others have proposed that it was Kartvelian (Trombetti 1902, Fähnrich 1981) or Austronesian (Diakonoff 1997, 1999, but see the criticism of Akulov 2016).

Komoróczy (1976a and b) has described the countless attempts, mostly by amateurs, to associate Sumerian with Hungarian, often driven by nationalistic and political motives; such attempts continue to this day as exemplified by a recent study purporting to identify the old Mesopotamian language as the ancestor of Etruscan, Turkish, Mongolian and Hungarian (Tóth 2007). Braun (2001, 2004) has revived an old idea (Ball 1913, 1918), hypothesizing that Sumerian was a member of the Tibeto-Burman family, although most of his examples come from Tibetan. The most recent comparative project – and one of the few initiated by someone who knows the language – belongs to Simo Parpola (2010, 2012), who has revived the longstanding hypothesis that Sumerian belonged to the Uralic family.

1.3 Kassite

The word that we render as "Kassite" referred to an ethnic group, in Babylonian terms, as well to the language associated with these people (Brinkman 1976–1980, Sassmannshausen

1999, Zadok 2015). The modern term derives from the Akkadian ethnicon *kaššû*, which is thought to have been an adaptation of Kassite *galdu*, or the like. There is no trace of anyone named thus or bearing an identifiable Kassite personal name before ca. 1800 BCE, when they first appear in northern Babylonia and towards the west, settling in rural areas and fortresses. People referred to as Kassites then begin to appear in Babylonian texts, usually as hostiles living in groups referred to as "houses" associated with eponymous ancestors or totemic names (e.g., the place name *Bīt-Hašmar* "House of Falcon," Beaulieu 1988; the word *bītu* is Babylonian). As Babylonia descended into chaos during the late seventeenth century, some of these groups established local power centers. In the wake of a political vacuum after a Hittite army raided Babylon in 1595 BCE, one such Kassite group was able to take the throne of the city. This Kassite royal family would rule the land until ca. 1155, and even after that, Kassite officials were prominent in some parts of the polity until the eighth century, and some of the "houses" continued to serve as administrative units (Brinkman 1976–1980: 466). They appear sporadically in texts until the end of the Assyrian empire ca. 612 BCE. Classical writers described a warlike group/people named Cossaei (and variants) in western Iran, but it is only speculation that this had anything to do with the earlier Kassites.

The members of the Kassite dynasty – the longest such reign in Babylonian history – may have carried Kassite names, but like so many foreign ruling families in the area, they quickly took on local identities. Contemporary writings, be they epistolary, inscriptional, administrative or literary, bear no traces of any new Kassite influence, although a few Kassite gods were added to the pantheon. As noted by Brinkman (1976–1980: 467), "there is no obvious trace of either a Kassite ruling caste of officials or even of a disproportionately large Kassite population within Babylonia." Unlike the rulers, many people identified as Kassites in administrative texts bore Babylonian names, even if their fathers and grandfathers had Kassite names.

Where the Kassites came from before they appeared in Babylonia is unknown. After the twelfth century BCE, they are primarily attested in the eastern highlands (Reade 1978). This, and their mastery of equid breeding and handling, suggests an origin in the eastern mountains, but that is only speculation.

1.3.1 Kassite language

There is not a single text written in Kassite. The language is known to us from a) personal and geographical names, b) loanwords in Babylonian, c) entries in Babylonian vocabularies explained as "Kassite" and d) two Babylonian lists of Kassite words. The personal names were short sentences, usually a verb and noun or two nouns, sometimes a noun and an adjective. Unfortunately, it is not always easy to identify such names as specifically Kassite (Zadok 1987: 16–20). The loanwords in Babylonian (Streck 2011: 375–376) were often connected with equid breeding, mostly involving terms for colors and other characteristics of horses, possibly of other equids as well, with chariotry and more rarely with irrigation, but also included some plant names and various sundry words. Entries in wordlists include plant and divine names. Kassite personal names are listed in Hölscher (1996: 277–278). The groundwork on Kassite, which still remains the main source of information on the language, was laid down by Balkan (1954). For subsequent reinterpretations, see Jaritz (1957), Ancillotti (1981) and Iosad (2010).

Two Babylonian lists of Kassite words have survived (Balkan 1954: 2–11). The first, known in two Assyrian copies from the eighth century BCE, contains personal names, including names of Mesopotamian kings, translated into Babylonian, mainly from Sumerian, but also including nineteen Kassite names. The second is a unique first-millennium glossary from Babylonia of 48 words, 16 of which are divine names, translated into Akkadian (Balkan 1954: 2–3, Brinkman 1977). The date of the original composition of these texts is difficult to establish, and there are discrepancies between them concerning the rendition of certain words, but the glossary seems to be the more reliable source (Balkan 1954: 4–11, Brinkman 1969: 242).

1.3.1.1 Phonology and morphology

For obvious reasons, we know very little about Kassite grammar. The phonological inventory, as filtered through the cuneiform script, looks very much like what is reconstructed for Hattic (see below), in Balkan's (1954) view, at least. Balkan additionally proposed that Kassite had a nasal that he represented as /r/, but this has been questioned by Paper (1955: 253). Paper also doubted the feature of voice in stops, noting that voiced stops are rare word-initially and seem to occur after nasals or intervocalically. For a more complex speculative inventory of phonemes, including long vowels and additional consonants, see, e.g., Jaritz (1957), which is highly speculative. Most scholars reconstruct only four vowels (/a/, /u/, /i/, /e/), possibly also /o/ (Ancillotti 1981: 39, also noting that the existence of /e/ is uncertain).

The order of constituents can only be detected in personal names. It is important to observe, however, that the identification of such names as Kassite is often subjective, and some of them may be Hurrian, hypocoristic or misunderstood by ancient scribes, or may simply belong to another unidentified language. Be that as it may, the names seem to indicate that Kassite was a verb-initial language and that it was exclusively or primarily suffixing. It is difficult to establish the status of gender and number in Kassite: it is impossible to detect any distinction between masculine and feminine, or between animate and inanimate for that matter. The only recognizable number morpheme is a plural adjectival morpheme -am (Balkan 1954: 250, van Soldt 1980: 78). Case markers have likewise not been definitely identified. Possessors apparently proceeded possessed, but a genitive marker seems to be lacking (e.g., the royal name Hašmar-galšu, "falcon Kassite" = "Kassite Falcon" (Balkan 1954: 55, 221, Boese 2010: 71 n. 2, Sassmannshausen 2014: 177).

1.3.1.2 External affiliation

Attempts have been made over the years to link Kassite with Indo-European, Elamite, Hattic and most recently to Dravidian by Braun (2009) and Hurro-Urartean by Schneider (2003) and Fournet (2011). An Indo-European connection was strongly argued by Ancillotti (1981), who insisted that it was related to Indian Prakrits. The speculative nature of such projects is evident in view of the paucity of the evidence.

Some Kassite words have been identified as Indo-European, among the divine names Šurijaš, Maruttaš and possibly Buriaš. The first two have been associated with Vedic Sanskrit *sūryaḥ*, "sun, sun god" and Maruts, while some have sought to connect the third with Greek Boreas. The same may hold for certain technical terms such as the Kassite loan in Babylonian *sakrumaš*, a military title, possibly connected with chariotry, that has been associated with Sanskrit *cakrá-* and Avestan *čaxra-*, both meaning "wheel" (Gamkrelidze and Ivanov 1995: 631). This may indicate that at some time certain "Kassites" may have lived in proximity to an early Indo-European speaking population.

1.4 Hattic

The Hattic (Hattian) language is documented in almost 360 texts from the Hittite archives in Hattusha (modern Boghazköy) and Sapinuwa (modern Ortaköy), both in central Turkey. The Hittite polity was a major power in the Near East, ruling most of central and eastern Anatolia, often expanding into parts of Syria. Its archives, totaling more than 30,000 cuneiform tablets in seven languages (Hittite, Luwian, Palaic, Hurrian, Akkadian, Sumerian, Hattic), span a period from ca. 1650–1200 BCE. The majority of texts were written in Indo-European Hittite, which is well understood, and therefore the 15 extant Hattic-Hittite bilingual texts provide important data for the reconstruction of the Hattic language. The rest of the documentation consists of monolingual Hattic texts and of passages in the language embedded in Hittite rituals without translation. The modern name of the language derives from Hittite *hatt-ili*, "in Hattic," with the Hittite comparative and language designation adverbial suffix *-ili*.

Almost all extant Hattic texts or textual passages relate to the cult, and there can be no doubt that early Hittite (Old Kingdom) religion was strongly influenced by Hattic practices: this is evident in the mythology and in the names of deities, many of which were Hattic. It has often been assumed that Hattic was an older language that served as the substrate for Hittite and related languages. Goedegebuure (2008) has argued that it was the other way around: Indo-European Luwian served as a substrate for Hattic within the complex sociolinguistic context of early second millennium BCE Anatolia. It is difficult to know who still spoke Hattic in Hittite times, but it is possible that the language was still alive as late as the fourteenth century BCE. For descriptions of the grammar, see Diakonoff (1967b), Kammenhuber (1969), Dunajevskaja and Diakonoff (1979), Girbal (1986), Soysal (2004), Klinger (2005), Kassian (2010), and the succinct description by Goedegebuure (2013).

1.4.1 Some typological features

There is still much disagreement on some of the basic structural properties of Hattic and on the forms and meanings of various morphological features and about its vocabulary (less than 200 words are known). Like some other ancient Near Eastern languages, it was agglutinative, but uncharacteristic for the area were the V(S)O basic word order for transitive clauses and the predominance of prefixing morphology. The issue of basic word order in Hattic is actually somewhat complex: while VSO order was the norm in mid-text transitive clauses, text-initial transitive clauses were always SOV, and intransitive clauses generally followed SV order (Goedegebuure 2008: 157). Adjectives preceded nouns, possessors preceded possessed and the latter were marked; subordinate clauses preceded main ones. According to Goedegebuure (2008: 157–159), Hattic was both a head and dependent marking language. There have been various interpretations of the basic alignment strategies of Hattic. Some scholars (e.g., Dunajevskaja and Diakonoff 1979, Taracha 1995: 354, 1998: 15, Braun 1994: 16, Chirikba 1996: 407, Braun and Taracha 2007: 196) were convinced that it was ergative. Kammenhuber (1969: 502), followed by others, wrote about nominative and accusative alignment. Most recently, Goedegebuure (2010: 978) concluded, in the context of a thorough analysis of verbal indexing morphology, that Hattic was "an active, or semantically aligned language with an ergative base" that moved more towards ergative alignment in middle Hittite times (fourteenth century).

1.4.2 Phonology

Information on Hattic phonology must be retrieved from the simplified syllabic/logographic system of Babylonian cuneiform adopted by the Hittites and which may not have had the resources to represent the full phonological inventory of Hattic. Moreover, it is apparent that Hittite scribes who copied or wrote down Hattic passages often had problems with the representation of the language in writing, as evidenced by much variation in the writing of the same words. The minimal inventory, as reconstructed by Soysal (2004: 70), is shown in Table 2.7 and Table 2.8, although some would recognize vowel length in Hattic.

Dunajevskaja and Diakonoff (1979) also recognized the existence of glides (/w/, /j/) and possibly /c/; Kassian (2010: 312–313) would add the affricates /ts/ and /č/, or an interdental fricative /θ/; rather than /ḫ/, he and others suggest a velar/uvular spirant /h/.

1.4.3 Morphology

Hattic had two genders, masculine and feminine, as well as two numbers, singular and plural. As already noted, the language was almost exclusively prefixing. Nouns had at least five prefix slots and one for case suffixes (nominative, accusative, genitive, dative and locative, although there are disagreements about the actual morphology). Verbal roots carried prefixes and one or two suffix slots. Soysal (2004: 189), for example, reconstructed six slots before the root, marking person, number, various spatial categories and main argument indexing, as well as one suffix slot, containing tense or modal morphs, which could also be followed by clitic particles such as the conjunctive. The imperative consisted of the stem followed by -a, as in miš-a "take," but could also take locative prefixes. There is no consensus on the number of morphological slots or on the meaning of all morphemes. For an example of such differing opinions, see the review of Soysal (2004) by Braun and Taracha (2007) or compare the charts of infixes in Dunajevskaja (1959: 26) and Soysal (2004: 189).

Nominal possession was marked by the case ending -(V)n. Most occurrences of nominal possession resemble left-dislocated, topicalized constructions in other languages, e.g.,

TABLE 2.7 HATTIC VOWELS

i		u
(e)		
	a	

TABLE 2.8 HATTIC CONSONANTS

p	t			k
(b)	d			(g)
	s	š		ḫ
	z			
		r	l	
		m	n	

TABLE 2.9 ELAMITE CONSONANTS

	Plosives		Fricatives		Affr.	Sonantes		
	Fortis	Lenis	Fortis	Lenis		Lat.	Tril	Nasal
Labiale	p	P' (b)	f or v					m, m'(?)
Dentale	t	t'(d)						n, n'(?)
Vélaire	k	k' (g)						
Palato-Alvéolaire			š		č			
Alvéolaire			s	s' (z)	ts	l	r	
Laryngale			(h)					
Latérale								
Rétroflexe						ll	rr	

Source: Tavernier 2011: 320.

tabarna-n le-wuur, "king-OBL PRO-land," "of the king, his land=king's land." Nouns were apparently not flagged for subject and object, but these were indexed in the verb.

1.4.4 External affiliation

For a language that is not well documented, Hattic has been the subject to an impressive number of attempts to link it with various linguistic groups. Already in the 1920s, soon after it had been identified as a separate language within the Hittite archives, attempts were made to identify it as Caucasian and, in more recent times, most often as West Caucasian (e.g., Diakonoff 1967b: 170–176, see Klinger 1994: 24–26, Chirikba 1996) and less often as Kartvelian (see Taracha 2000: 233 and Kassian 2009: 316, 321 for references). Kassian (2009) has proposed that Hattic constituted a separate branch of the putative Sino-Caucasian or Dene-Sino-Caucasian macrofamily.

1.5 Elamite

Elamite was a language of southwestern Iran, attested in writing from ca. 2200 to 300 BCE, in administrative texts, building and dedicatory inscriptions, a diplomatic treaty, personal names, items marked as Elamite in wordlists and a few loanwords in Mesopotamian writings. The geographical range of spoken Elamite is difficult to establish based on the written record and undoubtedly changed over time, but may have encompassed the area delimited as Fars, Khuzestan and southern Luristan in modern Iran. The documentation is discontinuous and is documented in relatively limited registers, known mainly from administrative texts and royal inscriptions, but also from a handful of entries in Meso-potamian wordlists and from personal names in Mesopotamian documents (Zadok 1987: 1–16). Traditionally, the language has been divided into four phases: Old Elamite (OE, a treaty from ca. 2200, a somewhat later text from southern Mesopotamia, and then two economic texts from Iran and a handful of magical charms from Mesopotamia from ca. 1800 BCE, and a few, mostly unpublished, royal inscriptions); Middle Elamite (ME, ca. 1500–1000 BCE, approximately 175 royal building and dedicatory inscriptions, mainly from Susa and Choga Zanbil, but also from other sites, administrative and legal texts from Susa and Anshan); Neo-Elamite (mainly seventh/sixth centuries BCE, royal inscriptions, 25 fragmentary letters from Nineveh, a few from Susa and one from Armavir Blur in Armenia, as well as some scattered unprovenanced ones, ca. 300 early sixth-century administrative texts, an omen text and a hemerological [favorable and unfavorable days for activities] text from Susa, some seal inscriptions); and Achaemenid Elamite (AE, 539–300 BCE, administrative texts, Elamite versions of mainly multilingual royal inscriptions).

The latest phase is the best attested, documented by royal inscriptions, some of them multilingual, and by large administrative archives. Such archives, written in a number of languages, but mainly in Elamite, were probably kept in many places at the time. They are known today from two large collections from Persepolis (Stolper 2014) and from a single tablet from Susa and one or two fragments from Kandahar, in Afghanistan (Fisher and Stolper 2015), demonstrating that the use of written Elamite extended over an enormous territory but apparently only for administrative purposes. There are many differences between the linguistic remains from these periods, with particular changes observable in AE, some of them attributable to language interference from Old Persian. Apparently, most of the administrative scribes were Iranophone who had learned Elamite with various degrees of accuracy; as a result AE acquired not just Iranian loanwords but also important contact induced morpho-syntactic calques and other forms of restructuring (Henkelman 2011).

There are disparate and conflicting opinions on many aspects of Elamite grammar that cannot be easily summarized here. The more comprehensive studies of the language include Diakonoff (1967a), Reiner (1969), Grillot-Susini and Roche (1987), Khačikjan (1998, 2010), Stolper (2008), Krebernik (2006), Tavernier (2011) and Bavant (2014: 235–336). For the Elamite lexicon, see Hinz and Koch (1987) and Zadok (1984, 1995).

1.5.1 Phonology

The language was written with a syllabic version of Mesopotamian cuneiform script and therefore the phonology at first glance very much resembles what is found in Akkadian, but this, once again, is probably an illusion founded on phonetic underrepresentation in the script. The only full study of the subject is found in Paper's (1955) analysis of AE, often referenced with some minor additions or subtractions. There are differing opinions on the nature of Elamite stops, as already noted by Labat (1951: 28). Paper recognized only voiceless /p/, /t/, /k/; Reiner (1969: 111–115) observed that spelling conventions indicated some distinction between two series of stops, possibly a tense/lax opposition, perhaps realized intervocalically as voiced/voiceless. Tavernier (2002, 131–138, 2011: 320) built on this analysis. He agreed that Elamite had no voiced stops but recognized a tense/lax (*fortis/lentis*) distinction, expressed in writing by reduplication of consonants, reconstructing /p'/, /t'/, /k'/ rather than /b/, /d/, /g/ and /s'/ rather than /z/, but also raising the possibility of tense /m'/ and /n'/, following Reiner and Khačikjan, but this is doubtful. He also recognized the existence of an alveolar affricate /ts/ and palato-alveolar affricate /č/ and retroflex sonorants /ll/ and /rr/. See also Stolper (2008: 58–59), who provides this inventory of consonants, observing that the status of possible glides, a vocalic /r/, the true phonetic nature of /h/ (which is lost in AE), etc. are not clear at present.

It is generally agreed that Elamite had four vowels, /a/, /e/, /i/ and /u/, no diphthongs and that vowel length was not phonemic. Tavernier (2011: 320) posited the nasalization of vowels and also the possibility of an additional vowel /ə/.

1.5.2 Morphology

Elamite morphology was agglutinative. There were two genders, animate and inanimate, and two numbers, singular and plural. Most words consisted of one or two syllables (CV, VC, VCV, CVCV), with only a very small number of CVCCV lexemes (Tavernier 2011: 320). Basic word order was verb final; SOV, in the earlier phases, but more flexible in AE. Nouns were not marked for case but could be followed by locational particles or clitics (it is often difficult to determine word boundary), but pronouns were signaled with suffixes that separately marked subject/indirect object and transitive object. Adjectives followed nouns. The morphology was exclusively suffixing, and it was postpositional, although there was a preposition *kuš*, "to(ward), until," in ME and AE (Stolper 2008: 71).

Because of the lack of direct marking of arguments, there are conflicting opinions on the basic typological description of alignment. Diakonoff (1967a: 99), and others claimed it was ergative, but this has been strongly critiqued by Wilhelm (1978, 1982). According to Khačikjan (1998: 65), it was an accusative language with traces of ergative features.

Elamite had a series of suffixes that were attached to nominals (including numerals), nominalized verbal forms, pronouns, and even an independent negative particle; entire phrases could be nominalized ("grain for women-who-have-been-sent-hither-from-Susa"). These suffixes have been the subject of much debate and have been described as class, or as gender/person/number suffixes (Reiner 1969: 77, Stolper 2008: 60, Tavernier 2011: 321–322); the animate distinguished three persons and two numbers, but there was only one person (most likely only third) in the inanimate, which was not marked for number (the terminology was introduced by Reiner 1969: 77):

1st s locutive (speaker)	*-k*
2nd s allocutive (addresses)	*-t*
3rd s animate delocutive (person/thing spoken about)	*-r*
pl "	*-p*
3rd inanimate delocutive	*-me (-n/-0/-t)*

The second person is attested only with certain verbal forms, never with nouns; indeed, there are clear examples in which the animate third person delocutive was used for second person address. The variants of the inanimate are somewhat problematical; *-n* may simply be an allomorph of *-me*, and *-t* may have been an older collective marker (W. Henkelman, personal communication). A bewildering array of functions has been ascribed to these suffixes: possessive, appositive, derivational, syntactic agreement, etc. Thus, for example, with *sunki* "king," the forms are: *sunki-k* "I, the king," *sunki-r* "he, the king," *sunki-p* "they, the kings," but *sunki-me* "kingship, kingdom." Bavant (2014: 249, 314), who has thoroughly analyzed these suffixes, confirms only an attributive possessive function, as in e.g.:

siyan pinikir-me
temple Pinigir-SUFF
"temple of (divine) Pinigir"

taki-me u-me
life-3.IN I-SUFF
"my life"

menik hatamti-k
ruler Elam-SUFF
"(I) ruler of Elam"

menik hatamti-r
ruler Elam-SUFF
"ruler of Elam"

napip hatamti-p
gods Elam-SUFF
"the gods of Elam"

In this reconstruction, *-me* was used when the possessed was inanimate; *-k*, when it was the speaker; *-r*, when it was an animate noun different from the speaker; and *-p*, when it was a plural animate (Bavant 2014: 314). The derivational function of some of these markers would follow from the possessive function, e.g. *hatamti-r*, "of Elam" = "Elamite." Moreover, because these class morphemes were used with adjectives, Elamite was a language in which adjectives were essentially denominal, e.g. *napi-r riša-r*, "god-SUFF great-SUFF" = "great god" (Tavernier 2011: 323). The fact remains that these suffixes were used to mark a variety of attributive relations: adjectival, dative, locative, etc.

Possession in Elamite took many forms and in some cases may have distinguished alienable versus inalienable possession, as described by Bavant (2014: 303). There were two series of possessive suffixes (Tavernier 2011: 325–326). In NE and AE, there was a suffix *-na* that is generally described as a genitive, but may have been a composite of *n* + relative *a*, that replaced the entire suffix system, hence a sign of reduction of syntactical complexity under Iranian influence (W. Henkelman, personal communication). Elamite verb forms made a distinction between perfective and imperfective aspects as well as distinguishing indicative, imperative, prohibitive and optative moods.

1.5.3 External affiliation

Some of the first attempts at classifying Elamite linked it with certain Caucasian families (e.g., Bleichsteiner 1928 with earlier literature). Moreover, already in the nineteenth century, attempts were made to connect Elamite with Dravidian, reinvigorated in modern times by Diakonoff (1967a: 108–112) and most prominently by McAlpin (1974, 1975, 1981, 2003, 2015), and lately by Southworth (2011). Blažek (2002) suggested that Elamite belonged to the Afroasiatic family. Both proposals have been criticized by Starostin (2002), who preferred to classify the language as a "bridge" between putative Nostratic and Afroasiatic (his terminology).

2 UNCLASSIFIED ANCIENT NEAR EASTERN LANGUAGES

A number of ancient Near Eastern languages can best be described as unclassified in that they "lack sufficient data for them to be compared meaningfully with other languages [and] therefore their possible kinship remains unknown" (Campbell, this volume p. 4). Some involve undeciphered or undecipherable early scripts, such as the early writings from Iran. Then there are examples like the highland Iranian Guti(um) and Lullubi, ethno-political labels that shifted over time, or the language of Marhashi, further southeast in Iran, that are known only as labels and exemplified only by personal names.

A poet had the Mesopotamian King Shulgi of Ur (Rubio 2006) claim to speak at least four languages, among them Sumerian, Elamite and the language of the "Black Land," which is generally assumed to refer to Marhashi and a later text mentions a "Marhashian translator," but the few personal names of people designated as coming from there seem to be Elamite, Akkadian, Hurrian, or unclassifiable (Glassner 2005), and this tells us nothing about the language(s) of Marhashi, now thought to be in the general area of Jiroft in the Kerman province of southeastern Iran (Steinkeller 2006, 2014, see Section 2.3).

The consequences of such ambiguity are perhaps best illustrated by the case of the Kashka "people" or language. Hittite sources from the second millennium BCE mention a group or polity labeled as Kashka, who occupied the northern frontier in north-central Anatolia (Singer 2007). A study of the ethnogenesis of the Kashka shows that, while they had their own political and military role to play, they were not otherwise distinct from the Hittites, and there is no convincing evidence for a separate Kashka language (Gerçek 2012: 55–56). Singer (2007) argued that they were essentially Hattians.

Mesopotamian documents as well as historical and literary texts include words that referred to human groups in a manner that may be roughly described as ethno-linguistic. They also preserve an enormous number of personal names in a variety of languages, many of which cannot be ascribed to any known tongue. Moreover, persons from other lands sometimes took on Sumerian or Babylonian names, and in certain times and places, visitors have been registered in Mesopotamian documents using local appellations rather than their original native names. Terms used for geographical areas did not necessarily describe languages, so that even mentions of translators for people of a certain area did not necessarily define separate languages. It is also important to keep in mind that people in the ancient world often wrote in languages that were not their mother tongues and that the practical use of writing was often linked with issues of prestige, power and display.

2.1 Proto-Cuneiform

The earliest notational system of Western Asia that is considered, by some scholars at least, as writing was proto-cuneiform, known from more than 6,000 clay tablets from southern Mesopotamia, most of them from the metropolis of Uruk, dating to ca. 3350–3000 BCE (Englund 1998, Woods 2010). The script was invented towards the end of a period of rapid multifarious economic expansion reflected in massive urban growth in Uruk itself, which had expanded to an area of ca. 250 hectares and may have housed between 25,000 and 50,000 inhabitants (Algaze 2012, Nissen 2016). All the Uruk tablets were discovered in trash deposits and fill associated with majestic architectural remains in the very heart of the city in an area later occupied by temples and named Eanna. Thus, the tablets have no precise functional provenienve. This complex script was developed solely for the recording of economic transactions and used a fluctuating number of signs, 600 in its earliest documented phase, at some points numbering more than 900. Meaning was conveyed through signs standing for specific goods, for semantic classifiers, accounting activities, as well as complex numerical and metrological signs, but also through use of distinct tablet shapes and sizes as well as rulings and divisions used to format the tablets. The signs were made with a reed stylus on clay tablets. During the earliest documented phase, labeled Uruk IV, the signs were curvilinear, drawn on the tablets with multiple stokes, but in the later Uruk III stage the contours became straight as each line was impressed with a limited repertoire of strokes using a differently designed reed stylus, leading to more abstract stylized representations, and this was the writing technique that would be used for cuneiform for millennia, down to the first centuries of the Common Era (the Roman numbers are used to designate archaeological levels in the Eanna district). The second phase is also characterized by an increased number of goods and transaction types as well as new information such as time notation, but also by more complex organization of information on tablets. The fact that the Uruk III documents registered more data and more complex information loads may be due to changes in administration, internal developments of the registration system or both. The distinction between earlier and later text groups is not stratigraphic but epigraphic because the discarded tablets were not associated with any archaeological levels. To date, Uruk IV type tablets have not been discovered outside of the city, but during later phases, the use of proto-cuneiform is documented from at least seven cities from both southern and northern Babylonia.

The earlier history of the script is unknown. Some of the sign shapes and numerical concepts were influenced by or even borrowed from earlier accounting techniques such as small clay tokens or tablets with purely numerical signs, but proto-cuneiform as a complex system was undoubtedly a novel invention. Among the 600 signs of the earlier tablet group, more than half of the signs were either combinations or graphically altered versions of simple signs. Among the simple signs, 98 were totally abstract and 114 were naturalistic drawings, such as a picture of a head or a boat, or somewhat abstracted versions of such depictions (Nissen 2016: 44). Therefore, while pictography played an important role in the creation of proto-cuneiform, it cannot be classified as a pictographic system.

This bookkeeping system was used to register movement of various dry goods such as grain, flour, bread, dried fruits, beer, oils, textiles, as well as animals and their products, rationing and organization of laborers and/or slaves etc. Distinctions were made between kinds of animals and humans, marking various terminological categories such as age or gender.

A small percentage of proto-cuneiform tablets consists of multiple copies of standardized lists of words of various classes such as names of professions, of metals or of types of pottery that were used to teach the writing system to prospective scribes; while most of these were already in use during the earlier phase, most of the extant manuscripts date from Uruk III times. In essence, this system, which was devised only for bookkeeping, consisted of things and ways of counting them, with rudimentary notations concerning the actors and activities involved and did not encode any morphological information. Some signs or sign combinations were used to convey personal names, but these have proven difficult to analyze. Many of the proto-cuneiform symbols resemble later cuneiform word signs that can be read in Sumerian or Akkadian, and therefore it is possible to understand the recorded transactions without recourse to any specific language.

Thus, to a large degree proto-cuneiform was an autonomous semiotic system based on and parallel to natural language and therefore cannot be classified as a writing system in the narrow sense of the term. One schooling composition may have been an attempt to record the outlines of a story, but it did so without any overt notation of morphological information (Civil 2013). Most of the signs can be defined as logograms, with very limited recourse to phonetic values used almost exclusively as phonetic complements (Woods 2010: 43). There are conflicting opinions on the language that may have been associated with the documents and wordlists. Because of certain gloss-like phonetic elements, many Sumerologists assume that it was Sumerian (e.g. Rubio 2005, Wilcke 2005), but Englund (2008: 81, 2009: 7–27), who has worked on this material more than anyone else, has been agnostic on the matter but has also insisted on occasion that there are no traces of the Sumerian language in any Mesopotamian inscriptional material prior to the so-called Archaic Texts from the city of Ur that are approximately one or two centuries younger than the last proto-cuneiform tablets.

2.2 Proto-Elamite

The late fourth millennium BCE Proto-Elamite tablets evidence the earliest writing in Iran, although simpler commodity-recording devices were used there prior to the invention of this script. More than 1,700 Proto-Elamite clay tablets have been discovered from 8 sites, spanning most of the Iranian plateau, from Susa in the west to a single tablet from Shahr-e Sokhta in the east, all but approximately 200 from Susa (Desset 2016: 69), with a distribution over a much larger area than Proto-Sumerian script ever achieved. The script remains undeciphered.

The known tablets recorded economic activities using 17 numerical and approximately 1,400 (or 1,900, depending on interpretation) non-numerical signs drawn with a stylus on clay tablets dating from the end of the fourth and the very beginning of the third millennium BCE (Dahl 2009, 2013). It is generally recognized that initially, at least, the inventors of Proto-Elamite were influenced by fourth millennium Mesopotamian proto-cuneiform and even borrowed specific signs (including the numerical ones) from the older system or from some common source. Desset (2016: 90) suggested that the beginnings of Proto-Cuneiform and Proto-Elamite were roughly contemporary, but Pittman (2013: 328–329) has persuasively argued on stratigraphic, iconographic and other grounds that the earliest examples of an early phase of Proto-Elamite writing were discovered in contexts that are later than the time of the first Uruk tablets.

With the possible exceptions of two mathematical exercises, all the known Proto-Elamite texts recorded complex bookkeeping activities and included headings and subscripts as well as commodities (foodstuffs, animals, types of workers, tools etc.), followed by numerical signs, and the context appears to be restricted to agricultural production, labor and animal management (Dahl 2013: 252). A small group of signs may have designated proper names (owners, geographical names, professional designations etc.) using syllabic signs (Dahl 2005), but it is difficult to ascertain the levels of linguistic encoding in Proto-Elamite, and it is impossible to know what language or languages may have been involved, as is the case with contemporary proto-cuneiform. The modern name is a misapprehension: it was coined in conjunction with the geographical term Elam, originally in the labeling of archaeological strata in the city of Susa, without any linguistic connotation and no links have been established between recordings in Proto-Elamite script and the Elamite language. In addition to the scholarly resources cited here, see now the detailed survey by Desset (2012: 3–92).

2.3 Linear Elamite and related tablets

There is yet another undeciphered Iranian script, conventionally designated as Linear Elamite, that was used in parts of Iran towards the end of the third millennium and the beginning of the second millennium BCE (Desset 2012: 93–128). The exact number of examples of this script is sometimes disputed: some may be forgeries and others may belong to different writing systems or represent owner marks or even ornamental patterns. Of the approximately 30 known Linear Elamite texts, 18 monumental exemplars were discovered in the city of Susa, in southwestern Iran (Dahl 2009: 26–31, 2013: 257–260), 1 on a pot from a grave in Shadad in eastern Iran, and possibly 3 or 4 in southeastern Iranian Konar Sandal. Moreover, currently ascribed to this script are texts on an unprovenienced seal in a style imitating Harappan design with a few Linear Elamite signs, a silver vase reportedly found close to Persepolis, and eight unprovenienced metal objects of dubious authenticity. Because of differences in the repertoire and form of signs in some texts, it is difficult to establish the levels of synchronic and/or diachronic variation within the system.

Ten of the eighteen monumental texts from Susa can be attributed to the reign of King Puzur-Inshushinak, who ruled in Susa ca. 2150 BCE (André and Salvini 1989). Almost half are closely related pseudo-duplicates of a royal inscription of some kind, two of which are accompanied by perfectly understandable Akkadian inscriptions, but this has proven to be of little help, and Linear Elamite remains undeciphered. Even though this was a time when Elamite was presumably spoken in Susa, there are no clues to identify the language of these inscriptions and it is possible that the Linear Elamite could have been used for different languages in places such as Shadad or Konal Sandal.

Nevertheless, most attempts at deciphering Linear Elamite have identified the underlying language as Elamite. Desset (2012: 104–127, with description of earlier attempts at decipherment) has recently proposed, more narrowly, that the Puzur-Inshushinak inscriptions, at least, were written in a form that language, but seemingly does not exclude the possibility that some of the other Linear Elamite inscriptions might be in Elamite as well. The fact that so many of the Susa texts were associated with the reign of this king has led many scholars to assume that Linear Elamite was used for a very short time, perhaps even limited to the reign of one ruler. Some recent work suggests that only a few generations of scribes were involved (Dahl, Petrie and Potts 2013: 375), but Desset (Desset 2012: 98, 2016: 93–95) argued that the script was in use for several centuries, from ca. 2500 to ca. 1900 BCE if the somewhat problematical Konar Sandal texts are taken into consideration.

The total inventory of signs in Linear Elamite numbered between 61 to over 200, depending on how one counts them, suggesting a syllabary mixed with logograms (Moqaddam 2009: 55–56, Desset 2012: 99–100). Dahl (2009: 30) has suggested that the non-display texts, which often have very different glyphs and patterns, were a form of pseudo-writing, mimicking a script that could no longer be understood for various cultural reasons.

The Linear Elamite enigma has become even more complicated with the discovery of four inscribed clay tablets in Konar Sandal South (Moqaddam 2009, Madjidzadeh 2011, Desset 2014), in the southeastern part of Iran that the Mesopotamians designated as Marhashi (Steinkeller 2006, 2014). The tablets, dating from the second half of the third millennium BCE, seem to contain at least two different scripts, although it must be noted that the circumstances of their discovery have prompted some skepticism, not all of which has dissipated (Lawler 2007; for a more precise description of the circumstances and context of their discovery, see Madjidzadeh 2011: 236–241). Two of them are covered on the obverse with Linear Elamite, with a small number of symbols in another system, described as "geometric," on the reverse. A third tablet is also covered with Linear Elamite on the obverse, but with a line of "geometric" symbols at the end. The fourth tablet is only a fragment with only remnants of six symbols remaining and while these might be Linear Elamite, it is also possible that it only contains ornamental designs. If these two sets of designs were in fact writing, then at least two different systems, and perhaps two different languages were involved.

In addition, objects with a few designs that have been identified as Proto-Elamite have been found in Gonur Tepe in Turkmenistan (a potsherd with two incised designs, Klochkov 1999) and at the site of Ra'as al-Junays in Oman (two stamp seals, a seashell ring; Glassner 1999: 137–140, 2002: 363–368). It is highly doubtful that these designs are in any way related to Proto-Elamite writing (Desset 2012: 94 n 4).

2.4 Gutian

People described as Guti/Gutium first make an appearance in Mesopotamian texts from ca. 2200 BCE during a time of weakening central control and appear sporadically in texts into the late first millennium BCE (Foster 2013). Some documents mention the names of kings of Gutium who presumably held some form of hegemony over local rulers in certain cities. The longest lists of such names are found in a literary text known as *The Sumerian King List* that describes, often in fictional terms, the kings of cities that held hegemony over Mesopotamia in early periods. The earliest known manuscript, from ca. 2100 BCE (Steinkeller 2003), refers to this as a time when a horde, or army (Akkadian *ummānum*) ruled the land. Only six names of such rulers are preserved before a break, two of which are probably Akkadian, and only three have some resemblance to those enumerated in eighteenth-century manuscripts, which refer to this period as the time of the "troops/horde of the land of *Gu-tu-um*," but even in these, no two versions have the same list of rulers in the same order (Michalowski 1983: 247–248). There are also names of persons, mostly from the Zagros Mountains to the east that some have identified as Gutian, although only rarely labeled as such in texts.

It is impossible to know if all these names belonged to one language, how many of them were garbled and which may have been invented in antiquity. Nevertheless, Henning (1978) and Gamkrelidze and Ivanov (1989, 1995: 786–787 n. 30, 2013: 119–120) have proposed links between Gutian and the Tocharian branch of Indo-European, known from sixth to eighth century AD texts found in the Tarim Basin in China, but much of this spurious (Zadok 1987: 21).

2.5 Lullubean

Much the same can be said about groups such as the Lullubi or Lul(l)u, who are first documented in the western Zagros Mountains in the general area around Suleimaniyah, in present-day Kurdistan, but also moved into northern Mesopotamia, between the Syrian Jebel Sinjar and Tur Abdin ranges in the second millennium BCE (Eidem 1992: 50–54, Schrakamp 2013) but were still attested in the Zagros during the first millennium BCE (Zadok 2005). The language of these groups – and it is unlikely that they were linguistically homogeneous – is once again known only from a small number of personal names (some of which are Mesopotamian) and an entry in a late Assyrians wordlist claims that their word for "god" was *kiurum*, or the like (Zadok 2005). The terms Guti (Quti) and Lullu were sometimes used in Mesopotamian writings as general terms for eastern/mountain dwelling/foreign plunderer or barbarian. Indeed, it is possible that the name Lullu(bi) might have been related to Hurrian/Urartean *lul(l)u*, "foreigner" (Rubio 2007b: 103).

2.6 Language(s) of the Harappan civilization

Further east, over 4,000 tablets, seals, sealings, gold ornaments, jewelry, pottery jars, tools, weapons, domestic and architectural items, stone as well as faience and terracotta tablets and bronze bars with symbols have been recovered by archaeologists from large cities in the far-flung Harappan civilization that flourished in the Indus Valley and beyond (A. Parpola 1996). Most these designs were recovered from archeological levels dated to ca. 2600–1900 BCE, and it seemed that the script appeared fully developed during this urban phase of the civilization (Possehl 1990: 273), but more recent excavations (Meadow and Kenoyer 2005) have revealed inscriptions from contexts that go back 200 years or so (Early Indus script), and it is possible that the origins of this symbolic system can be traced even earlier in the city of Harappa (Kenoyer and Meadow 2000: 68, Kenoyer 2006). The use of the script on seals and prestige objects disappears after ca. 1900 but seems to have been used occasionally on pottery in some parts of the civilization. More than a hundred published attempts at decipherment or identification of the putative language of these markings as Indo-European or Dravidian have not borne fruit (for a history of many of these, see LeBlanc 2013). While most scholars argue that the Indus symbols were used to convey some aspect of Indus language (Kenoyer and Meadow 2010: xliv, n. 1), Farmer et al. (2004) and Sproat (2014, 2015) have used statistical methods to argue that the Indus symbols were not used for the registration of natural language. This idea has been met with much resistance by those who believe that the Indus system was used to convey linguistic segments (Vidale 2007, Rao et al. 2010, 2015).

Many Indus script writings consist of a single sign; the average inscription runs to 5 signs, and the longest has 28. Seals provide the largest body of data for study because they were relatively well preserved and contain longer script sequences. However, recent excavations at Harappa have shown that they comprise only around 3% of the total sample of inscribed objects (J. M. Kenoyer, personal communication), with many more inscriptions preserved on incised tablets, molded terracotta tablets and inscribed pottery. The number of discrete signs is disputed, but probably around 400 were in use, many of them compound (A. Parpola 1996: 169–169).

Stamp seals and sealings resembling Harappan types have also been found in western Iran, Mesopotamia and, most important, on the Persian Gulf island of Bahrain, which was an important trade entrepôt in antiquity. There were innovations in the Harappan symbols used on the locally made Gulf Style seals from ca. 2100; Laursen (2010: 130) suggests that acculturated Harappans adjusted their script to accommodate writing in another language.

2.7 The Byblos Syllabary

Excavations in the Syrian coastal town of Byblos between 1928 and 1932 brought to light objects inscribed with an unknown script that has defied decipherment to this day (Dunand 1945: 71–138, 1978). The Byblos finds consisted of 12 inscribed clay tablets, stone fragments and bronze spatulas; subsequently some have proposed that another 8 or more objects with similar writing from Israel, the Sinai, Egypt, Greece and Italy should be added to this corpus (Colless 1998: 29), but this is not generally accepted. Dunand (1945) identified 114 distinct signs in these materials and therefore suggested that the writings found at Byblos were inscribed with a syllabary, which has variously been labeled as the Byblos Syllabary, as the Pseudo-hieroglyphic script or as Proto-Byblian. Others have suggested a slightly smaller repertoire of graphemes, but this does not change the general definition of the script. The dating of the use of this writing system, if indeed all the 20 or so exemplars belong to one and the same syllabary, is not well established, with the objects ascribed to ca. 1700–1400 BCE. Various attempts have been made to decipher Byblos Syllabic, mostly as some form of Semitic, but all of them have been critically received (Daniels 1996). The most comprehensive attempt to decipher these texts as Semitic was presented by Mendenhall (1985), but his methods and results did not convince mainstream scholars (e.g., Hamilton 1987, Izre'el 1988, Moran 1988, S. Kaufman 1989). The script remains undeciphered, and its language or languages remain unidentified.

2.8 Philistine

One other ancient Near Eastern unclassifiable language requires mention here, namely Philistine. The Philistines (*Plšt*) were first mentioned in Egyptian texts from the reign of Ramses III (1186–1155 BCE) as one element of a group of "sea peoples" with whom the Egyptians claimed to have fought a large naval battle and who then appear in various books of the Hebrew Bible (*Pelešet*) as outsiders who settled in southwestern Israel on the Mediterranean coast and created polities that acted as major forces in the area down to the sixth century BCE (Machinist 2000). Philistine ethnic identity was transcultural in origin, resulting from the entanglement of various sub-groups of the "sea peoples" with local populations and underwent dynamic changes once they settled on the Mediterranean coast (Davis, Maeir and Hitchcock 2015, Knapp and Manning 2016), some of whom might have been pirate in origin (Hitchcock and Maeir 2014). Recent excavations at Tell Tayınat in southwestern Turkey (Harrison 2014), probably the central city of a kingdom named P/Walastin or Patin (Weeden 2015), have revealed large amounts of locally made pottery that has been associated with Philistines and have strengthened suggestions (e.g., Singer 2013) that at least some of these people first settled north of Canaan and assimilated with local Luwian (Indo-European) speakers before moving south.

No texts in a putative Philistine language have survived, and the only traces that remain are personal names and a handful of loanwords that are assumed to be Philistine only because they have no good Semitic etymology, even though in the Bible Philistines – and their gods – have good Semitic names (the most recent collection of Philistine loanwords in Hebrew is Niesiołowski-Spanò [2012: 427–428; see now 2016]).

The six known inscriptions from the area they controlled are difficult to classify (Davis, Maeir and Hitchcock 2015: 142–143); one from Ashdod has been identified as Cypro-Minoan and another from Tell Aphek has been interpreted as similar to Linear A, but these ascriptions are not quite secure (Maeir, Hitchcock and Horwitz 2013: 11). Indeed, it has been suggested that the Philistines used a variety of written scripts and languages to negotiate public identity, but at least some of them at some point spoke "one or more creoles based on Late Bronze age and/or Iron Age trade language(s)" (Davis, Maeir and Hitchcock 2015: 157). Some inscriptions may have been written in a modified version of the Hebrew alphabet (Rollston 2014: 204 n. 5).

Machinist (2000: 64) has suggested that, whatever language(s) these people may have spoken earlier, by the time they came in contact with Israel, they had largely assimilated into the surrounding Semitic language context (see also Schneider 2011). Even though the remains of Philistine language(s) are scarce and uncertain, there is a long tradition of attempts to identify it as Indo-European on the basis of the etymology of a few loans such as Hebrew *seren* (attested as plural *serenim*), which reflected Philistine *trn*, "ruler." Recent studies (Giusfredi 2009, Davis, Maeir and Hitchcock 2015) have plausibly linked this term (and later Greek *tyrannos*) with the Luwian royal title *tarwanis* and therefore such words are of little help in identifying the languages of Phoenicia.

Ultimately, it is difficult to reconstruct a unified Philistine identity; the origins of various groups in the area were heterogeneous, from various foreign and local populations and the resulting new groups and identity formations were in constant flux (Maeir and Hitchcock 2017), and this suggests that the linguistic situation was equally mixed, fluid and complex.

Scholarly research on issues relating to "Philistines" continues at a rapid pace. Among the most recent publications one may mention Stockhammer (2017) and Ben-Dor Evian (2015, 2017). The former, who in other publications has argued for Cypriot connections of the "Philistines," provides evidence requiring a rethinking of the use of Aegean-type pottery to identify specific groups of actors in late 13th and early 12th century BCE Southern Levant. The latter has undermined the utility of the modern term "sea peoples," which has been used to render an Egyptian word thr that must probably be rendered as "allied troops." She suggests that these were warrior groups that were displaced in the wake of the collapse of the Hittite empire in Anatolia; some of them settled in northern Syria, while others moved further south. She concludes (Ben-Dor Evian 2015: 71): "it is from the Levant itself, and not from the 'sea' that some of the 'Sea-Peoples' actually came."

3 ANCIENT EUROPEAN UNCLASSIFIABLE LANGUAGES

3.1 The so-called Danube script

Discussions of evidence for early writing and language in Europe often invoke three clay tablets found in 1961 at the Rumanian site of Tartaria with symbols that some have described as early writing or proto-writing. These objects were found in a pit that may have been of ritual significance, but the archaeological context is somewhat murky, and therefore dating is insecure. They may have come from ca. 4000 BCE or ca. 2500, but the issue is still debated (for reassessment of the archaeological context and much of ensuing debate, see Zanotti 1983, Merlini and Lazarovici 2008). Many other objects with similar marks, although mostly one or two at a time, have been recovered from the Danube area, leading to sometimes contentious debates about the existence of early writing in Europe, the earliest traces of which supposedly go back as far as 6000 BCE, in some instances fueled by nationalistic or phantasmagoric impulses. But as noted by Schmandt-Besserat (1984), such markings on pots, figurines, spindle whorls etc., which are widely attested in many cultures, hardly constitute a system of writing. While some maintain that the Tartaria tablets prove that early European civilization was literate, others have insisted that the symbols they bear should be classified as proto-writing or precursors of writing (see the discussion by Hooker 1992, who also dismisses any putative relationship between this "script" and Linear A).

The tablets remain enigmatic, as do a few more recent finds, most prominently wood and clay objects bearing signs that were excavated at the mainland Greek site of Dispilio, on the western shore of Lake Kastoria. The partial draining of the lake revealed a middle Neolithic site that had been waterlogged and therefore preserved wooden objects such as cedar posts and a cedar "tablet" covered with ten rows of symbols, which was subsequently dated by carbon-14 analysis to ca. 5324–5079 BCE; see Facorellis, Sofronidou and Hourmouziadis (2014) for a summary of these inscribed or decorated objects. Whatever one thinks of these finds, the languages of the people who produced all these markings will never be identified, even if some have speculated that it might have been early Indo-European (Owens 1999).

3.2 Basque and Etruscan

During the last few thousand years, Europe has been dominated by Indo-European, Finno-Ugric and Semitic languages (i.e. Hebrew and Arabic) and Semitic elements in mixed languages such as Yiddish and Ladino. The two commonly cited exceptions that do not fit into any of these families are Basque, spoken in northern Spain and southern France and by immigrants in the US, and Etruscan, the long dead pre-Latin language of Italy, attested in inscriptions from ca. 700–ca. 25 BCE. Basque is often prominently mentioned in lists of isolates, but it is undoubtedly related to the ancient Aquitanian language, known only from personal and divine names cited in Latin funerary inscriptions from Gaul (see Lakarra, this volume; Campbell, this volume pp. 2–4); together they are sometimes referred to as Vasconic. There have been many speculations on the languages of Europe before the spread of Indo-European; in recent years, Vennemann (2003) has proposed a complex relationship between Vasconic and Afroasiatic speakers in prehistoric Europe, based principally on the analysis of hydronyms and various place names. For informed critiques of such hypotheses, see the essays in Udolph (2013) and the comments of Baldi and Page (2006).

Etruscan has long been considered an isolate, but it is now generally recognized that it was related to two other poorly attested ancient European languages, Raetic (Schumacher 1998c) and Lemnian (known from a single stele with two different texts from the island of Lemnos; Schumacher 1998b, Eichner 2012, 2013) sometimes subsumed under the general term Tyrrhenian. Still another language, known as Camunic, may belong with these three, but some would identify it as Indo-European (Schumacher 1998a, Zavaroni 2005). This language, written in a script derived from the Etruscan alphabet, is documented by more than 125 very short rock inscriptions (most of them 1 or 2 words, the longest had 8) from the Valcamonica Valley in northwestern Italy that have been dated between ca. sixth/fifth century BCE and the turn of the millennium.

3.3. Northern Picene/Picean

A stone stele supposedly discovered in Novilara, just outside of Ravenna in Italy, bears a sixth-century BCE twelve-line inscription written in a version of the Etruscan alphabet but in an unidentified language. Although the text cannot be understood, the language it was written in has been called Northern Picean. Texts on other fragmentary inscriptions have also been ascribed to the same language, but in-depth investigation reveals that only one other, which was found in regular excavations in a tomb in Novilara, can be linked to the stele (Di Carlo 2006). Although both these inscriptions can be transliterated, no one has presented a plausible translation, even if attempts have been made to connect Nothern Picean with the Italic Indo-European languages, most recently, each in their own way, by Blažek (2008–2009) and Harkness (2011).

3.4 Unclassifiable languages of the Iberian Peninsula and southern France

There are other inscriptions from Europe in various derivatives from the Phoenician, Greek, or Greek-derived Etruscan scripts that may provide clues to ancient languages, but most of them offer very little material to work with and yet have been subject to much speculation and controversy.

3.4.1 Tartessian

One such hypothetical language is Tartessian, documented in inscriptions from southern Portugal and southwestern Spain (Untermann 1997) that date to ca. 750–500 BCE. These were written in a Paleohispanic script based on the Phoenician alphabet. Some would ascribe almost a hundred such inscriptions on stele, rocks and potsherds to this language or language group, but not everyone agrees as to which of these actually belong to Tartessian. Opinions are divided on the language of these inscriptions: most view it as unclassified, but some have insisted that it was an Indo-European Celtic language. See, most recently, the debate published in the *Journal of Indo-European Studies* between Koch (2014), the main proponent of the Celtic hypothesis, and Eska (2014), as well as Valério

(2014a), who provide strong critiques of this ascription. T. Kaufman (2015), however, presented compelling evidence that Tartessian is an otherwise undocumented/unattested Celtic language in conjunction with an analysis of all unbroken texts.

3.4.2 Iberian

Another group of inscriptions from northeastern Spain and southern France, dating perhaps from the fifth to the first centuries BCE, or even perhaps somewhat later, written in Paleohispanic scripts may bear witness to still another language or group of languages labeled as Iberian (Untermann 1980, 1990). The inscriptions are found on a broad range of objects and materials, including stone monuments, funerary stele and blocks, ceramics, tiles, loom weights, coins, mosaics and bronzes as well as lead strips. The latter often contain the longer texts, but many of these may be forgeries (Doménech-Carbó et al. 2015).

3.5 Unclassifiable languages of Crete and Cyprus

The Mediterranean islands of Crete and Cyprus were home to many different writing systems during the second and first millennia BCE, culminating in the use of diverse alphabetic and syllabic scripts encoding various Greek dialects (Davies and Olivier 2012). There are earlier writing systems that have been discovered on these islands that cannot be read at present, and therefore, it is impossible to identify the languages that were being used there in written communication.

3.5.1 Cretan hieroglyphs

The earliest such undeciphered group of symbols consists of Cretan Hieroglyphs, thus far discovered on the island at Knossos, Malia and Poursat (Olivier and Godart 1996). The symbols are both abstract and naturalistic, and the term "hieroglyphic" is misleading, bringing to mind unfounded connections with Egyptian writing. There are approximately 270 such inscriptions on clay bars, tablets and other objects such as pottery and even one on stone, dated between ca. 1700 and 1550 BCE. More than half are on seals or seal impressions (Olivier 1986: 384; Olivier 1990: 12). There are earlier seals, perhaps as early as 2100 BCE with symbols (the so-called Archanes seals) that have been the subject of some controversy but they are most likely part of the same general system (Perna 2014: 253). It is possible to identify approximately 120 discrete symbols, but it is not at all certain that all examples belonged to a single system of signs, possibly a logo-syllabic writing system.

3.5.2 Linear A

The Linear A system consisted of 65 signs, written on tablets and on a variety of objects numbering almost 1500. As noted by Kober (1948: 88), "this is the only one of the Minoan scripts found regularly on objects which must have had a religious function, like libation tables and votive ladles, etc.," although many of the tablets are obviously administrative records. Linear A was mostly written on tablets and sealings, less often on pottery, stucco, stone and metal objects (Olivier 1986: 384). Because two-thirds of the symbols were also utilized as consonant-vowel syllabograms in the similar Linear B script that was used to write an early Greek dialect, it is assumed that this was also a syllabary. The oldest exemplar is from ca. 1800 BCE, but the first group comes from the palace at Knossos from a century later; it was used until ca. 1450 BCE. An outlier is a painted inscription from ca. 1350 (Perna 2014: 254). Although the use of Linear A overlapped with Cretan Hieroglyphics – indeed there are deposits that contain writings in both systems – unlike the latter it was never used on seals, with one possible exception (Perna 2014: 256). There is some evidence to suggest that the script – and possibly also Cretan Hieroglyphic – was also used on parchment and therefore our picture of Minoan writings is skewed by the chance survival of more permanent surfaces (Perna 2014: 258).

The similarity with Linear B notwithstanding, Linear A has not been deciphered, and it is not possible to establish whether the inscriptions were used for one language or more. Nevertheless, according to Davis (2013), there are indications that it utilized VSO word order. There have been many suggestions to as to its identity, often focusing on Indo-European (see discussion in Egetmeyer 2004: 235–236).

3.5.3 Phaistos Disc

The Phaistos Disc (Olivier 1975) was discovered in 1908 in a building in a Minoan palace (ca. 1850–1600 BCE) during an evening inspection of the site by a foreman and therefore without exact archaeological context (Hnila 2009: 60). The thin baked clay disk was inscribed with 241 tokens of 45 discrete symbols that were impressed from separate stamp seals on both sides, apparently to be "read" from the outer edges inward in counter-clockwise order. The use of such "stamps" is unique in the Aegean, and the only parallels can be found in far-off Mesopotamian inscriptions with short dedicatory texts impressed on bricks. Over the years, decipherment claims have included various Indo-European languages, Sumerian, Phoenician, Hurrian, Egyptian, Basque and even Chinese while others have deemed it a solar calendar or simply as a forgery (Duhoux 2000). Subsequent discoveries in Crete have revealed three objects with designs that might provide parallels to some of the symbols on the disk: on a bronze double-headed axe found in the Arkalo-chori cave, a stone block from Malia with 16 tokens of engraved symbols and a sealing on a piece of clay from Phaistos with a single "comb" symbol that also occurs on the disk (Hnila 2009: 64–65). As argued by Knapp and Voskos (2008: 679), between the thirteenth and eleventh centuries BCE, Cyprus underwent profound changes due to the hybridization of Phoenician, Aegean, native Cypriot and other elements that created a new society that maintained continuity in material culture and social practices. It is impossible to ascertain how these processes impacted linguistic practice on the island.

3.5.4 Eteocretan

The evidence for this language consists of five incomplete stone inscriptions excavated at Dreroes and Praisos on eastern Crete, ranging in date from the late seventh century/early sixth to the third centuries BCE. There are three more fragmentary texts from Praisos, but some of them may be in Greek (Duhoux 1982). The monuments were written in various forms of the Greek alphabet and the two early items from Dreros, cut into the wall of the temple of Apollo, together with Greek texts, were Eteocretan-Greek bilingual texts, but only a few lines of each have survived, and the language has defied interpretation. Gordon (1975 and elsewhere) insisted that Eteocretan (and Linear A) was North-West Semitic, but this is hardly a mainstream view, even if has been revived recently by Magnelli and Petrantoni (2013). It is highly unlikely, however, that the languages encoded in Linear A and Eteocretan writings would have been the same.

3.5.5 Cypro-Minoan scripts

Second millennium BCE Cyprus was a multilingual island. Besides the indigenous undeciphered writing systems described here, archaeology has revealed inscriptions in Phoenician and Greek (Steele 2013). Moreover, cuneiform letters to and from Alashiya, in a version of Babylonian that was utilized as a written *lingua franca* at the time, have been found in Egypt and at Ugarit on the Mediterranean coast, and there is no longer any doubt that Alashiya was an ancient name for some part of eastern Cyprus, or perhaps for the whole island (Goren et al. 2003). Personal names of Alashiyans preserved in second millennium BCE texts from elsewhere are difficult to analyze, but some of them are clearly Semitic, and one or two may be Hurrian.

People on the island of Cyprus used a variety of scripts during the second and first millennia BCE before they adopted the Greek alphabet, first attested there in the sixth century BCE (Phoenician is attested in Cyprus earlier in the ninth century). Some of these were used to write local varieties of Greek, but the early writing system(s) known as Cypro-Minoan remain undeciphered. At present, approximately 250 such inscriptions are known (Steele 2014: 129 n. 1; for the corpus, see Ferrara 2012–2013, Olivier and Vandenabeele 2007, Steele 2013: 9–97, and Valério 2014b). These have been classified into four groups (e.g. recently Davis 2011): C0, an early inscribed loom weight, cylinder seal and tablet from Enkomi and a few signs on a jug from Kathydhata (sixteenth/ fifteenth century BCE), an inscribed cylinder seal; C2, three later tablets from the same site (twelfth century BCE); C3, a dozen tablets found in the port city of Ugarit (Ras Shamra, thirteenth century BCE) on the Syrian coast; and finally C1, which contains all the other Cypro-Minoan writings (fifteenth–eleventh centuries BCE). Moreover, there are many potters' marks and similar brandings with one or two signs that resemble symbols used in Cypro-Minoan from objects throughout the Mediterranean area that should probably not be considered as true writing (Hirschfeld 2014).

The Cypro-Minoan script is usually described as a descendant of a version of Minoan Linear A, presumably adapted from a Cretan prototype, although Sherratt (2013) has recently questioned this assumption, suggesting that its ancestors may have had Anatolian roots. In turn, it was the model for the Cypriot Syllabic script, although the details of the relationship are rather vague at present (Egetmeyer 2013). On the basis of this history, it is evident that Cypro-Minoan must also have been a syllabary with open (consonant-vowel) symbols. Because some groups of inscriptions used signs that are not present in other groups, there are reasons to subdivide the Cypro-Minoan corpus into two or more scripts (Duhoux 2009, Steele 2014) used to record an unknown number of languages (for differing opinions on this matter see the articles in Steele, ed. 2013). The current state of our knowledge is simply insufficient to decipher these scripts and to identify the languages that they encoded (Steele 2013:79).

3.5.6 Eteocypriot (Amathousian/Golgian, Cypriot Syllabic script)

From the seventh to the first centuries BCE still another syllabary, descended from Cypro-Minoan, as noted earlier, was used to write a local Arcado-Cypriot variety of Greek and one or more unknown languages, sometimes referred to as Eteocypriot, documented in more than 1,360 texts. The temporal break between the last Cypro-Minoan writings, which may have already been adapted to Greek (ca. 1050–1950 BCE, Olivier 2013: 16), and Cypriot Syllabic may be due to chances of discovery or represents a break in traditions of literacy.

While most of the Cypriot Syllabic inscriptions were written in Greek, at least 26 of these, give or take a few, cannot be understood and are presumed to be in another language (or languages), which, for lack of a better word has been named Eteocypriot, although any connection between this putative language and the language(s) of the Cypro-Minoan texts is a matter of speculation. Four of them are bilingual, accompanied by a Greek version. Even though the remains of "Eteocypriot" are so sparse, unsuccessful attempts have been made to connect this putative language with Indo-European (Lydian, Illyrian, etc.); Semitic (Akkadian, Phoenician); and Hurrian/Urartean languages (Steele 2013: 103).

Egetmeyer (2008, 2009, 2012, 2013) through an analysis of both vocabulary and grammar has made a strong case for a hypothetical distinction between the languages of the non-Greek Cypriot Syllabic texts from the southwestern part of the island, which he calls Amathousian, and those from the east, which would be Golgian.

REFERENCES

Akulov, Alexander. 2016. Whether Sumerian Language Is Related to Munda? *Cultural Anthropology and Ethnosemiotics* 2: 23–29.

Algaze, Guillermo. 2012. The End of Prehistory and the Uruk Period. *The Sumerian World*, ed. by Harriet Crawford, 68–94. London: Routledge.

Ancillotti, Augusto. 1981. *La lingua dei Cassiti*. (Unicoplil Univesitario, 103). Milan: Unicopli.

André, Beatrice and Mirjo Salvini, 1989. Réflexions sur Puzur-Inšušinak. *Iranica Antiqua* 29:53–78.

Aristar, Anthony Rodrigues. 1995. Binder-Anaphors and the Diachrony of Case Displacement. *Double Case: Agreement by Suffixaufnahme*, ed. by Frans Plank, 431–447. Oxford: Oxford University Press.

Arnaud, Daniel. 1995. Les traces des 'Arabes' dans les textes syriens du début du IIe millénaire à l'époque néo-assyrienne: esquisse de quelques themes. *Présence arabe dans le croissant fertile avant l'Hégire. Actes de la table ronde internationale organisée par l'Unité de recherche associée 1062 du CNRS, études sémitiques, au Collège de France, le 13 novembre 1993*, ed. by Hélène Lozachmeur, 19–22. Paris: Editions Recherche sur les Civilisations.

Attinger, Pascal. 1993. *Eléments de linguistique sumérienne. La construction de $du_{11}/e/di$ "dire."* (Orbis biblicus et orientalis, Sonderband). Fribourg: Academic Press/Göttingen: Vandenhoeck & Ruprecht.

Baldi, Philip and B. Richard Page. 2006. Review of Vanneman 2003. *Lingua* 116: 2183–2220.

Balkan, Kemal. 1954. *Kassitenstudien 1. Die Sprache der Kassiten*. (American Oriental Series, 37). New Haven: American Oriental Society.

Ball, Charles James. 1913. *Chinese and Sumerian*. London: Humphrey Milford.

Ball, Charles James. 1918. The Relation of Tibetan to Sumerian. *Proceedings of the Society of Biblical Archaeology* 40: 95–105.

Bavant, Marc. 2014. *A Case Study of Basque, Old Persian and Elamite*. Doctoral dissertation, University of Amsterdam.

Beaulieu, Paul-Alain. 1988. Swamps as Burial Places for Babylonian Kings. *N.A.B.U.: Nouvelles Assyriologiques Brèves et Utilitaires* 1988: 36–37.

Benedict, Warren C. 1960. Urartians and Hurrians. *Journal of the American Oriental Society* 80: 100–104.

Ben-Dor Evian, Shirly. 2015. *"They were* thr on land, *others at sea . . ."* The Etymology of the Egyptian Term for "Sea-Peoples." *Semitica* 57: 57–75.

Ben-Dor Evian, Shirly. 2017. Ramesses III and the 'Sea-peoples': Towards a New Philistine Paradigm. *Oxford Journal of Archaeology* 36: 267–285.

Blažek, Václav. 2002. Elam: A Bridge between Ancient Near East and Dravidian India? *Mother Tongue* 7: 123–146.

Blažek, Václav. 2008–2009. On the North Picenian Language. *Talanta* 40–41: 173–180.

Bleichsteiner, Robert. 1928. Beiträge zur Kenntnis der elamischen Sprache. *Anthropos* 23: 167–198.

Boese, Johannes. 2010. Ḫašmar-galšu. Ein kassitischer Fürst in Nippur. *Festschrift für Gernot Wilhelm anläßlich seines 65. Geburtstages am 28. Januar 2010*, ed. by Janette C. Fincke, 71–78. Dresden: ISLET.

Bomhard, Allan R. 1997. On the Origin of Sumerian. *Mother Tongue* 3: 1–16.

Bomhard, Allan R. 2008. *Reconstructing Proto-Nostratic: Comparative Phonology, Morphology, and Vocabulary*. (Leiden Indo-European Etymological Dictionary Series, 6). Leiden: Brill.

Bomhard, Allan R. 2015. *A Comprehensive Introduction to Nostratic Comparative Linguistics with Special Reference to Indo-European*, vol. 1 (2nd ed.). Charleston.

Bomhard, Allan R. and John C. Kerns. 1994. *The Nostratic Macrofamily: A Study in Distant Linguistic Relationship*. Berlin: Mouton de Gruyter.

Braun, Jan. 1994. Chattskij i abchazo-adygskij. *Rocznik* Orientalistyczny 49: 15–23.

Braun, Jan. 2001. *Sumerian and Tibeto-Burman*. Warsaw: Agade.

Braun, Jan. 2004. *Sumerian and Tibeto-Burman: Additional Studies*. Warsaw: Agade.

Braun, Jan. 2009. *Kassite and Dravidian*. Warsaw: Agade.

Braun, Jan and Piotr Taracha. 2007. Review of Soysal 2004. *Bibliotheca Orientalis* 114: 193–200.

Brinkman, John A. 1969. The Names of the Last Eight Kings of the Kassite Dynasty. *Zeitschrift für Assyriologie und Vorderasiatische Archäologie* 59: 231–246.

Brinkman, John A. 1976–1980. Kassiten. *Reallexikon der Assyriologie und Vorderasiatischen Archäologie*, vol. 5, ed. by E. Ebeling et al., 464–473. Berlin: Harrassowitz.

Brinkman, John A. 1977. Notes on the Kassite-Akkadian Vocabulary (BM 92005 = 82–89–18,5637). *N.A.B.U.: Nouvelles Assyriologiques Brèves et Utilitaires* 1977: 102.

Chirikba, Viacheslav A. 1996. *Common West Caucasian: The Reconstruction of Its Phonological System and Parts of Its Lexicon and Morphology*. Leiden: Research School CNWS.

Civil, Miguel. 2013. Remarks On AD-GI$_4$ (A.K.A. "Archaic Word List C" or "Tribute"). *Journal of Cuneiform Studies* 65: 13–67.

Cogan, Mordechai and Haim Tadmor. 1977. Gyges and Ashurbanipal: A Study in Literary Transmission. *Orientalia, Nova Series* 46: 65–85.

Colless, Brian. 1998. The Canaanite Syllabary. *Abr Nahrain* 35: 26–46.

Dahl, Jacob L. 2005. Complex Graphemes in Proto-Elamite. *Cuneiform Digital Library Journal* 2005/3: 1–15.

Dahl, Jacob L. 2009. Early Writing in Iran: A Reappraisal. *Iran* 47: 23–31.

Dahl, Jacob L. 2013. Early Writing in Iran. *Oxford Handbook of Ancient Iran*, ed. by Daniel T. Potts, 233–263. Oxford University Press.

Dahl, Jacob L., Cameron A. Petrie, and Daniel T. Potts. 2013. Chronological Parameters of the Earliest Writing System in Iran. *Ancient Iran and Its Neighbours: Local*

Developments and Long-Range Interactions in the 4th Millennium BC, ed. by Cameron A. Petrie. (British Institute of Persian Studies Archaeological Monographs Series, 3), 353–378. Havertown: Oxbow Books.

Daniels, Peter T. 1996. The Byblos Syllabary. *The World's Writing Systems*, ed. by Peter T. Daniels and William Bright, 29–30. Oxford: Oxford University Press.

Davies, Anna Morpurgo and Jean-Pierre Olivier. 2012. Syllabic Scripts and Languages in the Second and First Millennia BC. *Parallel Lives: Ancient Island Societies in Crete and Cyprus: Papers Arising from the Conference in Nicosia Organized by the British School at Athens, the University of Crete and the University of Cyprus, in November-December 2006*, ed. by Gerald Cadogan, Maria Iacovou, Katerina Kopaka, and James Whitley. (British School at Athens Studies, 20), 105–118. London: British School at Athens.

Davis, Brent. 2011. Cypro-Minoan in Philistia? *Kubaba* 2: 40–74.

Davis, Brent. 2013. Syntax in Linear A: The Word-Order of the 'Libation Formula.' *Kadmos* 52: 35–52.

Davis, Brent, Aren M. Maeir, and Louise A. Hitchcock. 2015. Disentangling Entangled Objects: Iron Age Inscriptions from Philistia as a Reflection of Cultural Processes. *Israel Exploration Journal* 65: 140–166.

Del Olmo Lete, Gregorio. 2012. Ugaritic and Old(-South)-Arabic: Two WS Dialects? *Dialectology of the Semitic Languages: Proceedings of the IV Meeting on Comparative Semitics, Zaragoza, 06/9–11/2010*, ed. by Federico Corriente, Gregorio del Olmo Lete, Ángeles Vicente and Juan-Pablo Vita. (Aula Orientalis, Supplementa, 27), 5–23. Sabadell: AUSA.

Desset, François. 2012. *Premières écritures iraniennes: les systèmes proto-élamite et élamite linéaire*. (Dipartimento di Studi Asiatici, Università degli Studi di Napoli "L'Orientale," Series Minor, 76). Naples: Università degli Studi di Napoli "L'Orientale."

Desset, François. 2014. A New Writing System Discovered in 3rd Millennium BCE Iran: The Konar Sandal 'Geometric' Tablets. *Iranica Antiqua* 49: 83–109.

Desset, François. 2016. Proto-Elamite Writing in Iran. *Archéo-Nil* 26: 67–104.

Di Carlo, Pierpaolo. 2006. *L'enigma nord-piceno: saggi sulla lingua delle stele di Novilara e sul loro constesto culturale*. (Università degli Studi di Firenze: Studi, Quaderni del Dipartimento di Linguistica, 7). Florence: Dipartimento di Linguistica – Università di Firenze.

Diakonoff, Igor M. 1967a. Elamskij jazyk (The Elamite Language). *Jazyki drevnej perednej Azii* (Languages of the Ancient Near East), ed. by Igor M. Diakonoff, 85–112. Moscow: Nauka.

Diakonoff, Igor M. 1967b. Chattskij ("Protochettskij") jazyk (The Hattic ["Protohattic"] Language). *Jazyki drevnej perednej Azii* (Languages of the Ancient Near East), ed. by Igor M. Diakonoff, 166–176. Moscow: Nauka.

Diakonoff, Igor M. 1997. External Connections of the Sumerian Language. *Mother Tongue* 3: 54–62.

Diakonoff, Igor M. 1999. More on External Connections of the Sumerian Language. *Mother Tongue* 5: 141–144.

Doménech-Carbó, Antonio, María Teresa Doménech-Carbó, Monserrat Lastras Pérez, Miquel Herrero-Cortell. 2015. Detection of Archaeological Forgeries of Iberian Lead Plates Using Nanoelectrochemical Techniques: The Lot of Fake Plates from Bugarra (Spain). *Forensic Science International* 247: 79–88.

Duhoux, Yves. 1982. *L'Étéocrétois: les textes – la langue*. Amsterdam: J. C. Gieben.

Duhoux, Yves. 2000. How Not to Decipher the Phaistos Disc: A Review. *American Journal of Archaeology* 104: 597–600.

Duhoux, Yves. 2009. Eteocypriot and Cypro-Minoan 1–3. *Kadmos* 48: 39–75.

Dunajevskaja, Irina M. 1959. Porjadok razmeschtschenija prefiksov chattskogo glagola (The Order of the Prefixes of the Hattic Verb). *Vestnik Drevnej Istorii* 67: 20–37.

Dunajevskaja, Irina M. and Igor M. Diakonoff. 1979. Chattskij ("Protochettskij") jazyk (The Hattic ["Protohattic"] Language). *Jazyki Azii i Afriki, 3. Jazyki drevnej perednej Azii: nesemitskie, iberijsko-kavkazskie jazyki, paleoaziatskie jazyki*, ed. by G.D. Sanžeev, 79–83. Moscow: Nauka.

Dunand, Maurice. 1945. *Byblia Grammata. Documents et recherches sur le développement de l'écriture en Phénicie.* Beirut: République Libanaise, Ministère de l'Éducation National des Beaux-Arts.

Dunand, Maurice. 1978. Nouvelles inscriptions pseudo-hiéroglyphiques découvertes à Byblos. *Bulletin de Musée de Beyrouth* 30: 52–58.

Edzard, Dietz Otto. 2003. *Sumerian Grammar*. (Handbuch der Orientalistik, Erste Abteilung, Nahe und der Mittlere Osten, 71). Leiden: Brill.

Egetmeyer, Markus. 2004. À propos des inscriptions égéennes découvertes au Levant. *Antiquus Oriens. Mélanges offerts au professeur René Lebrun*, vol. I, ed. by Michael Mazoyer and Olivier Casabonne. (Collection Kubaba, Série Antiquité, 5), 229–248. Paris: L'Harmattan.

Egetmeyer, Markus. 2008. Langues et écritures chypriotes: nouvelles perspectives. *Comptes rendus des séances de l'Académie des inscriptions et Belles-Lettres* 152: 997–1020.

Egetmeyer, Markus. 2009. The Recent Debate on Eteocypriot People and Language. *Pasiphae* 3: 69–90.

Egetmeyer, Markus. 2012. "Sprechen Sie Golgisch?" Anmerkungen zu einer übersehenen Sprache. *Études mycéniennes 2010. Actes du XIIIe colloque international sur les textes égéens, Sèvres, Paris, Nanterre, 20–23 septembre 2010*, ed. by Pierre Carlier, Charles De Lamberterie, Markus Egetmeyer, Nicole Guilleux, Françoise Rougemont, Julien Zurbach. (Biblioteca di "Pasiphae," 10), 427–434. Pisa: Fabrizio Serra editore.

Egetmeyer, Markus. 2013. From the Cypro-Minoan to the Cypro-Greek Syllabaries: Linguistic Remarks on the Script Reform. *Syllabic Writing on Cyprus and Its Context*, ed. by Philippa M. Steele, 107–131. Cambridge: Cambridge University Press.

Eichner, Heiner. 2012. Neues zur Sprache der Stele von Lemnos (Erster Teil). *Journal of Language Relationship* 7: 9–32.

Eichner, Heiner. 2013. Neues zur Sprache der Stele von Lemnos (Zweiter Teil). *Journal of Language Relationship* 10: 1–42.

Eidem, Jesper. 1992. *The Shemshāra Archive 2: The Administrative Texts*. (Historisk-filosofiske Skrifter, 15). Copenhagen: Munksgaard.

Englund, Robert K. 1998. Texts from the Late Uruk Period. *Mesopotamien: Späturuk-Zeit und Frühdynastische Zeit*, ed. by Pascal Attinger and Marcus Wafler. (Orbis Biblicus et Orientalis, 160/1), 15–233. Freiburg: Academic Press/Göttingen: Vandenhoeck and Ruprecht.

Englund, Robert K. 2008. The Smell of the Cage. *Cuneiform Digital Library Journal* 2009/4: 1–27.

Eska, Joseph F. 2014. Comments on John T. Koch's Tartessian-as-Celtic Enterprise. *Journal of Indo-European Studies* 42: 428–438.

Facorellis, Yorgos, Marina Sofronidou, and Giorgos Hourmouziadis. 2014. Radiocarbon Dating of the Neolithic Lakeside Settlement of Dispilio, Kastoria, Northern Greece. *Radiocarbon* 56: 511–528.

Fähnrich, Heinz. 1981. Das Sumerische und Kartwelsprachen. *Georgica* 4: 89–101.

Fane, Hannah. 1980. Sumerian – Dravidian Interconnections: The Linguistic, Archeological and Textual Evidence. *International Journal of Dravidian Linguistics* 9: 286–305.

Farmer, Steven, Richard Sproat, and Michael Witzel. 2004. The Collapse of the Indus-Script Thesis: The Myth of a Literate Harappan Civilization. *Electronic Journal of Vedic Studies* 11: 19–57.

Ferrara, Silvia. 2012–2013. *Cypro-Minoan Inscriptions*, 2 vols. Oxford: Oxford University Press.

Fisher, Michael T. and Matthew W. Stolper. 2015. Achaemenid Elamite Administrative Tablets, 3: Fragments from Old Kandahar, Afghanistan. *Arta* 2015.001: 1–26.

Foster, Benjamin R. 2013. Guti. *The Encyclopedia of Ancient History*, ed. by Roger S. Bagnall, Kai Brodersen, Craige B. Champion, Andrew Erskine, and Sabine R. Huebner, 3004. Malden: Blackwells.

Fournet, Arnaud. 2011. The Kassite Language in a Comparative Perspective with Hurrian and Urartean. *The Macro-Comparative Journal* 2: 1–19.

Frame, Grant. 2013. The Political History and Historical Geography of the Aramean, Chaldean, and Arab Tribes in Babylonia in the Neo-Assyrian Period. *Arameans, Chaldeans, and Arabs in Babylonia and Palestine in the First Millennium B.C.*, ed. by Angelika Berlejung and Michael P. Streck. (Leipziger altorientalistische Studien, 3), 87–121. Wiesbaden: Harrassowitz.

Gamkrelidze, Tamaz V. 2006. *Selected Writings: Linguistic Sign, Typology and Language Reconstruction.* (Innsbruker Beiträge zur Sprachwissenschaft, 122). Innsbruck: Institut für Sprachen und Literaturen der Universität Innsbruck.

Gamkrelidze, Tamaz V. and Vyacheslav V. Ivanov. 1989. Pervyye indoyevropeytsy na arene istoriĭ: prototokhary v Peredney Azii ("The Earliest Indo-Europeans in the Historical Arena: Prototokharians in the Near East"). *Vestnik drevney istoriĭ* 190: 14–39. French translation: Les premiers Indo-Européens de l'histoire. Gamkrelidze 2006: 122–153.

Gamkrelidze, Tamaz V. and Vyacheslav V. Ivanov. 1995. *Indo-European and the Indo-Europeans: A Reconstruction and Historical Analysis of a Proto-Language and Proto-Culture.* (Trends in Linguistics. Studies and Monographs 80). Berlin: De Gruyter Mouton.

Gamkrelidze, Tamaz V. and Vyacheslav V. Ivanov. 2013. Indoyevropeĭskaya prarodina i rasseleniye indoyevropeĭtsev: polveka issledovaniĭ i obsuzhdeniĭ ("The Indo-European Homeland and Migrations: Half a Century of Studies and Discussions"). *Journal of Language Relationship* 9: 109–136.

Gerçek, Nebahat Ilgi. 2012. *The Kaška and the Northern Frontier of Ḫatti.* Doctoral dissertation, University of Michigan.

Girbal, Christian. 1986. *Beiträge zur Grammatik des Hattischen.* Frankfurt am Main: P. Lang.

Giusfredi, Federico. 2009. The Problem of the Luwian Title *tarwanis. Altorientalische Forschungen* 36: 140–145.

Glassner, Jean-Jacques. 1999. Dilmun et Magan: la place de l'écriture. *Languages and Cultures in Contact: At the Crossroads of Civilizations in the Syro-Mesopotamian Realm. Proceedings of the 42th RAI*, ed. by Karel van Lerberghe and Gabriela Voet. (Orientalia Lovaniensia Analecta, 96), 133–144. Leuven: Peeters.

Glassner, Jean-Jacques. 2002. Dilmun et Magan: le peuplement, l'organisation politique, la question des Amorrites et la place de l'écriture. Point de vue de l'assyriologue. *Essays on the Late Prehistory of the Arabian Peninsula*, ed. by Serge Cleuziou, Maurizio Tosi and Juris Zarins. (Serie Orientale Roma, 93), 337–381. Rome: Istituto italiano per l'Africa e l'Oriente.

Glassner, Jean-Jacques. 2005. L'onomastique de Marhashi. *N.A.B.U.: Nouvelles Assyriologiques Brèves et Utilitaires* 2005/1: 11–14.

Goedegebuure, Petra. 2008: Central Anatolian Languages and Language Communities in the Colony Period: The Luwian Substrate of Hattian and the Independent Hittites. *Anatolia and the Jazira during the Old Assyrian Period*, ed. by J.G. Dercksen. (Old Assyrian Archives, Studies, 3), 137–180. Leiden: The Netherlands Institute for the Near East.

Goedegebuure, Petra. 2010. The Alignment of Hattian. An Active Language with an Ergative Base. *Proceedings of the 53e Rencontre Assyriologique Internationale, July 2007, vol. 1*, ed. by Leonid E. Kogan (Babel und Bibel, 4.1), 949–981. Winona Lake: Eisenbrauns.

Goedegebuure, Petra. 2013. Hattic. *The Encyclopedia of Ancient History*, ed. by Roger S. Bagnall, Kai Brodersen, Craige B. Champion, Andrew Erskine, and Sabine R. Huebner, 3080–3081. Malden: Blackwells.

Gordon, Cyrus H. 1975. The Decipherment of Minoan and Eteocretan. *Journal of the Royal Asiatic Society of Great Britain and Ireland* 2: 148–158.

Goren, Yuval, Shlomo Bunimovitz, Israel Finkelstein, and Nadav Na'Aman. 2003. The Location of Alashiya: New Evidence from Petrographic Investigation of Alashiyan Tablets from El-Amarna and Ugarit. *American Journal of Archaeology* 107: 233–255.

Grillot-Susini, Françoise and Claude Roche. 1987. *Éléments de grammaire élamite*. Paris: Editions Recherche sur les Civilisations.

Hamilton, Gordon J. 1987. Review of Mendenhall 1986. *Journal of Biblical Literature* 106: 693–695.

Harkness, John. 2011. The Novilara Stele Revisited. *Journal of Indo-European Studies* 39: 13–32.

Harrison, Timothy P. 2014. Recent Discoveries at Tayinat (Ancient Kunulua/Calno) and Their Biblical Implications. *Congress Volume Munich 2013*, ed. by Christl M. Maier, 396–425. Leiden: Brill.

Henkelman, Wouter F.M. 2011. Cyrus the Persian and Darius the Elamite: A Case of Mistaken Identity. *Herodot und das Persische Weltreich: Akten des 3. Internationalen Kolloquiums zum Thema "Vorderasien im Spannungsfeld klassischer und altorientalischer Überlieferungen." Innsbruck, 24.–28. November 2008*, ed. by Robert Rollinger, Brigitte Truschnegg and Reinhold Bichler. (Classica et Orientalia, 3), 577–634. Wiesbaden: Harrassowitz.

Henning, Walter Bruno. 1978. The First Indo-Europeans in History. *Society and History: Essays in Honor of Karl August Wittfogel*, ed. by Gary L. Ulmen, 215–230. The Hague: Mouton.

Hinz, Walther und Heidemarie Koch. 1987. *Elamisches Wörterbuch*. (Archäologische Mitteilungen aus Iran, Ergänzungsband, 17). Berlin: Reimer-Verlag.

Hirschfeld, Nicolle. 2014. Signs of Writing? Red Lustrous Wheelmade Vases and Ashkelon Amphorae. *KE-RA-ME-JA: Studies Presented to Cynthia W. Shelmerdine*, ed. by Dimitri Nakassis, Joann Gulizio and Sarah A. James. (Prehistory Monographs, 46), 261–269. Philadelphia: INSTAP Academic Press.

Hitchcock, Louise A. and Aren M. Maeir. 2014. Yo-ho, Yo-ho, a *Seren*'s Life for Me! *World Archaeology* 46: 624–640.

Hnila, Pavel. 2009. Notes on the Authenticity of the Phaistos Disk. *Anodos* 9: 59–66.

Hölscher, Monica. 1996. *Die Personennamen der kassitenzeitlichen Texte aus Nippur*. (IMGULA, 1). Münster: Rhema.

Hooker, James. 1992. Early Balkan 'Scripts' and the Ancestry of Linear A. *Kadmos* 31: 97–112.

Høyrup, Jens. 1992. Sumerian: The Descendant of a Proto-Historical Creole? An Alternative Approach to the Sumerian Problem. *AIΩN. Annali del Dipartimento di Studi del Mondo Classico e del Mediterraneo Antico. Sezione linguistica. Istituto Universitario Orientale, Napoli* 14: 21–72.

Iosad, Pavel. 2010. Kassistkii jazyk ("The Kassite Language"). *Jazyki Mira. Drevnie reliktovye jazyki Perednej Azii* (Languages of the World: Ancient Languages of the Near East), ed. by N.N. Kazanskii, A.A. Kibrik and J.B. Korjakov, 184–187. Moscow: Academia.

Izre'el, Shlomo. 1988. Review of Mendenhall 1986. *Journal of the American Oriental Society* 108: 519–521.

Jagersma, Bram. 2010. *A Descriptive Grammar of Sumerian*. Doctoral dissertation, Universiteit Leiden.

Jaritz, Kurt. 1957. Die kassitische Sprachreste. *Anthropos* 52: 850–898.

Kammenhuber, Annalies. 1969. Das Hattische. *Altkleinasiatische Sprachen*, ed. by Johannes Friedrich. (Handbuch der Orientalistik, Erste Abteilung, II. Band: Keilschriftforschung und alte Geschichte Vorderasiens, 1. Und 2. Abschnitt, Lieferung 2), 428–546, 584–588. Leiden: E. J. Brill.

Kaneva, Irina Trofimovna. 2006. *Shumerskii iazyk* ("The Sumerian Language") (2nd ed.). St. Petersburg: Tcentr Peterburgskoe Vostokovedenie.

Kassian, Alexei. 2009. Hattic as a Sino-Caucasian Language. *Ugarit-Forschungen* 41: 309–447.

Kassian, Alexei. 2010. Chattski jazyk (The Hattic Language). *Jazyki Mira. Drevnie reliktovye jazyki Perednej Azii* (Languages of the World: Ancient Relict Languages of the Near East), ed. by N.N. Kazanskii, A.A. Kibrik and J.B. Korjakov, 168–184. Moscow: Academia.

Kaufman, Stephen A. 1989. Review of Mendenhall 1986. *Bulletin of the American Schools of Oriental Research* 276: 85–86.

Kaufman, Terrence. 2015. *Notes on the Decipherment of Tartessian as Celtic*. (Journal of Indo-European Studies Monograph Series, 62). Washington, DC: Institute for the Study of Man.

Keetman, Jan. 2005. Die altsumerische Vokalharmonie und die Vokale des Sumerischen. *Journal of Cuneiform Studies* 57: 1–16.

Kenoyer, Jonathan Mark. 2006. The Origin, Context and Function of the Indus Script: Recent Insights from Harappa. *Proceedings of the Pre-Symposium of RIHN and 7th ESCA Harvard-Kyoto Roundtable*, ed. by Toshiki Osada and Noriko Hase, 9–27. Kyoto: Research Institute for Humanity and Nature.

Kenoyer, Jonathan Mark and Richard H. Meadow. 2000. The Ravi Phase: A New Cultural Manifestation at Harappa. *South Asian Archaeology, 1997: Proceedings of the Fourteenth International Conference of the European Association of South Asian Archaeologists, Held in the Istituto italiano per l'Africa e l'Oriente, Palazzo Brancaccio, Rome, 7–14 July 1997*, vol. 1. ed. by Maurizio Taddei and Giuseppe De Marco. (Serie Orientale Roma, 90), 55–76. Rome: Istituto italiano per l'Africa e l'Oriente.

Kenoyer, Jonathan Mark and Richard H. Meadow. 2010. Inscribed Objects from Harappa Excavations: 1986–2007. *Corpus of Indus Seals and Inscriptions, Vol. 3: New Material, Untraced Objects, and Collections Outside India and Pakistan*, ed. by Asko Parpola, B.M. Pande and Petteri Koskikallio. (Memoirs of the Archeological Survey of India, 96), xliv-lviii. Helsinki: Suomalainen Tiedeakatemia.

Khačikjan, Margaret. 1998. *The Elamite Language*. (Documenta Asiana, 4). Rome: Consiglio Nazionale delle Ricerche, Istituto per gli Studi Micenei ed Egeo-anatolici.

Khačikjan, Margaret. 2010. Elamskij jazyk (The Elamite Language). *Jazyki Mira. Drevnie reliktovye jazyki Perednej Azii* (Languages of the World: Ancient Relict Languages of the Near East), ed. by N.N. Kazanskii, A.A. Kibrik, and J.B. Korjakov, 95–118. Moscow: Academia.

Klinger, Jörg. 1994. Hattisch und Sprachverwandtschaft. *Hethitica* 12: 23–40.

Klinger, Jörg. 2005. Hattisch. *Sprachen des Alten Orients*, ed. by Michael P. Streck, 128–134. Darmstad: Wissenschaftliche Buchgesellschaft.

Klochkov, I. S. 1999. Signs on a Potsherd from Gonur (On the Question of the Script Used in Margiana). *Ancient Civilizations from Scythia to Siberia* 5: 165–175.

Knapp, A. Bernard and Ioannis Voskos. 2008. Cyprus at the End of the Late Bronze Age: Crisis and Colonization, or Continuity and Hybridization? *American Journal of Archaeology* 112: 659–684.

Knapp, A. Bernard and Stuart W. Manning. 2016. Crisis in Context: The End of the Late Bronze Age in the Eastern Mediterranean. *American Journal of Archaeology* 120: 99–149.

Kober, Alice E. 1948. The Minoan Scripts: Fact and Theory. *American Journal of Archaeology* 52: 82–103.

Koch, John T. 2014. On the Debate over the Classification of the Language of the South-Western (SW) Inscriptions, also Known as Tartessian. *Journal of Indo-European Studies* 42: 335–427.

Komoróczy, Géza. 1976a. On the Idea of Sumero-Hungarian Linguistic Affiliation: Critical Notes on a Pseudo-Scholarly Phenomenon. *Annales Univerisitatis Scientarium Budapestinensis de Rolando Eötvös nominatae. Sectio historica* 17: 259–303.

Komoróczy, Géza. 1978. Das Rätsel der sumerischen Sprache als Problem der Frühgeschichte Vorderasiens. *Festschrift Lubor Matouš, I. Teil*, ed. by Blahoslav Hruška and Géza Komoróczy. (Assyriologia, 4–5), 225–252. Budapest.

Komoróczy, Géza. 1976b. *Sumer és magyar?* Budapest: Magvetö Kiadó.

Krebernik, Manfred. 2006. Elamisch. *Sprachen des Alten Orients*, ed. by Michael P. Streck, 159–182. Darmstad: Wissenschaftliche Buchgesellschaft.

Labat René. 1951. Structure de la langue élamite (état présent de la question). *Conférences de l'Institut de Linguistique de Paris* 9: 23–42.

Lambert, Wilfred G. 1987. A Vocabulary of an Unknown Language. *M.A.R.I. Annales de Recherches Interdisciplinaires* 5: 409–413.

Laursen, Steffen Terp. 2010. The Westward Transmission of Indus Valley Sealing Technology: Origin and Development of the 'Gulf Type' Seal and Other Administrative Technologies in Early Dilmun, c.2100–2000 BC. *Arabian Archaeology and Epigraphy* 21: 96–134.

Lawler, Andrew. 2007. Ancient Writing or Modern Fakery? *Science* 317, no. 5838: 587–589.

LeBlanc, Paul D. 2013. *Indus Epigraphic Perspectives: Exploring Past Decipherment Attempts and Possible New Approaches*. MA Thesis, University of Ottawa.

MacGinnis, John. 2012. Evidence for a Peripheral Language in a Neo-Assyrian Tablet from the Governor's Palace in Tušhan. *Journal of Near Eastern Studies* 71: 13–20.

Machinist, Peter. 2000. Biblical Traditions: The Philistines and Israelite History. *The Sea Peoples and Their World: A Reassessment*, ed. by Eliezer D. Oren. (University Museum Monograph, 108), 53–83. Philadelphia: University Museum of the University of Pennsylvania.

Madjidzadeh, Youssef. 2011. Jiroft Tablets and the Origin of the Linear Elamite Writing System. *Cultural Relations between the Indus and the Iranian Plateau during the Third Millennium BCE: Indus Project, Research Institute for Humanities and Nature, June 7–8, 2008*, ed. by Toshiki Osada and Michael Witzel (Harvard Oriental Series, Opera Minora, 7), 217–243. Cambridge: Department of South Asian Studies, Harvard University.

Maeir, Aren M., Louise A. Hitchcock, and Liora Kolska Horwitz. 2013. On the Constitution and Transformation of Philistine Identity. *Oxford Journal of Archaeology* 32:1–38

Maeir, Aren M., Louise A. Hitchcock. 2017. The Appearance, Formation and Transformation of Philistine Culture: New Perspectives and New Finds. *The Sea Peoples Up-To-Date: New Research on the Migration of Peoples in the 12th Century BCE*, ed. by Peter M. Fischer and Teresa Bürge, 149–162. Vienna.

Magnelli, Adalberto and Giuseppe Petrantoni. 2013. L'eteocretese di Dreros e il semitico: nuove considerazioni. *Myrtia* 28: 17–29.

McAlpin, David W. 1974. Toward Proto-Elamo-Dravidian. *Language* 50: 89–101.

McAlpin, David W. 1975. Elamite and Dravidian: Further Evidence of Relationship. *Current Anthropology* 16: 105–115.

McAlpin, David W. 1981. *Proto-Elamo-Dravidian: The Evidence and Its Implications.* (Transactions of the American Philosophical Society, 71/3). Philadelphia: American Philosophical Society.

McAlpin, David W. 2003. Velars, Uvulars, and the North Dravidian Hypothesis. *Journal of the American Oriental Society* 123: 521–546.

McAlpin, David W. 2015. Brahui and the Zagrosian Hypothesis. *Journal of the American Oriental Society* 135: 551–586.

Meadow, Richard H. and Jonathan Mark Kenoyer. 2005. Excavations at Harappa 2000–2001: New Insights on Chronology and City Organization. *South Asian Archaeology 2001: Proceedings of the Sixteenth International Conference of the European Association of South Asian Archaeologists, Held in Collège de France, Paris, 2–6 July 2001*, ed. by Catherine Jarrige and Vincent Lefèvre, 207–225. Paris: Editions Recherche sur les Civilisations.

Mendenhall, George E. 1985. *The Syllabic Inscriptions from Byblos.* Beirut: American University of Beirut.

Merlini, Marco and Gheorghe Lazarovici. 2008. Settling Discovery Circumstances, Dating and Utilization of the Tărtăria Tablets. *Acta Terrae Septemcastrensis* 7: 111–195.

Michalowski, Piotr. 1983. History as Charter: Some Observations on the Sumerian King List. *Journal of the American Oriental Society* 103: 237–248.

Michalowski, Piotr. 2008. Sumerian. *The Ancient Languages of Mesopotamia, Egypt, and Aksum*, ed. by Roger D. Woodard, 19–46. Cambridge: Cambridge University Press.

Michalowski, Piotr. In press. The Sumerian Language. *Handbook of Ancient Mesopotamia*, ed. by Gonzalo Rubio. De Gruyter.

Moqaddam, Azhideh. 2009. Ancient Geometry and "*Proto-Iranian" Scripts: South Konar Sandal Mound Inscriptions, Jiroft. *From Daēna to Dîn. Religion, Kultur und Sprache in der iranischen Welt. Festschrift für Philip Kreyenbroek zum 60. Geburtstag*, ed. by Christine Allison, Anke Joisten-Prushke and Antje Wendtland, 53–103. Wiesbaden: Harrasowitz Verlag.

Moran, William L. 1988. Review of Mendenhall 1986. *The Catholic Biblical Quarterly* 50: 508–510.

Niesiołowski-Spanò, Łukasz. 2012. Dziedzictwo Goliata. Filistyni i Hebrajczycy w cza-sach biblijnych (Goliath's Legacy: Philistines and Hebrews in Biblical Times, in Pol-ish). Toruń: Wydawnictwo Uniwersytetu Mikołaja Kopernika.

Niesiołowski-Spanò, Łukasz. 2016. *Goliath's Legacy: Philistines and Hebrews in Bibli-cal Times* (Philippika, 83). Wiesbaden: Harrassowitz.

Nissen, Hans. 2016. Uruk: Early Administration Practices and the Development of Proto-Cuneiform Writing. *Archéo-Nil* 26: 33–48.

Olivier, Jean-Pierre. 1986. Cretan Writing in the Second Millennium B.C. *World Archae-ology* 17: 377–389.

Olivier, Jean-Pierre. 1975. Le disque de Phaistos. *Bulletin de correspondance hellénique* 99: 5–34.

Olivier, Jean-Pierre. 1990. The Relationship between Inscriptions on Hieroglyphic Seals and those Written on Archival Documents. *Aegean Seals, Sealings and Administra-tion: Proceedings of the NEH-Dickson Conference of the Program in Aegean Scripts and Prehistory of the Department of Classics, University of Texas at Austin, Janu-ary 11–13, 1989*, ed. by Thomas G. Palaima. (Aegaeum, 5), 11–24. Université de Liège, Histoire de l'art et archéologie de la Grèce antique.

Olivier, Jean-Pierre. 2013. The Development of Cypriote Syllabaries from Enkomi to Kafizin. Steele, ed. 2013, 7–26.

Olivier, Jean-Pierre, and Louis Godart. 1996. *Corpus Hieroglyphicarum Inscriptionum Cretae*. (Études Crétoises, 31). Paris: De Boccard.

Olivier, Jean-Pierre and François Vandenabeele. 2007. *Édition holistique des textes chy-pro minoens*. (Biblioteca di "Pasiphae," 6). Pisa and Rome: F. Serra.

Owens, Gareth A. 1999. Balkan Neolithic Scripts. *Kadmos* 38: 114–120.

Paper, Herbert H. 1955. *The Phonology and Morphology of Royal Achaemenid Elamite*. Ann Arbor: University of Michigan Press.

Paper, Herbert H. 1956. Review of Balkan 1954. *Journal of Near Eastern Studies* 15: 251–254.

Parpola, Asko. 1996. The Indus Script. *The World Writing Systems*, ed. by Peter T. Dan-iels and William Bright, 165–171. Oxford: Oxford University Press.

Parpola, Simo. 1975. Transliteration of Sumerian: Problems and Prospects. *Studia Ori-entalia* 46: 239–257.

Parpola, Simo. 2010. Sumerian: A Uralic Language, I. *Language in the Ancient Near East, Volume 1: Compte rendu de la 53ᵉ Rencontre Assyriologique Internationale, 23–28 July 2007*, ed. by Leonid Cogan (Bibel und Bibel, 4/1), 181–209.Winona Lake: Eisenbrauns.

Parpola, Simo. 2012. Sumerian: A Uralic Language, II. *Babel und Bibel 6: Annual of Ancient Near Eastern, Old Testament and Semitic Studies*, ed. by Leonid Kogan, 269–322. Winona Lake: Eisenbrauns.

Payne, Annick. 2012. *Iron Age Hieroglyphic Luwian Inscriptions*. (Writings from the Ancient World, 29). Atlanta: Society of Biblical Literature.

Perna, Massino. 2014. The Birth of Administration and Writing *KE-RA-ME-JA* in Minoan Crete: Some Thoughts on Hieroglyphics and Linear A. *KE-RA-ME-JA: Studies Pre-sented to Cynthia W. Shelmerdine*, ed. by Dimitri Nakassis, Joann Gulizio, and Sarah A. James. (Prehistory Monographs, 46), 251–259. Philadelphia: INSTAP Academic Press.

Peust, Carsten. 2011. *Sumerian Grammar Bibliography*. www.peust.de/SumerianBiblio graphy.pdf.

Pittman, Holly. 2013. Imagery in Administrative Context: Susiana and the West in the Fourth Millennium BC. *Ancient Iran and Its Neighbours: Local Developments and*

Long-Range Interactions in the 4th Millennium BC, ed. by Cameron A. Petrie. (British Institute of Persian Studies Archaeological Monographs Series, 3), 293–336. Havertown: Oxbow Books.

Poebel, Arno. 1923. *Grundzüge der sumerischen Grammatik*. Rostock: Selbstverlag des Verfassers.

Possehl, Gregory L. 1990. Revolution in the Urban Revolution: The Emergence of Indus Urbanization. *Annual Review of Anthropology* 19: 261–282.

Rao, Rajesh P.N., Nisha Yadav, Mayank N. Vahia, Hrishikesh Joglekar, Ronojoy Adhikari, and Iravatham Mahadevan. 2010. Entropy, the Indus Script, and Language: A Reply to R. Sproat. *Computational Linguistics* 36: 795–805.

Rao, Rajesh P.N., Rob Lee, Nisha Yadav, Mayank Vahia, Philip Jonathan, and Pauline Ziman. 2015. On Statistical Measures and Ancient Writing Systems. *Language* 91: e189–e205.

Reade, Julian E. 1978. Kassites and Assyrians in Iran. *Iran* 16: 137–143.

Reiner, Erica. 1969. The Elamite Language. *Altkleinasiatische Sprachen*, ed. by Johannes Friedrich. (Handbuch der Orientalistik, Erste Abteilung, II. Band: Keilschriftforschung und alte Geschichte Vorderasiens, 1. Und 2. Abschnitt, Lieferung 2), 54–118. Leiden: E. J. Brill.

Rollston, Christopher A. 2014. Northwest Semitic Cursive Scripts of Iron II. *"An Eye for Form": Epigraphic Essays in Honor of Frank Moore Cross*, ed. by Jo Ann Hackett and Walter E. Aufrecht, 202–234. Winona Lake: Eisenbrauns.

Rubio, Gonzalo. 1999. On the Alleged Pre-Sumerian Substratum. *Journal of Cuneiform Studies* 51: 1–16.

Rubio, Gonzalo. 2005. On the Linguistic Landscape of Early Mesopotamia. *Ethnicity in Ancient Mesopotamia: Papers Read at the 48th Rencontre Internationale, Leiden, 1.-4. July 2002*, ed. by Wilfred H. van Soldt. (PIHANS, 102), 316–332. Leiden: Nederlands Instituut voor het Nabije Oosten.

Rubio, Gonzalo. 2006. Shulgi and the Death of Sumerian. *Approaches to Sumerian Literature: Studies in Honour of Stip*, ed. by Piotr Michalowski and Niek Veldhuis. (Cuneiform Monographs, 35), 167–179. Leiden: Brill.

Rubio, Gonzalo. 2007a. Sumerian Morphology. *Morphologies of Asia and Africa*, vol. 2, ed. by Alan S. Kaye, 1327–1379. Winona Lake: Eisenbrauns.

Rubio, Gonzalo. 2007b. The Languages of the Ancient Near East. *A Companion to the Ancient Near East*, ed. by Daniel Snell, 79–109. Oxford: Blackwell.

Sassmannshausen, Leonhard. 1999. The Adaptation of Kassites to the Babylonian Civilization. *Languages and Cultures in Contact: At the Crossroads of Civilizations in the Syro-Mesopotamian Realm; Proceedings of the 42th RAI*, ed. by Karel van Lerberghe and Gabriela Voet. (Orientalia Lovaniensia Analecta, 96), 409–424. Leuven: Peeters.

Sassmannshausen, Leonhard. 2014. *Kassitische herrscher und ihre Namen. He Has Opened Nisaba's House of Learning: Studies in Honor of Åke Waldemar Sjöberg on the Occasion of His 89th Birthday on August 1st 2013*, ed. by Leonhard Sassmannshausen. (Cuneiform Monographs, 46), 165–199. Leiden: Brill.

Sathasivam, Arumugam. 1965. *Sumerian: A Dravidian Language* (Sumerian Studies, 1). Berkeley.

Sathasivam, Arumugam. 1969. Linguistics in Ceylon (II): Tamil. *Linguistics in South Asia: Current Trends in Linguistics, Volume 5*, ed. by Thomas Albert Sebeok, 752–759. The Hague: Mouton.

Schmandt-Besserat, Denise. 1984. Review of Shann W.W. Winn, *Pre-Writing in Southeastern Europe: The Sign System of the Vinca Culture CA. 4000 B.C. American Journal of Archaeology* 88: 71–72.

Schneider, Thomas. 2003. Kassitisch und Hurro-Urartäisch. *Altorientalische Forschungen* 30: 372–381.

Schneider, Thomas. 2011. The Philistine Language and the Name "David." *Ugarit-Forschungen* 43: 569–580.

Schrakamp, Ingo. 2013. Lullubi. *The Encyclopedia of Ancient History*, ed. by Roger S. Bagnall, Kai Brodersen, Craige B. Champion, Andrew Erskine, and Sabine R. Huebner, 4166–4167. Malden: Blackwells.

Schumacher, Stefan. 1998a. Camunic. *Encyclopedia of the Languages of Europe*, ed. by Glanville Price. Malden: Blackwell.

Schumacher, Stefan. 1998b. Lemnian. *Encyclopedia of the Languages of Europe*, ed. by Glanville Price. Malden: Blackwell.

Schumacher, Stefan. 1998c. Raetic. *Encyclopedia of the Languages of Europe*, ed. by Glanville Price. Malden: Blackwell.

Sherratt, Susan. 2013. Late Cypriot Writing in Context. *Syllabic Writing on Cyprus and its Context: Proceedings of the Conference Held in Cambridge, 12th–13th December 2008*, ed. by Philippa M. Steele, 77–105. Cambridge: Cambridge University Press.

Singer, Itamar. 2007. Who Were the Kaška? *Phasis* 10: 168–181.

Singer, Itamar. 2013. 'Old Country' Ethnonyms in 'New Countries' of the 'Sea Peoples' Diaspora. *AMILLA: The Quest for Excellence. Studies Presented to Guenter Kopcke in Celebration of His 75th Birthday*, ed. by R.B. Koehl. (Prehistory Monographs, 43), 321–333. Philadelphia: INSTAP Academic Press.

Smith, Eric J.M. 2007. [-ATR] Harmony and the Vowel Inventory of Sumerian. *Journal of Cuneiform Studies* 59: 19–38.

Southworth, Franklin. 2011. Rice in Dravidian. *Rice* 4: 142–148.

Soysal, Oğuz. 2004. *Hattischer Wortschatz in hethitischer Textüberlieferung*. Leiden: Brill.

Sproat, Richard. 2014. A Statistical Comparison of Written Language and Nonlinguistic Symbol Systems. *Language* 90: 457–481.

Sproat, Richard. 2015. On Misunderstandings and Misrepresentations: A Reply to Rao et al. *Language* 91: e206–e208.

Starostin, George. 2002. On the Genetic Affiliation of the Elamite Language. *Mother Tongue* 7: 147–170.

Steele, Philippa M. 2013a. *A Linguistic History of Ancient Cyprus: The Non-Greek Languages and Their Relations with Greek, c.1600–1300 BC*. Cambridge: Cambridge University Press.

Steele, Philippa M, ed. 2013b. *Syllabic Writing on Cyprus and Its Context: Proceedings of the Conference Held in Cambridge, 12th–13th December 2008*. Cambridge: Cambridge University Press.

Steele, Philippa M. 2014. Distinguishing between Cypriote Scripts: Steps towards Establishing a Methodology. *Kadmos* 53: 129–148.

Steinkeller, Piotr. 2003. An Ur III Manuscript of the Sumerian King List. *Literatur, Politic und Recht in Mesopotamien: Festschrift für Claus Wilcke*, ed. by Walther Sallaberger et al. (Orientalia Biblica et Christiana, 14), 267–292. Wiesbaden: Harrassowitz.

Steinkeller, Piotr. 2006. New Light on Marhaši and its Contacts with Makkan and Babylonia. *Journal of Magan Studies* 1: 1–17.

Steinkeller, Piotr. 2014. Marhasi and Beyond: The Jiroft Civilization in a Historical Perspective. *'My Life is like the Summer Rose': Maurizio Tosi e l'Archeologia come modo di vivere: Papers in Honour of Maurizio Tosi for His 70th Birthday*, ed. by C.C.

Lamberg-Karlovsky, B. Genito and B. Cerasetti. (BAR International Series, 2690), 691–707. Oxford: Archeopress.

Stockhammer, Philipp W. 2017. How Aegean is Philistine Pottery? The Use of Aegean-type Pottery in the Early 12th Century BCE Southern Levant. *"Sea Peoples" Up-To-Date: New Research on Transformation in the Eastern Mediterranean in the 13th–11th Centuries BCE*, ed. by Peter M. Fischer and Teresa Bürge. (Denkschriften der Gesamtakademie 81), 379–387. Vienna: Österreichische Akademie der Wissenschaften.

Stolper, Matthew W. 2008. Elamite. *The Ancient Languages of Mesopotamia, Egypt, and Aksum*, ed. by Roger D. Woodard, 60–95. Cambridge: Cambridge University Press.

Stolper, Matthew W. 2014. Case in Point: The Persepolis Fortification Archive. *Archaeologies of Text: Archaeology, Technology, and Ethics*, ed. by Matthew T. Rutz and Morag Kersel. (Joukowsky Institute Publications, 6), 14–30. Havertown, PA: Oxbow Books.

Streck, Michael P. 2011. Babylonian and Assyrian. *The Semitic Languages: An International Handbook*, ed. by Stefan Weninger. (Handbücher zur Sprach- und Kommunikationswissenschaft, 36), 359–396. Berlin: De Gruyter Mouton.

Taracha, Piotr. 1988: Zu den syntaktischen Verknüpfungen im Hattischen. *Altorientalische Forschungen* 15: 59–68.

Taracha, Piotr. 1995. Zum Stand der hattischen Studien: Mögliches und Unmögliches in der Erforschung des Hattischen. *Atti del II Congresso Internaziomale di Hittitologia*, ed. by Onofrio Carruba, Mauro Giorgieri, and Clelia Mora. (Studia mediterranea, 9), 351–358. Pavia: Gianni Iuculano Editore.

Taracha, Piotr. 1998. Neues zu Sprache und Kultur der Hattier. *Orientalistische Literaturzeitung* 93: 8–18.

Taracha, Piotr. 2000. More on the Hattic Sentence-Building: Does the Category of Tense Exist in Hattic? *The Asia Minor Connexion: Studies on the Pre-Greek Languages in Memory of Charles Carter*, ed. by Yoël L. Arbeitman. (Orbis/Supplementa, 13), 223–243. Leuven: Peeters.

Tavernier, Jan. 2002. *Iranica in de Achaemenidische Periode (ca. 550–330 v. Chr), Taalkundige studie van Oud-Iraanse eigennamen en leenwoorden, die geattesteerd zijn in niet-Iraanse Teksten*. Doctoral dissertation, Faculteit Letteren, Departement Oosterse en Slavische Studies, Katholieke Universiteit Leuven.

Tavernier, Jan. 2011. Élamite. Analyse grammaticale et lecture de textes. *Res Antiquae* 8: 315–350.

Thompsen, Marie-Louise. 1984. *The Sumerian Language: An Introduction to Its History and Grammatical Structure*. (Mesopotamia, 10). Copenhagen: Akademisk Forlag.

Tóth, Alfréd. 2007. *Etruscans, Huns and Hungarians*. The Hague: Mikes International.

Trombetti, Alfredo. 1902. Delle relazioni delle lingue caucasiche con le lingue camito-semitiche e con altri grupi linguistici, I. *Giomale della Societa Asiatica Italiana* 15: 177–201.

Udolph, Jürgen, ed. 2013. *Europa vasconica – Europa semitica? kritische Beiträge zur Frage nach dem baskischen und semitischen Substrat in Europa*. (Beiträge zur Lexikographie und Namenforschung, 6). Hamburg: Baar.

Untermann, Jürgen. 1980. *Monumenta Linguarum Hispanicarum. Band II: Die Inschriften in iberischer Schrift aus Südfrankreich*. Wiesbaden: Dr. Ludwig Reichert.

Untermann, Jürgen. 1990. *Monumenta Linguarum Hispanicarum. Band III.1/2: Die Iberischen Inschriften aus Spanien*. Wiesbaden: Dr. Ludwig Reichert.

Untermann, Jürgen. 1997. *Monumenta linguarum Hispanicarum. Band IV: Die tartessischen, keltiberischen und lusitanischen Inschriften*. Wiesbaden: Dr. Ludwig Reichert.

Valério, Miguel. 2014a. The Interpretative Limits of the Southwestern Script. *Journal of Indo-European Studies* 42: 439–467.

Valério, Miguel. 2014b. Seven Uncollected Cypro-Minoan Inscriptions. *Kadmos* 53: 111–127.

Van Soldt, Wilfred H. 1980. MA and ḪUR in Kassite Texts. *Revue d'Assyriologie et d'archéologie orientale* 74: 77–80.

Vennemann, Theo. 2003. *Europa Vasconica, Europa Semitica*, ed. Patrizia Noel and Aziz Hanna (Trends in Linguistics, Studies and Monographs, 18). Berlin: Mouton de Gruyter.

Vidale, Massimo. 2007. The Collapse Melts Down: A Reply to Farmer, Sproat and Witzel. *East and West* 57: 333–366.

Weeden, Mark. 2015. The Land of Walastin at Tell Tayınat. *N.A.B.U. Nouvelles Assyriologiques Brèves et Utilitaires* 2015: 65–66.

Whittaker, Gordon. 2008. The Case for Euphratic. *Bulletin of the Georgian National Academy of Sciences* 2: 156–168.

Whittaker, Gordon. 2012. Euphratic: A Phonological Sketch. *The Sound of Indo-European: Phonetics, Phonemics, and Morphophonemics*, ed. by Benedicte Nielsen Whitehead, Tomas Olander, Birgit Anette Olsen, and Jens Elmegård Rasmussen. (Copenhagen Studies in Indo-European, 4), 577–606. Copenhagen: Museum Tusculanum Press.

Wilcke, Claus. 2005. ED Lú A und die Sprache(n) der archaischen Texte. *Ethnicity in Ancient Mesopotamia: Papers Read at the 48th Rencontre Internationale, Leiden, 1.-4. July 2002*, ed. by Wilfred H. van Soldt. (PIHANS, 102), 430–445. Leiden: Nederlands Instituut voor het Nabije Oosten.

Wilhelm, Gernot. 1978. Ist das Elamische eine Ergativsprache? *Archäologische Mitteilungen aus Iran* 11: 7–12.

Wilhelm, Gernot. 1982. Noch einmal zur behaupteten Ergativität des Elamischen. *Archäologische Mitteilungen aus Iran* 15: 7–8.

Woods, Christopher. 2010. The Earliest Mesopotamian Writing. *Visible Language: Inventions of Writing in the Ancient Middle East and Beyond*, ed. by Christopher Woods. (Oriental Institute Museum Publications, 32), 33–50. Chicago: The Oriental Institute of the University of Chicago.

Zadok, Ron. 1984. *The Elamite Onomasticon*. (ANNALI supplemento, 40). Naples: Istituto universitario orientale.

Zadok, Ron. 1987. Peoples from the Iranian Plateau in Babylonia during the Second Millennium B.C. *Iran* 25: 1–26.

Zadok, Ron. 1995. On the Current State of Elamite Lexicography. *Studi Epigrafici e Linguistici sul Vicino Oriente Antico* 12: 241–252.

Zadok, Ron. 2005. Lulubi. *Encyclopedia Iranica*. www.iranicaonline.org/articles/lulubi (31 January 2016).

Zadok, Ron. 2015. Kassites. *Encyclopedia Iranica*. www.iranicaonline.org/articles/kassites (31 January 2016).

Zanotti, David G. 1983. The Position of the Tărtăria Tablets within the Southeast European Copper Age. *American Journal of Archaeology* 87: 209–213.

Zavaroni, Adolfo. 2005. The Camunic Inscriptions: A Phonological Framework. *General Linguistics* 43: 87–105.

Zólyomi, Gábor. 2006. Sumerisch. *Schriften und Sprachen des Alten Orients* (2nd ed.), ed. by Michael Streck, 11–43. Darmstadt: Wissenschaftliche Buchgesellschaft.

CHAPTER 3

BASQUE AND THE RECONSTRUCTION OF ISOLATED LANGUAGES

Joseba A. Lakarra

1 INTRODUCTION[1]

> I think it's appropriate to ask what the purpose of our genetic classification is. I believe that most historical linguists value the classifications because they help us find out about the histories of the languages in a family. We reconstruct parts of their common protolanguage and then use those reconstructions to study and compare the changes that have occurred in the various daughter languages. In other words, *to be useful to a historical linguist, a hypothesis of genetic relationship must be fruitful: a valid genetic grouping will permit reconstruction and thus lead to be a better understanding of the member languages and their histories. If a genetic hypothesis does not lead to new insights of these kinds, therein it is sterile and, within linguistics, useless.*
>
> (Thomason 1993, p. 494; emphasis added [JAL])

The classification and comparison of languages is *not* the ultimate goal of diachronic linguists. Their main task is to describe and explain the development of languages or families studied in their different phases (whether documented or not). Comparison[2] is of no scientific interest except when, undertaken in strict conditions, its objective is to illuminate the structure of the languages under study and the changes produced within them, especially irregularities, exceptions, *fases sparitas* (stages with little or no attestation, impossible or difficult to investigate in the language (or dialect) itself).

In language families with a long developed tradition of diachronic research, such as Indo-European (IE), Uralic, or Semitic, demonstration of genetic relationships has not signified the culmination of comparativists' work[3] but rather the start of their true vocation as historical linguists. Their work must be based on the regularity of phonetic change and on homologies, not on analogies, similarities, and superficial or casual resemblances, such as the spurious "similarities", that, as Trask (1996: 220) shows, one could find between Ancient Greek and Hawaiian or between Hungarian and Basque (1997: 412–415), which only make for an amateur entertainment.

That the Basque language is genetically isolated has been an obvious statement for a long time now: its structural differences with respect to other languages, whether geographically close or not (Romance, Germanic, Semitic, and so on), are clear for all to see. In the past, when Bascophiles or Basque apologists have sought to transform historical, political, or religious issues into linguistic questions they often claimed that in ancient times Basque (B) was spoken in the whole of the Iberian Peninsula (more so than in Gaul or elsewhere in Europe), generally without attempting to establish genetic relationships (see Tovar 1981, Madariaga 2008).

After the development of comparative-historical linguistics, only very unorthodox linguistics, like Schuchardt, Uhlenbeck, Trombetti, or Tovar,[4] have attempted to relate B to other languages; those more aware of the limits of this method have avoided fantasizing impossible historical scenarios and chronologies as well as improper and ridiculous comparative "tricks".

Since having no proven genetic relationships implied imbuing the language with an ancient aura, non-Basque amateurs[5] have searched for such relationships with all kinds of other languages, from Iberian to Na-Dene, by way of all kinds of "bright" ideas.[6] In general, specialists in the relevant languages or families have not felt too concerned about such attempts or have refuted them as implausible, unfounded, ignorant of the data, based on erroneous analysis, and so on. Similar problems are typically found when these comparisons are judged from the perspective of Basque linguistics or even from a consideration of the basic principles of linguistic comparison (see Section 3).

2 SOME BASIC DATA FOR THE HISTORY OF THE LANGUAGE[7]

2.1 Context of Basque

There are just over 800,000 speakers of Basque (*euskara*, variants *heuskara, üskara, euskera, eskuera, eskuara*, etc.) on both sides of the Pyrenees, bordering the Bay of Biscay, in the territory – almost 27,000 km^2 – known in B as *Euskal Herria* (Country of the B Language). This area coincides in general terms with the historical provinces of Lapurdi (Labourd), Behenafarroa (Basse Navarre), and Zuberoa (Soule) in the North and the Kingdom of Navarre (Nafarroa/Navarra) and the provinces of Bizkaia (Vizcaya), Gipuzkoa (Guipúzcoa), and Araba (Álava) in the South.

In the latter three provinces (which together make up the Basque Autonomous Community, BAC) the language has been co-official since 1982 with Spanish, and its introduction into the education and administrative systems[8] has led to more people knowing it, especially among the younger generations – although not so much to a significant increase in its use – and a clear improvement in expectations for its future. In Navarre it only enjoys co-official status (and in a restricted way) in the B-speaking zone – north of Pamplona (B *Iruña* or *Iruñea*) – following a major decline in B-speakers between the 19th and 20th centuries. In the continental territories to the north, Basque is clearly declining toward a likely near extinction, led by the fairly typical encouragement of linguistic genocide of postrevolutionary France (see Calvet 1981).

Historically, the language was spoken in those territories (although there are no testimonies from parts of the Encartaciones area of Bizkaia or southern Navarre) and their surroundings during the Middle Ages (Rioja, Burgos) and even farther afield (from the Pyrenees to the Mediterranean according to Corominas, though not so extensively according to most; cf. Salaberri 2011a, Manterola 2015) in Late Antiquity (see Map 3.1).

2.2 Basque prehistory

The prehistory of the language – a period lacking any direct or indirect information – ends at the beginning of the Common Era, thanks to the Aquitanian inscriptions (between the 1st and 3rd centuries AD), which contain some 300 to 400 anthroponyms and theonyms.[9]

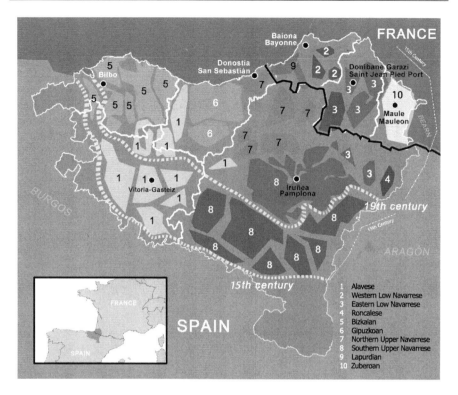

MAP 3.1 BASQUE MAP

Here we enter into protohistory, a period without any texts written in Basque but with abundant information, especially in the medieval era, thanks to the large number of names and toponyms included in Latin and Romance (Navarrese, Gascon, Castillian) texts; here, Luchaire was a pioneer, as Mitxelena (1964) points out.

2.3 Basque historical periods

The historical period of the Basque language is usually said to begin with the publication of *Linguae Vasconum Primitiae* (Bordeaux 1545) by Bernard Etxepare, even though there are a couple of 11th-century glosses[10] and the odd poetic fragment or letters dating from before 1500. It would seem preferable (cf. Mounole and Lakarra 2017) to move the beginning of this period back to 1400, given that recent philology has demonstrated that the language of texts collected from the oral tradition (sayings, ballads, and elegies) in the late 16th century and first half of the 17th century correspond to much older periods.

The typical periodization, in eight stages (Lakarra 1997a), combines internal linguistic criteria with other references to sources or phenomena in the literary language:

1   Up to the 1st century of the Common Era: Proto-Basque (PB)
2   1st–3rd centuries: Basque in Antiquity

3   10th–14th centuries: Medieval Basque
4   1400–1600: Archaic Basque
5   1600–1745: Old and Classical Basque
6   1745–1876: First Modern Basque
7   1876–1968: Second Modern Basque
8   1968–: Contemporary Basque

Thus, for example, some phonetic changes in composition and derivation and the presence of the article in the Middle Ages separate (2) and (3); the nature of the (secondary/primary) corpus distinguish (3) and (4); archaic verb forms (aorist and other extinct tenses and moods, more numerous synthetic forms) serve to separate (4) and (5); the consequences of Larramendi's work – 1729, Grammar, 1745 Sp-B-Latin Dictionary – mark the boundary between (5) and (6); and the unification or standardization of the language is the landmark between (7) and (8).

Dialectal differences,[11] which to uneducated enthusiasts and speakers may appear great, are few for comparativists (cf. Mitxelena 1964, 1981), so that the origins of the initial dialectal divergence must be dated close to its early documentation. Mitxelena dated Old Common Basque (OCB), toward the 5th–6th centuries (see 9th section), a thousand years after Late Proto-Basque (LPB), which is a stage of language defined as "the language that the Romans encountered".

3 CRITIQUE OF COMPARISONS

The Basque language has been the object of many attempts to link it genetically to languages nearby and distant in both space and time. However, none of them has achieved the standards demanded by the comparative method, and above all, they have not achieved the objectives of diachronic comparison; namely, such attempts have been of no use when it comes to illuminating aspects of the structure and evolution of the language, and therefore, they are inadmissible by the comparative method as it has been developed in truly established language families (see, inter alia, Campbell 2013, Trask 1996, Watkins 1990 and Meillet 1925 and Mitxelena 1963); see Campbell 2011 and supra chapter 1 about Basque-Aquitanian relation.

No standard evidence of genetic relationship has ever been provided (nor attempted) discovering phonetic rules (sound correspondences) relating – for example – Iberian and Basque or elaborating the historical grammar, and the few "promising" cognates (homophones) have dwindled to such an extent that they have all but disappeared from the literature (cf. de Hoz 2010–2011), either as a result of changes in reading and/or interpretation within Iberian or because of advances in Basque linguistics and philology that make them impossible; See also chapter 2, section 3.4.

The different hypotheses regarding the genetic relationships of Basque – classic ones such as Basque-Iberian, Basque-Caucasian, more recent ones as Basque-Uraloaltaic, Vasconic, Basque-Indo-European, etc. (see Mitxelena 1964, Trask 1997 and Lakarra 2017: Section 2) – share multiple characteristics that discredit them immediately:

1)   They start from the simple yet false idea according to which, given that neither Basque nor other isolate language belongs to IE, Semitic, Uralic, or other well-stablished families – with known histories and acceptably reconstructed protolanguages, i.e., impossible to be manipulated on the whim of the amateur of the moment – all of them, and particularly B and one or another of the remaining languages, must belong to the

same family. Since the demonstration of this a priori assumption is a something good, a goal in itself, the objectives, methods, and criteria of comparative-historical linguistics are not sufficient to cause such "discoverers" to desist.

2)   In cases in which a minimum attempt has been made to prove an argument, analyzing alleged cognates in B and one or more other language, the Basque part of the argument (as well as often the other part, of course) is strewn with errors: erroneous, dialectal, or later meanings and forms; nonexistent loanwords, words, or variants; flawed and arbitrary morphemic analyses; and so on (cf. Campbell 1988 and 2013).[12]

3)   No attention is paid to the body of work on Basque historical linguistics or the existing literature on the language(s) that are compared with it.

4)   As a consequence, after many decades of such comparative efforts, no light has been shed on any aspect of the historical phonology or grammar of B (nor of the other languages).

5)   Frequently, the false illusions or statements derived from those essays are perpetuated in later works: thus, for example, a claim was still recently made about the supposed abundance of initial vowel in B (cf. Odriozola 2016) that, explained arbitrarily as old articles, Schuchardt used to underpin his B-Hamitic-Semitic edifice, which had already been demolished 90 years before.[13]

6)   In the search for "explanations" for languages compared to Basque, numerous things are overlooked such as significant variants, underused archaic testimonies, irregularities, generalizations and clarifications about phonetics or grammar, and, in general, the most important data for reconstructing B: if the relationship of $hiri_1$ 'city' and $hiri_2$ 'close, near' (cf. *her, her(t)si 'to close' and Sp $cerca_1$ 'closure' and $cerca_2$ 'near'; see Corominas and Pascual 1980–1991, s.u.) is not examined, this can only be due to the age-old and false belief that $hiri_1$ derives from the family of Iberian ILTIR.[14]

Altogether, not only is there bad comparative practice in much of this work, but the true nature of comparison is either misinterpreted or ignored. Comparison cannot be a goal in itself and even less so when the universal standards its practice requires are not fulfilled (see Section 1).

4 THE CLASSIC RECONSTRUCTIVE PARADIGM OF PROTO-BASQUE

4.1 Martinet and the plosives

Following diverse prestructuralist essays (by Campión, Azkue, Schuchardt, Gavel, Uhlenbeck, and others), Martinet (1950) approached the study of B in order to test diachronic phonology with a specific case – the well-known voicing of initial plosives in B – just as he had done with other language – Semitic, IE, Slavic, Celtic, and Romance languages. In calling for the need for a structural view of the problem – not the change of isolated sounds but of the system as a whole – he transformed the bases of research in this field. Likewise, he also realized that the situation of prolonged bilingualism and uninterrupted contact between dialects was an obstacle for distinguishing variants derived from regular sound change from other types of variants.[15]

Latin-Romance loanwords offered the surest support, given that we know both their origin and their Romance evolution, in contrast to what happens with the inherited lexicon. The use of loanwords, allows us to determine the chronology of many internal changes in the language that have taking place during the last thousand years based on what is known about the evolution of the Romance languages (Mitxelena 1974, Echenique 1984).[16]

The changes in Basque plosives had been addressed previously: according to Uhlenbeck, word-initial voiceless consonants were voiced through dissimilation from other intervocalic consonants. The problem with this hypothesis was that, in addition to the uncommon character of this phenomenon, there is also voicing in words without an intervocalic voiceless consonant (*gerezi* 'cherry', *gela* 'room' < Lat *ceresia(m)*, *cella(m)*, etc.). Gavel (1920: 314ff) suggested that all word-initial plosives voiced regularly in a period subsequent to the adoption of the oldest loanwords, because in B there are no word-initial voiceless consonants, except in recent loanwords, phonosymbolism, after the loss of vowels, regressive assimilations, and so on.

Martinet[17] accepted the important part of Gavel's explanation: Ancient B had only voiced plosive phonemes in word-initial position, whereas word-finally only voiceless plosives were allowed. On the other hand, both voiced and voiceless plosives were found in intervocalic environment. Nevertheless, the treatment of loanwords demonstrates that something more than voicing is necessary to characterize the old system. For Martinet, the starting point would not be the voiceless/voiced opposition, but another very different one, a *fortis/lenis* contrast as in Danish, which he had previously studied. There would, thus, be two series of plosives, strong /P, T, K/ and weak /p, t, k/. The strong plosives would be realized as aspirated $[p^h, t^h, k^h]$ word-initially and as plain [p, t, k] intervocally. The weak plosives would be produced as soft voiceless $[p_o, t_o, k_o]$ in word-initial position, and as fricative $[\beta, \delta, \gamma]$ between vowels.

Thus, the initial plosives in Latin loanwords, both voiced and voiceless, were adapted to PB as *lenis* phonemes, given that the aspirated allophones of the *fortis* ones were very different from the Latin sounds. In intervocalic position, each Latin plosive would have its corresponding PB phoneme: voiceless ones strong and voiced ones weak. Word-initially the strong phonemes would not be used in the adaptation of any Latin loanwords, and later they would disappear through the influence of surrounding languages.[18]

4.2 The reconstruction of the phonological system by Mitxelena

Mitxelena (1951) accepted Martinet's hypothesis, adding important observations in its support regarding (1) the development of geminates and clusters of voiced and voiceless consonants, (2) the sound [f], and (3) Aquitanian and medieval graphic testimonies.

The development of geminates would be the clearest sign that Basque speakers paid attention to the strength of sounds (geminates = long, i.e. strong) rather than sonority, because voiced geminates were adapted as (voiceless) *fortis* plosives just like voiceless geminates: Lat *-bb-* > B *p*, cf. Lat *abbas*, *ad valle(m)*, *sabbatu(m)* > B *apaiz* 'priest', *apal* 'humble', *zapatu* 'Saturday' versus Sp *abad*, *sábado*. Romance voiced groups have also given simple voiceless ones: *cobdiçia* > B *gutizia* 'whim' versus Sp *codicia*.

The testimony of the sound *f* – nonexistent in the phoneme inventory of PB – would corroborate such a phenomenon, because it was at certain point a variant of *b* (*nafar/ nabar* 'multi-colored', *afari/abari* 'dinner'), then *p* (*alfer/alper* 'idle', *ifini/ipini* 'to place, put'). In ancient times, sonority was not the main distinction between *b* and *p*, but rather its strong or weak pronunciation, so that because the fricative *f* was weak, it was replaced by *b*. If in PB the voiced/voiceless distinction had been pertinent, [f] would have been replaced by one or the other, not by both, for that reason we should assume that this opposition was not the basic one.[19]

Lastly, Mitxelena points out that the data on Aquitanian inscriptions coincide with this analysis: the written symbols and <CC> represent strong plosives (vs. <TH>, aspirated). Likewise, the distribution of the plosives shows that *p* was infrequent and a variant of *b* in strong position (i.e. on initial in the second member of the compound (Aquit *Seniponnis* vs. usual *-bon(n)*) and after the sibilant: cf. Aquit *Andoxponni*.

Mitxelena (1957) extended Martinet's argument to the whole system, believing that the strong/weak opposition affected all the consonants, except /h/. The complete reconstruction would be as follows (where, as in modern Basque orthography, *z* represents a voiceless pre-dorso-alveolar or dental fricative [s̪] and *s* is a voiceless apico-alveolar fricative [s̺]):

Strong	—	T	K	TZ	TS	N	L	R	
									h
Weak	b	d	g	z	s	n	l	r	

The fact that more phonemes do not appear does not mean that there were no more sounds but rather that it is impossible or unnecessary to reconstruct them with the available data for the nuclear phonological inventory. Mitxelena dispensed with (subsequently phonologized) sounds such as the strong bilabial, palatals, historically expressive or automatically generated (secondary) sounds, the /m/, nonexistent outside loanwords and phonosymbolisms, except as an allophone in /b/ in nasal contexts. Vowels are not mentioned either in the original argumentation (1957) or in the summary of the *Fonética histórica vasca* (*FHV*, since they had hardly changed since Aquitanian: cf. *Nescato, Cison, Sembe, Ummesahar. . . .*). Thus the five vowels of modern B are reconstructed as such, with three levels of height and with no distinction based on quantity; the additional vowel [y] of Zuberoan comes from **u*. The approximants [j] and [w] are later, emerging in different places: [j] from *e-* in old verbs (*joan* 'to go' < **e-oan*; cf. *ebili* 'to walk' < **e-bil-i*) and [w] in loanwords when it is not a case of a final diphthong.

The plosive and sibilant subsystems seem to coincide in neutralization points (in initial and final position, after a sonorant and before a consonant), reflecting the same opposition: we would have two series of sibilants opposed to one another by point and means of articulation: apical and laminal, fricative and affricate.

The weak/strong distinction persists historically in rhotics (trill and tap), but in contrast to what happens with all other consonants, these do not appear word-initially. The existence of /L/ and /N/ is guaranteed by their behavior in the intervocalic context and by Aquitanian and medieval written symbols. Intervocalically not all the *n*'s and *l*'s behave the same way as one can see clearly in loanwords, and traces remain in inherited words; thus, if from Lat *angelu, gula* and *caelu*, we get *aingeru* 'angel', *gura* 'desire', and *zeru* 'sky' (Z *zelü*); we could have a weak *-l-* in the causative (*-ra-*) but not in *ilhe/ule* 'hair' (> ***irhe/**ure*) from **enon-le* > **e.ole* > **eule*, etc. With *ahate* 'duck' and *lehoi* (< **leohe*) 'lion', the result of Lat *anate(m)* and *leone(m)*, a strong /N/ would be needed by both *arrano* 'eagle' and *baino* 'than . . . (comparative)', but not **ardano* 'wine' (> *ardao, arno, ardan-*) or **bini* 'grain' (> *bihi*), or **seni* 'child' (> *sehi, sein*) or *bai(n) a* 'but'.[20] There is prosthesis before initial *r* in late Lat *ropam* > *arropa*, late Lat *ratonem* > *arratoi*, etc. (as in Aragonese and Gascon via Basque substrate); the *muta cum liquida* consonant clusters are broken up, with a vowel before /r/ – *garau* 'grain', *daraturu* 'drill', *boronte* 'front' < Lat *granu(m)*, *taratru(m)*, *fronte(m)*, etc., and with the plosive deleted before the lateral: cf. *laket* 'pleasant', *loria*, *lau* 'flat' < Lat *placet, gloria(m), planu(m)*, etc.[21]

Since PB, there has been a tendency to neutralize the fortes/lenes opposition in sibilants and sonorants except intervocalically, in favor of lenis in initial position and fortis in final position:[22] cf. *gorputz*, *bake* < Lat *corpus*, *pacem*, and *zeru* < Rom *tselu*; in inherited words cf. *gazi* 'salty, savory'/*gatz* 'salt'.

Mitxelena recognized a phonemic character to aspiration in PB, /h/ being the only consonant outside the strong/weak opposition. Gavel (1920) had a different opinion, arguing in favor of an adventitious late character of /h/, which would not have existed in southern dialects. Analyzing Aquitanian and other medieval peninsular testimonies – and the then recently discovered inscription in Lerga (Navarre) – Mitxelena observed that the old /h/ (a clear difference with respect to its neighbor languages) appeared throughout the historical territory and that, although already lost in Navarre by the 10th century through Romance influence,[23] it was attested until the 13th–14th centuries in Alava and Rioja, and even in Bizkaia and Gipuzkoa.

Therefore, *zahar* 'old', *ahuntz* 'goat', *zuhur* 'wise, prudent', etc. are more archaic than *za(a)r*, *a.untz* (*awntz*, *ajntz*), *zur*, etc., since they retain the structure and number of syllables of a previous stage, in the same way as *ahate* 'duck', *ohore* 'honor', etc. are older than the corresponding contracted forms (*a(a)te*, *ôre*, etc.).[24] Mitxelena established four etymological origins for the historical /h/: (1) PB plosives in absolute initial position, (2) Latin-Romance *f*-, (3) intervocalic lenis *n*, and (4) PB *h.[25] Many etymological *h*'s disappear in historical periods of the language (cf. *FHV* 525 and 219–220), for example, those situated after the accent, or the first of two *h*'s within a root. Historically, there is no *h* beyond the second syllable, but there is in Aquitanian and even a thousand years later in Medieval Basque.

The accent is a difficult point in the reconstruction of LPB. The most common pattern in modern B is phrasal, rather than word-level and only weakly contrastive. This system cannot be very old, given that the evolution of consonants depends on whether they appear in initial or in medial position. There have been two main proposals regarding the old accentual system:

1   Martinet: demarcative accent on the initial syllable, which would explain the distribution of plosives.
2   Mitxelena: accent on the 2nd syllable, to explain the modern distribution of *h* (never after the 2nd, nor two *h*'s in the same word).[26]

Later (1995 and ff.) Hualde has placed the old accent on the last syllable of the phrase (lexically contrastive accent arising later in borrowings and morphologically complex words), but his argument seems to correspond more to OCB than to LPB.[27]

Mitxelena (1979, *FHV²*) proposed for PB the syllabic structure (C)V(W)(R)(S)(T), similar to that observed in Iberian. He established two restrictions: (1) in word-initial position only one of the following consonants could appear: *b*-, *g*-, *s*-, *z*-, *n*-, *l*-; (2) most likely, not all the segmental slots in a syllable were ever filled (*geurtz* 'next year' would be the closest).[28]

As regards morphemes, Mitxelena assumed that the Canonical Root Structure (CRS) of Iberian onomastic compounds and derivatives was "[2 + 2]" and "[2 + 1]" and that the maximum size of roots was two syllables and proposed a similar structure for Old Basque.

4.3 Morphosyntactic reconstruction

As in other languages and language families, morphosyntactic reconstruction of Basque is less advanced. The relationship and organization of elements, which is evident in phonological reconstruction, is difficult to observe in morphosyntax. Furthermore, if in the reconstruction of the phonology, elements belonging to different periods are sometimes mixed together, as we have seen, this applies even more to morphemes, such as derivative suffixes[29]; plural verbal markers (cf. *gaitean* 'let us be, we should be', *gara* 'we are' versus *gatoz* 'we are coming', *gabiltza* 'we are walking'); elements in first- and second-level declension; and so on.

In the study of diachronic Basque morphology, one must mention the names of Schuchardt and Lafon (see 1943 and 1999), although in the case of the former, his war against the sound laws of the Neogrammarians was damaging for Basque studies, as Mitxelena pointed out time and again. Several works by Mitxelena are indispensable, even if they are not specifically morphological, among them *Fonética Histórica Vasca* and *Apellidos Vascos*; others that address toponymy (1971), old texts (1954a, etc.), and scattered studies on the form of suffixes, postpositions, or the history of the verb (1977).

Yet, in our opinion, the work of Trask (1977) on the structure of the verb and historical syntax is the most important contribution in the last 60 years. It established that *da-* (cf. *dator* 'is coming', *dakar* 'is bringing') was not originally a marker of person or time, but was aspectual, and that its position to the left of the root does not favor SOV order of agglutinative languages, but another order altogether, VO (SVO according to him, VSO for Gómez 1994 and Gómez and Sainz 1995). In the same work, Trask clarifies the later character of the dative markers and the origins of ergativity, making it a starting point for later works on Basque diachronic morphosyntax.

5 ANALYSIS OF THE CANONICAL ROOT STRUCTURE

5.1 Antecedents in other languages

An important topic in IE diachrony is that of the CRS, particularly since Benveniste (1935). He reproached his predecessors for having reconstructed for the protolanguage, not a system, but a disjointed amalgam of polymorphous roots. Exploring the economy of the root, he established a general outline from which all those would derive. The results of this line of inquiry have been splendid (cf. Watkins 1984) in morphology, phonology, and the lexicon of the protolanguage and derived languages.

More recently, the CRS has been studied diachronically in other families such as Semitic (del Olmo Lete 2003), Uralic (Bakrò-Nagy 1992), Japanese (Janhunen 1997), Sinitic (Sagart 1999), and others. All these studies have demonstrated significant results for the phonology, morphology, and structure of the core lexicon – especially the reconstruction of old families of words (as well as those cited, see Schuh 2013 on Hausa) – and in some cases (see Elmendorf 1997 on Yuki – Wappo) may contribute evidence about more profound genetic relationships beyond the protolanguages.

5.2 First results of the new paradigm

Until recently little attention was paid to the CRS in Basque. Azkue (1923–1925) dedicated only 20 lines to it in a book of a thousand pages and did not observe that the root was monosyllabic in ancient times. There is barely anything else until Uhlenbeck (1947 [1942]) and Lafon (1950). One can scarcely say anything positive about the latter, since he ignores internal reconstruction and proclaims that comparison with the Caucasian languages – supposed relatives – is the only existing recourse for analyzing B roots. Mitxelena, in *FHV*, does not use this term, nor does he derive any important or clear consequences derived from it, though he notices, for example, the restriction against homorganic consonants in rhotics and sibilants within the root: *erur* 'snow' > *elur/edur, berar* 'grass' > *belar/bedar*, and *sasoi* < Sp *sazón, frantses* < *francés* as *sinetsi* 'to believe' < *zinhetsi* (1545), but, across morpheme-boundaries, *erro-aren* 'of the root'. Uhlenbeck deserves praise for calling for an analysis of root models, although he did so in order to buttress his theory of the polygenesis of the B language, where Biz and the other dialects would stem from different languages. Perhaps for this reason, he did not have any followers in the study of the structure of the root.

In Lakarra (1995), we point out various restrictions on historical B roots – **VC and **CV in autonomous monosyllabic lexemes, **TVTV in disyllables were not permitted – and we suggest that they could be explained as originating from the root CVC; thus important lexical and morphological results were achieved:

A1) additional combinations with known roots:

- **bel* (before *harbel* 'blackboard', *ubel* 'bruised', *orbel* 'fallen leaf', etc.): *sabel* 'belly', *gibel* 'liver, behind', etc.

A2) new roots (historically fossils):

- **ger*: *okher* 'mischievous, twisted', *akher* 'male goat', *puzker* 'fart'.
- **han*: *ahuntz* 'goat', *(h)andots* 'ram', *ahari* 'ram'.

A3) previously unknown loanwords: *zemai* 'threat' (Old Sp *menaza*), *alu* 'vulva' (Lat. *aluus*).

B1) reduplication:

- *adar* 'horn, branch' < **da-dar, eder* 'beautiful' < **de-der, odol* 'blood' < **do-dol*.
- *ahal* 'to be able' < **na-nal* (Mitxelena **anal*), *ohol* 'board' < **no-nol* (Mitxelena **onol*).
- *zezen* 'bull' (< **ze-zen*) cf. *gi-zen* 'fatty part of meat' (see below), etc., similar to *go-gor* 'hard', etc.[30]

B2) prefixes

- **gi*: *gibel, gizen* 'fatty part of meat', *gihar* 'lean', *gizon* 'man', etc.
- **la*: *labar* 'cliff, precipice', *labur* 'short', *lagun* 'friend, companion', *labain* 'slippery'.
- **sa*: *sabel* 'belly', *samin* 'bitter, pain', *samur* 'tender', *sabai* 'attic, loft'.

5.3 Canonical root structure and formal etymology

In a language isolate with relatively late and limited documentation, tracing the etymology of inherited terms is much more complicated than tracing that of loanwords. For that reason, the study of phonotactic restrictions of roots, the structure of families of words, and the "etymologies of the root models", as Uhlenbeck (1942) suggested, may contribute to a safer and deeper reconstruction than the atomism that underlies the slogan "every word has its own history".

For the study of root models, we classify (Lakarra 2008d) the words documented historically – not reconstructions, even those clearly and universally accepted like *e-*thor* 'to come', *e-*dan* 'to drink', *e-*khar* 'to bring', etc. – in five groups: (1) loanwords, (2) later variants, (3) compounds and derived forms, (4) forms due to onomatopoeia and phonosymbolism, and (5) of unknown etymology. Later, productivity, phonotactic, and geographical filters are applied to those included in (5), the only ones potentially belonging to the oldest stages of the language.

In the last 15 years, disyllabic forms have been reclassified from (5) to (1) or (3) – rarely to (2) or (4) – and progress in research is moving in this direction. Adding the non-controversial reconstructions to the list of roots, we would obtain the result that monosyllables of unknown etymology would increase by almost 100% – with hardly any loanwords or derived words – in contrast to disyllabic cases. Thus, the clear difference between CVC and the other models is increased even more, ruling out any disyllabic forms CRS for Old Proto-Basque (OPB). In reality, given that the geographical filter is established based on distribution in modern dialects, the results correspond *at the earliest* to OCB or to later stages, since we have been very lenient when it comes to filtering innovations (cf. Lakarra 2008d and here Section 9).[31]

A formal etymology does not provide the exact origins of specific words, but its value as an initial diagnosis seems clear: if, for example, *fede* belongs to the CVCV type, which is a root type with multiple loanwords and very few inherited words (none with *f-*), it is difficult for this word to be included in (3) or (5); if *otso* 'wolf' is VCV and *-so* '*big, older' is repeated in *amaso* 'grandmother', *alabaso* 'granddaughter', and *atso* 'old woman', it is highly likely that it derives from **hortz-so* ['fang' + __], with loss of *r* in the consonant cluster: cf. **hertz-bu(n) > esku* 'hand' or **intzaurtzedi > intsausti* 'walnut grove', etc.

5.4 CVC canonical root structure and the phonology of old Proto-Basque

Phonological analysis of the monosyllabic root leads to the proposal of a new consonant system for OPB (cf. Martínez Areta 2006, Lakarra 2011b, 2017). Mitxelena (*FHV*) suggested that strong consonants in PB could come from old groups, but only the research related to CRS has provided sufficient proof (= etymologies) based on sonorants and sibilants to think that this is the correct direction in which to go.

On the one hand, in a CVC root, there is no internal position for consonants, precisely that in which the Mitxelenian system maintained the fortes/lenes opposition; namely, in OPB the sibilants would have had four allophones and two phonemes (one dorsal and the other apical), not four phonemes as in the later system, since there is no contrast but rather complementary distribution between fricatives and affricates. In reality (cf. Section 4.2), alternations like *gatz* 'salt'/*gazi* 'salty' show that previously there were fricatives also in final position, and Latin loanwords like *gorputz* (< *corpus*) are witness to the fact that, at the start of the Common Era (i.e., after LPB), affrication applied in final position. Insofar as we know, word-medial affricates come from consonant clusters – see *otso* earlier – or from affrications in final position of the first element: *atzo* 'yesterday' < *hatz* 'trace, behind' (cf. *haz-i* 'to grow, seed') + *-o* 'COMPLETIVE'.

The argument is similar for liquids and nasals, with the exception that there are no rhotics in word-initial position: cf. *baiNo* 'but'/*baina* 'except, save' < **ba(da)(d)in* 'if it were' + *-no* 'until'/+ *-a* to *beLe* 'crow, raven' < **bel-le* (cf. *bel-tz* 'black'); *erro* 'root, teat' [< *to 'hang up'] < **e-ra-don* [with *nr* > *R*] (**eradon* > **edaron* > **enaron* > **eanron* > *erro(n)*; cf. *errun* [to 'lay eggs'], *arrau(n/l)tza* 'egg'); see Lakarra 2017, in progress-b and Begiristain in progress).

The consonant system of OPB would then be as follows: *th, kh, b, d,*[32] *g, l, n, r, s̰, s̤, h*, i.e., five plosives, two sibilants, tree sonorants, and *h*.[33] Insofar as vocalism is concerned, we find no reason to modify Mitxelena's reconstruction (*a, e, i, o, u*); with respect to diphthongs, it is possible that in OPB there were none since in LPB much fewer would be reconstructed than those documented historically, with it being plausible to see previous hiatuses emerging as a result of the deletion of old consonants for almost all of them (cf. Lakarra 2010). There could be many more diphthongs arising from the loss of inter-vocalic consonant than those Mitxelena reconstructed, such as in *-do.i/lohi*. See the end of Section 6.3 on the development of consonants from LPB onward.

5.5 The Proto-Basque lexicon

Although there is interesting etymological information dating from the Middle Ages (*Izpea* 1051 'subtus penna', etc.) together with lines of argument like *Andalucía* < *Landaluzea* 'country, field (*landa*) long (*luze*)' or *alabanza* 'similar (*anza*) to the daughter (*alaba*)' (Larramendi 1745), etc., scholarly B etymology begins with Mitxelena (1950) and the establishing of B sound laws in the late 1950s (see also Mitxelena 1973). Previously, B words were mentioned or utilized improperly in comparisons between Basque and multiple other languages, but the study of their formation and evolution was never even a secondary goal, so that today their value is almost exclusively historiographical (see Agud and Tovar 1988–1995 and Section 5).

The collection of Mitxelenian etymologies by Arbelaiz (1978) and vol. 15 of Mitxelena's *Collected Works* (2012) are still the best available etymological repertories. M is the author of some 1,400–1,500 etymologies, including both loanwords and inherited words. These etymologies established the foundation of his later diachronic work, as well as of any alternative proposals to Mitxelena's reconstruction. Unfortunately, Trask's (2008) dictionary remains far from complete after his untimely death, and even if he had completed it, there was little new to be expected beyond Mitxelena, of whom Trask always remained indebted, a popularizer of Mitxelena's work.[34]

The *EHHE* (= Lakarra, Manterola, and Segurola 2017) includes over 2,500 entries, organized into 200 word families. The *EHHE* is a modular work designed to expand according to the percentage of words historically corresponding to each letter. Entries are selected and examined hierarchically according to criteria like age of documentation, historical and modern use, extent of dialectal distribution, abundance of compounds and derivations, particular historical-philological reasons (such as *hapax legomena* or literary language), and so on. The historical part of the microstructure includes, besides the information in the *Diccionario general vasco* (*DGV*) and other lesser sources, copious information on the protohistorical era – essentially medieval – absent or much scarcer in the *DGV* and other Basque dictionaries. As regards etymology, it goes much farther than the Mitxelenian paradigm thanks to the use of advances in phonological and morphological analysis and in philological documentation but, above all, thanks to the use of formal (see Section 5.3) and comparative etymology (later in this section).

Although problematic as in any protolanguage, we can attempt to establish when and where PB was spoken. It is impossible to determine what the language spoken by the Paleolithic or Neolithic tribes (nor even by one of them) in the area was, but nor is there any evidence that the remote ancestor of B was ever spoken outside the historical territory of the B language described in Section 2.[35] Meanwhile, if *haitz* 'rock, crag' appears to be in the word family *aizto* 'knife', *aitzur* 'hoe', etc., this does not sustain the old-fashioned idea that Basque is a Neolithic language: as Gorrochategui (1998, 2002) explained, there would be no more reason for this than for any other languages, like German, in which the same sort of thing is found. What is more, it is very likely that 'rock, crag, etc.' were not the old meanings of *haitz*, which appears to be a compound of **han* 'big', cf. *han-di* 'big' [< '*to become big'] and animal names like *ahari* 'ram', *akher* 'male goat', *ahuntz* 'goat' (see details earlier), etc.

Many plant and tree names have been taken from Latin or Romance (*porru* 'leek', *kipula* 'onion', *piper* 'pepper', *baba* 'bean', *leka* green bean, pod', *olho* 'oat', *gerezi* 'cherry', *mertxika* 'peach', etc.) but not other plants or trees such as *haritz* 'oak', *arte* 'holm oak', *gari* 'wheat', *garagar* 'barley', *ardantze* 'vineyard', and animals such as *behi* 'cow', *ahuntz* 'goat', *asto* 'donkey', *zezen* 'bull', *behor* 'mare', *zaldi* 'horse', *idi* 'ox', *ardi* 'sheep, (dialectal) flea', *ahardi* 'sow', or *txerri* 'pig', and not just wild ones like *hartz* 'bear', *otso* 'wolf', *orein* 'deer', *orkatz* 'roe deer', etc. It is worth emphasizing that in the names of colors – the peak of Dixon's (1977) adjective hierarchy – we find participles (*gorr-i* 'red', *zur-i* 'white', *hor-i* 'yellow' [cf. *e-thorr-i* 'come', *har-i-tu* 'take' (1545) with a pleonastic participial suffix], derivatives (*bel-tz* 'black'), compounds (*ur-din* 'grayish' [<'*to become water']) and loanwords (*berde* 'green', *marroi* 'brown', *azul* 'blue', *gris* 'gray'), i.e. ways of substituting for adjectives in languages with closed-class types; see Dixon (1977).

The same critique of IE languages by Benveniste (1935) can be applied to Mitxelena's etymologies: i.e., we find monosyllables, disyllables, and polysyllables; protoforms with initial and final vowels and consonants, with and without consonant clusters; etc. It is difficult to find a system in them or to believe that many of his etymologies are contemporary.

New analyses have explored the phonology and morphology (phonetic changes, restrictions, relative chronologies, etc.) of the words reconstructed by Mitxelena more deeply. Thus, his reconstructed **ardano* 'wine' and **enazur* 'bone', trisyllabic forms – recall that he thought that the OB roots were disyllabic – may lead even further: to **e-dara-dan-o* and **berna-zur*, respectively. In the former, we get **dan* from the verb *e-dan* 'to drink' and the same prefixal amalgam (*ar-*) in *arbin, arran-, arrats*, etc., old verbs with applicative/directional + causative. In the latter, insufficiently considered phonetic changes such as R – R > Ø – R (cf. *ezker* 'left (hand)'/*eskuin* 'right' in **herz-bu(n)-ger/*herz-bu(n)-on(e)* (**erskuin* after assimilation and simplification) or **b-* > Ø – not just in front of *o/u* as Mitxelena contended – would lead us to identify a first disyllabic element taken in a loanword (*berna* 'leg' < Lat *perna* 'ham'; cf. Eng *bone* = Ger *Bein* 'leg'), as well as the inherited root *zur* 'lumber', both autonomously known.

Comparative etymology – parallels in the formation and development of B words –[36] may lead us to discover the longed for "motivation" of Benveniste (cf. de Lamberterie 2000). Thus, for example, *bi* could not always have been 'two' but, rather, something like 'above, over' or, even better, 'franchissement' as Benveniste (1954) saw it in the family of Lat *pons-pontis*, etc.;[37] cf. *zubi* 'bridge' [< ***'lumber-over'], *azpi* 'beneath' [< **hatz-bi* 'traces/fingers-over'], *ibi* 'ford' [< **hur-bi* ***'water-over'], etc. (cf. Lakarra 2015c). It is strange that different domestic animal names – *zaldi* 'horse', *idi* 'ox', *ardi* 'sheep' (dialectically 'flea'), *ahardi* 'sow' – are formed based on *di-/-di* (<**din*) 'to come', as in certain African languages (cf. Dimmendaal 2011).[38]

The development of Monosyllabic Root Theory (Lakarra 1995) facilitates the discovery of very old morphological processes of word formation, like reduplication and

prefixation, and allows one to broaden old lexical families – a crucial instrument in reconstruction – or the establishment of other unknown ones:

*das	:	lats	:	adats	:	aldats	:	jatsi	:	arrats
		'stream'		'mane'		'incline'		'to descend'		'dusk'
*den	:	lehen	:	eden	:	ezten	:	eten	:	arren
		'before'		'poison'		'sting'		'to break'		'please'
*dur	:	lur	:	___	:	(h)andur	:	urri	:	(tx)inaurri
		'land'			'	'cruel'		'scarce'		'ant'

Naturally, the products of these processes belong to strata prior to, for example, the
transparent *goibel* 'sad' or *ikertzaile* 'investigator' (composition and suffixation); see
Section 8 on the *a quo* of prefixation and reduplication. New loanwords have been
discovered, sometimes such apparently pure words as *alu* 'vulva', *eskatu* 'to ask for',
zemai 'threat', *alhatu* 'to graze', *alhaba* 'daughter', *ilhoba* 'grandchild; niece/nephew'
(both of the last two with the suffix *-ba* of family words), *oihu* 'shout', *aupa* 'go!',
etc. (the latter five from Gascon; cf. Lakarra 2015a), the families of other previously
known ones (such as the cited *berna*) have been extended, and other ones assumed by
Mitxelena have been confirmed (*abagada-une* 'occasion' < Sp *vegada*, *dollor* 'bad,
poor' < Rom *trollo* 'bad fish,' etc.), obtaining the exact and previously unknown origin
(cf. Lakarra 2008d).[39] There is no doubt that more loanwords are yet to be discovered,
although the main line of research should not be in that direction, as Mitxelena already
intuited 50 years ago.

6 TYPOLOGICAL CHANGE AND CHANGE IN THE CANONICAL ROOT STRUCTURE

6.1 Monosyllabism and the need for a new typology

A monosyllabic root, with reduplications and – above all – with prefixes, is not what
we expect of a language like historic Basque, typically associated with an agglutinative
structure, SOV order, abundant suffixation on noun, and very rich verb agreement. In fact,
in similar languages such as the Turkic or Australian languages – with the well-known
exception of grammatical forms and phonosymbolisms – disyllabic roots are clearly in
the majority, reaching 100% in the case of Uralic languages (cf. Bakrò-Nagy 1992).[40]

The situation in OPB and much later stages – the geographical filter that monosyllables
but not most disyllables go through corresponds at most to OCB (see Section 5.4) – is
very different, with scarcely any inflection and VO order. Authors such as Trask (1977) –
although later he may have recanted in his 1997 text, but not in the appendix of his "Grammar" chapter – and Gómez (1994) and Gómez and Sainz (1995) gave clear indications
that PB was VO (SVO according to Trask, VSO according to Gómez & Sainz), as well
as providing arguments for the existence of an "impersonal" phase without agglutinative
personal agreement nor TAM in the verb.

6.2 Irregularities and new typology

It is easy to show that the characterization of Basque as a perfect agglutinative SOV-type
language (as in Trask 1997, 1998) only corresponds to recent phases in its evolution, but
not to previous (prehistoric) others or the oldest reconstructable periods.

Irregularities for an SOV language have been pointed out (cf. Lakarra 2005, 2006a) such as the Noun-Adjective order (which, however, Greenberg 1963 and follower typologists considered irrelevant).[41] We may add that we do not have single CVC roots until late, quite distinct from the CV(C)CV pattern in Uralic (see Bakrò-Nagy 1992), there is no vowel harmony as in Uralic and other agglutinative families, and there are indications of VO order, in contrast to the SOV of Uralic, Turkic, Mongol, etc. Nor does the first-syllable accents of these language families appear to be old in B, which explains the scarcity and late character of suffixes and postpositions (cf. Lakarra 1997a, Sarasola 1997).

In the oldest part of the case system (the "indeterminate declension")[42] a biunivocal relationship between form and function does not appear to have existed, unlike in Dravidian and other agglutinative languages, but rather, as in Tibeto-Burman (cf. Bhat 2000) there was a kind of general locative (modern inessive marker *-n*) that can be found in archaisms like *barru-a-n-goak* (15th c.) *Be-n-goa* (onomastic); and deictics like *ha-n-dik* 'from there', *heme-n-dik*, 'from now on' etc.

The final-syllable accent, i.e. on the monosyllabic root of old disyllables, implies the existence of prefixes, too, in the noun phrase, besides those on the verb pointed out by Trask (1977), together with a few others like the already mentioned **da-*. It is not just that, at a certain point, the previously prefixal language became suffixal, but rather that some of these prepositions and prefixes – *za-*, *le-*, *da-*, *de-*, etc.: cf. *basa-tza* 'muddy place', *saltzai-le* 'sell-er', *etxe-r-a(t)* '(to go) home', *elur-te* 'snowfall', have cognates in just as many other words where they are suffixes (cf. Lakarra 2006b), so that we must conclude that they emigrated to the right before becoming fossilized.

Perhaps more attention than that received in Basque grammars (it does not appear in any of them) should be given to the structure of the sociative coordination X-COMITATIVE (*-gaz/-kin*) Y-case = "X-case₁ *and/with* Y-case₁", as in the following examples:

- Gloria Patri/*Biz gloria Aitearekin semearentzat/*Biz gloria espiritu santuarentzat. 'Gloria Patri/Glory be to Father and Son/Glory be to the Holy Ghost' (lit. 'with the Father for the Son') (16th-century Gipuzkoan Psalm Miserere: modern ed. by L. Akesolo, *Olerti* 1982).
- *Oguiagaz hura oragaz heroen elicatura*, 'Water and bread, sustenance for the madmen and dogs' (lit. 'with bread, water. . . with dogs for madmen') (*RS* 1596, no. 246, ed. Lakarra 1996).

According to Stassen (2000)[43] the following generalizations are universal:
Tendencies in the casedness – *and/with* correlation:

1   If a language is Cased, it will tend to have *and*-status.
2   If a language has *with*-status, it will tend to be Non-Cased (44).

Tendencies in the tensedness – *and/with* correlation:

3   If a language is Tensed, it will tend to have *and*-status.
4   If a language has *with*-status, it will tend to be Non-Tensed (p. 46).

This fits perfectly what, by other means, we reconstruct for OPB (and perhaps later): monosyllabic words, without a case system, or verb inflection, with prepositions and prefixes and without postpositions or suffixes; VO order, not SOV, a closed adjective category, impersonal verb and without TAM, etc., i.e., much more close to the isolate than to the agglutinative type. This is all very different from what we find in present and historical Basque.

Since 2005 we have argued that diachronic holistic typology can give us some indication about the existence in the history of Basque – as in Munda (Donegan 1993; Donegan and Stampe 1983, 2004) or Tani (Post 2006, 2009) – of a drift from a structure similar to the Mon-Khmer toward one approximating more that of the modern Munda languages:

MUNDA *Phrase Accent*: Falling (initial); *Word Order* : Variable – SOV, AN, Postpositional; *Syntax* : Case, Verb Agreement; *Word Canon* : Trochaic, Dactylic; *Morphology* : Agglutinative, Suffixing, Polysynthetic; *Timing* : Isosyllabic, Isomoric; *Syllable Canon* : (C)V(C); *Consonant* : Stable, Geminate Clusters; *Tone/Register* : Level Tone (Korku only); *Vocalism* : Stable, Monophthongal, Harmonic.

MON-KHMER *Phrase Accent*: Rising (Final); *Word Order* : Rigid – SVO, NA, Prepositional; *Syntax* : Analytic; *Word Canon* : Iambic, Monosyllabic; *Morphology* : Fusional, Prefixing or Isolating; *Timing* : Isoaccentual; *Syllable Canon* : (C)V- or (C)(C)'V(C)(C); *Consonantism* : Shifting, Tonogenetic, Non-Geminate Clusters; *Tone/Register* : Contour Tones/Register; *Vocalism* : Shifting, Diphthongal, Reductive

(Donegan and Stampe 2004: 3, 16)

As in other instances of drift, the phonological evolution is consistent with the morphology and basic syntax of the language (see Lakarra 2005): development of nasal vowels, voiceless plosives in initial position, word-initial vowels and open syllables, and so on. Finally, in the same way as Dravidian – which doubles its consonantal inventory in the drift from the protolanguage to modern languages – we go from 11 consonants in Old Proto-Basque to 16 in Late Proto-Basque, and to some 20–22 in the modern dialects.

6.3 Changes in the canonical root structure

In order to arrive at the disyllabism of the majority of roots in modern B, in the drift referred to, we have to assume multiple phonological and morphological processes that conspired to erase and alter the monosyllabic constraints in favor of other larger ones (Lakarra 2009a): V-metatheses (**ha(t)s-la(b)ur* > **hasnaur* > *hausnar* 'to chew, ruminate') or C-metatheses (**edazun* > **ezadun* > *eza.un* > *ezagun* 'known'); dissimilations (**buru-bar* > *burar* > *bular* 'breast, chest'); and assimilations (*zin-hets-i* > *sin-hetsi* 'to believe') – especially against sibilant homorganic consonants and rhotics in roots – as well as contractions of polysyllables (*jabe* 'owner' < **e-da-dun-e*); additions of the hiatus-breaking -*g*- (*hogen* 'lack' < **ho.en* < Lat *offende(re)*, *eza.un* > *ezagun* 'to known'); neutralizations and deletions in final position in the first element (*larre* 'field' + *mendi* 'mountain' > *Larramendi* (topon.), *buru* 'head' + *hezur* 'bone' > *burhezur* 'skull'; and so on.

Moreover, noun prefixes (*sabel* 'belly' < **sa-* 'within' + -*bel* 'black') and verb prefixes (**e-da-ra-dan-* 'PREP.' + 'DIRECTIONAL' + 'CAUSATIVE' + ROOT + -o 'COMPLETIVE' > **ardano* > *ardo* 'wine') became fossilized, and reduplications stopped being productive (**zen* > *zezen* 'bull' but ***bebehi* < *behi* 'cow' or ***babalea* < Lat *ballena*), and there is other proof – not just formal indications – of prefix > suffix change (see Section 6.2).

While the morphological changes appear to be older – the fossilization of reduplication is prior to **d-* > *l-*, which, in its turn, is older than LPB, there are no traces of prefixation in old Latin loanwords (although there are in inherited words of lVC shape [*sarats* 'sauce' < **sa-latz*, [Lat *salicem* > B *zarika*]; cf. Lakarra 2015b) – phonological changes seem to be more recent or even later than OCB. That is consistent with what we have seen about the later character of disyllabic roots and the survival of multiple CVCs after OPB.[44]

7 GRAMMATICALIZATION AND RECONSTRUCTION OF PROTO-BASQUE

7.1 Introduction

Meillet, Kurylowicz, and other leading diachronic linguists pointed out the importance for linguistic reconstruction of the development from lexical to grammatical morphemes and from grammatical morphemes to even more grammaticalized forms. Whether it is to be understood as a primary process or as following from more basic phenomena, and whether or not it is always unidirectional (cf. Campbell ed. 2001, Fischer et al. eds. 2004, etc.), grammaticalization is takes place in languages everywhere, and its study may contribute greatly to Basque historical linguistics, as it has contributed to knowledge of the history of many other languages.

Certain grammaticalizations are known to have taken place in Basque. Among relatively well-understood phenomena, we find the development of articles from demonstratives (see Manterola 2015), the more recent development of the Gipuzkoan interrogative particle *al* and the quite diverse and interesting evolution of the auxiliary verbs, etc.

The holism of the phenomenon (phonetic and semantic erosion) and multiple parallels in different geographical and genetic languages (see Heine and Kuteva 2002) leads us to acknowledge its effects on markers like those of the dative (*-i* < **nin* 'GIVE'); unfinished aspect (*da-* < *dar* 'SIT'), the plural *-de* < **den* 'FINISH'); the prosecutive/ablative and adjectival suffix (*-ti* < **din*[45] 'COME'); superiority comparison (*-ago* < **ha* 'demostr. of 3rd level' + *-go* 'TO PASS'); and the adverbial suffixes of mood (completive) *-to* and *-ro* as well as the causative *ra-* (< **lo-*), from **don* 'PUT'; the old comparative and distant familiarity suffix (*-so* < **san* 'TO SAY'); the conjunction (*da*); the modal (*-la*); and the coordinations (*e-ta* 'and', *e-do* 'or'); etc. (cf. Lakarra 2013b, 2017).

It is obvious that without the help offered by analyzing grammaticalization, many of these reconstructions would still be unknown.

7.2 Serial verbs in Proto-Basque?

It seems difficult to accept that, in a language in which *aita-ren-tza-ko-a-k Bermio-ko-e-i har d-i-e-za-z-ki-e-ke-gu* ("we can get those that are for father from those from Bermeo") is a typical sentence, there would be no verbal or noun inflection at an earlier stage in its history. Nevertheless, we have more evidence besides that already cited (Sections 6.1 and 6.2) to defend the proposal that Basque lacked morphology in an earlier period: thus, the analysis of *dago* or *dakar* not as *d-* '3rd pers.' + *a* 'pres.' + *go(n)* 'to be' and *d-* '3rd pers.' + *a* 'pres.' + *kar* 'to bring' but as ø '3rd p.' + *da* 'IMPERF' + *go(n)* 'to be', etc. plus the testimony of *nago* 'I am' (< **ni-dago, ni* 'I') and *nakar* 'he brings me' (< **ni-dakar*) made Trask (1977) and Gómez (1994) assume that at some point the verb was "impersonal" (**dago, *dakar*) and that only later did personal markers agglutinate.

Trask stated that *da-go* and *da-kar* should be analyzed like that, with the root preceded by a prefix or auxiliary of indeterminate aspect, in a very different way from other SOV languages. We may add that *da-* (cf. Section 7.5) can be taken to be the grammaticaliza-tion of **dar* 'SIT' (**e-darr-i > jarri* 'to sit'), the best-known source of this type of marker in verb and the locative on the NP (B *-a/-t: Zarautz-a* 'to Zarautz', *hibaira-t* 'to the river'). Therefore, *da-go* [< **dar-*gon* 'SIT'-'STAY'] came to be a kind of asymmetric serial verb (see Aikhenvald 2006). We have testimonies of grammaticalization of typical serial verbs (cf. Lakarra 2008a, 2017) in many nominal cases: dative *-i*, ergative *-k* < **ga* < **gon* 'to stay', locative *-a* < **dar* 'SIT', *raino* 'until' < **r-a-(d)in-no* [epenthesis-SIT-COME-GO], etc.

7.3 Irregularities in the CRS, old root extensions, and reconstruction of the verb

Lafon (1943) in his work on the Archaic Basque verb (see now Mounole 2011) offered a long series of root structures, including monosyllables in V *da* 'copula', VC *utz-i* 'to leave', and CVC *e-thorr-i* 'to come', disyllables CVCVC *jakin* 'to know', CVCV *jagi* 'to get up', and trisyllables VVCCVCV *aurtiki* 'to throw', etc.

In reality (cf. Lakarra 2008c, 2017), the CRS of verbs was CVC and to that root one could add at least two prefixes (causative *ra-* and directional/applicative *da-*) or combi-nations of both,[46] as well as the 'initial vowel' (mirror image of the Bantu "final V").[47] Besides this, contracted forms of these exist:

> *e-thorr-i* 'to come', **e-(d)utz-i > utzi, itxi* 'to leave'
> **e-da-khin > jakin* 'to know', **e-da-duts-i > jautsi* 'to go down'
> *e-ra-bil-i* 'to use'
> **e-da-ra-don-tz-i > jarauntsi* 'to inherit', **e-da-ra-gotz-i > urgatzi* 'to help'

The prefixes on these verbs are fossils and have not extended to new roots since the prehistoric era (the end of LPB?) – there are none in verbs taken from Latin – and in the case of the causative it was substituted before the first texts by the suffix *-erazo/-arazi*. There are those who have seen in the destinative *-ra* (*mendi-ra* 'to the mountain', *egite-ra* 'to do', etc.) the origin of the causative (*e-ra-bil-i* 'to use' < '**to make walk*'), but this is unlikely: the two categories do not correspond to the same network of grammaticalization (cf. Heine and Kuteva 2002) and, what is more, we would have a case of suffix (active) > prefix (fossil) in a language with drift toward agglutination and SOV order. It is, moreover, unnecessary because the old auxiliary PUT **lon* (> *i-ro-*) is enough to explain causative *-ra* after *-o* > *-a* in composition and derivation, and regular VlV > VrV in loanwords and inherited words until the Early Middle Age.[48]

As we have seen (in Sections 7.1 and 7.2), *da-* (< **dar*) had locative and (indeter-minate) aspectual value, typical in the grammaticalization of SIT. Trask (1977) found this morpheme in conjugated forms (*dago, dakhar*, etc.), but it is also present in some non-conjugated ones, which explains the enormous abundance of *-a-* after yod in those pointed out by Mitxelena (*FHV*) and also in certain adjective root and nouns like *la-bur* 'short', *la-bar* 'edge of cliff', etc.

The reconstruction of elements preceding the old verb root shows the value of com-bining the notions of CRS and grammaticalization: we are able to reduce the polyform-ism assumed by Lafon and others and we are able to get a more precise idea of the old morphology and syntax, which functioned to the left and not to the right[49] as in historical times (see Trask 1977, Lakarra 2008c, 2017).

7.4 The Proto-Basque verb as a closed class

There has been a fairly widespread belief that the synthetic Basque verb, with multiple tense and agreement markers, has gradually deteriorated since its Golden Age in favor of periphrastic structures borrowed from neighboring languages. While archaic attestations (prior to 1600) document conjugated forms matching some six dozen (synthetic) verbs, currently there are no more than a dozen: *ekarri* 'to bring', *etorri* 'to come', *eroan-eraman* 'to take', *ibili* 'to walk', *egon* 'to be', *joan* 'to go', *jakin* 'to know', and little more in addition to the auxiliaries. This has led to the notion (cf. Gómez and Sainz 1995) that, if we were to go back in time, we would come across many more synthetic verbs and perhaps that all the verbs were conjugated synthetically at some more or less remote time.

However, we can state with some certainty that this idea is implausible. To start with, only some of the verbs with the prefix **e-* (> *e-, i-, j-* in known phonological conditions) are documented in conjugated forms: *ekarri* → *dakart, zekarren*, etc., does, but not *erosi* 'to buy', *iritsi* 'to arrive' or *jarri* 'to put (down), sit down', etc. Nor does any verb without that prefix have synthetic forms: *apurtu* 'to break', *bidali* 'to send', *hartu* 'to take', *sartu* 'to enter', etc. According to Mitxelena-Sarasola (1987–2005), we would have around 200 inherited words with *e-, i-, j-* and that is the maximum number of candidates for being old Basque verbs. Nevertheless, most of them do not reflect synthetic forms, and they even have serious problems in their structure for being considered old verbs: for example, *itsusi* 'ugly' or *itzali* 'to turn off, put out' cannot be analyzed as ***i-tsus-i* 'ugly', ***i-tzal-i* 'to be out', with root-initial affricates. On the other hand, we do see that over a dozen synthetic verbs only have conjugated forms in the imperative (still productive modern agglutinations), that many others have never developed more than just a small part of their potentialities (*dario* 'he/she/it flows' from *jario* but not ***zenerizkidakeen* (perhaps interpretable, if it existed, as 'they can flow to me from you'), etc. nor even more simple forms outside the 3rd pers.), and, if we pay attention to the internal structure of the verbs (Section 7.3) – prefix *da-, ra-* or combinations of them – we can assume that no more than two or three dozen roots were possibly ever conjugated. This is similar to what Pawley (2006) and others have described for a lot of Australian languages, as well as other languages of New Guinea, Siberia, and the Americas, i.e., that there is not an open class of inflected verbs with PERSON and TAM markers, but a few semantically basic verbs with such a structure besides several auxiliaries used with abundant "converbs" for the rest.

This is consistent with what was observed in Sections 6.2 and 7.2 and is additional evidence for the isolate > agglutinative evolution.

7.5 Grammaticalization and (pre)history of Basque morphemes

If we define as "primary grammaticalization" (PG) the conversion of lexical roots into grammatical morphemes and as "secondary grammaticalization" (SG) any other later change of the grammaticalized morphemes into more grammatical morphemes, bearing in mind that CVC was the CRS of the old lexemes, there are important consequences for the history of morphemes. It is, in addition, one of the strongest pieces of evidence for the existence of a CRS CVC in lexical roots. Thus, for example, we find that:

1   There can be no disyllabic or polysyllabic PG: *-tate* and *-tasun* are loanwords (Latin *-tatem*) or secondary amalgams (*-tasun* < *-t-ar-zu-n*). Likewise, *-heta* (archaic variant of the toponymic suffix *-eta*) and *-zaha* (the same for *-za*) are not PG but fusions of other morphemes: $*he + -ta$ (< *da*), $*-za + -ha$, etc.

2   There are no simple PGs with codas: $*-gan$ was not the old inessive morph, but an amalgam *-ga + -n* (*pace* Jakobsen, Trask, and de Rijk); sociative *-kin* < $*-k-i-de + -n$, etc.

3   There are no CV lexical morphemes but rather this is the Canonical Morpheme Structure of the PGs: *lo* (< $*don$) 'to sleep', *su* 'fire' (< *sun-/sur-*), etc. have lost $-C_2$ in composition or for other reasons (e.g. reanalysis).

4   All CV morphemes come from CVC, i.e. they are PGs. E.g. *da-/-da* < $*dar$ 'to sit', *-di/-ti* < $*din$ 'to come', etc.

5   V-, -V < CV and C-, -C < CV. The suffix and prefix in the dative *-i/i-* come from $*ni-$ (< $*nin$ 'to give') and *-t* '1st per.sing.', *-k* '2nd per.sing.' in *-da*, *-ga*. The *e-* in old verbs comes from $*Ce-$ ($*he-$), cf. *(h)eta, *her* 'close, closed'. The instrumental marker *-z* is reconstructed as $*-zV$ (cf. *za* 'pl.' and $*zan$ 'to be', plus the pleonastic *-zaz* < $*-za + za$) and the agreements *n-* '1st per.sing', *z-* '2nd per.pl.' in the pronouns *ni, zu*, etc.

6   -VC < $*(C)V\#C(V)$. This is a subcase of (2) and (5); thus *-ak* (nom.pl., ERG.sg. and ERG.pl[50] is *-(h)a + g(a)*. Manterola (2015) reconstructs as $*ha$ (without coda, not $*har$, as it has been to date) as the demonstrative and third-level article. The finals on -VC that Uhlenbeck (1942) took to be suffixes (*-ats, -ar*, etc.) are roots that have lost C- in composition (cf. *adats* 'mane', *aldats* 'incline', *ordots* 'male', etc.), not suffixes or amalgams.

7   In -rV (DAT. *-ri*, adlative *-ra*, GEN. *-ren*, etc.), the *-r* is epenthetic between a stem in -V and a case marker V-. It would apparently enter into (4), but *r-* is impossible in roots and words, and it is unlikely that all the -rVs in declension come from -lV(C) by $*VlV > VrV$. -V (< $*CV$ < $*CVC$) is the true suffix with later epenthetic *r*. Note that the stems in -V necessary for the change mentioned could only be developed later in a language with CVC Canonical Root Structure.

8   Postpositions and other morphemes may be differentiated: morpheme < CVC root/postposition < words (and constructions greater than CVC: *buru* 'head', *begi* 'eye', *aurre* 'front', *atze* 'back', *ondoren* 'after'). They could also be based on disyllables, and their internal structure (composition, derivation, as well as loanwords) is much more obvious compared to other morphemes; the degree of grammaticalization and the antiquity of postpositions is very little (cf. Hualde & Ortiz de Urbina 2003).

The combined study of CRS and CMS and grammaticalization may offer yet more advances in the reconstruction of PB (see Lakarra 2013b, 2016, 2017, 2018).

8   ADVANCES IN CHRONOLOGY AND PREHISTORICAL PERIODIZATION

Unfortunately, Basque lacks any known relatives, which makes it impossible to use for comparative history (see Section 3). This does not make the study of the history of the language an impossible task, as has sometimes been claimed, but it does require developing other means for doing so. Basque historical linguists were late in embracing the most productive approach in any language isolate, internal reconstruction (which practically began with Mitxelena), both because the necessary philological work has only been undertaken recently (publication of important texts after 1975, *DGV* in 1987–2005, for example) and because important developments in historical linguistics have had very little impact in the field of Basque studies until quite recently.

Still, we do have important prehistorical and protohistorical phenomena (reduplication, prefixes) and changes (*$*d-$ > $l-$, $T-$ > $D-$, $-n-$ > $-h-$, $*h_{2/3}$ > h_1, prefix → suffix, etc. (see supra) that we can attempt to connect in a relative chronology, thereby making some progress in establishing periods and strata in the development of Basque (cf. Lakarra 2015b). Thus, the existence of reduplication for patterns such as *dVC, *nVC, *zVC and *gVC (see Section 5.4) but not for *lVC is probably related to the prehistorical change (already noted by Mitxelena 1957) *$d-$ > $l-$: i.e., reduplication had ceased to be productive before that rule came into force. If *sarats* 'willow' comes from *$*sa$-$latz$,[51] with the prefix *sa-* and root *latz* 'rough, coarse, harsh' (< *$*datz$), then clearly that type of prefixation survived until a more recent time than reduplication and subsequent to *$d-$ > $l-$, but neither of these phenomena was in force when Basque-Latin contact began, since they are not present in any loanword, however old it may be.

Bearing in mind that there are only aspirated voiceless plosives in initial position in old verb roots – not plain voiceless or pure aspiration: *ekharri* 'to bring', *ekhusi* 'to see', *ethorri* 'to come', not **ekarri*, or **eharri*, etc. –[52] it is possible that such consonants are archaic, maintained without suffering *$T^{h\text{-}}$ > $h\text{-}$ by the addition of the prefix and not later aspirations like those of many loanwords (*khoroa* 'crown', *phike* 'tar, pitch' < Latin *coronam, picem*, etc.) or inherited words (*khal-te* 'loss' < *gal-du* 'to lose'). As verbs with the prefix *$e-$ (> $e-$, $i-$, $j-$ according to known contexts) can only be conjugated, we can infer that the prefix ceased to be added to the CVC bases before $T^{h\text{-}}$ > $h\text{-}$, so that the verbs that developed thereafter, whatever the C- and both in loanwords and inherited words, lack any synthetic form and are conjugated periphrastically.

Given the characteristics of the corpus of the language (Lakarra 1997a, Ulibarri 2013), absolute internal chronologies are scarce and uncertain. Thanks to the *DGV*, we have many interesting lexical and some morphosyntactic clues: e.g. the first appearance of the interrogative particle *al*, the *antequem* of the Aresti-Linschmann Law on neutral or intensive possessives – widespread up to the 18th century, which then disappeared in diverse ways among the different dialects – and the placing of *oso* 'very' (after the adjective or at the end of the phrase up to the same century).[53]

In phonology, when it comes to studying loanwords, the use of the chronological sequences elaborated by Straka (1954–57) and others in the evolution of Latin-Romance offer a good number of absolute and relative chronologies; cf. Guiter (1989):

200	300	400	1000	1100	1200
p- > b-	n > Ø, nt > nd	l > r		ll > l	
t- > d-	mp > mb, nd > n			nn > n	
k- > g-					
mb > m					

Research regarding chronology in the inherited lexicon has been more limited although it may progress with works such as that of Hualde (in press). For instance, based on the phonetic changes established in *FHV* and other work by Mitxelena and others, we can try to establish that $-n-$ > $-h-$ must be prior to $h_{3/2}$ > h_1 (Lat *arena* > OCB *$*areha$ > *harea* 'sand', OCB *$*enuskara$ > *$*ehuskara$ > *heuskara* > *euskara* 'Basque language')[54] and prior to those nasal vowels reconstructable for the OCB (*ardâô* 'wine', *gaztâá* 'cheese', etc.). In turn, *arrâî* 'fish' (still attested at the end of the 16th century) predates *arrai(n)*, as does **lukâîka* 'sausage' (< Lat *lucanica*) to *lukai(n)ka*. And **hVh > ØV(h)* is prior to $h_{3/2}$ > h_1 (**hur-bar-bi > *huhbah(b)i > *uhbahi > ibahi > hibai* 'river').

The old strata and variants are easier to recognize in loanwords (see Mitxelena 1974): *gela* 'room' < Lat *cellam* is older than *zeru* 'sky' (< *tselu* < Lat *caelum*) due to the fact that the palatalization of *k-* is a Romance phenomenon, so that *gela* must have already existed in B when *caelum* 'sky' was first palatalized and went on to become an affricate sibilant later. *Zeru* has *-l- > -r-* in contrast to its later variant *zelü*, but in *gela* the *-l-* comes from a fortis lateral (= Lat geminate) like PB **beLe* 'crow, raven', not from a singleton Lat *-l-* (*gula* > B *gura* 'to want') or B lenis (toponym *Araba*, cf. Rom *Álava*). In *baradizu/ paradisu* 'paradise', there is a voiced/voiceless C in line with the antiquity of the dorsal/ apical sibilant (this in recent loanwords); if we add *paraiso* we would have the modern *-o* with *p-* and *s-* but older *-u* with *-z-* and with *b-*.

The words *sabel* 'belly' and *zezen* 'bull' (prefixation and reduplication; cf. Section 5.2.2) are much less transparent in their structure than *ogibide* 'job' < ***'bread'- 'way'[55] (later composition) and *Hirutasun* ['Trinity' < *hiru* '*three' + *-tasun* '-ity'] (modern suffixation). Prefixation and reduplication are not just fossilized by the time of the first texts written in B, but they do not even apply to the oldest known loanwords. Derivative suffixes, on other hand, are scarce outside the highest literary language still in the 18th century (cf. Lakarra 1997a, Sarasola 1997).

In verbal inflection, the older nature of prefixes with respect to suffixes is clear. Regarding nominal inflection, the number and size of case markers in the noun phrase has grown substantially, due in part to the phenomenon known as *surdeclinaison* (*zaldi-ar-en-tzat* = horse-the-GEN-for; cf. Lafitte 1944). In the transitive auxiliaries of periphrastic forms in irrealis moods, *iron* 'can' (from the same root as the causative prefix *-ra-*) appears to have been more widespread at some time, although in modern times it has only survived in eastern areas; **ezan* (today central-eastern) is documented in the far western and southern areas in the 16th and 17th centuries; *egin* 'to do, make' is of general use as a main verb, but only in western varieties (Biz, A, G) is it used as an auxiliary. Among the transitive auxiliaries used with dative agreement (**nin, *edutsi, *eradun*) the first appears to be the oldest and most grammaticalized (widespread but barely attested in Biz), the second is an innovation from Biz and A, and the third is documented not just in eastern areas, as in the present, but also in G and A, even if only in plural in these latter dialects (cf. Ariztimuño 2013).[56]

As for the article – on which the singular and plural case systems are based – not only was it missing in LPB but also in Aquitanian and in Pyrenean Basque (see Manterola 2015). Its grammaticalization is more recent than in Hispanic Romance languages (after the 8th century).

9 ON OLD COMMON BASQUE[57]

Perhaps as a result of the limited development of many diachronic issues in B or because of the deep-rooted myth of the immovable nature of B, we know much more about the modern dialects than about their origin or about the changes that Post-Medieval B underwent in these dialects. In practice if not in theory, the B dialects are conceived of by many as old or eternal, as if the dialects have not changed at all – despite changes in structure and different changes according to territory, Moreover, the testimony of the old southern dialect (Landucci's vocabulary, Lazarraga's texts), the history of Biz and L (with abundant old evidence and without any continuity until Contemporary B), and the R attestations of 1615–1617 (see Lakarra 2014), as well as the practice of standard diachronic linguistics, have still not put an end to opinions based mainly on the modern situation of the language.

The dialects established by Bonaparte (1866), Mitxelena (1964), and Zuazo (1998) are recent, and there is little difference among them, without offering the possibility of taking us back to the speech of the old Vasconic or Vascoid tribes (at the beginning of the Common Era or the end of the previous age) or to LPB. Mitxelena (1981) postulated the notion that convergence of the most differentiated forms of speech beginning in PB – which Aquitanian and the Pyrenean B did not undergo – could have taken place in centuries after the weakening and fall of the Roman Empire, when the B-speaking populations resisted Visigoths and Franks.

It is clear that all B dialects have shared many innovations after PB in phonology (voicing of initial consonants, lenition of sonorants, metathesis of /h/, development of nasal vowels, neutralizations and deletion of vowels in final position in the first element of compound and derived words, etc.) and grammar (the article – initially including three degrees of deixis –, intensive personal pronouns, the plural, most definite declension and almost all indefinite declension, the tense system, the distribution of synthetic and periphrastic forms, most of the auxiliaries, the allocutive, verb periphrasis, the development of -zu 'you' from plural to singular, etc.). We must assume that if all B dialects came directly from PB, their differences would be much greater, almost certainly having become different languages.[58] We would have to assume therefore that the historical dialects known to us are the result of fragmentation of a common language dating from approximately the 5th to 6th centuries in the Common Era, which would have been the product of a convergence process among distinct and previously more disperse B forms of speech.

Yet Mitxelena based his ideas essentially on non-linguistic arguments – i.e., that conditions after the fall of the Roman Empire would be those most suited to reducing the dependency on foreign powers and reinforcing cohesion and internal organization (following the historical model of Barbero and Vigil (1965), which most historians currently reject) – in order to demonstrate the need to assume an OCB, without attempting a precise definition of such a protolanguage, and in particular its differences (relevant innovations) with regard to LPB, an indispensable task for its justification from a linguistic point of view and something that has only recently received some attention.

We tentatively present here a series of phonological innovations that could have occurred between LPB and OCB or, at the very least, prior to the fragmentation of the latter and that perhaps may serve to differentiate both protolanguages:

1 T- > D- ;
2 *-n- > -h-;
3 Nasal vowels;
4 Diphthongs;
5 *-n- > -n;
6 *-r > -h;
7 *hVh > øVh and *hC > øC);
8 *e- > j/__ V

9 *d_1 > ø/V__V;
10 a – o > o – a in the verb;
11 -n > -r/__#
12 *b-, *k- > ø-;
13 -l- > -r-;
14 – i_1/-u_2 > ø/__#;
15 -V_3 > ø/__#

On the other hand, without refuting the existence of horizontal innovations among the B varieties – which have never ceased to be in contact – it is obvious that the flat dialectal tree commonly used the field of B linguistics is implausible and antihistorical (cf. Austronesian or IE). Furthermore, it impedes the establishment of historical and geographical timelines[59] and hierarchies in the evolution of features and varieties.

Dialectal classification must be based on the oldest innovations and the bipartite branchings that they produce. It cannot depend on the number of traits that could be used to separate one dialect from another. Unquestionably, the dating of all the historical dialects of B – Biz, NHNa, and Z, for example – cannot be the same insofar as the particular innovations that each one of them shows are very different in their age (old in the case of Z, more recent in the case of NHNa). Thus, for example, considering phenomena like (a) voicing (or devoicing) of plosives after *l/n*, (b) palatalizations after *(V)i*, (c) dissimilation *a + a > ea*, and (d) grammaticalization of *egin* as AUX, it would appear that:

(1) is – against what is usually thought – an innovation of R and Z as opposed to the Central-Western voiced consonants (old lenis) and Pyrenean Romance forms of speech, further east than R and Z;
(2) is a particular and later innovation of Biz; and
(3)–(4) are innovations that, as well as Biz, affect A and most of G.[60]

The tree derived from these and other innovations would be closer to (2) (below) than to (1), despite the fact that this is the partition with the greatest number of followers (cf. Bonaparte, Lacombe, Uhlenbeck, etc.), especially among enthusiasts who do not make excessive use of the existing philological documentation on old Biz and A (cf. Lakarra 1996, Mounole 2015, Mounole and Lakarra 2017;[61] Mitxelena rejected this classification explicitly on many occasions (1958, 1964, 1981) and there are still no arguments to change this opinion.

Following a suggestion by Mitxelena (*FHV*), in Lakarra (2014) we defended the idea that voicing after *l* and *n* (*alde* 'side', *handi* 'big') is an archaism and that the innovation is the devoicing found in R and Z. For this, in addition to Mitxelena's observations, we are supported by the B substrate in Gascon (cf. Rohlfs 1977) and the parallel of sibilants in an identical context, which are realized as fricative (= lenis) and not as affricate (=

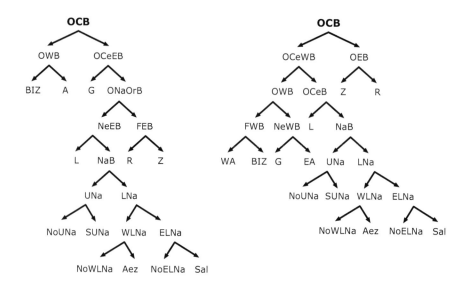

FIGURE 3.1 CLASSIFICATION OF BASQUE DIALECTS

fortes) unlike in the modern Western dialects. For that reason, R and Z are the innovators – this is perhaps the earliest dialectal innovation (= right tree in figure 3.1) that we know of – bearing in mind that affricates were opposed to fricatives and voiceless plosives to voiced plosives as fortes and lenis, respectively, in the previous system; cf. Section 4.2).[62]

As for the question of the OCB homeland, we believe we must locate innovations chronologically and geographically rather than considering the quantity of existing modern dialects in this or that territory (cf. Janhunen 2009 for Uralic, for example). In particular, in the territory of Bizkaia, Gipuzkoa, and Araba, the dialectal division seems much simpler than in Navarre, in the geographical area that runs from Pamplona toward the north, up to the modern French border. Perhaps that would be the area where OCB developed and from which it spread. It is not advisable to interpret the most modern forms of speech, situated at the lowest level of the tree, as decisive. We should look instead to the root of the tree when searching for the homeland of OCB, given that the first fragmentations are found in the highest branches: see Janhunen's (2009) conclusions on the homeland of Proto-Uralic.

Returning to our case, the place of Samoyedic, Finno-Ugric, and Proto-Uralic would be occupied, respectively, by Zuberoan-Roncalese (= Old Eastern Basque), Eastern Low Navarrese-Salazarese (= Easternmost Navarrese), and OCB, with the oldest isogloss situated between Z-R and NoELNa-Sal – during an era that, for the moment, we cannot specify – so that we should locate in that specific place[63] the proto-homeland of OCB, as shown in Figure 3.1 above.

10 CONCLUSIONS

The main proof for genetic relationship among languages lies in the help it offers for the reconstruction of a common protolanguage and for studying the history of the languages in the family. The strength of the demonstration cannot be based on the quantity of alleged superficial analogies without regular phonetic connections or the reconstruction of homologies.

We consider it essential that specialists in Basque, distancing themselves from unjustified allegiance to remote agendas, analyze the facts of B diachrony according to the best philology and the most productive theories and methods of linguistic change and reconstruction, as Meillet and Mitxelena asserted.[64] Any advances via the expansion of materials – languages or protolanguages related to ours, pre-Latin loanword strata – do not appear any nearer, than they were some decades ago, so it is reasonable and necessary to opt for the application of more efficient theories and methods (cf. Haas 1969), in order to arrive at a more complete and deeper reconstruction of PB and the prehistory of the language. We defend the notion that – besides the usual internal reconstruction methods masterfully used by Mitxelena a half century ago – research on the Canonical Form of roots and morphemes; Diachronic Holistic Typology (subordinate to the search for homologies, not dedicated to pure analogies); and Grammaticalization processes may continue to contribute important advances in reconstruction. Finally, the elaboration of chronologies and periodizations – including the establishment of a minimum number of necessary (intermediate) protolanguages for the reconstruction of the prehistory of the language (as is the case with Old Common Basque, Late Proto-Basque, and Old Proto-Basque) – are unavoidable topics, as we find in any other language or family.

NOTES

1 Work connected to the projects "*Monumenta Linguae Vasconum* (IV): Textos Arcaicos Vascos y Euskera Antiguo" (FFI2012–37696) and "*Monumenta Linguae Vasconum* (V)" [FFI2016-76032-P], Consolidated Research Group "Historia de la Lengua Vasca y Lingüística Histórico-Comparada" by the Basque Government (GIC.IT698–13) and UFI (Training and Research Unit) UFI 11/14 at the UPV/EHU.

Acknowledgements: I thank Borja Ariztimuño, Joaquín Gorrochategui, José Ignacio Hualde, Julen Manterola, and Blanca Urgell for numerous and interesting observations and corrections of form and content, although I have not necessarily accepted all of their suggestions; all remaining errors are my own. The map and the dialectal genealogies were produced by Adur Larrea, with the collaboration of Céline Mounole, with important observations from Gidor Bilbao and Ricardo Gomez. I have found Lyle Campbell as rigorous and generous an editor as anyone could want.

Abbreviations: C = consonant, R = sonorant, S = sibilant, T = plosive, V = vowel, p = person, sing = singular, pl = plural, ERG = ergative, DAT = dative, ABS = absolutive, GEN = genitive, part = participle, TAM = Tense-Aspect-Mode, PREP = preposition(al), PG = primary grammaticalization, SG = secondary grammaticalization. *Languages:* B = Basque (language), OPB = Old Proto-Basque, LPB = Late Proto-Basque; OCB = Old Common B; IE = Indo-European, Rom = Romance; Lat = Latin, Sp = Spanish, Eng = English, Ger = German; *Basque dialects*: A = Alavese, Aez = Aezkoan, Biz = Bizkaian, EA = Eastern Alavese, ELNa = Eastern Low Navarrese, G = Gipuzkoan, FEB = Far Eastern B, FWB = Far Western B, L = Lapurdian, LNa = Low Navarrese, NaB = Navarrese B, NeEB = Near Eastern B, NeWB = Near Western B, NoELNa = North-Eastern Low Navarrese, NoUNa = North-Upper Navarrese, NoWLNa = North-Western Low Navarrese, OCeEB = Old Central-Eastern B, ONaORB = Old Navarrese-Oriental B, OCeB = Old Central B, OCeWB = Old Central-Western B, OEB = Old Eastern B, OWB = Old Western B, R = Roncalese, Sal = Salazarese, SUNa = South Upper Navarrese, UNa = Upper Navarrese, WA = Western Alavese, WLNa = Western Low Navarrese, Z = Zuberoan. Others: DGV = *Diccionario general vasco* (Mitxelena & Sarasola 1987–2005), *FHV* = *Fonética Histórica Vasca* (Mitxelena 1961).

Symbols: * = *reconstructed form;* ** = *Undocumented and impossible.*

2 Following Ringe (2003), we understand that the comparison between dialects is not internal but rather comparative reconstruction. In our case, its result would be OCB (see Section 9), but it is far from being approached systematically, most likely because internal reconstruction is much more compelling on almost all fronts.

3 It is impossible to demonstrate that languages are not related, that there is *no* genetic relationships, and therefore, it is the "believers" – as Mitxelena used to say – who are obliged to offer proofs (standard ones, and not just any old thing).

4 All of them defended the polygenesis of *all* languages, like Boas and Trubetzkoy as well (Lakarra 2008d).

5 That is, not non-professionals in linguistics but people who are unfamiliar with the methods and aims of historical linguistics and philology and those who have no experience as regards the real history of any language or family, whether they are linguists by profession or not: this is not uncommon.

6 For Vovin (1994), Japanese had the dubious honor of having been the language on whose origins the most ridiculous things had been said; we do not know if he had thought about B when he argued this. In Campbell's (2013) extensive list of non-proven genetic relationship hypotheses, the extremely high proportion of combinations in which B appears is striking.

7 For the current sociolinguistic situation see Barreña et al. (2013); Hualde and Ortiz de Urbina (2003) is the most complete grammar in English on contemporary Basque; Mitxelena-Sarasola (1987–2015) the obligatory lexicographical, historical, and dialectal source; and Hualde, Lakarra, and Trask (1995), Trask (1997), and Martínez Areta (2013) are the most up-to-date monographs on the history of the language (particularly prehistory and internal developments). Gorrochategui, Igartua and Lakarra (eds. 2017), besides being an examination of prehistory and protohistory, is the most complete available treatment of strictly speaking historical eras.

8 In the school system, the "D" teaching model (in Basque with Spanish as a subject) is the most common choice now whereas the "A" model (instruction in Spanish with B as a subject) is fairly marginal. The University of the Basque Country awards degrees in both B and Spanish, with B being used at the university level for the first time in 1978; there are both television and radio stations (in the BAC) wholly in B as well as local television and radio stations in the language, which moreover is used increasingly on the Internet.

9 Studied in the last third of the 19th century by Luchaire and later by Mitxelena (1954b) and Gorrochategui (1984, etc.). In the southern part, one should add an important inscription found in Lerga (Navarre) and a few others discovered in the historical Vascons' territory, as well in La Rioja and Soria (cf. Gorrochategui 2011a).

10 Rico (1982) points out the curious syntactic order of many Romance glosses, more befitting B than Romance.

11 The two best-known dialectal classifications are that of Bonaparte (B, G, SHNa, NHNa, L, WLNa, EaLNa, and Z dialects) and that of Zuazo (1998); see Martínez Areta (2013). These two classifications refer to situations around 1860 and 1990 and were not done from a diachronic point of view. The observations of Mitxelena (1958, 1961–1977, and 1964) are interesting insofar as he distances himself from Bonaparte by differentiating (as Azkue had done previously) Z and R; he also separates, for phonetic reasons, Aez and Sal from LNa and adds the southern dialect (documented in Landucci 1562 and Lazarraga [~1600]). See Section 9 and Lakarra (2014), Mounole (2015), Mounole and Lakarra (2017).

12 See Blust (2014) on the Proto-Ongan-Austronesian hypothesis of Blevins (2007); it is difficult not to see similarities among diverse errors revealed there and those committed in her B-IE hypothesis (Blevins 2013).

13 Nor does the supposed existence of two datives -o/-a in 3rd p., which would come from those old articles, have any real foundations – (*pace* Rijk 1981); actually, *o* → *a/__C*; cf. *deutso* '3p.ERG-3p.DAT' : *deutsala* '3p.ERG-3p.DAT + -la', *jako* '3p. ABS-3p.DAT' : *jakan* '3p.ABS-3p.DAT + -la', etc. (Mitxelena 1954a).

14 Attempts have been made to justify other details but not the *h*-, despite the fact that this is etymologically present (cf. Lakarra 2009b, 2015a, etc.). Moreover, an internal explanation exists (**her* 'to close' + -*i* 'part.', cf. Lakarra 2010, 2013c), and ILTIR could mean 'river', not 'city' (cf. De Hoz 2010–2011).

15 The influence of a lack of clear and persistent fragmentation in the process of the dialectalization of Basque remains to be studied (cf. IE and Austronesian languages, for example); see Section 9.

16 For example, the -*n*- > -*h*- change that Mitxelena understood as simply prior to the first medieval onomastical testimonies (9th–10th centuries) can be taken back at least six centuries (cf. Lakarra 2014) from the dating by Chambon and Greub (2002) of Proto-Gascon in the 5th century, which shares this and other features with its Aquitanian substrate, as has been acknowledged since Luchaire (cf. Gorrochategui 1984).

17 Martinet also addressed sibilants, although his argument, which was complex and yielded few results, has not had any followers. On his ideas about old accentuation, see Section 4.2.5.

18 Although Martinet and his successors attributed the disappearance of aspirated *fortes* to external influence, this is unnecessary and unlikely, hypercharacterization being sufficient to explain it (*th-, *kh- > h : *b°, *d°, *g° → b-, d-, g-) after centuries of the weak phoneme systematically adapting loanwords. The rare exceptions (*cauea > habia* 'nest', *kar > harri* 'stone') are very problematic; nor are the *g-* and *k-* in deictics in Navarrese speech forms (*gau, gori, gura* and *kau, kori, kura* 'this', 'that' (close), and 'that' (far) versus common *hau, hori, hura*) obviously archaic but, rather, much later innovations (cf. Lakarra 2014, 2017); See Egurtzegi (2018) for more arguments on behalf of [aspirated = fortes] vs [non-aspirated = lenes] plosives and Lakarra (2017) for some new cases for *T^h- > h-*.

19 This argument should now be revised: Hualde (1997a) proposed *f < *wh* (see some of the etymologies in Lakarra 2009a) and, therefore, the chronology of these forms would be later, even subsequent to the change *au > ai* in Z and R: cf. Z *aihairi* 'dinner', *gaiherdi* 'midnight' versus general *afari, gauerdi*.

20 *Ba(d)in + -a / *ba(d)in + -no > bai(n)a* 'but, yet' / *baino* 'only, but' and *arran + -i / *arran + -no > arrain* 'fish' / *arrano* 'eagle'. *-no < *non* 'to move' as in comparisons in other languages (cf. Heine and Kuteva 2002).

21 Mitxelena mentioned it occasionally, but little importance has been given to another change (CrV- > CVr): cf. Rom. *trollo* (a little regarded fish, see Corominas-Pascual, s.u.) > *torllo > *dorllo > B *dollor* 'bad, poor'.

22 The same thing occurs in older testimonies with occlusives. Such a tendency is much less complete in final position than in initial position, and in sibilants and vibrants than in laterals and nasals. See *FHV* and now Begiristain (2015) and Lakarra (2017).

23 See the new southern (peninsular) data on /h/ in demonstratives with a later chronology in Manterola (2015).

24 Not all intervocalic *h*'s are, however, etymologically prior. *Lur* 'ground, soil, earth' has a late and very minor variant *luur* in Biz (cf. *zoor* 'debt' in this same dialect). In the DGV, *luhur* appears as attested in the modern LNa dialect of Baigorri, but not in any other modern or old dialect with /h/. It is thus extremely unlikely that these are old forms (pace Blevins 2013).

25 Only this latter one is *h < *h*. As Janhunen (2007) demonstrates, it is typical for /h/ to originate in different sources ("secondary laryngeals"), both in Uralic and in other languages. Lakarra (2015a) adds three other sources of /h/: (5) *-r > -h*, (6) /h/ in Gasconisms, and (7) *hVR- > VRh-* in Gasconisms and inherited words. There are, also, some *-b-, -d-, -g- > -h-* in Contemporary Low Navarrase (cf. Camino 2014) and *-r- > -h-* in Modern and Contemporary Zuberoan.

26 For the OPB and LPB accent, it should be remembered that the monosyllabic root (accentuated at the outset) was not initial but final with the important typological consequences that this implied (prefixes, not suffixes, etc.); cf. Section 6.2 ff.

27 In Hualde (1997b), one finds a synthesis of many of Hualde's works on accentology of the modern dialects (particularly the western ones) that revolutionized studies on the subject. Hualde (2012) himself later continued with studies on accents in varieties such Goizueta (Navarre). Other recent essays on the history of the accent are Martínez Areta (2009), Elordieta (2011a-b), and Egurtzegi and Elordieta (2013).

28 Artiagoitia's (1990) model is much more restrictive (CVC plus a extrametrical -C). Forms with CC-, -CC, and -VV- are common in phonosymbolisms (*brast* 'abrupt start', *dzaust* 'dive', etc.). Given that the canonical form of these usually (cf. IE, etc.) approaches the mirror image of lexemes, we have here additional proof of the CVC structure of the oldest B lexicon.

29 The expansion of derivation is a later phenomenon and belongs in great measure to literary B; see Lakarra (1997a), Sarasola (1997), etc.

30 Of great interest – although it corresponds to a much later stage – is the type of complex reduplication *ikusi-makusi* examined by Igartua (2013), whose distant origins could be in Turkish and surrounding languages and which would have been transmitted via Arabic and Romance.

31 See the results there corresponding to fossils and loanwords in the most common patterns.

32 Mitxelena pointed out that *$*d$- > l,* prior to LPB, may explain the lack of d- in inherited terms; now (cf. Lakarra 2006b) we reconstruct multiple *$*dVC$* roots: apart from the already known, *$*dun$* 'must, to have to' and *$*din$* 'to become', *$*don$* 'to put, to hang', *$*dar$* 'to sit, to get', *$*den$* 'to finish', *$*dats$* 'to go down', etc.

33 As Meillet and Mitxelena demonstrated on multiple occasions, the number of reconstructed phonemes is the minimum necessary to account for the morphemes in the protolanguage and its historical cognates. There could, of course, have been other phonemes that have not left sufficient traces or evidence of their existence. Of more interest are Igartua's works on aspiration (/h/), beginning with Igartua (2002), in which he brilliantly related the change of aspiration and the root, or that of Igartua (2008, 2015) on rhinoglottophilia, completing the known etymological character of /h/ – derived from intervocalic /n/ – with numerous typological parallels.

34 The work of Morvan (2009) is a parody of proper etymological method: he is unaware of testimonies and previous philological efforts, as well as the potentialities of internal reconstruction, which he attempts to replace by a recourse to supposed Siberian, Dravidian, Uralo-Altaic, and Amerindian genetic relationships, on his whim (see Lakarra 2017).

35 Probably in a much-reduced area; see Janhunen (1982 and 2009) on Proto-Uralic.

36 To which one should add everything related to grammaticalization; see Section 7.

37 In Lakarra (2010), we arrive at similar conclusions in another way: analyzing the formation of numerals in B, in the same way as in many other languages, we observe that counting began on the index finger, ignoring the thumb and, therefore, the middle finger, that which is "uppermost," was the second one; cf. Epps (2006) for Amazonian languages, de Lamberterie (2000) for IE languages, etc.

38 There are insufficiently researched or unknown others like *hor-tz* 'fang' (cf. Sp *canino*), *ipurdi* 'bottom' < *$*ibi-erdi$* 'central ford', *laur* 'four' < *labur* 'short', *zur* 'wood' and its derivative *zuhur* 'wise' or *aretx* 'oak/tree' in Old Biz, with parallels in IE (cf. de Lamberterie 2000).

39 Blanco (2014) marks the beginning of lexicological analysis of the archaic corpus (up to 1600); this analysis of the lexicon in the old and classic eras (1600–1745) is extended by Blanco in his thesis (in progress).

40 See Dixon (2002) for the Australian languages and Austerlitz (1976) for the definition of "agglutinative" in the Uralic, Turkic, Mongolic, and other languages of Eurasia: these languages share common features such as suffixation, SOV order, vowel harmony, etc., as well as disyllabism of roots

41 Yet, as in English (AdjN), a more harmonic previous order (SOV in Old English, SVO/VSO in PB: Trask 1997 / Gómez 1994). Add to this the lack of an adjective open class, as in Tibeto-Burman (as opposed to the Dravidian agglutinative, see Bhat 2000). As pointed out in Section 5.5, there are reasons to think that the adjective was not an open class in Tibeto-Burman, but, on the contrary, in modern Tani – and in historical B –, adjectives do belong to an open class (cf. Post 2006).

42 The two determinate declensions are based on the grammaticalization of the article (after the 8th century for the singular, later for the plural); cf. Mitxelena (1971) and Manterola (2015).

43 Stassen, by the way, contends that in B there are no "WITH-language" structures and is therefore badly informed by his B sources: as a *fase sparita* it appears in Old

Biz, A, G, and, at least, in Na and L oral ballads (see Lakarra 2008a). See Lakarra (in progress-b) for more consequences of the reconstruction of the COMITATIVE for PB morphology and syntax (sociative, modal adverbs, 'abstracts objects', dative flags, etc.); for parallels, see Lord (1973, 1993: West African languages) and Chapell et al. (2011: Chinese).

44 Note that the existence of disyllables and polysyllables in Aquitanian inscriptions does not demonstrate widespread root disyllabism; only later – after disyllabic inputs (not outputs) became the majority in word formation – could we speak of disyllabism as widespread CRS. Cf. Feng (1997) and Duanmu (1999) for monosyllabic to disyllabic change in the history of Chinese. See Lakarra (2018) for a preliminar analysis of some *–n / -r / -l / -h / -ø* alternations (and derived etymologies) in archaic CVC-word formation.

45 The oldest allomorph (present as *fase sparita* in adjectives like *hordi* 'drunk', *geldi* 'still', *handi* 'big', etc.) also concurs with the remote future/potential *-di* (*daidi*, *leidi*, etc.) as in other languages; cf. Heine and Kuteva (2002 s.u. COME) for parallels of all these grammaticalizations.

46 Combinations of applicative/directional prefixes + causative are polymorphous (*ar-*, *jar-*, *inar-*, *ihar-* or *ur-*, as well as *eroan/eraman* 'to take') as in Bantu but with the difference that in that family both suffixes and their combinations are not very old fossils as in B but instead are completely functional (cf. Good 2005, etc.).

47 Considered of unknown origin; it could come from a preposition similar to the English *to* and similar forms in other languages. Of identical origin seem to be the V- in the negation **eze*, the supposed epenthetic *-e-* in local cases of consonant declension or the conjunction *e-ta*, mentioned above; see Lakarra (in progress-b).

48 There are more than enough reasons for the destinative *-ra* to be an epenthetic *-r- + -a* 'case marker', in the same way as *-ri* (< **-r-i*) in DAT or *-ren* in GEN (<**-r-e-n*), i.e., such allomorphs are later reanalyses; see Section 7.5.

49 That is, it had prepositions and prefixes (both in verbs and in nouns, but not postpositions and suffixes) as in the historical period.

50 The *split ergativity* in plural of demonstratives shows (cf. Manterola 2015) that the distinction erg.pl./nom.pl. is secondary (Late Medieval), given that the article – the base of both the singular and the plural in declension – is also a later development among them (almost certainly after the 9th century).

51 Although this looks similar to Latin *salix* 'willow', it is not a loanword in Basque: 1) the sibilant in old Latin loans is *z-* (not the *-tz* of this case); 2) Latin-Romance words borrowed are nearly alwasy borrowed in the accusative form, which would be *salice(m)* in this case; 3) *-ice* or *-icV* does not palatalize (nor change to a sibilant nor change the sound of the voiceless stop in words that pass into Basque); and 4) there already exists a completely regular loan in Basque from that Latin or Indo-European form, *zarika* 'willow'. There are other arguments as well, but in short, Latin cannot be the source of this Basque word.

52 Although *e-ho(n)* 'to grind, crush' does exist, though from **e-non*, with **-n- > -h-*, subsequent to **Tʰ- > h-*; this verb does not possess any synthetic forms in contrast to what happens with *ekharri* 'to carry', *ekhusi* 'to see', *ethorri* 'to come'.

53 These last two chronological results clash directly with the "testimony" of the Iruña-Veleia inscriptions (dating from the 3rd–4th centuries according to their supposed "discoverers". They are not, of course, the only (linguistic, epigraphic, or any other type) oddities present in what constitutes one of the greatest modern European hoaxes; see Gorrochategui (2011a and 2011b). Gorrochategui (2002) offers some interesting approaches to dating Basque.

54 The name of the language – from *enausi 'to speak' (Irigoyen 1977), perhaps better *enotsi-hara – has nothing to do with the old ethnonym *Auscii* as has been suggested. The nasal vowels in [êûskera] (< enusquera >, Esteban de Garibay, 16th century) confirm the etymological character of the *h-* in *heuskara* 'B language': cf. Z *harea*, R *âria* 'sand', *ainzto* 'knife', etc.

55 The connection between 'job' and 'bread' has to do with 'the way to get bread' extending in meaning to 'to earn money'.

56 As is argued in Lakarra (2014), converting supposed "elections" like B *egin* 'make' : Central *ezan* 'can' : Eastern *iron* 'can' or B *eutsi* 'to hold up': Central *nin* 'give': Eastern *eradun* 'to have for', etc. into a series of innovations contributes to dating and to giving history to features that have usually been addressed as belonging to the timeless essences of the dialects. Thus in the first case, Biz shares the first three processes with the language as a whole, in the fourth with most of the forms of speech (all of them except Eastern ones), in the fifth with the Western ones as a whole, and in the sixth with some parts of A and G: it does not appear that, diachronically, such a choice confers it with a distinct personality, neither within the Western forms of speech nor within all of them as a whole.

57 See a fuller treatment of the methodological questions explored here in Lakarra (2014); we are far from having achieved the treatment that the numerous aspects and implications of the issue demand.

58 We can supose a family of two elements (PB and Aquitanian; cf. Campbell 2011) through a series of similar considerations, including parallels in the languages like the Germanic languages (see now Stiles 2013); however, in reconstructive practice such an option has not been especially important; it seems preferable to assume that Aquitanian is the brother of OCB and Pyrenean B and not LPB, the source of all of them.

59 The lack of attention to the chronology of innovations is noticeable in the case of G, whose existence prior to Larramendi (18th c.) is debatable; nevertheless, it is typical to find it counterposed to Biz, as if their modern differences were *ab initio* and not much greater in recent centuries than in earlier ones.

60 There has been no research on dating the origin of G as a distinct dialect, but clearly it is one of the most recent ones, based on the defining features of Zuazo (1998: 217):

1 Instability of the organic -*a*;	5 Change *f* > *p*;
2 Root -*e*- in pres. of *edun* '(to) have';	6 *nor* 'who'/*zein* 'which' > *zein* 'who, which';
3 Root -*e*- in present of *izan* 'to be';	7 Conjugated forms as *nijoa* 'I'm going' from *joan* 'to go';
4 Change *d* > *r* [intervocalic];	8 Interrogative particle *al*.

G shares with A (2), (3), (4), and (5), and (8) does not appear until 1785; (1) also appears to have spread in the 18th–19th centuries, the point of becoming a differentiating and marking characteristic with respect to the other Southern dialects. However, the innovations shared by G and A and with B are much older.

61 The bipartite classifications of Bonaparte and Lacombe (synchronic) and Uhlenbeck (linked to supposed polygenesis) – both similar to our left tree – have little to do with the conduct of diachronic dialectology and linguistics; see Mitxelena (1964), Lakarra (1996 and 2014), among others.

62 Lately, Camino (2011, 2014, etc.) has also maintained that the first split involves eastern forms of speech and has offered some indications of proof in this regard.

63 This hypothetical model of fragmentation of OCB could be compatible with ongoing historical work (cf. Pozo 2016) that contends that, in the 5th century, an important

political entity emerged between Pamplona and the Pyrenees, directly related to the later Kingdom of Pamplona.

64 Although for reasons of space I have only referred tangentially here to the philological part, the importance of its development for advances in B diachrony is essential. Besides the monumental Mitxelena and Sarasola (1987–2005) and Lakarra, Manterola and Segurola (2017), see among others Mitxelena (1958), Gorrochategui (1984), Lakarra (1997a), Mounole and Lakarra (2017), Ulibarri (2013), and Urgell (2013).

REFERENCES

Agud, Manuel and Antonio Tovar. 1988–1995. *Materiales para un diccionario etimológico de la lengua vasca (A-Orloi)*. Donostia-San Sebastián: Supplements of the *Anuario del Seminario de Filología Vasca Julio de Urquijo – International Journal of Basque Linguistics and Philology*, 7 vols.

Aikhenvald, Alexandra Y. 2006. Serial Verb Constructions in Typological Perspective. *Serial Verb Constructions. A Cross-Linguistic Typology*, ed. by Alexandra Y. Aikhenvald and Robert M. W. Dixon, 1–68. Oxford: Oxford University Press.

Arbelaiz, Juán José 1978. *Las etimologías vascas en la obra de Luis Michelena*. Tolosa: Kardaberatz.

Ariztimuño, Borja. 2013. Finite verbal morphology. In Martínez Areta, 359–427.

Artiagoitia, Xabier. 1990. Sobre la estructura de la sílaba en (proto)vasco y algunos fenómenos conexos. *Anuario del Seminario de Filología Vasca Julio de Urquijo - International Journal of Basque Linguistics and Philology* 24, no. 2: 327–349.

Austerlitz, Robert. 1976 [1970]. L'aglutination dans les langues de l'Eurasie septentrionale. *Études Finno-ougriennes* 13: 7–12.

Azkue, Resurrección María de. 1923–1925. *Morfología vasca*. Reed. Bilbao: La Gran Enciclopedia Vasca.

Bakrò-Nagy, Marianne Sz., 1992, *Proto-Phonotactics. Phonotactic investigation of the Proto-Uralic and Proto-Finno-Ugric consonant system*. Wiesbaden: Studia Uralica 5, Harrassowitz Verlag.

Barbero, Abilio and Marcelo Vigil. 1965. Sobre los orígenes sociales de la Reconquista: cántabros y vascones desde fines del Imperio Romano hasta la invasión musulmana. *Sobre los orígenes sociales de la Reconquista*, ed. by Abilio Barbero and Marcelo Vigil, 13–103. Ariel: Barcelona 1974.

Barreña, Andoni, Ane Ortega, and Estibalitz Amorrortu. 2013. The Basque Language Today: Achievements and Challenges. In Martínez Areta, 11–29.

Begiristain, Alazne. 2015. Gogoetak Mitxelenaren erronbo sistemaz eta honen historiaurreaz. Ikuspegi berri baterantz. BA Thesis, UPV/EHU.

Begiristain, Alazne. In progress. *FHV-ko kontsonante-taldeekiko atalaz*. MA Thesis, UPV/EHU.

Benveniste, Émile. 1935. *Origines de la formation des noms en indo-européen*. Paris: Maisonneuve.

Benveniste, Émile. 1954. Problémes sémantiques de la réconstruction. Reed. *Problèmes de linguistique générale*, ed. by Émile Benveniste, 289–307. Paris: Gallimard, 1966.

Bhat, D. N. Shankara. 2000. Dravidian and Tibeto-Burman: A Typological Comparison. *International Journal of Dravidian Linguistics* 29: 9–40.

Blanco, Endika. 2014. *Euskara Arkaikoaren Lexikoiaz*. Master Thesis, UPV/EHU.

Blevins, Juliette. 2007. A Long Lost Sister of Proto-Austronesian? Proto-Ongan, Mother of Jarawa and Onge of the Andaman Islands. *Oceanic Linguistics* 46: 154–198.

Blevins, Juliette. 2013. Advances in Proto-Basque reconstruction. *International Congress of Historical Linguistics* (Oslo).

Blust, Robert. 1988. *Austronesian Root Theory: Essay on the Limits of Morphology*. Amsterdam: Benjamins.

Blust, Robert. 2014. Recent Proposals Concerning the Classification of the Austronesian Languages. *Oceanic Linguistic* 53: 300–391.

Brandstetter, Renward. 1916. *An Introduction to Indonesian Linguistics*. London: The Royal Asiatic Society.

Calvet, Jean-Louis. 1981. *Lingüística y colonialismo*. Madrid: Ed. Jucar.

Camino, Iñaki. 2011. Pirinioak, ekialdea eta euskal mintzoak. In Sagarna et al., 773–822.

Camino, Iñaki. 2014. Ekialdeko euskararen iraganaz. In Epelde, 87–153.

Campbell, Lyle. 1988. (Art.-Review) *Language in the Americas* by Joseph H. Greenberg. *Language* 64: 591–615.

Campbell, Lyle. (ed.). 2001. *Grammaticalization: a critical assessment.* (Special issue of *Language Sciences*, vol. 23, numbers 2–3.).

Campbell, Lyle. 2011. La investigación histórica de las lenguas aisladas, o ¿es raro el vasco? In Lakarra, Gorrochategui and Urgell, 23–40.

Campbell, Lyle. 2013 [1998], *Historical Linguistics: An Introduction*. Edinburgh: Edinburgh University Press.

Chambon, Jean-Piérre and Yan Greub. 2002. Note sur l'âge du (proto)gascon. *Revue de Linguistique Romane* 66: 473–495.

Corominas, Joan and José Antonio Pascual. 1980–1991. *Diccionario crítico etimológico castellano e hispánico*, 6 vols. Madrid: Gredos.

De Hoz, Javier. 2011. *Historia lingüística de la Península Ibérica de la Península Ibérica en la Antigüedad. II. El mundo ibérico prerromano y la indoeuropeización*. Madrid: CSIC.

de Rijk, Rudolf P. G. 1981. Euskal morfologiaren zenbait gorabehera. In de Rijk 1998, 211–224.

de Rijk, Rudolf P. G. 1992. 'Nunc' Vasconice. *Anuario del Seminario de Filología Vasca Julio de Urquijo – International Journal of Basque Linguistics and Philology* 26, no. 3, 695–724. In de Rijk 1998, 347–376.

de Rijk, Rudolf P. G. 1998. *De lingua uasconum: Selected Writings*. Donostia-San Sebastián: Supplements of the *Anuario del Seminario de Filología Vasca Julio de Urquijo – International Journal of Basque Linguistics and Philology*.

Dimmendaal, Gerrit J. 2011. *Historical Linguistics and the Comparative Study of African Languages*. Amsterdam and Philadelphia: John Benjamins.

Dixon, Robert M. W. 1977. Where Have All Adjectives Gone. *Where Have All the Adjectives Gone and Other Essays in Semantics and Syntax*, ed. by Robert M. W. Dixon, 1–62. Berlin: Mouton 1982.

Dixon, Robert M. W. 2002. *Australian Languages*. Cambridge: Cambridge University Press.

Donegan, Patricia. 1993. Rhythm and Vocalic Drift in Munda and Mon-Khmer. *Linguistics in the Tibeto-Burman Area* 16: 1–43.

Donegan, Patricia and David Stampe. 1983. Rhythm and the Holistic Organization of Language Structure. *Papers from the Parasession of Phonology, Morphology and Syntax*, ed. by John F. Richardson et al., 337–353. Chicago: Chicago Linguistic Society.

Donegan, Patricia and David Stampe. 2004. Rhythm and the Synthetic Drift of Munda. *The Yearbook of South Asian Languages and Linguistics 2004*, ed. by Rajendra Singh, 3–36. Berlin and New York: de Gruyter.

Duanmu, Sam. 1999. Stress and the Development of Disyllabic Words in Chinese. *Diachronica* 16: 1–36.

Echenique, Maria Teresa. 1983. *Historia lingüística vasco-románica* (2nd ed.). Madrid: Paraninfo, 1987.

Egurtzegi, Ander. 2014. *Towards a Phonetically Grounded Diachronic Phonology of Basque*. PhD, UPV/EHU.

Egurtzegi, Ander. 2018. *Herskarien ustezko ahoskabetasun asimilazioa eta euskal herskari zaharren gauzatzea*. Forthcoming in a festschrift edited by Joseba Lakarra & Blanca Urgell.

Egurtzegi, Ander and Gorka Elordieta. 2013. Euskal azentueren historiaz. In Gómez et al., 163–186.

Elmendorf, William. 1997. A Preliminary Analysis of Yukian Root Structure. *Anthropological Linguistics* 39: 74–91.

Elordieta, Gorka. 2011a. Euskal azentuaren bilakaera: hipotesiak eta proposamenak. In Sagarna et al., 989–1014.

Elordieta, Gorka. 2011b. Euskal azentu eta intonazioari buruzko ikerketa: status quaestionis. In Lakarra et al., 389–428.

Epelde, Irantzu. (ed.). 2014. *Euskal dialektologia: lehena eta oraina*. Bilbo: Supplements of the *Anuario del Seminario de Filología Vasca Julio de Urquijo – International Journal of Basque Linguistics and Philology*, no. 69.

Etxepare, Bernat. 1545. *Linguae Vasconum Primitiae*. Edition by Patxi Altuna, Bilbao: Euskaltzaindia.

Epps, Patience. 2006. Growing a Numeral System: The Historical Development of Numerals in a Amazonian Language Family. *Diachronica* 23: 259–288.

Feng, Shengli. 1997. Prosodic Structure and Compound Words in Classical Chinese. *New Approaches to Chinese Word Formation: Morphology, Phonology and the Lexicon in Modern and Ancient Chinese*, ed. by Jerome L. Packard, 197–260. Berlin: Mouton de Gruyter.

Fischer, Olga, Muriel Norde, and Harry Perridon (eds.). 2004. *Up and Down the Cline – The Nature of Grammaticalization*. Amsterdam and Philadelphia: John Benjamins.

Forni, Gianfranco. 2013. Evidence for Basque as a IE Language. *Journal of Indo-European Studies* 41, nos. 1–2: 39–180.

García Uriz, Eneko. 2016. Hitz hasierako herskari ahoskabeak euskararen historian. BA Thesis, UPV/EHU.

Gavel, Henri. 1920. *Éléments de phonétique basque*. Paris: *Revue Internationale des Études Basques* 12.

Gómez, Ricardo. 1994. Euskal aditz morfologia eta hitzordena: VSO-tik SOV-ra. *La langue basque parmi les autres*, ed. by Jean-Baptiste Orpustan, 93–114. Baigorri: Izpegi.

Gómez, Ricardo and Koldo Sainz. 1995. On the Origin of the Finite Forms of the Basque Verb. In Hualde, Lakarra and Trask, 235–274.

Gómez, Ricardo, Joaquín Gorrochategui, Joseba Andoni Lakarra, and Céline Mounole (eds.). 2013. *Koldo Mitxelena Katedraren III. Biltzarra (Gasteiz, 8–11/X/2012)*. Vitoria-Gasteiz: UPV/EHU.

Good, Jeffry. 2005. Reconstructing Morpheme Order in Bantu: The Case of Causativization and Applicativization. *Diachronica* 22: 3–57.

Gorrochategui, Joaquín. 1984. *Estudio sobre la onomástica indígena de Aquitania*. Bilbao: UPV/EHU.

Gorrochategui, Joaquín. 1985. Historia de las ideas acerca de los límites geográficos del vasco antiguo. *Anuario del Seminario de Filología Vasca Julio de Urquijo – International Journal of Basque Linguistics and Philology* 19: 571–594.

Gorrochategui, Joaquín. 1987. Vasco-céltica. *Anuario del Seminario de Filología Vasca Julio de Urquijo – International Journal of Basque Linguistics and Philology* 21: 951–959.

Gorrochategui, Joaquín. 1998. *Euskararen historiaurreaz zenbait gogoeta. Algunas reflexiones sobre la prehistoria de la lengua vasca*. Vitoria-Gasteiz: UPV/EHU.

Gorrochategui, Joaquín. 2002. Planteamientos de la lingüística histórica en la datación del euskara. *XV Congreso de Estudios Vascos*, 103–114. Donostia-San Sebastián: SEV.

Gorrochategui, Joaquín. 2011a. Las armas de la filología. In Lakarra, Gorrochategui and Urgell, 41–70.

Gorrochategui, Joaquín. 2011b. *Hic et nunc*. Falsificaciones contemporáneas. El caso de Iruña-Veleia. *El monumento epigráfico en fuentes secundarias. Procesos de reutilización, interpretación y falsificación*, ed. by Jordi Carbonell, Helena Gimeno, and José Luis Moralejo, 241–261. Barcelona: Universitat Autonoma.

Gorrochategui, Joaquín. 2017. "El vasco en la Antigüedad." In Gorrochategui, Igartua & Lakarra (eds.). Forthcoming.

Gorrochategui, Joaquín, Iván Igartua, and Joseba Andoni Lakarra (eds.). 2017. *Historia de la lengua vasca*. Vitoria-Gasteiz: Gobierno Vasco. Forthcoming.

Gorrochategui, Joaquín and Joseba Andoni Lakarra. 2013. Why Basque Is Not, Unfortunately, an IE Language? *Journal of Indo-European Studies* 41, nos. 1–2: 203–237.

Greenberg, Joseph. 1963 [1990]. Some Universals of Grammar With Particular Reference to the Order of Meaningful Elements. Reed. *On language: Selected Writtings of Joseph H. Greenberg*, ed. by Keith Denning and Suzanne Kemmer, 40–70. Stanford, CA: Stanford University Press.

Guiter, Henri. 1989. Elementos de cronología fonética del vascuence. *Anuario del Seminario de Filología Vasca Julio de Urquijo – International Journal of Basque Linguistics and Philology* 23, no. 3: 797–800.

Haas, Mary. 1969. *The Prehistory of Languages*. The Hague: Mouton.

Heine, Bernhard and Tania Kuteva. 2002. *World Lexicon of Grammaticalization*. Cambridge, NY: Cambridge University Press.

Holmer, Nils M. 1970. A Historic-Comparative Analysis of the Structure of the Basque Language: The Principal Linguistic Types. *Fontes Linguae Vasconum. Studia et Documenta* 2: 5–47.

Houis, Maurice. 1970. Reflexion sur une double correlation typologique. *Journal of West African Languages* 7: 59–68.

Hualde, José Ignacio 1991. *Basque Phonology*. London and New York: Routledge.

Hualde, José Ignacio. 1995. Reconstructing the Ancient Basque Accentual System: Evidence and Hypotheses. In Hualde, Lakarra and Trask, 171–188.

Hualde, José Ignacio. 1997a. Aitzineuskararen leherkariak. *Anuario del Seminario de Filología Vasca Julio de Urquijo – International Journal of Basque Linguistics and Philology* 31: 411–424.

Hualde, José Ignacio. 1997b. *Euskararen azentuerak*. Donostia-San Sebastián: Supplements of the *Anuario del Seminario de Filología Vasca Julio de Urquijo – International Journal of Basque Linguistics and Philology*.

Hualde, José Ignacio. 2006. Laringalak eta euskal azentuaren bilakaera. *Andolin Eguzkitza gogoan. In honor to Professor Eguzkitza*, ed. by Beatriz Fernández and Itziar Laka, 497–511. Bilbao: UPV/EHU.

Hualde, José Ignacio. 2008. Acentuación y cronología relativa en la lengua vasca. *Oihenart* 23: 199–217.

Hualde, José Ignacio. 2012. Two Basque Accentual Systems and the Notion of Pitch-Accent Language. *Lingua* 122: 1335–1351.

Hualde, José Ignacio. (forthcoming). Dialektologia dinamikoa. In a volume of *Lapurdum* edited by Irantzu Epelde.

Hualde, José Ignacio, Joseba Andoni Lakarra, and Larry Trask (eds.). 1995. *Towards a History of Basque Language*. Amsterdam and Philadelphia: John Benjamins.

Hualde, José Ignacio and Jon Ortiz de Urbina (eds.). 2003. *A Grammar of Basque*. Berlin: Mouton de Gruyter.

Igartua, Iván. 2002. Euskararen hasperena ikuspegi tipologiko eta diakronikotik. *Erramu Boneta: Festschrift for Rudolf P.G. de Rijk*, Supplements of the *Anuario del Seminario de Filología Vasca Julio de Urquijo – International Journal of Basque Linguistics and Philology* no. 44, ed. by Xabier Artiagoitia, Patxi Goenaga, and Joseba Andoni Lakarra, 366–389. Bilbao: UPV/EHU.

Igartua, Iván. 2008. La aspiración de origen nasal en la evolución fonológica del euskera: un caso de rhinoglottophilia. *Anuario del Seminario de Filología Vasca Julio de Urquijo - International Journal of Basque Linguistics and Philology* 42: 171–189.

Igartua, Iván. 2013. La reduplicación compleja en euskera: notas acerca de su formación y sus paralelos en otras lenguas. *Fontes Linguae Vasconum. Studia et Documenta* 45: 5–30.

Igartua, Iván. 2015. Diachronic Effects of Rhinoglottophilia, Symmetries in Sound Change, and the Curious Case of Basque. *Studies in Language* 39, no. 3: 635–663.

Irigoyen, Alfonso. 1977. Geure hizkuntzari euskaldunok deritzagun izenaz. *Euskera* 22, no. 2: 513–538.

Janhunen, Juha. 1982. On the structure of Proto-Uralic. *Finnisch-ugrische Forschungen* 44: 23–42.

Janhunen, Juha. 1997. Problems of Primary Root Structure in Pre-Proto-Japonic. *International Journal of Central Asian Studies* 2, (ed. in chief Choi Hab-Woo). The International Association of Central Asian Studies Institute of Asian Culture and Development.

Janhunen, Juha. 2007. The Primary Laryngal in Uralic and Beyond. *Sámit, sánit, sátnehámit. Riepmočála Pekka Sammallahtii miessemánu 21. beaivve 2007*, 253, 203–227. Helsinki: Suomalais-Ugrilaisen Seuran Toimituksia = Mémoires de la Société Finno-Ougrienne.

Janhunen, Juha. 2009. Proto-Uralic: What, Where, and When? *The Quasquicentennial of the Finno-Ugrian Society*, ed. by Jussi Ylikoski, 57–78. Helsinki: *Mémoires de la Société Finno-Ougrienne* 258.

Krajewska, Dorota. In progress. *Historical syntax of relatives in Basque*. PhD, UPV/EHU.

Lafitte, Pierre. 1944. *Grammaire basque (navarro-labourdin littéraire)*. Facsimil, Donostia-San Sebastián: Elkar 1979.

Lafon, Réné. 1943. *Le système du verbe basque au XVIème siècle*. Donostia-San Sebastián: Elkar 1980.

Lafon, Réné. 1948. Sur les suffixes casuels *-ti/-tik* en basque. In Lafon 1999, 199–207.

Lafon, Réné. 1999. *Vasconiana*. Bilbao: Iker 11, Euskaltzaindia.

Lakarra, Joseba Andoni. 1995. Reconstructing the Root in Pre-Proto-Basque. In Hualde et al., 189–206.

Lakarra, Joseba Andoni. 1996. *Refranes y Sentencias: ikerketak eta edizioa*. Bilbao: Euskaltzaindia.

Lakarra, Joseba Andoni. 1997a. Euskararen historia eta filologia: arazo zahar, bide berri. *Anuario del Seminario de Filología Vasca Julio de Urquijo – International Journal of Basque Linguistics and Philology* 31: 447–535.

Lakarra, Joseba Andoni. 1997b. Gogoetak aitzineuskararen berreraiketaz: konparaketa eta barneberreraiketa. *Anuario del Seminario de Filología Vasca Julio de Urquijo - International Journal of Basque Linguistics and Philology* 31: 537–616.

Lakarra, Joseba Andoni. 2005. Prolegómenos a la reconstrucción de segundo grado y al análisis del cambio tipológico en (proto)vasco. *Palaeohispanica* 5: 407–470.

Lakarra, Joseba Andoni. 2006a. Protovasco, munda y otros: reconstrucción interna y tipología holística diacrónica. *Oihenart* 21: 229–322.

Lakarra, Joseba Andoni. 2006b. Notas sobre iniciales, cambio tipológico y prehistoria del verbo vasco. In Lakarra and Hualde, 561–621.

Lakarra, Joseba Andoni. 2008a. Aitzineuskararen gramatikarantz malkar eta osinetan zehar. *Gramatika Jaietan. Patxi Goenagari Omenaldia*, ed. by Xabier Artiagoitia and Joseba Andoni Lakarra, 451–490. Bilbao: Supplements of the *Anuario del Seminario de Filología Vasca Julio de Urquijo – International Journal of Basque Linguistics and Philology* no. 51, UPV/EHU.

Lakarra, Joseba Andoni. 2008b. *Vida con/y libertad*: sobre una coordinación arcaica y la autenticidad de "Urthubiako Alhaba." *Anuario del Seminario de Filología Vasca Julio de Urquijo – International Journal of Basque Linguistics and Philology* 42: 83–100.

Lakarra, Joseba Andoni. 2008c. Irregularidades radicales y antiguas extensiones a la izquierda: Para la reconstrucción del verbo vasco. Ms. UPV/EHU.

Lakarra, Joseba Andoni. 2008d. Forma canónica, etimología y reconstrucción en el campo vasco. *Anuario del Seminario de Filología Vasca Julio de Urquijo – International Journal of Basque Linguistics and Philology* 37: 261–391.

Lakarra, Joseba Andoni. 2009a. Forma canónica y cambios en la forma canónica en la prehistoria de la lengua vasca. *X. Congreso de Lenguas y Culturas Paleohispánicas, Palaeohispanica* 9: 557–609.

Lakarra, Joseba Andoni. 2009b. Adabakiak /h/-aren balio etimologikoaz. *Anuario del Seminario de Filología Vasca Julio de Urquijo – International Journal of Basque Linguistics and Philology* 43, nos. 1–2: 565–596.

Lakarra, Joseba Andoni. 2010. Haches, diptongos y otros detalles de alguna importancia: notas sobre numerales (proto)vascos y comparación vasco-ibérica (Apéndice sobre *hiri* y *bat-bi*). *Veleia* 27: 191–238.

Lakarra, Joseba Andoni. 2011a. Erro monosilabikoaren teoria eta aitzineuskararen berreraiketa: zenbait alderdi eta ondorio, *Fontes Linguae Vasconum. Studia et Documenta* 113, 5–114.

Lakarra, Joseba Andoni. 2011b. Aitzineuskara: egindakoak eta eginkizunak. In Andoni Sagarna, Joseba Andoni Lakarra, and Patxi Salaberri (eds.), *Pirineoetako hizkuntzak: lehena eta oraina*, Iker 26, Bilbao: 617–694.

Lakarra, Joseba Andoni. 2012. Mailegaketa eta berreraiketa euskararen historiaurrean ikerketan. In Igartua, 17–74.

Lakarra, Joseba Andoni. 2013a. Monosyllabic root theory and the reconstruction of Proto-Basque: some aspects and consequences. In Martinez Areta, 173–221.

Lakarra, Joseba Andoni. 2013b. Aitzineuskararen berreraiketa sakonagorantz: forma kanonikoa, tipologia holistikoa, kronologia eta gramatikalizazioa. In Gómez et al., 274–324.

Lakarra, Joseba Andoni. 2013c. Gramática histórica vasca o vasco-iberismo. *Palaeohispanica* 13: 567–592.

Lakarra, Joseba Andoni. 2014. Gogoetak euskal dialektologia diakronikoaz: Euskara Batu Zaharra berreraiki beharraz eta haren banaketaren ikerketaz. In Epelde, 155–241.

Lakarra, Joseba Andoni. 2015a. Hiru hasperen haboro. *Eridenen du zerzaz kontenta. Sailkideen omenaldia Henrike Knörr irakasleari*, ed. by Ricardo Gómez and Maria Jose Ezeizabarrena, 349–378. Bilbao: UPV/EHU.

Lakarra, Joseba Andoni. 2015b. *Saratsola* eta (aitzin)eusk(ar)en geruzak. In Beatriz Fernández and Pello Salaburu (eds.), *Ibon Sarasola. Gorazarre. Homenatge. Homenaje*, Donostia-San Sebastián: UPV/EHU, 419–439.

Lakarra, Joseba Andoni. 2015c. *Bi* eta bere askazia. Forthcoming in a festschrift.

Lakarra, Joseba Andoni. 2016. Gramatikalizazioa, morfemen forma kanonikoak eta berreraiketa morfologikoaren bide berriak. *Txipi Ormaetxea omenduz. Hire bordatxoan*, ed. by Gotzon Aurrekoetxea, Jesus Mari Makazaga, and Patxi Salaberri, 175–192. Leioa UPV/EHU.

Lakarra, Joseba Andoni. 2017. Prehistoria de la lengua vasca. In Gorrochategui, Igartua and Lakarra. Forthcoming.

Lakarra, Joseba Andoni. 2018. CVC berreraikiaz: aurretik eta atzetik. Forthcoming in a festschrift ed. by Joseba A. Lakarra and Blanca Urgell.

Lakarra, Joseba Andoni. In progress-a. Prehistoria del comitativo e implicaciones para la reconstrucción de la morfología y la sintaxis protovasca. Ms. UPV/EHU.

Lakarra, Joseba Andoni. In progress-b. Protogenitivo, protolocativo y sintaxis del protovasco. Ms. UPV/EHU.

Lakarra, Joseba Andoni, Joaquín Gorrochategui, and Blanca Urgell (eds.). 2011. *II Congreso de la Cátedra Luis Michelena*. Bilbao: UPV/EHU.

Lakarra, Joseba Andoni and José Ignacio Hualde (eds.). 2006. *Studies in Basque and Historical Linguistics in Memory of Robert Larry Trask* (=*Anuario del Seminario de Filología Vasca Julio de Urquijo – International Journal of Basque Linguistics and Philology* XL, 1–2). Bilbao: UPV/EHU.

Lakarra, Joseba Andoni, Julen Manterola, and Iñaki Segurola. 2016. Los estudios etimológicos vascos: historia y perspectivas. *Etimología e historia en el léxico del español. Estudios ofrecidos a José Antonio Pascual (Magister bonus et sapiens)*, ed. by Mariano Quirós, 843–869. Madrid/Frankfurt: Iberoamericana/Vervuert.

Lakarra, Joseba Andoni, Julen Manterola, and Iñaki Segurola. 2017. *Euskal hiztegi historiko etimologikoa*. Bilbao: Euskaltzaindia.

Lamberterie, Charles de. 2000. Problèmes sémantiques de la reconstruction en indoeuropéen. *Théories contemporaines du changement sémantique*, ed. by Jacques François, 109–134. Leuven: Peeters.

Larramendi, Manuel de. 1729. *El imposible vencido. Arte de la lengua bascongada*. Salamanca. Facsimil Hordago, Donostia-San Sebastián, 1979.

Larramendi, Manuel de. 1745. *Diccionario Trilingüe del castellano, bascuence y latín*, Donostia-San Sebastián. Facsimil Txertoa, Donostia-San Sebastián, 1984.

Lord, Carol. 1973. Serial verbs in transitions. *Studies in African Linguistics* 4, no. 3, 269–296.

Lord, Carol. 1993. *Historical Change in Serial Verb Constructions*. Amsterdam: John Benjamins.

Madariaga, Juán. 2008. *Apologistas y detractores de la lengua vasca*. Donostia-San Sebastián: Fundación para el estudio del Derecho Histórico y Autonómico de Vasconia.

Manterola, Julen. 2015. *Euskararen morfologia historikorako. Artikuluak eta erakusleak. Towards a history of Basque morphology: articles and demonstratives*. PhD, UPV/EHU.

Martinet, André. 1950. De la sonorisation des occlusives initiales en basque. *Word* 6: 224–233.

Martinez Areta, Mikel. 2006. *El consonantismo protovasco*. PhD, UPV/EHU.

Martinez Areta, Mikel. 2009. El acento protovasco. *Anuario del Seminario de Filología Vasca Julio de Urquijo - International Journal of Basque Linguistics and Philology* 38: 135–206.

Martinez Areta, Mikel. (ed.). 2013. *Basque and Proto-Basque*. Frankfurt: Peter Lang.

Meillet, Antoine. 1925, *La méthode comparative en linguistique historique*, Paris. Reed. Klincksieck 1970.

Michelena, Luis = Koldo Mitxelena.

Mitxelena, Koldo. 1950. De etimología vasca. In Mitxelena 1988, 439–444.

Mitxelena, Koldo. 1951. La sonorización de las oclusivas iniciales. In Mitxelena 1988, 203–211.

Mitxelena, Koldo. 1954a. Nota sobre algunos pasajes de los *Refranes y Sentencias* de 1596. In Mitxelena 1988, 792–798.

Mitxelena, Koldo. 1954b. De onomastica aquitana. In Mitxelena 1987, 409–445.

Mitxelena, Koldo, 1956, La lengua vasca como medio de conocimiento histórico, *Zumarraga* 6, 49–70.

Mitxelena, Koldo. 1957a. Las antiguas consonantes vascas. Reed. in Mitxelena 1988, 166–189.

Mitxelena, Koldo, 1957b, Basque et roman. Reed. in Mitxelena 1988, 106–115.

Mitxelena, Koldo. 1958. Introducción [a Landucci (1562)]. In Mitxelena 1988, II, 762–782.

Mitxelena, Koldo. 1961/77. *Fonética histórica vasca* (2nd revised ed.). Donostia-San Sebastián: Supplement of the *Anuario del Seminario de Filología Vasca Julio de Urquijo – International Journal of Basque Linguistics and Philology* no. 4.

Mitxelena, Koldo. 1963. *Lenguas y protolenguas*. In Mitxelena, Donostia-San Sebastián: Supplement of the *Anuario del Seminario de Filología Vasca Julio de Urquijo – International Journal of Basque Linguistics and Philology* no. 20, 1990.

Mitxelena, Koldo. 1964. Sobre el pasado de la lengua vasca. In Mitxelena 1988, 1–73.

Mitxelena, Koldo. 1971. Toponimia, léxico y gramática. In Mitxelena 1987, 141–167.

Mitxelena, Koldo. 1973. *Apellidos vascos* (3rd ed.). Donostia-San Sebastián: Txertoa.

Mitxelena, Koldo. 1974. El elemento latino-románico en la lengua vasca. In Mitxelena 1987, 195–219.

Mitxelena, Koldo. 1977. Notas sobre compuestos verbales vascos. In Mitxelena 1987, 311–335.

Mitxelena, Koldo. 1979. La langue ibère. Reed. in Mitxelena 1985, 341–356.

Mitxelena, Koldo. 1981. Lengua común y dialectos vascos. In Mitxelena 1987, 35–55.

Mitxelena, Koldo. 1987. *Palabras y Textos*, ed. Joaquín Gorrochategui. Bilbao: UPV/ EHU.

Mitxelena, Koldo. 1988, *Sobre historia de la lengua vasca*, ed. Joseba Andoni Lakarra. Donostia-San Sebastián: Supplements of the *Anuario del Seminario de Filología Vasca Julio de Urquijo – International Journal of Basque Linguistics and Philology* 10, 2 vols.

Mitxelena, Koldo. 2011–2012. *Luis Michelena. Obras Completas*, ed. Joseba Andoni Lakarra and Iñigo Ruiz Arzalluz, Bilbao/Donostia-San Sebastián: Supplements of the *Anuario del Seminario de Filología Vasca Julio de Urquijo – International Journal of Basque Linguistics and Philology*, 15 vols.

Mitxelena, Koldo and Ibon Sarasola. 1987–2005. *Diccionario general vasco. Orotariko Euskal Hiztegia*. Bilbao: Euskaltzaindia.

Morvan, Michel. 2009. *Dictionnaire étymologique basque-français-espagnol*. www. lexilogos.com/basque_dictionnaire.htm.

Mounole, Céline. 2006. Quelques remarques à propos de l'histoire des périphrases basques. In Lakarra and Hualde, 723–738.

Mounole, Céline. 2011. *Le verbe basque ancien: étude philologique et diachronique.* PhD UPV/EHU. Forthcoming in *Anuario del Seminario de Filología Vasca Julio de Urquijo – International Journal of Basque Linguistics and Philology.*

Mounole, Céline. 2015. Lazarragaren gramatika. Ms., UPV/EHU.

Mounole, Céline and Joseba Andoni Lakarra. 2017. Euskara Arkaikoa. In Gorrochategui, Igartua and Lakarra. Forthcoming.

Odriozola, Aitor. 2016. Hitz hasierako bokalismoa: *e-* hitzen berreraiketa eta bilakabide diakronikoa. BA Thesis, UPV/EHU.

Olmo Lete, Gregorio del. 2003. *Questions de linguistique sémitique. Racine et lexème. Histoire de la recherche (1940–2000).* Paris: Jean Maisonneuve, "Librairie d'Amerique et d'Orient".

Pawley, Andrew. 2006. Where Have All the Verbs Gone? Remarks on the Organisation of Languages with Small, Closed Verb Classes. *11th Biennial Rice University Linguistic Symposium, 16–18 March.* Unpublished.

Post, Mark W. 2006. Compounding and the Structure of the Tani Lexicon. *Linguistics in the Tibeto-Burman Area* 29: 40–60.

Post, Mark W. 2009. Prosodic and Typological Drift in Austroasiatic and Tibeto-Burman: Against "Sinosphere" and "Indosphere." Ms., The Cairns Institute, James Cook University.

Pozo, Mikel. 2016. *Vasconia y los vascones, de la crisis del Imperio Romano a la llegada del Islam (siglos V–VIII).* PhD Thesis, UPV/EHU.

Rico, Francisco. 1982. *Primera cuarentena y tratado general de literatura.* Barcelona: El festín de Esopo.

Ringe, David A. 2003. Internal reconstruction. *The Handbook of Historical Linguistics,* ed. by Brian D. Joseph and Richard D. Janda, 244–261. Oxford: Blackwell.

Rohlfs, Gerhard. 1977. *Le gascon. Études de philologie pyréneenne* (3rd ed.). Niemeyer: Tubinga.

Sagarna, Andoni, Joseba Andoni Lakarra and Patxi Salaberri (eds.). 2011. *Pirineoetako hizkuntzak: lehena eta oraina* (= 16. Biltzarra. *Iruñea 6–10/X/2008*). Bilbo: Iker 26, Euskaltzaindia.

Sagart, Laurent. 1999. *The Roots of Old Chinese.* Amsterdam and Philadelphia: John Benjamins.

Salaberri, Patxi. 1991. Toponimia, dialektologiaren ikerbide. *Nazioarteko dialektologia Biltzarra,* 619–645. Bilbao: Euskaltzaindia.

Salaberri, Patxi. 2011a. Pirinioetako euskal toponimoak: direnak eta diratekeenak. *Pirineoetako hizkuntzak: lehena eta oraina* (= 16. Biltzarra. *Iruñea 6–10/X/2008*), ed. by Andoni Sagarna, Joseba Andoni Lakarra, and Patxi Salaberri, 977–1005. Bilbo: Iker 26, Euskaltzaindia.

Salaberri, Patxi. 2011b. El sufijo occidental *-ika* y otras cuestiones de toponimia vasca. *Fontes Linguae Vasconum. Studia et Documenta* 43: 139–176.

Salaberri, Patxi. 2013. *Apellidos Vascos* eta Mitxelenaren onomastika lanak. In Gómez et al., 673–697.

Sarasola, Ibon. 1997. Euskal hitz altxorraz. *Anuario del Seminario de Filología Vasca Julio de Urquijo – International Journal of Basque Linguistics and Philology* 31: 617–642.

Schuh, Russell. 2013. Word Families in Hausa. *Language, Literature and Culture in a Multilingual Society. A festschrift for Abubakar Rasheed,* ed. by Ozo-Mekuri Ndimele,

M. Ahmad, and H.M. Yakasai, 579–598. Port Hardcourt: M. and J. Grand Orbit Communications.

Stassen, Leon. 2000. AND-languages and WITH-languages. *Linguistic Typology* 4: 1–54.

Stiles, Patrick V. 2013. The Pan-West Germanic Isoglosses and the Sub-Relationships of West Germanic to Other Branches. *NOWELE* 66: 1, 5–38.

Straka, Georges. 1951–1954. Observations sur la chronologie et les dates de quelques modifications phonétiques en roman et en français prélittéraires. *Revue des Langues Romanes* 71: 247–307.

Thomason, Sandra G. 1993. Copying with Partial Information in Historical Linguistics. *Historical Linguistics 1989: Papers from the Ninth International Conference on Historical Linguistics*, ed. by Henk Aertsen and Robert J. Jeffers, 485–496. Amsterdam: John Benjamins.

Thomason, Sandra G. 2001. *Language Contact: An Introduction*. Edinburgh: Edinburgh University Press.

Tovar, Antonio. 1981. *Mitología e ideología sobre la lengua vasca*. Madrid: Alianza Editorial.

Trask, Robert Larry. 1977. Historical Syntax and Basque Verbal Morphology. *Anglo-American Contributions to Basque Studies: In Honor of Jon Bilbao*, ed. by William A. Douglass, Richard W. Etulain, and William H. Jacobsen Jr., 203–217. Reno: University of Nevada.

Trask, Robert Larry. 1996. *Historical Linguistics*. London and New York: Arnold.

Trask, Robert Larry. 1997. *The History of Basque*. London: Routledge.

Trask, Robert Larry. 1998. The Typological Position of Basque: Then and Now. *Language Sciences* 20: 313–324.

Trask, Robert Larry. 2008. *Etymological Dictionary of Basque*, ed. by Max W. Wheeler. Sussex: University of Sussex.

Uhlenbeck, Cornelius. 1942. Les couches anciennes du vocabulaire basque. *Eusko-Jakintza* 1 (1947): 543–581. French translation of Dutch original by Georges Lacombe.

Ulibarri, Koldo. 2013. External History. Sources for Historical Research. In Martínez Areta, 89–117.

Urgell, Blanca. 2013. Euskal filologia: zer (ez) dakigu 25 urte beranduago? In Gómez et al. (eds.), 533-570.

Vovin, Anatoly. 1994, (Art.-Review) Long Distance Relationships, Reconstruction Methodology and the Origins of Japanese, *Diachronica* 11: 1, 95–114.

Watkins, Calvert. 1984. L'apport d'Émile Benveniste à la grammaire comparée. *Émile Benveniste aujourd'hui. Actes du Colloque international du CNRS*, ed. by Guy Serbat, I, 3–11. Louvain: Peeters.

Watkins, Calvert. 1990. Etymologies, Equations, and Comparanda: Types and Values, and Criteria for Judgment. *Patterns of Change, Change of Patterns: Linguistic Change and Reconstruction Methodology*, ed. by Philip Baldi, 289–304. Berlin and New York: Mouton de Gruyter.

Zuazo, Koldo. 1998. Euskalkiak gaur. *Fontes Lingua Vasconum. Studia et Documenta* 30: 191–233.

CHAPTER 4

AINU

Thomas Dougherty

1 INTRODUCTION

Ainu (アイヌイタク *Aynu Itak*) is a dormant language isolate previously spoken on the northernmost Japanese island of Hokkaidō, as well as southern half of the Russian island of Sakhalin, and in the disputed Kuril Islands. Map 4.1 depicts the historically attested range of the Ainu language in Northeast Asia. See Vovin (2009) for discussion of its suspected range in to the south on the Japanese main island of Honshū based on toponymical evidence.

This chapter primarily provides a typological overview of the Hokkaidō varieties of Ainu, highlighting some salient morphosyntactic phenomena found in Ainu. It focuses mainly on data from Ainu oral literature, as it is the most well-preserved genre of Ainu usage. In addition, proposed relationships and language contact are touched upon, as well as a brief discussion of the extant scholarly materials and primary sources of Ainu.

2 PROPOSED GENETIC RELATIONSHIPS AND LANGUAGE CONTACT

There have been a large number of proposed relationships between Ainu and other language families. The following list is not exhaustive but includes most of the major claims and some of the notable works:

- Austronesian (Stenberg 1929, Dahl 1977)
- Tai-Kadai (Li 1977)
- Austroasiatic (Vovin 1993)
- Hmong-Mien (Vovin 1993)
- Altaic (Street 1962, Patrie 1982)
- Ainu-Koreo-Japonic as a genetic unit under the Eurasiatic macrofamily (Greenberg 2000, 2002)
- Indo-European (Naert 1958, Lindquist 1960)

None of these claims has been accepted by the scholarly community at large. Vovin (1993) specifically argues against several and proposes very initial (but likely possibly spurious) comparisons for the two affiliations he suggests, with Austroasiatic and/or Hmong-Mien (Vovin 1993: 190–209).

While most of the claims with regards to a genetic relationship are questionable, language contact between Ainu and Japanese on the one hand and Ainu and Nivkh on the other are well-substantiated, albeit understudied.

Ainu has had a relatively close contact relationship with Japanese throughout the recorded history of both languages. Vovin's (2012 and 2013) translations of Old Japanese poetry dating to the 700s CE detail some proposed Ainu loans in Eastern Old

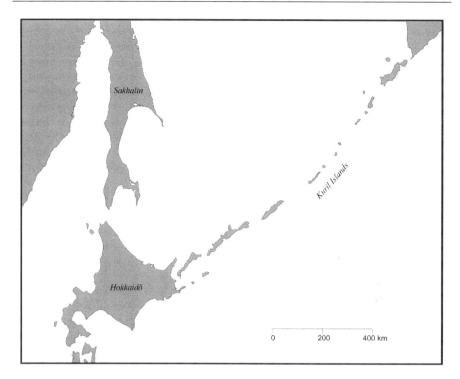

MAP 4.1 AINU MAP

Source: Map created by the author using R and the packages *maps* and *mapdata*.

R Core Team. 2016. *R: A language and environment for statistical computing*. R Foundation for Statistical Computing, Vienna, Austria. URL www.R-project.org/.

Brownrigg, Ray. 2016a. *maps: Draw Geographical Maps*. R package version 3.1.1. Original S code by Richard A. Becker, Allan R. Wilks. Enhancements by Thomas P. Minka and Alex Deckmyn. URL *https://CRAN.R-project.org/package=maps*.

Brownrigg, Ray. 2016b. *mapdata: Extra Map Databases*. R package version 2.2–6. Original S code by Richard A. Becker and Allan R. Wilks. URL *https://CRAN.R-project.org/package=mapdata*.

Japanese poetry (Vovin 2012: 11–12 et passim; Vovin 2013: 13–15 et passim). Among these are place names, for instance, Eastern Old Japanese (henceforth EOJ) *Tōya* [təja] < Ainu *to ya* 'lake shore' – but some involve even function words, including the relativizer EOJ *siNda* [siⁿda] 'when' < Ainu *hi-ta* 'time-LOC' (Vovin 2012: 12).

    Other, more well-known examples of loanwords from Ainu into Japanese are the kind of lexical items we might expect to enter a language of higher prestige from a language of lower status: animals found in areas traditionally inhabited by the Ainu and not colonized by the Japanese until quite late in the history of Japan, such as the 'sea otter' (*Enhydra lutris*): Ainu *rakko* > Japanese ラッコ *rakko*. By and in large, though, the direction of contact seems to be from Japanese into Ainu. For example, material items not found traditionally among the Ainu but important for Ainu-Japanese trade, such as 'tobacco' (Ainu *tabako* < Japanese たばこ *tabako*) are common and expected loanwords from Japanese into Ainu.

Similar, but less well-studied contact exists between Ainu and Nivkh. For instance, the reindeer (*Rangifer tarandus*) is not found in areas traditionally inhabited by the Ainu. The Nivkh, however, living at the mouth of the Amur River on the Asian mainland and in the north of Sakhalin, encountered various Tungusic peoples (such as the Ul'ta [or Orok]) who herd domesticated reindeer. Thus, the Sakhalin Ainu word *tunakay* 'reindeer' is a loan from Nivkh. Compare the Amur Nivkh form чолҳу [cʰolŋi] 'reindeer' and Sakhalin Nivkh form тлаҳу [tlaŋi] 'reindeer'. Note also that this word has been subsequently borrowed from Ainu into Japanese, as トナカイ *tonakai*.

3 MATERIALS AND PREVIOUS SCHOLARSHIP

This section addresses previous works on Ainu, focusing on notable dictionaries, grammars, and collections of materials. It also details the typical orthographies used to write Ainu.

3.1 Orthographies

Ainu is written in two orthographies: one based on the Latin alphabet, the other based on a modified version of the Japanese *katakana* syllabary. Some materials, such as Nakagawa and Nakamatsu (2004 and 2007) – textbooks for basic instruction in Ainu – are written in parallel in both the *katakana* script and the Latin script. Scholarly work tends to be only in the Latin script (e.g., Nakagawa 2000).

Although extended *katakana* for Ainu are a part of the Unicode standard, many fonts do not support them, and workarounds (such as using a smaller font for the half-size *katakana* used to write final stop consonants) are often needed.

3.2 Dictionaries

The earliest dictionary of Ainu is the *Moshiogusa*, compiled in 1792 by Chōshaburō Abe and his interpreter, Uehara Kumajirō. Several manuscripts of this dictionary survive, though little modern scholarship has examined it (see, for instance, Sato 2007). Of special interest is an appendix of Ainu texts, which, to the best of my knowledge, remains untranslated and unanalyzed.

The Rev. John Batchelor's dictionary, first compiled in 1889, is well known but has many mistaken translations and transcriptions, as well as "ghost lexemes" which do not appear in any other source and should mostly be avoided in favour of the other dictionaries mentioned here. The most widely available version is the second edition (Batchelor 1905), which has been digitized, though there were two later editions, for four total.

Mashiho Chiri produced what is likely the most important dictionary of Ainu, *Bunrui Ainugo Jiten* (*Categorical Ainu Dictionary*). Chiri's intention was to publish this in several volumes, but unfortunately, only two volumes (Chiri 1953 and 1954) were published before he passed away. An additional volume, Chiri (1962) was published posthumously. Shirō Hattori and Mashiho Chiri published an Ainu dialect dictionary, *Ainugo Hōgen Jiten*, in 1964. This work builds on some of the last fieldwork done in consultation with speakers of Ainu and forms the basis for the two reconstructions of Proto-Ainu (see below). Additionally, this work has not only Japanese glosses of the Ainu vocabulary, but English glosses as well, and will be of interest to non-Japanese-speaking researchers.

Finally, *I/Yay-Pakasnu*, compiled by Katsunobu Izutsu in 2006, is one of the most recent Ainu dictionaries and is a result of a corpus linguistics project focusing on the Asahikawa dialect of Ainu. The dictionary itself contains some limited information on other dialects.

3.3 Grammars

There are several grammars of Ainu. The early Japanese-language grammars (Kindaichi 1931, Chiri 1942, and Chiri 1974) are short – what today might be considered sketch grammars – but are still valuable due to the fact that the authors were in consultation with native speakers. Chiri and Kindaichi (1973) provide a brief grammatical sketch of Sakhalin Ainu, while Murasaki (1977 and 1978) describe the Raychiska variety of Sakhalin in more detail.

Refsing (1986) is a much longer grammar of Ainu, focusing primarily on the Shizunai dialect of southern Hokkaidō, as spoken by consultants Refsing worked with in 1980 and 1981 (Refsing 1986: 65). The grammar itself is idiosyncratic, lacking a phonological and phonetic analysis and instead focusing on a peculiar compromise of grammatical approaches based on the early work by the likes of Chiri and Kindaichi, as well as on later work on Japanese (not Ainu) by Bruno Lewin (1959) and Samuel E. Martin (1975).

In addition to these, the first half of Shibatani (1990) is a description of the Ainu language. However, it is mostly compiled from secondary sources, and while it does serve as a valuable English-language resource on Ainu, there are some issues especially with regards to Ainu morphology which perhaps more recent works approach differently and more comprehensively.

Tamura (2000) is the most recent English-language grammar of Ainu. While not quite as long as Refsing (1986), it is perhaps the compromise first choice for scholars who do not speak Japanese but are interested in starting to work with Ainu.

3.4 Collections of materials

There are a number of collections of Ainu materials. Two of the most notable collections are Kindaichi and Kannari (1959–1975) and Izutsu (2004–2005). Both collections focus almost exclusively on various types of folklore and are significant corpora of Ainu. Piłsudski (1912) is a collection of Sakhalin Ainu folklore, collected during Piłsudski's exile to Sakhalin. This work has recently been reprinted (although without some additional materials found in some earlier versions). Piłsudski includes extensive anthropological notes and, unlike contemporary works by explorers and missionaries, provides a relatively "modern" academic view of the Ainu people of Sakhalin at the time. A selection of additional early materials by European authors on the Ainu language has been compiled in Refsing (1996).

Audio materials, such as Tamura (1984, et seq), have been published, but often there are accessibility issues, either stemming from the fact that they have since ceased to be sold or made available or are only available in the Japanese market. Collections online are limited and are mostly confined to dictionaries, such as the *Topical Dictionary of Conversational Ainu* (Kokuritsu Kokugo Kenkyū-jo [NINJAL] 2015).

Some private collections of materials exist, such as those held by the *Hokkaidō Ainu Kyōkai* (Hokkaidō Ainu Society). In part due to privacy concerns over on-going discrimination that may be faced by descendants of Ainu people whose textual and other materials that are held in these collections, access is generally restricted to those doing scholarly work.

4 INTERNAL DIVERSITY

Ainu is primarily divided into three groups: varieties found on Hokkaidō, varieties found in the Kuril Islands, and varieties found on Sakhalin Island. From the sources, Vovin (1993) identifies and deals with data from the following dialects:

- Hokkaidō dialects: Yakumo, Horobetsu, Saru, Obihiro, Bihoro, Asahikawa, Nayoro, Sōya, and Chitose
- Sakhalin dialects: Raychiska (modern Krasnogorsk, Sakhalin Oblast) and Nairo (modern Gastello, Sakhalin Oblast)
- Kuril Island dialects: Shumshu

It is unclear if the varieties were mutually unintelligible with one another, thus perhaps more properly rendering them into two or more separate Ainu languages (Hokkaidō Ainu and Sakhalin Ainu), rather than a single Ainu language isolate. Claims have been made in both directions. For example, Refsing (1986: 53) remarks that Sakhalin and Hokkaidō varieties of Ainu are not generally mutually intelligible. But by and large, this is mostly an academic issue, as sometimes the decisions about whether we are dealing with dialects of a single language or with distinct but closely related languages is a very difficult and uncertain one. It is therefore also the case that often the difference between a language isolate (with its varieties) and a language family is not clear (see Campbell, this volume), especially in the case of those that lack a standardized variety. This is true even more so given that Ainu is a dormant language, making the testing of mutual intelligibility no longer possible.

There are two reconstructions of Proto-Ainu, based on applying the comparative method to forms from the various dialects. The earlier of the two works is Vovin (1993), which, as mentioned above, also entertains a number of hypotheses about long-distance relationships between Ainu and other languages but does not accept any of them as conclusive (Vovin 1993: 210–211). Additionally, it includes a partial English translation of I. G. Voznesenskii's Ainu-Russian glossary (Vovin 1993: 215). Alonso de la Fuente (2012) is the more recent reconstruction, and builds in part on Vovin's reconstruction.

In addition to Vovin's (1993) and Alonso de la Fuente's (2012) reconstructions of Ainu, there are also a handful works applying computational methods to the problem of sub-grouping Ainu. These include a lexicostatistical study by Hattori and Chiri (1960), a unique clustering algorithm developed by Asai (1974), and a more recent article using Bayesian maximum likelihood methods of phylogenetic inference borrowed from biology by Lee and Hasegawa (2013).

5 TYPOLOGICAL OVERVIEW

This section gives a typological overview of Ainu, beginning with its phonology, then moving on to several typologically salient morphosyntactic phenomena found in Ainu.

5.1 Phonology

The phonology of Ainu is in and of itself relatively unremarkable, with a typically sized inventory of consonants and vowels, and no cross-linguistically uncommon sounds, but in comparison to the two proposed language areas which it borders (the Siberian language area and the Altaic language area),[1] this "normality" of Hokkaidō Ainu (as well as other varieties of Ainu and the reconstructions of Proto-Ainu) is typologically unusual.

5.1.1 Vowels

Ainu has five vowels, /i/, /e/, /a/, /o/, /u/, detailed in Table 4.1.

5.1.2 Consonants

Ainu has 11 consonants, detailed in Table 4.2. Its consonantal and phonotactic system is unusual in comparison to the Altaic and Siberian language areas. For instance, Siberian-type languages tend to have a four-way nasal contrast, between /m/, /n/, /ɲ/, and /ŋ/ (Anderson 2006: 268–272). Ainu only has a two-way nasal contrast, between /m/ and /n/. Similarly, in Altaic-type languages, rhotics cannot appear in absolute word-initial position. They may do so freely in Ainu, for example, the word *rakko* 'sea otter'.

5.1.3 Pitch accent

Audio recordings of Ainu are extant but limited. Additionally, the usual transcription schemes for Ainu (with the notable exception of Hattori and Chiri's (1964) dialect dictionary of Ainu) do not include any transcription of pitch accent. These extant recordings and descriptions, however, are sufficient for the description and even a partial reconstruction of word-level intonation (e.g., Vovin 1993: 83–96) and some limited description of sentence-level prosody (e.g., Simeon 1968: 8–12).

All of the Ainu varieties of Hokkaidō (except Bihoro) have a system of pitch accent (Vovin 1993: 83). Data on Kuril Ainu varieties is extremely limited due to their early extinction, but they appear likely to have had a system of pitch accent as well (Vovin 1993: 83). Sakhalin varieties, on the other hand, do not possess pitch accent but do possess a phonemically distinctive length contrast that corresponds to pitch accent in the Hokkaidō variety (Vovin 1993: 83).

TABLE 4.1 AINU VOWELS

	Front	Central	Back
Close	i		u
Mid	e		o
Open		a	

TABLE 4.2 AINU CONSONANTS

	Bilabial	Alveolar	Alveolo-Palatal	Palatal	Velar	Glottal
Nasal	m \<m\>	n \<n\>				
Stop	p \<p\>	t \<t\>			k \<k\>	
Affricate			t͡ɕ \<c\>			
Fricative		s \<s\>				
Tap		ɾ \<r\>				
Approximant				j \<y\>	w \<w\>	h \<h\>

Ainu pitch accent is based on a relative rise in pitch, unlike Japanese, for instance, where pitch accent is characterized by a fall in pitch (McCawley 1968). In the Chitose dialect of Hokkaidō, for example, there is always a rise in pitch from a relatively low pitch in the preceding unaccented syllable to a relatively high pitch in the accented syllable (Nakagawa and Nakamoto 2004: 15). Further rules, such as closed syllables and stems attracting accent, have been proposed (see, for instance, Nakagawa and Nakamoto 2004: 15–17), but significant counter-examples exist, meaning that there is no consensus on the phonological reality of these rules (see discussion in Vovin (1993) on the reconstruction of the Ainu prosodic system).

5.2 Morphosyntax

Ainu has several salient morphosyntactic features which merit some extended discussion, including its system of verbal agreement, noun incorporation, three applicative morphemes, and its system of marking evidentiality.

5.2.1 Morphosyntactic alignment

In terms of word order, Ainu intransitive clauses are SV, while transitive are AOV, as shown in example (1):

(1)   a   *Seta   Ø-arpa*   [SV]
          dog   3.s-go.SG
          'The dog went.' (constructed)

      b   *Seta   eper   Ø-Ø-nospa*   [AOV]
          dog   bear   3.A-3.O-chase
          'The dog chased the bear.' (Izutsu 2006: 8)

      c   *Eper   seta   Ø-Ø-nospa*   [AOV]
          bear   dog   3.A-3.O-chase
          'The bear chased the dog.' (Izutsu 2006: 8)

Relative clauses, and other diagnostic tools, all point towards Ainu being a typical nominative-accusative language with a relatively fixed SV/AOV word order.

Note that Ainu verbal agreement markers – described in more detail below – show several different alignment patterns. First person singular agreement markers are in a nominative-accusative pattern, with a prefix shared by first person singular subjects of intransitive and transitive verbs, and a separate prefix for first person singular direct objects of transitive verbs. Second person singular and plural core arguments (subjects of intransitive and transitive verbs, as well as direct objects of transitive verbs) display a neutral pattern, distinguishing only plurality. Third person singular and plural core arguments are null-marked and thus can be analyzed as neutral. First person plural and inclusive person agreement markers are in a tripartite pattern, with unique markers for subjects of intransitive verbs, subjects of transitive verbs, and direct objects of transitive verbs.

5.2.2 Possession

Ainu has three strategies for expressing possession. The first of these is a possessive suffix, which denotes not only possession but also definiteness. The second, a morphological strategy, uses the equivalent to verbal agreement markers directly on a noun to express inalienable possession. Third, Ainu uses a periphrastic construction with the verb *kor* 'to have' to express alienable possession.

5.2.2.1 Possessive/definite suffix

Ainu nouns may take a possessive/definite suffix. This suffix takes three basic forms: *-V*, *-hV*, and *-VhV*. Generally, this includes the meaning of (inalienable) possession but also includes definiteness (Alonso de la Fuente 2012: 69–70). These include body part terms; some kinship terms; a few specific personal belongings (Refsing 1986 includes *mip* 'garment', *muor* 'undergarment', *cise* 'house', and *kotan* 'village' in this category); and parts of a whole (Refsing 1986: 81–89).

In consonant-final nouns – which are generally of the shape CVC, this is often simply the vowel found in the root repeated (for instance, *tek* 'hand' ~ *tek-e* 'hand-POSS'). However, nouns may also have an associative form of the shape *-i* or *-u* (for instance, *ak* 'younger.brother' ~ *ak-i* 'younger.brother-POSS', *kotan* 'village' ~ *kotan-u* 'village-POSS'). There is an exception with forms ending in the glides *y-* and *w-*, which lower high vowels to their mid vowel counterparts (**i* → *e* and **u* → *o*, respectively; for instance: *haw* 'voice' ~ *haw-e* 'voice-POSS'). And finally, they may have the longer form *-VhV* (for instance, *may* 'echo' ~ *may-ehe* 'echo-POSS').

Vowel-final nouns generally take the form *-hV*, where *V* is an echo vowel (for example, *sa* 'older.sister' ~ *sa-ha* 'older.sister-POSS', *etu* 'nose' ~ *etu-hu* 'nose-POSS', etc.).

This likely reflects an older, three-way noun class distinction that has been lost in the surviving varieties of Ainu (Alonso de la Fuente 2012: 80–81).

5.2.2.2 Inalienable possession

Inalienable possession is additionally expressed morphologically by the use of a set of prefixes and suffixes otherwise identical to the verbal agreement markers described in Section 5.2.3.

(2) *ku-tek-ehe*
     1SG.POSS-hand-POSS
     'my hand' (Refsing 1986: 81; glossing altered to match my own)

5.2.2.3 Alienable possession

Alienable possession is expressed periphrastically, by use of the verb *kor* 'to have' forming a relative clause with the possessed, along with appropriate pronominal agreement displayed on the verb for expressing the possessor.

(3) e-Ø-kor   seta
     2sg.a-3.o-have   dog
     'your dog' (Nakagawa and Nakamoto 2004: 48)

5.2.3 Verbal agreement

Ainu has a complex system of subject and object agreement on verbs, with different sets of markers showing different morphosyntactic alignments. Note that, based on word order alone, Ainu is an accusative type language, and these different alignments are apparently secondary phenomena.

First person singular markers have an accusative morphosyntactic alignment, with the markers for the single argument of intransitive verbs and for the Agent-like argument of transitive verbs being identical, and with a separate marker for Patient-like argument of transitive verbs, as seen in examples (4) and (5).

(4) **Ku**-*hepun-i*   *wa*   *en-enka=un*   **ku**-*i-nkar*   *akusu,*
     1SG.S-raise.head-SG   and   1SG.POSS-above=DIR 1SG.S-INDF.O-see   when
     nitek   *ka=ta*   *Ø-a*   *wa*   *Ø-an*   *ruwe*   *Ø-Ø-ne.*
     branch   top=LOC   3.S-sit   and   3.S-PFV   FACT   3.A-3.O-COP
     'When I raised my head and looked above me, it was sitting on top of a branch.'
     (Nakagawa and Nakamoto 2004: 112)

(5) *Kamuy*   *Ø-Ø-ne*   *manu=p*   *Ø-en-sikkasma*   *wa*
     deity   3.A-3.O-COP call.AUX=NMLZ   3.A-1SG.O-watch.over   and
     Ø-en-kor-e   *yan*
     3.A-1SG.O-have-CAUS   POL.IMP
     'Please, [those] who are called deities protect me.' (Nakagawa and Nakamoto 2007: 39)

First person plural and indefinite person markers are tripartite in their alignment, with the single argument of intransitive verbs, the Agent-like argument of transitive verbs, and the Patient-like argument of transitive verbs all having separate agreement markers. As in (6b), the indefinite person markers often have a passive-like reading. Further, in story-telling contexts, the indefinite person takes on a logophoric function, where the speakers co-references themselves (a second/third person) with the original participant in the quotation (see Bugaeva 2008).

(6) a *Pet*   *ot=ta*   *rap-**as***   *wa*   *cep*   *Ø-poron=no*
        river   place=LOC go.down.PL-**1PL.S** and   fish   3.S-be.big=ADVZ
        ci-Ø-koyki   *wa*   *arki-**as***   *ruwe*   *Ø-Ø-ne*
        1PL.A-3.O-catch and   come.PL-**1PL.S**   FACT   3.A-3.O-COP
        'We went down to the river and caught many fish and came [back].' (Nakagawa
        and Nakamoto 2004: 42)

     b **A-un**-*kor-e*   *ka*   *somo*   *Ø-Ø-ki*   *ruwe*   *Ø-Ø-ne*   *wa.*
        INDF.A-**1PL.O**-have-CAUS even   not   3.A-3.O-do   FACT   3.A-3.O-COP EMPH
        'It was the case that we weren't even given [any].' (Nakagawa and Nakamoto 2004: 72)

(7) *Cise*   *okari*   *Ø-apkas* *Ø-apkas* *humi*   **a**-*Ø-nu=wa* . . .
     house   around   3.A-walk   3.A-walk   sound   INDF.A-3.O-hear=and
     'And because she heard a noise walking around and around the house. . . .'
     (Nakagawa 2000: 58)

Second person singular and plural makers are neutral in their alignment, with one marker shared by the single argument of intransitive verbs, the Agent-like argument of transitive verbs, and the Patient-like argument of transitive verbs all sharing one agreement marker.

(8) a **E**-*Ø-kor*   *seta*   *e-Ø-tura*   *ruwe?*
        2SG.A-3.O-have   dog   **2SG.A**-3.O-be.with FACT?
        'Were you with your dog?' (Nakagawa and Nakamoto 2004: 48)

     b *Sine-n=ne*   *e-ek*   *siri*   *Ø-Ø-ne*   *ya?*
        one-person.CLF=DAT   2SG-come.SG   VIS   3.A-3.O-COP   Q
        'It seems you've come alone?' (Nakagawa and Nakamoto 2004: 102)

(9)   *Hunak=un eci-paye?*
      where=DIR 2PL-go.PL
      'Where are you going to?'

Third person singular and plural markers are also neutral in their alignment, with the single argument of intransitive verbs, the Agent-like argument of transitive verbs, and Patient-like argument of transitive verbs all sharing zero marking.

(10)   ***Ø**-mik   kor   paskur **Ø-Ø**-ko-terke   korka. . .*
       3.s-bark PROG   crow   **3.**A**-3.**o-toward.APL-leap   but . . .
       'Barking, it leapt at the crow, but. . . . ' (Nakagawa and Nakamoto 2004: 92)

(11)   *u   **Ø**-tek-tur-i   u   **Ø**-tek-yoni   kor,   **Ø**-i-ku-pa   kane*
       oh   3.A-arm-extend-SG   oh   3.A-arm-flex   PROG   3.S-APASS-drink-PL   PFV.PROG
       ***Ø**-okay   kor*
       3.S-exist.PL PROG
       'Oh, they were posing and oh they were flexing, [and] they were drinking.' (Izutsu and Tezuka 2006: 84)

A summary of these markers is given in Table 4.3.

Though it varies from variety to variety, in practice, some Ainu varieties, such as Saru Ainu, have so-called "portmanteau markers", with one marker serving to indicate both subject and object agreement, as shown in Table 4.4.

For the areas in Table 4.4 marked by dashes (first person subject-first person object agreement marking, second person subject-second person object agreement marking, etc.) the appropriate subject agreement marker and the reflexive *yay-* are used, rather than two agreement markers.

TABLE 4.3 AINU VERBAL SUBJECT AND OBJECT AGREEMENT MARKERS

	A	*S*	*O*
1SG	k(u)-		en-
1PL	c(i)-	-as	un-
2SG	e-		
2PL	eci-		
3SG	Ø-		
3PL	Ø-		
INDF	a(n)-	-an	i-

TABLE 4.4 POSSIBLE COMBINATIONS OF AGREEMENT MARKERS IN SARU AINU

	*1*SG.O	*1*PL.O	*2*SG.O	*2*PL.O	*3*SG.O *3*PL.O
1SG.A					k(u)-Ø-
1PL.A	-		eci-		c(i)-Ø-
2SG.A	en-	un-			e-Ø-
2PL.A	eci-en-	eci-un-	-		eci-Ø-
3SG.A					
3PL.A	en-	un-	Ø-e-	Ø-eci-	Ø-Ø- or -

Source: After Nakagawa and Nakamoto 2007: 45.

5.2.4 Pluriactionality

Ainu has a closed class of verbs that express pluriactionality, also called verbal number. At first blush, this system appears to have an absolute alignment, as it tends to coincide with the single argument of intransitive verbs and the Patient-like argument of transitive verbs in terms of number, but it can instead represent the number of times an action is done, either one (singular) or many (plural).

Verbs that display pluriactionality fall into two classes: suppletive verbs (where suppletion distinguishes the singular and plural form of the verb, as shown in (12a) and (b)) and regular verbs (where suffixes distinguish the singular and plural form of the verb, as shown in (12c) and (d)). Note that the majority of Ainu verbs are not marked for pluriactionality (shown in (12e) and (f)), and it is one of the grammatical features of Ainu which, at the time Ainu became dormant, appears to have been undergoing attrition.

(12)   a   *arpa* 'go.SG' ~ *paye* 'go.PL'

   b   *ek* 'come.SG' ~ *arki* 'come.PL'

   c   *ahu-n* 'enter-SG' ~ *ahu-p* 'enter-PL'

   d   *hosip-i* 'return-SG' ~ *hosip-pa* 'return-PL'

   e   *kira* 'run.away' (no pluriactionality)

   f   *hok* 'buy' (no pluriactionality)

Both suffixes display significant allomorphy. For the singular suffix, vowel-final verb stems take the allomorph *-n*. Consonant-final verb stems, except those ending in *y-* or *w-*, take the allomorph *-i*. Finally, glide-final verb stems take the allomorph *-e*. For the plural suffix, vowel-final verb stems take the allomorph *-p*, while consonant-final verb stems take the allomorph *-pa*.

5.2.5 Noun incorporation

The patient-like argument of transitive verbs (including verbs made transitive through causativization or applicativization) may be incorporated into verbs. Ainu verbs have a clear morphological template, as discussed in the previous section on verbal agreement. The object agreement slot may be occupied, not only by object agreement morphemes, but also by incorporated nouns. For instance:

(13)   a   *mokor-an*   (basic intransitive)
          sleep-INDF.S
          'We are sleeping.' (Nakagawa 2000: 58)

   b   *a-Ø-nukar*   (basic transitive)
          INDF.A-3.O-see
          'I saw it.' (Nakagawa 2000: 58)

   c   *toy-ta-an*   (intransitive derived by noun incorporation)
          ground-gather-INDF.S
          'I gathered from the ground.' (Nakagawa 2000: 55)

   d   *an-Ø-e-toy-ta*   (intransitive derived by NI, re-transitivized by applicative)
          INDF.A-3.O-from.APL-ground-gather
          'I gathered it from the ground.' (Izutsu and Tezuka 2006: 58)

Further, there are examples of incorporated numerals with numeral classifiers, as in (14), as well as nouns with oblique case (locative *-ne* and *-un*), as in (15) and (16).

(14)   *isimne   utarpa patek   Ø-nitan=kur   patek   Ø-pikan=kur   patek*
       next.day chief   only   3.s-be.quick=AGNT only   3.s-be.quick=AGNTonly
       *Ø-u-e-**tu-n**-us   wa. . .*
       3.A-RECP-APL-**two-person.CLF**-become   and. . .
       'The next day, only chiefs who were fast and fleet made pairs with each other, and. . .'
       (Nakagawa 2000: 61)

(15)   *Ø-Ø-ne=no   sir-an   kor   anakne,   somo*
       3.A-3.O-COP=ADVZ   weather-exist.SG PROG   TOP   NEG
       *Ø-e-**kim-ne**-an=pe   Ø-Ø-ne.*
       3.S-APL-**mountain-LOC**-exist.SG=NMLZ   3.A-3.O-COP
       'As for the weather being like [this], it was that he didn't go into the mountains.'
       (Nakagawa 2001: 82)

(16)   *o-tu   kes   pa-ta   /   o-re   kes   pa-ta   /*
       APL-two   after   year-LOC   /   APL-three after   year-LOC   /
       *Ø-e-**kim-ne**-an   kor*
       3.S-APL-**mountain-LOC**-exist.SG PROG
       'After two years,/after three years,/he was in the mountains, [and. . . .]'
       (Nakagawa 2008: 296)

See Kobayashi (2008) for further discussion of noun incorporation in Ainu.

5.2.6 Applicatives

Ainu has three applicative morphemes, *e-*, *ko-*, and *o-*. Applicative constructions are signalled by an overt morphological marker on the verb, which increases its valency by one, allowing for the coding of a syntactically and semantically peripheral argument as a new core argument (Bugaeva 2010: 752). The most widely attested kind of applicative construction cross-linguistically promotes a beneficiary argument to direct object, and these do occur in Ainu, as seen in (17):

(17)   *pirka   Ø-usike   a-i-**ko**-numke*
       good   3.POSS-piece   INDF.A-INDF.O-**for.APL**-choose
       'They chose the good pieces for me' (Nakagawa 2002: 138)

However, this is only one function of the morpheme *ko-*, and as described in the following sections, not just beneficiaries but many other obliques – including some typologically unusual ones – may become objects marked applicatively as core arguments of the verb, and many do so more frequently than do beneficiaries.[2]

Bugaeva (2006 and 2010) surveys applicative constructions in Ainu. She finds that the applicative *e-* is more frequent than the applicative *ko-*, and both are more frequent than the applicative *o-* (Bugaeva 2010: 756).

The applicative *e-* most commonly co-occurs with the semantic roles of Content (the counterpart of Experiencer in verbs of perception, emotion, cognition, and utterance; it is the thing that is experienced); Location; Instrument; Theme; and Cause/Purpose, with uncommon usages of Path, Beneficiary, Comitative (specifically Co-Agent), and Manner (Bugaeva 2010: 763, 772). Examples of Content and Theme are given below in (18) and (19), respectively. These examples are taken from Bugaeva (2010), but their glossing has been modified to match my own style.

(18)   *a-Ø-hoppa*   *wa*   *yan-an*   *hi*   *ney*   *pak=no*   *ka*   (Content)
        INDF.A-3.O-leave   and   go.up.SG-INDF.S   COMP   ever   until=ADVZ   even
        a- Ø-e-kewtum-wen   *kor*   *an-an*
        INDF.A-3.O-**about.**APL-feeling-be.bad   and   exist.SG-INDF.S
        'I'll always feel bad **that I returned having left (my son).**' (Bugaeva 2010: 764)

(19)   *Ito*   *Anna*   *Ø-or-o*   *wa*   *amip*   *Ø-Ø-e-so-uk*   (Theme)
        Ito   Anna   3.POSS-place-ASOC   from   dress   3.A-3.O-**THEME.**APL-debt-take
        wa   *Ø-an.*
        and   3s-exist.SG
        'Ito has borrowed **a dress** from Anna.' (Bugaeva 2010: 769)

Special note should be given to the use of *e-* as an applicative marker to promote new Themes to a verb. This does not resemble a prototypical applicative, as Theme is not a peripheral thematic role, which is what applicatives usually promote into core thematic roles (Bugaeva 2010: 769).

The applicative *ko-* most frequently co-occurs with the semantic roles of Addressee, Goal, Recipient/Beneficiary, Comitative (Co-Patient), and Malefactive Source (Bugaeva 2010: 759). Examples of applied Addressee objects and Comitative (Co-Patient) applicative objects are given in (20) and (21), respectively. Again, these examples have been modified to match my own glossing style and interpretation.

(20)   *Haru*   *kamuy*   *newannpe*   *Ø-i-ko-ruka.*   (Addressee)
        food   deity   that   3.A-INDF.O-**at.**APL-be.angry
        'The goddess of crops got angry **at me** for that.' (Bugaeva 2010: 776)

(21)   *A-Ø-kor*   *ekasi*   *po-kor-an*   *siri*   *ka*   (Comitative)
        INDF.A-3.O-have   grandfather   child-have-INDF.S   COMP   even
        Ø-Ø-nukar   *kane*   *pak=no*   *Ø-i-ko-onne.*
        3.A-3.O-see   as   until=ADVZ   3.A-INDF.O-**with.**APL-live.long
        'My grandfather lived **with me** so long that he saw that I had children.' (Bugaeva 2010: 780)

Applicative addressee objects with *ko-* are similar to Content applied objects with *e-* but contrast in the fact that Addressee applicative objects tend to be animate, while Content applicative objects tend to be inanimate (Bugaeva 2010: 782). However, this is only a tendency (Bugaeva 2010: 782).

The applicative *o-* co-occurs with the semantic roles of Location and Goal (Bugaeva 2010: 759). Again, these examples have been modified to match my own glossing style and interpretation.

(22)   *a-ar-serke-he*   *toy*   *tum*   *Ø-Ø-o-rer*   (Location)
        INDF.POSS-one-part.POSS-ASOC   earth   middle   3.A-3.O-**in.**APL-sink
        'Half of my body sank **in the earth.**' (Bugaeva 2010: 783)

(23)   *Ø-nupur-i*   *hontom*   *Ø-Ø-o-hemesu*   *wa . . .*   (Goal)
        3.POSS-mountain-ASOC   middle   3.A-3.O-**to.**APL-climb   and
        '[The fox] climbed **halfway up the mountain** and. . . .' (Bugaeva 2010: 783)

5.2.7 Evidentiality

Ainu has several evidential markers that come from grammaticalized nouns. These include *hawe*, 'voice; reportative evidential'; *humi* 'sound; nonvisual sensory evidential'; *ruwe* 'inferential/factual evidential' (perhaps from *ru* 'path, tracks' Chiri 1974: 155); and *siri* 'appearance; visual sensory evidential'.

(24) a *Apto   as.*
          rain   fall
          'Rain is falling.' (constructed)

      b *Apto   as   hawe.*
          rain   fall   REP
          'I am told rain is falling.' (constructed)

      c *Apto   as   humi.*
          rain   fall   NVIS
          'I hear that rain is falling.' (constructed)

      d *Apto   as   ruwe.*
          rain   fall   FACT
          'It is a fact that rain is falling.' (constructed)

      e *Apto   as   siri.*
          rain   fall   VIS
          'I see that rain is falling.' (constructed)

Abbreviations

1	first person	IMP	imperative
2	second person	INDF	indefinite person
3	third person	LOC	locative
A	Agent-like argument of transitive verbs	NEG	negative
ADVZ	adverbializer	NMLZ	nominalizer
AGNT	agentifier	NVIS	nonvisual sensory evidential
APL	applicative	O	Patient-like argument of transitive verbs
ASOC	associative plural	PFV	perfective aspect
AUX	auxiliary	PL	plural
CAUS	causative	POL	polite
CLF	classifier	POSS	possessive
COMP	comparative	PROG	progressive aspect
COP	copula	Q	question particle
DAT	dative	REP	reportative evidential
DIR	directive	S	single argument of intransitive verbs
EMPH	emphatic	SG	singular
FACT	factual evidential	VIS	visual sensory evidential

NOTES

1 We note that "Altaic language area" refers to the languages of this zone that show areal similarities. This in no way implies acceptance of the disputed and mostly discarded "Altaic hypothesis" of a genetic relationship shared by these languages.

2 Note that Bugaeva (2010: 776) also cites the example in this passage, but her and my interpretation of the second word differ enough that I have cited Nakagawa (2002) here directly.

REFERENCES

Alonso de la Fuente, José Andrés. 2012. *The Ainu Languages: Traditional Reconstruction, Eurasian Areal Linguistics, and Diachronic (Holistic) Typology.* PhD dissertation, Universidad de País Vasco-Euskal Herriko Unibersitatea.

Anderson, Gregory. 2006. Towards a Typology of the Siberian Linguistic Area. *Linguistic Areas: Convergence in Historical and Typological Perspective*, ed. by Yaron Matras, April McMahon, and Nigel Vincent, 266–300. Houndmills, UK and New York: Palgrave Macmillan.

Asai, Tōru. 1974. Classification of Dialects: Cluster Analysis of Ainu Dialects. *Hoppō Bunka Kenkyū [Northern Cultures Research]* 8: 66–135.

Batchelor, John. 1905. *An Ainu-English-Japanese Dictionary: Including a Grammar of the Ainu Language* (2nd ed.). Tōkyō: Methodist Publishing House.

Bugaeva, Anna. 2006. Applicatives in Ainu. *Chiba Daigaku Yūrashia Gengo Bunka Ron Kōza [Chiba University Journal of Eurasian Language and Culture]* 9: 185–196.

Bugaeva, Anna. 2008. Reported Discourse and Logophoricity in Southern Hokkaido Dialects of Ainu. *Gengo Kenkyū* 133: 31–75.

Bugaeva, Anna. 2010. Ainu Applicatives in Typological Perspective. *Studies in Language* 34, no. 4: 749–801.

Chiri, Mashiho. 1942. Ainu Gohō Kenkyū [A Study of Ainu Grammar]. *Karafuto-chō Hakubutsukan Hokōku (Karafuto Museum Report)*, 4.

Chiri, Mashiho. 1953–1962. *Bunrui Ainugo Jiten [Categorical Ainu Dictionary]*. Tōkyō: Nihon Jōmin Bunka Kenkyū-jo.

Chiri, Mashiho. 1974. Ainu Gohō Gaisetsu [An Outline of Ainu Grammar]. *Chiri Mashiho Chosakushū [Mashiho Chiri Collection]*, vol. 4, 3–197. Tōkyō: Heibonsha.

Chiri, Mashiho and Kyōsuke Kindaichi. 1973. Ainu Gohō Kenkyū – Karafuto Hōgen o Chūshin ni Shite [Ainu Grammar Research – With a Focus on the Sakhalin Dialect]. *Chiri Mashiho Chosakushū [Mashiho Chiri Collection]*, vol. 3, 457–586. Tōkyō: Heibonsha.

Dahl, Otto C. 1977. *Proto-Austronesian* (Scandinavian Institute of Asian Studies Monograph Series 15). Lund: Studentlitteratur.

Greenberg, Joseph. 2000. *Indo-European and Its Closest Relatives: The Eurasiatic Language Family 1: Grammar.* Stanford: Stanford University Press.

Greenberg, Joseph. 2002. *Indo-European and Its Closest Relatives: The Eurasiatic Language Family 2: Grammar.* Stanford: Stanford University Press.

Hattori, Shirō and Chiri Mashiho. 1964. *Ainugo Hōgen Jiten [Ainu Dialect Dictionary]*. Tōkyō: Iwanami Shoten.

Hattori, Shirō and Mashiho Chiri. 1960. Ainugo shohōgen no kisogoi-tōkeigaku-teki kenkyū [A lexicostatistical study of Ainu dialects]. *Minzokugaku Kenkyū [Journal of Ethnology]* 24, no. 4: 307–342.

Izutsu, Katsunobu. 2004–2005. *Ainugo Asahikawa Hōgen Shiryō Shūsei*, vols. 1–2. Asahikawa: Hokkaidō Kyōiku Daigaku Asahikawa-kō.

Izutsu, Katsunobu. 2006. *I/Yay-Pakasnu: Ainugo no Gakushū to Kyōiku no Tame ni*. Asahikawa: Hokkaidō Kyōiku Daigaku Asahikawa-kō.

Izutsu, Katsunobu and Tezuka Yoritaka. 2006. *Kiso Ainugo [Basic Ainu]*. Sapporo: Sapporo Dōshoten.

Kindaichi, Kyōsuke. 1931. *Ainu Jojishi* Yūkara *no Kenkyū [Research on Ainu Epic Yukar]*. Tōkyō: Tōkyō Bunko.

Kindaichi, Kyōsuke and Matsu Kannari. 1959–1975. *Ainu Jojishi Yūkara Shū*, vols. 1–9. Tōkyō: Sanseidō.

Kobayashi, Miki. 2008. Ainugo no Meishihōgō [Noun Incorporation in Ainu]. *Chiba Daigaku Jinbun Shakaikagau Kenkyū [Chiba University Humanities and Social Science Research]* 17: 199–214.

Kokuritsu Kokugo Kenkyū-jo [National Institute for Japanese Language and Linguistics (NINJAL)]. 2015. *A Topical Dictionary of Conversational Ainu.* http://ainutopic. ninjal.ac.jp.

Lee, Sean and Toshikazu Hasegawa. 2013. Evolution of the Ainu Language in Space and Time. *PLoS One* 8, no. 4: e62243. DOI: 10.1371/journal.pone.0062243

Lewin, Bruno. 1959. *Abriss der japanischen Grammatik auf der Grundlage der klassischen Schriftsprache [Summary of the Grammar of Japanese on the Basis of the Classical Written Language].* Wiesbaden: Harrassowitz.

Li, Fang-kuei. 1977. *A Handbook of Comparative Tai* (Oceanic Linguistics Special Publications 15). Honolulu: University of Hawai'i Press.

Lindquist, Ivar. 1960. Indo-European Features in the Ainu Language (With Reference to the Theory of Pierre Naert). *Acta Universitatis Lundensis*, n.s., pp. not given.

Martin, Samuel E. 1975. *A Reference Grammar of Japanese.* New Haven: Yale University Press.

McCawley, James D. 1968. *The Phonological Component of a Grammar of Japanese.* The Hague: Mouton.

Murasaki, Kyōko. 1977. *Karafuto Ainugo: Shiryō-hen [Sakhalin Ainu: Texts and Glossary].* Tōkyō: Kokushokankōkai.

Murasaki, Kyōko. 1978. *Karafuto Ainugo: Bunpō-hen [Sakhalin Ainu: Grammar].* Tōkyō: Kokushokankōkai.

Naert, Pierre. 1958. *La situation linguistique de l'aïno I: Aïnou et indoeuropéen.* Lund: Gleerup.

Nakagawa, Hiroshi. 2000. Ainu Kōshōbungei Tekisuto Shū 1 Shirasawa Nabe Kōjutsu Ōkami kara Nogareta Musume [Ainu Folklore Text 1: Shirasawa Nabe's "The Girl Who Escaped from Wolves"]. *Chiba Daigaku Yūrashia Gengo Bunka Ron Kōza [Chiba University Journal of Eurasian Language and Culture]* 3: 52–66.

Nakagawa, Hiroshi. 2001. Ainu Kōshōbungei Tekisuto Shū 2 Shirasawa Nabe Kōjutsu Shujin wo Tasukarenakatta Inu [Ainu Folklore Text 3: Shirasawa Nabe's "The Dog Who Couldn't Save His Master"]. *Chiba Daigaku Yūrashia Gengo Bunka Ron Kōza [Chiba University Journal of Eurasian Language and Culture]* 4: 77–94.

Nakagawa, Hiroshi. 2002. Ainu Kōshōbungei Tekisuto Shū 3 Shirasawa Nabe Kōjutsu Topattumi kara Nogareta Uraiushinai no Shōnen [Ainu Folklore Text 3: Shirasawa Nabe's "The Urayusnay Boy Who Escaped from Topattumi"]. *Chiba Daigaku Yūrashia Gengo Bunka Ron Kōza [Chiba University Journal of Eurasian Language and Culture]* 4: 111–143.

Nakagawa, Hiroshi. 2008. Ainu Kōshōbungei Tekisuto Shū 8 Shirasawa Nabe Kōjutsu Yukara Irupaye – Shinutapuka-jin, Ishikarai-jin to Tatakau [Ainu Folklore Text 8: Shirasawa Nabe's Yukar Irupaye "The Sinutapka Man Battles with the Iskar Man"]. *Chiba Daigaku Yūrashia Gengo Bunka Ron Kōza [Chiba University Journal of Eurasian Language and Culture]* 10: 291–313.

Nakagawa, Hiroshi and Mutsuko Nakamoto. 2004. *CD Ekusupuresu Ainugo [CD Express Ainu].* Tōkyō: Hakusuisha.

Nakagawa, Hiroshi and Mutsuko Nakamoto. 2007. *Kamuy Yukar de Ainugo o Manabu [Learn Ainu by Kamuy Yukar].* Tōkyō: Hakusuisha.

Patrie, James T. 1982. *The Genetic Relationship of the Ainu Language.* PhD dissertation, University of Hawai'i.

Piłsudski, Bronisław. 1912. *Materials for the Study of the Ainu Language and Folklore.* Cracow: Imperial Academy of Sciences.

Refsing, Kirsten. 1986. *The Ainu Language: The Morphology and Syntax of the Shizunai Dialect.* Aarhaus: Aarhaus University Press.

Refsing, Kirsten (ed.). 1996. *The Ainu Library Collection 1: Early European Writings on the Ainu Language.* 10 vols. Richmond: Curzon Press.

Sato, Tomomi. 2007. *Moshiogusa* no issatsubon ni tsuite [On the One Volume Edition of the *Moshiogusa*], 157–170. Hokkaidō Daigaku Bungaku Kenkyū-ka Kiyō [Hokkaidō University Graduate School of Letters Bulletin] 121.

Shibatani, Masayoshi. 1990. *The Languages of Japan.* Cambridge: Cambridge University Press.

Simeon, George. 1968. *The Phonemics and Morphology of Hokkaido Ainu.* PhD dissertation, University of Southern California.

Stenberg, Leo. 1929. The Ainu Problem. *Anthropos* 24: 755–799.

Street, John. 1962. Review of Vergleichende Grammatik der Altaischen sprachen, by Nikolaus Poppe. *Language* 38, no. 1: 92–99.

Tamura, Suzuko. 1984. *Ainugo Onsei Shiryō [Sound Materials for the Ainu Language].* Tōkyō: Waseda Daigaku Gogaku Kyōiku Kenkyū-jo.

Tamura, Suzuko. 2000. *The Ainu Language.* Tōkyō: Sanseido.

Uehara, Kumajirō and Chōsaburō Abe. 1792. *Moshiogusa [Seaweeds].* Manuscript: Waseda Library edition: http://archive.wul.waseda.ac.jp/kosho/ho02/ho02_05038/

Vovin, Alexander. 1993. *A Reconstruction of Proto-Ainu.* Leiden and New York: E. J. Brill.

Vovin, Alexander. 2009. Man'yōshū to Fudoki ni Mirareru Fushigi na Kotoba to Jōdai Nihon Rettō ni Okeru Ainugo no Bunpu [Strange Words in the Man'yōshū and Fudoki and the Distribution of the Ainu Language in the Japanese Islands in Prehistory]. *Nichibunken Fooranu Hōkokusho [Nichibunken Forum Reports],* 215. URI: http://publications.nichibun.ac.jp/ja/item/foru/2009-03-12/pub

Vovin, Alexander. 2012. *Man'yōshū: Book 14.* Folkestone: Global Oriental.

Vovin, Alexander. 2013. *Man'yōshū: Book 20.* Folkestone: Global Oriental.

CHAPTER 5

BURUSHASKI

Alexander D. Smith

1 INTRODUCTION

The aim of this chapter is to outline key typological aspects of Burushaski, including phonology, verb and noun morphology, and syntax. Section 1 (below) describes the geographical context and earlier work on the language and reviews claims of possible genetic affiliations. Section 2 describes Burushaski's rich phonological inventory, with 36 consonants, a large number of distinctive fricatives and affricates, and five vowels plus a length distinction. Section 3 focuses on sentences including constituent order and some aspects of syntax. Section 4 focuses on Burushaski's complex verbal morphology, and Section 5, on case marking. Burushaski marks case with both verb and noun morphology. Verb suffixes agree with the nominative subject, while verb prefixes show differential object marking, which agree with nouns under certain semantic restrictions. This sometimes causes double agreement where verb prefixes and suffixes both agree with the same noun. Section 6 focuses on the noun, which has a split ergative alignment that typically appears on the agent in non-future tenses (sentences with a future tense have no ergative marker), but which may also be used pragmatically to show volition in an intransitive sentence.[1]

Burushaski is a language isolate spoken in four areas: three in the northern Gilgit-Baltistan area of Pakistan and one in the Indian state of Jammu and in Indian Kashmir. The three dialects of Pakistan are Yasin, Hunza, and Nagar, each named after the valleys in which they are spoken. The Hunza and Nagar dialects are closely related, while the Yasin dialect is more divergent and isolated from the others. Jammu and Kashmir Burushaski is also isolated and divergent. Most of the documentation for Burushaski focuses on the Hunza dialect, but several works on the Yasin and Nagar dialects are also available. Jammu and Kashmir Burushaski is the least documented dialect of Burushaski. In all there are approximately 100,000 speakers of Burushaski, and of those speakers, only 300 speak the Jammu and Kashmir dialect, which is highly endangered. The *Catalogue of Endangered Languages* (http://endangeredlanguages.com) lists Burushaski as "threatened", meaning that the language is under pressure from Urdu and surrounding languages but is not yet at risk of being lost in the very near future.

1.1 Burushaski, the isolate

Burushaski is an isolate. Although numerous attempts have been made to link Burushaski to known language families, none has been successful at convincing most linguists. A number of proposals claim a genetic relationship between Burushaski and Proto-Indo-European (PIE) or Pre-Proto-Indo-European (see Berger 1956 for one example). These proposals involving Indo-European (IE) merit serious consideration. The exact nature of the proposed Burushaski-Indo-European relationship, however, is not clear, even amongst supporters. For example, Hamp (2013) proposes a sister language relationship between Proto-Indo-European-Hittite and Burushaski. Furthermore, he speculates, without supporting evidence, that Burushaski was creolized early in its history possibly due to prolonged contact with an ancient Indo-European dialect. Čašule, in several publications (1998, 2003a, 2003b, 2009a, 2009b, 2010, 2012, 2016), proposed an Indo-European (non-Indo-Iranian) connection with Burushaski, with connections to the Balkan languages, especially to Phrygian. However, Čašule makes several conflicting claims (see especially Čašule 2012), including the following:

1   There is either a genetic *or* contact history between Burushaski and the Aegean branch of IE.
2   Burushaski is connected to Northern and Western IE.
3   There is a Balkan substratum of shepherd terms.
4   Burushaski subgroups with Macedonian and Balkan-Slavic.
5   Burushaski has been transformed through language contact.
6   Burushaski might form part of a larger Indo-European-Anatolian-Burushaski family.

These claims involve contradictory hypotheses regarding Burushaski's possible connections with Indo-European. Čašule (2012) even contains two very different IE family tree diagrams: one (p. 123) places Burushaski as a primary branch of Pre-IE and another (p. 124) places Burushaski in a North-Western branch of IE, along with Baltic, Slavic, Albanian, Phrygian, Germanic, Italic, and others. Additionally, the liberal use of "creolization" and "language-contact" as explanations for Burushaski's apparent divergence lack supporting evidence. It is difficult to imagine how creolization, dating back thousands of years to the time of PIE, could possibly be shown to have existed using evidence from the modern language. These various IE proposals remain distinct from one another, and all lack mainstream acceptance. Additionally, some proposals have attempted to link Burushaski with Ket or Yeniseian, though unsuccessfully (see for example Toporov 1971, Bashir 2000b, and van Driem 2001:1186).

A number of proposals have involved hypothesized connections of one form or another with diverse language groups of the Caucasus (see for example Bleichsteiner 1930, Bashir 2000b, Holst 2015, 2016, among a number of others). Tuite (1998) had noted what he called quasi-genetic resemblances between Burushaski and Northeastern Caucasian (Nakh-Dagestanian). Bengtson and Blažek (1995), Bengtson (2008), Ruhlen 1994, Starostin (1991), and others proposed that Burushaski belongs with the hypothesized Dene-Caucasian (or Sino-Caucasian) macro-family, said to be most closely related to Basque and languages of the Caucasus. It can be noted also that scholars who favor some sort of Dene-Caucasian (or Sino-Caucasian) macro-family tend also to throw Yeniseian in as a branch along with all the others, including also Burushaski. Most historical linguists familiar with these languages, however, reject the Dene-Caucasian super-family proposal altogether (Campbell 1997, Goddard 1996, Sagart 1993, 1994,[2] and Lakarra, this volume, for example). Any link between Burushaski and any Caucasian or the larger putative Dene-Caucasian (Sino-Caucasian) macro-family is thus on shaky ground at best and is not likely to be taken seriously by the majority of mainstream historical linguists.

Recently Jan Henrik Holst (2015, 2016) has proposed a narrower connection with some languages of the Caucasus and also with Nahali; he argues that there is evidence to support a genetic relationship linking Burushaski and Kartvelian (South Caucasian). He proposes a larger "Kartvelo-Inean," which has two branches, Kartvelian and what he calls "Inean." His "Inean" links Burushaski and Nahali. While this hypothesis may be plausible, we await a presentation of the fuller evidence for it to be evaluated.

The only classification of Burushaski which is generally accepted maintains that Burushaski is a language isolate. The comparative method does not seem to show a link between Burushaski and any other language family. If any connection does exist, it is likely so ancient that time has obscured the evidence to the point that a genetic relationship becomes impossible to prove.

1.2 Documentation

In recent years, efforts to document and describe Burushaski have produced a rather large number of resources, the most widely available of which is arguably the *Burushaski Language Documentation Project* (Munshi 2015), an online database containing a grammatical sketch of the Hunza dialect, wordlists in ten semantic categories with audio recordings for each word in the singular and plural, stories in the four dialects with audio recordings, video recordings, and transcriptions, and a Burushaski orthography using the Latin alphabet. Larger works documenting Burushaski include Lorimer (1935–1938), a large three-volume work documenting the Yasin dialect, and Berger (1998), a massive grammar with texts and dictionary of the Hunza and Nagar dialects, and Munshi (2006) on the Jammu and Kashmir dialect of Burushaski. Other works on Burushaski are more focused and less documentary in nature; they include Anderson (1997) on Burushaski phonology; Anderson (2007) on its morphology; Bashir (1985, 2000a) on the semantics of Burushaski verbs and the *ḍ*-prefix; Morin and Tiffou (1988) on the Burushaski passive; Smith (2012) on case marking on the verb and noun; Tiffou and Morin (1982) on split ergativity; and Karim (2013) on middle voice. Holst (2014) is an important and recent publication on Burushaski, addressing dialect variation, internal reconstruction, person marking on the verb, and the Burushaski lexicon and semantics. Numerous other works which include Burushaski stories and proverbs are widely available.

2 PHONOLOGY

Burushaski has a rich inventory of consonants, including contrasts between dental and retroflex stops, eight affricates, seven fricatives, thirteen plosives, and a retroflex rhotacized fricative. Table 5.1 lists the consonant phonemes of Burushaski. The phonemes t^h, *t*, and *d* are between alveolar and retroflex (Munshi 2006: 59), but I have adopted the standard of marking the dental series of contrasting stops with a diacritic but with no diacritic for the near retroflex alveolar stops, similar to the system used in Munshi (2006).

The vowels of Burushaski are more straightforward. It has five vowels, including the vowel "triangle" *i, a*, and *u*, plus *o* and *e*. Burushaski also distinguishes long and short vowels.

2.1 Intervocalic devoicing

Because of space constraints, this paper addresses only one aspect of the synchronic phonology of Burushaski, but one of special phonetic interest. At morpheme boundaries, there is an alternation between voiced and voiceless obstruents, which can be analyzed as undergoing devoicing. In some examples, devoicing takes place between vowels, while in others, it takes place in consonant clusters. All the examples that I have found show devoicing after the addition of a prefix. In example (3), it is in the auxiliary that the initial consonant becomes voiceless when between vowels, *bim > a-pim*, and in example (4), the prefix *ḍ*- becomes voiceless when prefixed with the negative. Note that example (4) contains the Ø-stem verb 'come'; see Section 4.4. for discussion.

TABLE 5.1 BURUSHASKI CONSONANTS

	Labial	Dental	Palato-alveolar	Retroflex	Velar	Uvular	Glottal
Nasal	m	n			ŋ		
Aspirated voiceless plosive	pʰ	t̪ʰ		tʰ	kʰ		
Voiceless plosive	p	t̪		t	k	q	
Voiced plosive	b	d̪		d	g		
Aspirated voiceless affricate		cʰ [tsʰ]	čʰ [ʧʰ]	ċʰ [tʂʰ]			
Voiceless affricate		c [ts]	č [ʧ]	ċ [tʂ]			
Voiced affricate			ǰ [dʒ]	ż [dz]			
Voiceless fricative		s	š [ʃ]	ṣ [ʂ]	x		h
Voiced fricative		z			ɣ		
Trill		r					
Approximate		l	y [j]	ɻ	w		

TABLE 5.2 BURUSHASKI VOWELS

	Front	Central	Back
High	i/iː		u/uː
Mid	e/eː		o/oː
Low		a/aː	

(1) ɡaɣa-umo
   hide-3s.F.N.PST
   'She hid.'

   moo-s-t̪aq-am
   3s.F.CAUS-TRN-hide-1s.PST
   'I made her hide.'

(2) ɡuuɻ-imi
   melt-3s.PST
   'it melted.'

   ɡe-s-t̪uɻ-am
   d̪-TRN-melt-1s.PST
   'I melted it.'

(3) a-ar   lel   a-pim
   1s.GEN-DAT   know   NEG-AUX.3s.PST
   'I did not have knowledge.' (Baadil Jamal 70)

(4) *je*   *ḍaru-e*   *gane*   *a-ṭ-aa-Ø-ya*   *baa*
      1s   hunting-GEN   for   NEG-ḍ-1s-come-1s AUX.1s.PRF
      'I have not come for hunting.' (Baadil Jamal 34)

In languages generally, stops may undergo any number of assimilatory changes in medial position, the most common of these is arguably medial voicing of voiceless stops, or the weakening of medial voiced stops to a non-obstruent manner of articulation. Burushaski, however, shows the opposite change. It should be noted however, that intervocalic devoicing occurs only at morpheme boundaries and that voiced stops do appear in intervocalic position in roots. The alternations do not seem to be motivated by stress or other prosodic factors, since they occur invariably at morpheme boundaries regardless of stress.

3 SENTENCES

Burushaski is a typical head-final language, with agglutinative verb morphology, subject agreement, and pronoun drop. The basic word order is SOV, although the verb alone can often convey meaning without an overt subject or object noun phrase. Example (5) shows typical SOV word order, and (6) shows the same statement expressed without overt subject and object NPs. Example (7) shows the position of a subject in an intransitive sentence, while (8) shows a transitive sentence exhibiting SOV order without using pronoun.

(5) *je-e*   *un*   *mo-s-pal-am*
      1s-ERG   3s.F   3s.F-TRN-hid-1s.PST
      'I lost her.'

(6) *mo-s-pal-am*
      3s.F-TRN-hid-1s.PST
      'I lost her.'

(7) *hin*   *kaniiz-an*   *ḍuus-umo*
      one   maid-INDF   come out-3s.F.PAST
      'A maid came out.' (Baadil Jamal 31)

(8) *čumu-sel-aŋ-e*   *je-e*   *gatu-nc*   *xeša-m*
      fish-hook-PL-ERG   1-GEN cloth-PL   tear-PTCP
      bica
      AUX.3.Past (bila class)
      'The fish hooks tore the clothes.' (Morin and Tiffou 1988: 511) (YB)

Other constructions in Burushaski strictly conform to head-final order, including adjective-noun order, genitive-noun order, and the use of postpositions, as in the following examples where (9) shows adjective-noun order and (10) shows both a possessive and dative postposition.

(9) *burum*   *laqpis*
      white   handkerchief
      'white handkerchief' (Baadil Jamal 90)

(10) *cʰar-e*   *cat-ar*
      mountain-GEN crack-DAT
      into the crack of the mountain.' (Baadil Jamal 69)

3.1 Questions

Burushaski is a language where content question words (so-called *wh*-question words) remain in situ and are not fronted, as in many languages. Question words appear in the same slot as the real nouns that they replace or represent. Yes/no questions are formed by adding the suffix -*a* to the end of the verb, after the subject agreement suffix. Examples of both kinds of questions follow.

(11)   *un-e   besan ṣi-uma*
       2s-erg   what eat-2s.n.pst
       'What did you eat?'

(12)   *in-e   amul-ar   ni-umo*
       3s-erg   where-dat   go-3s.f.n.pst
       'Where did she go?

(12)   *mi-e   ṣi-om-a*
       1s-erg   eat-1p.n.imp-Q
       'Shall we eat?'

3.2 Conjunction reduction

In constructions with conjoined clauses where the subject of clauses is co-referential, the identical co-referential subject does not need to appear, as for example, in English *Bob$_j$ came home and – $_j$ hit Bill*. Here, the gapped subject of *hit* in the second clause is co-referential with the subject *Bob* in the first clause. In Burushaski, in this kind of sentence, the first verb cannot be formed with regular verbal morphology but must instead take either an *n*- prefix or *ḍ*-prefix (see Section 4.3) combined with an agreement suffix -*n*. These are likely nominalized forms of the verb, and the actual verb appears at the end of the sentence, with regular morphology and a suffix that agrees with the subject in both clauses, as seen in (13) and (14).

(13)   *tʰaan   n-eṭ-an   ḍuus-u   bo*
       shove   ptcp-do-ptcp   come.out-3s.f   aux.3s.f.prf
       'i.e. 'she$_1$ shoved (him) and (she$_1$) came out'.' (Limpi Kiser 152)

(14)   *mu-yi   čap   ne   ḍuus-u   bo*
       3.F-son hide   PTCP   come out-3.F   AUX.3.F.PERF
       'She hid her son and came out.' (Limpi Kiser 143)

3.3 Relative clauses

Relative clauses in Burushaski are also head final. The head noun that is modified by the relative clause appears at the end of the relative sentence, followed by the main clause. All head nouns modified by the relative clause are introduced with a deictic 'this' or 'that'. These also act as articles, marking a definite and specific NP. They might also be interpreted as relative connectors. The following examples are from Munshi (2015).

(15)   *cʰil   min-um   ine   hir*
       water   drink-nom   that   man
       'the man who drank the water'

(16)   *sadap-e   karim-ar   yuu-m   ise   baalt   ja-e   ṣi-am*
       Sadaf-erg   Karim-dat   give-nom   that   apple   1s-erg   eat-1s.n.pst
       'I ate the apple that Sadaf gave to Karim.'

4 THE VERB

The verb in Burushaski is morphologically rich, with numerous prefixes and suffixes that can be attached to it. In this section I will go over some of the basics of Burushaski verbal morphology, including special verbs, verbs with a Ø stem (where morphemes are attached to an invisible stem), causative constructions, a transitivising prefix, and negation.

4.1 Causatives

Causative constructions in Burushaski are marked with a transitivising prefix -*s* (discussed more below) and by lengthening the vowel of a verb prefix which agrees with the cause. Thus, a verb like *o-ṭ-imi* 'he chose them' is made causative by lengthening the vowel in the prefix *o-*, creating the causative sentence *oo-ṭ-imi* 'he made them choose'. In these cases, vowel lengthening is the sole indicator of causation as shown in examples (17)–(19):

(17)　*garkuy-anc*　　　*n-u-man-in*　　　　　*yuwa*　　*ḍamši*
　　　 Marriageable-pl　 ptcp-3pl -become-ptcp　 sons　　 choose
　　　 oo-ṭ-imi
　　　 3pl.CAUS-do-3s.pst
　　　 'Becoming marriageable, he made his sons choose.' (Baadil Jamal 15)

(18)　*es*　　*mo-qaṭ*　　*yaare*　　***moo-yan-ai***
　　　 that　 3-armpit　 down　　 **3s.f.caus** -take-3
　　　 'He put it under her armpit.' (he made her take it) (Limpi Kiser 99)

(19)　*leel*　　　　　*a-**moo**-ṭ-um*
　　　 find.out　　　 neg-**3s.f.caus** -do-nom
　　　 'Not letting her know that.' (Limpi Kiser 100)

The *s*- prefix may signal a causative in intransitive constructions and is analyzed as a transitivizer. When the *s*- transitivizer is affixed to an unergative verb – i.e. an intransitive verb whose subject is agent-like (as in 'the boy hid') and not patient-like (as in 'the window broke') – the result is a transitive causative where the verb prefix agrees with the causee of the construction. Example (20) shows a regular unergative construction, and (21) shows the prefix appearing in the corresponding causative.

(20)　*ḍaγa-umo*
　　　 hide-3s.f.pst
　　　 'She hid.'

(21)　*moo-s-ṭaq-am*
　　　 3s.f.caus-trn-hide-1.pst
　　　 'I made her hide.'

If the verb is made transitive with the *s*- transitivizer, the construction can no longer be classified as unergative (applicable only to intransitive verbs). The pronominal prefix appears, and the vowel is lengthened to show causation. The *s*- prefix may also be attached to unaccusative verbs – intransitive verbs whose subject is patient-like (as in 'the door closed'), and the result is consistent with other transitive forms where the animate causee is marked on the prefix of the verb through vowel lengthening. Compare example (22) with (23) and example (24) with (25) for contrasts between unaccusative verbs without the *s-* transitivizer and unaccusative verbs with the *s-* transitivizer:

(22)   *ḍ-i-man-am*
       ḍ-3s-become-3.prf
       'He was born.' (Limpi Kiser 114)

(23)   *in-e   hiles-an*   *ḍ-e-s-man-umo*
       3s.f-erg   boy-indf   ḍ-3s-trn-become-3s.f.pst
       'She gave birth to a boy.'

(24)   *mu-waal-umo*
       3s.f-lose-3s.f.pst
       'She was lost.'

(25)   *mo-s-pal-am*
       3s.f-trn-hid-1s.pst
       'I lost her.'

Note that, in this example, the transitivizing *s-* is combined with the verb prefix *mo-* to derive a transitive sentence. If the vowel were to be lengthened, as in *moospalam*, the reading would be something along the lines of 'I made her become lost'. So a derivation of causative from an intransitive verb must first add the *s-* transitivizer and later lengthen the vowel of the obligatory agreement prefix to form the causative.

4.2 Negation

Negative clauses in Burushaski take the verbal prefix *a-*, which appears before the *ḍ-* prefix (see Sections 4.3) and any pronominal agreement prefixes. Alternatively, the negative can be attached to the phrase-final auxiliary (*-bim*), although it does not appear that this is a strict requirement, as negatives can also appear prefixed to the verb despite the presence of an auxiliary. Some examples are given here:

(26)   *je-e   ma-yeen-am*   *a-pim*
       1-erg   2pl-know-1   Neg-aux.3s.pst
       'I did not know you.' (Baadil Jamal 70)

(27)   *a-ar   lel   a-pim*
       1-dat   know   neg-aux.3s.pst
       'I did not have knowledge.' (Baadil Jamal 70)

(28)   *je   ḍaru-e*   *gane*   *a-ṭ-aa-Ø-ya*   *baa*
       1   hunting-gen   for   neg- ḍ-1-come-1   aux.1s.prf
       'I have not come for hunting.' (Baadil Jamal 34)

4.3 The *ḍ-*prefix

Certain verbs in Burushaski take the prefix *ḍ-* which has a varying degree of semantic impact on the verbs that it is attached to. Phonologically, it is followed by an ambiguous vowel which is subject to vowel harmony (Anderson 2007: 1248–1250, Anderson 1997, Munshi 2006: 194–197). The exact function of the *ḍ-*prefix remains somewhat unclear. On both transitive and intransitive verbs, Bashir (1985: 21, 2000a: 4–11) claims that it brings a focus to the result and defocuses the actors. In my data the ḍ-prefix has two main functions. The first is associated with a slight change in meaning, such as in adding focus or transitivity, and the second is associated with the derivation of a completely different word. The contrast exemplified in (29) and (30) shows the first type, and that of (31) and (32) shows the second type. Also note that the ḍ-prefix does not create an intransitive verb in (33), despite some claims in the literature that it is an intransitivizing prefix.

(29) ḍuu.ṭ-imi
      melt-3s.pst
      'it melted.'

(30) ḍe-s-ṭu.ṭ-am
      ḍV-trn-melt-1.pst
      'I melted it.'

(31) i-man-imi
      3-become-3s.pst
      'He became (something).'

(32) ḍ-i-man-imi
      ḍ-3s.m-become-3s.pst
      'He was born.'

(33) un-e   limpi kisar   ḍ-i-c-aa
      2-erg   Limpi Kiser   ḍ-3s.m-bring-2s
      'You brought Limpi Kiser.' (Limpi Kiser 108)

   A good list of verbs that occur in two forms, one with the ḍ-prefix and one without, along with their corresponding glosses, can be found in Bashir (1985: 21–23). Other comparative lists of ḍ-prefix verbs and analyses of the ḍ-prefix paradigm can be found in Munshi (2006:194–197), Anderson (2007: 1248–1250), and Bashir (2000a). It is important to remember that the ḍ-prefix appears semantically to be a bleached affix, and it is not clear if further investigation will help to specify its meaning more clearly, other than revealing further bleaching and loss of former function.

4.4 The verb 'to come', a verb with no form

The verb 'to come' presents an interesting hurdle to analysis. It is the only verb in Burushaski that is formed without a stem (has a Ø-stem). Instead, it is formed with the ḍ-prefix and a suffix agreeing with the subject, as shown in example (35). See Anderson (2007: 1264) for a list of different realizations of the verb 'to come'. The verb is written as -Ø in glosses, as shown in example (34).

(34) ḍa-Ø-a   baa
      ḍV-come-1s.pres aux.1s.pres
      'I come.'

   The verb 'to come', a verb formed without a stem where the ḍ-prefix and suffix are affixed to /Ø/, is one of the stranger oddities in Burushaski. It would seem that the ḍ-prefix alone is responsible for conveying the meaning of the Ø-stem verb 'to come' while the suffix attaches itself to a stem that is not phonologically analyzable.

5 CASE MARKING

Morphologically, case marking differentiates between subject and object in transitive sentences in two different ways in Burushaski. The first is through use of the ergative marker which appears on the agent noun phrase. The second way that Burushaski differentiates agent from object is through its verb agreement patterns which mark the subject of the sentence. Nouns are marked as ergative or absolutive, while verbs have agreement suffixes that agree with the nominative subject. This type of difference has been described in Mallinson and Blake (1981), Kroeger (2004: 283), and Simpson (1983; 1991: 155–161). Specifically, Mallinson and Blake identify twelve theoretical types of case marking in languages. Their type eight, where noun marking is ergative and verbal agreement is nominative, is similar to the type seen in Burushaski. Suffix agreement on the verb is described in Anderson (2007:1258 and Wilson 1996: 4) as being in agreement with the grammatical subject of the sentence. Verbal suffixes agree with the intransitive subject and with the transitive agent. I discuss first the different agreement affixes on the verb and how they align with participants. After, I discuss the case marking of nouns.

5.1 Verbal subject agreement suffixes

The agreement suffixes are listed in Tables 5.3 and 5.4. Data are taken from Anderson (2007) in my analysis of verb suffixes. Third person here is broken into four classes: male animate, female, *bi* inanimate, and *bila* inanimate classes. *Bi* class nouns typically involve concrete and tangible items, sometimes described as countable, while the *bila* class nouns are typically non-concrete items, sometimes referred to as non-countable

TABLE 5.3 VERBAL AGREEMENT SUFFIXES IN PERFECTIVE, FUTURE, PAST, AND PERFECT

	Perfective		*Future*		*Past*		*Perfect*	
	sng	pl	sng	pl	sng	pl	sng	pl
1st	-a	-an	-am	-an	-am	-uman	-a baa	-aan
2nd	-a	-an	-uma	-een	-uma	-uman	-aa	-aan
3rd M	-i	-an	-(im)i	-een	-imi	-uman	-ai	-aan
3rd F	-o	-an	-(um)o	-een	-umo	-uman	-u bo	-aan
3rd (bi)	-i	-ien	-(im)i	-ie(n)	-imi	-imie	-i bi	bien
3rd (bila)	-i	-i	-(im)i	-(im)i	-imi	-imi	-ila	bica

TABLE 5.4 VERBAL AGREEMENT SUFFIXES IN PRESENT, PLUPERFECT, AND IMPERFECT

	Present		*Pluperfect*		*Imperfect*	
1st	-a baa	-oon	-a bayam	-am	-a bayam	-om
2nd	-oo	-oon	-am	-am	-om	-om
3rd M	-oi	-oon	-am	-am	-om	-om
3rd F	-u bo	-oon	-u bom	-am	-u bom	-om
3rd (bi)	-i bi	bien	-i bim	-i bim	-i bim	-i bim
3rd (bila)	bila	bica	-i bilum	-i bicum	-i bilum	-i bicum

(Munshi 2006: 185, Munshi 2015, Lorimer 1935, Berger 1998: 144–158). Tables are followed by several examples which show the suffixes and how they agree with the grammatical subject of the clause with nominative-accusative alignment.

(35)   *ye*   *minaš-in* *ke*   *kaafi*   *et-**a***   ***baa***
        dm   story-pl comp   enough do-**1s**   **aux.1s.prf**
        'I have told many stories.' (Baadil Jamal 3)

(36)   *je*   *daru-e*   *gane*   *a-ṭa-a-Ø-**a***   ***baa***
        1   hunting-gen   for   neg- ḍV-1-come-**1s**   **aux.1s.prf**
        'I have not come here for hunting.' (Baadil Jamal 34)

(37)   *nu-sen*   *šootkum*   *no*   *u-cʰarkan-**uman***
        ptcp-say   insult   ptcp   3pl-beat-**3pl.pst**
        'Insulting them, they beat them.'(Mattum Ke Burum Looto 41from Munshi 2015)

(38)   *garkuy-anc*   *u-man-**uman***   *yuwa*
        Marriageable-pl   3pl-become-**3pl.pst**   sons
        'His sons became marriageable.' (Baadil Jamal 14)

(39)   *parišaan*   *mu-man-**umo***
        worried   3s.f-become-**3s.f.pst**
        'She was worried.' (Baadil Jamal 63)

(40)   *ite*   *minas*   *go-ar*   *eč-**am***
        That   story   2s-dat   do-**1s.ft**
        'I will tell you that story.' (Baadil Jamal 8)

(41)   *je*   *hole*   *ḍuuš-**am***
        1   outside   come.out-**1s.ft**
        'I will come outside.' (Baadil Jamal 52)

(42)   *in-e*   *paaḍša buċ*   *ḍel-**imi***
        3-erg   king   oriental plane   cut-**3s.pst**
        'He cut the king's oriental plane.' (Limpi Kiser 74)

(43)   *niin-in*   *i-kʰaran-**imi***
        go-ptcp   3-late-**3s.pst**
        'He was late.' (Limpi Kiser 61)

These examples show that the agreement suffixes in Burushaski agree with the subject, that is, with the agent of a transitive sentence and with the subject of an intransitive sentence. Noun phrases, on the other hand, have an ergative system of case marking and are described in more detail in Section 6.1.

5.2 Verbal agreement prefixes

Burushaski verbs are also equipped with agreement in the form of verbal prefixes. This means that Burushaski routinely has double agreement marked on the verb. In fact, Burushaski routinely has a verbal prefix and a verbal suffix which agree with the *same* NP. There is disagreement in the literature on the exact nature of the person marking verbal prefixes. For example, Munshi (2006: 129–141, 2015) states that these prefixes agree with the absolutive subject and appear in agreement only with animate noun phrases.

TABLE 5.5 VERBAL AGREEMENT PREFIXES

	Singular	*Plural*
1st	a-	mi-/me-
2nd	gu-/go-	ma-
3rd M/bi/bila	i-/e-	u-/o-
3rd F	mu-/mo-	u-/o-

Bashir (1985: 9–12) claims that the prefixes follow active language patterns of agreement. Smith (2012) analyzes the verbal prefixes as differential object markers. Table 5.5 lists the agreement prefixes followed by several examples that show the prefixes in use.

(44)   *garkuy-anc*   *u-man-uman*
       Marriageable-pl   3pl-become-3pl.pst
       'They became marriageable.' (Badil Jamal 14)

(45)   *sa*   *ʈʰalekuc ʈʰap*   *ʈʰalekuc e-yay*   *bim*
       sun   seven.days   night   seven.days   3s-sleep aux.3s.pst
       'He (the monster) slept for seven days and seven nights.' (Limpi Kiser 96)

(46)   *a-kayuwa*   *ye*   *ĵe*   *a-war-a*   *baa*
       1s-children   VOC   1s   1s-tired-1s.   aux.1s.pres
       'My children, I am tired.' (Daddo Puno 47)

(47)   *mu-ci-ate*   *i-waal-imi*
       3s.f-com-on   3s-lost-3s.pst (Mattum ke Burum 39)
       'He was lost on her.' ('He became lost in her.')

(48)   *alʈiʈ*   *raʈ-ulo*   *go-rš-a*   *baa*
       Altit   plain-loc   2s-drunk-2s   aux.2s.pres
       'You are drunk in the Altit plain.' (Matum ke Burum 31)

These examples all show intransitive verbs, where the prefix agrees with the intransitive subject. Other examples show that the prefix also often agrees with the patient in transitive constructions. This is why the prefix has sometimes been analyzed as absolutive agreement. Examples (49) through (51) show transitive sentences with patient agreement on the verb.

(49)   *ĵe-e*   *ma-yeen-am*   *a-pim*
       1-erg   2pl-know-1s   Neg-aux.3s.pst
       'I did not know you.' (Lit: 'I knew you, not.') (Baadil Jamal 70)

(50)   *un-e*   *buk*   *gu-xulĵ-i*   *bi*
       2s-gen   throat   2s-hurt-3s   aux-3s.pres
       'Your throat hurts.' (lit: 'your throat is hurting you.')

(51)   *ĵe-e*   *a-u-e*   *ke*   *żap*   *a-ko-č-i*
       1-gen   1-father-erg   comp spare neg-2-do-3s.ft
       'My father will not spare you.' (Baadil Jamal 75)

There are also constructions where the prefix agrees with the agent itself. Take for example the instance of experiencer marking in example (52). The prefix agrees with the subject of the sentence which is also marked directly as ergative. When asked to change the prefix to agree with the absolutive, the sentence becomes ungrammatical, as shown in example (53). This would not be expected if the prefix showed true absolutive alignment, since it is agreeing with an agent.

(52)   *u-e*   *je-e*   *čaɣa*   *ḍ-o-yal-uman*
            3 pl-erg   1-gen   word   ḍ-3pl-listen-3pl.pst
            'They heard me.' (They listened to me.)

(53)   **u-e*   *je-e*   *čaɣa*   *ḍ-i-yal-uman*
            *3pl-erg   1-gen   word   ḍ-3s-listen-3pl.pst
            *They heard my words

Verb prefixes typically only agree with animate arguments. Verbs such as 'eat' are almost always associated with inanimate patients and thus do not trigger verb agreement. However, when the patient is changed from inanimate to animate with the same verb, the prefix appears, agreeing with the animate patient. Munshi uses the following examples to show how the animacy constraint on patients works to deny prefix realizations with inanimate patients but allows animate prefix agreement on the same verb:

(54)   *mi-e*   *pʰiti*   *ṣi-uman*
            3pl-erg   bread   eat-3pl.pst
            'We ate bread.' (Munshi 2006: 136) (J&K)

(55)   *muuṭu*   *um-e*   *ja*   *a-ṣi-ċu*   *ba*
            Now   2-erg   1s   1s-eat-2s   aux.2s.pres
            'Now that you are eating me.' (Munshi 2006: 136) (J&K)

In recipient constructions (where the dative is used to mark the recipient), the verbal agreement prefix agrees with the dative and not with the absolutive. In these constructions, the absolutive has no agreement marking on the verb (Munshi 2006: 138–140). Example (56) shows this type of recipient agreement. In the second example (57), attempting to remove the prefix (which is expected if the prefix must agree with the inanimate absolutive 'book' as Ø) creates an ungrammatical sentence.

(56)   *in-e*   *in-e-re*   *kiṭaab-an*   *e-uč-umo*
            3-erg   3-gen-dat   book-indf   3-give-3s.pst
            'She gave him a book.' (Munshi 2006 139) (J&K)

(57)   ** in-e*   *in-e-re*   *kiṭaab-an*   *Ø-uč-umo*
            *3-erg   3-gen-dat   book-indf   give-3s.pst
            *She gave him a book

All intransitive constructions from the texts which have prefix agreement with the subject are either sate of being constructions or changes in state of being constructions.

However, when the verb involves an event; something happening; describing an action that the animate subject of an intransitive sentence is actively doing; something along the lines of walking, running, going, flying; etc., there is no prefix on the verb and thus no double marking. Consider the following examples (58) through (62), where the subject is an active participant in the action and cannot be labeled as being affected by the verb in question. There is no prefix in these cases.

(58)   *i-gurč-imi*
       3-submerge-3s.pst
       'He drowned.' (Bashir 1985: 16) (YB)

(59)   *gurč-imi*
       Submerge-3s.pst
       'He dived (to clean his body).' (Bashir 1985: 16) (YB)

(60)   *in   ḍaya-mo*
       3s.f   hide-3s.f.pst
       'She hid.'

(61)   *je   muarar   akʰole   huruš-a   baa*
       1   forever here   stay-1   AUX.1s.pres
       'I stay here forever.' (Baadil Jamal 38)

(62)   *um-e   šugulo   gaarc-imi*
       2-gen   friend   run-3s.pst
       'Your friend ran.' (Munshi 2006: 130) (J&K)

In these examples, the presence or absence of the verb prefix is determined by whether the sentences are unergative or unaccusative. The prefix in intransitive sentences appears on the verb and agrees with the subject of unaccusative verbs, but it does not appear on the verb or agree with the subject of unergative verbs. Unaccusative verbs are intransitive verbs where the subject is not an agent, and unergative verbs are intransitive verbs where the subject acts as an agent or has some sort of intent or initiation with the action being performed.[3] There are four rules that determine whether these prefixes appear on the verb, which are shown below:

1   The prefix agrees with the animate patient or unaccusative subject.
2   In theme/recipient constructions, the prefix agrees with the animate recipient.
3   In stimulus/experiencer constructions, the prefix agrees with the animate experiencer.
4   If none of these conditions hold, there is no prefix.

From these examples, it is clear that the classic analysis where the pronominal prefixes are analyzed as agreeing with the absolutive is not satisfactory. It fails to explain why the prefix does not agree with the absolutive if an experiencer or recipient argument is present, and it does not explain why the prefix fails to appear if the subject of an intransitive sentence in unergative. Differential object marking (Escandell-Vidal 2009, Haspelmath 2005, Hoop and Malchukov 2007, McGregor 1998, Aissen 2003) seems to be a better description of the Burushaski pronominal prefixes. Differential object marking is a means by which languages mark unexpected noun phrases. Speakers expect that most often objects will be inanimate, that subjects will not be the affected party of a construction, and that the subject will be the agent (Haspelmath 2005: 9). If these expectations are not met (if the object is animate, or if the subject is the experiencer, recipient, or if the subject is unaccusative), then the verb will have a prefix that agrees with the unexpected participant.

6 THE NOUN

This section addresses the rich morphology of Burushaski nouns. Nouns can take a number of affixes, including pronominal prefixes and case suffixes. They are separated into four classes, and are inflected for number (singular and plural). I begin with about case marking on the noun, then continue the discussion from the previous section on case and agreement affixes on the verb.

6.1 Nominal case marking

Although the verbal suffixes agree with the subject in nominative alignment, an ergative suffix appears on agentive NPs. Note that the ergative suffix, -e, is homophonous with the genitive suffix, a feature typical of many ergative languages. Phonologically, the ergative marker appears as the suffix -e on nouns that end in consonants. On nouns that end in a short vowel, the ergative marker is vowel lengthening. Finally, when the ergative marker is used on nouns that end in a long vowel, there is no overt ergative marking, although some analyze this as null marking (Munshi 2015: 173). In example (63), there is no ergative marking on the intransitive subject *je*, but in example (64), *jee* has ergative vowel lengthening.

(63)   *a-kayuwa*   *ye*   *je*   *a-war-a*   *baa*
       1-children   voc   1   1s-tired-1s   sux.1s.pres
       'My children, I am tired.' (Daddo Puno 47)

(64)   *je-e*   *dasin*   *mu- yeec –am*
       1-**erg**   girl   3s.f-see- 1s.pst
       'I saw the girl.'

(65)   *un-e*   *buk*   *gu-xulj-i*   *bi*
       2-**gen**   throat   2-hurt-3   aux-3s.pres
       'your throat hurts.' (lit: 'your throat is hurting you.') (HB)

According to Tiffou and Morin (1982) and Lorimer (1935: 65), Burushaski is said to have split ergativity between non-future versus future tenses. The split system itself can be seen in noun morphology, where the ergative marker /-e/ appears only after agents in past and present tenses and is absent in future tense. Past tense 'I saw the girl' displays the ergative marker on the first person singular pronoun /je/, /je-e/, while future tense 'I will see the girl' does not have this marker. Examples (68) and (69) come from Lorimer (1935) and show the same pattern on the second person singular pronoun /un/.

(66)   *je-e*   *ḍasin*   *mu-yeec-am*
       1s-erg   girl   3s-see-1s.pst
       'I saw the girl.'

(67)   *je*   *ḍasin*   *mu-yeš-am*
        1s   girl   3s-see-1s.ft
        'I will see the girl.'

(68)   *un-e*   *in*   *mu-cuč-aa*
        2s-erg   her   3s-marry-2s.pres
        'You marry her.' (Lorimer 1935: 65) (YB)

(69)   *un*   *in*   *mu-cuč-uma*
        2s   3s   3s-marry-2s.fut
        'You will marry her.' (Lorimer 1935: 65) (YB)

The ergative marker also appears in contexts where its usage is pragmatic, e.g. to distinguish between volitional and non-volitional actions. The ergative marker can both appear unexpectedly in intransitive sentences and can be absent in transitive sentences. In examples (70) and (71), the ergative marker alone is used to denote a volitional action, even though the sentence is intransitive in both examples. In example (72), the ergative marker is absent on the agent, though this may be because the agent is not animate. But in at least one example, shown in example (73), in the Yasin dialect, the ergative appears on an intransitive agent.

(70)   *hiles-e*   *har(a)-imi*
        baby-**erg**   pee-3s.pst
        'The baby peed.' (volitionally)

(71)   *hiles-Ø*   *har(a)-imi*
        baby-**Ø** pee-3s.pst
        'The baby peed.' (non-volitionally)

(72)   *je-e*   *žame- Ø*   *ḍ-a-c-i*   *bi*
        1s-gen   arrow- **Ø** ḍ-1s-bring-3s   aux-3s.pres
        'My arrow brought me here.' (Baadil Jamal 70)

(73)   *čumu-sel-aŋ-e*   *je-e*   *gatu-nc*   *xeša-m*   *bica*
        fish-hook-pl-erg   1s-gen   cloth-pl   tear-ptcp   aux.3s.pst (bila class)
        'The fish hooks tore the clothes.' (Morin and Tiffou 1988: 511) (YB)

Apart from ergative case, the noun can also take dative, genitive, locative, instrumental, and ablative case marking suffixes. As stated above, the genitive is homophonous with the ergative marker, except for genitive feminine pronouns which take the special -*mo* suffix. Table 5.6 below lists all of the Burushaski nominal case markers. Note that the absolutive is listed in some works as a Ø suffix, but I have chosen to simply exclude the absolutive from this chart, since it has no phonetic form.

TABLE 5.6 NOMINAL CASE MARKING

Ergative	-*e*, -*V:*
Genitive	-*e*, -*V:*, -*mo*
Locative	-*ulo*, -*ate*
Instrumental	-*ate*
Ablative	-*um*, *cum*
Dative	-*ar*

The behavior of the dative case morpheme is very interesting. It can be used to mark the subject noun phrases of so-called experiencer constructions (see Munshi 2006: 133–134, Bhatia 1990, Masica 1976, Mishra 1990, Verma and Mohanan 1990 for more on dative subjects in South Asia). Some examples of this phenomenon follow (from Munshi 2006: 133–134).

(74) *je-e-re*   *in*   *šua*   *yan-umo*
      1-gen-dat   3s.f   good   feel-3s.f.pst
      'I liked her.' (Literally, 'to me she feels good'.)

(75) *je-e-re*   *šuriyaar*   *ḍila*
      1-gen-dat   happiness   be.3s.pres
      'I am happy.' (Literally, 'to me is happiness'.)

However, whether or not the dative in these constructions is actually the subject is still a matter of debate. Smith (2012) argues that dative arguments are not the actual subjects and that the NP that bears on overt morphological marking, which agrees with the verbal subject agreement suffix, is the actual subject ('she' and 'happiness' in these examples). If the dative were truly the subject in these constructions, then it is not clear why the verb suffix, which should agree with the subject, does not.[4] Yet the argument against interpreting these dative subjects as actual subjects in Smith (2012) lack supporting evidence and cannot be verified without specifically testing for subject in these dative subject constructions.

6.2 Pronominal prefixes on the noun

The possessive pronominal prefixes are used as an alternative way to show possession and are homophonous with verbal pronominal prefixes which, as discussed next, agree with the affected argument of a construction, or in some analyses, with the absolutive argument. The nominal prefixes are listed in Table 5.7, and several examples are given after the table, showing how the prefixes are attached to possessed nouns.

(76) *mu-riin-um*
      3s.f-hand-ptcp
      'her hand'(Baadil Jamal 90)

(77) *i-riin-um*
      3-hand-ptcp
      'his hand.' (Baadil Jamal 71)

(78) *a-kayuwa*
      1-children
      'my children' (Daddo Puno 47)

TABLE 5.7 POSSESSIVE PRONOMINAL PREFIXES ON NOUNS

	Singular	*Plural*
1st	a-	mi-/me-
2nd	gu-/go-	ma-
3rd M/bi/bila	i-/e-	u-/o-
3rd F	mu-/mo-	u-/o-

The pronominal prefixes can attach to postpositions, indicating a position in relation to the person in question. For example, *ṭik yaare* 'below ground' is formed with the post-position *yaare*. The phrase 'below me' however, is not *ja yare* as might be expected, but rather, *a-yaare*, literally, 'my below'. Additional examples of this type of positional are: *gu-yate* 'on you', *mu-yar* 'before her', *o-paci* 'near them', and *i-lji* 'behind him'. Munshi (2015) has an exhaustive list of positionals and possible combination with the pronominal prefixes.

6.3 Plural

Burushaski nouns can also take plural suffixes, which vary depending on the class and phonetics of the noun. Tiffou (1993) claims that there are close to 50 suffixes for marking plural in Burushaski. As stated earlier, there are four classes: male human; female human; *bi* class (for animals and tangible, countable items); and *bila* class (for nouns which are typically non-concrete items, sometimes referred to as non-countable) (Munshi 2006: 185, Munshi 2015, Lorimer 1935, Berger 1998: 144–158). Munshi (2015) contains a list of the most common suffixes, which is reproduced in Table 5.8, and the class of each noun is marked. Note that the plural suffixes come in three types: (1) male and female; (2) male, female, and *bi* class; and (3) *bila* class. Thus, there is no male-only or female-only class of nouns, since classes (1) and (2) can include both male and female nouns.

7 CONCLUSION

Although this chapter is focused mainly on the morphology of Burushaski, a number of other topics were also considered, though many others remain. Burushaski has been the topic of a large and growing number of works dealing mostly with its interesting morphosyntax. Projects such as the *Burushaski Language Documentation Project* show a strong interest in long-term documentation. The language is still in need of a comprehensive grammar (Lorimer 1935 is outdated, and the *Burushaski Documentation Project* as well as Berger 1998 have a Hunza/Nager focus). Despite some claims to the contrary,

TABLE 5.8 BURUSHASKI PLURAL SUFFIXES

	Singular	*Plural*
boy (male)	hiles	hilešo
sheep (*bi* class)	belis	belišo
stone (*bi* class)	ḍa:n	ḍayo
wood (*bi* class)	toq	toquc
sun (*bi* class)	sa	samuc
monkey (*bi* class)	šaḍi	šaḍimuc
sword (*bila* class)	yaṭenċ	yaṭa:ŋ
oxen (*bi* class)	har	haro
stream (*bila* class)	bul	bulyaŋ
vine (*bi* class)	šun	šunaync
polo stick (*bi* class)	finč	finčko
wine (*bila* class)	mel	melmiŋ
school (*bila* class)	suku:l	suku:liŋ

Burushaski is best considered a language isolate. It has a rich phonological inventory with 36 consonants, a large number of distinctive fricatives and affricates, but a less remarkable system of 5 vowels, plus a length distinction. Burushaski is a typical head-final language, with SOV word order, and it has a complex morphology. Burushaski has nominative alignment of verbal suffixes which agree with the subject NP. It has differential object marking in the form of verbal prefixes which agree with the differential object NP and which sometimes causes double agreement with the verbal subject suffix, pronominal prefix, and the subject NP. It also shows split nominal ergative marking, which typically appears on the agent in non-future tenses, but which may also be used pragmatically to show volition in an intransitive sentence. It has a null root verb 'to come', which is formed with the ɡ́-prefix and a suffix, but no root. Burushaski is a fascinating language with some very interesting properties which warrant further discussion and future research.

NOTES

1 Data used in this paper comes from two main sources. First, many examples come from texts available online at the *Burushaski Language Documentation Project*. Those examples come from several texts, "Baadil Jamal", "Limpi Kiser", "Daddo Puno", "Chine Maghuyo", "Mattum Ke Burum", and "Hamale Khattun." In this paper, examples from these texts are cited by story and line number. Other examples have no citation and were elicited directly from Piar Karim, a native Burushaski speaker and friend, who was working and studying at the University of North Texas while I was writing my master's thesis. Data from other sources is cited accordingly. The majority of this material is from the Hunza dialect, but some examples are from Yasin, Nagar, and Jammu and Kashmir Burushaski. Examples from a dialect other than the Hunza dialect are marked accordingly.
2 Sagart's response to Sino-Caucasian was to propose Sino-Austronesian, which itself was criticized in Blust 1995. Overall, neither the Sino-Caucasian, Dene-Caucasian, nor Sino-Austronesian hypotheses are widely accepted by historical linguists specializing in any of these specific language families. Burushaski seems to have been taken along for the ride in an argument between distant genetic relationships involving Sinitic.
3 See Wilson (1996) for another discussion of unaccusative and unergative influence in Burushaski.
4 It has been brought to my attention that dative subjects in Germanic languages have good support for being treated as subjects, but don't necessarily satisfy agreement. This also casts doubts on the conclusions of Smith (2012), which does not treat dative subjects as true subjects in Burushaski.

REFERENCES

Aissen, Judith. 2003. Differential Object Marking: Iconicity vs Economy. *Natural Language and Linguistic Theory* 21: 435–483.

Anderson, Gregory. 1997. Burushaski Phonology. *Phonologies of Asia and Africa (Including the Caucasus)*, ed. by A. Kay and P. Daniels, 1021–1041. Winona Lake: Eisenbrauns.

Anderson, Gregory. 2007. Burushaski Morphology. *Morphologies of Asia and Africa*, ed. by A. Kaye, 1233–1275. Winona Lake: Eisenbrauns.

Bashir, Elena. 1985. Toward a Semantics of the Burushaski Verb. *Conference on Partici-pant Roles: South Asia and Adjacent Areas*, ed. by A. Zide, D. Magier, and E. Schiller, 1–32. Bloomington: Indiana University Linguistics Club.

Bashir, Elena. 2000a. *The d-prefix in Burushaski: Viewpoint and Evidentuality*. Paper presented at the 36th international conference of Asian and North African studies, Montreal. August 27.

Bashir, Elena. 2000b. A Thematic Survey of Burushaski Research. *History of Language* 6: 1–15.

Bengtson, John D. 2008. Materials for a Comparative Grammar of the Dene-Caucasian (Sino-Caucasian) Languages. *Aspects of Comparative Linguistics* 3: 45–118.

Bengtson, John D. and V. Blažek. 1995. Lexica Dene – Caucasica. *Central Asiatic Jour-nal* 39: 11–50, 161–164.

Berger, Hermann. 1956. Mittelmeerische Kulturpflanzennamen aus dem Burushaski. *Indo-Iranian Journal* 3: 17–43.

Berger, Hermann. 1998. *Die Burushaski-Sprache von Hunza und Nager*. Wiesbaden: Harrassowitz.

Bhatia, Tej K. 1990. The Notion of 'Subject' in Punjabi and Lahanda. *Experiencer Sub-jects in South Asian Languages*, ed. by M. Verma and K.P. Mohanan, 181–194. Stan-ford: Center for the Study of Language and Information.

Bleichsteiner, Robert. 1930. *Die werschikisch-burischkische Sprache im Pamirgebiet und ihre Stellung zu den Japhetitensprachen des Kaukasus [The Werchikwar-Burushaski language in the Pamir region and its position relative to the Japhetic languages of the Caucasus]*. Wiener Beiträge zur Kunde des Morgenlandes 1: 289–331.

Blust, Robert 1995. An Austronesianist Looks at Sino-Austronesian. *The Ancestry of the Chinese Language*. Journal of Chinese Linguistics Monograph Series Number 8, ed. by William S-Y. Wang, 283–298. Berkeley.

Campbell, Lyle. 1997. *American Indian Languages: The Historical Linguistics of Native America*. Oxford: Oxford University Press.

Čašule, Ilija. 1998. *Basic Burushaski Etymologies. (The Indo-European and Paleobal-kanic Affinities of Burushaski)*. Munich-Newcastle: Lincom Europa.

Čašule, Ilija. 2003a. Burushaski Names of Body Parts of Indo-European Origin. *Central Asiatic Journal* 47: 15–74.

Čašule, Ilija. 2003b. Evidence for the Indo-European laryngeals in Burushaski and Its Genetic Affiliation with Indo-European. *The Journal of Indo-European Studies* 31(1–2): 21–86.

Čašule, Ilija. 2009a. Burushaski Shepherd Vocabulary of Indo-European Origin. *Acta Orientalia* 70: 147–195.

Čašule, Ilija. 2009b. Burushaski Numerals of Indo-European Origin. *Central Asiatic Journal* 53, no. 2: 163–183.

Čašule, Ilija. 2010. *Burushaski as an Indo-European "Kentum" Language: Reflexes of the Indo-European Gutturals in Burushaski*. Munich: Lincom.

Čašule, Ilija. 2012. Correlation of the Burushaski Pronominal System with Indo-European and Phonological and Grammatical Evidence for a Genetic Relationship. *The Journal of Indo-European Studies* 40(1–2): 59–153.

Čašule, Ilija. 2016. *Evidence for the Indo-European and Balkan Origin of Burushaski*. (LINCOM Etymological Studies, 5.) Munich: LINCOM GmbH.

Escandell-Vidal, Victoria. 2009. Differential Object Marking and Topicality: The Case of Balearic Catalan. *Studies in Language* 33, no. 4: 832–884.

Goddard, Ives 1996. The Classification of the Native Languages of North America. *Languages*. Vol. 17 of William Sturtevant, ed., *Handbook of North American Indians*, ed. by I. Goddard, 290–324. Washington, DC: Smithsonian Institution.

Hamp, Eric P. 2013. The Expansion of the Indo-European Languages: An Indo-Europeanist's Evolving View. *Sino-Platonic Papers* 239: 1–14.

Haspelmath, Martin. 2005. *Universals of Differential Case Marking*. Handout presented at the 2005 LSA Institute: *Dialogues in Grammatical Theory, Experiment, and Change*. http://wwwstaff.eva.mpg.de/~haspelmt/2.DiffCaseMarking.pdf.

Holst, Jan Henrik. 2014. *Advances in Burushaski linguistics*. Tübingen: Narr.

Holst, Jan Henrik. 2015. *The Origin of Burushaski – An Extremely Brief Report*. Unpublished paper, University of Hamburg.

Holst, Jan Henrik. 2016. *Typological Features of Burushaski and Their Context*. Abstract of paper to be presented at the "Workshop on typological profiles of language families of South Asia", Uppsala, Sweden, September 15–16, 2016.

Hoop, Helen and Andrej Malchukov. 2007. On Fluid Differential Case Marking: A Bidirectional Approach. *Lingua*, 117: 1636–1656.

Karim, Piar. 2013. *Middle Voice Construction in Burushaski: From the Perspective of a Native Speaker of the Hunza Dialect*. Unpublished M.A. thesis, Department of Linguistics, University of North Texas, Denton, TX.

Kroeger, Paul. 2004. *Analyzing Syntax*. Cambridge: Cambridge University Press.

Lorimer, David. 1935. *The Burushaski Language*. Oslo: H. Aschehoug.

Mallinson, Graham and Barry Blake. 1981. *Cross-Linguistic Studies in Syntax*. Amsterdam: North-Holland.

Masica, Colin P. 1976. *Defining a Linguistic Area*. Chicago: University of Chicago Press.

McGregor, William. 1998. "Optional" Ergative Marking in Gooniyandi Revisited: Implications to the Theory or Marking. *Leuven Contributions in Linguistics and Philology* 87: 491–571.

Mishra, Mithilesh K. 1990. Dative/Experiencer Subjects in Maithili. *Experiencer Subjects in South Asian Languages*, ed. by M. Verma and K. Mohanan, 105–118. Stanford, CA: Center for the Study of Language and Information.

Morin, Y.-Ch. and Etienne Tiffou. 1988. Passives in Burushaski. *Passives and Related Constructions*, ed. by M. Shibatani, 493–524. Amsterdam: John Benjamins.

Munshi, Sadaf. 2006. *Jammu and Kashmir Burushaski: Language Contact and Change* Unpublished doctoral dissertation. University of Texas, Department of Linguistics, Austin.

Munshi, S. 2015. *A Grammatical Sketch of Burushaski*. Burushaski language documentation project: www.ltc.unt.edu/~sadafmunshi/Burushaski/language/grammaticalsketch.html.

Ruhlen, Merritt. 1994. *On the Origin of Languages: Studies in Linguistic Taxonomy*. Stanford: Stanford University Press.

Sagart, Laurent. 1993. Chinese and Austronesian: Evidence for a Genetic Relationship. *Journal of Chinese Linguistics* 21: 1–62.

Sagart, L. 1994. Proto-Austronesian and Old Chinese Evidence for Sino-Austronesian. *Oceanic Linguistics* 33, no. 2: 271–308.

Simpson, Jane. 1983. *Aspects of Warlpiri Morphology and Syntax*. Cambridge: MIT University Press.

Simpson, J. 1991. *Warlpiri Morpho-Syntax: A Lexicalist Approach*. Dordrecht: Kluwer Academic.

Smith, Alexander D. 2012. *Burushaski Case Marking, Agreement, and Implications: An Analysis of the Hunza dialect*. Unpublished Master's Thesis, Department of Linguistics and Technical Communication, University of North Texas.

Starostin, Sergei. 1991. On the Hypothesis of a Genetic Connection between the Sino-Tibetan Languages and the Yeniseian and North Caucasian Languages. *Dene – Sino-Caucasian Languages: Materials from the First International Interdisciplinary Symposium on Language and Prehistory*, ed. by Vitaliy Shevoroshkin, 12–41. Ann Harbor: Bochum: Brockmeyer.

Tiffou, Etienne and Y.-Ch. Morin. 1982. A Note on Split Ergativity in Burushaski. *Bulletin of the School of Oriental and African Studies* 45, no. 1: 88–94.

Tiffou, Etienne and Y.-Ch. Morin. 1993. *Hunza Proverbs*. Calgary: University of Calgary Press.

Toporov, Vladimir. 1971. Burushaski and Yeniseian Languages: Some Parallels. *Travaux Linguistiques de Prague* 4: 107–125.

Tuite, Kevin. 1998. Evidence for Prehistoric Links between the Caucasus and Central Asia: The Case of the Burushos. *The Bronze Age and Early Iron Age Peoples of Eastern Central Asia, vol. 1: Archeology, Migration and Nomadism*, ed. by V.H. Mair, pp. 447–475. (*Journal of Indo-European Studies*, Monograph 26.) Washington, DC: The Institute for the Study of Man in collaboration with the University of Pennsylvania Museum Publications.

van Driem, George. 2001. *Languages of the Himalayas: An Ethnolinguistic Handbook of the Greater Himalayan Region*. Leiden: Brill.

Verma, M. K., and Mohanan, K. P. (Eds.). (1990). *Experiencer Subjects in South Asian Languages*. Stanford, CA: Center for the Study of Language and Information, Stanford University.

Wilson, Stephen R. 1996. Verb Agreement and Case Marking in Burushaski. *Working Papers of the Summer Institute of Linguistics (North Dakota Session)* 40: 1–71.

CHAPTER 6

OTHER ISOLATED LANGUAGES OF ASIA

Stefan Georg

1 ISOLATED LANGUAGES OF ASIA

The classification of Asian languages may seem, at first sight, fairly settled and uncontroversial, but a closer look reveals that some of the bigger families, which are mostly cited
in reference works and encyclopediae, are not without problems.

Uncontroversial families are *Uralic* (*Finno-Ugric* and *Samoyedic*) in Western Siberia (and Eastern and Northern Europe); the *Turkic* family, which spreads from Eastern
Europe to the far North of Asia and China; *Mongolic* in the heart of the continent; and
Tungusic in its Northern and North-Eastern parts. The Caucasus is home to a great number
of languages, but all of them are firmly placed in one of three autochthonous genealogical
groupings. The Indian and Iranian branches of Indo-European are far from isolated as
well, and the Southern regions of the continent show big and well-established language
families such as *Dravidian*, the discontinuously distributed *Austro-Asiatic*, the somewhat
compact *Hmong-Mien* in Southern China and Indochina, the *Tai-Kadai* languages, and
the enormous *Austronesian* language family. *Chinese* (or the *Sinitic* family of languages,
as some would prefer) has for more than a century been classified together with the vast
Tibeto-Burman stock as *Sino-Tibetan*, and this is the state-of-the art according to most
linguistic and non-linguistic encyclopediae, but it should be mentioned that this hypothesis has never been without its skeptics, and that voices of dissent are and continue to be
heard. This is even more true of much disputed *Altaic*, the by-now more than one and a
half centuries old hypothesis which claims that the already mentioned Turkic, Mongolic,
and Tungusic families (and sometimes also Korean and Japanese) should be regarded as
descendants of a common ancestor (cf. Section 2.3). True *isolates* are rare, but present in
Asia. Traditionally, the isolated languages of North Asia (and some small families) are,
ever since Shrenk (1883), referred to as the "*palaeoasiatic*" (or, since they are situated in
Siberia, "*palaeosiberian*") languages, which term implies that their communities represent remnants of populations, which perhaps once occupied wider territories of the continent, and which have been reduced to their current (usually small) speaker numbers and
their confined territories by the advancement of more recent intruders – mostly speakers
of Uralic and "Altaic" languages, not to mention, of course, the historically recent, but
culturally and linguistically overwhelming, advent of Russian in the region. The traditional *palaeoasiatic* languages are *Ket* (with its extinct *Yeniseian* relatives), *Nivkh*, and
Yukaghir, and the *Chukchi-Kamchatkan* family, as well as, although now not spoken any
longer in Siberia, (Sakhalin) *Ainu*, which is treated at greater length in the chapter in this
volume by Thomas Dougherty.

The other Asian macro-region where isolated languages are found is the Indian subcontinent, or *South Asia*, where *Burushaski* of Northern Pakistan (presented by Alexander

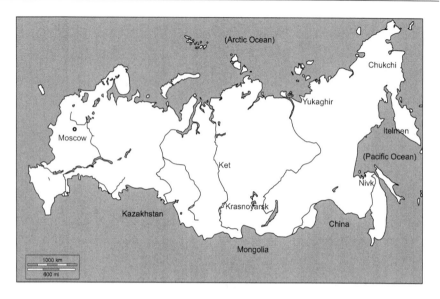

MAP 6.1 ISOLATED LANGUAGES AND MEMBERS OF SMALL FAMILIES OF NORTH ASIA

Source: Base map adapted from http://d-maps.com/carte.php?num_car=24964&lang=de.

Smith in this volume), *Kusunda* in Nepal, and the still enigmatic *Nahali/Nihali* language of West Central India have defied all attempts to subsume them in one of the bigger families of the world, although many such attempts have been undertaken and continue to be published. To these we might, with due caution, add the *Great Andamanese* language on the archipelago of this name, briefly discussed in Section 3.3.

2 ISOLATED LANGUAGES OF NORTH ASIA

2.1 Ket (Yeniseian)

The *Ket* language is the sole survivor of the *Yeniseian* (or *Yeniseic*) family of languages, which once occupied the better part of both sides of the *Yenisei* River, from its headwaters almost down to its estuary. Its true "island" position, in the middle of a typologically rather uniform "ocean" of Uralic (Samoyedic and Ob'-Ugric), Turkic, and Tungusic languages, made it the target of numerous, and mostly wildly speculative, attempts at classification, the number of which may perhaps only be rivalled by those for Basque. None of these can be regarded as successful, although no stone was left unturned in the Old World (including, of course, proposed connections with Basque, several – or all of the – Caucasian languages, Sumerian, Sino-Tibetan, Burushaski), and also in America (Dene/Athabaskan). Everything which can meaningfully be said about the classification of Ket is that it is part of a small family, which goes by the name of Yeniseic. The established family tree of those Yeniseic languages, for which some documentation is available, can be given in Figure 6.1.

As mentioned, all of these languages, with the sole exception of *Ket*, are completely extinct by now. Arin and Pumpokol died out already in the 18th century. *Kott* data (only

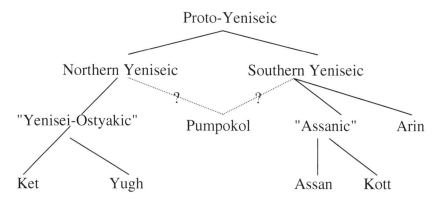

FIGURE 6.1 THE YENISEIC LANGUAGE FAMILY

words and paradigms, no texts) could still be collected by M.A. Castrén in the 1840s. *Assan* may have simply been identical with this language. Note that, in spite of the superficial resemblance, the name *Kott* is etymologically not connected with the name *Ket*; these two languages do not belong to the same subgroup of the family. *Yugh* is often referred to in the literature as *Sym-Ket*, as opposed to *Imbatsk-Ket*, after the names of two prominent rivers. It disappeared in the late 1980s. The number of persons with some degree of fluency in one of the still extant three dialects of Ket (Southern, Central, and Northern) can, with some optimism, be estimated at ca. 500 out of an ethnic population of ca. 1000. The name *Ket* is a Soviet neologism, based on the noun *keˀd* 'human'. Curiously, when using Russian, speakers often refer to their ethnic group as *ketó*, which is actually the vocative form of this noun. The name most often used for the language in Ket itself is *òstik(an) qà* 'Ostyak language', which gives some justification to the name 'Yenisei-Ostyak' found in the earlier literature; the name *Ostyak* has a variegated history as autonym and exonym in the region, and, without 'Yenisei-', *Ostyak* is mostly used for the Ob'-Ugric (Finno-Ugric, Uralic) ethnic group and language nowadays usually referred to as *Khanty*. Yugh differs from Ket mainly in terms of a handful of regular sound changes, whereas its grammatical system corresponds largely to that of Ket. Kott, the only other Yeniseian language for which more than very sketchy morphological data are available, shows a rather different typological makeup in many subsystems (e.g. a largely suffixing verbal morphology, as opposed to almost exclusively prefixing Yenisei-Ostyakic (Ket and Yugh)).

The Yeniseic family and its sole survivor stick out from their neighbouring languages, in fact from all languages and families of native Siberia, by a great number of typological peculiarities and areal singularities. These make present-day Ket a true island in this vast territory, which is mostly occupied by typically "Ural-Altaic" languages of the exclusively suffixing, agglutinative SOV type, which is so characteristic of Northern and Central Asia at large.

On the phonological level, a relatively unspectacular system of vocalic and consonantal segmental phonemes, with no "exotic" elements (but with some asymmetries in the distribution of the feature [+voice] among stops, cf. Tables 6.1 and 6.2), is accompanied by a system of *syllabic tones*, which is without parallel in all of Northern and Central Asia.

TABLE 6.1 THE CENTRAL KET VOWELS

i		*ɨ*	*u*
	e	*ə*	*o*
		a	

TABLE 6.2 THE CENTRAL KET CONSONANTS

	Labial	Alveolar	Lateral	Palatal	Velar	Uvular	Laryngeal
Stop	*b*	*t d*			*k*	***q***	
Fricative		*s*					*h*
Continuant			*l*	*j*			
Nasal	*m*	*n*			*ŋ*		

Note the absence of /p/, which is quite typical for Siberian (especially "Altaic") languages. The language lacks a phonemic /r/ (Southern Ket shows *phonetic,* flapped, [r] as the realization of intervocalic /d/). Ket phonotactics is further characterized by the avoidance of initial liquids (i.e. /l/) and the near-absence of initial nasals (/n/ and /m/), which closely resembles the similar constraint found in (the native vocabulary of) *Turkic* languages.

Ket syllabic tones manifest themselves only on monosyllabic words, most of which are nominative forms of nouns; the system consists of four tonal units, which can be symbolized as V̄ (half-long, level or slightly rising); Vʔ (short rising-falling, with glottal constriction or "creakiness"); VV (long rising-falling, lower than Vʔ); and V̇ (short, sharply falling), respectively. When suffixes are added, the distinctive prosodic quality of the root vowel is lost and gives way to a stress-like system involving the first two syllables of the phonological word (noted as V̇-V or V̇-V, for details cf. Georg 2007:47–61, and Vajda 2000).

Ket nouns show a typically Eurasian case system, with the exception that personal possession is expressed by prefixes. A representative case paradigm is that of the feminine noun *qīm* 'woman' (Table 6.3, cf. Georg 2007:104). Note that the dative, benefactive, ablative, and adessive are based on the genitive – this is found in all genders and numbers. This kind of 'two-story' case system resembles similar phenomena in some Uralic languages or, then, in Indo-European *Tokharian.* Animate nouns do not take a locative; the suffix found on inanimate nouns is *-ka.*

Grammatical gender is covert in nominative/citation forms and manifests itself in the genitive and the cases based on it: *-da* in masc. sg.; *-di* in fem. sg., neuter sg., and neuter pl.; and *-na* in masc. and fem. (= animate) pl.

Ket case suffixes are often described as *clitics,* rather than true suffixes, because they may "float", i.e. they can occur without being attached to a noun or pronoun, when this "head" is present in the immediately preceding discourse context, cf.:

suul   Ø-dīta   d[u]⁸-b³-il²-i/bed, ásle-ŋ   Ø-dīta bōn d[u]⁸-b³-il²-i/bed
sledge Ø-BENf 3-3n-Pst-make   ski-PL Ø-BENf NEG 3-3n-Pst-make
He made a sledge for her, he didn't make skis for her.

Noun plurals are mostly formed by means of the phonotactically altering suffixes *-n* and *-ŋ,* but many idiosyncratic and, for the macro-region, quite unusual techniques of

TABLE 6.3 KET NOUN INFLECTION (NOUN OF FEMININE CLASS)

	SG	PL
Nominative	qīm	qím-n
Genitive	qím-di	qím-n-a
Dative	qím-diŋa	qím-n-naŋa
Benefactive	qím-dita	qím-n-nata
Ablative	qím-diŋal	qím-n-naŋal
Adessive	qím-diŋta	qím-n-naŋta
Prosecutive	qím-bes	qím-n-bes
Instrumental	qím-as	qím-n-as
Abessive	qím-an	qím-n-an
Translative	qím-esaŋ	qím-n-esaŋ
Vocative	qim-ɔ́	qím-n-ɔ́

TABLE 6.4 POSSESSIVE PREFIXES IN KET

	SG	PL
1	b-	na-
2	k-	na-
3m	da-	na-
3f	d-	na-
3n	d-	d-

TABLE 6.5 PERSONAL PRONOUNS IN KET

	1SG	2SG	3SGm
Nominative	ād	ū(k)	bū
Genitive	āb	ūk	bú-da

plural-formation exist, including the change of root vowels ($di^{\text{ʔ}}$, pl. $da^{\text{ʔ}}n$ 'log'); tones (ēj, pl. èj 'tongue', áluk, pl. àluk 'yoke'); both (tēd, pl. tátn 'husband'); or complete suppletion (ōks, pl. $a^{\text{ʔ}}q$ 'tree'); all of these techniques are highly exceptional for languages of the Siberian and Central Asian linguistic area. This is also true of the use of prefixes for possessors (Table 6.4), which are historically and etymologically connected with the personal pronouns (Table 6.5).

   The verb is the most salient, and complicated, part of speech in Ket, and it has taken scholarship a long time to disentangle most of its intricacies. Only a rough sketch of Ket verbal morphology can be given here. Any Ket verb (cf. Table 6.6) will contain a lexical root (R), found at the end of the morpheme chain (and only followed by a subject plural marker, PL). The lexical core of the verb may be compounded, in which case one of the elements is found further left in the morpheme chain (at position P^7; this position also hosts *incorporated* elements, which may be patients/(effected) objects/targets of change or, most frequently, instruments; the highly productive *causative* marker /q/ also occupies this position). Also part of the lexical makeup of verbs are *determiners* (also known as *preverbs* or *adpositions*, in position P^5), morphemes consisting of a single consonant (k, n, h etc.), with sometimes vaguely determinable functions, but often simply lexicalized.

TABLE 6.6 THE MORPHEME POSITIONS OF KET VERBS

P^8-p^7-p^6-p^5-p^4-p^3-p^2-p^1-R-PL

P^8	subject person
P^7	lexical incorporate
P^6	subject or object person (sometimes + /determiner)
P^5	lexical determiner
P^4	subject/object person or "thematic" vowel, partially sensitive to tense
P^3	(neuter object) person (or - petrified - applicative/intensive)
P^2	tense (preterite)
P^1	subject or object person (or petrified resultative marker)
R	lexical root
PL	subject plural

The positions P^6, P^4, P^3, and P^1 host actant markers, indicating at least the person (and, sometimes, the gender) of the main actant (subject, agent), or the object/patient of transitives. However, a verb with two actant markers may cross-reference the sentential subject twice in its morpheme chain. The choice of actant markers and their distribution over the morpheme chain is largely lexically determined and leads to the classification of Ket verbs into five different *conjugations*. P^4 may also contain the "thematic" vowel /a/, whose function is unclear, but which is, when present, routinely labialized to /o/ in past tense forms. The past tense morpheme itself, in most cases /il/ or /in/, occupies position P^2, which, since P^1 is only filled in a small subset of verbs, more often than not occurs immediately before the root (R).

No Ket verb form can be correctly parsed (or formed) without recourse to one of the numerous morpho-phonotactic (sometimes referred to as "morphotactic" in the specialist literature) rules of the language. Such rules determine the *deletion* or *insertion* of vowels and/or consonants, governed by the actual presence of morphological material in a certain (and lexically defined) subset of the ten morpheme slots (and not by any purely phonological feature of the verb form). The detection of morphotactical rules by Vajda (2001a) allowed for the first time a full understanding of the surface realizations of the absolute majority of Ket verb forms, while earlier descriptions often had to go as far as to call practically every Ket verb "irregular". Georg (2007, 203–215) enumerates 11 *truncation* rules, 5 *vowel insertion* (*anaptyxis*) rules, and 12 *separator rules*. Only examples for such rules can be given here, cf. *Truncation Rule 1* (Georg 2007: 205):

> *Any P^8 subject marker (≠ 3SGf. /da-/)) loses its vowel when immediately standing before the preterite marker /il/, /in/, i.e. in the configuration P^8-P^2* – truncated material marked by []:

> *di^8-loqŋ* 'I shiver' vs. *d[i]^8-il^2- loqŋ* 'I shivered'

Another example is *Separator Rule 1* (Georg 2007: 210):

> *Any P^8 subject marker standing immediately before a R morpheme, which begins with either a vowel, or a labial, velar or uvular consonant, triggers a (j)-separator* – inserted material marked by ():

> *di^8-(j)-aq* 'I go', *di^8-(j)-bed* 'I make' vs. *di^8-təəl* 'I freeze'

The following sample paradigms illustrate an intransitive verb of "conjugation I" (Table 6.7), with only P^8 subject markers (*-loqŋ* 'shiver'); an intransitive verb of "conjugation IV" (Table 6.8), with P^8 subject markers and "coreferential" (not "reflexive") subject markers in P^1 (*-tan* 'to stop, remain standing'); and finally a partial paradigm of a transitive verb of conjugation IV with subject marking in P^8 and P^1 and object markers in P^6 (*-qa* 'to sell', all forms are 2nd person subject 'you sell me, him, her, us etc.').

The imperative forms, here and everywhere else in the language, always contain the preterite morpheme (here /il/ and its morphotactic variants).

TABLE 6.7 SAMPLE PARADIGM OF A KET INTRANSITIVE VERB OF CONJUGATION I

	Present tense	*Past tense*
1SG	di^8-*loqŋ*	$d[i]^8$-il^2-*loqŋ*
2SG	ku^8-*loqŋ*	$k[u]^8$-il^2-*loqŋ*
3SGm	du^8-*loqŋ*	$d[u]^8$-il^2-*loqŋ*
3SGf	$də^8$-*loqŋ*	da^8-il^2-*loqŋ*
1PL	di^8-*loqŋ-in*	$d[i]^8$-il^2-*loqŋ-in*
2PL	ku^8-*loqŋ-in*	$k[u]^8$-il^2-*loqŋ-in*
3PL	du^8-*loqŋ-in*	$d[u]^8$-il^2-*loqŋ-in*
	imperative singular	imperative plural
	il-loqŋ	il^2-*loqŋ-in*

TABLE 6.8 SAMPLE PARADIGM OF A KET INTRANSITIVE VERB OF CONJUGATION IV WITH TWO SUBJECT MARKERS

	Present tense	*Past tense*
1SG	$d[i]^8$-a^4-$d[i]^1$-*tan*	$d[i]^8$-o^4-$[i]l^2$-di^1-*tan*
2SG	$k[u]^8$-a^4-ku^1-*tan*	$k[u]^8$-o^4-$[i]l^2$-ku^1-*tan*
3SGm	$d[u]^8$-a^4-(j)-a^1-*tan*	$d[u]^8$-o^4-$[i]l^2$-a^1-*tan*
3SGf	da^8-a^4-(j)-a^1-*tan*	da^8-o^4-$[i]l^2$-a^1-*tan*
1PL	$d[i]^8$-a^4-$daŋ^1$-*tan*	$d[i]^8$-o^4-$[i]l^2$-$daŋ^1$-*tan*
2PL	$k[u]^8$-a^4-$kaŋ^1$-*tan*	$k[u]^8$-o^4-$[i]l^2$-$kaŋ^1$-*tan*
3PL	$d[u]^8$-a^4-(j)-$aŋ^1$-*tan*	$d[u]^8$-o^4-$[i]l^2$-$aŋ^1$-*tan*

TABLE 6.9 SAMPLE PARADIGM OF A KET TRANSITIVE VERB OF CONJUGATION IV WITH TWO SUBJECT MARKERS AND ONE OBJECT MARKER IN P^6 (SUBJECT 2ND SG.)

	present tense	*past tense*
1SG	$k[u]^8$-*bo*/k^6-ku^1-*qa*	$k[u]^8$-*bo*/$[k]^6$-$[i]l^2$-ku^1-*qa*
2SG	–	–
3SGm	$k[u]^8$-*o*/k^6-ku^1-*qa*	$k[u]^8$-*o*/$[k]^6$-$[i]l^2$-ku^1-*qa*
3SGf	$k[u]^8$-*u*/k^6-ku^1-*qa*	$k[u]^8$-*o*/$[k]^6$-$[i]l^2$-ku^1-*qa*
1PL	$k[u]^8$-*dəŋ*/$[k]^6$-ku^1-*qa*	$k[u]^8$-*dəŋ*/$[k]^6$-il^2-ku^1-*qa*
2PL	–	–
3PL	$k[u]^8$-*o*/*ŋ*/$[k]^6$-ku^1-*qa*	$k[u]^8$-*o*/*ŋ*/$[k]^6$-il^2-ku^1-*qa*

This notation includes, for transparency's sake, phonetic material elided by morphotactic rules in square brackets and material added by such rules in round brackets; thus, the surface realization of the 3PL form in the present tense column of Table 6.8 is /dajaŋtan/ and that of the 3SGf form in the past tense is /dolatan/.

A comprehensive guide to the literature on Yeniseian is Vajda (2001b), and descriptive grammars of Ket include Werner (1997a), Vajda (2004), and Georg (2007). The lexical stock of all known Yeniseic languages, past and present, is collected in Werner (2002), with an English index). Data on Yugh are practically only found in Russian and German publications, an exception is Werner (2012), which also contains verbal paradigms. Castrén's Kott data from the 1840s are analyzed and discussed in Werner (1997b).

2.2 Nivkh

Nivkh – ethnic autonym ñivxgu (Amur), ñiɣvŋun (Eastern Sakhalin) – or *Gilyak*, as it used to be called in the earlier literature, is a small cluster of two fairly divergent variants, which may or may not be viewed as separate languages; for those who see these varieties as separate languages, the name *Amuric* has been proposed as that of the small family.

The two main variants, *Amur Nivkh* (in the vicinity of the estuary of the Amur River in the Russian Far East) and (*Eastern*, *Northern*, and *Southern*) *Sakhalin Nivkh* (on Sakhalin Island in the Sea of Okhotsk), are reported as mutually unintelligible; differences pervade all linguistic subsystems; Table 6.13 below shows some cognates and non-cognates of these two main variants.

Out of a population of ca. 5,000 ethnic Nivkhs, at most 700 individuals still use the language (ca. 200 on the mainland/Amur and ca. 500 on Sakhalin), which translates into a language retention rate of only ca. 14% (data from 1926 report a language retention rate until then of approximately 100%).

Phonologically, Nivkh sticks out from all its neighbours (Ainu, Tungusic languages, Japanese) by a particularly rich consonant system with an areally unusual contrast of voiced, voiceless, and voiceless aspirated stops and an unusually large inventory of voiced and voiceless continuants, cf. Table 6.10.

TABLE 6.10 THE CONSONANT PHONEMES OF AMUR NIVKH

	Labial	Labiodental	Dental	Palatal	Velar	Uvular	Laryngeal
Voiceless stop	p		t	t'	k	q	
Voicel. asp. stop	p'		t'	č'	k'	q'	
Voiced stop	b		d	d'	g	ġ	
Voiceless fricative		f	s		x	χ	h
Voiced fricative		v	z		γ	ĝ	
Nasal	m		n	ñ	ŋ		
Sonant			l	j			
Voiceless trill			ř				
Voiced trill			r				

Source: After Gruzdeva 1998: 10.

The (Eastern) Sakhalin dialect adds to this the bilabial approximant /w/.

Another areally salient feature of Nivkh phonology is its tolerance for word-initial and, especially, word-final consonant clusters (cf. Eastern Sakhalin *p 'riɣŋ azmt'* 'lover', *mχokr muɣf* 'holiday', *řəřkř* 'key').

Nivkh is widely known for its system of initial consonant mutations, which require the systematic alternation of initial consonants in reaction to the final consonant of a preceding morpheme. The consonants (all consonant phonemes, except the nasals, sonants and the laryngeal /h/) are grouped into *alternation series* like /t ~ r ~ d/ (there are about 20 of such series). A noun or verb which (outside of any syntactic context, as "citation form") begins with the first member of such a set changes this anlaut in syntactic constructions (not in accidental juxtapositions) with preceding morphemes (attributes in the case of nouns, direct objects in the case of verbs) to one of the other members of the set. The operating rules are originally assimilatory in nature, but the loss of final consonants and other processes have partly obscured the original contexts. Examples for such alternations are, from the Amur variant (Gruzdeva 1998, 14; cf. also Mattissen and Drossard 1998, 9f., Comrie 1981, 267, Beffa 1982, 60–64 for more in-depth treatments and attempts to rationalize the system):

/p ~ v ~ b/

　　pəñx 'soup' –

　　t'us pəñx 'beef soup', *čo vəñx* 'fish soup', *ova bəñx* 'flour soup' (cf. East Sakhalin *ofaŋ*)

/z ~ t' ~ d'/

　　zosq- 'to break' –

　　laq zosq- 'break a ski', *luvr t'osq-* 'break a spoon', *ŋir d'osq-* 'break a cup' (East Sakhalin *ŋirŋ*)

A peculiar consequence of this system is that all transitive verbs begin with a fricative phoneme, obviously due to the generalization of the form with preceding object, cf. *pəkz-* 'to get lost' versus *vəkz-* 'to lose' (Gruzdeva 1998, 12).

The personal pronouns of Nivkh are given in Table 6.11.

TABLE 6.11 PERSONAL PRONOUNS IN THREE NIVKH DIALECTS

	Amur	*East Sakhalin*	*North Sakhalin*
1SG	*ñi*	*ñi*	*ñi*
2SG	*či*	*či*	*či*
3SG	*if*	*jaŋ*	*i*
1DU exclusive	*megi/mege*	*meŋ*	*memak*
1PL exclusive	*ñəŋ*	*ñiŋ*	*ñəŋ*
1PL inclusive	*mer/mir*	*meřn/miřn/min*	*mer/mir*
2PL	*čəŋ*	*čin*	*čin*
3PL	*imŋ/ivŋ/imɣ*	*iřn*	*in*

Source: Gruzdeva 2001, 361.

Nivkh nouns distinguish, by suffixes, up to ten cases, as shown in Table 6.12.

TABLE 6.12 NIVKH NOUN CASES (∂T(∂)K 'FATHER')

	Amur	East Sakhalin
Nominative	ətək-Ø	ətk-Ø
Dative-accusative	ətək-aχ	ətk-aχ
Comparative	ətək-ək	ətk-ak
Dative-allative	ətək-roχ	ətk-roχ
Locative	ətək-uin	-
Ablative	ətək-ux	ətk-ux
Limitative ('until')	ətək-roχo, ətək-řəxə	ətk-roχo
Prosecutive ('along')	ətək-uχə	-
Instrumental	ətək-xir	ətk-xir, ətk-xis
Vocative	ətək-a	ətk-a

Source: Savel'eva/Taksami 1970, 514–515.

The plural suffix -ku/-γu precedes the case markers.

TABLE 6.13 LEXICAL COGNATES AND NON-COGNATES IN THE MAIN NIVKH VARIANTS

	Amur Nivkh	Eastern Sakhalin Nivkh
'nest'	ŋəvi	ŋavi
'reindeer'	č'olŋi	tlaŋi
'wolf'	liγs	liγř
'child'	oγla	eγlŋ
'search'	ŋəŋd'	ŋanγd
'man'	utku	azmət'
'woman'	umgu	řaŋy
'snow'	ŋaqr	q'avi
'who'	aŋ	nař
'what'	sid'	nud

Nivkh has an unusually complex numeral system, which distinguishes at least 24 series of numerals according to the type of the counted objects. Thus, the numeral 'three' has the surface forms (Amur):

t'em (boats)
t'ar (dried fish)
t'a (fathoms)
t'ŋaq (crops)
t'for (nets)
t'eu (eyes of the fishing net)
t'eřqe (strips)
t'e(γ)it (fingers when measuring the thickness of fat)
t'la (poles)
t'fasq (paired objects)
t'rax (thin, flat objects)
t'aqr (people)

t'eř (sledges)
t'ma (a measure, span)
t'əγvi (bundles of dog food)
t'χos (crops, diff. kind)
t'fat (ropes for hunting)
t'eo (fishing nets)
t'laj (a. k. o. ropes)
t'ezču (families)
t'avr (places)
t'et' (wooden boards)
t'ex (long objects)
t'or (animals)
(after Panfilov 1968, 414–415)

In some, but by no means in all, of these numerals, the noun for the counted object can still be discerned in the rhyming portion of the word.

TABLE 6.14 IMPERATIVE SUFFIXES IN AMUR NIVKH

1SG	*-nəkta/-əxta*
1DU	*-nəte/-nte*
1PL	*-da*
2SG	*-ja/-j*
2PL	*-ve/-be-/-pe*
3SG/PL	*-ġaro* (East Sakhalin has a separate 2PL: *-ġarġaro*)

Source: Gruzdeva 1998, 34.

The Nivkh verb is morphologically complex and predominantly suffixing (object, reflexive, and reciprocal markers are prefixed) and has morphological markers for various categories of *mode* (indicative, imperative), *aktionsart* (completive, habitual, progressive, iterative etc.), *tense, causative, evidentiality, number, person*, and a particularly rich inventory of non-finite forms or *converbs*. Person marking is typologically peculiar, since it is not found in finite (indicative) verb forms, but only in imperatives and, which is areally and generally quite unusual, in a subset of the numerous Nivkh converb forms. Table 6.14 shows the person-inflected imperative paradigm (Amur, dual number is only found with 1st person).

The most comprehensive grammar of Nivkh is still Panfilov (1962–1965). Gruzdeva (1998) is a more accessible, but shorter and somewhat eclectic, treatment. The standard dictionary is Savel'eva and Taksami (1970) (Amur dialect with Eastern Sakhalin equivalents). A comprehensive treatment of Nivkh syntax with much information beyond this, is Nedjalkov and Otaina (2013).

2.3 Problematic or controversial cases – Yukaghir, Itel'men, Korean, Japanese

The highly endangered *Yukaghir* language of North-Eastern Siberia is routinely included among the (mostly isolated) Palaeoasiatic languages as well. While it is true that the hypothesis of a (possibly only very distant) relationship with the *Uralic* (Finno-Ugric and Samoyedic) family of languages is often mentioned in the literature ("Uralo-Yukaghir"), the recent thorough study by Aikio (2014) shows that this has little basis in fact and should probably be abandoned.

Apart from this, the two main variants of Yukaghir are very often regarded as two different languages, *Kolyma* Yukaghir (or *Odul*) and *Tundra* Yukaghir (or *Wadul*), both today with less than 100 speakers, and Kolyma Yukaghir with a mere 30, and the small family is, then, sometimes called *"Odulic"*. In terms of morphology, the unity of the two Yukaghir variants is quite obvious and justifies the treatment as dialects of a single language, but great differences separate the lexical makeup of both, as evidenced by the following examples from basic vocabulary (Table 6.15, after Nikolaeva and Khelimskij 1997: 155). Table 6.16 shows the basic nominal case suffixes (after Krejnovich 1958: 36), which are clearly cognate.

The typological hallmark of both Yukaghir (or Odulic) dialects/languages is an intricate system of (subject, object, verb) *focus*, with morphological marking on nouns and verbs, cf. (Kolyma, Nikolaeva and Khelimskij 1997: 160, focussed constituent highlighted):

TABLE 6.15 LEXICAL DIFFERENCES IN KOLYMA AND TUNDRA YUKAGHIR BASIC VOCABULARY

	Kolyma Yukaghir	Tundra Yukaghir
one	irkēj	mōrqōñ
two	ataqlōj	kijōñ
five	iñhañbōj	imd'ald'añ
many	niŋel	pojōl
all	t'umu	jawnə
day	pod'erqə	t'ajləŋ
sun	jelōd'ə	jerpəjəŋ
water	ōd'ī	lawjəŋ
fish	anil	al'həŋ
reindeer	at'ə	il'eŋ
dog	pubel	laməŋ
person	šoromə	ködeŋ
people	omnī	t'īŋ
eye	aŋd'ə	jōd'īŋ
tooth	todī	sal'hərīŋ
night	emil	t'iŋit'əl
foot	nojl	t'ohul
name	ñū	kirijəŋ
to sit	modo-	sahañe-
to kill	kuledə-	puñī-
to die	amdə-	jabə-
to know	leidī-	kurilī-
to drink	ožə-	law-

TABLE 6.16 NOMINAL CASE SUFFIXES IN THE TWO MAIN VARIANTS OF YUKAGHIR

	Kolyma Yukaghir	Tundra Yukaghir
Nominative	(zero)	(zero)
Dative	-ŋin	-ŋin'
Instrumental	-le	-lek
Locative	-ge	-γa
Prolative	-gen	-γan
Ablative	-get	-γat

mət modojə	'I *am sitting*.'
mətək modol	'*I* am sitting.'
mēmēt'en šoromələ kudedəm	'The bear *killed* the person.'
mēmēt'en šoromələk kudedəmlə	'The bear killed *the person*.'
mēmēt'elək šoromələ kudedəl	'*The bear* killed the person.'

The rather complicated system of Yukaghir focus has been repeatedly, and extensively, treated in the linguistic literature, cf. Maslova (1997), Schmalz (2012).

Another *Palaeoasiatic* group, this time certainly a family, are the *Chukchi-Kamchatkan* languages, comprised of *Chukchi*, *Koryak*, *Alyutor*, and (extinct) *Kerek* in the far North-East of Russia (with Chukchi as the northeasternmost language of Eurasia, facing Alaska over Bering Strait, and the other languages found further south, centering on Kamchatka). In Georg and Volodin (1999), it was argued that its fifth member, *Itel'men* (or *Kamchadal*, in the southwest of Kamchatka), should, perhaps, be taken out of this family and given the status of a language isolate. Though the differences between Itel'men and the *Chukchi-Koryak* (Chukchi, Koryak, Kerek, Alyutor) languages remain significant and deserve further study, it is possibly safe to say that our skepticism was not justified, and that Itel'men is best regarded as a – highly aberrant – member of this family after all.

The status of *Korean* and *Japanese*, both of course major languages of the world (with upwards of 78 and 127 million speakers, respectively) and well studied from all angles, needs to be briefly discussed here.

First of all, it should be mentioned that both are actually members of (small) language families – Japanese forms, together with the languages of the *Ryukyuan Islands* (with *Okinawan* being the best-known variant, cf. Michinori and Pellard 2010), the *Japonic* family, and the highly aberrant characteristics of the Korean "dialects" of the island of *Jeju* in the south and the *Hamkyeng Mountains* in the nort-east justify their treatment as languages in their own right and thus speaking of a "Koreanic" language family. Japanese may have a linguistic relative on the Asian continent, but the language of the *Koguryo* empire (37 BCE – 668 CE) is only known from small wordlists, and the controversial discussion about their linguistic interpretation is still going on (for the position that the Koguryo language is an early form of *Japonic* cf. Beckwith 2004, and for the opinion that it is *Koreanic* instead, cf. Vovin 2005a).

Apart from this, it is true that both languages or small families have often been regarded as genealogically related to each other or, more frequently, as members of a larger grouping, "*Altaic*", which is said to consist of the *Turkic*, the *Mongolic*, and the *Manchu-Tungusic* languages. If validated, this would be one of the major language families of Eurasia, ranging from Eastern Europe (with the westernmost fringes of Turkic) to the Pacific Ocean. However, for many specialists, it is by no means validated, and for a sizable number of informed observers, the Altaic hypothesis is outright wrong and the numerous commonalities between the languages involved are best explained in an areal framework. The debate, often hotly conducted, continues with unabated vigour. General-interest (and also some linguistic) encyclopediae and handbooks very often treat "Altaic" (with or without Korean and Japanese) as an unquestioned given, but the reality is certainly much more complex.

For a first approximation to this highly complicated and involved scholarly discussion of the classificatory issues surrounding Korean and Japanese (and, of course, the other "Altaic" languages), readers may turn to Martin (1966, *pro* Korean-Japanese); Miller (1996, *pro* Korean and Japanese as Altaic); Starostin (1991, *idem*); Robbeets (2005, *idem*); Georg (2008, a review of the latter, *contra* Altaic); Vovin (2005b, *contra* Altaic); Vovin (2010, *contra* Korean-Japanese); and Georg (2011, *contra* Altaic). If anything, the case of Japanese and Korean shows that isolated languages are by no means always obscure, hardly known, and receding languages in difficult-to-access regions of the world.

3 ISOLATED LANGUAGES OF SOUTH ASIA

Apart from *Burushaski* in the Karakorum, at least two more languages (and perhaps a third one) of the Indian Subcontinent must be mentioned as linguistic isolates here, *Kusunda* of Nepal and *Nahali* of Madhya Pradesh and Maharashtra (India), and possibly *Great Andamanese*.

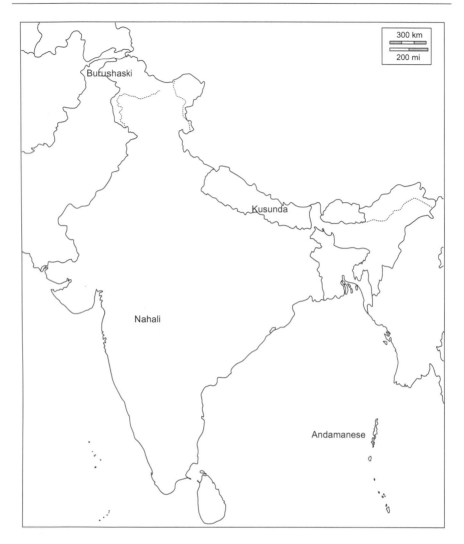

MAP 6.2 ISOLATED LANGUAGES OF SOUTH ASIA

Source: Base map adapted from http://d-maps.com/carte.php?num_car=285&lang=de.

3.1 Kusunda

The elusive *Kusunda* (or *Ban Raja* 'Forest King') language is spoken in Nepal's mid-Western Gorkha district by, today, at best a handful of persons (certainly less than ten). It has been known at least since the mid-19th century (Hodgson 1848, 1857–1858), but the first usable study of it became only available in the late 20th century (Reinhard and Toba 1970).

No linguist was able to establish any contact with Kusunda speakers for some decades to follow this, and the language and its speakers were widely regarded as extinct. In 2004, a team led by David E. Watters managed to locate some still competent speakers of Kusunda, which led to the publication of a book-length treatment of this hitherto virtually unknown language (Watters 2006), which is the source of all information and examples given here.

No attempt to find linguistic relatives for Kusunda has been successful (and those which were published did not go beyond typically macro-comparativist claims that what is – somehow – similar must be related, mostly involving some vague notion of a connection with putative "Indo-Pacific" or the like). The sudden increase of available linguistic data in the early years of this century did not change this situation – Kusunda is a linguistic isolate and also a language with an areally highly unusual typological makeup.

Tables 6.17 and 6.18 illustrate the phonological system of the language.

Kusunda nouns have no gender/class system and no marker of plurality. Table 6.19 illustrates the suffixal noun case system of the language (Watters 2006: 50–56, cf. also Kausen 2013: 605).

TABLE 6.17 KUSUNDA VOWEL PHONEMES

i			*u*
	ə		
e			*o*
	a		

Source: Watters 2006: 24.

TABLE 6.18 KUSUNDA CONSONANT PHONEMES

	Labial	Apical	Laminal	Velar	Uvular	Glottal
Voiceless stop	*p*	*t*		*k*	*q*	*ʔ*
Voiceless aspir. stop	*pʰ*	*tʰ*		*kʰ*	*qʰ*	
Voiced stop	*b*	*d*		*g*	*ɢ (ʕ)*	
Voiced aspir. stop	*bʰ*	*dʰ*		*gʰ*		
Fricative		*s*			*(χ)*	
Voiceless affricate		*ts*	*(tʃ)*			
Voiceless aspir. affr.		*tsʰ*				
Voiced affricate		*dz*				
Voiced aspir. affricate		*dzʰ*				
Nasal	*m*	*n*	*(ɲ)*	*ŋ*	*ɴ*	
Lateral		*l*				
Rhotic		*r*				
Semi-vowel	*w*		*y*			

Source: Watters 2006: 32, elements in brackets are of somewhat doubtful phonemic status.

TABLE 6.19 KUSUNDA CASE MARKERS

Nominative	*(zero)*
Genitive	*-yi/-ye; -i/-e*
Accusative-dative	*-da*
Locative I	*-da*
Locative II	*-ga/-gə*
Ablative	*-əna*
Allative	*-a*
Comitative	*-ma*

The "locative I" suffix is formally identical with the accusative-dative marker but routinely used as a locative with some nouns, such as 'road' (*un-da* 'on the road') or 'forest'. The "locative II" seems to be the general locative marker. The *-a/-ə* contrast follows an as-yet only imperfectly understood pattern of (high-low) vowel harmony.

Although surrounded by (Indo-Aryan and Tibeto-Burman) languages with at least some degree of ergativity, there seems to be no trace of this alignment pattern in Kusunda.

Kusunda verbs are inflected according to two fundamentally different patterns, of which one ("class I") marks the category of (subject) person by *prefixes*, and the other ("class II") by *suffixes* – all other categories (number, realis/irrealis, tense) are exclusively suffixal. Class I verbs have no tense marking but have a *realis* form which covers present and past time reference, as opposed to an *irrealis* form, which covers future time and possibility. Class II verbs have a third form for *past tense* only. The realis-irrealis distinction is perceived by Watters as the older and more fundamental dichotomy, whereas class II "past" gives the impression of having been secondarily added to the system. *Past* forms have an "unequivocal past-completive reading, while *realis* is used more frequently in utterances with a kind of 'neutral' or 'timeless' sense" (Watters 2006, 66–67), cf. the following example (*ņ* marks a 'syllabic' articulation of the apical nasal, which is not given phonemic status but routinely written as such by Watters and his colleagues):

(a)   *pyana   tsi wi a-t-ņ   təīna ts-ip-du*
       yesterday I house build-1-REAL today 1-sleep-IRREAL
       'Yesterday, I built a house, today I will sleep.'

(b)   *pyana   tsi wi a-d-i   təīna ts-ip-du*
       yesterday I house build-1-PAST today 1-sleep-IRREAL
       'Yesterday, I built (finished) a house, today I will sleep.'

The two basic patterns of person marking, prefixing in class I and suffixing in class II, are illustrated in Tables 6.20 and 6.21; the order of affixes in class I is: *person marker*-ROOT-(*plural marker*: -*da*-)-*mode marker*; in class II verbs, which are always transitive, it is: ROOT-*transitiviser* (-*a*-, identical with the verbal root for 'to make')-*person marker-mode/number (portmanteau) marker*.

The *irrealis* mode is distinguished from realis by changing the final morpheme of the chain to -*du* (SG) and -*dak* (PL) in class I and to -*u* (SG) and -*ək* (PL) in class II. The distinct *past tense* suffixes in class II are -*di* (SG) and -*dei* (PL).

Some highly frequent verbs like 'go' and 'come', all of class I, distinguish irrealis from realis by a process called *mutation* (Watters 2006: 68). This is a non-segmental process, by which "all consonants and vowels used for the irrealis form are shifted back one point of articulation – apical becomes laminal, velar becomes uvular, *ə* becomes *a*, and *u* becomes *o*", cf.:

(a)   Realis   *tsi ts-əg-ən*   'I went'
       Irrealis   *tʃi tʃ-aG-an*   'I am going'

(b)   Realis   *nu n-əg-ən*   'you went'
       Irrealis   *nu ɲ-aG-an*   'you are going'

This process is mainly found in the realis-irrealis distinction of some verbs but does occur also elsewhere in the grammar of the language.

TABLE 6.20 KUSUNDA PERSON AND NUMBER MARKING IN CLASS I VERBS (*REALIS MODE*)

	'to eat'	'to sleep'	'to come'	'to go'
1SG	t-əm-ən	ts-ip-ŋ	t-ug-un	ts-əg-ən
1PL	t-əm-da-n	ts-ip-da-n	t-ug-da-n	ts-iʔ-da-n
2SG	n-əm-ən	n-ip-ŋ	n-ug-un	n-əg-ən
2PL	n-əm-da-n	n-ip-da-n	nug-da-n	n-iʔ-da-n
3SG	g-əm-ən	g-ip-ŋ	ug-ən/ugi	d-əg-ən/d-əg-əi
3PL	g-əm-da-n	g-ip-da-n	u-dəi	d-əg-əi

Source: Watters 2006: 60.

TABLE 6.21 KUSUNDA PERSON AND NUMBER MARKING IN CLASS II VERBS

	'to buy'
1SG	dza-a-t-ŋ
1PL	dza-a-d-ən
2SG	dza-a-n-ŋ
2PL	dza-a-n-ən
3SG	dza-əg-ən
3PL	dza-əg-ən

Source: Watters 2006: 61.

Apart from Watters (2006), Pokharel (2005) contains useful information on Kusunda.

3.2 Nahali

The *Nahali* (or *Nihali*) language is severely underdescribed. While works (of varying quality) on its possible external relations are available, a thorough description of its phonology and morphology is still lacking. It is not even possible to present a full account of the affixes and processes that make up the Nahali verb. The language is spoken by, perhaps, ca. 2,000 individuals of the ca. 5,000 members of the ethnic group (which refers to itself as *Kalto*) in the Gawilgarh Hills in Madhya Pradesh and Maharashtra, Central India. Most remaining speakers are bilingual in *Korku* (Munda) and/or *Marathi* (Indo-Aryan) or local variants of *Hindi*. The Nahali language has so far resisted all attempts to classify it with other languages of the Indian subcontinent and beyond (Munda/Austroasiatic being the grouping mentioned most often), and the very complicated (and at times possibly traumatic) sociolinguistic history of its speakers led to a linguistic system which gives a patchwork-like impression of Munda, Dravidian, and also Indo-Aryan elements. This goes so far that it has been claimed that Nahali is no "natural" language at all, but nothing more than an "argot," composed of heterogeneous elements, and not transmitted as a first language. The recent summary by Zide (2008: 772ff) concludes, not without due caution, that (my rephrasing, SG) (a) Nahali goes back to an autochthonous language in Western Central India, which was not related to any known family of the continent and which first (b) underwent some influence from early (pre-Korku or non-Korku) Munda, when the ancestors of the present *Kalto* were still a vigorous and belligerent community. In phase (c), which may have begun around 1800 CE, their society underwent a catastrophic breakdown due to intentional violent acts by the Moghul state and/or other regional powers against the Kalto but also due to diseases and famines, which forced the survivors of this ethnic group into an asymmetric symbiosis with the Munda speaking Korku, on whom they are almost completely dependent with respect to their economy. This process may have led to the breakup of the original morphosyntax of Nahali and opened the gates for a now massive influx of foreign lexical elements, mostly from Southern Munda. Phase (d) would, then, be characterized by a "creole-like" restructuring of the language, with foreign morphological elements and a continuing heavy relexification from Korku/Munda. The resulting Nahali language, then, may have been used as a secret speech by some of its speakers, and it may also have undergone "argot-style speech deformation in some of the lexicon" – note that this assumption does not make the Nahali language "simply an argot, and not a 'natural' language".

At any rate, the lexicon (and the little that is known of the morphology) of Nahali shows an unusually extensive influence of practically all historically and contemporarily adjacent language families. Kuiper (1962) estimates that the Nahali lexicon is composed of approximately 40% Munda (mostly Korku) elements, 9% come from Dravidian, 2% from Tibeto-Burman (this number can probably be dismissed, the comparisons mentioned being most likely spurious), 20% Indo-Aryan (Hindi and Marathi), and 25% "unknown." This last figure would then represent the truly autochthonous Nahali lexical stock. Table 6.22 lists a few of these lexical items (from Kuiper 1962, cf. Kausen 2013: 621).

Nahali has a system of suffixal noun cases, which may be summarized as in Table 6.23 (Kuiper 1962: 20).

TABLE 6.22 POSSIBLY   AUTOCHTHONOUS NAHALI LEXICAL ITEMS

'to die'	betṭo-
'to give'	ma-
'to kill'	paḍa-
'today'	bay
'finger'	akhaṇḍi
'eye'	jiki
'water'	joppo
'egg'	kãllen
'woman'	kõl
'fish'	cãn

TABLE 6.23 NAHALI NOMINAL CASE SUFFIXES

Nominative	(zero)
Genitive-accusative	-n(a)
Dative	-ke/-ki/-ge
Ablative	-kon

Some of these suffixes may or may not have comparanda in Munda and possibly in Dravidian. The personal pronouns clearly show the influence of Dravidian languages (Table 6.24, Kuiper 1962: 27ff), which otherwise seem to have contributed relatively little to the Nahali lexicon.

TABLE 6.24 NAHALI PERSONAL PRONOUNS (SINGULAR ONLY)

	1SG	*2SG*
Nominative	*j(u)ō*	*nē*
Genitive	*eṅge*	*nē, nēne*
Accusative	*(h)eṅgen*	*nēne-n*
Dative	*eṅg-ke*	*nē-ke*
Ablative	*eṅge-kon*	-

All forms in this paradigm, with the exception of the Nominative 1SG, very closely resemble (and 1SG oblique forms are practically identical with) the respective pronominal forms in the North Dravidian languages *Kurukh* and *Malto*. By way of an analogy, the case of Samoyedic *Enets* in Northern Siberia may be mentioned, which clearly borrowed its second and third person pronouns from *Ket* (cf. Siegl 2008) but shows little influence from that language in other parts of its lexicon.

The morphology of the Nahali verb is hardly known, and the available data allow only tentative identifications; thus, the language seems to have (Kuiper 1962: 31–35) a causative suffix *-en-*, an imperative marker *-ki* (also found in Dravidian *Kurukh*), a habitual present in *-ka/-ke*, a future tense marker *-ken*, as yet poorly understood past tense markers (*-ya*, *-(y)i*, *-ka* (?)), and an absolutive (converb) suffix in *-ḍo*.

For any progress on the understanding of, first, the synchrony and then, possibly, the history of Nahali, the availability of fresh and coherent data is absolutely indispensable. Kuiper's (1962) comparative study had to base itself on the problematic, and partly certainly incorrect, material of the *Linguistic Survey of India* (with a single biblical text, cf. Grierson 1906) and the short paper by Bhattacharya (1957). It may be safe to say that Nahali has possibly received more work which tried to pigeonhole it into one of the established or hypothetical language families of the world than descriptive work or field studies, which alone would allow us to speak about these questions in an informed way.

3.3 Great Andamanese

The autochthonous languages of the *Andaman Islands* in the Indian Ocean are today spoken by approximately 530 persons (Abbi 2006). Of these, *Jarawa* (Rutland, South Andaman, and Middle Andaman Islands, approximately 250 speakers) and *Onge* (Little Andaman Island) form an uncontroversial language family (called the *Ang* family by Abbi 2008). *Great Andamanese* is, historically, a group of at least ten tribal languages (*Aka-Cari, Aka-Kora, Aka-Bo, Aka-Jeru* on North Andaman; *Aka-Kede, Oko-Juwoi, Aka-Kol* on Middle Andaman; *A-Pucikwar* and *Aka-Bea* on South Andaman; and *Akar-Bale* on Ritchie's Archipelago). This family has been repeatedly declared extinct in the past, but according to Abbi (2008: 792), eight speakers, not all of them fluent, spoke, at the time of her fieldwork, what she calls "a kind of mixed language derivative of these varieties" or, more precisely, of at least the four variants/dialects/languages: *Kora, Jeru, Cari,* and *Bo*. On the basis of her own field materials and available older data, Abbi concludes that this "Great Andamanese" cluster is genetically unrelated to the *Ang*-languages and that it has to be regarded as another linguistic isolate of South Asia. Apart from showing wide-reaching typological differences from *Angic*, which as such of course cannot support a negative judgement on genetic relatedness, Great Andamanese shows a very different lexicon as opposed to Jarawa and Onge and offers little which could be

TABLE 6.25 PERSONAL PRONOUNS IN JARAWA, ONGE, AND GREAT ANDAMANESE

	Onge	Jarawa	Great Andamanese
1SG	*mi̇*	*mi ~ ma ~ m*	*tʰu*
1PL	*eṭi*	-	*ma*
1PL incl.	*eṭa-koṭoṭ*	-	*meŋ*
2SG	*ɲi*	*ɲi ~ ɲa ~ ni ~ na*	*ŋu*
2PL	*ni*	-	*ŋilie*
3SG	*gi*	*li ~ hi ~ h*	*ḍu* (distal), *kʰudi* (prox.)
3PL	*ekʷi*	-	*ḍuniyo* (distal), *diya* (prox.)

Source: Abbi 2008, 803–805.

meaningfully compared in defence of a wider Andamanese family. Table 6.25 shows the personal pronouns of Jarawa, Onge, and Great Andamanese (Jarawa has no distinct plural forms of pronouns; Great Andamanese has actually a larger system, with distal/ proximative, visible/invisible and honorific forms) to illustrate some of the differences, but it goes without saying that a claim of non-relationship must be backed up by more, and deeper, investigations.

Whatever the ultimate status of Great Andamanese may be, it is quite certain that the Andaman Islands are, apart from the languages mentioned, home to perhaps the "most isolated language of them all", *Sentinelese*. The island of *North Sentinel* is known to be inhabited by people anthropologically close to the population of the other Andaman Islands, yet they fiercely refuse to be contacted by any outsiders, and the Indian government has decided to respect this demonstrated wish and to disallow all attempts to change this state of affairs. The number of the Sentinelese is estimated at about 150 individuals, and the default assumption is that they speak a single language. This language is (and will probably remain) unknown, as are, consequently, its possible relationships to other languages of the world. It may, thus, be just another Andamanese language, it may be exclusively related to Great Andamanese, it may be related to some other language of the greater region, or, then, to none at all.

A comprehensive overview of the Andamanese languages is Abbi (2006).

Abbreviations:

1	first person
2	second person
3	third person
affr.	affricate
aspir.	aspirated
BEN	benefactive
f/fem.	feminine
DU	dual
incl.	inclusive
m/masc.	masculine
n	neuter
NEG	negation
P	position class
PL/pl.	plural

prox.   proximal
Pst   past
R   root
SG/sg.   singular
voicel.   voiceless

REFERENCES

Abbi, Anvita. 2006. *Endangered Languages of the Andaman Islands*. München/ Newcastle: LINCOM EUROPA

Abbi, Anvita. 2009. Is Great Andamanese Genealogically and Typologically Distinct from Onge and Jarawa? *Language Sciences* 31: 798–812.

Aikio, Ante. 2014. The Uralo-Yukaghir Lexical Correspondences: Genetic Inheritance, Language Contact or Chance Resemblance? *Finnisch-Ugrische Forschungen* 62: 7–76

Beckwith, Christopher. 2004. *Koguryo, the Language of Japan's Continental Relatives: An Introduction to the Historical-Comparative Study of the Japanese-Koguryoic Languages with a Preliminary Description of Archaic Northeastern Middle Chinese*. Leiden/Boston: Brill.

Beffa, Marie-Lise. 1982. Présentation de la langue nivx. *Études mongoles et sibériennes* 13: 40–98.

Bhattacharya, Sudhibhushan. 1957. Field-Notes on Nahali. *Indian Linguistics* 17: 245–258.

Comrie, Bernard. 1981. *The Languages of the Soviet* Union. Cambridge: Cambridge University Press.

Georg, Stefan. 2007. *A Descriptive Grammar of Ket (Yenisei Ostyak)*. Folkestone: Global Oriental.

Georg, Stefan. 2008. Review of Robbeets 2005. *Bochumer Jahrbuch für Ostasienforschung* 32: 247–278.

Georg, Stefan. 2011. *The Poverty of Ataicism*, online publication, www.academia. edu/1638942/The_Poverty_of_Altaicism

Georg, Stefan and Aleksandr P. Volodin. 1999. *Die itelmenische Sprache. Grammatik und Texte*. Wiesbaden: Harrassowitz.

Grierson, G.A. (ed.). 1906. *Linguistic Survey of India, Vol. IV: Muṇḍā and Dravidian Languages*. Calcutta: Government of India Printing Office.

Gruzdeva, Ekaterina. 1998. *Nivkh*. München/Newcastle: LINCOM EUROPA.

Gruzdeva, Ekaterina. 2001. Nivkhskij jazyk. *Jazyki rossijskoj federacii i sosednykh gosudarstv. Enciklopedija, Vol. II (K – R)*, ed. by V.A. Vinogradov et al., 357–366. Moskva: Nauka.

Hodgson, Brian Houghton. 1848. On the Chépáng and Kúsúnda Tribes of Nepal. *JASB* 17: 650–658.

Hodgson, Brian Houghton. 1857–1858. Comparative Vocabulary of the Languages of the Broken Tribes of Népal. *JASB* 26: 317–522, 27, 393–442.

Kausen, Ernst. 2013. *Die Sprachfamilien der Welt. Bd. 1: Europa und Asien*. Hamburg: Buske.

Krejnovich, E.A. 1958. *Jukagirskij jazyk*. Moskva/Leningrad: Nauka.

Kuiper, F.B.J. 1962. *Nahali. A Comparative Study*. Amsterdam: Noord-Holland.

Martin, Samuel E. 1966. Lexical Evidence Relating Korean to Japanese. *Lg* 42: 185–251.

Maslova, Elena. 1997. Yukagir Focus in a Typological Perspective. *Journal of Pragmatics* 27: 457–475.

Mattissen, Johanna and Werner Drossard. 1998. *Lexical and Syntactic Categories in Nivkh (Gilyak)*. Düsseldorf: Heinrich-Heine-Universität (Theorie des Lexikons. Arbeiten des SFB, 282).

Michinori, Shimoji and Thomas Pellard. 2010. *An Introduction to Ryukyuan Languages*. Tokyo: ILCAA.

Miller, Roy Andrew. 1996. *Languages and History. Japanese, Korean, and Altaic*. Bangkok: White Orchid Press.

Nedjalkov, Vladimir P. and Galina A. Otaina. 2013. *A Syntax of the Nivkh Language. The Amur Dialect*. Amsterdam: John Benjamins.

Nikolaeva, Irina A. and Evgenij A. Khelimskij. 1997. Jukagirskij jazyk. *Jazyki Mira. Paleoaziatskie jazyki*, ed. by V.N. Jarceva et al., 155–168. Moskva: Indrik.

Panfilov, Vladimir Z. 1962–1965. *Grammatika nivkhskogo jazyka, Vol. 1–2.* Moskva/ Leningrad: Nauka.

Panfilov, Vladimir Z. 1968. Nivkhskij jazyk. *Jazyki Narodov SSSR. Vol. 5: Mongol'skie, tunguso-man'chzhurskie i paleoaziatskie jazyki*, ed. by Skorik P. Ja. et al., 408–434. Leningrad: Nauka.

Pokharel, P. 2005. Strategies of Pronominalization in Kusunda. *Contemporary Issues in Nepalese Linguistics*, ed. by Yadava, Y. et al., 189–192. Kathmandu: Linguistic Society of Nepal.

Reinhard, Johan and Sueyoshi Toba. 1970. *A Preliminary Linguistic Analysis and Vocabulary of the Kusunda Language*. Kathmandu: Summer Institute of Linguistics.

Robbeets, Martine. 2005. *Is Japanese Related to Korean, Tungusic, Mongolic and Turkic?* Wiesbaden: Harrassowitz.

Savel'eva, V.N. and Ch.M. Taksami. 1970. *Nivkhsko-russkij slovar'*. Moskva: Sovetskaja enciklopedija.

Schmalz, Mark. 2012. Towards a Full Description of the Focus System in Tundra Yukaghir. *Linguistic Discovery* 10, no. 2: 53–108.

Shrenk, L.I. 1883. *Ob inorodcakh Amurskago kraja, Vol. I.* Sankt Peterburg: Imperatorskaja Akademija Nauk.

Siegl, Florian. 2008. A Note on Personal Pronouns in Enets and Northern Samoyedic. *Linguistica Uralica* 44/2: 119–130.

Starostin, Sergej A. 1991. *Altajskaja problema i proiskhozhdenie japonskogo jazyka.* Moskva: Nauka.

Vajda, Edward. 2000. *Ket prosodic Phonology*. München: LINCOM EUROPA.

Vajda, Edward. 2001a. The Role of Position Class in Ket Verb Morphophonology. *Word* 52, no. 3, 369–436.

Vajda, Edward. 2001b. *Yeniseian Peoples and Languages*. Surrey: Curzon.

Vajda, Edward. 2004. *Ket.* München: LINCOM EUROPA.

Vovin, Alexander. 2005a. Koguryŏ and Paekche: Different Languages or Dialects of Old Korean? *Journal of Inner and East Asian Studies* 2, no. 2, 34–64.

Vovin, Alexander. 2005b. The End of the Altaic Controversy. *Central Asiatic Journal* 49, no. 1: 71–132.

Vovin, Alexander. 2010. *Koreo-Japonica: A Re-Evaluation of a Common Genetic Origin.* Honolulu: University of Hawai'i Press.

Watters, David E. 2006. Notes on Kusunda Grammar: A Language Isolate of Nepal. *Himalayan Linguistics Archive* 3: 1–182.

Werner, Heinrich. 1997a. *Die ketische Sprache*. Wiesbaden: Harrassowitz.

Werner, Heinrich. 1997b. *Abriß der kottischen Grammatik*. Wiesbaden: Harrassowitz.

Werner, Heinrich. 2002. *Vergleichendes Wörterbuch der Jenissej-Sprachen*, 3 vols. Wiesbaden: Harrassowitz.
Werner, Heinrich. 2012. *Dictionary of the Yugh Language*. München: LINCOM-EUROPA.
Zide, Norman. 2008. On Nihali. *The Munda Languages*, ed. by Gregory D.S. Anderson, 764–776. London and New York: Routledge.

CHAPTER 7

AFRICAN LANGUAGE ISOLATES

Roger Blench

1 INTRODUCTION

One of the notable differences between Africa and most other linguistic areas is its relative uniformity. With few exceptions, all of Africa's languages have been gathered into four major phyla, and most recent progress in classification has been in resolving details (Greenberg 1963; Blench 2016). The number of undisputed language isolates is very small. By contrast, Australia, Papua and the New World are extremely diverse at the phylic level, and all have substantial numbers of isolates or very small phyla. Eurasia is hard to classify since Europe is universe and is characterised by a small number of geographically extensive languages, but Siberia and Northeast Asia are diverse on a level with the Amazon. Southeast Asia, on the other hand, is somewhat similar to Africa, in having a relatively small number of phyla, each with many languages and almost no isolates. Given the time-depth of human settlement in Africa, this is somewhat surprising. If the *ex Africa* hypothesis for the origin of modern humans is accepted, then we have to assume that *Homo sapiens sapiens* originated some 150–200 kya and spread to Eurasia from Northeast Africa, largely displacing, but perhaps also interbreeding with, the hominids already *in situ*. Looking at the worldwide pattern of isolates, they are apparently very unevenly distributed, assuming standard references such as the *Ethnologue* reflect true diversity and not just differences in research traditions across regions. There is almost a gradient from west to east, with few in Europe and the greatest number in the New World.

The explanation for this is unclear, and indeed for some authors, this is based on a mistaken analysis of the genetic affiliation of individual families or specific subgroups. The identification of isolates in Africa has not been without controversy. Joseph Greenberg, whose classification of African languages remains the principal framework in use today, was a committed 'lumper' and was inclined to ensure every language found a classificatory home, sometimes on the basis of extremely tenuous evidence. Recent years have seen a sceptical counter-trend, to consider that some of the languages or branches classified by Greenberg and formerly accepted, are isolates. If this is so, then Africa may be the home of many more isolates than are usually listed. This chapter[1] describes the controversies over the identification of African isolates, covers in more detail those generally accepted, and deals more briefly with controversial cases. For some languages, fragmentary data makes an uncontroversial resolution impossible. The chapter also considers briefly the identification of substrates and claims about residual foragers which may well point to a prior, more diverse Africa.

2 METHODOLOGICAL ISSUES

2.1 Traditions of classificatory research in Africa

The perceived diversity of a linguistic region is not entirely the result of a rigorous scientific process; it also reflects strongly the patterns established in the early period of scholarship. In African studies, the intellectual tradition has been characterised from an early period by continent-spanning hypotheses. The discovery that Bantu languages from Cameroun to South Africa were related dates back to the seventeenth century (Doke 1961), and the discovery of noun-classes in West African languages led some nineteenth-century scholars to speculate on their relation to Bantu. Wilhelm Bleek (1862, 1869) went so far as to include a West African division in the family he named Bantu. Diedrich Westermann (1911) posited a 'Sudanic' family divided into 'East' and 'West', corresponding to Meinhof's work on Bantu (Meinhof 1910), bringing together what we would now consider Nilo-Saharan and Niger-Congo.

Joseph Greenberg took a fresh look at the classification of African languages in a series of articles published between 1949 and 1954, later collected and updated in book form in Greenberg (1963). He combined 'West Sudanic' and Bantu into a phylum he named Niger-Kordofanian [but now usually referred to as Niger-Congo (Bendor-Samuel 1989)], while he treated 'East Sudanic' as a different phylum. In the latest version he gathered together several groups previously treated as distinct into Nilo-Saharan and renamed the 'Hamito-Semitic' languages 'Afroasiatic'. Greenberg re-iterated the hypotheses of Dorothea Bleek (1956), who assumed, not only that all the Khoesan languages were related to one another, but that the languages with clicks in East Africa were also part of a presumed Macro-Khoesan. The effect of this was to tidy up the linguistic picture of the whole continent – every language was theoretically 'placed' (Blench 1999a). Greenberg's desire not to admit any isolates has been enormously influential on succeeding generations of Africanist scholars. Indeed Greenberg's later publications, first on Indo-Pacific (Greenberg 1971a), then gathering all the languages of the Americas into three phyla (Greenberg 1960, 1987) and bringing together Eurasian languages into 'Eurasiatic' (Greenberg 2000, 2002), a macrophylum with considerable overlap with Nostratic, show that he was a committed 'lumper'.

These views remain very much at odds with more conventional scholarly opinion on the languages of Papua, Australia and the New World. In these regions, linguists have generally entered the field with few preliminary assumptions about relatedness or macro-groupings – and so progress has been much more 'bottom-up'. Small groups have been derived from data and gradually built into larger ones. But, unlike Greenberg's proposals for Africa, Amerind and other intellectual constructs have gained almost no assent from the scholarly community. The intellectual tradition of a region is thus extremely powerful in determining the pattern of phyla, families and isolates. If Africa were in Melanesia, as it were, its linguistic geography might well be represented as a few larger phyla and many isolates characterised by complex contact phenomena. Figure 7.1A is a schematic model of lumpers and splitters which tries to visualise the impact they have on our perception of the linguistic geography of a region.

Is the conclusion that we might also be wrong about Africa? That Nilo-Saharan, Niger-Congo or Khoesan are no more than networks of isolates, or much smaller phyla, and the supposed cognates simply borrowings or chance? If we depended only on

LUMPERS

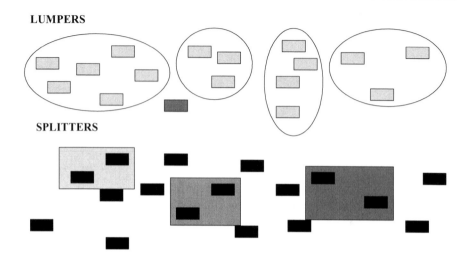

SPLITTERS

FIGURE 7.1A SCHEMATIC MODEL CONTRASTING LUMPERS AND SPLITTERS

Greenberg's 'mass/multilateral comparison', this might indeed be the case, since it is now all too apparent how significant borrowing can be between languages. For Niger-Congo, Greenberg depended on a mass of prior work which he rarely cited but which provided much of the evidence for his proposals. The comparative nominal morphology of Niger-Congo was first laid out in detail by Westermann (1935), and it is largely one of the accidents of history that this is not cited as the key paper in establishing the phylum. Recent publications (beginning with Dixon 1997 but characterising some of the papers in Heine and Nurse 2008) and conferences with titles such as 'Beyond Niger-Congo' have used geographical and typological mapping of traits to suggest that Niger-Congo in particular is somehow not a valid phylum. As an example of this type of construct, consider 'Macro Sudanic' (Güldemann 2008a, 2011). This consists of a series of maps and tables showing that particular phenomena (labial-velars, logophoricity, vowel harmony) have quite similar distributions across a wide area of northern Sub-Saharan Africa. Güldemann concludes from this that the historical linguists are wrong and that 'the Macro-Sudan belt is genealogically highly heterogeneous'. He underlines this scepticism in Güldemann (2014) which treats 'Khoesan' as a 'negative entity' and compares its typological traits to other hypothetical African language phyla. In other words, this is a reprise of the arguments of Dalby (1970) concerning a 'Fragmentation Belt' across Africa. But to imagine that demonstrating that widespread phenomena can be partly attributed to genealogical characteristics and partly to contact is not in any way to discredit the findings of historical linguistics. The point, and it is an important one, is that some linguistic phenomena are more prone to diffusion than others. Linguistic geography is highly contingent; it depends on the phenomena you decide to map, the literature you consult and the state of linguistic description, which itself may reflect politics and financial resources. It has little to do with the argument about whether cognate morphemes in Niger-Congo affixing systems constitute proof or otherwise of the reality of the phylum.[2]

2.2 Doubts over the major phyla

The situation with the other proposed phyla is more complex. Greenberg (1971b) is largely responsible for the concept of Nilo-Saharan as a construct, and there was neither a body of existing scholarship binding together its putative subgroups nor was the case self-evident. Indeed publications such as Tucker and Bryan (1956) had treated many of the groups falling within Nilo-Saharan as 'isolated units'. Widespread doubts over the affiliation of languages claimed to be Nilo-Saharan inevitably reflect the way historical linguistics is conventionally conducted. Compared with other African phyla, the difficulties of demonstrating the reality of Nilo-Saharan have typically propelled authors into methodological excursuses (Bender 1997; Ehret 2001; Blench 2002). It seems highly unlikely that Nilo-Saharan will ever pass the tests of regular sound correspondences and possibly an agreed internal structure that are now part of the formula for the usual textbooks on historical linguistics. In other words, Nilo-Saharan will never look like Austronesian or Dravidian. There are simply not enough undisputed lexical cognates to set up secure correspondences or develop clouds of isoglosses illustrating particular subgrouping hypotheses. This has led various linguists either to dismiss it wholesale (Dixon 1997) or to exclude individual subgroups on unspecified grounds (Dimmendaal 2011). The extreme form of this is the online resource Glottolog.org 3.0, the major non-*Ethnologue* resource for global languages, which treats all the branches of Nilo-Saharan as isolates or their affiliations as unproven.

In the case of Afroasiatic, in its avatar as Hamito-Semitic, it has been generally considered a phylum since Cohen (1947) with many earlier precursors. The major controversy arose over the identification of Omotic, a complex ensemble of little-known languages in southwestern Ethiopia, previously considered Cushitic. The first monograph on Omotic is Bender (1975), and Omotic has generally found acceptance as a genealogical unit (e.g. Hayward 1990; Bender 1988, 2000, 2003; Amha 2012). Nonetheless, persistent doubts both as to its Afroasiatic affiliation and its internal coherence remain in the literature (e.g. Theil 2012).

Finally, Khoesan is undoubtedly a case where a single typological feature has overridden the usual canons of historical linguistics. The presence of clicks led most researchers to suppose all languages with clicks were related (e.g. Bleek 1956; Greenberg 1963). This is demonstrably not so with the Cushitic language Dahalo, which has clicks (Tosco 1991). The contrary case was put by Westphal (1963) who broke up Khoesan into seven unrelated families, a notion which lives on implicitly in recent syntheses (Voßen 2013; Güldeman 2014). However, the incorporation of the East African click languages, Hadza and Sandawe, was shown to be based on poor transcription of clicks and wishful semantics (Sands 1998). Currently Hadza is treated as an isolate, whereas Sandawe is argued to be linked to the Khoe subgroup of Khoesan (Güldemann and Elderkin 2010). More problematic are two languages Kwadi and Eastern Hoã. Kwadi is extinct and its affiliation cannot be resolved, although Güldemann (2004, 2008b) treats its as Khoe Similarly Eastern ǂHoã, a living language, was first considered an isolate but has been shown to have systematic correspondences with the Northern Khoesan (Ju) family (Traill 1973; Heine and Honken 2010).

2.3 Excluding chance resemblances

The identification of isolates depends on the tools used to classify languages. If a language shows only a small number of problematic cognates with its proposed relative, then its genetic affiliation will inevitably be questioned. Nilo-Saharan and Khoesan in particular include languages whose inclusion in the phylum remains debated. Several of the languages of the Ethio-Sudan borderland, such as Shabo and Gumuz within Nilo-Saharan and the 'Mao' languages, particularly Ganza, within Omotic, not only have very low lexical cognate count with their relatives but lack tidy correspondences. Three explanations are possible:

a)   The putative branches have been diverging away from the rest of the phylum for sufficiently long for natural vocabulary erosion to be responsible for low lexical counts.
b)   Apparent similarities with the other branches of the phylum are due to borrowing.
c)   Apparent similarities are due entirely to chance.

Linguistic analysis, the demonstration of regular sound correspondences or the detection of loanword phonology should be sufficient to show whether a) or b) are probable. But what about chance? There is a literature suggesting that lexical lists of any two languages in the world might show up to 5% resemblances of CVC stems (Bender 1969). Calculations by Ringe (1992, 1999) have applied a great deal of energy to algorithms illustrating the difficulties of showing languages are related. So the suggestion that the resemblances leading to a proposal of a relationship are 'chance' appears at first sight persuasive. But the calculations made by Bender assumes that languages have no structure, that in principle any combination of CV phonemes may arise. In practice of course this is not true. Most languages are extremely constrained in their permissible phonotactic structures. If two languages are related, then the set of lexemes said to be cognate should have constraints on both phonology and canonic forms. The assumption of chance is thus an unusable tool. We can draw up tables of more or less likely cognates, and whether these are accepted by other linguists is a function of the credibility of the sound-meaning correspondences and demonstration that these are not borrowings. A good example of how marked are the differences between linguists' assessment of credibility is shown by the debate over the coherence of Altaic. In their etymological dictionary of Altaic, Starostin et al. (2003) claim there are thousands of reconstructible roots, whereas Janhunen (1994) discards all putative Altaic etymologies as borrowings or chance.

   Attributing resemblance to 'chance' is thus a virtually worthless heuristic, because it is an untestable proposition, since no empirical data can ever be adequate to exclude it. Amassing evidence may make any linguistic proposition more likely, but a negative can never be demonstrated. In other words, often it cannot be shown that the apparent relation between two lexemes is *not* due to chance. Clearly, it is always possible to find unrelated languages where individual items show close sound/meaning correspondences. Our assumption that the languages in question are unrelated is partly determined by geography, partly by the lack of a regular relationship. But the regularity of a relationship can really only be determined by comparative data. If one language shows lookalikes and its genetic relatives do not, borrowing or chance may be the explanation. But if languages have no close relatives, then it is problematic to exclude these alternatives.

3   LANGUAGE ISOLATES IN AFRICA AND ELSEWHERE

3.1   African isolates and claimed isolates

The list of African isolates remains controversial and few have not been the subject of some proposal as to their affiliation. The quality of the evidence is in almost inverse proportion to the speculation about their classification. For example, neither of the two languages for which there are only written sources, Meroitic and Guanche, have enough core vocabulary to establish their relationships following the usual canons of historical linguistics. They could be treated as unclassifiable, following a distinction made elsewhere in this book. At least one language, Oropom, is almost certainly spurious, and two others, Kwadi and Mpra, died out in the twentieth century before an adequate amount of data could be collected. I have not reviewed all the fragmentary reports of unknown languages, for which there are sometimes ten words or less. Table 7.1 lists the languages about which few doubts exist.

Jalaa may well be extinct; although individuals claiming Jalaa ethnicity are still present in the Cham-speaking area, none now remember any words of the language.

There are further languages which have been reported initially as isolates but which seem to be affiliated to known phyla or can otherwise be excluded. A list of these is given in Table 7.2.

TABLE 7.1 AFRICAN LANGUAGE ISOLATES NOT GENERALLY DISPUTED

Language name	Location	Source	Speakers
Bangi Me	Mali	Blench (2007a), Hantgan (2013)	2000–3000 est.
Jalaa (= Cuŋ Tuum)	Nigeria	Kleinwillinghöfer (2001)	Probably extinct
Hadza	Tanzania	Sands (1993), Kirk Miller (personal communication)	800
Laal	Chad	Boyeldieu (1977), Faris (1994), Lionnet (2010)	800?

TABLE 7.2 AFRICAN ISOLATES: REPORTED, SUGGESTED, CONTROVERSIAL

Name	Location	Source	Comments
Bēosi	Madagascar	Birkeli (1936), Blench and Walsh (n.d.)	Austronesian with unknown ? Southern Cushitic substrate
Dompo	Ghana	Painter (1967), Blench (n.d. a)	Guang language with unknown substrate
Guanche	Canaries	Wölfel (1965)	Extinct. Absence of basic vocabulary makes classification impossible to resolve
Gumuz	Ethiopia	Bender (2005), Ahland (2004, 2012)	Nilo-Saharan isolate branch
Kujarge	Sudan	Doornbos and Bender (1983); Lovestrand (2012), Blench (2013)	Probably Chadic
Kwadi	Angola	Westphal (1963), Güldemann (2004)	Perhaps Khoesan
Meroitic	Ancient Sudan	Rilly and De Voogt (2012)	Probably a close relative of Nubian
Mpra	Ghana	Cardinall (1931), Blench (n.d. c)	Extinct. Kwa language
Ongota	Ethiopia	Fleming et al. (1992), Sava and Tosco (2000)	Probably Afroasiatic
Oropom	Uganda	Wilson (1970)	Probably spurious (Heine pers. comm.)
Sandawe	Tanzania	Sands (1998), Güldemann and Elderkin (2010)	Probably Khoesan
Shabo	Ethiopia	Bender (1977), Fleming (1991), Teferra (1991, 1995), Tsehay (2015)	Nilo-Saharan isolate branch

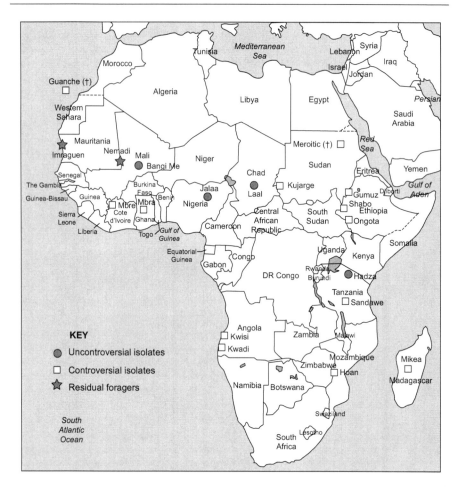

MAP 7.1 AFRICA: LANGUAGES ISOLATES AND RESIDUAL FORAGERS

Meroitic and Guanche became extinct long ago, while for Bēosi, Kwadi and Mpra, it is unlikely that further data can be collected, so the question cannot be resolved. The status of Kujarge is unknown, but no speakers have been encountered since Doornbos' original record, and the civil war that has passed over their homeland may well have finalised their demise. Map 7.1 shows a composite map locating the language isolates, the controversial cases given in Table 7.2, and the location of residual foragers who might represent former isolates.

3.2 African isolates, undisputed

3.2.1 Bangi Me

The Bangi Me (Bangi-me) language is spoken in Mali, in seven villages east of Karge, reached by turning off the Sevare-Douentza road 38 km north of Sevare. The population

of Bangi Me speakers (pictured in Figure 7.1B) is likely to be 2000–3000 (2005 estimate). Its existence was first reported in Bertho (1953) and later in Hochstetler et al.
(2004). Both these surveys considered it to be part of the surrounding network of Dogon
languages, and speakers consider themselves Dogon. Blench (2007a) conducted new
fieldwork and first argued that this was a language isolate. The deceased Dutch linguist
Stefan Elders conducted further fieldwork which has been salvaged.[3] Hantgan (2012,
2013) is an extended wordlist and grammar of Bangi Me. The current situation in Mali
has made fieldwork very difficult, but there is no immediate reason to consider Bangi Me
endangered.

3.2.1.1 Phonological features

CONSONANTS
Table 7.3 shows the consonants of Bangi Me. Marginal phonemes are shown in grey.

/y/ is used for the palatal approximant, corresponding to IPA /j/. /ʋ/ is an allophone of /b/.

VOWELS
Bangi Me vowels are given in Table 7.4.

Nasalisation is predictable and non-contrastive. Vowel length is largely predictable, with
few words contrasting on the basis of vowel length alone. Permissible diphthongs are:

[ie iɛ ɛe eɛ aɛ ɔo oɔ]

FIGURE 7.1B BANGI ME SPEAKERS AT NIANA

TABLE 7.3 BANGI ME CONSONANTS

	Bilabial	Alveolar	Palatal	Alveolo-palatal	Velar	Labial-palatal	Labio-velar	Glottal
Plosives	p b	t d			k g			
Prenalised	ᵐp ᵐb	ⁿt ⁿd			ᵑk ᵑg			
Nasals	m	n	ɲ		ŋ			
Fricatives		s	ʃ ʒ	ɕ	ɣ			h
Affricates				ʧ				
Approximants	[ʋ]	r	y			ɥ	w	
Nasal approximant		r̃	ỹ				w̃	
Lateral		l						

Source: Hantgan (2013).

TABLE 7.4 BANGI ME VOWELS

	Front	Central	Back
Close	i		u
Close-mid	e		o
Open-mid	ɛ		ɔ
Open		a	

3.2.1.2 Tone

Bangi Me is tonal language, with two tones, high and low, with the mora the tone-bearing unit. On monosyllabic words with two morae, level tones can combine to create rising or falling melodies. Rising tones may appear on monomoraic syllables in word-initial position. Rising tones on monomoraic words usually appear after a velar consonant. A phonetic mid tone which is the result of a non-automatic downstep.

3.2.1.3 Morphology

One of the main attributes of Bangi Me that differentiates it from the Dogon languages is its lack of segmental, bound morphology. Like many Niger-Congo languages, Dogon languages are agglutinating, whereas Bangi Me is isolating. Bangi Me has no evidence for noun class markers or even remnants, although there is a diminutive suffix and an opaque frozen [–r] suffix. Bangi Me also differs from the Dogon languages in that tense, aspect and mood markers are unbound morphemes. Verbs in Bangi Me are divided into different classes based on transitivity, phonological shape and semantic category, whereas most verbs in Dogon take the same inflection, with the exception of change-of-state verbs.

3.2.1.4 Syntax

Although at the phrase level Bangi Me is head initial, with noun-postposition and noun-modifier word order (except DEF N and POSS N), at the clause level, the basic constituent order is either SVO, SOV or OSV. The ordering of constituents in the sentence depends on the tense/aspect/mood of the clause. A feature not shared by any surrounding language is the use of tonal marking on the verb and object if present. Subject and TAM are marked by a combination of segmental and autosegmental features.

3.2.2 Hadza

The Hadza (Tindiga) language is spoken by about 800 individuals close to Lake Eyasi in Northern Tanzania. It has been the subject of intensive anthropological research with more than a thousand references, mostly focusing on the persistence of hunting and gathering.[4] The presence of clicks in Hadza encouraged earlier researchers to classify Hadza together with Sandawe (also in Tanzania) and the Khoesan languages of Southern Africa. This idea may first have been argued by Bleek (1956) in her 'Comparative Bushman Dictionary' and was then picked up in Greenberg (1963). Since Sands (1998) it is generally accepted that Hadza is an isolate, despite the presence of clicks and that the connections with Khoesan were based on unreliable transcriptions. Kirk Miller (personal communication) has been working on a grammar and dictionary of Hadza, but these are not yet in the public domain.

Hadza phonology is complex and the history of descriptions is marked by considerable variation between different accounts. The earliest modern description is Tucker et al. (1977), but the most complete overview of Hadza phonology is Sands et al. (1993), reformulated in Sands (2013a). Table 7.5 is adapted from Sands et al. (1993).

Hadza has the five cardinal vowels: /i/, /e/, /a/, /o/ and /u/ (Table 7.6). A few words show contrastive /ĩ/ and ũ/. Vowel length, pharyngealisation, glottalisation and breathiness are not contrastive.

Whether Hadza is tonal is the subject of some uncertainty. Tucker et al. (1977) transcribe both stress and three level tones. However, subsequent investigations have not

TABLE 7.5 HADZA CONSONANTS

	Bilabial	Labio-dental	Dental	Alveolar	Palatal	Velar	Labialised velar	Glottal
Plosive	pʰ p b			tʰ t d	dʒ	kʰ k g	kʰʷ kʷ gʷ	ʔ
Ejective	(p')					k'	k'ʷ	
Central oral click			k|	k!				
Lateral oral click					k‖			
Nasal	m			n	ɲ	ŋ	ŋʷ	
Nasal central click			ŋ|' ŋ|	ŋ!' ŋ!				
Nasal lateral click					ŋ‖' ŋ‖			
Prenasal plosive	mpʰ mb		ntʰ nd			ŋkʰ ŋg		
Prenasal affricate			nts ndz		ndʒ			
Central affricate			ts dz		ʧ dʒ			
Lateral affricate					tɬ̬			
Ejective central affricate			ts'		ʧ'			
Ejective lateral affricate					tɬ̬'			
Fricative		f		s	ʃ			
Lateral fricative				ɬ				
Approximant					y		w	ɦ
Lateral				l				

TABLE 7.6 HADZA VOWELS

	Front	*Central*	*Back*
High	i (ĩ)		u (ũ)
Mid	e		o
Low		a	

confirmed this. Sands et al. (1993) and Sands (2013a) conclude that Hadza shows a simple two-way contrast and might well be considered a pitch-accent language.

Morphology

Hadza divides nouns into masculine and feminine and marks both gender and number with suffixes. Table 7.7 shows number and gender marking for *n!e* 'leopard'. Hadza verbs are inflected with suffixes, although initial reduplication can mark emphasis. Hadza also has plural verbs, or distributives, which are marked with infixes.

Syntax

The basic constituent order of Hadza is VSO. For example:

'ela-ta-ta	mulinga-ko	ne-ta	gundida-ko
build-3F.sg.DO-	beehive-3F.sg	INST-F	hammer-3F.sg
1F.sg.UT			

I will build a beehive with a hammer

However, Sands (2013c: 265) provides examples of the great variability in word order and concludes, 'Hadza is best described as a pronominal argument language'.

3.2.3 Jalaa

The Jalaa (also Jalabe, Jaabe) live in a single settlement, Loojaa, in Balanga Local Government Area, southern Bauchi State, Nigeria. One person is *níí jàlàà*, and the people are *jàlààbè*. They are also known locally as Cèntûm or Cùntûm, from a name for their former settlement. The only information available on the Jalaa language is the wordlist in Kleinwillinghöfer (2001: 243) which gives lexical comparisons with neighbouring languages but states that 'old people were able to remember and provide additional words and phrases from their former language'. Kleinwillinghöfer (2001: fn. 8) mentions that it is possible Jalaa is still used in ritual performances but that his informants were unwilling to disclose information about this. The Jalaa are surrounded by Adamawa-speaking peoples, such as the Cham and Dadiya, and they have been almost completely absorbed linguistically by the Cham.

Not much can be said of the phonological features, but the basic sound-system can be inferred from the data in Kleinwillinghöfer (2001). Table 7.8 shows the consonants of Jalaa.

TABLE 7.7   HADZA NUMBER AND GENDER MARKING

Gender	Number	Hadza	Gloss
M.	sg.	n!eø	single male leopard, many leopards
M.	pl.	n!e-bi'I	few leopards (paucal)
F.	sg.	n!e-ko	single female leopard
F.	pl.	n!e-be'e	few female leopards (paucal)

Source: Sands 2013b.

TABLE 7.8 JALAA CONSONANTS

	Bilabial	Alveolar	Post-alveolar	Alveolo-palatal	Velar	Labio-velar	Glottal
Plosives	p b	t d			k g	kp	
Nasals	m	n		ɲ	ŋ		
Fricatives	f	s					h
Affricates				ʧ dʒ			
Approximants		r	y			w	
Lateral		l					

Source: Extracted from Kleinwillinghöfer (2001).

Jalaa permits labialised consonants /sʷ/, kʷ/, /bʷ/ as well as a palatal /dʸ/.

Vowels

Kleinwillinghöfer does not give the vowel system explicitly and uses the Nigerian convention of subdots to represent – ATR vowels. On this basis there is a ten-vowel system, in Table 7.9.

Three level tones are transcribed, as well as a falling tone. Some long vowels are transcribed, for example *yúú* 'sesame', but whether length is systematic remains difficult to discern.

Jalaa has a number-marking system with alternating suffixes for nouns, like the surrounding Adamawa languages. Whether this is original or borrowed is unclear. For example, Jalaa often has an identical suffix alternation for similar meanings to Cham, the language with which it has a strong borrowing relationship, despite quite different segmental material. Table 7.10 illustrates this.

As Kleinwillinghöfer (2001) points out, the similarities of nominal affix alternation with its Adamawa neighbours combined with the striking rarity of shared lexemes lead to the speculation that these number marking strategies were borrowed.

3.2.4 Laal

The Laal (Gori, Laabe) language is spoken in Central Chad in the Moyen-Chari Region, Barh Kôh department, between Korbol and Dik, Gori (centre), Damtar and Mailao

TABLE 7.9 JALAA VOWELS

	Front	Central	Back
Close	i		u
	ɪ		ʊ
Close-mid	e	ə	o
Open-mid	ɛ		ɔ
Open		a	

TABLE 7.10 JALAA NUMBER MARKING IN COMPARISON TO CHAM

Gloss	sg.	pl.	Gloss	sg.	pl.
mouth	bɔɔ	bɔɔní	mouth	ɲii	ɲiini
tree	gwìiràŋ	gwìitè	tree	riyaŋ	riitɛ
meat	lìbò	lìbòté	meat	nàm	nàmtɛ
hole	suroŋ	suroŋte	crocodile	kùlɔŋ	kùlɔ̀ŋtɛ
nose	yamər	yaməta	nose	dʒòr	dʒòtɛ
leg	kobər	kobta	knot	fúbər	fúbtɛ
fish	fui	fuuta	dog	dʒɔil	dʒɔɔte
wife	ʧùwì	ʧùùbó	stranger	(nii) fui	fùbɛ
person	nətâ	nətaaba	person	nii	nàb

Source: Adapted from Kleinwillinghöfer (2001).

villages. There were 750 speakers in the year 2000. Damtar village was said to have its own dialect called Laabe with three speakers left in 1977. The Laal do not have an autonym but refer to themselves as:

muǎŋ lá	people from Gori
muǎŋ 6uāl	people from Damtar

The language name, *yəw láàl*, is 'language' + Gori.nominal suffix. The Laal are not hunter-gatherers, but today have an economy based on fishing and farming and may have formerly been pastoralists.

Preliminary work on Laal was conducted by Boyeldieu (1977, 1982a, 1982b, 1987, n.d.) who first drew attention to the difficulties of classifying it. Faris (1994) confirmed that the Laal had survived the civil war in Chad and Lionnet (2010, 2013) has begun a description of Laal. Boyeldieu shows that, although Laal incorporates elements of the neighbouring Chadic and Adamawa languages, it has a large corpus of unetymologisable lexemes.

Phonological features

The consonant inventory of Laal is characteristic of the Southern Chad area, except perhaps for the palatal implosive [ʄ] (Table 7.11). The vowels are represented by Lionnet (2010) as in Table 7.12. The type of system this is intended to represent is slightly opaque, at least to me. Boyeldieu (1977) transcribes three tone heights and a rising and falling tone.

Morphology

Number marking on nouns is extremely diverse. Table 7.13 shows examples of the different number-marking strategies.

TABLE 7.11 LAAL CONSONANTS

	Bilabial	Alveolar	Palatal	Alveolo-palatal	Velar	Labio-velar	Glottal
Plosives	p b	t d	c j [ɟ]		k g		ʔ
Prenalised	ᵐb	ⁿd			ⁿg		
Nasals	m	n	ɲ		ŋ		
Implosives	ɓ	ɗ	ì [ʄ]				
Fricatives		s					h
Flap		r					
Lateral		l					
Approximants			y [j]			w	

Source: Extracted from Lionnet (2010).

TABLE 7.12 LAAL VOWELS

	Front	Central		Back
Close	i ü [y]	ɨ		u
Mid	e üo [ɥo]	ə		o
Open	i̧a (~ɛ) üa [ɥa]	a	ɥa	(~ɔ)

TABLE 7.13 LAAL NOMINAL NUMBER MARKING

Gloss	sg.	pl.
mahogany	círám	cúrmú
bag	bwālāg	bólgó
mat	sún	súnà
cock	kògòr	kwāgrā
hyena	ŋyāāl	ŋēē
ear	sìgál	sìgíy
elephant	ɲé	ɲwáɲá
dog	ɓyāāg	ɓīīgāɲ
bird	ndíí	ndírmá
pigeon	lóóg	lwágmí
water	sū	sùgá
sheep	ɗēē	ɗwāārī

Source: Compiled from Boyeldieu (1977).

The striking feature of Laal which marks it out from all neighbouring languages is its threefold gender system marked, not on nouns, but on pronouns, and the 'connective' particle. The three classes are masculine (human male), feminine (human female) and neuter (non-human).

The subject pronouns are as presented in Table 7.14.

Although the usual comparisons for Laal are with Chadic and Adamawa languages, this gender system is strongly reminiscent of Nilo-Saharan languages, such as Krongo (Reh 1985), although there is no other evidence for a Nilo-Saharan affiliation.

TABLE 7.14 LAAL SUBJECT PRONOUNS

		Masculine	*Feminine*	*Neuter*
Singular	1	já	jí	–
	2		ʔò	–
	3	ʔà	ʔìn	ʔàn
Plural	1 ex		ʔùrú	–
	1 inc		ʔăŋ	–
	2		ʔùn	–
	3		ʔì	ʔuàn

Source: Boyeldieu (1982a).

Syntax

Basic constituent order of Laal is SVO. For example:

ʔà   sìr   sū
he   drinks   water

nììnàn   sáá   kìndì
wife.his   take   zither

Every verb has three forms:

1   simplex: simplest, more frequent, unmarked for tense/aspect/mood
2   'centripetal' form: marking movement towards the speaker in space or time
3   'participative' (instrumental) form: usually in complex utterances

These are marked by tone and occasionally by segmental morphology, as exemplified in Table 7.15.

3.3 African isolates, controversial or undecidable

3.3.1 Bēosi

The island of Madagascar is today entirely the province of an Austronesian language, Malagasy, divided into a large number of dialects. However, there is strong archaeological and palaeo-environmental evidence for hunter-gatherer settlement prior to the coming of the Austronesians (Blench 2007c). Today there are number of forager groups scattered across Madagascar, bearing the names Mikea, Vazimba and Bēosi or their variants. All these people speak Malagasy today, and genetic studies of the Mikea have not indicated any unusual profile (Pierron et al. 2014). Nonetheless, some Mikea groups, particularly the Bēosi, have non-standard lexical items in their lect of Malagasy and also retain songs which cannot be interpreted. This suggests that, although this speech would be classified as a variant of Malagasy, today it may retain a substrate of an isolate or unknown language. The only record of these is Birkeli (1936) although more recent reports show that some of these terms are still in use (Stiles 1994). Unfortunately the lexical data reflects such items as useful plants or poetic terms rather than core vocabulary. Blench and Walsh (n.d.) have analysed this idiosyncratic material and suggest there is a possible

TABLE 7.15 LAAL VERB FORMS

Gloss	1	2	3
take	tō	tòò	tòó
do	ká	kárá	kárá
refuse	pāl	pàlà	pàlá

Source: Lionnet (2010).

Southern Cushitic substrate. This would not be unreasonable since the nearest forager group today on the adjacent mainland are the Southern Cushitic Aasax, whose language has unfortunately now been lost, but for which a reasonable record remains (Fleming 1969). However, many other lexical items are of unknown origin, and since it seems unlikely further data can be collected, the question of the original affiliation of Bēosi will never be resolved with certainty.

3.3.2 Gumuz

The Gumuz language is situated on the Ethio-Sudan borderland and has 179,000 speakers in Ethiopia according to the 2007 census. It is dialectally heavily divided (Ahland 2004). Reports in 2014 show that there is a previously unreported language apparently related to Gumuz, Dasin (Ahland, personal communication). Bender (1979, 1997) is the first published record of Gumuz although his work is a recension of earlier Italian and other sources and he treated Gumuz as a branch of Nilo-Saharan. However, Gumuz lacks many characteristic Nilo-Saharan features such as 'moveable k-' and three-term number marking (Ahland 2010, 2012). In his final statement on the subject, Bender (2005) suggested Gumuz was an isolate. Ahland (personal communication) has prepared a comparative wordlist illustrating cognate items shared between the two families, and the present author considers that Gumuz *is* Nilo-Saharan and indeed related to the Koman languages.

3.3.3 Shabo

The Shabo language is spoken by the *Sabu* (Shabo, Chabu) people of southwestern Ethiopia. The name found in earlier sources, *Mekeyer*, is used by the Majang people (Jordan et al. 2007). The Shabo live in what used to be the Kafa Region, between Godere and Masha, among the Majang and Shekkacho. According to the current administrative divisions, most Shabo people now live in the Sheka Zone of the Southern Nations, Nationalities and Peoples Region (SNNPR) and the Majangir Zone of Gambela Region.

Under the name Mikeyir, Harvey Hoekstra seems to have been the first to report this language, and using his data, Bender (1977) classified it as possibly Surmic. Shabo is still spoken by some 400–500 individuals, although it is losing ground to Majang and latterly Amharic. The forms then identified as cognates are now seen to be the result of extensive loans from the Majang language rather than an indication of true genetic affiliation. Since that date there have been a variety of attempts to classify Shabo, including Teferra and Unseth (1989); Fleming (1991, 2002); Ehret (1995); Bender (1983, 1997); and Schnoebelen (2009). None of these is conclusive, in part because of the small amount of available data. Bender's treatment of Shabo as an isolate branch of Nilo-Saharan is a reasonable inference from the existing data. Teferra (1991, 1995) was for a long time almost the only descriptive work on the phonology and grammar of Shabo, but more detailed treatment of Shabo lexicon and grammar has recently become available (Tsehay 2015). Like Gumuz, Shabo lacks 'classic' features of Nilo-Saharan such as three-term number marking or moveable *k-*. Nonetheless it seems most likely that Shabo is related to its close neighbours Koman and Gumuz. Although these are close to one another geographically, they are surprisingly dissimilar; nevertheless, they have enough common aspects to tentatively propose that they form a subgroup of Nilo-Saharan. Some typical items shared are given in Table 7.16.

Shabo is undoubtedly a language of considerable significance in the larger picture of African languages.

3.3.4 Ongota

The Ongota (Birale) people live in a single village in southwestern Ethiopia, in the South Omo zone, on the west bank of Weyt'o River. *Ethnologue* (Simons and Fennig 2017) reports ten speakers, but recent visitors suggest there may be as few as six who are competent (Mikeš, personal communication). Nearly all adults have switched to the Cushitic Tsamay or other regional languages such as Konso and Hamer. The first report of this language is in Fleming et al. (1992), and since then, it has had considerable publicity, although in terms of actual data there is only an extended wordlist and sketches of aspects of the grammar. Key references are Fleming et al. (1992), Fleming (2006), Sava and Tosco (2000), Yilma[5] (ined.) and Blažek (2007). These authors come to very different conclusions on the affiliation of Ongota. These views can be summarised as in Table 7.17.

None of these support the notion that Ongota is a true isolate, although the different conclusions concerning its affiliation make any definitive assignment problematic. It could indeed be an isolate with differing levels of influence from different languages. The present author considers Fleming's proposal for an Afroasiatic affiliation the most reasonable.

TABLE 7.16 KOMAN, SHABO AND GUMUZ SHARED LEXICAL ITEMS

	Shabo		Gumuz		Koman	
head	Shabo	ƙoy	Common Gumuz	*kʷa	PK	kup
breast	Shabo	kowan	Common Gumuz	*kúá	PK	*koy
horn	Shabo	kulbe	Guba dialect	k'əla	Kwama	kwaap
sun	Shabo	ukʰa, oxa	Yaso dialect	oka	Komo	kʰaala

TABLE 7.17 HYPOTHESES CONCERNING THE CLASSIFICATION OF ONGOTA

Author	Summary
Fleming	Ongota is a separate branch of Afroasiatic, parallel with Cushitic and others, following the primary split of Omotic.
Sava & Tosco	Ongota is a type of Dullay, albeit with heavy regional influences.
Yilma	Ongota is a creole and thus cannot be classified.
Blažek	Ongota is Nilo-Saharan. (Author's conclusion is not definitive.)

3.3.5 Meroitic

Meroitic was the language of a substantial urban polity that existed on the Nile between eighth century BC until about 350 AD, when it was destroyed by Axumite armies. The inhabitants of Meroe used hieroglyphs and initially wrote in the Egyptian language. By the first century BC, hieroglyphs gave way to a Meroitic script that adapted the Egyptian writing system to an indigenous language. Meroitic is an alphabetic script with 23 signs used in a hieroglyphic form (mainly on monumental art) and in a cursive. The cursive version was widely used; so far some 1,278 texts are known. The most up-to-date review of what is known about Meroitic script is in Rilly and De Voogt (2012). The new alphabet was phonetic, assigning syllabic values to hieroglyphs and occasionally using hieroglyphs in their original sense to explicate the texts, rather as Chinese ideograms are still printed alongside Japanese today.

Meroitic inscriptions, which have proven problematic to decipher, have fuelled a string of poorly supported and indeed fringe hypotheses as to its genetic affiliation. Some of these are very bizarre, such as the proposal that Meroitic was Tocharian, the extinct Indo-European language of north-west China. The Web has created a new forum for individuals to publish their attempts at decipherment without the usual constraints of scholarship. Meroitic was previously considered to be degraded Egyptian, but it was then unclear why it could not easily be read. Most serious attempts at decipherment assumed that the original language is Afroasiatic, although there was no particular reason to think this was the case. The proposal that Meroitic was Nilo-Saharan was first made in the 1960s, and Greenberg (1971b) and Bender (1981) both supported this. However, since 2000, considerable progress has been made, and there are now more than 40 Meroitic terms transcribed with some certainty. Rilly and De Voogt (2012) argue that it was a close relative of Nubian, and this has gained general acceptance among Nilo-Saharan scholars.

3.3.6 Oropom

The Oropom language, said to be spoken among the Karamojong in northeast Uganda, is recorded in a single source, Wilson (1970). Wilson claimed that the Oropom were a subset of the Karamojong who used stone tools until the recent past. He recorded a 97-word list of the language, transcribed orthographically. Some ten years after Wilson's report, Bernd Heine (personal communication) went to seek rememberers of Oropom and could find no individuals who would even admit to this ethnic identity. For this reason he regarded the language as spurious, perhaps constructed on the spot by an informant. Souag (2004) re-analysed the vocabulary and found much of it borrowed from neighbouring languages, although with a core of unexplained lexical items. With no further reports, the safest conclusion is that Heine was correct in regarding Oropom as bogus.

3.3.7 Sandawe

The Sandawe are a people in the Kondoa district of Dodoma region in central Tanzania, notable for their non-Bantu click language. They were predominantly foragers and pastoralists before Europeans colonised Africa. In 2000, the Sandawe population was estimated to be 40,000. Sandawe ethnography and language was first described in Dempwolff (1916) and later in Ten Raa (1986). Sandawe grammar has been relatively well described (Van de Kimmenade 1954; Eaton 2010; Eaton et al. 2007; Steeman 2012), and there are two lexicons (Kagaya 1993; Ehret et al. 2012). The presence of clicks in Sandawe led Bleek (1956) and Greenberg (1963) to assume a relationship with Southern African Khoesan. More recent analyses have also reached the same conclusion although most of the earlier proposed cognates were compromised by poor transcription (Elderkin 1983; Sands 1998; Güldemann and Elderkin 2010). Nonetheless, if this is correct, the relationship is not close. Surprisingly, given that both are click languages in the same region of East Africa, Sandawe and Hadza seem to show no common lexicon.

3.3.8 Kwadi

The Kwadi (Bakoroka, Cuanhoca, Cuepe, Curoca, Koroka, Makoroko, Mucoroca) are a group of former pastoralists who live in the remote area in the extreme southwest of Angola. Strikingly, despite speaking a click language, they do not have the typical phenotype of Khoesan speakers. They were first reported by Capello-Ivens (1886) and described in more detail by the ethnographer Estermann (1956, translation Gibson 1976). Tape recordings of spoken Kwadi were made by the ethnographer Almeida, but these have never been released. Westphal (1963) made a field trip to the area and made extensive notes on Kwadi, which remain in the archive of the University of Cape Town. However, for some reason he never published an analysis of this data although he considered Kwadi an isolate (Westphal 1963, 1971). Güldemann (2013a, 2013b, 2013c) has written up the linguistic element of Westphal's notes. Güldemann (2004, 2008b) argues that Kwadi is part of Khoe, i.e. Central Khoesan, although the argument for this is complex, as the pronominal system and person marking seem to be very different from Khwe. The lexical cognates, however, seem to be at a level of near identity (Table 7.18).

Kwadi also shares a common Khwe root for 'cattle'.

Khwe	góɛ́
Naro	gòè
//Ana	gúè
Kwadi	goe-

TABLE 7.18 KWADI-KHOE LEXICAL CORRESPONDENCES

Kwadi	Gloss	Proto-Khoe	Gloss	Comment
guu-	sheep	*gu	sheep	
ha	to come	*ha	to come	
pa-	to bite	*pa	to bite	
pi-/ bi-	milk, breast	*pi	milk, breast	Also in Southern African Bantu
kho-	person	*khoe	person	
kõ	to go	*!ũ, *kũ	to go	(Kalahari East)
kuli-	year	*kudi, also kuri	year	
kum (also kũŋ)	to hear	*kum	to hear	(Kalahari)
kxo-	skin, fur	*kho, also kxo	skin, fur	
k''o- [= /kx'o/]	male	*kx'ao	male	
k''o- [= /kx'o/]	meat	*kx'o	to eat (meat)	
so-	medicine	*tso, *so	medicine	(Khoekhoe)
tame-	tongue	*dam	tongue	

Source: Güldemann (2008b).

Since the morphosyntax of Kwadi is very different from the Khwe languages, the near identity of the forms where the words *are* cognate suggests to the present author the possibility that the Kwadi language is an isolate displaying a borrowing relationship with Khwe. Since Güldemann (2008b) notes that the Kwadi were former pastoralists it might be that at least the livestock vocabulary was an early borrowing from Kwadi into Khwe. Unfortunately, even in the 1950s, there were few speakers of Kwadi, and it seems the language has now vanished completely, so this question can probably no longer be resolved.

3.3.9 Kujarge

The Kujarge language is, or was, spoken on the Chad-Sudan border by a small and scattered group of hunter-gatherers. The fate of these people, whose homeland is exactly in the centre of the recent civil conflicts, is unknown, but prognostications cannot be good.[6] The only published information on this language is Doornbos and Bender (1983). On the basis of 100 words, they concluded that the language was East Chadic, although its cognacy rate with other East Chadic languages is very low. In the 2000s an unpublished manuscript containing additional words collected by Paul Doornbos has been circulated, together with some etymological commentary. Nonetheless, the sample remains small, and the transcription and reliability of some forms can be questioned. Kujarge is clearly an important language, however, and the exiguous nature of the dataset is to be regretted. The present author has listed Kujarge as an isolate in various publications (e.g. Blench 2006) based on its low cognacy counts with its neighbours. Lovestrand (2012) has established additional lexical resemblances to East Chadic languages, and Blench (2013) now considers it to belong with East Chadic, although a highly divergent branch. Lovestrand classifies it as B1.3, a parallel branch to the Bidiya and Kajakse groups. The unlikelihood that more data will become available may mean that the definitive classification of Kujarge will remain unresolved.

3.3.10 Dompo

The Dompo language is spoken in West-Central Ghana in a settlement adjacent to Banda, the main town of the Nafaanra people. Painter (1967) gives a map reference as 8° 09′ N 2° 22′ W. Banda is reached from Wenchi by going northwards from the main road to Bondoukou in Côte d'Ivoire, south of the Black Volta. A visit by the present author in April 1998 established a longer wordlist. Dompo has a striking lexicon for wild fauna which is of unknown origin (cf. Table 7.19), but the main lexicon is undoubtedly Guan, and its closest relative is probably Gonja (Blench n.d. a). Either the names for animals

TABLE 7.19 MPRA-DOMPO RESEMBLANCES

Species	Mpra	Dompo
donkey	kwimi	kunumɔ
hartebeest	dʒunga	ʧɔŋ
hippopotamus	ʧaji	ʧa
kob	volo	fulofulo
oribi	wulo	wuloŋ
roan antelope	bruguni	buruŋ 'waterbuck'

constitute some sort of lexical avoidance or honorific system (Blench 2007b) or Dompo is a relic hunting group almost completely assimilated by the Guan.

3.3.11 Mpra

Cardinall (1931) reported the existence of a language, Mpre (correctly Mpra), spoken in Central Ghana, which had nearly disappeared in his time. Goody (1963) revisited the settlement in 1956 and was able to add a few more lexical items. Mpra has been listed in some sources as an isolate (e.g. Dimmendaal 2011). To see whether any speakers still existed, the present author visited the village of Butei (Bute in Goody) on February 28th, 2007. Butei is some 20 km from the main Tamale-Kintampo road, branching east towards Mpaha shortly after the Fulfulso junction leading to Damongo, and between the two branches of the Volta. By 2007, although former speakers still acknowledged their ethnic identity, only personal names and a few songs in Mpra remained (Blench n.d. c).

Blench (n.d. c) tabulates possible external sources of the lexicon. Overall, a large proportion of the vocabulary of Mpra has no evident source. The most notable parallels are with Avikam, a language spoken along the coastal lagoons of Cote d'Ivoire west of Abidjan (Hérault 1983b). Some lexical similarities are only shared with Avikam, to judge by Hérault (1983a); others are also found in other coastal languages such as Eotile, Adyukru and Nzema. The similarities to Lagoon languages might be ancient loans rather than true

FIGURE 7.2 LAST REMEMBERERS OF THE MPRA LANGUAGE

genetic cognates, particularly as many are extremely close in form and there are no obvious regular sound changes. There are also a few very specific parallels with the names of animals in the Dompo language (Table 7.19), a Guan language spoken near the Cote d'Ivoire border (Section 3.3.10). This is particularly surprising, as Mpra otherwise shows no Guan influence and is quite remote from Banda, where the Dompo live.

This may be evidence of the sharing of technical vocabulary between roaming hunters in their long-distance sweeps of the bush in the dry season. In the absence of further data, Mpra can probably be accepted as Niger-Congo, but whether it was an isolate branch or affiliated to a larger grouping can no longer be resolved.

3.3.12 Guanche

The Guanche were the ancient people of the Canary Islands, which were apparently settled around 3000 BP. The name originally applied to the inhabitants of Tenerife but has come to refer to what were probably at least four distinct languages. Modern European contact probably dates from the fourteenth century, and the first record of the Guanche language appears in the work of the Genoese mariner Nicoloso da Recco in 1341. The Castilian conquest of the Canaries began in 1402, and Guanche disappeared as a spoken language in seventeenth century, though rememberers may have persisted somewhat later. Virtually all the existing language materials are collected in Wölfel (1965). Rock inscriptions in the Canaries include short sentences in both Libyco-Berber and Punic languages. Unfortunately these include hardly any basic lexicon, except numbers, and many items of unknown origin. It is generally considered that Guanche is related to Berber, mostly on the basis of numbers (Pietschmann 1879). However, it is equally likely that it was an old North African language of unknown genetic affiliation and that similarities to Berber are later borrowings.

3.4 Residual foragers

An issue which warrants brief discussion is the question of whether the residual foragers of the Sahara and the equatorial rainforest represent the remnants of populations who spoke isolate languages. Two Saharan populations have been identified in this regard, the Imraguen fishermen of the coast of Mauretania and the Nemadi, who migrate between eastern Mauretania and Mali (locations shown on Map 7.1). The literature contains a certain amount of misleading information concerning these populations, including the speculation that they spoke a 'special' language among themselves (Hermans 2013). As is often the case, foragers in contact with major languages often adopt an accent which makes them difficult to understand (this is also true of the pygmies of the equatorial forest) (Hewlett 2014). However, although the Nemadi retain special vocabulary in relation to hunting with dogs, they speak standard Hassaniya Arabic, and there is no real evidence of any other language (Taine-Chcikh 2013). Similarly, the Imraguen have idiosyncratic terms for the fish they catch, but this would be expected, given that the Moors are not fishing people. But again they speak only Hassaniya (Taine-Cheikh 2013). Similar arguments have been advanced concerning specialised vocabulary of some pygmy groups in Central Africa (Letouzey 1976; at greater length Bahuchet 1992, 1993; Hewlett and Fancher 2014). Other residual foragers have been described from Chad (I. Nicolaisen 2011, J. Nicolaisen 1968; Matthey 1966) but in no case has significant evidence for a residual lexicon been given. The question is whether idiosyncratic vocabulary among

FIGURE 7.3 GUANCHE TERRACOTTA FIGURE

populations with a highly specialised knowledge of the environment constitutes evidence for a former substrate language. Blench (1999b) argues strongly that this is not the case.

4 CONCLUSIONS

This chapter has covered the complex methodological issues concerning the identification of language isolates in Africa and established a reference list of the most likely candidates, which are briefly described from a linguistic point of view. A longer list covers languages which have sometimes been considered isolates, but which are either undecidable for lack of adequate data or now have a fairly certain genetic affiliation. It should be underlined that a spectrum of views exists, from a position where languages are considered isolates until their affiliation is proven to a very high standard of evidence, to a position linking almost all known languages to larger phyla. The author has tried to tread a middle road and give a flavour of the debate. It is certain, however, that almost all candidates have only very small numbers of speakers, and living languages such as Laal, Bangi Me and Hadza deserve more description and analysis. Language isolates can provide clues to the language situation of Africa in the Pleistocene and enriching this sparse but valuable evidence must surely be a high priority.

NOTES

1 This chapter draws on the presentations and discussions at a workshop held in Lyon December 3 and 4, 2010, and a presentation circulated for that meeting. I am grateful to Harald Hammarström for helping me to get access to a variety of scarce documents and for insightful comments on the first version. I was subsequently invited to review the classificatory work of Joseph Greenberg for a special session of the Linguistic Society of America, held in Washington, January 2016. The text from that session is available at www.academia.edu/20110452/ Greenberg_s_Universal_Project_the_classification_of_the_world_s_languages.
2 Larry Hyman (2011) has also presented a detailed critique of Güldemann's methods and results, although using very different examples from those given here.
3 http://dogonlanguages.org/bangime.cfm
4 According to Woodburn (personal communication, May 2014), there are still Hadza who live almost entirely from foraging, despite the encroachment on their lands by herders and national parks.
5 This document is referred to in Fleming (2006), but it seems never to have been published, nor is a full bibliographic reference available.
6 Lovestrand (personal communication) conducted a search for Kujarge speakers in 2015 but without success.

REFERENCES

Ahland, Colleen A. 2004. *Linguistic Variation within Gumuz: A Study of the Relationship between Historical Change and Intelligibility*. MA Linguistics. Arlington: UTA.

Ahland, Colleen A. 2010. Noun Incorporation and Predicate Classifiers in Gumuz. *Journal of African Languages and Linguistics* 31, no. 2: 159–203.

Ahland, Colleen A. 2012. *A Grammar of Northern and Southern Gumuz*. Ph.D. University of Oregon.

Amha, Azeb. 2012. Omotic. *The Afroasiatic Languages*, ed. by Z. Fajzyngier and E. Shay, 423–504. Cambridge: Cambridge University Press.

Bahuchet, Serge. 1992. *Dans la forêt d'Afrique Centrale: les pygmées Aka et Baka*. Histoire d'une civilisation forestière, I. Paris: Peeters-SELAF.

Bahuchet, Serge. 1993. *La rencontre des agriculteurs: les pygmées parmi le peuples d'Afrique centrale*. Histoire d'une civilisation forestière, II. Paris: Peeters-SELAF.

Bender, Marvin Lionel. 1969. Chance CVC Correspondences in Unrelated Languages. *Language*, 45, no. 3: 519–531.

Bender, Marvin Lionel. 1975. *Omotic: A New Afroasiatic Language Family*. Carbondale, IL: University Museum Studies 3.

Bender, Marvin Lionel. 1977. The Surma Language Group: A Preliminary Report. *Studies in African Linguistics* 7:11–21.

Bender, Marvin Lionel. 1979. Gumuz: A Sketch of Grammar and Lexicon. *Afrika und Übersee*, 62: 38–69.

Bender, Marvin Lionel. 1981. The Meroitic Problem. *Peoples and Cultures of the Ethio-Sudan Borderlands*, ed. by M.L. Bender. Northeast African Studies 10, 5–32. East Lansing, MI: Michigan State University.

Bender, Marvin Lionel. 1983. Remnant Languages of Ethiopia and Sudan. *Nilo-Saharan Language Studies*, ed. M.L. Bender. Michigan State University Press.

Bender, Marvin Lionel. 1988. Proto-Omotic: Phonology and Lexicon. *Cushitic-Omotic: Papers from the International Symposium on Cushitic and Omotic Languages*, ed. by M. Bechhaus-Gerst and F. Serzisko, 121–162. Hamburg: Buske Verlag.

Bender, Marvin Lionel. 1997. *The Nilo-Saharan Languages: A Comparative Essay* (2nd ed.). Munich: Lincom Europa.

Bender, Marvin Lionel. 2000. *Comparative Morphology of Omotic Languages*. München: Lincom Europa.

Bender, Marvin Lionel. 2003. *Omotic Lexicon and Phonology*. Carbondale, IL: Southern Illinois University.

Bender, Marvin Lionel. 2005. Gumuz. *Encyclopaedia Aethiopica*, ed. by Siegbert Uhlig, 3: 914–916.. Wiesbaden: Harrassowitz Verlag.

Bendor-Samuel, John (ed.). 1989. *The Niger-Congo Languages*. Lanham: University Press of America.

Bertho, J. 1953. La place des dialectes dogon de la falaise de Bandiagara parmi les autres groupes linguistiques de la zone soudanaise. *Bulletin de l'IFAN* 15: 405–441.

Birkeli, Emil 1936. *Les Vazimba de la cote ouest de Madagascar: notes d'ethnologie*. Mémoires de l'Académie malgache. Tananarive: Imprimerie moderne de l'Emyrne, Pitot de la Beaujardière.

Blažek, Václav. 2007. Nilo-Saharan Stratum of Ongota. *Advances in Nilo-Saharan Linguistics. Proceedings of the 8th Nilo-Saharan Linguistics Colloquium, University of Hamburg, August 22–25, 2001*, ed. by Mechthild Reh and Doris L. Payne, 1–10. Köln: Rüdiger Köppe Verlag.

Bleek, Dorothea 1956. *A Bushman Dictionary*. New Haven: American Oriental Society.

Bleek, Wilhelm H.I. 1862, 1869. *A Comparative Grammar of South African Languages*. (1862: Part I; 1869: Part II). London: Trübner & Co.

Blench, Roger M. 1999a. The Languages of Africa: Macrophyla Proposals and Implications for Archaeological Interpretation. *Archaeology and Language, IV*, ed. by R.M. Blench and M. Spriggs, 29–47. London: Routledge.

Blench, Roger M. 1999b. Are the African Pygmies an Ethnographic Fiction? *Hunter-Gatherers of Equatorial Africa*, ed. by K. Biesbrouyck, G. Rossel, and S. Elders, 41–60. Leiden: Centre for Non-Western Studies.

Blench, Roger M. 2002. Besprechungsartikel. The Classification of Nilo-Saharan. *Afrika und Übersee* 83: 293–307.

Blench, Roger M. 2006. *Archaeology, Language and the African Past*. Lanham: Altamira Press.

Blench, Roger M. 2007a. Bangi Me: A Language of Unknown Affiliation in Northern Mali. *Mother Tongue* XII: 147–178.

Blench, Roger M. 2007b. Lexical Avoidance Taboos and the Reconstruction of Names for Large Animals in Niger-Congo, an African Language Phylum. *Le symbolisme des animaux – l'animal "clef de voûte" dans la tradition orale et les interactions homme-nature*, ed. by Edmond Dounias, Elisabeth Motte-Florac, and Margaret Dunham, 545–569. unpaginated appendices. Paris: Editions IRD.

Blench, Roger M. 2007c. New Palaezoogeographical Evidence for the Settlement of Madagascar. *Azania* XLII: 69–82.

Blench, Roger M. 2013. Links between Cushitic, Omotic, Chadic and the position of Kujarge. *Proceedings of the 5th International Conference of Cushitic and Omotic languages*, ed. by M. van Hove, 67–80. Köln: Rüdiger Köppe.

Blench, Roger M. 2016. *Greenberg's Universal Project: The Classification of the World's Languages*. Paper presented at the Symposium of Joseph Greenberg, Linguistic Society of America, Washington, 2016.

Blench, Roger M. n.d. a. *Wordlist and Etymological Analysis of Dompo*. Electronic ms.

Blench, Roger M. n.d. c. Recovering Data on Mpra [=Mpre] a Possible Language Isolate in North-Central Ghana. Electronic ms.

Blench, Roger, M. and M. Walsh n.d. *The Vocabularies of Vazimba and Beosi: Do They Represent the Languages of the Pre-Austronesian Populations of Madagascar?* Electronic ms.

Boyeldieu, Pascal. 1977. Eléments pour une phonologie du laal de Gori (Moyen-Chari). *Etudes phonologiques tchadiennes*, 186–198. Paris: SELAF (Bibliothèque, 63–64).

Boyeldieu, Pascal. 1982a. *Deux Etudes laal (Moyen-Chari, Tchad)*. Berlin: Dietrich Reimer Verlag.

Boyeldieu, Pascal. 1982b. Quelques questions portant sur la classification du laal (Tchad). *The Chad Languages in the Hamitosemitic-Nigritic Border Area (Papers of the Marburg Symposium, 1979)*, ed. by H. Jungraithmayr, 80–93. Berlin: Dietrich Reimer.

Boyeldieu, Pascal. 1987. Détermination directe/indirecte en laal. *La maison du chef et la tête du cabri: des degrés de la détermination nominale dans les langues d'Afrique centrale*, ed. by P. Boyeldieu, 77–87. Paris: Geuthner.

Boyeldieu, Pascal. n.d. *Presentation du láà:l ou "Gori" (Moyen-Chari, Tchad)*. ms. CNRS, Paris.

Cardinall, A.W. 1931. A Survival. *Gold Coast Review* 5, no. 1: 193–197.

Cohen, M. 1947. *Essai comparatif sur le vocabulaire et la phonétique du Chamito-Sémitique*. Paris: Honoré Champion.

Dalby, David. 1970. Reflections on the Classification of African Languages: With Special Reference to the Work of Sigismund Wilhelm Koelle and Malcolm Guthrie. *African Language Studies* 11 147–171.

Dempwolff, Otto. 1916. *Die Sandawe: linguistisches und ethnographisches Material aus Deutsch-Ostafrika*. (Abhandlungen des Hamburger Kolonial-Institutes, Bd 34. Reihe B: Völkerkunde, Kulturgeschichte und Sprachen, Bd 19.) Hamburg: Friederichsen.

Dimmendaal, Gerrit J. 2011. *Historical Linguistics and the Comparative Study of African Languages*. Amsterdam: John Benjamins Publishing.

Dixon, R.M.W. 1997. *The Rise and Fall of Languages*. Cambridge: Cambridge University Press.

Doke, C.M. 1961. The Earliest Records of Bantu. *Contributions to the History of Bantu Linguistics*, ed. by C.M. Doke and D.T. Cole, 1–26. Johannesburg: Witwatersrand University Press.

Doornbos, P. and M.L. Bender. 1983. Languages of Wadai-Darfur. *Nilo-Saharan Language Studies*, ed. by M.L. Bender, 43–79. East Lansing: Michigan State University Press.

Eaton, Helen. 2010. *A Sandawe Grammar*. (SIL e-Books, 20.) Dallas, TX: SIL International. www.sil.org/silepubs/index.asp?series=941

Eaton, Helen, Daniel Hunziker, and Elisabeth Hunziker. 2007. *A Sandawe Dialect Survey*. SIL Electronic Survey Reports, 2007–2014. Dallas, TX: SIL International. www.sil.org/silesr/2007/silesr2007-014.pdf.

Ehret, Christopher. 1995. Do Krongo and Shabo Belong in Nilo-Saharan? *Proceedings of the Fifth Nilo-Saharan Linguistics Colloquium, Nice, 1992*, R. Nicolai and F. Rottland, 169–193. Köln: Rudiger Köppe.

Ehret, Christopher. 2001. *A Historical-Comparative Reconstruction of Nilo-Saharan.* Köln: Rudiger Köppe.

Ehret, Christopher, Patricia Ehret, and Eric ten Raa. 2012. *A Dictionary of Sandawe: The Lexicon and Culture of a Khoesan People of Tanzania.* Köln: Rüdiger Köppe Verlag.

Elderkin, E.D. 1983. Tanzanian and Ugandan Isolates. *Nilotic Studies: Proceedings of the International Symposium on Languages and History of the Nilotic Peoples,* ed. by Rainer Vossen and Marianne Bechhaus-Gerst, vol. 2, 499–521. Berlin: Dietrich Reimer.

Estermann, Carlos [ed. and trans. Gordon G. Gibson] 1976. *The Ethnography of South-western Angola, Volume I.* New York: Africana Publishing Company. [original dated 1958]

Faris, David. 1994. *In-House Summary of the Laal/Gori language.* Electronic ms. SIL: Chad.

Fleming, H.C. 1969. Asa and Aramanik: Cushitic Hunters in Masai-land. *Ethnology,* 8(1): 1–36.

Fleming, Harold C. 1991. Shabo: Presentation of Data and Preliminary Classification. *Proceedings of the Fourth Nilo-Saharan Conference. Bayreuth, 1989,* ed. by M.L. Bender, 389–402. Hamburg: Buske.

Fleming, Harold C. 2002. Shabo: A New African Phylum or a Special Relic of Old Nilo-Saharan? *Mother Tongue,* VII: 1–37.

Fleming, Harold C. 2006. *Ongota: A Decisive Language in African Prehistory.* Mainz: Harassowitz.

Fleming, Harold C., A. Yilma, A. Mitiku, R. Hayward, Y. Miyawaki, P. Mikesh, and J.M. Seelig. 1992. Ongota or Birale: A Moribund Language of Gemu-Gofa (Ethiopia). *Journal of Afroasiatic Languages* 3, no. 3:181–225.

Goody, J.R. 1963. Ethnological Notes on the Distribution of the Guang Languages. *Journal of African Languages* 2, no. 3: 173–189.

Greenberg, Joseph H. 1960. The General Classification of Central and South American Languages. *Men and Cultures: Selected Papers of the Fifth International Congress of Anthropological and Ethnological Sciences, Philadelphia, September 1–9, 1956,* ed. by Anthony F.C. Wallace, 791–794. Philadelphia: Pennsylvania University Press.

Greenberg, Joseph H. 1963. *The Languages of Africa.* The Hague: Mouton.

Greenberg, Joseph H. 1971a. The Indo-Pacific Hypothesis. *Current Trends in Linguistics, Volume VIII – Linguistics in Oceania,* ed. by T.A. Sebeok, 807–871. The Hague: Mouton.

Greenberg, Joseph H. 1971b. Nilo-Saharan and Meroitic. *Current Trends in Linguistics Vol. 7, Sub-Saharan Africa,* ed. by J. Berry and J.H. Greenberg, 421–442. The Hague: Mouton.

Greenberg, Joseph H. 1987. *Language in the Americas.* Stanford, CA: Stanford University Press.

Greenberg, Joseph H. 2000, 2002. *Indo-European and Its Closest Relatives: The Eurasiatic Language Family.* [2 vols] Stanford, CA: Stanford University Press.

Güldemann, Tom. 2004. Reconstruction Through 'de-construction': The Marking of Person, Gender and Number in the Khoe Family and Kwadi. *Diachronica* 21, no. 2: 251–306.

Güldemann, Tom. 2008a. The Macro-Sudan Belt: Towards Identifying a Linguistic Area in Northern Sub-Saharan Africa. *A Linguistic Geography of Africa,* ed. by Bernd Heine and Derek Nurse, 151–185. Cambridge: Cambridge University Press.

Güldemann, Tom. 2008b. A Linguist's View: Khoe-Kwadi Speakers as the Earliest Food-Producers of Southern Africa. *Southern African Humanities* 20, no. 1: 93–132.

Güldemann, Tom. 2011. Proto-Bantu and Proto-Niger-Congo: Macro-Areal Typology and Linguistic Reconstruction. *Geographical Typology and Linguistic Areas*, ed. by O. Hieda, C. König, and H. Nakagawa, 109–142. Amsterdam and Philadelphia: John Benjamins.

Güldemann, Tom. 2013a. Phonology: Kwadi. *The Khoisan Languages*, ed. by Rainer Voßen, 87–88. Routledge Language Family Series. London: Routledge.

Güldemann, Tom. 2013b. Morphology: Kwadi. *The Khoisan languages*, ed. by Rainer Voßen, 261–264. Routledge Language Family Series. London: Routledge.

Güldemann, Tom. 2013c. Syntax: Kwadi. *The Khoisan Languages*, ed. by Rainer Voßen, 431–433. Routledge Language Family Series. London: Routledge.

Güldemann, Tom. 2014. 'Khoisan' Linguistic Classification Today. *Beyond 'Khoisan': Historical relations in the Kalahari Basin*, ed. by Tom Güldemann and Anne-Maria Fehn, 1–40. Amsterdam: Benjamins.

Güldemann, Tom and Edward D. Elderkin. 2010. On External Genealogical Relationships of the Khoe Family. *Khoisan Languages and Linguistics: Proceedings of the 1st International Symposium, January 4–8, 2003, Riezlern/Kleinwalsertal.* (Quellen zur Khoisan-Forschung, 24), ed. by M. Brenzinger and C. König, 15–52. Köln: Rüdiger Köppe.

Hantgan, A. 2012. *Bangime Dictionary*. Manuscript previously published online.

Hantgan, A. 2013. *Aspects of Bangime Phonology, Morphology, and Morphosyntax*. Ph.D., Indiana University.

Hayward, R.J. (ed.). 1990. *Omotic Language Studies*. London: School of Oriental and African Studies.

Heine, Bernd and Derek Nurse (eds.). 2008. *A Linguistic Geography of Africa*. Cambridge: Cambridge University Press.

Heine, Bernd and Henry Honken. 2010. The Kx'a Family. *Journal of Asian and African Studies* 79: 5–36.

Herault, G. 1983a. *Atlas des langues Kwa de Côte d'ivoire, Tome 2*. Abidjan: ILA.

Herault, G. 1983b. Avikam. *Atlas des langues Kwa de Côte d'ivoire, Tome 1*, ed. by G. Hérault, 255–276. Abidjan: ILA.

Hermans, Jean-Michel. 2013. *Les Némadis, chasseurs-cueilleurs du désert mauritanien: les derniers chasseurs-cueilleurs de race blanche*. s.l.: Édilivre.

Hewlett, B.S. (ed.). 2014. *Hunter-Gatherers of the Congo Basin: Cultures, Histories, and Biology of African Pygmies*. Piscataway, NJ: Transaction Publishers.

Hewlett, B.S. and J.M. Fancher. 2014. Central African Hunter-Gatherer Research Traditions. *Oxford Handbook of the Archaeology and Anthropology of Hunter-Gatherers*, ed. by Cummings, Jordan, and Marek Zvelebil, 936–957. Oxford: Oxford University Press.

Hochstetler, J. Lee, J.A. Durieux, and E.I.K. Durieux-Boon. 2004. *Sociolinguistic Survey of the Dogon Language Area*. SIL International. www.sil.org/silesr/2004/silesr2004-004.pdf.

Hyman, L.M. 2011. The Macro-Sudan Belt and Niger-Congo Reconstruction. *Language Dynamics and Change* 1, no. 1: 3–49.

Janhunen, Juha. 1994. Additional Notes on Japanese and Altaic [1 and 2]. *Journal de la Société Finno-Ougrienne* 85: 236–240, 256–260.

Jordan, L., H. Mohammed, and J. Netzley. 2007. *Sociolinguistic Survey of Shabo*. ms.

Kagaya, Ryohei. 1993. *A Classified Vocabulary of the Sandawe Language* (Asian and African lexicon, 26.) Tokyo: Institute for the Study of Languages and Cultures of Asia and Africa, Tokyo University of Foreign Studies (ILCAA).

Kleinewillinghöfer, U. 2001. The Language of the Jalaa: A Disappearing Language Isolate. *Sprache und Geschichte in Afrika* 16/17: 239–271.

Letouzey, R. 1976. *Contribution de la Botanique au problème d'une éventuelle langue Pygmée.* Bibliothèque de la SELAF, 57–58. Paris : SELAF.

Lionnet, Florian. 2010. *Laal: An Isolate Language?* Handout for the Workshop *Isolates in Africa* Lyon, 3 December 2010.

Lionnet, Florian. 2013. Doubly Conditioned Rounding in Laal: Conditional Licensing and Correspondence Chains. Abstract for *Berkeley Phonetics and Phonology Forum* (Vol. 8).

Lovestrand, J. 2012. *Classification and Description of the Chadic Languages of the Guéra (East Chadic B).* SIL Electronic Working Papers 2012–2004. Dallas, TX: SIL International.

Matthey, Piero. 1966. Brief Notes on the Nooy, a Former Tribe of Hunters and Fishers in Southern Chad. *Bulletin of the International Committee on Urgent Anthropological Ethnological Research* 8: 37–38.

Meinhof, Carl. 1910. *Grundriss einer Lautlehre der Bantusprachen.* Berlin: Dietrich Reimer.

Nicolaisen, Ida. 2011. *Elusive Hunters: The Haddad of Kanem and the Bahr el Ghazal.* Aarhus: Aarhus Universitetsforlag.

Nicolaisen, Johannes. 1968. The Haddad – a Hunting People in Tchad: Preliminary Report of an Ethnographical Reconnaissance. *Folk* 10: 91–109.

Painter, C. 1967. The Distribution of Guang in Ghana and a Statistical Pre-Testing on Twenty-Five Idiolects. *Journal of West African Languages*, 4, no. 1: 25–78.

Pierron, Denis, Harilanto Razafindrazaka, Luca Pagani, François-Xavier Ricaut, Tiago Antao, Mélanie Capredon, Clément Sambo, Chantal Radimilahy, Jean-Aimé Rakotoarisoa, Roger M. Blench, Thierry Letellier, and Toomas Kivisild. 2014. Genome-Wide Evidence of Austronesian – Bantu Admixture and Cultural Reversion in a Hunter-Gatherer Group of Madagascar. *Proceedings of the National Academy of Sciences* 111, no. 3: 936–941.

Pietschmann, Richard. 1879. Über die kanarischen Zahlwörte. *Zeitschrift für Ethnologie* 11: 377–391.

Reh, M. 1985. *Die Krongo-Sprache (nìino mó-dì)* : *Beschreibung, Texte, Wörterverzeichnis.* Kölner Beiträge zur Afrikanistik, 12. Berlin: Dietrich Reimer.

Rilly, Claude and Alex de Voogt. 2012. *The Meroitic Language and Writing System.* Cambridge: Cambridge University Press.

Ringe, Don A. 1992. On Calculating the Factor of Chance in Language Comparison. *Transactions of the American Philosophical Society* 82, no. 1: 1–110.

Ringe, Don A. 1999. Language Classification: Scientific and Unscientific Methods. *The Human Inheritance: Genes, Language, and Evolution*, ed. by Brian D. Sykes, 45–74 Oxford: Oxford University Press.

Sands, B. 1998. *Eastern and Southern African Khoisan: Evaluating Claims of a Distant Linguistic Relationships.* Quellen zur Khoisan-Forschung 14. Köln: Rüdiger Köppe.

Sands, B. 2013a. Phonetics and Phonology: Hadza. *The Khoisan Languages*, ed. by Rainer Voßen, 38–42. Routledge Language Family Series. London: Routledge.

Sands, B. 2013b. Morphology: Hadza. *The Khoisan Languages*, ed. by Rainer Voßen, 107–124. Routledge Language Family Series. London: Routledge.

Sands, B. 2013c. Syntax: Hadza. *The Khoisan Languages*, ed. by Rainer Voßen, 265–274. Routledge Language Family Series. London: Routledge.

Sands, B., I. Maddieson, and P. Ladefoged. 1993. The Phonetic Structures of Hadza. *UCLA Working Papers in Phonetics* 84: 67–87.

Savà, Graziano and Mauro Tosco. 2000. A Sketch of Ongota: A Dying Language of Southwest Ethiopia. *Studies in African Linguistics* 29, no. 2: 59–135.

Schnoebelen, T. 2009. Classifying Shabo: Phylogenetic Methods and Results. *Conference on Language Documentation and Theory*, Vol. 2, ed. by Peter K. Austin, Oliver Bond, Monik Charette, David Nathan, and Peter Sells, 275–284. London: SOAS.

Simons, Gary F. and Charles D. Fennig (eds.). 2017. *Ethnologue: Languages of the World, Twentieth edition*. Dallas, Texas: SIL International. Online version: http://www.ethnologue.com.

Souag, Lameen M. 2004. *Oropom Etymological Lexicon: Exploring an Extinct, Unclassified Ugandan Language*. ms. SOAS.

Starostin, S.A., Anna Dybo, and Oleg Mudrak. 2003. *Etymological Dictionary of the Altaic Languages*. Leiden/ Boston: Brill.

Steeman, S. 2012. *A Grammar of Sandawe: A Khoisan Language of Tanzania*. LOT-Netherlands Graduate School of Linguistics, Utrecht.

Stiles, D. 1994. The Mikea, Hunter-Gatherers of Madagascar. *Kenya Past and Present* 26: 27–33.

Taine-Cheikh, Catherine. 2013. Des ethnies chimériques aux langues fantômes: l'exemple des Imraguen et Nemâdi de Mauritanie. *In and Out of Africa: Languages in Question. In Honour of Robert Nicolaï. Vol. 1. Language Contact and Epistemological Issues*, ed. by Carole de Féral, 137–164. Louvain: Peeters.

Teferra, A. 1991. A Sketch of Shabo Grammar. *Studies in African Linguistics*, 7: 11–21.

Teferra, A. 1995. Brief Phonology of Shabo (Mekeyir). *Fifth Nilo-Saharan Linguistics Colloquium. Nice, 24–29 août 1992*, ed. by R. Nicolaï and F. Rottland, 169–193. Hamburg: Helmut Buske.

Teferra, A. and P. Unseth. 1989. Toward the Classification of Shabo (Mikeyir). *Topics in Nilo-Saharan Linguistics. Nilo-Saharan 3*, ed. by M.L. Bender, 405–418. Hamburg: Helmut Buske.

Ten Raa, Eric. 1986. The Acquisition of Cattle by Hunter-Gatherers: A Traumatic Experience in Cultural Change. *Sprache und Geschichte in Afrika* 7, no. 2: 361–374.

Theil, Rolf. 2012. Omotic. *Semitic and Afroasiatic: Challenges and Opportunities*, ed. by Lutz Edzard, 369–384. Wiesbaden: Otto Harrassowitz.

Tosco, Mauro. 1991. *A Grammatical Sketch of Dahalo Including Texts and a Glossary* (Kuschitische Sprachstudien/Cushitic Language Studies, Band 8). Hamburg: Helmut Buske Verlag.

Traill, A. 1973. "N4 or S7": Another Bushman Language. *African Studies* 32, no. 1: 25–32.

Tsehay, Kibebe. 2015. *Documentation and Grammatical Description of Chabu*. Ph.D., University of Addis Ababa.

Tucker, Archibald N. and M.A. Bryan. 1956. *The Non-Bantu Languages of North-Eastern Africa*. Published for the International African Institute by Oxford University Press.

Tucker, Archibald N., Margaret Bryan, and James Woodburn. 1977. The East African Click Languages: A Phonetic Comparison. *Zur Sprachgeschichte und Ethnohistorie in Afrika (Festschrift Oswin R.A. Köhler)*, ed. by W.J.G. Möhlig, F. Rottland, and B. Heine, 301–323. Berlin: Dietrich Reimer.

Van de Kimmenade, Martin. 1954. *Essai de grammaire et vocabulaire de la langue Sandawe*. Micro bibliotheca anthropos, no 9. Posieux (Switzerland): Anthropos-Institut.

Voßen, Rainer (ed.). 2013. *The Khoisan Languages*. Routledge Language Family Series. London: Routledge.

Westermann, Diedrich. 1911. *Die Sudansprachen*. Hamburg: Friederichsen.

Westermann, Diedrich. 1935. Nominalklassen in westafrikanischen Klassensprachen und in Bantusprachen. *MSOS* 38: 1–52.

Westphal, E.O.J. 1963. The Linguistic Prehistory of Southern Africa: Bush, Kwadi, Hottentot and Bantu Linguistic Relationships. *Africa* 33: 237–265.

Westphal, E.O.J. 1971. The Click Languages of Southern and Eastern Africa. *Current Trends in Linguistics*, Volume 7: Linguistics in Sub-Saharan Africa, ed. by T.A. Sebeok, 367–420. Berlin: Mouton.

Wilson, John G. 1970. Preliminary Observations on the Oropom People of Karamoja, Their Ethnic Status, Culture and Postulated Relation to the Peoples of the Late Stone Age. *Uganda Journal* 34, no. 2: 125–145.

Wölfel, D.J. 1965. *Monumenta linguae Canariae*. Austria: Akademische Druck.

CHAPTER 8

LANGUAGE ISOLATES OF NORTH AMERICA

Marianne Mithun

Approximately half of the language families indigenous to North America North of Mexico have been identified as isolates, families consisting of a single language. The figure is necessarily approximate for several reasons. The first is the quality of data. Some languages are represented by so little documentation, often of poor quality, that demonstrating genetic relationships to any other languages with confidence is difficult. A second is the continuum between dialects and languages. A third is the potentially deep impact of language contact. Ultimately, isolate status does not entail particular structural characteristics inherent in the language itself: it is more about their potential relatives.

1 LANGUAGE ISOLATES AND UNCLASSIFIED LANGUAGES

There is an important distinction between isolates, that is, languages with no known relatives, and unclassifiable languages, those for which it is difficult or impossible to identify relatives due to the quality and quantity of documentation. But the line between the two is not sharp. There are no written records of most North American languages comparable in time depth to those of some languages of Europe and Asia. While some groups in eastern and southeastern North America encountered Europeans as early as the sixteenth century, others in the West saw no Europeans until the mid-nineteenth century. In too many cases their languages did not survive long after contact. Some we know about only from brief mention in historical accounts; with no data, these are necessarily unclassifiable. For others, data are sparse, mixed in among notes from brief encounters.

A clear example of an unclassifiable language is **Aranama**, also known as **Tamique**, the language of two groups at the Franciscan mission of Espiritu Santo de Zúñiga, founded on the lower Guadalupe River in Texas in 1726 (Goddard 1979: 373). Our entire documentation of the language consists of one single word and one two-word phrase: *himiyána* 'water' and *Himiána tsýi!* 'Give me water!'. These were recorded by Albert Gatschet in 1884 from a Tonkawa man known as Old Simon, who also provided a short vocabulary of Karankawa, another Texas language. Old Simon himself identified the language as Hanáma or Háname (Gatschet 1884). The only people indigenous to that area with a similar name were those known as the Aranama, Saranames, or Jaranames.

Another example of an unclassifiable language is **Calusa**, once spoken in southern Florida. This language is represented by just a dozen words from the 1575 account of Escalante Fontaneda (1944), who had been a captive among the Calusa, and by 50–60 place names published in Swanton 1922 (Goddard 1996a: 17, Landar 1996: 725). Early accounts indicate that Calusa was distinct from other languages in the area, those spoken by the Timucua, Apalachee, Ais, Jeaga, Tequesta, Guale, and Yamasee (Marquardt 2004: 204), suggesting that it may have been an isolate. With such a small record, however, its status cannot be confirmed.

Only slightly more information is available on a language referred to as **Solano**: a sheet with 21 words found in the manuscript for Swanton's 1940 work on languages from southern Texas and northeastern Mexico (Goddard 1979: 371). The page bore the following description: "Near the end of the original book of baptisms of the San Francisco Solano Mission, 1703–1708, is a brief vocabulary, presumably of the Indians of that mission". It was apparently sent to Swanton by H. E. Bolton from Queretaro, Mexico, about 1909, who characterised it as the language of the Terocodame band cluster associated with the missions opposite present Eagle Pass, Texas, in the early eighteenth century. It was published in Swanton 1915: 34–35 and 1940: 54–55, but it has not been possible to link the language to any other.

An important aspect of documentation is whether the language was recorded from native speakers. **Cotoname**, also called Carrizo de Camargo, was indigenous to the lower Rio Grande Valley of south Texas and northeastern Mexico. It is known to us only from a vocabulary of 104 words recorded by Berlandier around 1829 (Berlandier and Chowell 1828–1829) and some additional words recorded by Gatschet in 1886 from Comecrudo speakers (Goddard 1979: 370), totaling around 150 words in all. Goddard comments:

> In view of its source it is perhaps not surprising that there is more similarity between Comecrudo and Cotoname in Gatschet's materials than in Berlandier's. Two significant examples suggest that Gatschet's informants used original Cotoname words in both languages.
>
> (Goddard 1979: 370)

After close inspection of the sources, Goddard concludes that "Coahuilteco, Comecrudo, and Cotoname must all be considered independent isolated languages whose genetic relationships are at present unknown, and the fragments of Solano and Aranama cannot be put in any language grouping with any confidence" (1979: 379).

Similar challenges are presented by **Karankawa**, once spoken on the Texas coast. The last Karankawa speakers died in 1858 on Padre Island at the hands of Texas Rangers and Mexican soldiers. All of the attested material, over 400 vocabulary items and some phrases, sentences, and translations of English nursery rhymes, is assembled in Grant (1994). It comes from the following sources: French brothers Jean-Baptiste and Pierre Talon, who had been part of La Salle's expedition and were captured by Karankawas around 1686, dictated to M. de Boissieu in Brittany in 1689; the French sea captain Jean Béranger, who collected vocabulary near Matagorda Bay in 1720–1721; the Mexican geologist Rafael Chowell, who collected vocabulary in south Texas or Coahuila, Mexico in 1828–1829; the Tonkawa man Old Simon (mentioned earlier as the source for Aranama), dictated to Albert Gatschet at Fort Griffin, Texas, in 1884; a blind Tonkawa woman, Sallie Washington, who had once lived with a Karankawa man, dictated to Gatschet in 1884; and Alice Williams Oliver, a White woman who had lived near the Karankawa in Texas as a child and made a list of around 600 forms, though that list was subsequently lost. Gatschet discovered Mrs. Oliver living in Lynn, Massachusetts, and worked with her in 1888–1889. Not surprisingly, Grant found considerable variation in the material, since the language was spoken by a number of bands and so much came from non-native speakers. Nevertheless Grant, like others, concludes that it was a single language.

In some cases classification of a language depends not only on the quantity and quality of the data available on that language, but also on our knowledge about potential relatives. A German philologist comparing German *Hund* and English *dog* might not see a relationship immediately, but with more extensive knowledge of English, the link to English *hound* would be clear, and further comparisons could confirm the connection. When Jacques Cartier first sailed into the Bay of Gaspé in 1534, he encountered fishermen from a settlement up the Saint Lawrence River at the site of present-day Quebec City. He took two captives back with him to France but returned with them the following summer, staying longer and going further upriver to a settlement at the site of present-day Montreal. When Champlain arrived in the region in 1603, these people had vanished from the area. But appended to the accounts of the first two Cartier voyages were vocabulary lists which together comprise a little over 200 words. From these lists it is possible to identify the language as Northern Iroquoian with certainty, in good part because the modern Northern Iroquoian languages are well known (Mithun 1982). It can even be seen that the words come from several different dialects or languages.

A group known as the **Adai** (also known as Adaizan, Adaizi, Adaise, Adahi, Adaes, Adees, or Atayos) was first encountered in what is now eastern Louisiana around 1530. Adai was the language of the Spanish Mission of Adayes founded in 1715 west of Natchitoches, but when that mission closed in 1792, the converts joined Caddoan groups in Texas. Their language is known only from a list of 275 words recorded around 1802 by John Sibley, the first Indian Agent of the United States (Sibley 1832: 722). The original manuscript has been lost, but a copy is in the American Philosophical Society Library, and vocabulary from it has been published in Adelung and Vater (1816: 3.2.278), Gallatin (1836, with errors), and Taylor (1963: 114). Sibley noted that the language "differs from all others, and is so difficult to speak or understand that no nation can speak ten words of it" (Powell 1891: 122). Gatschet saw some similarities to words of the neighboring Caddo. With better knowledge of Caddo, however, Wallace Chafe could determine with certainty that it is not Caddo (personal communication). This leaves us with a language which we can see is not related to the most likely neighbor and without demonstrable relationships to other well-known languages in the area, suggesting it is an isolate.

Knowledge about earlier stages of potential relatives can sometimes be useful. Slightly more documentation is available for **Beothuk**, once spoken in present-day Newfoundland. The Beothuk were first mentioned in the account of Cartier's 1534 voyage. Records of their language consist of 4 vocabularies together comprising over 400 items: one recorded by John Cline during the eighteenth century; one by John Leigh from a woman named Demasduit (Mary March) captured in 1819; one by a man named King; and one by W. E. Cormack from a voluntary captive named Shanawdithit (Nancy April), who died in 1829. All are published in Hewson 1978. Investigation into possible genetic relationships has focused on the surrounding Algonquian languages. A few similarities have been noted, but Voegelin and Voegelin (1946) concluded that the similarities were too close to be cognates and should rather be identified as loans. Hewson (1968, 1971, 1978, 1982) did see some similarities between the Beothuk vocabulary and certain Proto-Algonquian reconstructions. At present, however, the general consensus is that a relationship is unlikely though not impossible.

2 DIALECTS AND LANGUAGES

A second challenge for the identification of isolates is the continuum between dialects and languages. Technically two forms of speech are considered *dialects* if they are mutually intelligible, and separate *languages* if they are not. A group of dialects could together constitute a language isolate if there are no other relatives. Once the differences among them become so great as to interfere with intelligibility, they no longer constitute an isolate. (It should be noted that into the early twentieth century, the term *dialect* was often used to refer to all speech varieties known to be related at any level.) Particularly for languages no longer spoken, it can be difficult to assess precise degrees of mutual intelligibility. There are a number of such situations in North America.

Alsea, spoken along the central coast of Oregon, comprises either two dialects or closely related languages: Alsea and Yaquina. Frachtenberg, who worked with both in 1910, left a major manuscript grammar. There he reported on the recent history of the two, which he termed Yakonan:

> Until 1876 most of the Yakwina and Alsea Indians lived at the Yahatc reservation. Even at that time the number of Yakwinas still extant was limited. When, on the 26th day of April, 1876, this reservation was abolished, the remaining members of the Yakonan family were transferred to the newly established Siletz Agency (in 1913) but only one adult Yakwina and eight full-grown Alsea Indians were left, of whom only five may be said to have retained some knowledge of the language, traditions, and customs of their forefathers. With the demise of this handful the Yakonan group will have become a thing of the past.
>
> (Frachtenberg 1918 ms: 14)

Such proximity could have led to mutual intelligibility even if the two were not closely related, but further comments suggest that they were in fact close dialects:

> The differences between the Alsea and Yakwina dialects are very slight. As far as has been ascertained, there is only one phonetic deviation, and a limited number of stems are particular to each dialect. The Alsea combination of *al* appears in most instances in Yakwina as a *u* diphthong.
>
> (Frachtenberg 1918 ms: 15)

Frachtenberg provides four examples of pairs of words showing the phonological correspondence (among them *qalp-/qaup-* 'to roll'), and nine stems that differ (among them *pəlú:pəlu:/k'ins* 'beard'). His descriptions suggest that the two were indeed dialects, so together they would constitute a language isolate. (Distant relationships to neighboring Siuslaw and Coos have been proposed but are not considered established.)

Mutual intelligibility is of course a matter of degree and experience. **Yana**, spoken in central Northern California, was well documented by Sapir early in the twentieth century, but it disappeared not long afterward. Four dialects are generally recognised: Northern Yana, Central Yana, Southern Yana, and Yahi. Sapir characterised their relationships as follows:

> The probability is strong that Southern Yana was a link between the Central and Yahi dialects, with a leaning, I surmise, to Yahi rather than to Central Yana. The Central and Northern dialects, though neatly distinct on a number of phonetic points, are mutually intelligible without difficulty. Yahi is very close in all essential respects to the two Northern forms of Yana, but there are enough differences in phonetics, vocabulary, and morphology to put it in a class by itself as contrasted with the other two. It is doubtful if a Northern or Central Yana Indian could understand Yahi perfectly, but it is certain that he could make out practically all of it after a brief contact.
>
> (Sapir and Spier 1943, cited in Sapir and Swadesh 1960: 14)

Atakapa, once spoken by a number of small groups along the Gulf of Mexico from Vermillion Bay and Bayou Teche in Louisiana to Galveston Bay and up the Trinity River in Texas, presents a cloudier picture. It is sometimes said to comprise three languages, sometimes two, and sometimes one. Three varieties were recognised by Swanton. A list of 45 words, recorded in 1721 by the sea captain Jean Béranger from a captive taken at Galveston Bay, Swanton identified as Akokisa (published in Villiers du Terrage and Rivet 1919). Another list of 287 words collected by Martin Duralde in 1802 at modern Martinville, Louisiana, he identified as Eastern Atakapa (published in Vater 1820–1821 and Gallatin 1836). The most extensive documentation, consisting of around 2,100 words and sentences, as well as 9 texts, was obtained by Gatschet in 1885 at Lake Charles, Louisiana, from 2 of the last speakers to know the language well. This material Swanton identified as Western Atakapa. A grammatical sketch based on all sources is in Swanton 1929a, and a dictionary with texts in Gatschet and Swanton 1932. Swanton's classification may not actually have been meant as a linguistic one, however. Martin notes that "the relatively small and unsystematic variation seen in the data provide little support for these groupings" (2004: 79). If the three varieties are indeed very closely related, as it appears they are, together they comprise a language isolate. (Hypotheses of more remote relations once grouped it with neighboring languages in a Gulf superstock, described below.)

Ultimately the status of a language as an isolate depends more on possible relatives than on the language itself. The **Timucua** were first encountered by Ponce de León in 1513 near present-day St. Augustine, Florida. Their language was documented early by two priests who were in the area between 1603 and 1627, Francisco Pareja and Gregorio de Movilla. They left a grammar, three catechisms, a confessional, a *doctrina*, and other materials, with a total of about 2,000 pages of bilingual Timucua-Spanish text. The grammatical sketch, by Pareja, was published in Mexico between 1612 and 1627 and reprinted in 1886. Two catechisms by Movilla were published in Mexico in 1635. There are also two letters with Spanish translations, one written to the governor of Florida in 1636 by a Timucua chief, and another by six Timucua chiefs addressed to the king of Spain in 1688 (Crawford 1979: 326–327). By the early nineteenth century, few Timucua people remained. Granberry published a grammatical sketch (1990) and grammar (1993) based on these resources.

In 1707 a man named Lamhatty appeared at the estate of Colonel John Walker in Virginia, saying that he was from the village of Tawasa near the Gulf of Mexico but had been captured by the Tuscarora. Walker recorded 60 words of his language, but soon afterward Lamhatty disappeared. Swanton (1929b) noted resemblances in the wordlist to Timucua, as well as to some Muskogean languages. Since then, the status of Tawasa has been under discussion. The wordlist is reprinted in Granberry (1993: 10). A number of the Tawasa forms are so similar to Timucua as to suggest they are the same language, represented with different spellings: Tawasa *hĕmè*, Timucua *hime* 'come'; Tawasa *néăh*, Timucua *nia* 'woman'; and so on. Some differences could be attempts at representing sounds not in the native languages of the transcribers: Tawasa *soua*, Timucua *soba* 'meat' for something like [soβa], or Tawasa *héwah*, Timucua *hiba* 'sit down', for [hiβa]. There are also forms that match those in neighboring Muskogean languages, likely loans in one direction or the other: Tawasa *hássey*, Alabama *haši*, Timucua *ela* 'sun'. Martin (2004: 78) notes that most of these are probably loans from Creek. If Tawasa was actually Timucua itself or a dialect of that language, Timucua would remain an isolate, as it was identified by Powell (1891: 123) and Sapir (1921, 1929). If Tawasa was an unrelated language, Timucua would still be an isolate. (There is also a long history of attempts to link Timucua to other languages of the area as well as Middle and South America, discussed in Crawford 1979, 1988.)

The possibility of clear-cut distinctions between dialects and languages is also challenged by dialect chains, situations in which speakers of different varieties may be able to understand their immediate neighbors, but those at the edges may not understand each other. An example is **Keres**, with seven varieties spoken in pueblos in New Mexico. Two major groups can be distinguished: Eastern Keres, consisting of Cochiti, Santo Domingo, San Felipe, Santa Ana, and Zia, and Western Keres, consisting of Laguna and Acoma. Each dialect is mutually intelligible with its neighbors, but differences are greater between those of pueblos located at larger distances, such as Cochiti and Acoma. Davis (1959) estimates the time depth of the group at not more than 500 years, a period over which change can be slight or substantial. Keres is generally considered an isolate.

Apparent intelligibility can of course also come from exposure or bilingualism. **Cayuse** was spoken in the early nineteenth century in the plateau region of northeastern Oregon and southeastern Washington. Documentation consists primarily of nineteenth-century wordlists published in Rigsby 1969. For some time, Cayuse was linked to the neighboring Molala. Rigsby (1966: 369) traces the original idea of a relationship to an 1846 publication by Horatio Hale containing Cayuse and Molala vocabularies. Hale did not explicitly declare that the two were related, but he listed them together in a Waiilatpu family. Rigsby suspects that this grouping may have been stimulated by a remark from Marcus Whitman, who established a Presbyterian mission in the area in 1836, and assumed the languages were mutually intelligible when he heard Cayuse and Molala people speaking together. The grouping was retained in the Powell classification of 1891 and carried into the Sapir classifications of 1921 and 1929. After careful examination of the material from both languages, however, Rigsby concluded that the two are in fact not related:

> Cayuse and Molala do not appear to be genetically relatable, though there are obvious areal relations involved since they share a small number of identical or near-identical lexical items.
>
> (Rigsby 1966: 370)

In the situations observed by Whitman, the Cayuse speakers may have learned some Molala, the Molala speakers may have learned some Cayuse, or both may have simply acquired enough passive bilingualism to be able to understand the other, while still speaking their own languages. Cayuse is now considered an isolate.

3 DEEP GENETIC RELATIONSHIPS, CHANCE, AND CONTACT

Related languages are traditionally defined as those descended from a common ancestor. But a relationship cannot be simply proven or disproven. Evidence may be strong, weak, somewhere in between, or lacking. Where languages share sufficiently pervasive, systematic similarities that are clearly not due to contact, onomatopoeia, or chance, a relationship is considered established. Where they share just some such features, a common origin may be considered probable or possible. But there is no disproof of relationship: it can only be determined that there is insufficient solid evidence to posit one.

The history of classification of languages indigenous to North America is traced in detail in Goddard 1996b and Campbell 1997. Early schemes were in Gallatin in 1836 and 1848, though at that time some languages were still unknown or sparsely documented.

Later in the century, a comprehensive classification with 58 families including isolates was published in Powell (1891). Small changes were made in subsequent editions.

In 1903 Dixon and Kroeber noted typological similarities among language families of California:

> The main purpose of the paper is to point out that California languages may be classified into several groups. It must be clearly understood, however, that the classification that has been attempted deals only with structural resemblances, not with definite genetic relationships; that we are establishing not families, but types of families.
>
> (Dixon and Kroeber 1903: 3)

In 1913, however, they proposed some remote genetic relationships among California languages (1913a, 1913b). One they termed "Penutian" included Costanoan, Miwok, Maiduan, Yokuts, and Wintuan (1913b). As samples of evidence of relationship, they provided five lexical sets ('bow', 'three', 'fire', 'liver', 'forehead'); some case suffixes; and structural similarities, including elaborate vowel mutations, lack of prefixes, seven cases on nouns, absence of instrumental or locative affixes on verbs, and intransitive, inceptive, voice, mode, tense, and person suffixes. They concluded:

> There is available enough information on the structure of the five Penutian languages to prove their genetic affinity beyond a doubt even without recourse to lexical similarities.
>
> (Dixon and Kroeber 1913b: 649)

A second group they termed "Hokan" included Karuk, Chimariko, Shastan, Pomoan, Yana, Esselen, and Yuman (1913b). They illustrated their proposed relationship with another five sets of stems ('tongue', 'eye', 'water', 'stone', 'sleep'), as well as some structural similarities, including no plural form for most nouns, frequent pairs of distinct verb stems differing in number, verb prefixes denoting instruments and often pronominals, and verb suffixes marking plurality and location.

A flurry of work followed, aimed at uncovering deeper relationships among the Powell families and refining subgrouping. In 1919 Dixon and Kroeber presented lexical sets obtained from translations of 225 English terms into 67 languages, as well as some additional forms. For Penutian, they found 171 stem resemblances between two or more languages, proposed some sound correspondences, discussed phonological changes, and listed some structural similarities. To Hokan, they added Washo, Salinan, and Chumash in California and Seri and Chontal (Tequistlatecan) in Mexico, drawing in part on work by Sapir (1917a) which showed similarities among Yana and other possible Hokan languages.

Sapir continued the search for remote relations, ultimately proposing classifications of all of the languages into just six superstocks or phyla (1921, 1929): Eskimo-Aleut, Algonkin-Wakashan, Nadene, Penutian, Hokan-Siouan, and Aztec-Tanoan. With this scheme there were no isolates.

Some of Sapir's subgroups within the phyla are now generally accepted as families. One is the Tlingit-Athabaskan family, which was Sapir's Continental Nadene subgroup of his Nadene superstock (with the later addition of Eyak). Another is the Algic family, his Algonkin-Ritwan subgroup of his Algonkin-Wakashan superstock. (Wiyot and Yurok of California, linked as Ritwan, are no longer seen as a subgroup.) A third is the Utian family, his Miwok-Costanoan branch of his California Penutian subgroup of his broader Penutian hypothesis. A fourth is the Uto-Aztecan family, a subgroup of his Aztec-Tanoan. A fifth is the Kiowa-Tanoan family, another subgroup of his Aztec-Tanoan. Some other proposals appear promising to varying degrees but are not yet generally considered fully established, such as his Plateau Penutian subgroup (Sahaptin, Molala, Klamath-Modoc); Takelman (Takelma and Kalapuya, which he linked as two of three members of his Oregon Penutian subgroup); his Iroquoian-Caddoan; and his Siouan-Yuchi. Other proposals of his have been abandoned. In many cases the discovery of more remote relationships may never be possible because the languages are no longer spoken, and time depths would be so deep that few common inheritances remain.

In what follows, languages identified as isolates are surveyed by geographical area. There is insufficient space to list all references to unpublished and published documentation and comparative work on the languages, or to describe each language in full, but additional detail can be found in Goddard 1996a, 1996b, 1996c; Campbell 1997; Mithun 1999; and Golla 2011.

3.1 The Northwest

Haida is spoken on the Queen Charlotte Islands off the coast of British Columbia and to the north in Alaska. There is a Southern dialect (Skidegate, Ninstints) and a Northern dialect (Kaigani, Masset), both groups representing amalgamations of villages. The two dialects are only partially mutually intelligible, with practice (Krauss 1979: 838). Good documentation exists. Notable are a Kaigani dictionary with a substantial grammatical sketch by Leer (Lawrence 1977), a grammar of Skidegate in Levine 1977, and a grammar of both Masset and Skidegate in Enrico 2003. There are texts in Eastman and Edwards 1983, 1991; Edwards 1995; Edwards and Eastman 1995; and Enrico 1995, and additional works on specific aspects of the language.

The Haida consonant inventory is typical of the Northwest, with three series of stops and affricates. Enrico's (2003) practical orthography distinguishes unaspirated *b, d, j [dž], g, r [G], ʔ;* aspirated *t, ts, k, q;* and ejective: *t', ts', k', q'.* As in neighboring Tlingit-Athabaskan languages, there is a wealth of laterals: *dl, tl* [λ[, *tl'* [λ'], *hl* [ɬ], and *'l* (glottalised *l*). The Massett dialect also has a pharyngealised fricative *ħ.* There are two series of nasals: plain *m, n, ŋ,* and glottalised *'m, 'n.* Glides are *y, w, h,* and vowels *i, e* [ɛ], *a, o* [ɔ], *u,* with long vowels written as double. The Canadian dialects have distinctive tone, but it has a low functional load.

Pronominals show an agent/patient pattern: referents in control are generally identified by agent forms, and those not in control by patient forms, independently of aspect or transitivity. Paradigm choice is lexicalised with each verb. The pattern appears in first person forms in both dialects, and in second singular and third persons as well in Skidegate.

(1)   Haida: Enrico 2003: 24
      Tsiin-ee   'laangaa hl   dah   rujuu-ʔwa-gan.
      salmon-DEF 3PL.POSS 1SG.AGT buy   all-PL-PAST
      'I bought all their fish.' (Masset)

(2)   Haida: Enrico 2003: 1209
      Dii   st'i-gihl   tay-gan.
      1SG.PAT   sick-PUNC   lie.down-PAST
      'I got sick and lay down.' (Skidegate)

(3) Haida: Enrico 2003: 1254

'laa	dii	'la	kil	q'alasdla-gan.
3	1SG.PAT	3	vocally	get.suspicious.of-PAST

'He made me suspicious of him by what he said (about him).' (Masset)

There is a set of means/manner/instrumental markers with functions similar to the prefixes of many unrelated languages to the south. In Haida they are separate words which occur pre-verbally, but their combinations with the following verb are generally lexicalised. Among them are:

q'i	'with knife'	*gi*	'bending'
qii	'throwing down'	*stl'a*	'with fingernails'
ʔun	'lying on'	*cal*	'from heat'
ja	'using chisel, wedge'	*t'a*	'stepping on'
sda	'kicking'	*q'u*	biting'
sgi	'hitting with ax, chopping'	*ki*	'poking with stick'
qahl	'freezing'	*dang*	'pulling'
kun	'hitting with front of vehicle'	*gii*	'from wave action, tide'
xi	'sawing'	*hlri*	'digging'
ru	'sitting on, with buttocks'	*tl'a*	'squeezing between thumb and forefinger'
tl'ah	'slapping'	*xa*	'manipulating with hands'
tla	'manipulating with hands'	*k'a*	'pounding'
yah	'kicking'	*ra*	'moving'
da	'pushing with hand'	*cu*	'blowing'
q'u	'biting'	*ʔis*	'moving past'
t'a	'stepping'	*k'u*	'with lips'
ri	'with side of body'	*hlku*	'with cupped hand'
hlk'yaaw	'with broom'	*ts'a*	'using scissors'
qa	'slicing (fish fillet only)'	*xay*	'weaving'
tl'ii	'sewing'	*kyuu*	'tying'
kil	'by vocal action'		

(Enrico 2003: 1149–1150)

(4) Haida: Enrico 2003: 1148

Dam.an	raa	'la	sgi	jagii.a-gan.
very.much	PP	3	chopping	unable-PAST

'He was really unable to chop it.' (Masset)

(5) Haida: Enrico 2003: 1147

ʔaajii-ga-gu	dang	q'u	gwaawaa?
this-PP-Q	2	biting	not.want

'Don't you want to eat this?' (Masset)

Haida was listed as an isolate (Skittagetan) in Powell's (1891) classification, but grouped with Tlingit-Athabaskan by Sapir in his Nadene stock (1915, 1929). Eyak was later related to Tlingit and Athabaskan. There are some structural similarities between Haida on the one hand and Tlingit, Eyak, and Athabaskan languages on the other. Like Haida, those languages have rich consonant inventories. Tlingit, for example, has three series of stops and affricates: plain (written as voiced) *d, λ, ɜ [dz], ǯ [dž], g, gʷ, ɢ, ɢʷ, ʔ, ʔʷ*; aspirated *t, ƛ, c, č, k, kʷ, q, qʷ*; and ejective *t', ƛ', c', č'k', k'ʷ, q', q'ʷ*; plain fricatives *ł, s, š, x, xʷ, x̣, x̣ʷ, h, hʷ*; glottalised fricatives *ł', s', x', x'ʷ, x̣', x̣'ʷ*; and sonorants *n, y, ÿ* (rounded), and *w*. It also has a simple vowel system: *i, e, a, u* (Leer 1991a: 10). Tlingit also shows agent/patient patterning in pronominals, Tlingit verbs, like those in Athabaskan languages, contain incorporated nouns (or remnants of them) near the beginning of the template, which can indicate unspecified involvement of a kind of entity.

(6)   Tlingit: Story 1966: 98
      ǰi- 'hand'   du ǰín   'his hands'

      ǰi-yasádg   'he's quick with his hands'
      ǰi-waƛ'égʷ   'he dodged his fist'
      duʔìde **ǰi**-ndagú   'Go and beat him up!'

There are, however, conspicuously few lexical similarities apart from loans. The agent/patient patterning of Tlingit pronominals is likely an effect of contact from Haida, as the Eyak and Athabaskan cognates show nominative/accusative patterning (Mithun 2008). According to native tradition, the Kaigani Haida (Masset) moved from the Queen Charlotte Islands north into southeastern Alaska, formerly Tlingit territory, around 1700. Tlingit village names remain there (De Laguna 1990: 203). Story (1966: 10) notes that Tlingit people have intermarried extensively with other groups and moved to live with them. Pinnow (1964), Levine (1979), Leer (1990, 1991b), and Jacobsen (1993) have shown that the similarities that originally served as the basis for this grouping, mainly structural, are actually the result of misanalysis and contact. Haida is once again generally considered an isolate.

Kutenai (=Kootenai=Kootenay) is spoken in communities in British Columbia, Montana, and Idaho. It was the dominant community language until about the mid-twentieth century, when parents stopped passing it on to their children. During the nineteenth century, various visitors collected vocabulary. In 1891 Chamberlain worked with all of the dialects, collecting vocabulary, grammatical material, and texts (1893, 1894a, 1894b, 1894c, 1895a, 1895b, 1902, 1906, 1910). In 1894 the missionary Canestrelli published a grammar in Latin (republished in 1927 by Boas). Boas visited the Kutenai in 1888 and 1914, when he worked through the Chamberlain texts and collected additional material, which he published in 1918. Garvin published lexical material (1947, 1948a); a grammatical sketch (1948b, c, d, 1951a); a narrative text (1953) and conversation (1954); and articles on further topics (1951b). A major grammar with texts is by Morgan (1991).

Kutenai was listed as an isolate (Kitunahan) in Powell 1891. Sapir 1921, 1929 included it as one of three branches of his Algonkin-Wakashan superstock, beside Algonkin-Ritwan and Salish-Wakashan. An Algonquian language, Blackfoot, is spoken immediately to the east, and Salishan languages are spoken to the west and south.

The possibility of a remote relationship to Algonquian was further investigated by Haas (1965). Kutenai does show certain structural similarities to Algonquian languages, in particular obviation, a kind of ranking of third persons. In both Kutenai and Algonquian languages, if there is only one third person in a clause, this will be the unmarked proximate. If there is more than one, the more topical one is proximate, and all other subsidiary third persons are marked as obviative. In the sentence below, the man is proximate and the bee obviative.

(7) Kutenai: Morgan 1991: 432
N'itk'un**apsi**   titqat'   yuwat's.
n=i?t-k'u-?-n-**ap-s**=i   titqat'   yuwat'-s
PRED=become-by.point-TR-CONN-**INVERSE?-3OBVIATIVE**=IND   man   bee-**OBV**
'The bee (OBV) stung the man (PROX).' = 'The man got stung by a bee.'

Persons form a hierarchy, essentially echoing degrees of general topic-worthiness.

1, 2 > 3PROXIMATE > 3OBVIATIVE

If one participant acts on another to its left on the hierarchy, a special marker occurs in the verb. In the Kutenai sentence above, the obviative bee is acting on the proximate man, and the suffix -*ap* appears in the verb (3OBV > 3PROX). In the sentence below, a third person (the bee) is acting on a first person (me), and the suffix -*ap*- again appears in the verb (3 > 1).

(8) Kutenai: Morgan 1991: 433
N'itk'un**ap**ni   yuwat'.
n=?i?t-k'u-?-n-**ap**=n=i   yuwat'
PRED=become-by.point-TR-CONN-**INVERSE?**=1SG=IND   bee
'I got stung by a bee.'

Comparable verb suffixes in Algonquian languages are termed *inverses*. The Kutenai system differs slightly from its Algonquian counterparts, however. In Kutenai, first and second persons are equivalent on the hierarchy (1, 2 > 3PROX > 3OBV), while in Algonquian, second persons are ranked over first (2 > 1 > 3PROX > 3OBV). Morgan proposes that, though the Kutenai suffix -*ap* may have originally been an inverse marker, it now functions more like a first and third person singular object marker. The second person object suffix is -*is*, and the first person plural object suffix is -*awas*. (The actual forms of the morphemes show no similarities between Kutenai and Algonquian.)

Morgan (1991: 497) reexamined evidence of a distant relationship to Algonquian with lexical comparisons and identified only 14 Kutenai morphemes or, at the outside 24, that might be similar enough to Algonquian forms to suggest either cognate relations or borrowing. He concluded that the resemblances are likely due to chance. A common origin for Kutenai and Algonquian is no longer considered likely, though similarities like the proximate/obviative distinction and inverse system indicate that even very abstract structures can be transferred through language contact.

Both Algonquian and Salishan languages contain verbal suffixes with meanings much like lexical nominals, likely descendants of incorporated nouns. Kutenai shows such constructions as well, like -*q'anku*- 'firewood' in the verb 'pack-firewood' below.

(9) Kutenai: Morgan 1991: 517
?At   skikił   hucawisq'ahkusi   tiłnamu?is.
?at=   s-kik-i?ł=   hucawis-**q'anku**-s=i   tiłnamu?-?is
IPFV=   CONT-SUFFIX-ADV=   pack-**load.of.firewood**-3OBV=IND   old.woman-3POSS
'His wife would be bringing **wood** to their home.'

The phonological inventory of Kutenai is typical of the Northwest: consonants *p, t, c, k, q, ?; p', t', c', k', q'; s, ł, x, h; (l), y, w, m, n; m', n'*, and vowels *i, a, u; i:, a:, u:*. It is

strikingly similar to that reconstructed for Proto-Salishan: *p, t, c, k, kʷ, q, qʷ, ; pʼ, tʼ, ƛ',
cʼ, kʼ, kʼʷ, qʼ, qʼʷ; ł, s, x, xʷ, x̌, x̌ʷ, (h); m, n, l, y, (ɣ), w, ʕ, ʕʷ; mʼ, nʼ, lʼ, yʼ, (ɣ'), wʼ, ʕ',
ʕʼʷ* (Kroeber 1999: 7, after Thompson 1979). Reconstructed Salishan vowels are *i, a, u,
ə*. Morgan (1980, 1991: 494–498) investigated possible relationships between Kutenai
and the Salishan family and found 144 possible cognate sets, which he groups by recurring sound correspondences. He reports that of 99 Kutenai grammatical morphemes, 42
appear to be cognate with Salishan morphemes (1991: 494). Another 23 sets he identifies as the results of lexical borrowing, most from Salishan languages into Kutenai. He
predicts that additional sets are unlikely to be found, and that if there is a genetic link, it
is very remote:

> The more one chooses to see the linguistic connection between Kutenai and Salishan
> as diffusional, rather than genetic, the stronger the case can be for the idea that the
> Kutenai language was in sustained contact with a variety of Salishan languages,
> including not only the presently neighboring Interior Salishan languages, but also
> probably Proto-Interior Salish, and quite possibly also Proto-Salish itself. Both
> Proto-Interior Salish, and Proto-Salish were evidently spoken directly to the west of
> what is now Kutenai territory.
>
> (Morgan 1991: 497)

3.2 The West: Oregon and California

Oregon is home to a number of languages that have been identified as isolates: Siuslaw,
Takelma, Klamath-Modoc, Molala, and Cayuse (discussed earlier).

Siuslaw was spoken on the Oregon Coast, with closely related dialects Siuslaw proper
and Lower Umpqua. Major documentation of the language was carried out by Frachtenberg in 1911, when he worked with an elderly Lower Umpqua woman, Louisa Smith, and
her husband, William Smith. The work was challenging. Mrs. Smith knew no English:

> Her memory of old traditions was almost entirely gone, and she had lost the faculty
> of relating facts coherently and in consecutive order. Besides, her narratives, such as
> could be obtained, were too much interspersed with Chinook Jargon.
>
> (Frachtenberg 1914: 1)

William Smith was an Alsea man who knew Lower Umpqua as a second language. Nevertheless, Frachtenberg produced remarkable documentation, publishing a text collection
with vocabulary (1914) and a detailed grammatical sketch (1922). The language was
gone by the 1970s.

In the mid-nineteenth century, Latham (1848) and Gatschet (1884) recognised Siuslaw
and Lower Umpqua as dialects of an isolate. On the basis of a vocabulary he collected
in 1884, Dorsey linked the two with Alsea and Yaquina in a Yakonan stock, a grouping
adopted by Powell in his 1891 classification. After more intensive work, however, Frachtenberg disagreed:

> After a superficial investigation, lasting less than a month, Dorsey came to the con-
> clusion that Siuslaw and Lower Umpqua were dialects belonging to the Yakonan
> stock. This assertion was repeated by J.W. Powell in his "Indian Linguistic Families"
> (*Seventh Annual Report of the Bureau of American Ethnology*, p. 134), and was held
> to be correct by all subsequent students of American Indian languages. This view,
> however, is not in harmony with my own investigations. A closer study of Alsea

(one of the Yakonan dialects) on the one hand, and of Lower Umpqua on the other, proves conclusively that Siuslaw and Lower Umpqua form a distinct family, which I propose to call the Siuslawan Linguistic stock.

(Frachtenberg 1922: 437)

Frachtenberg did not entirely dismiss the possibility of more remote relations:

It is not at all impossible that this stock, the Yakonan, Kusan, and perhaps the Kalapuyan, may eventually prove to be genetically related. Their affinities are so remote, however, that I prefer to take a conservative position, and to treat them for the time being as independent stocks.

(Frachtenberg 1922: 437)

Sapir combined those languages in his Oregon Penutian subgroup, but at present, this grouping is not generally considered established.

Takelma was spoken in southern Oregon in the Rogue River Valley. There were at least four dialects (Kendall 1982). It was no longer spoken by the mid-twentieth century. Sapir published a collection of texts (1909) and impressive grammatical sketch (1922) on the basis of one and a half months of work with a single speaker, Frances Johnson, at the Siletz reservation. Further references are in Kendall (1977 and 1990).

The language was listed as an isolate in Powell (1891). In 1918 Frachtenberg suggested a relation to the Kalapuyan family to the north in what he termed Takelman:

While carding and indexing my Kalapuya field material (collected three years ago), preparatory to the writing of a grammatical sketch of these languages, I was forcibly struck by some marked correspondences in the lexicography of Kalapuya and Takelma, and of Kalapuya and Chinook. . . . The resemblances between Kalapuya and Takelma are much greater and far more numerous, although, as has been stated before, only part of the Kalapuya data have thus far been tabulated.

(Frachtenberg 1918: 178)

On the basis of 55 Takelma-Kalapuya lexical pairs, he posited sound correspondences. Sapir linked Takelma, Kalapuya, and his Coast Oregon Penutian (Coos, Siuslaw, Yakonan) into an Oregon Penutian branch of Penutian (1929). Since that time, various researchers have pursued the Takelman hypothesis. In 1956, Swadesh included Takelma with his Penutian stock and provided (mostly identical) consonant correspondences (1956: 36). In 1965, after work with Kalapuya speakers, he compared 100-word basic vocabulary lists from Takelma and the three Kalapuyan languages and estimated that they were 48% cognate, which he saw as 'equivalent to a minimum of 24 centuries of divergence' (1965: 237). He included additional comparisons and sound correspondences. In 1969 Shipley proposed a reconstruction of Proto-Takelman based on Sapir's phonemicised Takelma and his own reconstructed Proto-Kalapuyan. Berman (1988) assembled additional possible lexical similarities and sound correspondences. Kendall, who had done substantial work with Takelma, looked further into analysis and internal reconstruction of the language, which could facilitate comparisons to Kalapuyan (1982 and especially 1997). He reported:

Based on these works and my own investigation, it seems certain that Takelma and Kalapuyan share a common, though remote, origin. That the two languages belong to the same subgroup within Penutian must remain a working hypothesis.

(Kendall 1997: 1)

In 1998, however, Tarpent and Kendall reexamined the evidence and concluded that the similarities noted previously were erroneous and that Takelma is an isolate after all.

Klamath-Modoc (= Lutuamian) consists of two dialects, Klamath proper and Modoc. They were spoken in south central Oregon along the eastern slope of the Cascade Mountains, Klamath to the north and Modoc to the south. The last speaker died in 2003. Good documentation exists. Most important are a two-volume work containing a dictionary, grammatical sketch, and texts in Modoc by Gatschet (1890) and especially a dictionary, grammar, and texts by Barker (1963a, b, 1964). Additional work on particular aspects of the language has been published as well.

The language was listed as an isolate by Gallatin (1848) and Powell (1891). Others saw possible relationships to neighboring languages. Gatschet (1880) assembled 18 pairs of words in Klamath and Northern Sahaptin, noting:

> The Sahaptin and Wayíletpu [Klamath-Modoc] families are the only ones with whom a distant kinship is not altogether out of the question.
>
> (Gatschet 1880: lvi, cited in Aoki 1963: 107).

Frachtenberg also noted some similarities:

> [I have] gathered voluminous data supporting previously expressed contentions concerning the genetic relationship between Lutuamian [Klamath-Modoc], Wailatpuan [Molala-Cayuse], and Sahaptin, which will be published as soon as additional material from the Sahaptin field will be made available.
>
> (Frachtenberg 1918: 176)

Sapir considered a relationship among Klamath-Modoc, Sahaptian, and Molala-Cayuse 'either probable or very possible' and classified them as a Plateau subgroup of Penutian. In 1963 Aoki drew up a set of sound correspondences linking Klamath-Modoc to the two languages of the Sahaptian family, Nez Perce and Sahaptin. The correspondences were based on 99 lexical sets, 57 containing forms from Klamath and both Sahaptian languages, 35 with just Klamath (K) and Nez Perce (NP), and 7 with just Klamath and Sahaptin (S). Much of it is core vocabulary, such as K *ptisap*, S. *psit*, NP *pist* 'father'; K *č'ole:ks*, NP *cilá:kt* 'meat, flesh, body'; K *k'ek'e:č'* 'vein', NP *kiké?t* 'blood'; and K *č'moks* 'darkness', NS *cimúxcimux* 'black', S *cmúk* 'black'. In 1987, Rude pointed out some grammatical similarities among the languages. One is the Klamath genitive suffix *-am* and the Nez Perce genitive/ergative with kinship terms *-em*. On nouns, the Klamath genitive case is *-?am*, the Nez Perce *-nim*, and the Sahaptin *-nmí*. The Klamath accusative case suffix is *-n* on demonstratives and articles, and the general Sahaptian accusative **-ne*. There is a Klamath nominaliser *-s* comparable to Nez Perce *-s* and Sahaptin *-š*. Klamath *-waas* derives place names, as does Nez Perce *-niwees*. Personal pronouns are similar in shape: Klamath 1 *ni*, 2 *mi*, 3 *bi*; Nez Perce 1 *?iin*, 2 *?iim*, 3 *?ipi*; and Sahaptin1 *in*, 2 *im*, 3 *pən*. Various other similarities in grammatical markers are given as well. DeLancey, Genetti, and Rude (1988) identified further lexical similarities bringing the total to 293 (of varying quality, as they note). DeLancey (1992) draws attention to Klamath-Sahaptian similarities in the first four numerals and notes that the higher numbers in Klamath all have semitransparent etymologies, but he agrees with Rigsby (1965: 109–152) that they could be the result of ancient contact.

Molala was spoken in west central Oregon in the Cascade Mountains. The last speaker, Fred Yelkes, died in 1958 (Berman 1996). There is considerable documentation, most unpublished. In 1910–1911 Frachtenberg worked with speaker Stevens Savage, collecting vocabulary, some grammatical material, and texts. Between 1927 and 1930 Jacobs worked with speakers Kate Chantèle (Molala Kate), Fred Yelkes, and Victoria Howard, collecting vocabulary from Mr. Yelkes and texts from Mrs. Chantèle and Mrs. Howard, though most of these remain untranslated. Berman (1996) describes the phonology and morphology.

As noted above, Molala was earlier identified as a dialect of Cayuse, and on that basis, it was listed with it by Powell and Sapir. After a reexamination of the material, Rigsby (1966, 1969) concluded that any lexical similarities were due to contact. But Berman has found possible evidence of a relation to Klamath-Modoc and the Sahaptian languages Sahaptin and Nez Perce. Potential cognates are affixes: on nouns, a kinship prefix and genitive and locative suffixes; on pronouns, a distributive plural prefix and plural and accusative suffixes; on verbs, a causative prefix and benefactive applicative, celerative ('immediately'), and horative suffixes and a nominaliser. He notes that there are many shared lexical items, but the majority appear to be loanwords, chiefly names of birds and animals and other non-basic vocabulary. At present, relations among Klamath-Modoc, Sahaptian, and Molala are seen as promising.

Six isolates have been identified in California and adjacent Nevada: Yana (discussed above), Karuk, Chimariko, Washo, Esselen, and Salinan.

Karuk (= Karok) is spoken in northwest California along the Klamath River. It is no longer being acquired as a first language by children, and first-language speakers are few, but revitalisation work is underway. Various vocabulary lists were collected during the second half of the nineteenth century, and texts were recorded by Curtin in 1889 and Kroeber in 1902–1903. Harrington published a body of texts (1930, 1932a) and bilingual description of traditional tobacco use (1932b), and de Angulo and Freeland published a text collection with grammatical notes (1931). Bright produced a detailed grammar, dictionary, and text collection (1957) in addition to other more specific works. A website created at the Department of Linguistics at Berkeley in collaboration with the Karuk Tribe (http://linguistics.berkeley.edu/~karuk/index.php) contains an online dictionary, search functions for examples and texts, and a rich text collection which can be viewed a) in paragraph form with parallel columns for the Karuk and English, b) by sentences followed just by a free translation, c) by word-by-word glossing and free translation, or d) by morphological parsing and free translation. Some of the texts are accompanied by audio files.

Karuk was listed as an isolate (Quoratean) in the Powell 1891 classification, but it was linked to Chimariko, Shastan, Pomoan, Yana, Esselen, and Yuman by Dixon and Kroeber (1903, 1913a, 1913b, 1919) and included in Sapir's Hokan stock. Kroeber reported that speakers of one upriver dialect were bilingual in Shasta (1936: 35–37). Bright commented on possible relations:

> The Karok language is not closely or obviously related to any other. It has, however, been classified as a member of the northern group of Hokan languages, in a subgroup which includes Chimariko and the Shastan languages, spoken in the same general part of California as Karok itself. Considerable work remains to be done before the historical position of Karok can be properly clarified.
>
> (Bright 1957: 1)

The language is generally considered an isolate today.

To the south of Karuk still in northwestern California is **Chimariko**, spoken in the nineteenth century in a few small villages in Trinity County. The first encounter between Chimariko speakers and Europeans was in the 1820s or 1830s. The last speaker probably died in the 1940s. An excellent resource is in Jany (2009), based primarily on 3,500 pages of handwritten field notes collected by John Peabody Harrington in the 1920s. Jany (2009) contains both a grammatical description and typological comparison with other languages in the area.

Chimariko was listed as an isolate in the Powell (1891) classification. In 1910, on the basis of 57 lexical comparisons, Dixon suggested that it was related to Shasta, Achomawi, and Atsugewi (1910: 306). Jany points out that the Chimariko spent years in exile with the Shasta before becoming Dixon's consultants, so at least some similarities he noted may have been the result of contact (2009: 2). Sapir classified those languages as a sub-branch of his Northern Hokan.

Further south and east, in an area centering around Lake Tahoe into Nevada, is **Washo**. Major documentation includes a grammatical sketch in Kroeber (1907) and grammar and grammatical sketch in Jacobsen (1964, 1986); and texts in Dangberg (1927) and Lowie (1963). More recently Alan Yu and colleagues have created a website with online audio dictionary and bibliography of works on the language at https://lucian.uchicago.edu/blogs/washo/?page_id=90.

Examining early vocabularies, Gatschet (1882: 254–255) identified Washo as an isolate. On the basis of his own work with speakers in 1883, Henshaw echoed this judgment:

> From the fragmentary vocabularies of this tongue before accessible the Washo had been supposed to be the sole representative of a linguistic stock, a supposition which the present vocabulary sustains.
>
> (Henshaw 1887: xxx, cited in Jacobsen 1964: 11)

The language was accordingly listed as an isolate in Powell (1891). In 1917 Harrington announced similarities between Washo and the Chumashan languages to the south (1917: 154), which led Sapir to classify Washo as Hokan, since the Chumash family was already in that group (1917b: 449–450). (The proposed Hokan affiliation of Chumash has since been abandoned.) Dixon and Kroeber noted that originally Washo "was credited with remarkably few parallels to any other. Superficial examination indeed reveals very few similarities between it and Hokan tongues" (1919: 104). Stimulated by a comment from Sapir on a possible relationship, however, they assembled a list of lexical similarities between Washo and other languages hypothesised to be Hokan:

> The outcome is about sixty parallels of greater or less validity. This is not a wholly convincing showing. But the general plan of Washo structure is so similar to that of Hokan that material resemblances weigh more heavily.
>
> (Dixon and Kroeber 1919: 105)

The structural similarities were described in a note:

> For instance, the noun without cases but with numerous local suffixes and with possessive prefixes; the verb with pronominal and instrumental prefixes, local and modo-temporal suffixes; verb stems frequently different for singular and plural; composition in abundance.
>
> (Dixon and Kroeber 1919: 105)

In the same work they included a longer list of Washo-Hokan similarities assembled independently by Sapir, with lists of stems, pronouns, prefixes, noun suffixes, postpositions, local suffixes on verbs, and other verb suffixes. The subsequent history of classification of Washo is described in detail in Jacobsen (1964: 10–21). At present, Washo is still generally considered an isolate.

Further south on the California coast was **Esselen** (= Huelel), spoken by early converts at Mission Carmel. Shaul (1995a: 191) surmises that it was probably the first known California language to have become extinct. Because of its early demise, documentation is sparser than for some other California isolates. Sources are described in Beeler (1977, 1978); Turner and Shaul (1981); and Shaul (1995a). There is a list of 20 words (including 10 numerals), collected during the La Pérouse expedition of 1786, and a list of 107 words and a trilingual (Esselen/Spanish/English) catechism by Father Lasuén, collected during the Galiano-Malaspina expedition of 1792. The numerals were collected again in 1840–1842 by Duflot. The Franciscan missionary Felipe Arroyo de la Cuesta recorded 58 words and 14 phrases and sentences at the Soledad Mission in 1832 (Kroeber 1904). Later documentation comes from non-native speakers and rememberers. In 1878 Pinart collected about 140 items from a woman whose husband had been Esselen (Heizer 1952: 73–82), and in 1888, Henshaw collected 110 words and 50 phrases and sentences from a Rumsen speaker whose mother had been Esselen (Kroeber 1904: 49–57, Heizer 1955). After that time a few words were collected from people who were not speakers but remembered having heard the language (Shaul 1995b). Descriptions of Esselen phonology, morphology, and syntax are in Shaul (1995a), along with a transcription of the complete Galiano-Malaspina catechism.

Esselen was classified as an isolate in Powell (1891). In 1913 Dixon and Kroeber added it to their Hokan stock on the basis of three words plus an ending -*nax*, which they related to an ending -*na* in Yana: Esselen *a sa-nax*, Yana *ha-na* 'water'; Esselen *šie fe*, Yana *k'ai-na* 'stone'; Esselen *a tsi n*, Yana *sa m* 'sleep' (1913b: 651). Sapir adopted the proposal and linked Esselen with Yuman as a subgroup of Hokan. At present it is generally agreed that there is too little evidence to link Esselen to any other languages.

Immediately to the south of Esselen on the central coast was **Salinan**, with two documented closely related dialects, Antoniano (from Mission San Antonio, founded in 1771) and Migueleño (from Mission San Miguel, founded in 1797). The dialect situation may have been more complex before the mission period. A third dialect was mentioned in early accounts, Playaño (on the beach), but it was never documented. The language was last spoken around 1960. Sources are detailed in Turner (1987 and 1988). Franciscan priests at both missions apparently spoke the language and left important documentation (Golla 2011: 116). Fathers Buenaventura Sitjar and Miguel Pieras, who founded the San Antonio mission, assembled a bilingual dictionary (Sitjar 1861) and a *confesionario*. Later Father Pedro Cabot, who served there from 1804 to 1835, and Father Juan Sancho, there from 1804 to 1830, added to the dictionary and translated a number of religious texts. Additional material was collected through the nineteenth century and the first half of the twentieth. Kroeber collected some Migueleño vocabulary and grammatical material (1904: 43–49). J. Alden Mason worked with speakers of both dialects in 1910 and 1916 and published a grammatical sketch and texts in 1918. J. P. Harrington worked with speakers of both dialects in 1922 and 1931–1933, collecting over 5,000 words, much of it re-elicitation of earlier material. His nephew Arthur Harrington made audio recordings of hours of monolingual Miegueleño texts in the mid-1930s. Jacobsen worked with the last speakers of both dialects in 1954, 1955, and 1958. His field notes and recordings are archived in the Survey of California and Other Indian Languages at the University of California, Berkeley: http://linguistics.berkeley.edu/Survey/. The work by J. P. Harrington and Jacobsen is particularly valuable for its phonetic precision not always present in the earlier records. A longer grammar is in Turner (1987).

Salinan was identified as an isolate in the Powell classification of 1891. Dixon and Kroeber had noted some structural similarities to the Chumashan languages to the south and proposed a grouping of the two they termed Iskoman, but they recognised that lexical similarities were not 'conspicuous' (1913b: 652–653). When Harrington saw resemblances between Chumash languages and Yuman, already part of the Hokan hypothesis, Salinan was 'folded into' Hokan and remained part of this stock in the 1929 Sapir classification. As reported by Turner, further work has not unearthed compelling similarities to Chumashan languages (apart from loans) or other languages classified as Hokan:

> Attempts to discover genetic relationships with other languages or language families in California have been fruitless. The result of my earlier historical, typological and areal study of Salinan (Turner 1983) is that the Salinan language shows as much influence from its contacts with unrelated California languages as it does evidence of genetic affiliations with any other putative Hokan languages.
>
> (Turner 1987: 3)

Salinan is again considered an isolate.

The Oregon and California isolates were all grouped by Sapir into one of two phyla. In fact all of the Oregon isolates (Siuslaw, Takelma, Klamath-Modoc, Molala, Cayuse) were classified as Penutian, though his Penutian languages were spoken over an area extending from British Columbia with Tsimshianic, through Oregon and California (with the Wintun, Maidun, Utian, Yokuts families) and into Mexico (with Mixe-Zoque and Huave). All of the California isolates (Yana, Karuk, Chimariko, Washo, Esselen, Salinan) were classified with the Hokan subgroup of his proposed Hokan-Siouan phylum, which extended over California into Mexico with Seri and Tequistlatecan (Chontal). The West has long been recognised as a linguistic area, centered in Northern California (Haas 1976, Conathan 2004, O'Neill 2008). For a time it was thought by some that contact is generally limited to vocabulary, so that parallels in grammatical structure would be good indicators of deep genetic relationship. Structural parallels did indeed enter into many hypotheses of remote relations, including Penutian and Hokan. It is now recognised, however, that structure is often replicated in language contact as well. Most communities in this linguistic area have long been relatively small, so exogamy and multilingualism were the norm. People typically spoke the language of the community they were in, as a courtesy to their hosts. When bilinguals make a choice about which of their languages to use in a particular context, they tend to focus on those aspects of the language over which they have the most conscious control: vocabulary. More abstract structural patterns, and propensities to choose certain alternatives, are easily transferred unconsciously. Particularly early bilingualism can facilitate another kind of structural transfer. Bilinguals used to expressing a distinction in one of their languages often create constructions to express them in the other, using resources native to that language.

Contact effects are illustrated by Jany in her work on the isolate Chimariko, of Northern California. As Jany shows, Chimariko resembles its neighbors, many of which have never been proposed to be related. Sapir classified Chimariko in his Hokan superstock. Among its neighbors are Wintu (Wintun family, grouped by Sapir with Penutian); Hupa (Athabaskan, grouped by Sapir with Na-Dene); and Shasta (grouped by Sapir with Hokan). Chimariko has three series of obstruents: plain p, t, c, $\underset{\cdot}{t}$, $\check{c}$, k, q, $ʔ$; aspirated p^h, t^h, c^h, $\underset{\cdot}{t}^h$, $\check{c}^h$, k^j, q^h; and ejective p', t', c', $\underset{\cdot}{t}'$, $\check{c}'$, k'. This inventory matches that of its immediate neighbors Wintu and Hupa but not Shasta (which lacks an aspirated series). Its uvular series (q, q ', q^h) matches those of Wintu and Hupa but not Shasta. Other languages classified as Penutian show inventories similar to Chimariko, such as Takelma with *p, t, k, k^w,; p^h, t^h, k^h, k^{hw}; p', t', c', k', k'^{w}, ?; w, s, y, x, h; m, n; a, e, i, o, u, ü,* and Molala with *p, t, c, ƛ, k, q; p^h, t^h, k^h, q^h; p', t', c', k', q', ?; f, s, ł, x, h; m, n, l, ; w, y; i, a, u,* and *i:, a:, u:* (Berman 1996: 3).

Chimariko arguments are identified on the predicate by pronominal prefixes, which show agent/patient patterning with a hierarchical overlay. Just one argument is represented on the verb, according to a hierarchy (1, 2, > 3; Agent > Patient). In the sentences below, only first persons are identified in the verb, a grammatical patient *č-* in the first clause, and a grammatical agent *i-* in the last.

(10)   Chimariko: Jany 2009: 145
    No?ot   **č**-ušehe-**m**-de?w   k'oti-hu-t,
    1SG   1SG.PAT-take.along-**away**-INDEF.AGT   flee-CONT-PFV
    'They took **me off**, I fled,

    ?awa   hida   **i**-mam-da.
    house   lots   1SG.AGT-see-PFV
    '**I** saw lots of houses.'

Hierarchical systems can be seen to have developed through contact in the area, but from different resources in the different languages (Mithun 2012). They can be seen as well not only in Karuk and Yana (both isolates classified as Hokan by Sapir), but also in Hupa (Athabaskan) and Yurok (Algic). Possession in Chimariko is marked on the possessor (the head of possessive construction) as in Hupa but not Shasta (or Wintu).

One of the structural features originally cited as characteristic of Hokan languages is means/manner/instrumental prefixes on verbs. Chimariko contains such prefixes, among them *mitei-* 'with the foot', *wa-* 'by sitting on', *e-* 'with the end of long object', *a-* 'with a long object', *me-* 'with the head', *tsu-* 'with a round object', and *tu-* 'with the hand' (Jany 1009: 133).

(11)   Chimariko mean/manner/instrumental prefixes: Dixon 1910: 329, cited in Jany 2009: 133.
    n-**a**-klucmu   'knock over with a bat'
    ni-**e**-klucmu   'knock over with end of pole by thrust'
    ni-**mitci**-klucmu   'knock over with foot'
    ni-**mitci**-kmu   'roll log with foot'
    ni-**tu**-kmu   'roll log with hand'
    ni-**wa**-tcexu   'break by sitting on'

(The initial *ni-* prefix is likely an imperative.) Such prefixes appear not only in Chimariko, the isolate Karuk, and Achumawi (all classified by Sapir as Hokan), but also in the isolates Yana and Washo, and in the Pomoan, Yuman, and Chumashan languages, all in California and all classified at least at some point as Hokan. They do not, however, appear in other languages classified as Hokan, namely Shastan or the isolates Esselen, or Salinan, also in California. Furthermore they occur in languages not classified as Hokan. In California they appear in the Maidun languages (Maidu, Konkow, Nisenan) spoken at contact immediately to the south of Yana and Atsugewi and to the north of Washo, classified as Penutian. In Oregon they appear in the isolates Klamath and Takelma, and the Sahaptian languages, also classified as Penutian. But they do not occur in other languages classified as Penutian; there is no mention of them in descriptions of the Wintun, Utian, or Yokuts languages in California, nor the Oregon languages Coosan, Siuslaw, or Alsea (Mithun 2007). They also occur in neighboring languages classified as neither Hokan nor Penutian: Yuki and Wappo (Sapir's Yukian) and Uto-Aztecan (though at certain points there were attempts to add Uto-Aztecan to Penutian).

Another structural feature originally cited as characteristic of Hokan languages is an inventory of locative/directional suffixes in the verb. Chimariko shows just such an inventory: *-ktam/-tam* 'down', *-ema/-enak* 'itno', *-ha* 'up', *-hot* 'down', *-lo* 'apart', *-ro* 'up', *-sku* 'towards', *-smu* 'acrsoss', *-tap* 'out', *-tku/-ku* cislocative ('towards here'), *-tmu/-mu* translocative (towards there), *-kh* 'motion towards here', *-m* 'motion towards there', *-tpi* 'out of', *-xun/-xunok* 'in, into', *-aʰa* 'along', *-pa* 'off, away', *-qʰutu* 'itno water', *-č'ana* 'to, toward', *-čama* 'in, into'.

(12)   Chimariko locative suffixes: Jany 2009: 134

Č'imar	xotai	h-eṭahe-**sku**-t	uwa-**tku**-t,
man	three	3-flee-**towards**-PFV	go-**towards.here**-PFV

'Three men came as fugitives;

h-eṭahe-**sku**-t	č'utamdač.
3-flee-**towards**-PFT	Burnt.Ranch

they ran away to Burnt Ranch.'

As Jany notes, neighboring Shasta, Karuk, Yana, and Achumawi, all classified as Hokan, also have such suffixes, but the neighboring Maidu, classified as Penutian, does as well. Prefixes with similar functions occur in other languages of the area classified as Hokan: Yana, Washo, and Pomoan. But they also occur in other languages classified as Penutian: not only Maidu, but also the isolate Klamath and the Sahaptian languages. They do not appear in all members of either group, however. There is no mention of them in the Yuman family (classified as Hokan), or in the isolates Takelma or Siuslaw, nor in the Wintun, Utian, Yokuts, Coosan, or Alsea families (all classified as Penutian). They are not mentioned for Chumashan Yukian. Like the means/manner/instrumental prefixes, the locative/directional suffixes appear to be very old structures that were spread through contact.

The possibility of deeper relations among languages in the West remains to some extent an open question. Much of the structural evidence put forth for earlier groupings has turned out to be a likely result of longstanding contact. Identification of lexical cognates is hampered by the extensive phonological processes that many of the languages have undergone, such as ablaut and phonological reduction. At least some of the proposed deeper relations remain intriguing, however. Kaufman (1988ms, 1989) has pursued both lexical and structural similarities among hypothesised Hokan languages; has reconstructed consonants, phonotactics, and word structure; and has presented preliminary ideas on the reconstruction of vowels. He, like others, sees some of the original members more likely than others, including isolates Karuk, Chimariko, Yana, Washo, Esselen, Salinan, and Coahuiltecan. Others remain unconvinced.

3.3 The Southwest

Several languages indigenous to the Southwest have been identified as isolates. One is Keres, discussed earlier.

Another is **Zuni**, still with many speakers, some still in their twenties (Adrienne Tsikewa, personal communication, 2016). Most live at Zuni Pueblo in western New Mexico, but some are in eastern Arizona. There are grammars of the language in Bunzel (1934) and Newman (1965, 1996); a dictionary (Newman 1958); and texts (Bunzel 1932, 1933), as well as numerous works on individual topics.

Structurally Zuni is quite different from the other isolates discussed so far. It has just one series of obstruents, *p, t, c, č, k, k*^{w}*, ʔ; s, š, ł, h*, and five sonorants: *m, n, l, w, y*. Unlike many North American languages, it is primarily dependent marking: pronouns, which show nominative/accusative patterning, are independent words rather than affixes. Locative and directional relations are marked on nominal phrases rather than the predicate.

(13)   Zuni: Newman 1996: 500

ʔikʷʔałt   suski   powa=kʷin   ʔa:č   ʔi-ka.
back   coyote   rest.on.ground=ALLATIVE   they.two   come-PAST
'The two came to the place where ere Coyote was resting.'

Zuni was identified as an isolate in the Powell (1891) classification, but Sapir included it in his Aztec-Tanoan superstock. Similarities to Uto-Aztecan are generally attributed to contact, however. Suggestions of numerous other links have been proposed as well, including Penutian, Hokan, and Keres, but none are considered convincing. Zuni is again generally identified as an isolate.

3.4 Texas

A number of languages were spoken at contact in what is now Texas and adjacent Mexico. Troike (1996: 644) reports that so far as is known, all had become extinct by the mid-twentieth century. Some of those mentioned in historical sources are unclassifiable because there is little or no documentation. As seen earlier, Aranama, Cotoname, and Karankawa present challenges because of the limited quantity and quality of data from them. There are still others, however, which have been identified as isolates with more confidence.

Coahuilteco was spoken in south Texas and northeastern Mexico. It is described in detail in Troike (1996). The primary documentation is a confessor's manual apparently written by a Spanish Franciscan missionary, Bartolomé García, at Mission San Francisco de la Espada in San Antonio. A version published in 1760 in Mexico City includes 88 numbered pages of text with parallel columns of Spanish and Coahuilteco. Troike reports:

> The text consists primarily of short sentences or paragraphs. These include questions, statements, and commands, with questions predominating. . . . The total number morphs in the text is estimated at about 20,000. The short and often repetitious nature of the sentences in many cases facilitates analysis, but at the same time the limitations of the text sometimes make it impossible to determine the composition of certain unique constructions or to discern the semantic significance or contextual conditioning of particular functional elements.
>
> (Troike 1996: 646)

García, who spent 12 years at the mission and knew the language well, probably completed this polished version in 1738 (Troike 1978, 1996) An earlier, undated draft entitled *Confesonario de Indios* was discovered in 1962, accompanied by another document entitled *Cuadernillo de lengua de. . . Pajalates*. The *Cuadernillo* contains vocabulary and verb paradigms from the same dialect and was attributed to Father Gabriel de Vergara, president of the San Antonio missions from 1725 to about 1737.

The **Tonkawa** were first encountered in the eighteenth century in central Texas. Over the nineteenth century, travelers recorded vocabulary. In 1884 Gatschet recorded around 1,000 words and 50 pages of texts, still unpublished. From 1928 to 1931 Hoijer carried out major documentation, working primarily with speaker John Rush Buffalo. At that time only six elderly speakers remained. Hoijer published a grammar (1931–1933), grammatical sketch (1946), dictionary (1949), and texts (1972), in addition to work on specific topics.

Tonkawa was listed as an isolate in Powell (1891). In 1915 Swanton proposed a family consisting of two branches: Cotoname-Tonkawa and Coahuilteco-Comecrudo-Karankawa. In 1920 Sapir linked this group to Hokan and then included it in his Hokan-Siouan superstock. In 1940, however, after further examination and work by various other scholars, Swanton reconsidered. He wrote:

> In view of the marked divergences exhibited by three supposedly "Coahuiltecan" dialects, their almost equally close connection with the supposedly independent Karankawan, and the further divergence shown by the San Francisco Solano vocabulary, I am of the opinion that the present classification of the tongues of this region into Coahuiltecan, Karankawan, Tamaulipecan – and probably also Olivean and Janambrian – families is wholly artificial, and that we do not know how many stocks there were.
>
> (Swanton 1940: 144, cited in Troike 1996: 649)

Manaster Ramer (1996) proposed that Coahuilteco, Cotoname, Comecrudo, Garza, and Mamulique are all related in a family he termed Pakawan, related in turn to Karankawa and perhaps Atakapa to the east. After careful examination of the evidence presented by Manaster Ramer, Campbell (1996) concluded that at present, there are insufficient grounds for positing these relationships. Haas briefly explored the possibility of a relationship between Tonkawa and Algonquian (1959, 1967). Coahuilteco and Tonkawa are now considered isolates.

3.5 The Southeast

In addition to Atakapa and Timucua discussed earlier, the Southeast is home to the isolates Chitimacha, Natchez, Tunica, and Euchee (Yuchi).

The **Chitimacha** were first encountered in southern Louisiana in the late seventeenth century by the French. The last two speakers were Benjamin Paul, who died in 1934, and Delphine Ducloux, slightly less fluent, who died in 1940. Chitimacha vocabulary was recorded over the course of the nineteenth century. In 1881–1882 Gatschet collected vocabulary and texts. In 1907 Swanton collected more vocabulary and produced a manuscript dictionary. On subsequent visits he added more vocabulary and texts. Between 1932 and 1934 Swadesh carried out major documentation and produced numerous works, particularly a 1939 manuscript grammar with texts and vocabulary and a grammatical sketch (1946a).

The **Natchez** were near present-day Natchez, Mississippi, when La Salle's expedition came through in 1682. Over the next 50 years, their numbers were seriously diminished by wars with the French. Survivors took refuge among other Southeastern groups, particularly the Cherokee, Creek, and Chickasaw. When these groups were force to move to Oklahoma during the 1836 Removal, the Natchez accompanied their hosts. Some vocabulary was recorded during the eighteenth and nineteenth centuries, all reprinted in Van Tuyl 1979. In 1907, 1908, and 1915 Swanton collected lexical, grammatical, and textual material in Oklahoma from five of the last speakers. In 1934 and 1936 Haas collected much more from the last two, Watt Sam and Nancy Raven. The Swanton and Haas materials remain unpublished, but Haas produced a 1975 manuscript grammar sketch, which served as the basis for a shorter published sketch by Kimball (2005).

The **Tunica** were near present-day Vicksburg, Mississippi, when they first encountered the French in the late seventeenth century. A century later they were dispersed, and many moved to an area near present Marksville, Louisiana. In 1886 Gatschet collected vocabulary and texts. Twenty years later Swanton visited the group and ultimately produced a grammatical sketch (1921). Between 1933 and 1939 Haas worked with the last semi-fluent speaker, Sesostrie Youchigant, which resulted in a full grammar (1941), grammatical sketch (1946), text collection (1950), and dictionary (1953),as well as work on more specific topics. There is an active revitalisation program underway on the Tunica-Biloxi reservation at Marksville.

Atakapa, Chitimacha, Natchez, and Tunica were all identified as isolates in Powell (1891). During the first half of the twentieth century, various scholars noted similarities among these languages and those of the neighboring Muskogean family. Swanton linked Atakapa to Chitimacha and Tunica (1919), and Natchez to Muskogean (1907, 1924). Sapir classified these two larger groups, along with his Iroquoian-Caddoan and Siouan-Yuchi, as part of his Hokan-Siouan superstock (1929). Further work was directed at uncovering additional links among Atakapa, Chitimacha, Natchez, Tunica, and Muskogean. Swadesh presented 258 lexical sets with sound correspondences between Atakapa and Chitimacha (1946b, 1947). Haas assembled reconstructions for 'water' (1951) and 'land' (1952) for a stock she termed Gulf, consisting of Atakapa, Chitimacha, Natchez, Tunica, and Muskogean. She noted additional similarities between Natchez and Muskogean languages (1956). In 1969 Gursky published some lexical comparisons among Atakapa, Chitimacha, and Tunica, revising some earlier proposals by Swanton. In 1979, Haas reconsidered some of the relationships, and in 1994, Kimball detailed further difficulties with the Gulf hypothesis. Attempts have also been made to connect Gulf to other groups. In 1958 Haas sought evidence of links between the hypothesised Gulf stock and Algic, but evidence was weak and the hypothesis has since been abandoned. In 1994 Munro looked into possible connections to Yuki in California, but that proposal has not been pursued. Proposals involving they hypothesised Gulf and relations beyond the Southeast are assessed by Campbell (1997: 305–309).

The **Euchee** (= Yuchi) were encountered by Europeans in present-day Georgia at the beginning of the eighteenth century, but they were forced to move, along with the Shawnee and Lower Creeks, to eastern Oklahoma during the 1832–1834 Removal. There are now a very few speakers near Sapulpa, in northeastern Oklahoma. Several vocabulary lists were collected during the nineteenth century. Between 1904 and 1908 Speck recorded additional vocabulary as well as texts. During 1928 and 1929 Wagner worked with Yuchi speakers in Oklahoma and published a text collection (1931) and grammatical sketch (1933). A comprehensive grammar is in Linn (2000).

The language is not demonstrably related to any other. It was listed as an isolate (Uchean) in Powell (1891). Sapir suggested a relation to the Siouan family and then combined his Siouan-Yuchi group into his larger Hokan-Siouan superstock. Crawford, who worked with Yuchi speakers intermittently between 1969 and 1973, pursued the possibility of a link to Siouan, and concluded that evidence was insufficient to establish a relationship. He concluded:

> If Yuchi and Siouan are related, the time depth of separation is probably so great that it will be exceedingly difficult, if not impossible, to prove the relationship. I say this in spite of the fact that it is possible to find homophonous and nearly homophonous morphemes and segments of morphemes in Yuchi and Siouan. One would expect that languages, no matter how distantly related, might share a few identity correspondences and a certain number of homophonous or nearly homophonous cognates. But when all the evidence for a genetic relationship consists of nothing else and when the identity correspondences are not regular and recurrent, one is inclined to suspect that the similarities may be coincidental or due to borrowings. It is quite possible that borrowing may be the explanation for many of the Yuchi-Siouan similarities.
>
> (Crawford 1979: 342–343)

By 1979 Haas felt that Timucua, Atakapa, Chitimacha, Natchez, Tunica, and Yuchi are isolates. She reported:

> In the past, similarities among languages have often been considered explainable only on a genetic basis. This is true in spite of the fact that many of the earlier groupings were originally suggested by typological similarities. Moreover Boas' (1920, 1929) well-known objection to some of the genetic schemes of Kroeber, Radin, and Sapir were resisted at the time as representing an anti-historical bias. But in recent years an increasing amount of attention is being given to areal linguistics, i.e. the tracing of traits across the basic genetic boundaries. This is fast becoming a very promising field of investigation, especially since it is now generally recognised that genetic linguistics and areal linguistics are not antithetical but complementary. Consequently the proper delineation of linguistic prehistory requires us to take full advantage of both lines of investigation.
>
> (Haas 1979: 319)

It is now generally agreed that so far, resemblances among the hypothesised Gulf languages are due to contact, though a remote relationship between Euchee and Siouan is possible. The Southeast, like the Northwest and West, is a well-known linguistic area. Phonologically labial fricatives are rare across North America, but they occur in the isolates Atakapa, Chitimacha, Tunica, Yuchi, and Timucua. They are reconstructed for Proto-Muskogean, ancestor of the major language family of the Southeast (Booker 1980: 254). They also occur in Ofo and (marginally) Biloxi, languages of the Siouan family, as a result of a regular sound change Proto-Siouan $*s$ > Ofo fh (Robert Rankin, personal communication). Cognates in Siouan languages outside of the area show s or $š$ in their place. In the isolates, the fricatives tend to occur in loanwords.

Another structural feature shared by many languages of the area is agent/patient patterning of pronominal affixes. Such a pattern is reconstructed for Proto-Muskogean and Proto-Siouan, and it also appears in Atakapa, Chitimacha (in first person only), Natchez, and in variants in Tunica. There are several mechanisms by which such patterns can spread. In all of these languages, third persons are unmarked, intransitive and transitive verbs are not distinguished formally, and basic word order is predicate-final. It would thus be easy for speakers to reanalyze a nominative/accusative pattern as agent/patient and vice versa:

'(It) me.OBJECT scared.' < > 'Me.PATIENT scared.'

Another mechanism for transfer can be the reanalysis of transitive impersonal constructions as intransitives, a likely source for some Tunica constructions:

'Something me.OBJECT choked' > Me.PATIENT choked.'

Still another pervasive feature across languages of the Southeast is the propensity of speakers to specify the posture or position of entities, typically 'sitting', 'standing' (vertical), or 'lying' (horizontal). Because of their frequency, in most of the languages they have developed into aspectual auxiliaries or suffixes. Such constructions occur, not only in languages of the Siouan and Muskogean families, but also in the isolates Atakapa, Chitimacha, Natchez, and Tunica. It is easy to see how such structures could spread through long-term intensive contact. Bilinguals used to specifying position systematically in one of their languages could easily transfer this propensity to the other, since the lexical means would already be available. Rankin (1977, 1978, 2004, 2011) has demonstrated that the construction was apparently brought into the Southeast by speakers of Siouan languages (Quapaw, Osage, Biloxi, Ofo). It can be reconstructed for Proto-Siouan. It occurs in all of the modern Muskogean languages, but the forms are not cognate across the daughter languages. The construction has developed to varying degrees in the isolates (Mithun 2010, 2017).

4 IMPLICATIONS

In the end, isolate status is not an either/or matter: there are degrees of quantity and quality of documentation; of mutual intelligibility between dialects and separate languages; of likelihood of chance resemblance; and of identifiability of areal phenomena. Many isolates are represented by small, closed corpora. This is of course not a necessary feature of isolates: in North America, Zuni is known through a grammar, grammatical sketch, dictionary, and texts (though much more would be desirable), and it is still used by substantial numbers of speakers of nearly all ages. Often, however, apparent isolates are represented solely by data collected during brief encounters by scribes unfamiliar with the language, perhaps working through an interpreter, trying to render unfamiliar sounds in a writing system without equivalent categories. The speakers themselves may not have had native command of the language. Small vocabulary lists do tend to be heavy in basic vocabulary, of the kind most likely to remain in languages over long periods of time, but more data of better quality might reveal relationships to other languages.

Isolate status depends entirely on the existence of related but distinct languages. Identification of relatives can depend on the quantity and quality of documentation of potential candidates. And assessing the nature of the relationships can present challenges. If potential relatives are mutually intelligible, they can be considered dialects, and the group as a whole an isolate. If they are not, the language is no longer an isolate but a member of a larger family. Yet assessing degrees of mutual intelligibility is not always straightforward, particularly in the case of languages no longer spoken. Understanding can vary along a continuum and be facilitated by experience.

Perhaps the greatest challenge in identifying isolates is detecting remote relationships: spotting possible cognate vocabulary and structure, on the one hand, and distinguishing common inheritance from contact effects and chance, on the other. In North America, as elsewhere, the challenges persist, as more is learned about earlier stages of languages and language families and about the possible effects of language contact under various kinds of circumstances. Ultimately there is no proof of isolate status: we can only surmise that there is insufficient evidence for positing relationships to any other languages.

REFERENCES

Adelung, Johann Christoph and Johan Severin Vater. 1816. *Mithridates, oder allgemeine Sprachenkunde*. Berlin: Vossischen.

Angulo, Jaime de and L.S. Freeland. 1931. Karok Texts. *International Journal of American Linguistics* 6: 194–226.

Aoki, Haruo. 1963. On Sahaptian-Klamath Linguistic Affiliations. *International Journal of American Linguistics* 29, no. 2: 107–112.

Barker, M.A.R. 1963a. *Klamath Texts*. University of California Publications in Linguistics 30. Berkeley, CA: University of California, Berkeley.

Barker, M.A.R. 1963b. *Klamath Dictionary*. University of California Publications in Linguistics 31. Berkeley, CA: University of California, Berkeley.

Barker, M.A.R. 1964. *Klamath Grammar*. University of California Publications in Linguistics 32. Berkeley, CA: University of California, Berkeley.

Beeler, Madison. 1977. The Sources for Esselen: A Critical Review. *Berkeley Linguistic Society* 3: 37–45.

Beeler, Madison. 1978. Esselen. *Journal of California Anthropology Papers in Linguistics* 1: 3–38.

Berlandier, Jean Louis and Rafael Chowell. 1828–1829. Vocabularies of Languages of South Texas and the Lower Rio Grande. Additional Manuscripts no. 38720, in the British Library, London.

Berman, Howard. 1996. The Position of Molala in Plateau Penutian. *International Journal of American Linguistics* 62: 1–30.

Boas, Franz. 1918. *Kutenai Tales*. Bureau of American Ethnology vol. 59, pp. 1–387.

Boas, Franz. 1920. The Classification of American Languages. *American Anthropologist* 22: 367–376.

Boas, Franz. 1929. Classification of American Indian Languages. *Language* 5: 107.

Booker, Karen. 1980. *Comparative Muskogean: Aspects of Proto-Muskogean Verb Morphology*. Ph.D. dissertation, University of Kansas.

Bright, William. 1957. *The Karok Language*. University of California Publications in Linguistics 13. Berkeley, CA: University of California Press.

Bunzel, Ruth. 1932. Zuñi Origin Myths. *Bureau of American Ethnology Annual Report* 47, 545–609. Washington: Government Printing Office.

Bunzel, Ruth. 1933. *Zuni Texts*. Publications of the American Ethnological Society 15. New York: G E Steckert & Co.

Bunzel, Ruth. 1934. Zuni. *Handbook of American Indian Languages*, vol. 3, ed. by Franz Boas, 383–515. Gluckstadt: J.J. Augustin.

Campbell, Lyle. 1996. Coahuiltecan: A Closer Look. *Anthropological Linguistics* 38, no. 4: 620–634.

Campbell, Lyle. 1997. *American Indian Languages: The Historical Linguistics of Native America*. Oxford: Oxford University Press.

Canestrelli, Philippo. 1894. *Linguae Ksanka: Elementa Grammaticae*. Santa Clara, CA: N.H. Downing. Bound and offered for sale in 1959 as *A Kootenai Grammar* by the Oregon Province Archives, Crosby Library, Gonzaga University, Spokane, WA. Reprinted in 1927 as 'Grammar of the Kutenai language', *International Journal of American Linguistics*, vol. 4, pp. 1–84.

Chamberlain, Alexander. 1893. Einige Wurzeln aus der Sprache der Kitona'qa-Indianer von Britisch-Columbien. *Zeitschrift fur Ethnologie* 25: 419–425.

Chamberlain, Alexander. 1894a. Incorporation in the Kootenay Language. *Proceedings of the American Association for the Advancement of Science* 43: 346–348.

Chamberlain, Alexander. 1894b. New Words in the Kootenay Language. *American Anthropologist*, ns 7: 186–192.

Chamberlain, Alexander. 1894c. Words Expressive of Cries and Noises in the Kootenay Language. *American Anthropologist* 7: 68–70.

Chamberlain, Alexander. 1895a Kootenay Indian Personal Names. *Proceedings of the American Association for the Advancement of Science* 44: 160–161.

Chamberlain, Alexander. 1895b. Word-Formation in the Kootenay Language. *Proceedings of the American Association for the Advancement of Science* 44: 259–260.

Chamberlain, Alexander. 1902. Earlier and Later Kootenay Onomatology. *American Anthropologist* 4: 229–236.

Chamberlain, Alexander. 1906. Terms for the Body, Its Parts, Organs, etc. in the Language of the Kootenay Indians. *Boas Anniversary Volume*, ed. by B. Lanfer, 94–107. New York: G.E. Stechert.

Chamberlain, Alexander. 1910. Noun Composition in the Kootenay Language. *Anthropos* 5: 787–790.

Conathan, Lisa. 2004. *The Linguistic Ecology of Northwestern California: Contact, Functional Convergence, and Dialectology*. Ph.D. dissertation, University of California, Berkeley.

Crawford, James. 1979. Timucua and Yuchi. *The Languages of Native America: Historical and Comparative Assessment*, ed. by Lyle Campbell and Marianne Mithun, 327–354. Austin, TX: University of Texas Press.

Crawford, James. 1988. On the Relationship of Timucua to Muskogean. *Honor of Mary Haaw*, ed. by William Shipley, 157–164. Berlin: Mouton de Gruyter.

Dangberg, Grace. 1927. Washo Texts. *University of California Publications in American Archaeology and Ethnology*, 22: 391–443.

Davis, Irvine. 1959. Linguistic Clues to Northern Rio Grande Prehistory. *El Palacio* 66: 73–84.

De Laguna, Frederica. 1990. Tlingitm. *Handbook of North American Indians 7: Northwest Coast*, ed. by Wayne Suttles, 203–228. Washington: Smithsonian Institution.

DeLancey, Scott. 1992. Klamath and Sahaptian Numerals. *International Journal of American Linguistics* 58, no. 2: 235–239.

DeLancey, Scott, Carol Genetti, and Noel Rude. 1988. Some Sahaptian-Klamath-Tsimshianic Lexical Sets. *In Honor of Mary Haas: From the Haas Festival Conference on Native American Linguistics*, ed. by William Shipley, 195–224. Berlin: Mouton de Gruyter.

Dixon, Roland. 1910. The Chimariko Indians and Language. *University of California Publications in American Archaeology and Ethnology* 5, no. 5: 293–380.

Dixon, Roland and Alfred Kroeber. 1903. Native Languages of California. *American Anthropologist* 5: 1–26.

Dixon, Roland and Alfred Kroeber. 1913a. Relationship of the Indian Languages of California. *Science* 37: 225.

Dixon, Roland and Alfred Kroeber. 1913b. New Linguistic Families in California. *American Anthropologist* 15: 647–655.

Dixon, Roland and Alfred Kroeber. 1919. Linguistic Families of California. *University of California Publications in American Archaeology and Ethnology* 16: 47–118.

Eastman, Carol and Elizabeth Edwards. 1983. Qaao Qaao: A Haida Traditional Narrative, or Quoth the Raven "Nevermore". *International Conference on Salish and Neighboring Languages* 18: 64–79.

Eastman, Carol and Elizabeth Edwards. 1991. *Gyaehlingaay: Traditions, Tales, and Images of the Kaigani Haida.* Seattle: Burke Memorial Museum/University of Washington.

Edwards, Elizabeth. 1995. '"It's an ill wind"'. *Language and Culture in Native North America: Studies in Honor of Heinz-Jürgen Pinnow*, ed. by Michael Dürr, Egon Renner, and Wolfgang Oleschinsy, 245–252. Munich: LINCOM.

Edwards, Elizabeth and Carol Eastman. 1995. Fried Bread: A Recipe for the Structure of Haida Oral Narrative. *Language and Culture in Native North America*, ed. by Michael Dürr, Egon Renner, and Wolfgang Oleschinsy, 253–264. Munich: LINCOM.

Enrico, John. 1995. *Skidegate Haida Myths and Stories.* Skidegate, BC: Queen Charlotte Islands Museum.

Enrico, John. 2003. *Haida Syntax.* Lincoln: University of Nebraska Press.

Escalante Fontaneda, Hernando d'. 1944. Memoir of Do. d'Escalenta Fontaneda Respecting Florida, Written in Spain about the Year 1575. Trans. from the Spanish with Notes by Buckingham Smith (Washington, 1854), ed. David O. True, *University of Miami and the Historical Association of Southern Florida Miscellaneous Publications* 1. Miami.

Frachtenberg, Leo. 1914. Lower Upmqua Texts and Notes on the Kusan Dialect. *Columbia University Contributions to Anthropology* 4: 141–150. Reprinted in 1969 in New York: AMS.

Frachtenberg, Leo J. 1918. Comparative Studies in Takelman, Kalapuyan, and Chinookan Lexicography, a Preliminary Paper. *International Journal of American Linguistics* 1: 175–182.

Frachtenberg, Leo J. 1918ms, *Alsea Grammar.* Washington: Smithsonian Institution.

Frachtenberg, Leo J. 1922. Siuslawan (Lower Umpqua). *Handbook of American Indian Languages*, vol. 2, ed. by Franz Boas, pp. 431–629. Gluckstadt: J.J. Augustin.

Gallatin, Albert. 1836. *A Synopsis of the Indian Tribes within the United States East of the Rocky Mountains, and in the British and Russian Possessions in North America.* Transactions and Collections of the American Antiquarian Society 2. Worcester, MA: American Antiquarian Society.

Gallatin, Albert. 1848. The Families of Languages as Far as Ascertained. *Hale's Indians of North-West America, and Vocabularies of North America: With an Introduction*, xxiii–clxxxviii. Transactions of the American Ethnological Society 2. New York.

García, Bartolomé. 1760. *Manual para administrar los santos sacramentos. . . a los indios de las naciones: Pajalates, Orejones, Pacaos, Tilijayas, Alasapas, Pausanes, y otras muchas diferentes que se hallan en las misiones del Rio San Antonio, y Rio Grande.* Mexico.

Garvin, Paul. 1947. Christian Names in Kutenai. *International Journal of American Linguistics* 13: 69–77.

Garvin, Paul. 1948a. Kutenai Lexical Innovations. *Word* 4: 120–126.

Garvin, Paul. 1948b. Kutenai I: Phonemics. *International Journal of American Linguistics* 14: 37–42.

Garvin, Paul. 1948c. Kutenai II: Morpheme Variation. *International Journal of American Linguistics* 14: 87–90.

Garvin, Paul. 1948d. Kutenai III: Morpheme Distributions (prefix, theme, suffix). *International Journal of American Linguistics* 14: 171–178.

Garvin, Paul. 1951a. Kutenai IV: Word Classes. *International Journal of American Linguistics* 17: 84–97.

Garvin, Paul. 1951b. L'obviation en Kutenai: échantillon d'une catégorie grammaticale amérindienne. *Bulletin de la Société de Linguistique de Paris* 47: 166–212.

Garvin, Paul. 1953. Short Kutenai Texts. *International Journal of American Linguistics* 19: 305–311.

Garvin, Paul. 1954. Colloquial Kutenai Text: Conversation II. *International Journal of American Linguistics* 20: 316–334.

Gatschet, Albert S. 1880. The Numeral Adjective in the Klamath Language of Southern Oregon. *American Antiquarian and Oriental Journal* 2: 210–217.

Gatschet, Albert S. 1882. Indian Languages of the Pacific States and Territories and of the Pueblos of New Mexico. *Magazine of American History with Notes and Queries* 8: 254–263.

Gatschet, Albert S. 1884. Field Notes on Karankawa and Aranama, Collected at Fort Griffen, Texas. Smithsonian Institution National Anthropological Archive ms 506.

Gatschet, Albert S. 1890. *The Klamath Indians of Southwestern Oregon*. Contributions to North American Ethnology 2.1.

Gatschet, Albert S. and John R. Swanton. 1932. A Dictionary of the Atakapa Language, Accompanied by Text Material. *Bureau of American Ethnology Bulletin* 108, Smithsonian Institution, Washington. Reprinted by Scholarly Press, St. Claire Shores, MI, 1974.

Goddard, Ives. 1979. The Languages of South Texas and the Lower Rio Grande. *The Languages of Native America: Historical and Comparative Assessment*, ed. by Lyle Campbell and Marianne Mithun, 355–389. Austin, TX: University of Texas Press.

Goddard, Ives. 1996a. The Description of the Native Languages of North America before Boas. *Languages: Handbook of North American Indians*, vol. 17, 17–42. Washington: Smithsonian Institution.

Goddard, Ives. 1996b. The Classification of the Native Languages of North America. *Languages: Handbook of North American Indians*, vol. 17, 290–323. Washington: Smithsonian Institution.

Goddard, Ives. 1996c. Introduction. *Languages: Handbook of North American Indians*, vol. 17, 1–16. Washington: Smithsonian Institution.

Golla, Victor. 2011. *California Indian Languages*. Berkeley: University of California Press.

Granberry, Julian. 1990. A Grammatical Sketch of Timucua. *International Journal of American Linguistics* 56: 60–101.

Granberry, Julian. 1993. *A Grammar and Dictionary of the Timucua Language* (3rd ed.). Tuscaloosa: University of Alabama Press.

Grant, Anthony P. 1994. Karankawa Linguistic Materials. *Papers in Linguistics* 19: 1–56.

Gursky, Karl-Heinz. 1969. A Lexical Comparison of the Atakapa, Chitimacha, and Tunica Languages. *International Journal of American Linguistics* 35, no. 2: 80–107.

Haas, Mary R. 1941. Tunica. *Handbook of American Indian languages*, vol. 4, ed. by Franz Boas, 1–143. New York: J.J. Augustin.

Haas, Mary R. 1946. A Grammatical Sketch of Tunica. *Linguistics Structures of Native America*, ed. Harry Hoijer, vol. 6, 337–366. New York: Viking Fund.

Haas, Mary R. 1950. Tunica Texts. *University of California Publications in Linguistics* 6: 1–174.

Haas, Mary R. 1951. The Proto-Gulf Word for *Water* (with notes on Siouan-Yuchi). *International Journal of American Linguistics* 17, no. 2: 71–79.

Haas, Mary R. 1952. The Proto-Gulf Word for *Land* (with a Note on Proto-Siouan). *International Journal of American Linguistics* 18, no. 4: 238–240.

Haas, Mary R. 1953. Tunica Dictionary. *University of California Publications in Linguistics, Berkeley* 6, no. 2: 175–332.

Haas, Mary R. 1956. Natchez and the Muskogean Languages. *Language* 32, no. 1: 61–72.

Haas, Mary R. 1958. A New Linguistic Relationship in North America: Algonkian and the Gulf Languages. *Southwestern Journal of Anthropology* 14, no. 3: 231–264.

Haas, Mary R. 1959. Tonkawa and Algonkian. *Anthropological Linguistics* 1, no. 2: 1–6.

Haas, Mary R. 1965. Is Kutenai Related to Algonquian? *Canadian Journal of Linguistics* 10: 77–92.

Haas, Mary R. 1967. On the Relations of Tonkawa. *Studies in Southwestern Ethnolinguistics: Meaning and History in the Languages of the American Southwest*, ed. by Dell Hymes and William E. Bittle, 310–320. The Hague: Mouton.

Haas, Mary R. 1976. The Northern California Linguistic Area. *Hokan Studies*, ed. by Margaret Langdon and Shirley Silver, 347–359. The Hague: Mouton.

Haas, Mary R. 1979. Southeastern Languages. *The Languages of Native America: Historical and Comparative Assessment*, ed. by Lyle Campbell and Marianne Mithun, 299–326. Austin, TX: University of Texas Press.

Hale, Horatio. 1846. Ethnography and Philology. *United States Exploring Expedition during the Years 1838, 1839, 1840, 1841, 1842 under the Command of Charles Wilkes, U.S.N.*, vol. 6. Lea and Blanchard, Philadelphia. Reprinted in 1968 by Gregg Press, Ridgewood, N.J.

Harrington, John Peabody. 1917. Announcement of Genetic Relationship Between Washo and Chumashan. *American Anthropologist* 19: 154.

Harrington, John Peabody. 1930. Karuk Texts. *International Journal of American Linguistics* 6, no. 2: 121–161.

Harrington, John Peabody. 1932a. *Karuk Myths*. Bureau of American Ethnology Bulletin vol. 107, Government Printing Office, Washington.

Harrington, John Peabody. 1932b. *Tobacco Among the Karuk Indians of California*. Bureau of American Ethnology Bulletin 94. Washington, DC: Smithsonian Institution.

Heizer, Robert (ed.). 1952. *California Indian Linguistic Records: The Mission Indian Vocabularies of Alphonse Pinart*. Anthropological Records, University of California, vol. 15 no. 1.

Heizer, Robert (ed.). 1955. *California Indian Linguistic Records: The Mission Indian Vocabularies of HW Henshaw*. Anthropological Records, University of California, vol. 15, no. 2.

Henshaw, Henry. 1887. Notice of Linguistic Research on Washo in 1883. *Bureau of American Ethnology Report* 5: xxx.

Hewson, John. 1968. Beothuk and Algonkian: Evidence Old and New. *International Journal of American Linguistics* 34: 85–93.

Hewson, John. 1971. Beothuk Consonant Correspondences. *International Journal of American Linguistics* 37: 244–249.

Hewson, John. 1978. Beothuk Vocabularies. *Technical Papers of the Newfoundland Museum* vol. 2. St Johns, Newfoundland.

Hewson, John. 1982. Beothuk and the Algonkian Northeast. *Languages in Newfoundland and Labrador*, ed. by Harrold J. Paddock, 176–187. St. John's, Newfoundland: Department of Linguistics, Memorial University.

Hoijer, Harry. 1931–1933. Tonkawa: An Indian Language of Texas. Extract from the *Handbook of American Indian Languages* vol. 3, pp. 1–148, Distributed privately by the University of Chicago Libraries in 1931, Columbia University, New York.

Hoijer, Harry. 1946. Tonkawa. *Linguistic Structures of Native America*, ed. by Harry Hoijer, 289–311. Viking Fund Publications, New York.

Hoijer, Harry. 1949. *An Analytical Dictionary of the Tonkawa Language*, University of California Publications in Linguistics vol. 9, Berkeley.

Hoijer, Harry. 1972. *Tonkawa Texts*. University of California Publications in Linguistics vol. 73, Berkeley: University of California Press.

Jacobsen, William H. 1964. *A Grammar of the Washo Language*, Ph.D. dissertation, University of California, Berkeley.

Jacobsen, William H. 1986. Washoe Language. *Handbook of North American Indians 11: Great Basin*, ed. by Warren L. D'Azevedo, 107–112. Washington: Smithsonian Institution.

Jacobsen, William H. 1993. *Another Look at Sapir's Evidence for Inclusion of Haida in Na-Dene*. Paper presented at the Annual Meeting of the linguistic Society of America, Los Angeles.

Jany, Carmen. 2009. *Chimariko Grammar: Areal and Typological Perspective*. University of California Publications in Linguistics 142. Berkeley: University of California Press.

Kaufman, Terrence. 1988ms. A Research Program for Reconstructing Proto-Hokan: First Groupings. ms.

Kaufman, Terrence. 1989. Some Hypotheses Regarding Proto-Hokan Grammar. Paper presented at the Hokan-Penutian Workshop, University of Arizona, Tucson.

Kendall, Daythal. 1977. *A Syntactic Analysis of Takelma Texts*. Ph.D. dissertation, University of Pennsylvania.

Kendall, Daythal. 1982. Some Notes toward Using Takelma Data in Historical and Comparative Work. *Occasional Papers on Linguistics 10: Proceedings of the 1981 Hokan Languages Workshop and Penutian Languages Conference*, 78–81. Carbondale, IL: Southern Illinois University Department of Linguistics.

Kendall, Daythal. 1990. Takelma. *Handbook of North American Indians 7: Northwest Coast*, ed. by Wayne Suttles, 589–592. Washington: Smithsonian Institution.

Kendall, Daythal. 1997. The Takelma Verb: Toward Proto-Takelma-Kalapuyan. *International Journal of American Linguistics* 63, no. 1: 1–17.

Kimball, Geoffrey. 1994. Comparative Difficulties of the "Gulf" Languages. *Proceedings of the Meeting of the Society for the Study of the Indigenous Languages of the Americas, July 2–4, 1993, and the Hokan-Penutian Workshop, July 3, 1993*, ed. by Margaret Langdon, 31–39. Berkeley: Survey of California and Other Indigenous Languages Report 8, Department of Linguistics, University of California.

Kimball, Geoffrey. 2005. Natchez. *Native Languages of the Southeastern United States*, ed. by Heather K. Hardy and Janine Scancarelli, 385–453. Lincoln: University of Nebraska Press.

Krauss, Michael E. 1979. Na-Dene and Eskimo-Aleut. *The Languages of Native America: Historical and Comparative Assessment*, ed. by Lyle Campbell and Marianne Mithun, 803–901. Austin, TX: University of Texas Press.

Kroeber, Alfred S. 1904. Languages of the Coast of California South of San Francisco. *University of California Publications in American Archaeology and Ethnology* 2, no. 2.

Kroeber, Alfred S. 1907. The Washo Language of East Central California and Nevada. *University of California Publications in American Archaeology and Ethnology* 4, no. 5: 251–317.

Kroeber, Alfred S. 1936. Karok Towns. *University of California Publications in American Archaeology and Ethnology* 35, no. 4: 29–38.

Kroeber, Paul D. 1999. *The Salish Language Family: Reconstructing Syntax.* Lincoln: University of Nebraska Press.

Landar, Herbert J. 1996. Sources. *Languages: Handbook of North American Indians*, vol. 17, 721–761. Washington: Smithsonian Institution.

Latham, Robert G. 1848. On the Languages of the Oregon Territory. *Journal of the Ethnological Society of London* 1: 154–166.

Lawrence, Erma (ed.). 1977. *Haida Dictionary*, with grammatical sketch by Jeffry Leer. Alaska Native Language Center, Fairbanks.

Leer, Jeffry. 1990. Tlingit: A Portmanteau Language Family. *Linguistic Change and Reconstruction Methodology*, ed. by Philip Baldi, 73–98. Berlin: Mouton de Gruyter.

Leer, Jeffry. 1991a. *The Schetic Categories of the Tlingit Verb*, Ph.D. dissertation, University of Chicago.

Leer, Jeffry. 1991b. Evidence for a Northern Northwest Coast Language Area: Promiscuous Number Marking and Periphrastic Possessive Constructions in Haida, Eyak, and Aleut. *International Journal of American Linguistics* 57: 158–193.

Levine, Robert. 1977. *The Skidegate Dialect of Haida*, Ph.D. dissertation, Columbia University, New York.

Levine, Robert. 1979. Haida and Na-Dene: A New Look at the Evidence. *International Journal of American Linguistics* 45: 157–170.

Linn, Mary. 2000. *A Reference Grammar of Euchee (Yuchi)*, Ph.D. dissertation, University of Kansas.

Lowie, Robert. 1963. Washo Texts. *Anthropological Linguistics* 5, no. 7: 1–30.

Manaster Ramer, Alexis. 1996. Sapir's Classifications: Coahuiltecan. *Anthropological Linguistics* 38: 1–38.

Marquardt, William H. 2004. Calusa. *Handbook of North American Indians: Southeast*, vol. 14, ed. by Raymond D. Vogelson, 204–212. Washington: Smithsonian Institution.

Martin, Jack. 2004. Languages. *Handbook of North American Indians: Southeast*, vol. 14, 68–86. Washington: Smithsonian Institution.

Mason, J. Alden. 1918. The Language of the Salinan Indians. *University of California Publications in American Archaeology and Ethnology* 14, no. 1: 1–154.

Mithun, Marianne. 1982. The Mystery of the Vanished Laurentians. *Papers from the Fifth International Conference on Historical Linguistics*. Current Issues in Linguistic Theory 21, ed. by Anders Ahlqvist, 230–242. Amsterdam: John Benjamins.

Mithun, Marianne. 1999. *The Languages of Native North America.* Cambridge: Cambridge University Press.

Mithun, Marianne. 2007. Grammar, Contact, and Time. *Journal of Language Contact Thema* 1: 144–167.

Mithun, Marianne. 2008. The Emergence of Agentive Systems. *The Typology of Semantic Alignment Systems*, ed. by Mark Donohue and Søren Wichmann, 297–333. Oxford: Oxford University Press.

Mithun, Marianne. 2010. Contact in North America. *Handbook of Language Contact*, ed. by Raymond Hickey, 673–694. Oxford: Blackwell.

Mithun, Marianne. 2012. Core Argument Patterns and Deep Genetic Relations: Hierarchical Systems in Northern California. *Typology of Argument Structure and Grammatical Relations*, ed. by Pirkko Suihkonen, Bernard Comrie, and Valery Solovyev, Studies in Language Companion Series, 257–294. Amsterdam: John Benjamins.

Mithun, Marianne. 2017. Native North American Languages. *The Cambridge Handbook of Areal Linguistics*, ed. by Raymond Hickey, 878–933. Cambridge: Cambridge University Press.

Morgan, Lawrence. 1980. *Kootenay-Salishan Linguistic Comparison: A Preliminary Study*. M.A. thesis, University of British Columbia, Vancouver.

Morgan, Lawrence. 1991. *A Description of the Kutenai Language*. Ph.D. dissertation, University of California, Berkeley.

Movilla, Gregorio de. 1635. Forma Breve de administar los Sacramentos a los Indios, y Españoles que viuen entre ellos. Approbado por Autoridad Apostolica, y sacado del Manual Mexicano, que se usa en toda la nuena España y Pirù, mutatis mutandis, esto es, lo q̃ estua en légua Mexicana traducido en lengua Floridiana. Imprenta de Iuan Ruyz, Mexico.

Munro, Pamela. 1994. Gulf and Yuki-Gulf. *Anthropological Linguistics* 36, no. 2: 125–222.

Newman, Stanley. 1958. *Zuni Dictionary*. Indian University Research Center Publications vol. 6. Indiana University, Bloomington.

Newman, Stanley. 1965. *Zuni Grammar*. University of New Mexico Publications in Anthropology 14. University of New Mexico, Albuquerque.

Newman, Stanley. 1996. Sketch of the Zuni Language. *Handbook of North American Indians: Language*, vol. 17, ed. by Ives Goddard, 483–506. Washington: Smithsonian Institution.

O'Neill, Sean. 2008. *Cultural Contact and Linguistic Relativity Among the Indians of Northwestern California*. Norman: University of Oklahoma.

Pareja, Francisco [1612] 1886. Arte de la lengua timvqvana compvesto en 1614 por el Pe Francisco Pareja y publicado comforme al ejemplar original único por Lucien Adam y Julien Vinson. *Bibliothèque Linguistique Américane* 11. Paris.

Pareja, Francisco de 1612, 'Catechismo y breve exposición de la doctrina Christiana. Muy util y necessaria, asi para los Espanoles, como para los Naturales, en Lengua Castellana, y Timuquana, en modo de preguntas, y respuestas'. México: Viuda de Pedro Balli. Copy in Buckingham Smith Collection, New York Historical Society, New York City. Photostat, Manuscript No. 2401, "Codex A", National Anthropological Archives, Smithsonian Institution, Washington.

Pinnow, Hans-Jürgen. 1964. On the Historical Position of Tlingit. *International Journal of American Linguistics* 30: 155–164.

Powell, John Wesley. 1891 [1892]. Indian Linguistic Families of America North of Mexico. *Annual Report of the Bureau of [American] Ethnology 7 for 1885–1886*. Smithsonian Institution, Washington, vol. 7, 1–142. Reprinted 1966 University of Nebraska Press, Lincoln.

Rankin, Robert L. 1977. From Verb to Auxiliary to Noun Classifier and Definite Article: Grammaticalisation of the Siouan Verbs 'sit', 'stand', 'lie''. *Proceedings of the 1976 Mid-America Linguistics Conference*, 273–283, ed. by R.L. Brown, Jr., K. Houlihan, L.G. Hutchinson, and A. MacLeish. St. Paul: Department of Linguistics, University of Minnesota.

Rankin, Robert L. 1978. *On the Origin of the Classificatory Verbs in Muskogean*. Paper presented at the Annual meeting of the American Anthropological Association, Los Angeles.

Rankin, Robert L. 2004. The History and Development of Siouan Positionals with Special Attention to Polygrammaticalisation in Dhegiha. *Sprachtypologie und Universalien Forschung (STUF)* 2/3: 202–227.

Rankin, Robert L. 2011. The Siouan Enclitics: A Beginning. Paper prepared for the Comparative Linguistics Workshop, University of Michigan, Ann Arbor.

Rigsby, Bruce. 1965. *Linguistic Relations in the Southern Plateau*, Ph.D. dissertation, University of Oregon.

Rigsby, Bruce. 1966. On Cayuse-Molala Relatability. *International Journal of American Linguistics* 32: 369–378.

Rigsby, Bruce. 1969. The Waiilatpuan Problem: More on Cayuse-Molala Relatability. *Northwest Anthropological Research Notes* 3, no. 1: 68–146.

Rude, Noel. 1987. Some Klamath-Sahaptian Grammatical Correspondences. *Kansas Working Papers in Linguistics* 12, no. 1: 189–190.

Sapir, Edward. 1909. *Takelma Texts*. University of Pennsylvania University Museum, Anthropological Publications, vol. 2, 1–267. Berkeley: University of California Press.

Sapir, Edward. 1915. The Na-Dene Languages, a Preliminary Report. *American Anthropologist* 17: 534–558.

Sapir, Edward. 1917a. *The Position of Yana in the Hokan Stock*. University of California Publications in American Archaeology and Ethnology, vol. 13, 1–34. Berkeley: University of California Press.

Sapir, Edward. 1917b. The Status of Washo. *American Anthropologist* 19: 449–450.

Sapir, Edward. 1920. The Hokan and Coahuiltecan Languages. *International Journal of American Linguistics* 1, no. 4: 280–290.

Sapir, Edward. 1921. A Bird's Eye View of American Languages North of Mexico. *Science* n.s. 54, 408. Reprinted 1990 in *The Collected Works of Edward Sapir 5: American Indian Languages*, ed. by William Bright, Mouton de Gruyter, Berlin, pp. 93–94.

Sapir, Edward. 1922. The Takelma Language of Southwestern Oregon. *Handbook of American Indian Languages*, ed. by Franz Boas. Bureau of American Ethnology Bulletin vol. 40, no. 2, pp. 1–296. Washington: Government Printing Office.

Sapir, Edward. 1929. Central and North American Indian Languages. *Encyclopaedia Britannica* (14th ed.), vol. 5, 138–141. Reprinted 1949, 1963 in Mandelbaum, ed. pp. 169–178, and 1990 in *The collected works of Edward Sapir 5: American Indian Languages*, ed. William Bright, Mouton de Gruyter, Berlin, pp. 95–104.

Sapir, Edward and Leslie Spier. 1943. Notes on the Culture of the Yana. *Anthropological Records* 3, no. 3: 239–297.

Sapir, Edward and Morris Swadesh. 1960. *Yana Dictionary*, ed. Mary R. Haas. University of California Publications in Linguistics vol. 22. Berkeley: University of California Press

Shaul, David. 1995a. The Huelel (Esselen) Language. *International Journal of American Linguistics* 61, no. 2: 191–239.

Shaul, David. 1995b. The Last Words of Esselen. *International Journal of American Linguistics* 61: 245–249.

Shipley, William. 1969. Proto-Takelman. *International Journal of American Linguistics* 35: 226–230.

Sibley, John. 1832. Historical Sketches of the Several Indian Tribes in Louisiana, South of the Arkansas River, and Between the Mississippi and River Grande. Communicated to Congress by Thomas Jefferson, February 19, 1806. *American State Papers, Documents, Legislative and Executive, of the Congress of the United States* IV: 721–730.

Sitjar, Bonaventure. 1861. *Vocabulary of the Language of San Antonio Mission, California*, Shea's Library of American Linguistics vol. 6. New York: Cramoisy Press.

Story, Gillian. 1966. *A Morphological Study of Tlingit*, M.A. thesis, School of Oriental and African Studies, University of London, London.

Swadesh, Morris. 1946a. Chitimacha. *Linguistic Structures of Native America*, ed. by Harry Hoijer, 312–336. Viking Fund Publications in Anthropology 6. New York: Viking Fund.

Swadesh, Morris. 1946b. Phonologic Formulas for Atakapa-Chitimacha. *International Journal of America Linguistics* 12, no. 3: 113–132.

Swadesh, Morris. 1947. Atakapa-Chitimacha *kw. *International Journal of American Linguistics* 13, no. 2: 120–121.

Swadesh, Morris. 1956. Problems of Long-Range Comparison in Penutian. *Language* 32: 17–41.

Swadesh, Morris. 1965. Kalapuya and Takelma. *International Journal of American Linguistics* 31, no. 3: 237–240.

Swanton, John R. 1907. The Ethnological Position of the Natchez Indians. *American Anthropologist* n.s. 9, no. 3: 513–528.

Swanton, John R. 1915. Linguistic Position of the Tribes of Southern Texas and Northeastern Mexico. *American Anthropologist* 17: 17–40.

Swanton, John R. 1919. A Structural and Lexical Comparison of the Tunica, Chitimacha, and Atakapa Languages. *Bureau of American Ethnology Bulletin*, 68. Washington: Smithsonian Institution.

Swanton, John R. 1921. The Tunica Language. *International Journal of American Linguistics* 2: 1–39.

Swanton, John R. 1922. Early History of the Creek Indians and Their Neighbors. *Bureau of American Ethnology Bulletin*, Government Printing Office, Washington, 73. Reprinted 1970 by Johnson Reprint, New York.

Swanton, John R. 1924. The Muskhogean Connection of the Natchez Language. *International Journal of American Linguistics* 3, no. 1: 46–75.

Swanton, John R. 1929a. A Sketch of the Atakapa Language. *International Journal of American Linguistics* 5, no. 2–4: 121–149.

Swanton, John R. 1929b. The Tawasa Language. *American Anthropologist* 31: 435–453.

Swanton, John R. 1940. *Linguistic Material from the Tribes of Southern Texas and Northeastern Mexico*. Bureau of American Ethnology Bulletin, 127. Washington: Government Printing Office.

Tarpent, Marie-Lucie and Daythal Kendall. 1998. On the Relationship Between Takelma and Kalapuyan: Another Look at "Takelman". Paper presented at the annual meeting of the Society for the Study of the Indigenous Languages of the Americas, New York.

Taylor, Allan. 1963. Comparative Caddoan. *International Journal of American Linguistics* 29: 113–121.

Thompson, Laurence. 1979. Salishan and the Northwest. *The Languages of Native North America*, ed. by Lyle Campbell and Marianne Mithun, 692–765. Austin, TX: University of Texas Press.

Troike, Rudolph C. 1978. The Date and Authorship of the Pajalate (Coahuilteco) Cuardernillo. *International Journal of American Linguistics* 44, no. 4: 168–171.

Troike, Rudolph C. 1996. Sketch of Coahuilteco, a Language Isolate of Texas. *Handbook of North American Indians: Languages*, ed. by Ives Goddard, vol. 17, 644–665. Washington: Smithsonian Institution.

Turner, Katherine. 1983. Areal and Genetic Affiliations of the Salinan. *Kansas Working Papers in Linguistics* 8, no. 2: 215–246.

Turner, Katherine. 1987. *Aspects of Salinan Grammar*. Ph.D. dissertation, University of California, Berkeley.

Turner, Katherine. 1988. Salinan Linguistic Materials. *Journal of California and Great Basin Anthropology* 10: 265–270.

Turner, Katherine and David Shaul. 1981. John Peabody Harrington's Esselen Data and the Excelen Language. *Journal of California Publications in Linguistics* 3: 95–124.

Van Tuyl, Charles D. 1979. The Natchez: Annotated Translation from Antoine Simon le Page du Pratz's *Histoire de la Louisiane* and a Short English-Natchez Dictionary, with Ethnographic Footnotes, Natchez Transcription, Sound System, Kinship Terminology, and Kinship System by Willard Walker. *Oklahoma Historical Society Series in Anthropology* vol. 4. Oklahoma City, OK: Oklahoma Historical Society.

Vater, Johann Severin. 1820–1821. *Analekten der Sprachenkunde* 2 vols. Leipzig: Dyksche Buchhandlung.

Villiers du Terrage, Marc de and Paul Rivet. 1919. Les indiens du Texas et les expéditions françaises de 1720 et 1721 à la 'Baie Saint-Bernard.' *Journal de la Société des Américanistes de Paris*, n.s. 11, no. 2: 403–442.

Voegelin, Carl and Erminie Voegelin. 1946. Linguistic Considerations of Northeastern North America. *Man in Northeastern North America*, 178–194. Papers of the Robert S. Peabody Foundation for Archaeology 3. Andover, MA.

Wagner, Günther. 1931. *Yuchi Tales*. Papers of the American Ethnological Society 13. New York: AMS Press.

Wagner, Günther. 1933. Yuchi. *Handbook of American Indian Languages*, vol. 3, 293–384. Glückstadt/Hamburg/New York: JJ Augustin.

FURTHER READING

Campbell, Lyle. 1997. *American Indian Languages: The Historical Linguistics of Native America*. Oxford: Oxford University Press.

Goddard, Ives. 1996a. The Classification of the Native Languages of North America. *Languages: Handbook of North American Indians*, vol. 17, 290–323. Washington: Smithsonian Institution.

Goddard, Ives. 1996b. Introduction. *Languages: Handbook of North American Indians*, vol. 17, 1–16. Washington: Smithsonian Institution.

Mithun, Marianne. 1999. *The Languages of Native North America*. Cambridge: Cambridge University Press.

CHAPTER 9

LANGUAGE ISOLATES OF MESOAMERICA AND NORTHERN MEXICO

Raina Heaton

1 INTRODUCTION

This chapter discusses the four linguistic isolates spoken (or formerly spoken) in Meso-america and northern Mexico: Seri, Huave, Purépecha (Tarascan) and Cuitlatec. Although Cuitlatec is the only one which is no longer spoken, the other three are either threatened or endangered. This chapter provides basic information on each of these isolates, includ-ing their location, vitality and brief history. In an effort to demonstrate that each of these languages is indeed a linguistic isolate, also included is a discussion of the major pro-posals for genetic relationships involving these languages, as well as an evaluation of the evidence presented for each. The section on each language concludes with an overview of the typological characteristics of the language and some of the features it possesses which may be of general interest to linguists.[1]

Mesoamerica can be a particularly difficult region in which to determine genetic rela-tionship since it is recognised as a linguistic area, where features have been shared across language boundaries. This Mesoamerican linguistic area roughly aligns with the Meso-american cultural area and is considered to have, in addition to a large number of less-widely distributed linguistic features, the following diagnostic characteristics (Campbell et al. 1986: 555):

1 Nominal possession with the following structure: *his-dog the man*
2 Relational nouns (mandatorily possessed noun roots which express relational notions)
3 Vigesimal numeral systems
4 Non-verb-final basic word order
5 Widespread semantic calques, e.g. 'deer-snake' for boa constrictor

Some languages lack sufficient documentation to be accurately classified and therefore have been excluded from this chapter, such as Maratino and Naolan. These have long been extinct, with extremely scant attestations, so there is little hope of being able to classify them. Also not included here are those small language families which have occasionally been discussed as individual languages, but which are not true isolates. These include: Xincan (four languages of Guatemala: Yupiltepeque, Jumaytepeque, Chiquimulilla, Guazacapan); Lencan (two languages: Honduran Lenca, Salvadoran Lenca); Jicaquean (two languages of Honduras: Western Jicaque, Eastern Jicaque/Tol); and Tequistlatecan/

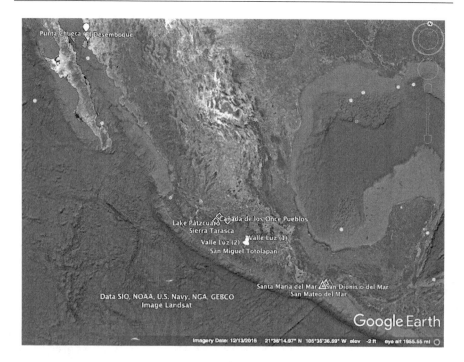

MAP 9.1 LOCATIONS OF THE SERI, PUREPÉCHA, CUITLATEC AND HUAVE LINGUISTIC COMMUNITIES

Chontal of Oaxaca (three languages: Lowland Chontal/Huamelultec, Highland Chontal, Tequistlatec) (after Campbell 1997).

The communities/areas where the four isolates which are the focus of this chapter are currently spoken or, in the case of Cuitlatec, have been spoken, are shown in Map 9.1. The northernmost isolate is Seri, represented by circles (Marlett 2006: 1); Purepécha is spoken in many towns in the Lake Pátzcuaro area of Michoacan, indicated by diamonds (Capistrán 2015: 8); just south of that are the towns which contained Cuitlatec speakers, indicated by a pin (Drucker et al. 1969: 566); finally, Huave is spoken in four towns in the Gulf of Tehuantepec, represented by triangles (Kim 2008: 1).

2 HUAVE

2.1 Basic information

Huave is a language isolate spoken in towns on three peninsulas extending into the Gulf of Tehuantepec in the state of Oaxaca. The designation 'Huave' is thought to be an exonym from the Zapotec for 'people who rot in the humidity' (e.g. Millán 2003) and is therefore dispreferred by some as a label. The preferred endonyms for the blanket designation 'Huave' are the equivalents in each dialect of 'our (INCLUSIVE) mouth'. However, in Spanish the Huaves are commonly referred to as *marenos* or 'people of the sea', and their language is referred to as 'Huave' (Kim 2008: 6).

There is some disagreement as to the number and status of the varieties which compose Huave. The general consensus appears to be that Huave is a single language with four dialects which have varying degrees of mutual intelligibility: Santa María del Mar, San Francisco del Mar, San Dionisio del Mar and San Mateo del Mar. *Ethnologue* lists each variety as a separate language but reports 88% mutual intelligibility between speakers in Santa María del Mar and San Mateo del Mar, but only 38% mutual intelligibility between speakers of San Francisco del Mar and San Mateo del Mar (Lewis, Simons and Fennig 2014). This low level of mutual intelligibility is apparently due largely to vowel shifts and prosodic differences (Kim 2008: 3), since these varieties share 91% of their basic vocabulary (Suaréz 1975: 1). In contrast, INALI (Instituto Nacional de Lenguas Indígenas de México) lists two Huave '*variantes*', West Huave and East Huave, where East Huave is composed of San Dionisio and San Francisco del Mar, and West Huave of San Mateo and Santa María del Mar (INALI: www.inali.gob.mx/). This grouping is at odds with other classifications, considering that Kim (2008: 3) reports that the San Dionisio dialect is most similar to that of San Mateo, and that the Santa María dialect is most similar to that of San Francisco, although this is complicated somewhat by a higher degree of contact between Santa María and San Mateo given their geographical proximity. She also reports that intelligibility between the San Francisco and San Mateo dialects requires significant exposure, which supports the 38% intelligibility rating given by *Ethnologue* (Kim 2008: 3).

In pre-colonial times, the Gulf of Tehuantepec area was made sociopolitically important by trade routes that lay between the central highlands and the Soconusco region in the state of Chiapas. At that time, Huaves occupied a large portion of the Chiapas coast, and their population centers were points of support for the Mexica traders who traveled the ancient salt route (Millán 2003: 7). There was therefore quite a bit of contact between Huave, Mixtec, Zapotec and Mixe-Zoquean languages for the purposes of trade. Most of the Huave way of life was also centered around fishing, and particularly shrimping, which supported their communities economically. This is still the case today, although the distribution of fishing activities between the towns is un equal, with San Dionisio and San Francisco accounting for 90% of the harvest, and only 10% from San Mateo (Griffin 2001).

In the 16th century, following the conquest of the area by the Spanish, the populations in the Tehuantepec region were decimated by disease such that the remaining residents were relegated to small towns hardly exceeding 100 people (Millán 2003: 8). Kim (2008: 3) speculates that this post-conquest separation of Huave populations into more isolated populations marked the beginning of the separation of the Huave dialects known today. This would give them no more than 500 years of divergence, during which time they were still in relatively close contact with one another, as well as with Zapotec. Interestingly, Huave speakers seem to have maintained a high degree of monolingualism into the 19th century, although this was less true in San Francisco del Mar, where there was a resident Zapotec population (Millán 2003: 10, Kim 2008:4).

These communities, like many other indigenous communities in Mesoamerica and around the world, have more recently been receiving pressure from globalization and modernization which threaten their language and their way of life (Kim 2008: 3). Reports from researchers and INALI put the total speakers of Huave at around 15,000: 10,000–15,000 from Kim (2008: 1), and 15,993 from the INALI 2008–2012 report. These numbers include semi-speakers and bilinguals/multilinguals, as most of the population has become bilingual or monolingual in Spanish, as it is the dominant language in the area. Reports indicate that there are very few monolingual speakers of Huave, with no remaining monolingual speakers of the San Francisco dialect as of 2008 (Kim 2008: 1), and about 1,550 monolinguals in San Mateo del Mar (Lewis, Simons and Fennig 2014). San Mateo is also the only dialect still being actively acquired by children, although most speakers are bilingual in Huave and Spanish.

Reports from San Dionisio indicate that younger people in the community are Spanish-dominant, and most adults are Spanish-Huave bilinguals. *Ethnologue* lists one monolingual speaker of the San Dionisio dialect, data ca. 2005 (Lewis, Simons and Fennig 2014). Kim (2008: 1–5) says of the San Francisco dialect that as of 2008 when she conducted her fieldwork, there were no more than 100 residents with a high degree of fluency in Huave. Most of these speakers were elderly and had not spoken Huave in some time, since the family members with whom they were accustomed to speaking had passed away. Adult individuals over the age of 40 were likely to understand and have passive knowledge of Huave if they grew up in a Huave-speaking household. However, those who grew up in Spanish-speaking households may only know a few Huave lexical items. There are no native Huave speakers in San Francisco under the age of 40.

Santa María is the smallest dialect in terms of population and is listed by UNESCO (Moseley 2010) as 'severely endangered'. The Expanded Graded Intergenerational Disruption Scale (EGIDS) (Lewis, Simons and Fennig 2014) lists all Huave dialects as 7 ('shifting'), except for San Mateo, which is 5 ('developing'). The *Catalogue of Endangered Languages* lists Huave as 'vulnerable', but only with 20% certainty ("Huave", Endangered Languages 2015). UNESCO (Moseley 2010) lists San Mateo as 'vulnerable', and all others as 'definitely endangered' to 'critically endangered'. This appears to be the most accurate characterization, since there is clearly a shift towards Spanish dominance in all dialects except perhaps San Mateo. There does seem to be some nascent interest in learning and/or preserving the language among the younger generations, and there is a group actively involved in cultural preservation efforts (Kim 2008: 5).

2.2 Relationship and documentation

There have been several proposals attempting to relate Huave to other languages and language families, primarily within in Mesoamerica. Radin (1916) proposed a relationship between Huave and Mixe-Zoquean languages, which was later incorporated by Sapir into his Mexican Penutian macrofamily. Radin (1924) then built on his earlier proposal and attempted to relate his Huave-Mixe-Zoquean to the Mayan languages. Morris Swadesh (1960) took a different approach and proposed that Huave is related to Otomanguean. However, according to Campbell (1997: 161), many of the items compared were Zapotecan loans. Suaréz (1975: 2) also criticizes Swadesh for only using a single dialect of Huave as his base of comparison.

There have also been several other geographically less plausible proposals attempting to relate Huave to languages outside of Mesoamerica. Suaréz (1975) proposed a relationship between Huave, Algonquian and the so-called 'Gulf' languages (cf. Haas 1951), which included Tunica, Chitimacha, Natchez (isolates) and Atakapan and Muskogean (families). Since the Gulf grouping is not widely accepted and has no demonstrable relation to Algonquian, it is even less feasible that Huave could then be connected with any of these groups. A decade prior to Suaréz, Bouda (1964; 1965) proposed an even more surprising relationship between Huave and the Uralic languages, which is likewise not supported today.

Suaréz (1975) notably used internal reconstruction and the comparative method based on the four modern Huave dialects to reconstruct Proto-Huave (which he further compared with Algonquian and Gulf). He reconstructed Proto-Huave with a series of plain stops and pre-nasalized stops, contrastive vowel length (only in penultimate syllables) and tone. There were several uncertainties, such as whether lexical tone should be reconstructed or could have arisen in San Mateo via other means. Also, it is possible that some segments that Suaréz reconstructed but which only occur in a few cognate sets are not true proto-phonemes (see Campbell 1997: 161). However, this attempt to apply internal reconstruction and the comparative method to dialects in order to elucidate the history of Huave is an important contribution to the historical study of isolates, as this method is principal among the very few techniques that allows us to recover previous stages for language isolates.

Of the four Huave dialects, the San Mateo del Mar variety is the most studied to date, with a grammar (Stairs and Stairs 1981) and a dictionary (Stairs and Hollenbach 1981) published through the work of the Summer Institute of Linguistics (SIL). There has also been work on particular aspects of San Mateo del Mar Huave morphology, most notably Stairs and Hollenbach (1969), Matthews (1972), Noyer (1993; 1997) and Cuturi and Gnerre (2005). There has also been some work on syntax, e.g. Pike and Warkentin (1961), Stolz (1996) and Pak (2007; 2010; 2014). Huave phonology has been of particular interest in the literature, with contributions by Noyer (1991; 2003), Davidson and Noyer (1997) and Evanini (2007).

The study of San Francisco del Mar Huave has been vastly improved in recent years due primarily to the work of Yuni Kim. Her dissertation in 2008 discussed in detail several aspects of Huave phonology and morphology, using primary data from the San Francisco del Mar dialect. She has since continued to work on Huave morphology and phonology, with articles on affix order, derivation, loan phonology and event structure (Kim 2009; 2010; 2011; 2013; *inter alia*). There remains very little linguistic work on the San Dionisio and Santa María dialects. The texts published in Radin (1929) are still the primary documentation of the San Dionisio dialect, and the Santa María dialect is represented mainly in Suaréz (1975). However, there is some recent work on vowels and palatalization in the Santa María dialect by Alberto G. Montoya Pérez (2014a; 2014b). There is also a conference, *Jornada de Estudios Huaves* (Conference on Huave Studies), which brings researchers together to discuss anthropological and linguistic work on all varieties of Huave. The first meeting was in 2010, the second in 2014.

2.3 Of typological interest

Huave can be characterized as a mildly agglutinating language, with marking on the verb for subject agreement, tense and subordination or gerundive status; nouns take possessive pronominal markers. Plurality is marked on determiners rather than on the noun itself (Kim 2008: 9). Huave is a head-marking language, and verb roots can be categorized in terms of those which take prefixes and those which take suffixes. Syntactically Huave is right-branching with VO basic word order, manifesting many of the patterns that correlate with VO order (e.g. relative clause following head noun, sentence-initial *wh-* question words). The basic order of S (Subject) is more difficult to discern, however, with both SV(O) and V(O)S readily attested. The position of S depends on discourse context and argument structure, among other things. Pak (2007) points out that there is a phonological difference between SV and VS orders, where preverbal subjects are phonologically separate from the predicate, but postverbal subjects are phonologically grouped with the verb.

In addition to prefixes and suffixes, Huave also has "mobile affixes," which have long been a topic of interest in the literature (cf. Matthews 1972; Noyer 1993; Kim 2010). These affixes can be either prefixes or suffixes depending on the context, i.e. the morphophonological properties of the base to which they attach. They also occur at a fixed distance from the root in the linear ordering of affixes. These mobile affixes are touted as being one of the few existing cases of phonologically conditioned affix ordering, the existence of which has theoretical ramifications for the study of the relationship between phonology and morphology. Kim (2010) proposes a hierarchical structure for affixes in Huave and accounts for the phonological conditioning of affix ordering in an Optimality-Theory framework where phonological well-formedness constraints outrank morphologic alignment constraints. However, true phonologically conditioned affix ordering is problematic for theories such as Lexical Phonology and Distributed Morphology (Halle and Marantz 1993) where morphology precedes phonology in the derivation of forms. Paster (2009: 34) suggests that these mobile affixes, since they consist only of single consonants, could potentially also be analyzed autosegmentally as floating features which then associate with the CV tier entirely within the realm of phonology.

Huave also has several interesting phonological features, including a contrast between a plain and a palatalized series of stops, diphthongization and vowel harmony. The San Mateo del Mar dialect also has contrastive vowel length, which corresponds to vowel "aspiration" (vowel plus postvocalic glottal fricative) in San Francisco del Mar (Kim 2008: 11). One of the more extensively researched topics in Huave, however, is lexical tone, which only exists in the San Mateo dialect. Tone in San Mateo del Mar Huave has a low functional load, and tonal contrasts are often neutralized by phrasal intonation patterns. Noyer (1991: 277) claims that low tone is assigned to all tone-bearing units which are not assigned tone lexically or metrically, and the distribution of high tones is based entirely on metrical constituency. High tone plateaus spread rightward across certain syntactic domains, making tone a factor in determining syntactic boundaries (cf. Pike and Warkentin 1961: 627; Pak 2007).

3 SERI

3.1 Basic information

Seri is spoken on the coast of Sonora in Mexico in two primary villages. The first, Punta Chueca, is located at 29°00'53" N, 112°09'45" W. The second is El Desemboque, located at 29°30'12" N, 112°23'46" W (Marlett 2006: 1). The Seri were traditionally largely nomadic, subsisting by hunting, gathering and fishing along the islands (particularly Tiburón Island) and margins of the Gulf of California (Sheridan 1979). According to Moser (1963), there were originally six bands of Seris who occupied Tiburón Island and the adjacent coastline, stretching northward around Puerto Lobos and southward to Guaymas. Although these six groups may have linguistically constituted three Seri dialects, there is today only one, with some minor internal variation (Marlett 2006). Although the Seris' ethnic pride, isolationism and location in the harsh desert landscape allowed them to maintain their language and culture longer than some other groups, external pressures of colonization, missionization and warfare significantly reduced their numbers, leaving fewer than 200 Seri speakers in 1920 (Moser 1963, Sheridan 1999). Today their numbers are increasing, and the land given to them as an *ejido* (communal lands) by the Mexican Republic in the 1970s has allowed them more control over their contact with non-Seri. Also, despite the 62 kilometers separating the two Seri villages, there is still regular contact between the Seris in both locations (Marlett 1981; 2006).

The Seri traditionally subsisted on fish and other sea life, particularly turtles, as well as berries, roots and whatever else they could gather from the desert landscape, which receives less than 10 inches of rain a year (Sheridan 1999: 8). However, the Seri diet was unique in that they did not have traditional grain staples, as the environment does not sustain traditional agriculture. Instead, their grain staple came from the seeds of *Zostera marina L.*, or eelgrass. The Seri are the only people known to have used a grain from the sea as a primary food source (Felger and Moser 1973; 1985; Sheridan and Felger 1977; Felger et al. 1980). The use of eelgrass as a grain staple was part of their lifestyle for a long time, which is evident in the amount of specialized vocabulary surrounding it. For example, the ripe eelgrass fruit is called *xnoois*,[2] whence comes the Seri term for April, '*xnoois* when there is moon', in which eelgrass becomes ready to harvest. There are also separate terms for those who harvest floating eelgrass (*capoee*) versus those that harvest growing eelgrass (*cotám*) (Felger and Moser 1973: 355).

Felger and Moser (1973) also argue that eelgrass has potential as a general food source for people globally, since it grows in abundance in the warm, shallow coastal areas of the Gulf of California, close to modern metropolitan areas. It also does not require fertilizers, pesticides or fresh water, and it has a nutritional profile similar to other grains. Additionally, it lacks any disagreeable flavors which might lead people to reject it (Felger and Moser 1973: 356). This discovery that eelgrass could be a major source of human sustenance is not only important in terms of food security but also in terms of endangered language advocacy. This discovery was made by studying the language and culture of a non-Western group of people whose language is endangered and whose traditional knowledge of their local ecosystem has expanded the reach of modern science. This is therefore a perfect case study as to the importance of the study of lesser-known language groups and how they can make significant, tangible contributions to human knowledge.

3.2 Naming and variation

The name 'Seri' is an exonym of unknown origin, although it is attested in records since 1692 (Di Peso and Matson 1965). As Marlett (2011b) clarifies, 'Seri' may have referred to only one or several of the original Seri bands, or an altogether unrelated group. Hypotheses about the etymology of 'Seri' include a suggested Spanish origin, from *sera* 'large basket' (Gatschet 1877–1892, 4: 3), an Opata origin, from a supposed Opata word meaning 'spry' (McGee 1898: 9), and a Yaqui origin, from a supposed Yaqui word/phrase meaning 'people of the sand'. Marlett (2011b: 3–5) demonstrates that all of these etymologies are quite likely spurious, and the only thing that is certain is that 'Seri' is an exonym, as the Seri language lacks a native /r/ phoneme. The Seri call themselves *Comcáac* /komˈkaːk/ [konˈkaːk], applied to ethnic Seri people (Marlett 2006: 1; 2011b: 5–10). However, this term cannot be applied to their language (unlike the term 'Seri', which has been applied to both the ethnic group and the language), which they call *Cmiique Iitom* [kw̃ĩkˈiːtom], 'Seri person's word' (Marlett 2011b: 1).

Although there is only one Seri dialect, there is some systematic linguistic variation between speakers involving phonetics, phonology, semantics and the lexicon. Several interesting aspects of this variation follow (see Marlett (2006) for a thorough discussion).

First, the language has a voiceless fricative which is labiodental for some speakers (/f/), but bilabial for others (/ɸ/) (Marlett et al. 2005: 117). /j/ ([y] in Americanist phonetics) is also sometimes pronounced as a voiced postalveolar affricate, which is a recent development due to contact with local Spanish (2005: 118), which has variation between [ʒ] and [dʒ] as a prestige pronunciation of /j/. In terms of the phonology, there is also variation in the application of a sibilant assimilation rule, where /s/ before /ʃ/ becomes postalveolar. However, some speakers systematically do not assimilate, e.g. *szatx aha* [ˈʃʃatχaʔa] ~ [ˈsʃatχaʔa] 's/he/it will have burs (alguates)' (Marlett 2006: 4). In addition, there is an asymmetry in the frequency of the two laterals in Seri, /l/ and the voiceless fricative /ɬ/, where plain, voiced /l/ appears in very few native words and some loans (Marlett et al. 2005: 117), but /ɬ/ is exceedingly common. Although for some speakers /l/ appears in a few lexical items where other speakers would use /ɬ/, apparently the fricative is gaining use (Marlett 2006: 4). This is interesting both because of typological expectations for voiced /l/ to be less marked and therefore more frequent and because of the phonetic transfer from Spanish influencing other sounds, but apparently not these laterals. In terms of inter-speaker variation in the lexicon, there are differences, not only in a few content words, but also in at least one function word, the determiner *cop* 's/he (standing)' which some systematically pronounce as *cap*, not only in isolation, but also derived forms such as *ticop* ~ *ticap*. There is also evidence of taboo avoidance, where the word *otác* 'frog, toad' ceased to be used after a woman known as *otác quiho* 'she who sees the frog' passed away (Marlett 2006: 5).

3.3 Status

Seri currently has between 800 and 900 speakers (Marlett et al. 2005; Marlett 2006), almost all of whom are ethnic Seri. That is, the language is closely tied to the ethic population, so that non-Seri do not speak Seri, and almost all Seri speak Seri (Marlett 2006: 1). The language is listed by *Ethnologue* as being in 'vigorous' use (Lewis, Simons and Fennig 2014), whereas the *Catalogue of Endangered Languages* lists it as 'threatened', with 80% certainty ("Seri", Endangered Languages 2015). Marlett (2006: 2) reports that Seri is still the language of everyday communication in Seri communities. Spanish exists in the community, but only in official domains such as in schools, with some use in religious services and official, commercial and tourism-related interactions with outsiders. Other adjacent language groups (primarily Uto-Aztecan) have not had more than minor lexical influences on Seri. There are also some cases of exogamy, where the children end up either Spanish-dominant bilinguals or Spanish monolinguals. However, this does not appear to be having a significant impact on language use amongst the youth in the community, since generally children of all ages are fluent in Seri (Marlett 2006: 2). Seri speakers generally have a positive opinion of their language, unlike in many other Mesoamerican and other Mexican indigenous communities. However, Seri is beginning to come under some of the same pressures from technology and globalization. More specifically, since both Seri villages now have consistent electricity, Spanish-language television programming has started to introduce Spanish into daily life where it was not formerly present. This has caused some concern relating to potential language loss in the future (Marlett 2006: 3).

Seri is extremely well documented for a small language of Mexico. The current favorable status of the documentation on Seri is due primarily to a large and thorough body of work published by Stephen Marlett over the past 35 years. Marlett's dissertation was

"The Structure of Seri" in 1981, and he has since continued to work on topics related to Seri linguistic structure and development (e.g. Marlett 1988; 1990; 2002; 2005; 2007; 2008a; 2008b; 2010b; 2012b; *inter alia*), including a full treatment of the grammar of the language (Marlett forthcoming). In addition to his scholarly work, he has also made the majority of his Seri information public, discussed in layman-friendly terms through his personal website. One particularly useful piece of documentation he has made available is a periodically updated comprehensive bibliography of sources on Seri for a wide variety of topics including ethnography, anthropology, archaeology, history, art, films, language, historical linguistics, literature, literacy materials and other 'popular' publications (Marlett 2013). He has also published two editions of a trilingual Seri-Spanish-English dictionary with Mary Moser (Moser and Marlett 2005; 2010), with an associated grammatical sketch. A full grammar of Seri (in English) is in preparation.

In addition to the solo and collaborative work on Seri conducted by Stephen Marlett, a large amount of information on Seri was also collected by Edward and Mary Moser under the auspices of SIL beginning in the 1950s. The research they compiled has been the foundation for much of the later work (cf. Marlett 1981: vii). They not only worked out an orthography (Moser and Moser 1965); published a bilingual vocabulary (Moser and Moser 1961); and compiled data for a grammar, they also published on specific aspects of the language such as switch-reference (Moser 1978) and pluralization (Moser and Moser 1976). In addition to strictly linguistic work, they also published on a number of anthropological topics involving the Seri culture, e.g. Mary Moser (1970a; 1970b; 1988), Edward Moser (1973) and the aforementioned work on Seri ethnobotany (e.g. Felger and Moser 1973; 1985; Felger et al. 1980). Prior to the Mosers, the linguistic work which had been done on Seri was minimal, consisting almost entirely of vocabulary lists (e.g. McGee 1898; Kroeber 1931).

More recently there have also been students and researchers working in Mexico who have contributed several theses and other publications to the linguistic literature on Seri. There is a growing body of work by Carolyn O'Meara (UNAM) relating to issues involving language, landscape and spatial relationships (O'Meara 2008; 2010; 2011a; 2011b; 2014a; 2014b; O'Meara and Bohnemeyer 2008; Bohnemeyer and O'Meara 2012). Additional contributions to the understanding of Seri structure come from Munguía Duarte (2005), a doctoral dissertation on morphophonology and applied linguistics, as well as from Munguía Duarte (2004; 2006) and Munguía Duarte and López Cruz (2009). There are also two master's theses from the University of Sonora, Larios Santacruz (2009) on ditransitive constructions and Martínez Soto (2003) on discourse and information structure.

3.4 Proposed genetic relationships

There have been numerous attempts to place Seri in larger proposed phylogenetic groupings, but thus far the evidence has been inconclusive (Campbell 1997: 160), leaving Seri, at least at present, best classified as an isolate. Marlett considers Seri to likely be related in some very distant fashion to some other languages in the Americas, but does not consider this relationship to be demonstrable (cf. Marlett 2007). The major proposals for genetic relationships have involved the Hokan hypothesis and various subdivisions within Hokan (Brinton 1891; Kroeber 1915; Lamb 1959; Voegelin and Voegelin 1965; and Kaufman 1988). A separate critique and revision of Greenberg's Seri data from Greenberg and Ruhlen's *An Amerind Etymological Dictionary* (2007) is available in Marlett (2011a).

The Hokan hypothesis has had proponents for over a century but still remains controversial. There are differing proposals for which languages may belong to 'Hokan', but generally Shastan, Chamariko, Karuk, Palaihnihan, Yana, Washo, Pomo, Esselen, Yuman, Chumash, Salinan, as well as Seri and Tequistlatecan, are included (Sapir 1917a; Dixon and Kroeber 1919; Voegelin and Voegelin 1965). The critiques of the larger Hokan hypothesis apply also to the suggestion of genetic affiliation between Seri and the other "Hokan" groups (cf. Olmsted 1964; Turner 1967; Klar 1977; Campbell 1997; *inter alia*). The primary criticisms revolve around a paucity of rigorous comparative data, where either little lexical or grammatical data is presented, or that the data that have been presented contain a number of flaws, including but not limited to incorrect forms, exceptional semantic latitude, inclusion of Pan-Americanisms, onomatopoeia, monosyllables and nursery forms (see Campbell 1997: 290–195, Chapter 7). As better data have become available on many of these putative 'Hokan' languages, researchers have been re-evaluating possible relationships among some languages within the larger proposal and have often rejected the association (e.g. Turner 1967 (Seri-Tequistlatic); Klar 1977 (Chumash)) or have come up with evidence that is at best suggestive of, but certainly not proof of, genetic relationship (e.g. Haas 1964b; McLendon 1964; Silver 1964).

There have been several less wide-reaching hypotheses which have examined a closer relationship between Seri and other Hokan groups which merit discussion here. Brinton (1891) grouped Seri, Tequistlatecan (Chontal of Oaxaca) and Yuman very early on. In a similar vein, Lamb (1959) included Seri in a Hokan subgroup 'Karok-Yuman', and Powell (1891) likewise grouped Seri with Yuman. Bright (1956) proposed a relationship between Seri and Salinan, and Bright (1970) defended the relationship of Seri to Tequistlatecan. However, Langdon (1974) supported a Southern Hokan group consisting of Seri, Chumash languages and Tequistlatican, while grouping Yuman and Pomoan (Langdon 1979). These various proposals have since been evaluated further, and comments on each proposed relationship are provided below.

3.4.1 Seri-Yuman

The putative Seri-Yuman connection, although a long-standing proposal, has suffered from the same a lack of data and comparative rigor as discussed above for Hokan generally. It appears to be based on minimal evidence and was opposed early on in Gatschet (1900b) and by Hewitt in McGee (1898). Years later, Crawford (1976) presented 227 points of comparison involving Seri and various Yuman languages, but this list unfortunately contains serious problems with respect to the Seri data which make it unconvincing (Marlett 2007: 3–4). Marlett (2007) also refers to an unpublished manuscript by Margaret Langdon which provides 34 putative Seri-Yuman cognates (although with no mention of regular sound correspondences) and other similarities which could be suggestive of a relationship. The possessive/subject agreement paradigms are nearly identical in Seri and Yuman, and although many Seri words are polysyllabic while the Yuman forms are monosyllables, Marlett (2007: Table 2) notes that the second, non-accented syllable in Seri appears to correspond to the Yuman form. He also notes that body part terms in Seri often have an initial *y-*, while many Yuman body part terms begin with the phonetically similar segment *i-* (Marlett 2007: 4). So while the evidence appears to be scarce and relationship has not been demonstrated, some of these types of similarities merit further careful investigation.

3.4.2 Seri-Tequistlatec

A possible relationship between Tequistlatecan (Chontal of Oaxaca) and Seri was investigated and subsequently rejected by Turner (1967). He argues that the 6 proposed cognates between Seri and Tequistlatec presented in Kroeber (1915) in a list of 27 pairs is a misrepresentation of the frequency of potential cognates when one considers the full set of 100 items from the Swadesh wordlist, or even a list of 500 words from each language. Of the larger dataset, only 8% of the Swadesh list and 4% of the extended list appeared to be matches, which, as Turner points out, is about the percentage of similarity one could expect from chance given two languages with similar phonemic inventories (Turner 1967: 236–237). There is also an apparent lack of similar forms with respect to kinship terms and numerals, lexical areas which are typically considered to be more conservative. What is more, the kinship systems of the languages do not make the same distinctions, and the Tequistlatec numeral system is vigesimal while Seri is decimal. Finally, Seri makes other lexical distinctions not present in Tequistlatec, e.g. demonstratives which indicate body position[3] (Turner 1967: 238–239).

Bright (1970) responded to the evidence in Turner (1967) by referring to the well-known maxim that it is impossible to prove non-relation, and he then questioned the method and semantic categories which Turner used to make the comparison. He contends that the meanings associated with kinship and numerical systems are "highly culture-bound" and are also subject to borrowing, and therefore are not sufficient to suggest non-relationship (Bright 1970: 289). He also cites a prior study (Bright 1956) in which he found 40 cognates in a 200-word Swadesh list, which would yield similarity on par with Kroeber's 20% possible cognate ratio. He argues that these 40 putative cognates are affirmed by the identification of nine regular phonological correspondences, each attested in three to six items (Bright 1970: 288). He admits, however, that some of these correspondences may be spurious and do not constitute sufficient evidence to convincingly demonstrate a genetic affiliation between Seri and Tequistlatec (1970: 289).

More recently, Marlett (2007) reports the preliminary results of a small study conducted using WordSurv (Wimbish 1989) and finds an "interesting" number of possible cognates (Marlett 2007: 12, Table 3.2), i.e. which were found to be to some extent phonetically similar. A very preliminary attempt to establish regular correspondence looked at the lateral fricative in Seri and Tequistlatec and attempted to find a pattern in their alternation. However, this likewise did not lead to any clear demonstration of regularity and relationship.

3.4.3 Seri-Salinan

In the same paper which provided data investigating a potential relationship between Seri and Tequistlatec (Bright 1956), Bright also provided similar data suggesting a possible relationship between Salinan and Seri. Out of 132 lexical comparisons, 39 pairs showed either what appeared to be sound correspondence or other phonetic similarity (only 26 of which were given in the publication) (Bright 1956: 46–47). He put forth nine putative sound correspondences: [Seri:Salinan] k:k, X:k, ʔ:k, ɬ:l, m:n, n:n, p:p, ɬ:t, k:ʔ, with no stated conditioning environments. Marlett (2008a) looked closely at the forms provided in Bright (1956) and brings the Seri data up to the present state of knowledge, given his own fieldwork on Seri and the forms in Moser and Marlett (2005). The result was that no previous Seri form remained without issue. In some cases the issues were comparatively minor (e.g. no indication of vowel length), but many are now known to be compositional forms and therefore are not individual, uninflected roots which previous comparisons had assumed them to be (true of at least 10 of the 26 forms; see the appendix to Marlett 2008a). This leaves the Seri-Salinan hypothesis even more tentative than it was previously, and a cursory look at the new correspondences does not reveal anything more promising. However, the question may bear revisiting with a different lexical set now that we have access to better information.

3.5 Of typological interest

Seri is a primarily head-marking language with complex verbal morphology. Like many other languages of the region, both subjects and objects are cross-referenced on the verb. Seri also has a wide array of derivational affixes, many of which encode valency, and therefore it has a robust distinction between intransitive and transitive verbs. This distinction is reinforced by separate sets of inflectional and derivational affixes which appear on verbs of each type, as shown in Table 9.1. Given this type of synthetic morphology, Marlett estimates that an intransitive verb can have more than 110 different forms, and a transitive verb more than 220 (2005: 65).

Seri shares several other morphological features of note with other Mesoamerican languages, including inflecting certain adpositional-type elements commonly called relational nouns. There are a number of these relational nouns in Seri which indicate spatial relationships (e.g. *ipac* 'place behind it', *iyat* 'place on top of it', *imac* 'place between them', among others). These forms only appear with possessive pronominal prefixes (see Table 9.2).

Another interesting feature of Seri is that it has a separate possessive series for kinship associations, which contrasts with the possessive prefixes used for body part terms, relational nouns, personal items and deverbal nouns (Marlett forthcoming: 330). The forms *ʔa* and *ma* only appear with a plural possessor before /j/ ([y] in Americanist phonetics). Alienable possession is expressed using a separate relative structure, equivalent to 'which X owns' (Marlett 1981: 69).

TABLE 9.1 TRANSITIVE VS. INTRANSITIVE MORPHOLOGY IN SERI

	Transitive	Intransitive
1st sg. subject agreement:	*h-*	*hp-*
Infinitive:	*iha-* (plus Ablaut)	*ica-*
Non-Fut/oblique nominalizer:	*h-*	*y-*

Source: Marlett 2005: 65.

TABLE 9.2 KINSHIP VS. OTHER INALIENABLE POSSESSIVE PREFIXES

	Kinship	Other possessed nouns
1st person	*hi-*	*hi-* (and *ha-*)
1st person emphatic	–	*hati-*
2nd person	*ma-*	*mi-* (and *ma-*)
3rd person	*a-*	*i-*

Source: Marlett forthcoming: 331.

Inalienable:
(1) **mi**-naail   'your skin'
    i-pxasi   'his/its flesh'   (Marlett 1981: 66)

Kinship:
(2) **ma**-paz   'your paternal grandfather'
    a-paac   'his older sister'   (Marlett forthcoming: 331)

Notice also that glottal stop (represented in the community orthography by *h*) appears to be phonemic in initial position (in addition to being phonemic elsewhere), which is less typical of Mesoamerica, although common in some Austronesian languages. See Moser and Marlett (1999) for more on Seri kinship.

Although Seri possesses several features which are present in other Mesoamerican languages, it is not considered part of the Mesoamerican linguistic area (cf. Campbell et al. 1986). While Seri has about 12 relational nouns, they are not based on body part terms; it has a decimal, not a vigesimal numeral system; it does not appear to share some of the common calques present in the Mesoamerican linguistic area; finally, it has SOV dominant word order and switch-reference which are characteristically lacking from the other languages of the linguistic area but are present in the neighboring languages (e.g. Seri, Jicaquean, Coahuilteco and Yuman) (Campbell 1997: 334).

Switch-reference in Seri has been the subject of several investigations (Moser 1978; Marlett 1984a; Farrell et al. 1991) as it differs somewhat from other switch-reference systems. In Seri, SS (Same Subject) is unmarked, and DS (Different Subject) is marked with two elements: *ta* in irrealis clauses and *ma* in realis clauses (Marlett 1981: 195). Switch-reference marking only appears in dependent clauses. However, the grammatical subject ("final subject", Farrell et al. 1991) is not the relevant reference point for dictating the use of switch-reference marking. For example, the following passive clause has the same grammatical subject in the first clause as in the second clause, and yet DS marking appears:

(3) Tpezi   **ma**, tatax,   yoque
    RLT:PASS:defeat[4]   **DS** RLT:go   RLYO:UNSP.SBJ:say
    'He was defeated and he went, it is said'   (Marlett forthcoming: 215)

This suggests that the language is instead indexing the semantic subject, or the deep structure subject argument ('initial subject'). However, the reference point for switch-reference marking does appear to be the 'final subject' in raising constructions, which Marlett (1981; 1984a; Farrell et al. 1991: 438) argue is because raising clauses are initially unaccusative and therefore have no 'initial subject'.

(4) Mi-Ø-p-azt[5]   quih im-p-ah-aatxo (***ta**) x **in**-s-ooha   a=ha
    2.POS-AN-PASS-tattoo   the **2SG.S**-IR-RA-many **DS** UT **2SG.S**-IR-cry   AUX=DCL
    'If you are tattooed many times, you will cry.'   (Farrell et al. 1991:438)

Switch-reference in Seri is therefore not exclusively governed by the grammatical status of the various arguments, and is somewhat unusual in requiring an appeal to other features to produce the appropriate pattern.

4 PURÉPECHA

4.1 Basic information

Purépecha (also known as Tarascan, Tarasco, P'urhépecha, sometimes also as Phurhepecha, Phorhé, Phorhépecha) is a language spoken in an area approximately 3,500 km² in the northwestern part of the state of Michoacán in Mexico (De Wolf 2013: 1). Like other languages in Mesoamerica, Purépecha is spoken in a large number of small towns, ranging in occupancy from less than 100 persons to more than 5,000 persons (Friedrich 1971b: 166). Although different authors provide different ways of grouping the dialects based on various criteria, the simplest categorization is provided by Capistrán (2015: 8, Map 2), which divides the region into three areas: Lake Pátzcuaro, the Sierra Tarasca and the Cañada de los Once Pueblos (Valley of the Eleven Pueblos). See Map 9.1 for the approximate locations of these towns.

As of the 1940s, the Sierra Tarasca region contained 66% of Purépecha speakers. Lake Pátzcuaro, despite being one of the major Purépecha political centers in earlier times, is one of the areas suffering from the greatest language loss, with many of the 26 towns and *rancherías* (hamlets) in the area having almost entirely lost the language, particularly around the southern edge. The Eleven Pueblos region is a small valley which is home to just 9% of Purépecha speakers. About 10% of the Purépecha-speaking population also lives in six towns northeast of Lake Pátzcuaro as well as in the following more isolated towns in the South: Cuanajo, San Angel Zurumucapio, Caltzontzin and Villa Silva (De Wolf 2013: 1).

Within the Purépecha cultural and linguistic area there are 116 towns which are or were recently home to some number of Purépecha speakers, which De Wolf (2013: 1) divides into 66 Purépecha towns and about 50 *rancherías*. Of these 116 towns, about 50 are composed almost entirely of Purépecha speakers (Friedrich 1971b: 166). Although most authors consider Purépecha to be a single language with a large amount of dialectal variation, *Ethnologue* divides it into western (the Sierra dialects) and eastern languages (roughly the lake dialects and dialects to the North and the South), which have 60%–80% mutually intelligibility (Lewis, Simons and Fennig 2014).

Although it is normal in the region for each small town or area to constitute its own dialect, Purépecha appears extreme in that none of the towns are more than a mile apart, and some are only separated by a single street. However, the dialectal differences are still sufficiently substantial that a given speaker can be identified as being from a given small town by their speech. It has also been reported that there is no real difference in prestige or importance among the dialects, i.e. that none has a more privileged sociopolitical status than another. The primary social valuation reflects local pride associated with the variety one grew up speaking. However, speakers do tend to label the Sierra varieties as 'better' or 'pure', and there is a general correlation between negative attitudes towards Purépecha and preference for Spanish (Friedrich 1971b: 166).

Both the terms 'Tarascan/Tarasco' and variant spellings of 'Purépecha' are commonly used in the literature on this language. 'Tarascan' is an exonym, considered pejorative by some, while Purépecha is an endonym. While the endonym is gaining use in the academic community, 'Tarascan' is still widely known as a designation for both the language and the ethnic population.

4.2 Endangerment

Prior to the arrival of the Spanish, the Tarascan kingdom was one of the important imperial states in Mesoamerica. The Purépecha were in competition for the control of land and resources with the Aztecs, leading to many armed conflicts (cf. Pollard 1993). However, after the arrival of the Spanish and the domination of the area in 1530, the region controlled by Purépecha speakers significantly decreased, and the population was integrated into Spanish colonial structure. Now Purépecha is under many of the same social and economic pressures from Spanish as other languages in the region, which is slowly causing its obsolescence.

The speaker numbers reported for Purépecha vary, and even appear to be increasing. Friedrich (1971a, 1971b, 1975) provides a figure of about 50,000 native speakers in the early 1970s, but by 2000, the Instituto Nacional de Estadística y Geografía de México (INEGI) reports 121,409 speakers over the age of 5. Based on his fieldwork experiences in the mid-1900s, Friedrich (1971b: 168) reported that in about two-thirds of the 50 Tarascan-speaking towns, children had little exposure to Spanish before going to school (post age 5). This led him to conclude that "the necessary sociolinguistic preconditions do exist for transmitting the Tarascan language in a relatively stable and continuous manner" (Friedrich 1971b:168). He also provides a very helpful list of 31 towns in relation to the general competence of the 5–6 year old residents of that town in Purépecha (T) or Spanish (S). Towns where children are exhibiting dominance in Spanish (9 of the 31) are the sites of language loss both in terms of declining numbers of speakers and a fall in its acquisition by children (see Friedrich 1971b: 168, Chart II).

However, by the 2000s when Alejandra Capistrán Garza was conducting her fieldwork in Puácuaro, one of the towns listed in Friedrich (1971b) as "essentially monolingual T [Tarascan]", she reports that most children are no longer learning Purépecha as a first language. In fact, only about 60% of the adult population of the town are speakers, and all are bilingual in Spanish (Capistrán 2015: 6). If this type of situation is representative of the other dialects, then the language is certainly endangered. Capistrán and Nava (1998: 144) also report that, although the Purépecha population has grown since 1940, when 27% of the population spoke the language, only 8.5% spoke it by 1996. Purépecha is currently listed in the *Catalogue of Engendered Languages* as 'threatened' (with 60% certainty) ("Purepecha", Endangered Languages 2015), by *Ethnologue* as 5 ('developing') (for both languages) (Lewis, Simons and Fennig 2014), and by UNESCO (Moseley 2010) as 'vulnerable'.

4.3 Documentation

Purépecha has been the topic of linguistic and cultural study since the early colonial era; the grammars and dictionaries of Bautista de Lagunas (1983 [1574]) and Gilberti (1987 [1559]) are well known. However, most of the linguistic work on the language was from the 1930s onward. Maxwell D. Lathrop of SIL published linguistic material on Purépecha beginning in the 1930s, which included some initial information about the language (Lathrop 1937) and short vocabularies (Lathrop 1973; 2007). Some descriptive work on the grammar was done by Alan Wares (1956) and Mary Foster (1969) (although see comments in Wares 1972; Friedrich 1973). Morris Swadesh (1969) also wrote a 190-page grammar sketch and dictionary (published posthumously), based primarily on colonial sources.

In the 1970s, Paul Friedrich made significant contributions to Purépecha phonology and dialectology (Friedrich 1971a; 1971b; 1975) and drew attention to its theoretical implications, e.g. in Friedrich (1969; 1970; 1971c). In the 1980s and 1990s, Paul De Wolf likewise dedicated many years of his life and scholarship to Purépecha, and most notably published a series of three books on the language (De Wolf 1989; 1991; 2013), the last of which was published posthumously. De Wolf worked primarily in Tarecuato (in the Eleven Pueblos area), which is a less well-studied dialect area, and dedicated a significant portion of his final book to Purépecha discourse, making his contribution rather unique (De Wolf 2013: v).

A considerable amount of work on Purépecha morphosyntax has been published in the last 20 years. Claudine Chamoreau, in addition to writing a grammar of the language (2000), has worked on a variety of grammatical topics, including transitivity and grammatical relations (1993; 1998; 1999b; 2008; 2012a) and language contact, variation and change (1995; 2007; 2012b; 2014). The literature on Purépecha has also been significantly expanded by recent doctoral dissertations and associated publications focusing on Purépecha morphosyntax (Maldonado and Nava 2002; Monzón 2004; Nava 2004; Capistrán 2004; 2006; 2010; 2011; 2015; Villavicencio 2006; Vázquez Rojas 2012). There is also community interest in Purépecha language and culture, with the stated goal of getting back to their pre-Hispanic roots (see www.purepecha.mx/). So while Purépecha is now rather well described for a Mesoamerican language, there is still a lot of work to be done beyond phonology and morphology, since that has been the nexus of most of the linguistic work to date.

4.4 Proposed genetic relationships

There have been surprisingly few serious proposals attempting to link Purépecha to other genetic groups in view of the number of proposals of distant genetic relationship for the other isolates discussed in this chapter. Purépecha was included as a member of Greenberg's putative Chibchan-Paezan phylum (Greenberg 1987: 106–107), which stretched from Florida to Mexico to South America and included such disparate groups as Timucua, Cuitlatec, Lenca, Xinka and Warrau (Warao). This proposal was not received well by linguists, and the evidence has been called both "scant" and "flawed" (Campbell 1997: 176).

Another hypothesis with little evidence is a Purépecha-Quechua hypothesis, in Swadesh (1967a). The only evidence put forth in favor of this relationship was 27 sets of phonetically similar words (not cognates), which fail to be convincing or even suggestive of relationship due to flaws such as the inclusion of onomatopoeic forms and pan-Americanisms (Campbell 1997: 325–326).

Swadesh had also previously proposed a relationship between Mayan and Purépecha (1966) which, although it presented more data, suffered from some of the same flaws. Swadesh provides over 300 forms for comparison which he claims illustrate 37 different phonological correspondences. Instead of using Proto-Mayan reconstructions as the point of comparison with Mayan, he uses data from Tseltal, Kaqchikel, Huastec and Yucatec. In addition to problems such as including onomatopoeic forms, loanwords and forms which exhibit a great degree of semantic latitude (Campbell 1997: 224–226), there are also 135 comparisons which only involve Purépecha and a single Mayan language. It is also not uncommon that the Mayan forms presented for a comparison are not themselves cognate. The following example from Swadesh's (1966: 195) comparisons illustrate this problem:

Language	Form	Meaning
Purépecha	aká-	'concave, below'
Yucatec	ak	'turtle, recipient'
Huastec, Tseltal	aka-n	'foot/leg, base'
Kaqchikel	aqa-n	'foot/leg, base'

Besides the semantic disparity between 'concave', 'turtle' and 'leg', only the Huastec, Tseltal and Kaqchikel forms are actually cognate, from Proto-Maya *-aqan 'leg'. The Yucatec áak 'turtle' can only be reconstructed back to western Mayan *ahk, whereas Proto-Mayan had *peets or *peety (cf. Kaufman 2003), which is hardly similar to aká-.

4.5 Of typological interest

There are several facets of Purépecha grammar which have received attention for their relative rarity with respect to other Mesoamerican languages. Purépecha is an agglutinating, nominative-accusative language which is entirely suffixing and is characterized by long words and consistent dependent-marking. Interestingly, Purépecha has a basic case system (nominative, accusative, genitive, comitative, instrumental, locative), the diachronic development of which is discussed at length in Villavicencio (2006). There are also some relevant issues surrounding transitivity. For example, Purépecha has differential object marking based on the animacy and definiteness of the patient argument (cf. Capistrán 2010). It also has various ways of increasing valency, not only by a causative suffix, but also by an applicative/benefactive suffix (Capistrán 2006). These devices allow the creation of tritransitive syntactic constructions, or verbs with four core arguments, which is typologically uncommon (Capistrán 2015: 249). Also, Chamoreau (2008) argues that it has an antipassive construction, although antipassives are more typically associated with ergative languages.

Other topics of typological interest involve how Purépecha deals with the classification of space. In addition to locative morphemes, Purépecha has more than 40 verbal morphemes which express spatial relationships and are akin to the lexical affixes in Salishan languages (Friedrich 1971a; Capistrán 2011). Some of these are related to body part terms, but others are not, and such an extensive system is not common in Mesoamerica. This system of locative affixes is complemented by a set of classificatory roots, which are sets of verbs which involve the same basic action, but which verb root is chosen depends on the physical characteristics or orientation of the noun in question. For example, the concept of being 'fat' or 'thick' gets expressed using different forms for longish objects (tepá-), flattish objects such as tortillas (tayá-) or roundish objects (toyó-, poré-) (Friedrich 1970: 388). In addition to these two means of shape classification, Purépecha also has numeral classifiers, which are well described but unfortunately are being lost (Friedrich 1970: 381–386; Chamoreau 1999a; 2013; Vázquez Rojas 2012). Nava (1994) posits that there may have originally been up to 18 numeral classifiers based on evidence in colonial texts, but modern speakers have only the following three: ichúkwa for flat objects, ichákwa for elongated objects and erhákwa for rounded objects (Vázquez Rojas 2012: 85–86). See Vázquez Rojas (2012: Chapter 4) for more on the grammar of numeral classifiers and Chamoreau (2013) for an evaluation of their obsolescence.

Finally, there is some remaining question about how Purépecha fits into (or does not fit into) the Mesoamerican cultural and linguistic area. Campbell et al. (1986) list Purépecha as a member of the Mesoamerican linguistic area, but Capistrán and Nava (1998: 146–150) argue that it lacks several of the core characteristics of Mesoamerican languages. Although it has a vigesimal numeral system, it lacks relational nouns and many of the calques common in the region, and it has a genitive construction which reflects the expected order for SOV syntax instead of the Possessor-Possessed structure common to Mesoamerican languages:

(5) Xwánu-iri wíchu
     Juan-GEN dog
     'Juan's dog' (Capistrán 2015: 23)

The issue of word order is also relevant: Purépecha has pragmatically determined word order, and there has been debate as to whether either SOV or SVO should be considered 'basic', or pragmatically unmarked. Capistrán (2002) argues that, at least for the dialect on which she works, SVO is pragmatically unmarked and SOV serves to emphasize the object. However, Vázquez Rojas (2012: 6) points out that this is likely only a regional effect and that the *Meseta* dialects have SOV order. Purépecha does appear to have several of the secondary typological characteristics of an SOV language, such as postpositions, genitive-noun (possessor-possessed) order as shown in (5) above, and overt case marking on nominals. However, if SOV were to be unmarked, this would be another strike against its inclusion in the Mesoamerican linguistic area, as the area is characterized by a lack of SOV order (Campbell et al. 1986: 547–548). However, Purépecha does share many of the non-diagnostic Mesoamerican linguistic traits, e.g. devoicing of final consonantal sonorants, voicing of obstruents after nasals, numeral classifiers and verbal directional morphemes (Campbell 1997: 345–346). This places the language in the interesting position of being outside of the Mesoamerican linguistic area, but still sharing many (but not all) of the relevant traits with the surrounding languages, which were presumably still obtained from areal diffusion.

5 CUITLATEC

5.1 Basic information

Cuitlatec is a now-extinct language formerly spoken in Guerrero, Mexico. The pre-contact Cuitlatec area stretched from the middle of the Balsas River Valley to the Pacific coast, but the modern Cuitlatec live in the *'tierra caliente'* (hot country) on the mid-point of the Balsas River, primarily in the area of Totolapan. The original Cuitlatec area included the municipalities of Ajuchitlan, Totolapan, Atoyac and Benito Juárez (see the maps in Drucker et al. 1969: 566).

The name "Cuitlatec(o)" was originally an exonym of Nahuatl origin, composed of $k^w itla$- 'excrement, feces' + -*te.ka*- '-ite, inhabitants of the place of' (Campbell 1997: 6), although others have given translations such as "bastard people" or "people of the place of gold" (Drucker et al. 1969: 565, referencing Brand 1943). However, according to Hendrichs Pérez, the Cuitlatec people called their language *ujpuné'zlu* (no etymology provided), about which he noted – giving no particular motivation as to why – that "this word and many others give the language a melancholy, tragic and funereal character" (1939: 346, my translation).

The Cuitlatec area borders not only on Nahuatl territory, but also on Purépecha and Matlaltzinca (Otomanguean) territory to the North and Northeast (Hendrichs Pérez 1939: 329). This was a contested locale, since they occupied the land which was in dispute during the wars between the Aztecs and the Purépecha, both large and powerful pre-colonial Mesoamerican states. The Cuitlatecs were conscripted as mercenaries to fight on behalf of either side, which most likely contributed to a decrease in their numbers (Hendrichs Pérez 1939: 333).

The territory which the modern Cuitlatec occupy is warm, dry and desert-like (Drucker et al. 1969: 567; see also the map on p. 568). The economy is primarily tied to agriculture, particularly to sesame. The Cuitlatecs also grow typical Central American fare, including corn, beans, chiles and squash (Drucker et al. 1969: 567–572). Although there is little documentation of Cuitlatec cultural beliefs and practices from pre-colonial times, Hendrichs

Pérez noted that evidence of some older beliefs were detectable in the stories he collected from some of the elderly people in 1939 (cf. Hendrichs Pérez 1939: 351–355).

5.2 Speakers and endangerment

Colonial sources mention that prior to the Spanish arrival in Mexico, the Cuitlatecs were a vibrant and strong people who lived in cities along the coast between the mouth of the Balsas River and Acapulco. One such city, Mexcaltepec, had a population at one point of 150,000. However, the number of inhabitants fell drastically with the arrival of the Spanish – to only about 1,000 – over the course of just a few years (Hendrichs Pérez 1939: 333). Hendrichs Pérez also speculated that the Cuitlatec way of life was not particularly compatible with Spanish rule, and therefore they had difficulty acclimating to the hard work and Western rule of law which the Spanish imposed. Indeed, the writings which we have from colonial governors and captains detail extensive resistance of the Cuitlatecs to their colonial overlords and that this resistance was still strong even after 60 years of subjugation (Hendrichs Pérez 1939: 331–332).

However, the massive reduction of the Cuitlatec population eventually took its toll on the language. By 1930, the Mexican census indicated that there were only 80 remaining speakers of Cuitlatec. By the time Hendrichs Pérez arrived in San Miguel Totolapan in 1939, he was dismayed to discover only about 20 elderly people who still knew the language sufficiently to form phrases. He discusses the large amount of variation in the forms that different consultants gave him and expressed frustration at the inability of most to provide a wide variety of grammatical forms, saying "De hecho, ya no existe ningún indio cuitlateco que sea capaz de dar todas las formas de la declinacíon de un sustantivo o de conjugar correctamente algún verbo" [In fact, there no longer exists any Cuitlatec who is able to provide all of the forms for the declension of a noun or correctly conjugate a given verb (my translation)] (Hendrichs Pérez 1946: 131). But by the conclusion of his fieldwork, Hendrichs Pérez had found four individuals who he felt had the most linguistic knowledge: Doña Constancia Lázaro de Robles (age ~70), Don Cristóbal Salgado (age ~60), Don Maclovio Aguirre (age 86) and Doña María Dolores Hernández (likely over 100 years old at that time) (Hendrichs Pérez 1946: 131). He was unable to locate a single family that was still actively using the language in the home, which had been his goal (Hendrichs Pérez 1939: 339–340).

Only a few years later, Norman McQuown reports in his paper on Cuitlatec phonetics that there were no more than 20 people who had any knowledge of Cuitlatec, yielding it severely moribund if not essentially extinct. Moreover, the language had ceased to be spoken actively at least 50 years ago, and Spanish had taken over as the language of the community (McQuown 1941: 239). By 1959–1961, when Escalante Hernández conducted his fieldwork, there was only one remaining speaker of Cuitlatec, Juana Can who had learned the language as a child from her grandmother. She had not actively used the language in the 40 years since her grandmother's death, and mostly was able to recall stories and conversations from when she was young. Escalante Hernández refers to Juana Can as the last speaker of Cuitlatec (Escalante Hernández 1962: 12–13).

Despite Escalante Hernández's claim that his consultant was the last speaker of Cuitlatec, there is some evidence that there were still some people who remembered some Cuitlatec well into the next decade. Although Drucker et al. (1969) do not state when exactly they conducted their fieldwork in San Miguel Totolapan, they do say that their ethnographic data came primarily from their own field investigation. One of the few notes they provide specifically on the language is that, at that time, the few who spoke any Cuitlatec used it for telling scatological jokes (Drucker et al. 1969: 575). Although this is a highly restricted domain, this shows that there was still a group of people who knew something of the language, and it had at least one use in the community as of the late 1960s. In the following years, the language lost all domains of use and was presumed extinct. However, a team of researchers who went to the Cuitlatec area in 1979 to study Nahuatl found two elderly women who could still remember some Cuitlatec vocabulary – Florentina Celso and Apolonia Robles. Interestingly, Apolonia Robles was the grand-daughter of Hendrichs' primary informant Constancia Lazaro de Robles. The researchers gathered what they could, which included 50 Cuitlatec words and some ethnographic information (Valiñas Coalla et al. 1984: 171). This appears to be the most recent source which cites original Cuitlatec data.

5.3 Documentation

The linguistic documentation available on Cuitlatec is very limited and, as noted by various researchers, appears to exhibit a great deal of inter-speaker variation. Both the limited corpus and the variation can almost certainly be attributed to the fact that the language was already moribund by the time anyone attempted to document it. This fact has also contributed to the difficulties in its classification. Works primarily pertaining to proposals for genetic affiliation are discussed in Section 4.4.

Although there were some short Cuitlatec wordlists and some ethnographic information collected prior to 1930 (e.g. León 1903), the earliest serious linguistic documentation of Cuitlatec comes from a pair of 1939 articles by Robert Weitlaner and Hendrichs Pérez, respectively. Both articles mention sounds and some aspects of Cuitlatec grammar. Hendrichs Pérez primarily provides verb conjugations and attempts to divide them into classes. He also lists possessive noun and pronoun paradigms and some information on syllable structure (1939: 355). Weitlaner included a wordlist which served as the starting point for the work of Norman McQuown shortly thereafter. In a later publication, Hendrichs Pérez (1946) discusses at greater length his methods of data collection, possible remnants of Cuitlatec in local Spanish and in toponyms, some data from Xinka and K'ichee' for possible genetic comparison and some additional points on the grammar. However, the most important contribution of Hendrichs Pérez (1946) is a vocabulary of 1,221 items, which includes some verb conjugations.

McQuown (1941) is a phonetic study of Cuitlatec and an attempt to make use of what little the speakers at that time could provide. He worked with Hendrichs Pérez's primary informant, Constancia Lazaro de Robles, who was 60–70 years old, and her sister who was present for some of the sessions. His data came from three sessions of approximately 2 hours, so only about 6 contact hours. He carefully transcribed 450 lexical items but notes that there was no opportunity to check his transcriptions (McQuown 1941: 240). These lexical items and short phrases are included in the publication. In addition to providing an inventory of 18 consonants, 8 vowels and an additional 3 sounds (/ɾ, r, s/) borrowed from Spanish, McQuown comments on accent/stress, the frequency of various sounds, and some phonological rules (e.g. /n/ assimilates to following velar stops (1941: 245), and vowels devoice optionally and word-finally in unaccented positions).

Most work for the next decade was primarily ethnographic (e.g. Hendrichs Pérez 1946), or concerned with genetic classification of the language (e.g. Osnaya 1959), and did not involve efforts to expand the linguistic documentation. Escalante Hernández's 1962 work, simply titled *El Cuitlateco*, was the next and probably most comprehensive effort to document the language before it disappeared. He revises some of the claims made by McQuown and provides an analysis of Cuitlatec phonetics, phonology and morphology. He gives little information on syntax, but does include two short texts and a vocabulary of approximately 900 items. In 1969, Escalante Hernández and others also published an ethnographic work on Cuitlatec (Drucker et al. 1969). Other work on Cuitlatec included papers by Ruth Almstedt (1974), which were apparently mainly based on unpublished data from H. V. Lemley. The last known effort to collect original data on Cuitlatec was in 1979, and the results are published as part of a larger study by researchers at UNAM to create a Cuitlatec database to facilitate archiving, to create alphabetized lists and to do searches for phonetic sequences (Valiñas Coalla et al. 1984). Some of the results of their analysis of Cuitlatec phonetic sequences led to a revision of previous claims about Cuitlatec, some of which are discussed in Section 5.5.

5.4 Proposed genetic affiliation

Like other Mesoamerican isolates, there have been many proposals attempting to link Cuitlatec to other linguistic groups in Mesoamerica, as well as broader proposals which include Cuitlatec in some superstock spanning large areas in the Americas. One of the first proposals was by Lehmann (1920), who suggested that Cuitlatec and Tlapanec belonged to a 'Californian group', but did not provide convincing comparative evidence (Osnaya 1959: 560). Weitlaner (1939) discussed similarities which Cuitlatec might have with Otomian languages, and Hendrichs Pérez mentioned briefly that Cuitlatec is not a bastardized version of Nahuatl, as thought by some at the time, and that it certainly qualifies as its own language (1939: 345). However, Hendrichs Pérez later suggested that Cuitlatec might be related to Mayan (1946: 137–139).

The only serious comparative work done on Cuitlatec to date was by Osnaya (1959), who used lexicostatistics to compare Cuitlatec to a variety of languages in the Americas with the goal of finding evidence in favor of or against Swadesh's "Paleo-American" hypothesis. She also made some attempt to provide more traditional evidence, with reconstructions and observations about possible phonological changes. She cautions that the results are preliminary and would need to be affirmed by attention to more lexical and morphological data (1959: 561). Her results indicate that Cuitlatec is not closely related to any other languages in her sample, but could be related to Nahuatl ('mexihca') and Paya at a time depth of 5,500 years minimum based on 18 or 19 supposed cognates out of a 100-item wordlist (Osnaya 1959: 563). For the broader comparison, Osnaya lists 25 proposed reconstructions using data from languages throughout the Americas, including Cuitlatec. Unfortunately there are a number of issues with the reconstructions. For example, 12 of 25 involve single syllables reconstructed from predominantly poly-syllabic words in the compared languages; 8 of 25 involve dashes or parentheses which separate off parts of the form, although there is no evidence of morphological divisions in the modern languages (e.g. *(?e)ye(we)* 'this'); and others involve wide semantic latitude such that her proposed reconstructed form has an unrealistic set of possible meanings, e.g. *hle(w)*: 'tree, plant, grass, head hair, horn'; *hlewna*: 'woman, man, people'; *(ke-) weli* 'feather, head hair, hand, arm'; *yaw-me*: 'walk, foot, swim'. These types of problems leave the hypothesis unconvincing. Cuitlatec is therefore at present best classified as a language isolate.

5.5 Of typological interest

So little is known about the details of Cuitlatec grammar that we must assume the language may have had interesting features that were not recorded. But, from the little that we do have, it is possible to give a basic typological profile of the language and to comment on features which it does or does not share with surrounding languages.

Cuitlatec is morphologically agglutinating and primarily suffixing. Like other languages in the area, it appears to be vigesimal, although the details of numeral composition are not clear (Valiñas Coalla et al. 1984: 182–185). Unlike other languages of the Mesoamerican linguistic area (cf. Campbell et al. 1986), Cuitlatec does not appear to have relational nouns or discernible locatives or directionals based on parts of the body (Valiñas Coalla et al. 1984: 195). Cuitlatec also has an interesting kinship system wherein gender is only distinguished for members of ego's generation and ascending generations, such that, for instance, for 'child of' and 'grandchild' no distinction is made equivalent to English 'son'/'daughter' or 'grandson'/'granddaughter' (Valiñas Coalla et al. 1984: 186).

There are also some interesting aspects of the phonology which merit mention. First, Valiñas Coalla et al. revised the phonetic inventory based on a phoneme distribution study and called into question some of the putative phonemes given in earlier works (McQuown 1941; Escalante Hernández 1962), namely /ʔ/ versus /h/, /k/ versus /kʷ/ and /l/ versus /ɬ/. The inventory which they provide excludes /h/ and /kʷ/ but does maintain both laterals (Valiñas Coalla et al. 1984: 179). Among the vowels, they support a single central vowel where McQuown had two (/ə/ and /ʌ/). In terms of interesting phonological features, Cuitlatec has vowel harmony as well as somewhat regular alternations between [i] and [e] and between [u] and [o] word-finally, and also between all vowels and [ə], although the conditioning environment is not clear (Valiñas Coalla et al. 1984: 180).

6 CONCLUDING REMARKS

Although all of the language isolates spoken in Mesoamerica and northern Mexico are in different stages of obsolescence, those that still have native speakers have been sufficiently well documented that they are no longer in danger of disappearing without record. While much more can and should be done to document and study these languages further, it is reassuring that much valuable information about what these unique languages contain has been made available to the world thanks to the dedicated efforts of scholars, particularly in the past 50 years.

The language isolates Huave, Seri and Purépecha are sufficiently well described that they can be compared with other languages to test for possible broader genetic relationships, and the unsuccessful result of the various attempts to date supports their current status as language isolates. While the documentation of Cuitlatec is more limited, it is also sufficient to place in doubt all the proposals to date for broader affiliations that would include it. However, some proposals may merit revisiting with more, updated data. Hopefully the work that points out the weaknesses of previous proposals may also point to directions for further research.

NOTES

1 I thank Lyle Campbell and Stephen Marlett for their very helpful comments on this chapter. Any remaining mistakes are my own.

2 The orthography has been updated throughout from how it appeared in older sources to be in line with the current orthographical standard used in Moser and Marlett (2010). Many thanks to Stephen Marlett for providing the updated versions of these items.

3 Turner (1967: 238–239) also claims that Seri has separate terms for 'blue' and 'green', separate terms for buying food versus buying non-food and separate terms for dying animals versus humans. However, more recent research does not support the existence of these lexical differences as such (Stephen Marlett, personal communication, 2015).

4 Glossing conventions: 2 = 2nd person, AUX = auxiliary, AN = action nominalizer, DCL = declarative, DS = different subject, GEN = genitive, IR = irrealis, PASS = passive, POS = possessive, RA = raising prefix, RLT = realis 't' form, RLYO = realis 'yo' form, SG.S = singular subject, UNSP.SBJ = unspecified subject, UT = unspecified time.

5 The orthography and glossing of this example have been modified by Stephen Marlett from the original publication to reflect the current community orthographical system used throughout this section.

REFERENCES

Almstedt, Ruth. 1974. *Cuitlatec: An Example of Linguistic Salvage*. Presentation at the *XIII Conferencia sobre las lenguas indígenas americanas*, sección VII, America Latina.

Bohnemeyer, Jürgen and Carolyn O'Meara. 2012. Vectors and Frames of Reference: Evidence from Seri and Yucatec. *Space and Time in Languages and Cultures: Language, Culture and Cognition*, ed. by Luna Filipović and Kasia Jaszczolt, 217–249. Amsterdam: John Benjamins.

Bouda, Karl. 1964. Huavestudien I: Uralisches im Huave. *Études Finno-ougriennes* 1: 18–28.

Bouda, Karl. 1965. Huavestudien II. *Études Finno-ougriennes* 2:167–175.

Brand, Donald. 1943. A Historical Sketch of Geography and Anthropology in the Tarascan Region: Part I. *New Mexico Anthropologist* 37–108.

Bright, William. 1956. Glottochronologic Counts of Hokaltecan Materials. *Language* 32: 42–48.

Bright, William. 1970. On Linguistic Unrelatedness. *IJAL* 36: 288–290.

Brinton, Daniel. 1891. *The American Race*. New York: D. C. Hodges.

Campbell, Lyle. 1997. *American Indian Languages: The Historical Linguistics of Native America*. Oxford: Oxford University Press.

Campbell, Lyle, Terrence Kaufman, and Thomas Smith-Stark. 1986. Meso-America as a Linguistic Area. *Language* vol. 62, no. 3: 530–558.

Capistrán, Alejandra. 2002. Variaciones de orden de constituyentes en p'orhépecha. *Del cora al maya yucateco: estudios lingüísticos sobre algunas lenguas indígenas mexicanas*, ed. by Paulette Levy, 349–402. UNAM: Mexico City.

Capistrán, Alejandra. 2004. Construcciones de doble objeto con verbos trivalentes en p'orhépecha. *VII Encuentro Internacional de Lingüística en el Noroeste*, t. I, ed. by Isabel Barreras Aguilar y Mirna Castro Llamas, 445–460. Hermosillo, Mexico: Universidad de Sonora.

Capistrán, Alejandra. 2006. Sufijos de aumento de participantes de tipo dativo. ¿Existen aplicativas en p'orhépecha? *Southwest Journal of Linguistics* 25, no. 1: 85–113.

Capistrán, Alejandra. 2010. *Expresión de argumentos, funciones gramaticales y transitividad en p'orhépecha*. Tesis de Doctorado. México, COLMEX.

Capistrán, Alejandra. 2011. Locative and Orientation Descriptions in Tarascan: Topological Relations and Frames of Reference. *Language Sciences* 33, no. 6: 1006–1024.

Capistrán, Alejandra. 2015. *Multiple Argument Constructions in P'orhepecha: Argument Realization and Valence-Affecting Morphology*. Leiden, The Netherlands: Koninklijke Brill.

Capistrán, Alejandra and E. Fernando Nava. 1998. Medio siglo de una lengua del Occidente de México: del tarasco de 1946 al p'urhépecha de 1996, *Antropología e Historia del Occidente de México*, México, SMA-UNAM, 143–163.

Chamoreau, Claudine. 1993. Quelques remarques à propos du sujet en phurhépecha. *Travaux du SELF* 3: 103–115.

Chamoreau Claudine. 1995. La comparaison en pʰurhépecha. Un exemple d'évolution syntaxique. *Faits de Langues* 5: 139–143.

Chamoreau, Claudine. 1998. Le système verbal du Phurhépecha. *Systemes Verbaux*, ed. by Fernand Bentolila, 55–69. Belgium, Peeters : Louvain-la-Neuve.

Chamoreau, Claudine. 1999a. Évolution des indices catégoriels en Purépecha. *Faits de Langues* 14: 143–152.

Chamoreau, Claudine, 1999b. Le marquage differentiel de l'objet en purépecha. *La Linguistique* 35, no.2: 99–114.

Chamoreau, Claudine. 2000. *Grammaire du purépecha parlé sur les iles du lac de Patzcuaro (Mexique)*. Lincoln Europa: München.

Chamoreau, Claudine. 2007. Grammatical Borrowing in Purepecha. *Grammatical Borrowing in Cross-Linguistic Perspective*, ed. by Yaron Matras and Jeanette Sakel, 465–480. Berlin: Mouton de Gruyter.

Chamoreau, Claudine. 2008. Voz antipasiva en lenguas nominativo-acusativas. El caso del purépecha. *Encuentro de Linguistica en el Noroeste* 9: 105–124.

Chamoreau, Claudine. 2012a. Constructions périphrastiques du passif en purepecha. Une explication multifactorielle du changement linguistique. *Changement linguistique et langues en contact: approches plurielles du domaine prédicatif*, ed. by Claudine Chamoreau and Laurence Goury, 71–99. Paris, CNRS Editions.

Chamoreau, Claudine. 2012b. Contact-Induced Change as an Innovation. *Dynamics of Contact-Induced Language Change*, ed. by Claudine Chamoreau and Isabelle Léglise, 53–76. Berlin, Mouton de Gryuter.

Chamoreau, Claudine. 2013. Classificateurs numéraux en purepecha: entre perte de vitalité et motivation pragmatique. *La Linguistique* 49, no. 2: 51–66.

Chamoreau, Claudine. 2014. Enclitics in Purepecha: Variation and Split Localization. *Patterns in Mesoamerican Morphology*, ed. by Jean-Léo Léonard and Alain Kihm, 119–143. Paris: Michel Houdiard éditeur.

Crawford, James. 1976. A Comparison of Chimariko and Yuman. *Hokan Studies: Papers from the First Conference on Hokan Languages*, ed. by Margaret Langdon and Shirley Silver, 177–191. The Hague: Mouton.

Cuturi, Flavia and Maurizio Gnerre. 2005. Concomitance in Huave. *Conference on Otomanguean and Oaxacan Languages (COOL)*, ed. by Rosemary Beam de Azcona and Mary Paster, Survey of California and Other Indian Languages Report 13, 51–86. Berkeley, CA: UC Berkeley Department of Linguistics.

Davidson, Lisa and Rolf Noyer. 1997. Loan Phonology in Huave: Nativization and the Ranking of Faithfulness Constraints. *Proceedings of WCCFL 15*, ed. by Brian Agbayani and Sze-Wing Tang, 65–80. Stanford, CSLI.

De Wolf, Paul. 1989. *Estudios Lingüísticos sobre la lengua P'orhé*. Mexico City: Colegio de Michoacán.

De Wolf, Paul. 1991. *Curso básico del Tarasco hablado*. Zamora/Morelia, El Colegio de Michoacán – Gobierno del Estado de Michoacán.

De Wolf, Paul. 2013. *El idioma tarasco: Sinopsis de la estructura gramatical*. LINCOM Studies in Native American Linguistics, 70, München, LINCOM.

Di Peso, Charles and Daniel Matson. 1965. The Seri Indians in 1692 as described by Adamo Gilg, S.J. *Arizona and the West* 7: 33–56.

Dixon, Roland and Alfred Kroeber. 1919. Linguistic Families of California. *University of California Publications in American Archaeology and Ethnology* 16, no. 3: 47–118.

Drucker, Susana, Roberto Escalante Hernández, and Roberto Weitlaner. 1969.The Cuitlatec. *Handbook of Middle American Indians: Ethnology: Part One*, ed. by Evon Vogt, 565–576. Austin, TX: University of Texas Press.

Escalante Hernández, Roberto. 1962. *El Cuitlateco*. Mexico: INAH.

Evanini, Keelan. 2007. The Phonetic Realization of Pitch Accent in Huave. *Proceedings of the 33rd Annual Meeting of the Berkeley Linguistics Society*, ed. by Zhenya Antić, Charles Chang, Clare Sandy, and Maziar Toosarvandani, 53–65. Berkeley, CA, Berkeley Linguistics Society.

Felger, Richard and Mary Moser. 1973. Eelgrass (Zostera marina L.) in the Gulf of California: Discovery of Its Nutritional Value by the Seri Indians. *Science* 181: 355–356.

Felger, Richard and Mary Moser. 1985. *People of the Desert and Sea: Ethnobotany of the Seri Indians*. Tucson: University of Arizona Press, Reprinted 1991.

Felger, Richard, Mary Moser, and Edward Moser. 1980. Seagrasses in Seri Indian Culture. *Handbook of Seagrass Biology: An Ecosystem Perspective*, ed. by Roland Phillips and C. Peter McRoy, 260–276. New York: Garland STPM Press.

Farrell, Patrick, Stephen Marlett, and David Perlmutter. 1991. Notions of Subjecthood and Switch Reference: Evidence from Seri. *Linguistic Inquiry* 22: 431–456.

Foster, Mary. 1969. *The Tarascan Language*. University of California publications in linguistics 56. Berkeley, University of California Press.

Friedrich, Paul. 1969. On the Meaning of the Tarascan Suffixes of Space. Indiana University publications in anthropology and linguistics, Baltimore: Waverly Press.

Friedrich, Paul. 1970. Shape in Grammar. *Language* 46, no. 2, Part 1: 379–407.

Friedrich, Paul. 1971a. *The Tarascan Suffixes of Locative Space: Meaning and Morphotactics*. Indiana University: Bloomington.

Friedrich, Paul. 1971b. Dialectal Variation in Tarascan Phonology. *IJAL* 37, no. 3: 164–187.

Friedrich, Paul. 1971c. Distinctive Features and Functional Groups in Tarascan Phonology. *Language* 47, no. 4: 849–865.

Friedrich, Paul. 1973. Review of: The Tarascan Language by Mary LeCron Foster. *Language* 49, no. 1: 238–245.

Friedrich, Paul. 1975. *A Phonology of Tarascan*. Chicago: University of Chicago, Department of Anthropology.

Gatschet, Albert. 1877. Der Yuma-Sprachstamm nach den neuesten handschriftlichen Quellen. *Zeitschrift für Ethnologie* 9: 341–350, 365–418.

Gatschet, Albert. 1883. Der Yuma-Sprachstamm nach den neuesten handschriftlichen Quellen. *Zeitschrift für Ethnologie* 15: 123–147.

Gatschet, Albert. 1886. Der Yuma-Sprachstamm nach den neuesten handschriftlichen Quellen. *Zeitschrift für Ethnologie* 18. 97–122.

Gatschet, Albert. 1892. Der Yuma-Sprachstamm nach den neuesten handschriftlichen Quellen. *Zeitschrift für Ethnologie* 24: 1–18.

Gatschet, Albert. 1900b. The Waikuru, Seri, and Yuman Languages. *Science* 12: 556–558.

Gilberti, Maturino. 1559. *Vocabulario en lengua de Mechuacan*, Transcripción paleográfica de Agustín Jacinto Zavala, 1997, Zamora, Michoacán, México, El Colegio de Michoacán.

Greenberg, Joseph. 1987. *Language in the Americas*. Stanford: Stanford University Press.
Greenberg, Joseph. and Merritt Ruhlen. 2007. *An Amerind Etymological Dictionary* (12th ed.). Stanford: Department of Anthropological Sciences, Stanford University.
Griffin, William. 2001. Camaron i cultura en Oaxaca. *Cuadernos del Sur*, vol. 16. Mexico: Oaxaca.
Haas, Mary. 1951. The Proto-Gulf Word for *Water* (With Notes on Siouan-Yuchi). *IJAL* 17: 71–79.
Haas, Mary. 1964b. California Hokan. *Studies in Californian Linguistics*, ed. William Bright, UCPL, vol. 34, 73–87. Berkeley: University of California Press.
Halle, Morris and Alec Marantz. 1993. Distributed Morphology and the Pieces of Inflection. *The View from Building 20*, ed. by Ken Hale and Samuel Jay Keyser, 111–176. Cambridge, MA: MIT Press.
Hendrichs Pérez, Pedro. 1939. Un estudio preliminar sobre la lengua cuitlateca de San Miguel Totolapan, Gro. *El México Antiguo* 4: 329–362.
Hendrichs Pérez, Pedro. 1946. *Por Tierras Ignotas: Viajes Y Observaciones en la Región Del Río de Las Balsas*, vol. 2. México: Editorial Cultura.
Huave, Endangered Languages 2015, The Linguist List at Eastern Michigan University and The University of Hawaii at Manoa. 2/15/2015. www.endangeredlanguages.com/lang/4292.
Instituto Nacional de Estadística, Geografía e Informática (INEGI). 2000. Tabulados Básicos, Estados Unidos Mexicanos, XII Censo General de Población y Vivienda.
Instituto Nacional de Lenguas Indígenas (INALI), México, Lenguas indígenas nacionales en riesgo de desaparición, Huave.
Kaufman, Terrence. 1988. *A Research Program for Reconstructing Proto-Hokan: First Groupings*, unpublished manuscript, University of Pittsburgh.
Kaufman, Terrence. 2003. *A Preliminary Mayan Etymological Dictionary, with the Assistance of John Justeson*, FAMSI report, www.famsi.org/reports/01051/index.html.
Kim, Yuni. 2008. *Topics in the Phonology and Morphology of San Francisco del Mar Huave*. Ph.D. thesis, University of California, Berkeley.
Kim, Yuni. 2009. Alternancias causativas y estructura de eventos en el huave de San Francisco del Mar [Causative alternations and event structure in S.F. del Mar Huave]. *Proceedings of CILLA IV*.
Kim, Yuni. 2010. Phonological and Morphological Conditions on Affix Order in Huave. *Morphology* 20, no. 1: 133–163.
Kim, Yuni. 2011 [to appear], Fuentes de rasgos fonológicos de préstamos castellanos en huave de San Francisco del Mar, Submitted to the *Proceedings of the I Jornada de Estudios Huaves*.
Kim, Yuni. 2013. Estrategias de pasivización en la morfología verbal del huave. *Amerindia* 37, no. 1: 273–298.
Klar, Kathryn. 1977. *Topics in Historical Chumash Grammar*. Ph.D. thesis, University of California, Berkeley.
Kroeber, Alfred. 1915. Serian, Tequistlatecan, and Hokan. *UCP AAE*, no. 11, Berkeley, University of California Press, pp. 279–290.
Kroeber, Alfred. 1931. The Seri. *Southwest Museum Papers* 6.
Lagunas, Juan Bautista de. 1574. *Arte y diccionario con otras obras en lengua Michuacana*, Intro. de J. Benedict Warren 1983, Morelia, Fimax.
Lamb, Sydney. 1959. Some Proposals for Linguistic Taxonomy. *AL* 1, no. 2: 33–49.
Langdon, Margaret. 1974. *Comparative Hokan-Coahuiltecan Studies: A Survey and Appraisal, Janua Linguarum* Series Critica no. 4. The Hague: Mouton.

Langdon, Margaret. 1979. Some Thoughts on Hokan with Particular Reference to Pomoan and Yuman. *The Languages of Native America: Historical and Comparative Assessment*, ed. by Lyle Campbell and Marianne Mithun, 592–649. Austin, TX: University of Texas Press.

Larios Santacruz, Maria Alfonsa. 2009. *Sistema de alineamiento en construcciones bitransitivas de la lengua de los Comcáac de Punta Chueca, Sonora*. Master's thesis, Universidad de Sonora.

Lathrop, Maxwell. 1937. Report of a Partial Study of the Tarascan Dialect. *Investigaciones Lingüísticas* 4: 111–129.

Lathrop, Maxwell. 1973. *Vocabulario del idioma tarasco* (compiler), Literatura Tarasca.

Lathrop, Maxwell. 2007. *Vocabulario del idioma purépecha* (compiler), Instituto Lingüístico de Verano, A.C.

Lehmann, Walter. 1920. *Zentral-Amerika*. Berlin: Museum fur Volkerkunde.

Lemley, H.V. 1949. Three Tlapanec Stories from Tlacoapa, Guerrero. *Tlalocan* III: 76–82.

León, Nicolás. 1903. Vocabulario en lengua Cuitlateca de Totolapam. *Anales del Museo Nacional: 1a época* 7: 304–307.

Lewis, Paul, Gary Simons, and Charles Fennig. (eds.). 2014. *Ethnologue: Languages of the World* (18th ed.). Dallas, TX: SIL International. Online version: www.ethnologue.com.

Maldonado, Ricardo. and E. Fernando Nava. 2002. Tarascan Causatives and Event Complexity. *The Grammar of Causation and Interpersonal Manipulation*, ed. by Masayoshi Shibatani, 157–195. Amsterdam: John Benjamins.

Marlett, Stephen. 1981. *The Structure of Seri*. Ph.D. thesis, University of California, San Diego.

Marlett, Stephen. 1984a. Switch-Reference and Subject Raising in Seri. *Syntax and Semantics 16: The Syntax of Native American Languages*, ed. by Eung-Do Cook and Donna Gerdts, 247–268. New York: Academic Press.

Marlett, Stephen. 1988. The Syllable Structure of Seri. *IJAL* 54, no. 3: 245–278.

Marlett, Stephen. 1990. Person and Number Inflection in Seri. *IJAL* 56: 503–541.

Marlett, Stephen. 2002. Reanalysis of Passive and Negative Prefixes in Seri. *Linguistic Discovery* 1, no. 1: 1–14.

Marlett, Stephen. 2005. A Typological Overview of the Seri Language. *Linguistic Discovery* 3, no. 1: 54–73.

Marlett, Stephen. 2006. La situación sociolingüística de la lengua seri en 2006. *Situaciones sociolingüísticas de lenguas amerindias*, ed. by Stephen Marlett, 1–6. Lima, SIL International y Universidad Ricardo Palma.

Marlett, Stephen. 2007. Las relaciones entre las lenguas hokanas en México: ¿cuál es la evidencia? *Memorias del III Coloquio Internacional de Lingüística Mauricio Swadesh*, ed. by Cristina Buenrostro et al., 165–192. Mexico City: Universidad Nacional Autónoma de México and Instituto Nacional de Lenguas Indígenas.

Marlett, Stephen. 2008a. The Seri and Salinan Connection Revisited. *IJAL* 74, no. 3: 393–399.

Marlett, Stephen. 2008b. Stress, Extrametricality and the Minimal Word in Seri. *Linguistic Discovery* 6, no. 1: 1–14.

Marlett, Stephen. 2010. A Place for Writing: Language Cultivation and Literacy in the Seri Community. *Revue Roumaine de Linguistique* 55, no. 2: 183–194.

Marlett, Stephen. 2011a. Corrections to and Clarifications of the Seri Data in Greenberg and Ruhlen's an Amerind Etymological Dictionary. *Work Papers of the Summer Institute of Linguistics*, University of North Dakota Session, vol. 51, pp. 1–9.

Marlett, Stephen. 2011b. The Seris and the Comcaac: Sifting Fact from Fiction about the Names and Relationships. *Work Papers of the Summer Institute of Linguistics*, University of North Dakota Session #51, pp. 1–20.

Marlett, Stephen. 2012b. Relative Clauses in Seri. In *Relative Clauses in Languages of the Americas: A Typological Overview*, ed. by Bernard Comrie and Zarina Estrada-Fernández, 213–242. Amsterdam: Benjamins.

Marlett, Stephen. 2013. *A Bibliography for the Study of Seri History, Language and Culture*. April 2013 revision. www.und.nodak.edu/instruct/smarlett/Stephen_Marlett/Publications_and_Presentations_files/SeriBibliography.pdf.

Marlett, Stephen. Forthcoming. *Cmiique Iitom: The Seri language* [provisional title].

Marlett, Stephen, F. Xavier Moreno Herrera, and Genaro G. Herrera Astorga. 2005. Illustrations of the IPA: Seri. *JIPA* 35, no. 1: 117–121.

Martínez Soto, Jorge Armando. 2003. *Seguimiento de la referencia en el cuento seri*. Master's thesis, Universidad de Sonora.

Matthews, Peter. 1972. Huave Verb Morphology: Some Comments from a Non-Tagmemic Standpoint. *IJAL* 38: 96–118.

McGee, William. 1898. *The Seri Indians: Seventeenth Annual Report of the Bureau of American Ethnology to the Secretary of the Smithsonian Institution*. Washington, DC. 1971 reprint by the Rio Grande Press, Glorieta, New Mexico.

McLendon, Sally. 1964. Northern Hokan (B) and (C): A Comparison of Eastern Porno and Yana. *Studies in Californian linguistics*, ed. by William Bright, UCPL, vol. 34, 126–144. Berkeley, University of California Press.

McQuown, Norman. 1941. La fonémica del cuitlateco. *El México Antiguo* 5: 239–254.

Millán, Saúl. 2003. Huaves. *Pueblos indígenas del México contemporáneo*. Mexico City, Comisión Nacional para el Desarrollo de los Pueblos Indígenas.

Montoya Pérez, Alberto. 2014a. *Sistema vocálico del huave de Santa María del Mar*, Presented at the *II Jornada de Estudios Huaves*, Instituto de Investigaciones Antropológicas, UNAM.

Montoya Pérez, Alberto. 2014b. *Palatalización en el Huave de Santa María del Mar*. Presented at the *X Coloquio de lingüística* at ENAH.

Moser, Mary and Stephen Marlett. 2010 (2005). *Comcáac quih yaza quih hant ihíip hac: Diccionario seri-español-inglés*, Hermosillo, Sonora, Universidad de Sonora and Plaza y Valdés Editores, Editions 1 and 2.

Moser, Edward. 1963. Seri Bands. *The Kiva* 28, no. 3: 14–27.

Moser, Edward. 1973. Seri Basketry. *The Kiva* 38: 105–140.

Moser, Edward. and Mary Moser. 1961, *Vocabulario seri: seri-castellano, castellano-seri*, Mexico City, Instituto Lingüístico de Verano.

Moser, Edward and Mary Moser. 1965. Consonant-Vowel Balance in Seri (Hokan) syllables', *Linguistics*, vol. 16, pp. 50–67.

Moser, Edward. and Mary Moser. 1976. Seri Noun Pluralization Classes. *Hokan Studies*, ed. by Margaret Langdon and Shirley Silver, 285–296. The Hague, Mouton.

Moser, Mary. 1970a. Seri Elevated Burials. *The Kiva* 35: 211–216.

Moser, Mary. 1970b. Seri: From Conception Through Infancy. *The Kiva* 35: 201–210.

Moser, Mary. 1978. 'Articles in Seri', *Occasional Papers on Linguistics*, vol. 2: 67–89.

Moser, Mary and Stephen Marlett. 1999. Seri kinship terminology. *SIL Electronic Working Papers* (1999–1005).

Monzón, Cristina. 2004. *Los morfemas espaciales del p'urhépecha; significado y morfosintaxis*. El Colegio de Michoacán, Zamora.

Moseley, Christopher (ed.). 2010. *UNESCO Atlas of the World's Languages in Danger*. UNESCO Publishing. www.unesco.org/culture/en/endangeredlanguages/atlas.

Moser, Mary B. 1988. Seri History (1904): Two Documents. *Journal of the Southwest* 30: 469–501.

Munguía Duarte, Ana Lidia. 2004. Relaciones de marcación y armonía relativa. *Memorias del VII Encuentro Internacional de Lingüística en el Noroeste*, Tomo 1, ed. by Isabel Barreras Aguilar and Mirna Castro Llamas, 65–84. Hermosillo: Universidad de Sonora.

Munguía Duarte, Ana Lidia. 2005. *Morfofonología del konkaak [sic]: Aplicación de la investigación lingüística en la educación indígena*. Ph.D. thesis, Universidad Autónoma de Sinaloa, Culiacán.

Munguía Duarte, Ana Lidia. 2006. 'Alternancias vocálicas en posición intermorfémica en el konkaak [sic]: control de predominancia morfológica' in *Memorias del VIII Encuentro Internacional de Lingüística en el Noroeste*, Tomo 2, ed. by Rosa María Ortiz Ciscomani, 295–320. Hermosillo: Universidad de Sonora.

Munguía Duarte, Ana Lidia and Gerardo López Cruz. 2009. De la fonología a la práctica ortográfica: Hacia un sistema de escritura en el konkaak [sic]. *Lexicografía y escritura en lenguas mexicanas*, ed. by Andrés Acosta Félix and Zarina Estrada-Fernández, 195–214. Editorial UniSon, Hermosillo.

Nava, E. Fernando. 1994. Los clasificadores numerales del p'urhépecha prehispánico. *Anales de antropología*, vol. 61, 299–309, UNAM, México.

Nava, E. Fernando. 2004. *La voz media en p'urhepecha un estudio de formas y significados*. Ph.D. thesis, FFL-UNAM, Mexico.

Noyer, Rolf. 1991. Tone and stress in the San Mateo dialect of Huave. *Proceedings of ESCOL 1991*, 277–288.

Noyer, Rolf. 1993. Mobile affixes in Huave: optimality and morphological well-formedness. *Proceedings of the Twelfth West Coast Conference on Formal Linguistics*, ed. by Eric Duncan, Donka Farkas, and Philip Spaelti, 67–82. Stanford: CSLI.

Noyer, Rolf. 1997. *Features, Positions and Affixes in Autonomous Morphological Structure*. Garland: New York.

Noyer, Rolf. 2003. *A Generative Phonology of Huave*, unpublished manuscript, University of Pennsylvania.

Olmsted, David. 1964. A History of Palaihnihan Phonology. *University of California Publications in Linguistics*, vol. 35, Berkeley: University of California Press.

O'Meara, Carolyn. 2008. 'Basic Locative Construction in Seri' in *Memorias del IX Encuentro Internacional de Lingüística en el Noroeste*, Tomo 2, ed. by Rosa María Ortiz Ciscomani, 253–269. Hermosillo: Universidad de Sonora.

O'Meara, Carolyn. 2010. *Seri Landscape Classification and Spatial Reference*. Ph.D. thesis, University at Buffalo.

O'Meara, Carolyn. 2011a. Frames of Reference in Seri. *Language Sciences* 33, no. 6: 1025–1046.

O'Meara, Carolyn. 2011b. The locative definite article *hac* in Seri. *Fonología, morfología y tipología semántico-sintática*, ed. by Ana Lidia Munguía Duarte, Estudios Lingüísticos 1, Hermosillo, Sonora, Mexico: Editorial Universidad de Sonora.

O'Meara, Carolyn. 2014a. Verbos de movimiento en seri y la expresión de trayectoria. *Verbos de movimiento en lenguas de América: Léxico, sintaxis y pragmática*, ed. by Lilián Guerrero, 207–236. México, Instituto de Investigaciones Filológicas, UNAM.

O'Meara, Carolyn. 2014b. Entre lugares, estrellas y vientos: Descripciones de rutas y narraciones del paisaje en seri. *Mapas del cielo y de la tierra. Espacio y territorio en la palabra oral*, ed. by Mariana Masera, 251–274. México, Instituto de Investigaciones Filológicas, UNAM.

O'Meara, Carolyn and Jürgen Bohnemeyer. 2008. Complex Landscape Terms in Seri. *Language Sciences* 30, no. 2–3: 316–339.

Osnaya, Evangelina Arana. 1959. Afinidades lingüísticas del Cuitlateco. *Actas del XXXIII Congreso Internacional de Americanistas*, 560–572. Lehmann: Costa Rica.

Pak, Marjorie. 2007. Phrasal tone domains in San Mateo Huave. *Proceedings of the 33rd Annual Meeting of the Berkeley Linguistics Society*, ed. by Thera Crane et al., 310–322. Berkeley Linguistics Society, CA.

Pak, Marjorie. 2010. Pre-nominal a in San Mateo Huave. Presented at the *I Jornada de Estudios Huaves*, UNAM, Mexico City.

Pak, Marjorie. 2014. Phonological Evidence for the Syntax of SVO and VOS in Huave. Presented at the *Workshop on Sound Systems of Mexico and Central America*, Yale University.

Paster, Mary. 2009. Explaining Phonological Conditions on Affixation: Evidence from Suppletive Allomorphy and Affix Ordering. *Word Structure* 2, no. 1: 18–37.

Pike, Kenneth and Milton Warkentin. 1961. Huave: A Study in Syntactic Tone with Low Lexical Functional Load. *A William Cameron Townsend en el vigésimo-quinto aniversario del Instituto Lingüístico de Verano*, 627–642. Mexico: Instituto Lingüístico de Verano.

Pollard, Helen Perlstein. 1993. *Taríacuri's Legacy: The Prehispanic Tarascan State*. The Civilization of the American Indian series, vol. 209. Norman: University of Oklahoma Press.

Powell, John Wesley. 1966 [1891], *Indian linguistic families of America north of Mexico*, Seventh annual report, Bureau of American Ethnology, Washington, D.C., Government Printing Office.

Purepecha, Endangered Languages 2015, The Linguist List at Eastern Michigan University and The University of Hawaii at Manoa. 6/21/2015. www.endangeredlanguages.com/lang/7569.

Radin, Paul. 1916. On the relationship of Huave and Mixe. *American Anthropologist* 18: 411–423.

Radin, Paul. 1924. The Relationship of Maya to Zoque-Huave. *Journal de la Société des Américanistes* XVI: 317–324.

Radin, Paul. 1929. Huave Texts. *IJAL* 5: 1–56.

Sapir, Edward. 1917a. The Position of Yana in the Hokan Stock. *University of California Publications in American Archaeology and Ethnology*, vol. 13, 1–34. Berkeley: University of California Press.

Seri, Endangered Languages 2015, The Linguist List at Eastern Michigan University and The University of Hawaii at Manoa. 3/10/2015. www.endangeredlanguages.com/lang/5846.

Sheridan, Thomas. 1979. Cross or Arrow? The Breakdown in Spanish-Seri Relations 1729–1750. *Arizona and the West* 21: 317–334.

Sheridan, Thomas. 1999. *Empire of Sand: The Seri Indians and the Struggle for Spanish Sonora, 1645–1803*. Tucson: University of Arizona Press.

Sheridan, Thomas and Richard Felger. 1977. Indian Utilization of Eelgrass (*Zostera marina L.*) in Northwestern Mexico: The Spanish Colonial Record. *The Kiva* 43, no. 2: 89–92.

Silver, Shirley. 1964. Shasta and Karok: A Binary Comparison. *Studies in Californian linguistics*, ed. by William Bright, University of California Publications in Linguistics, vol. 34, 170–181. Berkeley: University of California Press.

Stairs, Emily and Barbara Hollenbach. 1969. Huave verb morphology. *IJAL* 35: 38–53.

Stairs, Emily and Barbara Hollenbach. 1981. Gramática huave. *Diccionario huave de San Mateo del Mar*, ed. by Glen Stairs and Emily Stairs, 283–391. SIL, Mexico.

Stairs, Glen and Emily Stairs. 1981. *Diccionario huave de San Mateo del Mar*, Serie de vocabularios y diccionarios indígenas "Mariano Silva y Aceves" 24, SIL, Mexico.

Stolz, Thomas. 1996. Some Instruments Are Really Good Companions – Some Are Not. On Syncretism and the Typology of Instrumentals and Comitatives. *Theoretical Linguistics* 23, no. 1–2: 113–200.

Suaréz, Jorge. 1975. Estudios Huaves. *Collección Lingüistica* 22, INAH, Mexico.

Swadesh, Morris. 1960. The Oto-Manguean Hypothesis and Macro-Mixtecan. *IJAL* 26: 79–111.

Swadesh, Morris. 1966. Porhé y Maya. *Anales de Antropología* 3: 173–204.

Swadesh, Morris. 1967a. Lexicostatistic Classification. *Linguistics*, ed. Norman McQuown, vol. 5 of *HMAI*, ed. by Robert Wauchope, 79–115. Austin: University of Texas Press.

Swadesh, Morris. 1969. *Elementos del tarasco antiguo*. México: UNAM.

Turner, Paul. 1967. Seri and Chontal (Tequistlatec). *IJAL* 33, no. 3: 235–239.

Valiñas Coalla, Leopoldo, Mario Cortina Borja, and Miguel Mireles Padilla. 1984. Notas sobre el Cuitlateco. *Anales de Antropologia* 21, no. 1, Instituto de Investigaciones Antropológicas, UNAM.

Vázquez Rojas Maldonado, Violeta. 2012. *The Syntax and Semantics of Purépecha Noun Phrases and the Mass/Count Distinction*. Ph.D. thesis, New York University.

Villavicencio Zarza, Frida. 2006. *P'orhépecha kaso sïrátahenkwa: Desarrollo del sistema de casos del Purépecha*. Mexico: DF, Colegio de México, Centro de Investigaciones Superiores en Antropología Social.

Voegelin, Carl and Florence Voegelin. 1965. Classification of American Indian Languages. *AL* 7, no. 7: 121–150.

Wares, Alan. 1956. *Suffixation in Tarascan*. Master's thesis, Indiana University.

Wares, Alan. 1972. Review of: The Tarascan Language, by Mary L. Foster. *Journal of Linguistic*s vol. 8: 190–196.

Weitlaner, Robert. 1939. Notes on the Cuitlatec Language. *El México Antiguo* 4: 363–373.

Wimbish, John. 1989. 'WORDSURV: A Program for Analyzing Language Survey Word Lists. *Occasional Publications in Academic Computing*, vol. 13. Dallas: Summer Institute of Linguistics.

CHAPTER 10

LANGUAGE ISOLATES IN SOUTH AMERICA

Frank Seifart and Harald Hammarström

1 INTRODUCTION

South America is the continent with the highest proportion of language isolates: as much as 60% of the lineages are isolates (no other continent surpasses 50%) and more than 10% of South American languages are isolates (65 out of 574 languages), compared to an average of less than 2.5% on other continents (Table 10.1). But it is not only the number of isolates that is reflective of the genealogical diversity in South America. More generally, this continent exhibits more two-member families, more three-member families, fewer very large families and so on, compared to the other continents. Entropy (as in Table 10.1) is a systematic measure of the diversity of a distribution (here, the division of languages into lineages), and South America shows the highest entropy, which is also reflected in the average of only about 5 languages per lineage, compared to an average of about 25 languages per lineage in other continents.

The fact that the proportion of isolates (and linguistic diversity more generally) is so much greater in South America than on other continents becomes even more intriguing when considering that South America was the continent that was the last to be populated by humans, i.e. languages had less time to diverge there than on other continents. Nichols (1990) pushed the argument that diversity can only be the result of early settlement, implying that the Americas must have been settled several dozen millennia ago, i.e. much earlier than previously assumed. Specifically regarding South America, if one assumes that the Americas were settled first by passing through the Bering Strait and further into South America mainly via the land route whose most narrow stretch is in Panama, then this idea becomes incongruent with the linguistic diversity in South America, which is higher than in North America, yet with a strictly later settlement. Nettle (1999), on the other hand, argues that diversity is the expected result of a relatively recent migration into

TABLE 10.1 NUMBERS ON SOUTH AMERICAN ISOLATES AND LINEAGES COMPARED TO OTHER CONTINENTS

Macro-Area	# lgs	# isolates	# fam	% isolates	Entropy	Avg # lgs/ lineage
South America	574	65	44	60%	5.07	5.27
North America	618	31	40	44%	4.29	8.70
Eurasia	1654	12	23	34%	2.83	47.26
Africa	2207	17	33	34%	2.08	44.14
New Guinea Area	2139	55	72	43%	2.88	16.84
Australia	342	9	23	28%	2.21	10.69

Source: Figures taken from Hammarström et al. (2015).

an unoccupied area. In this model, diversity results from initial fissioning in a novel area rich in resources, and lack of diversity arises when there is sufficient time for later expansions to obliterate the diversity from the initial settlement. Blench (2012) is consistent with this scenario, arguing that the most powerful obliterative expansions are the ones linked to agriculture and that these happened relatively late in South America. Nettle's (1999) model is clearly more consistent with the linguistic as well as archaeological data for the Americas. But on a world-level, a simple equation of late settlement with high diversity is difficult to reconcile with the archaeological and linguistic facts of, e.g. the New Guinea area, so probably more parameters than settlement-depth need to be taken into account to explain the emergence of linguistic diversity on a global level.

Specifically regarding South American isolates, Dahl et al. (2011) propose a novel suggestion for their emergence. First, migration routes are calculated using detailed geographical/geomorphological datasets, such that, if entry into South America was in the northwest and the migrating humans were aiming to reach the southern tip, what would be the shortest/least cumbersome way to get there? This procedure yields a route through the Andes to the southern tip with various wrinkles along the way. Dahl et al. (2011) note impressionistically that the geographical distribution of language isolates seems to be concentrated along this route, as if they were 'dropped-off' on migrations along the route. While attractive, the assumption behind obtaining the route in question, namely that the migrations were destined to reach the southern tip, is more convenient than it is realistic. Also, objective measures as to the geographical concentration of isolates are still lacking, as are comparisons to even simpler geologically based co-variation than migration routes, e.g., simply being in a foothills area between the Andes and the rainforest.

In recent work, Epps (in press and personal communication) links South American linguistic diversity, and thus also the high number of isolates, to distinctly South American patterns of social organization. She argues that Amazonian people, and maybe South American people in general (at least prior to the Inca expansion), present particular dynamics of interaction and corresponding linguistic ideologies. Consistent with Eriksen (2011), who uses a Geographic Information System (GIS) to reconstruct ancient ethnogenetic processes from archaeology, linguistics, geography, and ethnohistory, Epps argues that Amazonian societies "developed a set of socio-economic practices in which different groups formed complementary parts of larger systems" rather than being organized in hierarchical, top-down social structures. A prototypical example of such a multiethnic and multilingual system is the Vaupés, which encompasses a couple dozen ethnolinguistic groups. Crucially for linguistic diversity, "differences are viewed as essential to the functioning of the articulated whole" within such systems. This is prototypically exemplified in the institutionalized linguistic exogamy in the Vaupés regional system but is consistent also with remarkably low rates of lexical borrowing across South America (at least Amazonia) (Bowern et al. 2011; Bowern et al. 2014). This distinctly South American indigenous social structure implies historically relatively little language shift (prior to the arrival of Europeans), which would wipe out linguistic diversity, and it provides a motivation for the maintenance of genealogical distinctions with little subsequent diversification, resulting in the long term in a high number of isolates.

If isolates are the result of purely historical processes of language expansions and language extinction, there is little reason to suspect that language isolates should be structurally different from non-isolates. But the historical processes may be conditioned by factors that leave structural commonalities of isolates as epiphenomena, for example, if isolates were more likely to be spoken by hunter-gatherers or if isolates are remnants of a linguistic area. However, these lines of research have yet to be systematically investigated for the South American continent.

In this chapter, we provide a brief synopsis of language isolates in South America. We define isolates by two criteria as a single language with (1) sufficient attestation, i.e. at least about 50 words of basic vocabulary (otherwise they are considered as "unclassified"), and (2) a language which has not been demonstrated in publication to be related to any other language by the comparative method (Campbell and Poser 2008). It is important that the 50 or so words comprise so-called basic vocabulary which has been found to be relatively resistant to borrowing (Tadmor, Haspelmath and Taylor 2010) and which has better prospects for comparison than, e.g., 50 items of flora-fauna vocabulary or toponyms of uncertain analysis.

For the sake of presentation, isolates are grouped into seven geographic areas, moving roughly from North to South: Orinoco and North (Section 2), Andes (Section 3), Western Amazon (Section 4), Guaporé-Mamoré (Section 5), Central Amazon (Section 6), Eastern Amazon (Section 7), and, finally, Chaco and the Southern Cone (Section 8). Within these sections, we first discuss living language isolates, i.e. with known living speakers, and then extinct language isolates, with no known living speakers. We provide ISO 639–3 codes for living isolates (and for extinct isolates where available), as well as selected references for all isolates. Full lists of bibliographical references can be found in Glottolog 2.5 (Hammarström et al. 2015), building on the fundamental bibliographical work of Fabre (1998). We use language names as given by Hammarström et al. (2015) and provide only the most common alternative names.

There have been innumerable proposals in the literature to link South American isolates to established language families or to other isolates, which we will not go through in full, but mention a few recent issues in the sections below. Compared to other continents, the level of description of South American languages is relatively good and has considerably increased over the past couple of decades. However, for many isolates of South America, especially the extinct ones, not much more than a wordlist is available, often just enough to identify the language as an isolate according to our criteria. The scarce documentation of so many isolates prompts the question whether we would have found the relative(s) of some of these isolates if only they were better documented than in a short wordlist or two? Surely, more documentation, when used properly, can only increase our knowledge about the historical relationships between languages. But in terms of finding deeper genealogical connections, empirical findings imply that knowing the basic vocabulary is just about as informative as knowing the basic vocabulary and the grammar. Hammarström (2014) shows that, for South America, the classification by Loukotka (1968), which was based solely on basic vocabulary comparison, is almost identical to that of Campbell (2012) who had access to a wealth of documentation of lexicon and grammar that appeared in the meantime. Not only is core vocabulary the basic probative instrument, there are also good prospects for automating the comparison, and still recover a high degree of accuracy (such as the ASJP program, see details in Hammarström 2014). Automated comparison has the advantage of being objective and of double checking that all potential connections are actually explored. Thus, even if we had richer documentation of the extinct isolates listed here as only attested with a wordlist or two, we should not expect a drastic change in the classificatory outcome.

2   ISOLATES IN THE ORINOCO AND NORTHERN SOUTH AMERICA

This area spans the basin of the Orinoco River and the Caribbean coast of South America. The main linguistic families of this area are Cariban and Arawakan, which used to occupy the Caribbean coast and islands, but there are also some Tupian languages, and a number of smaller families. This area hosts 13 isolates, 6 of which are extinct. Many of the isolates of this area were first mentioned, and often documented in more or less a short wordlist, by Theodor Koch-Grünberg, who travelled the area extensively in the early 20th century.

2.1 Arutani [atx]

Located in Southeastern Venezuela and across the border in Brazil, Arutani, also known as Awake, Auake, or Uruak, is a highly endangered (if not extinct) and poorly documented language (short vocabularies and a small amount of analyzed grammar), first mentioned by Koch-Grünberg (1913; 1922; 1928a). Hammarström (2010:181) rejects earlier proposals of a grouping with Sapé (Section 2.2), following the comments by Migliazza (1978; 1985), who collected first hand data on both languages, and thus both Arutani and Sapé are considered isolates here. Arutani appears to be an SOV language (Migliazza 1985:50).

2.2 Sapé [spc]

In the vicinity of Arutani, Sapé has even fewer, if any speakers left. Data from what appear to be the four last speakers (or semi-speakers or rememberers) appeared in Perozo et al. (2008). However, this data is limited to 33 words from one speaker, 11 from another, 6 from two other speakers, and 5 phrases. These phrases lack verbal morphology, so even these are likely not fluent speakers (Raoul Zamponi, personal communication, 2013). Sapé is even more poorly documented than Arutani. Published data is confined to short vocabularies and some phrases (Koch-Grünberg 1928b; de Matallana and de Armellada 1943; Migliazza 1978; Perozo et al. 2008) and a minuscule amount of analyzed grammar (Migliazza 1980; 1983; 1985). As with Arutani, Raoul Zamponi and Chris Rogers have been analyzing Migliazza's data and recordings and everything else on this language, to be published soon.

2.3 Puinave [pui]

Puinave is spoken by a relatively large community on the Colombian side of the Orinoco River. Recent work by Bolaños (2011) re-evaluates earlier claims starting from Rivet and Tastevin (1920) on the relation between Puinave, Kakua-Nukak, and the Nadahup languages. A lot of the earlier parallels need to be discarded with the appearance of high-quality data on all languages involved, and only a minuscule number of parallels remain, including however, pronoun similarities between Puinave and Kakua-Nukak. If they are related at all, the relation must be very distant, because of the near total divergence in basic vocabulary. Thus, to explain their relation in terms of simply deriving from a common ancestor seems to provoke more questions than it answers: if so, why did the two branches essentially only keep pronouns in near-identical forms while replacing the remainder? The structure of Puinave has been thoroughly described by Girón, especially in Girón (2008). Further documentation includes a description of Puinave musical traditions (Girón, Miraval and Miraval 2004). Girón (2008:336–338) describes Puinave as a relatively free constituent order language (agent role signalled by ergative case-marking) where only OSV is ungrammatical in the finite clause.

2.4 Pumé [yae]

Pumé, also called Yaruro or Yuapín, is a relatively vital language spoken in Western Venezuela. Linguistic data has been available since the late 18th century (Hervás y Panduro 1787). A certain amount of grammatical description is available from various sources (Hervás y Panduro 1971 [1799]; Mosonyi 1966; Obregón Muñoz and Pozo 1989; Mosonyi and García 2000), but there is no comprehensive grammar. Yaruro is an SOV language that distinguishes masculine/feminine gender on two levels; there is gender agreement according to the gender of a head noun as well as according to the interlocutor (Mosonyi and García 2000).

2.5 Taruma

The Taruma people lived near the mouth of the Rio Negro River in Brazil in the late 17th century (Rivière 1966) but subsequently moved to the Southern Guianas where the tribe diminished and ceased to exist as a separate ethnolinguistic group sometime around the 1920s. Without a separate ethnolinguistic identity, the language was presumed extinct until three surviving speakers were found living among the Wapishana (Carlin and Mans 2014:82–85). Only one speaker remains today who is no longer completely fluent (Sérgio Meira, personal communication, 2015). Eithne Carlin and Sérgio Meira have worked with the last (semi-)speakers and some unpublished textual data collected in the 1920s has survived, which promises that at least some of the grammatical characteristics of Taruma will be known. Until now, the only published data consists of wordlists (Loukotka 1949). An ISO 639–3 code for this language has recently been requested.

2.6 Warao [wba]

Warao is one of the largest languages of Venezuela with about 28,000 speakers along the Caribbean coast. Various grammatical descriptions are available (Vaquero 1965; Romero-Figeroa 1997; Granados 1998). These document that Warao has the exceedingly rare OSV word order in pragmatically neutral sentences (except for stative sentences) (Romero-Figeroa 1985; 1997:5–12), as in example (1). Note that we present language data throughout as given in the original sources, i.e. orthographically in most cases. This includes the use of apostrophe to represent glottal stops, as in example (7).

(1) Warao (Romero-Figeroa 1997:5)
erike   huba   abu-a-e
Enrique snake   bite-PUNTCUAL-PAST
'A snake bit Enrique.'

Warao has been hypothesized to belong to some constellation of macro-Chibchan (see Kaufman 1990:35, 50, 54 and references therein). Some versions of this hypothesis involve the extinct language Timucua in Florida, North America (Granberry 1993:15–16). Later evaluations of such proposals have dismissed the alleged similarities as chance resemblances (e.g., Sturtevant 2005:14, Arinterol 2000:118).

2.7 Yuwana [yau]

Yuwana is more commonly known as Hodï (Jotí, Hoti), sometimes also as Waruwaru, or Chikano (Chicano). Its several hundred speakers are monolingual hunter-gatherers in an inaccessible region in central Venezuela, contacted first only in the 1970s. There are descriptions of a number of Yuwana grammatical features (Vilera Díaz 1985; 1987; Quatra 2008a), and there is a dictionary (Quatra 2008b). Yuwana has a system of nominal classification reminiscent of the Sáliban languages, and once the Yuwana system has been sufficiently described, a systematic comparison can be undertaken. Jolkesky (2009) is an initial comparison involving lexical and some grammatical morphemes of Yuwana, Sáliban, Andoque (Section 4.1), and Tikuna.

2.8 Extinct isolates of the Orinoco and Northern South America

Six extinct isolates of this area have sufficient documentation (i.e. at least wordlist of about 50 words) to identify them as such according to our criteria. The **Betoi-Jirara** dialect cluster was once spoken in what is now the border between Colombia and Peru. Based on older materials, Zamponi (2002; 2003) produced a basic grammatical description. Betoi is an SOV language (Zamponi 2002:218–219). The extinct language **Guamo** was spoken near the Caribbean coast and is only known from a wordlist from the 18th century (Anónimo 1928a). **Jirajaran** was spoken by a number of groups (possibly speaking a different dialect, or closely related languages), **Jirajara** proper, **Ayomán**, and **Gayón**. They presented violent resistance against the first conquistadors of South America, and finally became extinct in the 20th century. Wordlists and very limited grammatical information is available (Oramas 1916; Jahn 1927; Querales 2008). In the vicinity of Jirajaran, **Otomaco** was spoken, it is essentially known only from one wordlist (de Luzena no date), which was sufficient for Rosenblat (1936) to draw up a phonemic inventory. Slightly more information, including some morphosyntactic facts, are known about the extinct isolate **Timote-Cuica** cluster, from the same region (Arrieta E. 1993; 1998), allowing a phonological analysis and discerning some grammatical characteristics such as SVO word order (Arrieta E. 1993:101–102).

The recently extinct isolate **Máku** in Southern Venezuela, whose last speaker remained in Brazil until about 2002, is not to be confused with the former name of the Nadahup linguistic family or the Maco language, or other Amazonian languages with similar names (Hammarström 2011). Vocabulary and basic grammatical description is available (Migliazza 1965; 1966; Maciel 1991). Raoul Zamponi is preparing a more extensive grammatical description based on all earlier materials (Raoul Zamponi, personal communication, 2014). Máku was an SOV language (Migliazza 2008).

3 ISOLATES OF THE ANDES

There are 12 known language isolates in the Andean region of South America, the majority of which (8) are extinct, reflecting the early penetration of the Andes by Europeans, which, on the one hand, left some early documentation but, on the other hand, lead to massive language loss (adding to a possible earlier wave of language loss due to the Inca expansion). Moving from North to South, the major language families (once) spoken this area are Chibchan and Quechuan (with Barbacoan nested between them), while the Southern Andes are dominated by Aymara and Mapudungun (see also Section 8).

3.1 Páez [pbb]

In the Northern Andes in Colombia, what Adelaar (2004) calls the "Chibchan sphere," Páez is the second largest language in numbers of speakers in Colombia (40,000 according to Crevels 2007) and may be the largest isolate in South America in terms of numbers of speakers. A number of good grammatical descriptions are available on this language (Slocum 1986, Jung 1989, Rojas Curieux 1998). Páez grammar is noteworthy, among other things, for its complex phoneme inventory, with various series of consonants (involving aspiration, prenasalization, and palatalization) and various series of vowels (involving length, glottalization, and aspiration).

3.2 Tinigua [tit]

Tinigua is a moribund (if not extinct) and understudied language in the Andean foothills, reaching into the Western Amazon. Very little is known about this language and its sister dialect/language Pamigua (Castellví 1940; Tobar Ortiz 2000), and it tends to be neglected either in surveys of their original habitat or their final location. The Tinigua suffered persecution throughout the last century. Tobar Ortiz (2000), who was able to work with the last two speakers, is the only significant source for grammatical data. Tinigua is described as an SVO language (Tobar Ortiz 2000).

3.3 Camsá [kbh]

In Southern Colombia, Camsá is an isolate that belongs to the "Quechuan sphere." There are a few descriptive studies on Camsá (Howard 1967; 1977), including studies authored by members of the speech community (Juajibioy Chindoy 1962; Jamioy Muchavisoy 1989, 1992, 1999). Camsá grammar is unlike those of surrounding language in that it has a number of prefixes, and it has an extraordinarily complex morphology.

3.4 Leco [lec]

A number of language isolates are or were spoken in the vicinity of Lake Titicaca, on the border between Peru and Bolivia. Leco is the only one of these with remaining (semi-) speakers, albeit very few. Van der Kerke (2000; 2002; 2006; 2009) provides descriptions of various aspects of its grammar.

3.5 Extinct isolates of the Andes

In a once large territory, encompassing lake Titicaca, **Puquina [puq]** was recognized as a 'general language' (along with Quechua), i.e. the lingua franca, also used by the Spanish administration, in the early colonial period, which implies a considerable number of speakers. However, it rapidly became extinct soon after (Adelaar 2004:350). Its earlier status left a multilingual religious text, *Rituale seu Manuale Peruanum* (de Oré 1607), as a principal source for the language, which was first analyzed by de la Grasserie (1894). A considerable amount of information on this language is available from this document, and from a limited number of other older sources (Adelaar 2004:350–362), including information on an unusual system of inverse marking (Adelaar 2004:354). Parts of Puquina lexicon survive in Callahuaya, a secret, mixed language with a Puquina lexical base and Quechua morphology and grammatical structure, still used by traditional healers (Muysken 1994; 1997).

Mochica [omc] (which has also been called Yunga) was spoken on the Pacific coast of what is now Northern Peru, where it came under pressure from European settlers early on and eventually became extinct in the early, 20th century. There is a certain amount of documentation of this language, e.g. Middendorf (1892), who did his own fieldwork, as well as Brüning (2004) and Hovdhaugen (2004) which are based on a more thorough analysis of older sources, which include the very early de la Carrera (1880 [1644]).

The **Andaqui [ana]** were once a numerous group in what is now Southern Colombia. They perished along with their language, of the same name, in fierce warfare against the Spaniards. Similarities with Chibchan languages (Rivet 1924) and with the neighbouring isolate Páez (see Section 3.1) have been noted (Adelaar 2004:140), but neither of these substantiate genealogical relatedness. Linguistic documentation is limited to two (rather extensive) wordlists (Anónimo 1928b; Vergara y Vergara and Delgado 1860).

Four extinct isolate languages were spoken on the slopes of the Andes: Atacame, Yurumanguí, Sechuran, and Tallán. **Atacame** or Esmeraldeño became extinct in the 19th century. The only available Atacame data was collected in 1877 by J. M. Pallares, which was reproduced and discussed in later publications (e.g., Seler 1902; Jijón y Caamaño 1945). Atacame had as an interesting grammatical feature classifying prefixes that refer to shape (example 2), a feature common in Amazonian language. By the time it was documented, the Atacame language was spoken by a population of predominantly African descent, which raises the possibility that it is an African language rather than an (adopted) Amerindian language. Cursory searches for resemblances with mainly West African languages (e.g., in terms of classifying prefixes) have been carried out by various individuals, so far without interesting results.

(2) Atacame (Adelaar 2004:158; citing Jijón y Caamaño 1941:435–436)
   a *ra-tuna*
      PROTRUDING.ELEMENT-mouth.area
      'beard'
   b *vil-tuna*
      WRAPPING-mouth.area
      'lips'
   c *di-sa*
      hand-1.POSSESSOR
      'my hand'
   d *ta-di-sa*
      LONG.OBJECT-hand-1.POSSESSOR
      'my arm'
   e *ta-kel-sa*
      LONG.OBJECT-bone-1.POSSESSOR
      'my back'
   f *mu-kil-sa*
      BULKY.OBJECT-bone-1.POSSESSOR
      'my bone'

The only record of **Yurumanguí** is one wordlist from the 18th century. It was used by Rivet (1942) to propose a genealogical relation with the putative Hokan languages of North America, a proposal which has since been rejected (e.g., Constenla Umaña 1991).

The main source for the extinct isolate **Sechuran** of the coastal plain of Northern Peru is a wordlist collected in 1863 by Richard Spruce and published by von Buchwald (1919). Even less material survives of neighbouring **Tallán** (Ramos Cabredo 1950). There are occasional lexical links between Tallán and Sechuran (Adelaar 2004:398–400), but the very limited data available is not compelling for a genealogical relationship. **Culli** was spoken in the Central Andes late into the 20th century (Adelaar 1988), surrounded by Quechua, and is documented in two wordlists, one of them published by Rivet (1949). Mutual influence of Culli with surrounding varieties of Quechua can be shown (Adelaar 2004:401–404).

4 WESTERN AMAZON

In the Western Amazon a number of Arawakan and Tupian languages are spoken, and it is the home of a number of (more or less) small families such as Jivaroan, Zaparoan, Witotoan, and Tucanoan. In this setting, there are also nine language isolates, which include three known extinct isolates. It is safe to assume that many more isolates existed but vanished without leaving traces, given the later onset of colonization in the lowlands, when compared to the Andes. Missionary sources contain long lists of ethnonyms which are never heard of in later accounts and are likely to include some isolates that disappeared without a discernible linguistic footprint.

4.1 Andoque [ano]

Andoque is spoken along the middle Caquetá River by approximately 350 speakers. It is part of one of the typical Amazonian regional cultural complex mentioned in Section 1, that of the Caquetá-Putumayo (autodenomination 'People of the Centre'), together with the two Boran and the three Witotoan languages, as well as the Arawakan language Resígaro (Seifart et al. 2009). Intense contacts among these languages has led to diffusion of a number of grammatical features, among them extensive systems of noun classifiers, which Andoque also has (Landaburu 1979; 2000).

4.2 Cofán [con]

Cofán is spoken near the Andean foothills in Northeast Ecuador and Southern Colombia by a few thousand speakers. It is relatively well described (Borman 1962; 1976; Tobar Gutiérrez 1995; Fischer 2007). A full descriptive grammar is in preparation by Rafael Fischer and Kees Hengeveld. The Cofán are one of the tribes famous for use of hallucinogenic Yagé (or Ayauasca).

4.3 Candoshi-Shapra [cbu]

In the Northern part of the Peruvian Amazon, Candoshi and Shapra are closely related varieties (one of them being extinct), considered here to be dialects of a single language. Correspondences with neighbouring Jivaroan languages are due to borrowing (Payne 1981). Available grammatical description of Candoshi-Shapra is limited to some specific grammatical features (Cox 1957; Anderson and Wise 1963), and there is a dictionary (Tuggy 1966). The language is still spoken by a sizeable population, and a full grammatical description is in progress by Simon Overall. A popular hypothesis is that Candoshi-Shapra will prove to be the closest relative of the large Arawakan language family after Payne (1989) uncovered some lexical correspondences that match better with reconstructed proto-Arawakan (or Maipuran Arawakan in his terminology) than with modern Arawakan languages.

4.4 Waorani [auc]

Like Candoshi-Shapra, Waorani (alternative names: Huaorani, Auca, Huao, Sabela, Auishiri) still has a considerable number of speakers (in Ecuador), possibly in addition to some uncontacted speakers in Peru. The Waorani have a history of violent resistance against outside contact (Yost 1981). After missionaries had succeeded in establishing contact, grammatical descriptions were produced, especially Peeke (1968). Noteworthy features of Waorani include an inverse pulmonic nasal /m</ and a labial inverse oral click (Pike and Saint 1962). Given the hostile relations to outsiders, the Waorani were monolingual, and the language, upon initial entrance in 1958, was reported to only have had two loanwords (Peeke 1973:4). If this assessment is correct, Waorani is the South American (if not the world) record holder of lack of borrowing.

4.5 Taushiro [trr]

Another language of Northern Peru, Taushiro, is now nearly extinct. Various proposals have been made to link it to other languages like Zaparoan, Kandoshi, and especially Omurano (Section 4.7), but none convincing. There is a basic grammatical description (Alicea 1975a; 1975b) which shows Taushiro to be a VSO language.

4.6 Urarina [ura]

Thanks to the work of Olawsky (2006), Urarina is one of the best described isolates of South America. It has about 3,000 speakers. It has the typologically rare OVS basic word order, as illustrated in example 3 (see also Olawsky 2005), which is otherwise attested in only a small number of other languages, mostly South American, and among these mostly Cariban.

(3)   Urarina (Olawsky 2006:655)
      nitoane-ĩ   *hetau=te*   *katça*   *lemɨ-e=lɨ*   *lomaj*
      be.like.that-PARTICIPLE HEARSAY=FOCUS   man   sink-3SG=PAST   Lomaj
      [ADV]   [O]   [V]   [S]
      'Lomaj sank the people in that way'

4.7 Extinct isolates of the Western Amazon

Omurano is one of the three known isolates of the Western Amazon that is extinct. Data on this language is limited to a wordlist collected by Tessmann (1930). In 2011, a few words (mostly ones already contained in the Tessmann list) were collected from a "rememberer" (O'Hagan 2011). Proposals (Kaufman 1994:63) of genealogical links with Taushiro (Section 4.5) are not convincing.

Muniche [myr], also in the Northern part of the Peruvian Amazon, is an extinct language with a number of semi-speakers in 2009 (Proyecto de Documentación del Idioma Muniche 2009). Some grammatical features have been documented in Gibson (1988; 1996) which shows Muniche to have been a suffixing genderless VSO language.

Aewa [ash], also known as Aʔɨwa (Aiwa), Tekiráka (Tequiraca), or Vacacocha or the ambiguous Abijira (with spelling variants), was spoken in the Northern Peruvian Amazon. Wordlists of Tekiráka appear in Tessmann (1930:475–485) and Villarejo (1959). These bear no significant relations to neighbouring languages (Loukotka 1968:156;

Adelaar 2004:456). The language is presumed to be extinct (Lewis, Simons and Fennig 2015), although Michael and Beier (2012) have located a few semi-speakers from whom they collected another wordlist and did a phonemic analysis.

5 ISOLATES OF THE GUAPORÉ-MAMORÉ AREA

The Guaporé and Mamoré area, in Southwestern Amazonia, encompasses the Eastern Bolivian and Western Brazilian lowlands and is drained by the Guaporé and Mamoré Rivers. This area is linguistically highly diverse, with language from 11 families, including Arawakan, Chapacuaran, Macro-Gé, Panoan, South Nambikaran, and Tupian. Adding to this diversity, there are 12 known isolates in this area, two of which are extinct. Crevels and Van der Voort (2008) describe structural similarities between unrelated languages within this area, such as evidentials, verbal number, directional, inclusive/exclusive distinctions, alienable/inalienable distinctions, lack of a grammaticalized gender system, etc.

5.1 Cayubaba [cyb]

In the western part of the Guaporé-Mamoré area, in the Beni department in Northern Bolivia, four isolates neighbour each other: Cayubaba, Itonama, Movima, and the extinct Canichana. Cayubaba (sometimes also spelled Cayuvava) is also already extinct according to some, but Crevels and Muysken (2012) have found a handful of speakers and produced a short grammatical description, based on earlier work by Key (1963; 1967; 1974; 1975) and to some extent on new data. Cayubaba is a VOS language.

5.2 Itonama [ito]

Itonama is moribund, with only two elderly speakers in 2011 (Crevels 2012a). It has an extensive set of classifiers that are typologically unusual because they occur on verbs as well as demonstratives and because they are a distinct set from another set of classifiers that occur on numerals. Table 10.2 illustrates the forms of the proximate demonstrative with these classifiers. Itonama has VSO basic word order (Crevels 2012a:51).

5.3 Movima [mzp]

Unlike Cayubaba, Itonama, and Canichana, Movima still has a considerable number of speakers (about 1,400). It has been comprehensively described by Haude (2006). A particularly noteworthy feature of its grammar is hierarchical alignment of core arguments, which determines the syntactic status of higher versus lower-ranked participants in terms of word order, cross-reference, etc. (see example 4). Semantic role assignment is carried out solely by direct and inverse marking on the predicate (see also Haude 2009).

(4)   Movima (Haude 2006:277)

a.   *tikoy-na=sne*   *os*   *mimi:di*
    kill-DIRECT=3.FEM.ABSOLUTIVE   ARTICLE.NEUTER.PAST   snake
    'She killed the/a snake.'

b.   *tikoy-kay-a=sne*   *os*   *mimi:di*
    kill-INVERSE-LINKER =3.FEM.ABSOLUTIVE   ARTICLE.NEUTER.PAST   snake
    'The snake killed her.'

TABLE 10.2 ITONAMA CLASSIFIERS

nota'na M, notahka F	ANIMATE + STANDING + SG [men, women, dogs, cats]
na-**dïlï**	ANIMATE + STANDING + PL [men, women, dogs, cats]
nu-**cha'u**	ANIMATE + SITTING + SG [men, women, dogs, cats]
no'o-**di**	ANIMATE + SITTING + PL [men, women, dogs, cats]
nu'u-**pu**	FLAT, ROUND, HORIZONTAL + SG [banana, canoe, cut tree, big leaf, fenced lot, Chaco, village]
no'o-**so**, no-**so**-he'ke	FLAT, ROUND, HORIZONTAL + PL [banana, canoes, cut trees, large leaves, large fields, clearings, villages]
nu'u-**du**	OVAL, CONTAINER + SG [pot, glass, egg, coconut, basket, gourd, grain (of rice)]
no'o'-**ye** no-'**e**-he'ke	OVAL, CONTAINER + PL [pots, cups, eggs, coconuts, baskets, tutumas, grains (rice)]
no-**chobo**	PLANTED, STANDING + SG [tree, house]
no'o-**bo**	PLANTED, STANDING + PL [trees, houses]
no'o-**tyo**	LIQUID [water, milk]
na'a-**chï** na'a-**chï**-he'ke (PL)	LONG, WINDING, HANGING, TIED [rope, hammock, snake]
no'o-**ba**, no'o-**ba**-he'ke (PL)	LONG, WINDING [rope, hammock, snake, small blade]
no'o-**lo**, no'o-**lo**-he'ke (PL)	FLUID [stream, river, road, snake]

Source: Crevels (2002:42–43).

5.4 Kanoê [kxo]

In the Eastern Guaporé-Mamoré area, on the Brazilian side of the Guaporé River, Kanoê, Kwaza, and Aikanã are three isolates that are spoken close to each other, all by very few speakers. Kanoê (5 speakers) is comprehensively described by Bacelar (2004). When contacted, the Kanoê and the neighbouring Akuntsu (who speak a Tupi language) had both been decimated in violent encounters with encroaching colonists and farmers (Aragon 2014:1–11). Both tribes were down to a handful of people each and were more or less forced to interact in a novel way, which is said to have given rise to a Kanoê-Akuntsu pidgin (Crevels and van der Voort 2008:156). One of the features of its grammar, which it shares with other languages of the Guaporé-Mamoré region, especially the directly neighbouring ones, is semantically empty noun-formative roots (*i-* or *e-*, glossed as 'Ø-') that combine with bound roots or classifiers (as in examples 5–6).

(5) Kanoê (Bacelar 2004:130)
  i-kuta
  Ø-head
  '(its) head'

(6) Kwaza (van der Voort 2004:397)
  e-'kai
  Ø-CLASSIFER:leg
  '(its) lower leg'

5.5 Kwaza [xwa]

Kwaza reportedly has seven remaining speakers. There is a comprehensive grammar by van der Voort (2004). Like many Amazonian languages – albeit not too many in this particular area – it has classifiers, and, related to this, it also has semantically empty elements that are used to form nouns from classifiers and from bound roots (see example 6, earlier).

5.6 Aikanã [tba]

In close contact with Kwaza, Aikanã is still spoken by about 200 speakers, but it has not been described to the same degree. A brief grammatical description is Vasconcelos (2004). Currently, further description is on-going by Hein van der Voort's team at the Museu Goeldi.

5.7 Mosetén-Chimané [cas]

Mosetén and Chimané are spoken in the western Bolivian lowlands along the Beni River. The varieties of Mosetén and Chimané form a dialect chain and are here considered one language, though there are also arguments for distinguishing Chimané as a separate language, especially on the grounds of ethnic identification. A comprehensive description of Mosetén is Sakel (2004). Sakel (2004:303) describes an unusual detransitivizing antipassive marker -ti- that contrasts with other antipassive markers of the language in that is primarily used with verbs expressing violence or aggression (as in example 7).

(7)   Mosetén (Sakel 2004:312; 2009:200)
      me'-si-si'   *aj*   *chhi-ti-'-in*
      SO-LINKER.FEM-REDUPLIATION   yet   grab-ANTIPASSIVE-FEM.SUBJECT-PLURAL
      jib-i-ti-'-in
      eat-VERBAL.STEMI-ANTIPASSIVE- FEMININE.SUBJECT-PLURAL
      'And then (the monster) grabbed her like this and ate her.'

5.8 Yuracaré [yuz]

Yuracaré is spoken by about 2,500 speakers in the eastern Beni and Cochabamba departments of Bolivia, primarily along Chapare River. A comprehensive grammar was written by van Gijn (2006). Analysis of a large Yuracaré corpus of conversational data revealed that Yuracaré has so-called *intersubjective evidential markers*, i.e., evidentials that not only express the speaker's information source but also convey the speaker's assumptions about the addressee's perspective on the information (Gipper 2011).

5.9 Chiquitano [cax]

Chiquitano is spoken by about 7,800 speakers in the central region of the Bolivian Santa Cruz department, on the limits of the Chaco area (see Section 8), and it is also well described with both missionary-era and modern descriptions (for a recent overview, see Galeote Tormo 2014). Chiquitano is one of the South American languages with male versus female registers, which is otherwise known mostly from Tupian languages (example 8).

(8)   Chiquitano (Galeote Tormo 2014:271)

MALE SPEECH	FEMALE SPEECH	
u-mases	*mases*	'squirrel'
u-pauches	*pauches*	'pig'
iñuma	*ni-xhupuxu*	'grandson'
yaiso	*nakarima*	'father-in-law'

5.10 Extinct isolates of the Guaporé-Mamoré area

We know of three more, now-extinct, isolates that were spoken in the Guaporé-Mamoré area, two of these in the vicinity of Kwaza, Kanoê, and Aikanã (see Sections 5.4–5.6). The first of these is **Canichana**, of which only three rememberers were encountered around the year 2000. The scarce information from historical sources is summarized in Crevels (2012b). The second one, **Mure**, has been extinct for longer and is documented solely by a *pater noster*, *ave maria*, and *credo* translation found in the archive of Cardinal Mezzofanti (Teza 1868:130), where it is called Moré. There at least two languages distinguished in the missionary writings from what is present-day Bolivia with a name similar to More. One is a Chapacuran language also known as Itén which is still spoken and has relatively ample documentation (e.g., Angenot-de-Lima 2002). The other Hervás y Panduro (1800:251) calls Mure and can likely be equated with the language in Teza (1868:130). Créqui-Montfort and Rivet (1913) provide a morphemic interpretation of the textual data in Teza (1868:130) and file the language as Chapacuran. We find the morphemic breakdown proposed by Créqui-Montfort and Rivet (1913) to be essentially sound, but the idea that the language is Chapacuran is difficult to sustain. The parallels with Chapacuran are limited to a few words (which are easily interpretable as loans due to joint missionization), while the remainder is very different. The Chapacuran specialist Birchall (2013:259) reached a similar conclusion when interpreting another text in Teza (1868) which can be satisfactorily analyzed as an otherwise unattested Chapacuran language (Rocorona). No other relation for the Mure data has been suggested or is apparent.

Finally, the **Ramanos** language was once spoken in the Moxos region in Central Bolivia. The only data on this language is a dozen or so words finally published by Palau and Saiz (1989 [1794]). The minuscule wordlist has the most important items of basic vocabulary and shows no significant resemblances to the surrounding languages so we treat it as an isolate here, although leaving it unclassified for scarcity of data would also be arguable.

6 CENTRAL AMAZON

The Central Amazon region is home to many Tupian languages, interspersed with, among others, six known isolated languages, two of which are extinct.

6.1 Guató [gta]

In Southwestern Brazil, near the Guaporé-Mamoré and the Chaco areas, Guató is down to extremely few speakers or has perhaps already lost its last fluent speaker (Postigo 2009). The language was first described by Schmidt (1905). The grammatical description by Palácio (1984) shows, among other things, that it has split ergativity.

6.2 Irántxe [irn]

Irántxe (or Mỹky) is a moribund language with about 40 speakers in the South-Central Amazon. A dictionary and grammatical description are available on this language (Monserrat and Amarante 1995; Monserrat 2000).

6.3 Pirahã [myp]

The Pirahã, now famous through the popular books and films by and about Daniel Everett, are located on the Maici River. They are the remnants of a once large group, mostly referred to as Mura, probably consisting of various dialects, that moved through a vast territory in Central and Western Amazonia, as far Northwest as the Caquetá River. Pirahã is known for its small phoneme inventory and complex prosody, which facilitates whistled and hummed speech (Everett 1985). Pirahã appears to have extremely simple clause structure and is also claimed to lack recursion, numerals, and colour terms (Everett 2005). Thomason and Everett (2001) argued that all of Pirahã personal pronouns are borrowed from Nhengatú (Tupian).

6.4 Trumai [tpy]

Trumai is a language isolate within the multilingual cultural complex of the Upper Xingu, together with Arawakan and Cariban languages. There is a comprehensive reference grammar by Guirardello (1999), showing that Trumai is basically an isolating language with ergative syntax.

6.5 Extinct isolates from the Central Amazon

Matanawí was spoken on the Upper Madeira River, where Nimuendajú (1925) collected a wordlist, which is the only data available on this language, and which shows no systematic resemblance to other languages. **Mato Grosso Arára [axg]** also known as Arara do Rio Branco still had a few people who remembered some words in 2001. It is surrounded mostly by Tupian languages. There is only a short wordlist (Hugo 1959; Hargreaves 2007) for which the majority of entries are not Tupi cognates. Cognates for these words have so far not been uncovered in other languages or families.

7 EASTERN AMAZON

The Eastern Amazon, along the Atlantic coast of Brazil, was once dominated by languages from the Macro-Gé family. Many of them became extinct during the relatively early occupation by Europeans. Consequently, only one of the five isolates that are known from this area now has any known living speakers.

7.1 Fulniô [fun]

Fulniô, with its closely related dialect Yatê, is the only isolate that is still spoken in Northeastern Brazil. Its grammatical structure is well described by, e.g., Lapenda (1968), Meland (1968), and da Costa (1999).

7.2 Extinct isolates of the Eastern Amazon

The four known extinct isolates of the Eastern Amazon, Tuxá, Xukurú, Pankararú, and Otí, all became extinct relatively early and are all poorly documented. Only short wordlists are available for **Tuxá [tud]**, **Xukurú [xoo]**, and **Pankararú [paz]** (Meader 1978; Loukotka 1955; Lapenda 1962), but even these are of dubious quality, elicited mostly from rememberers. Meader (1978) shows that Pankararú [paz] displays Tupian lexical influence. The only information available on **Oti [oti]** is also a few wordlists, collected before the last speakers died in the early 20th century (Quadros 1892; von Ihering 1907; Borba 1908).

8 CHACO AND THE SOUTHERN CONE

There are eight known isolates in the Chaco and the Southern Cone, i.e. in a region which spans from the (Gran) Chaco, a semi-arid lowland south of the Amazon, to Tierra del Fuego, the Southern tip of South America. The languages of the Chaco (including Guaycuruan, Mascoyan, Matacoan, Zamucoan, and Tupian languages) share some structural characteristics, but Campbell (2013:287) notes that they are overall limited and concludes that the "we should not declare the existence of a Chaco linguistic area". Only one of the isolates in the Chaco has known living speakers, as does also one isolate in Tierra del Fuego, reflecting the extinction of most indigenous languages in an area that has been colonized intensively by Europeans e.g. for cattle breeding.

8.1 Vilela [vil]

Once spoken in the Chaco, and still remembered by a few, Vilela shares some cultural vocabulary with the neighbouring extinct isolate Lule (Section 8.3) (Viegas Barros 2001), but otherwise the two are clearly distinct (Zamponi 2008:li–lv). Work is still on-going as to whether the two can be shown to be ultimately related on a very deep level. Aspects of Vilela grammar and lexicon have been described in, e.g. Balmori (1998), Lozano (2006), and Golluscio (2015).

8.2 Yámana [yag]

The Yámana language on Tierra del Fuego, also called Yaghan, has currently only one living native speaker. There are a number of grammatical descriptions, see Adelaar (2004:567–578) for a good overview. Yámana has an intriguing verb stem selection system. The object of a transitive clause and the subject of an intransitive clause determines the verb stem, i.e., in an ergative-like alignment.

8.3 Extinct languages of the Chaco and the South

Lule was spoken in the Gran Chaco, in contact with Vilela (see Section 8.1). There are a number of early descriptions which include grammatical information (Hervás y Panduro no date; Machoni de Cerdeña (1877 [1732]); Zamponi 2008 [1732]). **Guachi** was spoken in the Eastern Chaco and is poorly documented. The best case for Guachi relatedness is with Guaycurúan (Viegas Barros 2004), but the parallels are still insufficient. **Payagua** was spoken in the southern Chaco until about 1900. The best case for Payaguá relatedness is, again, with Guaycurúan and/or Guachi (Viegas Barros 2004), but again, the parallels are insufficient.

Puelche [pue] was spoken in Patagonia in central Argentina up to the early 20th century. A grammatical description, based on work carried out with the last speaker in the 1950s, is Casamiquela (1983). The parallels with Chon or Chon-Querandí (Viegas Barros 2005; 2006a; 2006b) are interesting but not conclusive. **Kunza [kuz]** (or Atacameño) was spoken in the Atacama desert in northern Chile. Its lexicon is well documented (e.g., Vilte Vilte 2004), and shows no significant resemblance to other languages. Its grammatical structure is poorly known. **Chono** was spoken on the Chilean Pacific coast and is also poorly documented, known only from short missionary translations, brought to light relatively recently (Bausani 1975). There are lexical parallels with Mapuche as well as Qawesqar (Trivero Ribera 2005:82), but the core is clearly unrelated.

9 CONCLUSION: NON-ISOLATES OF SOUTH AMERICA

To conclude we discuss evidence for genealogical relatedness of some South American languages that are often cited as isolates. The dialect survey by Croese (1985) shows that **Mapudungun [huh]** and **Huilliche [arn]** are distinct enough to be considered different languages. **Ticuna [tca]** is related to **Yurí** [no isocode], as documented in the 19th century (Orphão de Carvalho 2009; Goulard and Montes 2013; Seifart and Echeverri 2014), and both may be related to the language spoken by the uncontacted group **Carabayo [cby]** (Seifart and Echeverri 2014). Viegas Barros (1990) analyzed lexical data from **Kawesqar [alc]** and its extinct relatives and found reason to distinguish a Southern Kawesqar and a Central Kawesqar as separate languages. Torero (2002) attributed the lexical items shared between **Cholón [cht]** and the poorly documented **Hibito [hib]** to loans, but we prefer the interpretation that the majority represent inheritance (Adelaar 2004:461–463), in which case the two form a family.

REFERENCES

Adelaar, Willem F.H. 1988. Search for the Culli Language. *Continuity and Identity in Native America: Essays in Honor of Benedikt Hartmann*, vol. I, ed. by M. Jansen, Peter van der Loo and R. Manning, 111–131. (Indiaanse Studies). Leiden: E. J. Brill.

Adelaar, Willem F.H. 2004. *The Languages of the Andes*. Cambridge: Cambridge University Press.

Alicea, Neftalí. 1975a. Análisis fonémico preliminar del idioma taushiro. *Datos Etno-Lingüísticos* 23: 1–65.

Alicea, Neftalí. 1975b. *Análisis preliminar de la gramática del idioma Taushiro*. (Datos Etno-Lingüísticos 24). Lima: Instituto Lingüístico de Verano. www.sil.org/americas/peru/html/pubs/show_work.asp?id=3413.

Anderson, Loretta and Mary Ruth Wise. 1963. Contrastive Features of Candoshi Clause Types. *Studies in Peruvian Indian Languages* 1: 67–102. (Summer Institute of Linguistics: Publications in Linguistics 9). The Summer Institute of Linguistics and the University of Texas at Arlington.

Angenot-de-Lima, Geralda. 2002. *Description Phonologique, Grammaticale et Lexicale du Moré, Langue Amazonienne de Bolivie et du Brésil*. Leiden: Rijksuniversiteit te Leiden.

Anónimo. 1928a. Traduccion de algunas voces de la lengua Guama. *Lenguas de América* 6: 382–393. (Manuscritos de La Real Biblioteca, Vol. 1, Catálogo de La Real Biblioteca). Madrid.

Anónimo. 1928b. Vocabulario Andaqui-Español. *Lenguas de América* 6: 175–195. (Manuscritos de La Real Biblioteca, Vol. 1, Catálogo de La Real Biblioteca). Madrid.

Aragon, Carolina Coelho. 2014. *A Grammar of Akuntsú, a Tupían Language*. Mānoa: University of Hawai'i at Mānoa.

Arinterol, Basilio. 2000. Warao. *Manual de Lenguas Indígenas de Venezuela* (Serie Orígenes), Esteban Emilio Mosonyi and Jorge Carlos Mosonyi, 116–183. Caracas: Fundación Bigott.

Arrieta, Anita E. 1993. Tipología morfosintactica del timote. *Revista de Filología y Lingüística de la Universidad de Costa Rica* XIX, no. 2: 99–110.

Arrieta, Anita E. 1998. Tipología fonológica del timote. *Revista de Filología y Lingüística de la Universidad de Costa Rica* XXIV, no. 1: 85–100.

Bacelar, Laércio Nora. 2004. *Gramática da língua Kanoê*. Nijmegen, Netherlands: Katholieke Universiteit Nijmegen. http://webdoc.ubn.kun.nl/mono/b/bacelar_l/ gramdalik.pdf.

Balmori, Clemente Hernando. 1998. Diccionario vilela: a, b, c. *Clemente Hernando Balmori. Textos de un lingüista*, ed. by Diana Balmori, 139–252. La Coruña: Ediciós do Castro.

Bausani, Alessandro. 1975. Nuovi materiali sulla lingua chono. *Linguistica – Folklore – Storia americana – Sociologia*, vol. 3, Ernesta Cerulli and Gilda Della Ragione, 107–116. (Atti Del XL Congresso Internazionale Degli Americanisti (Roma – Genova, 3–10 Settembre 1972)). Roma/ Génova: Roma/ Génova: Genoa: Tilgher.

Birchall, Joshua. 2013. A look at the Rokorona language. *Sprachtypologie und Universalienforschung* 66, no. 3: 257–271.

Blench, Roger. 2012. The Role of Agriculture in Explaining the Diversity of Amerindian Languages. *The Past Ahead: Language, Culture and Identity in the Neotropics*, ed. by Christian Isendahl, 13–37. Uppsala: Acta Universitas Uppsaliensis.

Bolaños, Katherine. 2011. Evaluando la relación lingüística de Kakua y Puinave, dos lenguas del noroeste Amazónico, Colombia. CILLA V, 6 Octubre 2011.

Borba, Telemáco. 1908. *Actualidade Indígena (Paraná, Brazil)*. Curitiba: Impressora Paranaense.

Borman, M.B. 1962. Cofán phonemes. *Studies in Ecuadorian Indian Languages 1*, vol. 1, ed. by Benjamin F. Elson, 45–59. Norman: Summer Institute of Linguistics of the University of Oklahoma. www.sil.org/acpub/repository/10288.pdf.

Borman, M.B. 1976. *Vocabulario cofán: Cofán-castellano, castellano-cofán*. (Serie de Vocabularios Indígenas "Mariano Silva Y Aceves" 19). Quito: Instituto Lingüístico de Verano.

Bowern, Claire, Hannah Haynie, Catherine Sheard, Barry Alpher, Patience Epps, Jane Hill and Patrick McConvell. 2014. Loan and Inheritance Patterns in Hunter-Gatherer Ethnobiological Nomenclature. *Journal of Ethnobiology* 34, no. 2: 195–227.

Bowern, Claire, Patience Epps, Russell Gray, Jane Hill, Keith Hunley, Patrick McConvell and Jason Zentz. 2011. Does Lateral Transmission Obscure Inheritance in Hunter-Gatherer Languages? *PLoS ONE* 6, no. 9: 1–9.

Brüning, Hans Heinrich. 2004. *Mochica Wörterbuch: Diccionario Mochica: Mochica-Castellano, Castellano-Mochica*. Universidad de San Martín de Porres, Escuela Profesional de Turismo y Hotelería.

Buchwald, Otto von. 1919. Migraciones sudamericanas. *Boletín de la Sociedad Ecuatoriana de Estudios Históricos Americanos* 3: 227–236.

Campbell, Lyle. 2012. Classification of the Indigenous Languages of South America. *The Indigenous Languages of South America: A Comprehensive Guide*, ed. by Lyle Campbell and Verónica Grondona, 59–166. (The World of Linguistics 2). Berlin, Boston: De Gruyter Mouton.

Campbell, Lyle. 2013. Language Contact and Linguistic Change in the Chaco. *Revista Brasileira de Linguística Antropológica* 5, no. 2: 259–292.

Campbell, Lyle and William J. Poser. 2008. *Language Classification: History and Method*. Cambridge: Cambridge University Press.

Carlin, Eithne B. and Jimmy Mans. 2014. Movement Through Time in the Southern Guianas: Deconstructing the Amerindian Kaleidoscope. *In and Out of Suriname: Language, Mobility and Identity*, ed. by Eithne B. Carlin, Isabelle Léglise, Bettina Migge and Paul B. Tjon Sie Fat, 76–100. Leiden: Brill.

Carrera, Fernando de la. 1880. *Arte de la lengua Yunga de los valles del Obispado de Trujillo*. Lima: Imprenta Liberal.

Casamiquela, Rodolfo M. 1983. *Nociones de Gramática del Gününa Küne: Présentation de la langue des Tehuelche Septentrionaux Australs (Patagonie Continentale)*. Éditions du Centre National de la Recherche Scientifique.

Castellví, Marcelino de. 1940. La Lengua Tinigua. *Journal de la Société des Américanistes* XXXII: 93–101.

Constenla Umaña, Adolfo. 1991. *Las lenguas del áreas intermedia. Indroducción a su estudio areal*. San José: Editorial de la Universidad de Costa Rica.

Costa, Januacele da. 1999. *Ya:thê, a última língua nativa no Nordeste do Brasil: aspectos morfofonológicos y morfo-sintáticos*. Recife: Universidade Federal de Pernambuco.

Cox, Doris. 1957. Candoshi Verb Inflection. *International Journal of American Linguistics* 23: 129–140.

Créqui-Montfort, Georges de and Paul Rivet. 1913. Linguistique Bolivienne: La Famille Linguistique Čapakura. *Journal de la Société des Américanistes* X: 119–172.

Crevels, Mily. 2002. *Itonama o Sihnipadara, Lengua no Clasificada de la Amazonia Boliviana*. (Estudios de Lingüística 16). Departamento de Filología Española, Lingüística General y Teoría de Literatura, Universidad de Alicante.

Crevels, Mily. 2007. South America. *Encyclopedia of the World's Endangered Languages*, ed. by Christopher Moseley, 103–196. London and New York: Routledge.

Crevels, Mily. 2012a. Itonama. *Ambito Andino*, vol. 2, ed. by Mily Crevels and Pieter Muysken, 233–294. (Lenguas de Bolivia). La Paz: Plural Editores.

Crevels, Mily. 2012b. Canichana. *Amazonía*, vol. 2, Mily Crevels and Pieter Muysken, 415–449. (Lenguas de Bolivia). La Paz: Plural Editores.

Crevels, Mily and Hein van der Voort. 2008. The Guaporé-Mamoré Region as a Linguistic Area. *From Linguistic Areas to Areal Linguistics*, ed. by Pieter Muysken, 151–179. (Studies in Language Companion Series 90). Amsterdam, Philadelphia: John Benjamins.

Crevels, Mily and Pieter Muysken. 2012. Cayubaba. *Ambito Andino*, ed. by Mily Crevels and Pieter Muysken, vol. 2, 341–374. (Lenguas de Bolivia). La Paz: Plural Editores.

Croese, Robert A. 1985. Mapuche Dialect Survey. *South American Indian Languages: Retrospect and Prospect*, ed. by Harriet E. Manelis Klein and Louisa Stark, 784–801. Austin: Texas University Press.

Dahl, Östen, Christopher Gillam, David G. Anderson, José Iriarte and Silvia M. Copé. 2011. Linguistic Diversity Zones and Cartographic Modeling: GIS as a Method for Understanding the Prehistory of Lowland South America. *Ethnicity in Ancient Amazonia: Reconstructing Past Identities from Archaeology, Linguistics, and Ethnohistory*, ed. by Alf Hornborg and Jonathan D. Hill, 211–224. Boulder, CO: University Press of Colorado.

Epps, Patience. In press. Amazonian Linguistic Diversity and Its Sociocultural Correlates. *Language Dispersal, Diversification, and Contact: A Global Perspective*, ed. by Mily Crevels and Pieter Muysken. Oxford: Oxford University Press.

Eriksen, Love. 2011. *Nature and Culture in Prehistoric Amazonia: Using G.I.S. to Reconstruct Ancient Ethnogenetic Processes from Archaeology, Linguistics, Geography, and Ethnohistory*. Lund, Sweden: Lund University.

Everett, Daniel L. 1985. Syllable Weight, Sloppy Phonemes, and Channels in Pirahã Discourse. *Proceedings of the Eleventh Annual Meeting of the Berkeley Linguistics Society*, ed. by Mary Niepokuj, Mary van Clay, Vassiliki Nikiforidou and Deborah Feder, 408–416. Berkeley: Berkeley Linguistics Society.

Everett, Daniel L. 2005. Cultural Constraints on Grammar and Cognition in Pirahã: Another Look at the Design Features of Human Language. *Current Anthropology* 46, 4: 621–634.

Fabre, Alain. 1998. *Manual de las lenguas indígenas sudamericanas, I-II*. (LINCOM Handbooks in Linguistics 4–5). München: Lincom.

Fischer, Rafael. 2007. Clause Linkage in Cofán (A'ingae). *Language Endangerment and Endangered Languages: Linguistic and Anthropological Studies with Special Emphasis on the Languages and Cultures of the Andean-Amazonian Border Area*, ed. by Leo W. Wetzels, 381–399. (Lenguas Indígenas de América Latina (ILLA) 5). Leiden: Research School of Asian, African and Amerindian Studies (CNWS), Universiteit Leiden.

Galeote Tormo, Jesús. 2014. Chiquitano (Besïro). *Oriente*, vol. 3, ed. by Pieter Muysken and Mily Crevels, 259–301. (Lenguas de Bolivia). La Paz: Plural Editores.

Gibson, Michael. 1988. *The Muniche Language: With Partial Reference to Verb Morphology*. Reading, UK: University of Reading.

Gibson, Michael Luke. 1996. *El Munichi: Un idioma que se extingue*. (Serie Lingüística Peruana 42). Pucallpa: Instituto Lingüístico de Verano. www.sil.org/americas/peru/html/pubs/show_work.asp?id=596.

Gijn, Erik van. 2006. *A Grammar of Yurakaré*. Nijmegen, Netherlands: Radboud Universiteit. http://webdoc.ubn.ru.nl/mono/g/gijn_e_van/gramofyu.pdf.

Gipper, Sonja. 2011. *Evidentiality and Intersubjectivity in Yurakaré: An Interactional Account*. Radboud Universiteit Nijmegen Ph.D. dissertation.

Girón, Jesús Mario. 2008. *Una Gramática del Wãnsöhöt (Puinave)*. Utrecht: LOT.

Girón, Jesús Mario, Celestino Miraval and Moisés Miraval. 2004. *Recuperación de cantos de baile de la etnia puinave del Departamento de Guainía*. (Tradicions orales colombianos 2). Bogotá: Universidad de Los Andes : CESO : CCELA.

Golluscio, Lucía. 2015. Huellas de trayectorias y contactos en el sistema lingüístico: el vilela (Chaco). *Language Contact and Documentation*, ed. by Bernard Comrie and Lucía Golluscio, 77–120. Berlin: DeGruyter Mouton.

Goulard, Jean Pierre and María Emilia Rodríguez Montes. 2013. Los Yurí/Juri-Tikuna, en el complejo socio-lingüístico del noroeste amazónico. *LIAMES – Línguas Indígenas Americanas* 13: 7–65.

Granados, Héctor. 1998. *Lingüística indígena: la lengua waraw*. Caracas: Editorial Comisión Macuro 500 años.

Granberry, Julian. 1993. *A Grammar and Dictionary of the Timucua Language* (3rd ed.). Tuscaloosa, AL: Tuscaloosa: The University of Alabama Press.

Grasserie, Raoul de la. 1894. *Langue Puquina*. (Langues Américaines). Leipzig: F. Koehler.

Guirardello, Raquel. 1999. *A Reference Grammar of Trumai*. Houston, TX: Houston: Rice University. http://scholarship.rice.edu/handle/1911/19387.

Hammarström, Harald. 2010. The status of the least documented language families in the world. *Language Documentation and Conservation* 4: 177–212.

Hammarström, Harald. 2011. A Note on the Maco [wpc] (Piaroan) Language of the lower Ventuari, Venezuela. *Cadernos de Etnolingüística* 3: 1–11.

Hammarström, Harald. 2014. Basic Vocabulary Comparison in South American Languages. *The Native Languages of South America: Origins, Development, Typology*, ed. by Pieter Muysken and Loretta O'Connor, 56–70. Cambridge: Cambridge University Press.

Hammarström, Harald, Robert Forkel, Martin Haspelmath and Sebastian Bank. 2015. *Glottolog 2.5*. Leipzig: Max Planck Institute for Evolutionary Anthropology. http://glottolog.org.

Hargreaves, Inês. 2007. *Lista de palavras transcritas por Inês Hargreaves, de dois grupos ao norte do Parque Aripuanã, RO*.

Haude, Katharina. 2006. *A Grammar of Movima*. Nijmegen University Ph.D. dissertation. http://repository.ubn.ru.nl/bitstream/2066/41395/1/41395_gramofmo.pdf.

Haude, Katharina. 2009. Hierarchical Alignment in Movima. *International Journal of American Linguistics* 75, no. 4: 513–532.

Hervás y Panduro, Lorenzo. 1787. *Saggio Pratico delle lingue*. (Idea dell'Universo XXI). Cesena: Gregorio Biasini all'Insengna di Pallade.

Hervás y Panduro, Lorenzo. 1800. *Lenguas y naciones Americanas*. (Catálogo de Las Lenguas de Las Naciones Conocidas, Y Numeracion, Division, Y Clases de Estas I). Madrid: Imprenta de la Administración del real arbitrio de beneficencia.

Hervás y Panduro, Lorenzo. 1971. Elementos Grammaticales de la lengua Maipure [sic!]. *Aportes Jesuiticos a la Filología Colonial Venezolana: Tomo II Documentos*, vol. 4/5, ed. by José del Rey Fajardo, 277–288. (Lenguas Indígenas de Venezuela). Caracas: Universidad Católica Andres Bello.

Hervás y Panduro, Lorenzo. no date. *Lingua Lule*.

Hovdhaugen, Even. 2004. *Mochica*. (Languages of the World/Materials 433). München: Lincom.

Howard, Linda. 1967. Camsa Phonology. *Phonemic Systems of Colombian Languages*, ed. Viola G. Waterhouse, 73–87. Norman: Summer Institute of Linguistics.

Howard, Linda. 1977. Camsa: Certain Features of Verb Inflection as Related to Paragraph Types. *Discourse Grammar: Studies in Indigenous Languages of Colombia, Panama, and Ecuador, part 2*, ed. by Robert E. Longacre and Frances Woods, 273–296. (Summer Institute of Linguistics Publications in Linguistics and Related Fields 52(2)). Arlington: Summer Institute of Linguistics and University of Texas at Arlington. www.sil.org/acpub/repository/15975.pdf.

Hugo, Vítor. 1959. *Desbravadores*. São Paulo: Missão Salesiana de Humaitá.

Ihering, Hermann von. 1907. A anthropologia do estado de São Paulo. *Revista do Museu Paulista* VII: 202–257.

Jahn, Alfredo. 1927. *Los Aborígenes del Occidente de Venezuela: Su Historia, Etnografía y Afinidades Lingüísticos*. Caracas: Lit. y Tip. del Comerio.

Jamioy Muchavisoy, José Narciso. 1989. Morfología del verbo Kamëntsa. Santafé de Bogotá: Universidad de los Andes.

Jamioy Muchavisoy, José Narciso. 1992. Tiempo, aspecto y modo en kamentsa. *Memorias del II Congreso del CCELA*, vol. 2, 199–207. (Memorias). Bogotá: Universidad de los Andes, CCELA.

Jamioy Muchavisoy, José Narciso. 1999. Estructuras predicativas del kamëntsa. *Congreso de Lingüística Amerindia y Criolla. Lenguas Aborígenes de Colombia*, 251–284. (Memorias 6). Santafé de Bogotá: CCELA, UNIANDES.

Jijón y Caamaño, Jacinto. 1941. *El Ecuador interandino y occidental antes de la conquista castellana, vol. 2*. Quito: Editorial Ecuatoriana.

Jijón y Caamaño, Jacinto. 1945. Las lenguas del Ecuador preincáico. *Antropología prehispánica del Ecuador*, 69–94. Quito: La prensa catolica.

Jolkesky, Marcelo. 2009. *Macro-Daha: reconstrução de um tronco lingüístico do noroeste amazônico*. Paper presented at the ROSAE - I Congresso Internacional de Lingüística Histórica, Salvador do Bahia.

Juajibioy Chindoy, Alberto. 1962. Breve Estudio preliminar del grupo Aborigen de Sibundoy y su lengua Kamsa en el sur de Colombia. *Boletín del Instituto de Antropología [Universidad de Antioquia]* II, no. 8: 3–33.

Jung, Ingrid. 1989. *Grammatik des Paez: Ein Abriss*. Osnabrück: Universität Osnabrück.

Kaufman, Terrence. 1990. Language History in South America: What We Know and How to Know More. *Amazonian Linguistics. Studies in Lowland South American Languages*, ed. by Doris L. Payne, 13–73. (Texas Linguistics Series). Austin: University of Texas Press.

Kaufman, Terrence. 1994. The Americas. *Atlas of the World's Languages*, ed. by Christopher Moseley and R.E. Asher, 1–76. Cambridge: Cambridge University Press.

Kerke, Simon van de. 2000. Case Marking in the Leko Language. Ensaios sobre lenguas indígenas de las tierras bajas de Sudamérica: Contribuciones al 49o Congreso Internacional de Americanistas en Quito 1997, vol. 1, Hein van der Voort and Simon van de Kerke, 25–37. (Lenguas Indígenas de América Latina (ILLA)). Leiden: Research School of Asian, African and Amerindian Studies (CNWS), Universiteit Leiden.

Kerke, Simon van de. 2002. Complex Verb Formation in Leko. *Current Studies on South American Languages*, vol. 3, ed. by Mily Crevels, Simon van de Kerke, Sérgio Meira and Hein van der Voort, 241–254. (Lenguas Indígenas de América Latina (ILLA)). Leiden: Research School of Asian, African and Amerindian Studies (CNWS), Universiteit Leiden.

Kerke, Simon van de. 2006. Object Cross-Reference in Leko. *What's in a Verb?*, ed. by Grażyna J. Rowicka and Eithne B. Carlin, 171–188. (LOT Occasional Series 5). Utrecht: LOT.

Kerke, Simon van de. 2009. El Leko. *Ambito Andino*, vol. 1, Pieter Muysken and Mily Crevels, 287–332. (Lenguas de Bolivia). La Paz: Plural Editores.

Key, Harold. 1963. *Morphology of Cayuvava*. Austin: University of Texas.

Key, Harold. 1974. *Cayuvava texts*. (Language Data Amerindian Series 4). Dallas: Summer Institute of Linguistics.

Key, Harold. 1975. *Lexicon-Dictionary of Cayuvava-English*. (Language Data Amerindian Series 5). Dallas: Summer Institute of Linguistics.

Key, Harold H. 1967. *Morphology of Cayuvava*. (Janua Linguarum: Series Practica LIII). Berlin: Mouton de Gruyter.

Koch-Grünberg, Theodor. 1913. Abschluß meiner Reise durch Nordbrasilien zum Orinoco, mit besonderer Berücksichtigung der von mir besuchten Indianerstämme. *Zeitschrift für Ethnologie* 45: 448–474.

Koch-Grünberg, Theodor. 1922. Die Völkergruppierung zwischen Rio Branco, Orinoco, Rio Negro und Yapurá. *Festschrift Eduard Seler dargebracht zum 70: Geburtstag von Freunden, Schülern und Verehrern*, ed. by W. Lehmann, 205–266. Stuttgart: Stecker und Schröder.

Koch-Grünberg, Theodor. 1928a. Auake. *Sprachen*, 308–313. (Von Roroima Zum Orinoco: Ergebnisse Einer Reise in Nordbrasilien Und Venezuela in Den Jahren 1911–1913 4). Stuttgart: Strecker und Schröder.

Koch-Grünberg, Theodor. 1928b. Sapará, Purukotó, Wayumará. *Sprachen*, 257–272. (Von Roroima Zum Orinoco: Ergebnisse Einer Reise in Nordbrasilien Und Venezuela in Den Jahren 1911–1913 4). Stuttgart: Strecker und Schröder.

Landaburu, Jon. 1979. *La langue des Andoke*. 36: SELAF.

Landaburu, Jon. 2000. La Lengua Andoque. *Lenguas indígenas de Colombia: una visión descriptiva*, ed. by María Stella González de Pérez and María Luisa Rodríguez de Montes, 275–288. Santafé de Bogotá: Instituto Caro y Cuervo.

Lapenda, Geraldo. 1968. *Estrutura da Língua Iatê: Falada pelos índios Fulniôs em Pernambuco*. Recife: Imprensa Universitaria, Universidade Federal de Pernambuco.

Lapenda, Geraldo Calábria. 1962. O dialecto Xucuru. *Doxa (Revista Oficial do Departamento de Cultura do Diretório Acadêmico da Faculdade de Filosofia de Pernambuco da Universidade do Recife)*. X, no. 10: 11–23.

Lewis, M. Paul, Gary F. Simons, and Charles D. Fennig (eds.). 2015. *Ethnologue: Languages of the World, Eighteenth edition*. Dallas, TX: SIL International. www.ethnologue.com (13 June 2013).

Loukotka, Čestmír. 1968. *Classification of South American Indian Languages*, ed. Johannes Wilbert. Los Angeles: Latin American Center, University of California.

Loukotka, Čestmír. 1949. La Langue Taruma. *Journal de la Société des Américanistes* XXXVIII: 53–82.

Loukotka, Čestmír. 1955. Les langues non-Tupí du Brésil du Nord-Est. *Anais do XXXI Congresso Internacional de Americanistas 31, São Paulo, 1954*, vol. II, ed. by Herbert Baldus, 1029–1054. São Paulo: Anhembi.

Lozano, Elena. 2006. *Textos Vilelas (con notas gramaticales y etnográficas)*, ed. by Lucía A. Golluscio. Buenos Aires: Instituto de Lingüística, Universidad de Buenos Aires.

Luzena, Gerónimo Josef de. no date. *Traducion de la lengua española á la otomaca, taparita y yarura*.

Machoni de Cerdeña, Antonio. 1877 [1732]. *Arte y vocabulario de la lengua lule o tonocoté*. Buenos Aires: Coni.

Maciel, Iraguacema. 1991. *Alguns aspectos fonológicos e morfológicos da língua Máku*. Brasilia: Universidade de Brasília.

Matallana, Baltasar de and Cesareo de Armellada. 1943. Exploración del Paragua. *Boletín de la Sociedad Venezolana de ciencias naturales* VIII, no. 53: 61–110.

Meader, Robert E. 1978. *Indios do Nordeste: Levantamento Sobre Os Remanescentes Tribais do Nordeste Brasileiro*. (Série Lingüística 8). Brasília: Summer Institute of Linguistics.

Meland, D. 1968. *Fulniô Grammar*. (Arquivo Lingüístico 26). Brasilia: Brasilia: ILV.

Michael, Lev and Christine Beier. 2012. *Phonological sketch and classification of Aʔiwa [ISO 639: ash]*.

Middendorf, E.W. 1892. *Das Muchik oder die Chimu-Sprache mit einer einleitung über die culturvölker, die gleichzeitig mit den Inkas und Aimaraàs in Südamerika lebten und einem Anhang über die Chibcha-Sprache*. (Die Einheimischen Sprachen Perus). Leipzig: F. A. Brockhaus.

Migliazza, Ernesto C. 1965. Fonología Makú. *Boletim do Museu Paraense Emílio Goeldi, Série Antropologia* 25: 1–17.

Migliazza, Ernesto C. 1966. Esbôço sintático de um corpus da língua Makú. *Boletim do Museu Paraense Emílio Goeldi, Série Antropologia* 32: 1–38.

Migliazza, Ernesto C. 1978. Maku, Sape and Uruak Languages: Current Status and Basic Lexicon. *Anthropological Linguistics* XX, no. 3: 133–140.

Migliazza, Ernesto C. 1980. Languages of the Orinoco-Amazon Basin: Current Status. *Antropológica* 53: 95–162.

Migliazza, Ernesto C. 1983. Lenguas de la Región Orinoco Amazonas: Estado Actual. *América Indígena* 43: 703–784.

Migliazza, Ernesto C. 1985. Languages of the Orinoco-Amazon Region: Current Status. *South American Indian Languages: Retrospect and Prospect*, ed. by Harriet E. Manelis Klein and Louisa Stark, 17–139. Austin: Texas University Press.

Migliazza, Ernesto C. 2008. *Máku*. Paper presented at the 4th Conference on Endangered Languages and Cultures of Native America, University of Utah.

Monserrat, Ruth Maria Fonini. 2000. A língua do povo Mỹky. Rio de Janeiro: Universidade Federal do Rio de Janeiro.

Monserrat, Ruth Maria Fonini and Elizabeth R. Amarante. 1995. *Dicionário Mỹky-Português*. Rio de Janeiro: Editora Sepeei/SR-5/UFRJ.

Mosonyi, Esteban Emilio. 1966. *Morfología del verbo Yaruro*. Caracas: Universidad Central de Venezuela.

Mosonyi, Esteban Emilio and Jorge Ramón García. 2000. Yaruro (Pumé). *Manual de Lenguas Indígenas de Venezuela*, ed. by Esteban Emilio Mosonyi and Jorge Carlos Mosonyi, 544–593. (Serie Origenes). Caracas: Fundación Bigott.

Muysken, Pieter. 1994. Callahuaya. *Mixed Languages: 15 Case Studies in Language Intertwining*, Peter Bakker and Maarten Mous, 207–211. (Studies of Language and Language Use 13). Amsterdam: Amsterdam: IFOTT.

Muysken, Pieter. 1997. Callahuaya. *Contact Languages: A Wider Perspective*, Sarah Grey Thomason, 427–447. (Creole Language Library 17). Amsterdam: John Benjamins.

Nettle, Daniel. 1999. Linguistic Diversity of the Americas can be reconciled with a recent colonization. *Proceedings of the National Academy of Sciences of the USA* 96: 3325–3329.

Nichols, Johanna. 1990. Linguistic Diversity and the First Settlement of the New World. *Language* 66, no. 3: 475–521. doi:10.2307/414609.

Nimuendajú, Curt. 1925. As Tribus do Alto Madeira. *Journal de la Société des Américanistes* XVII: 137–172.

O'Hagan, Zachary J. 2011. Informe de campo del idioma omurano.

Obregón Muñoz, Hugo and Jorge Díaz Pozo. 1989. *Morfología Yarura*. Maracay: Instituto Universitario Pedagógico Experimental de Maracay.

Olawsky, Knut. 2005. Urarina – Evidence for OVS Constituent Order. *Leiden Papers in Linguistics* 2(2): 43–68.

Olawsky, Knut. 2006. *A Grammar of Urarina*. (Mouton Grammar Library 37). Berlin: Mouton de Gruyter.

Oramas, Luis. 1916. *Materiales para el estudio de los dialectos Ayamán, Gayón, Jirajara, Ajagua*. Caracas: Litografía del Comercio.

Oré, Luis Jerónimo de. 1607. *Rituale seu Manuale Peruanum*. Napels.

Orphão de Carvalho, Fernando. 2009. On the Genetic Kinship of the Languages Tikúna and Yurí. *Revista Brasileira de Linguística Antropológica* 1, no. 2: 247–268.

Palácio, Adair P. 1984. *Guató: a língua dos índios canoeiros do rio Paraguai*. Campinas: São Paulo: Universidade Estadual de Campinas. http://libdigi.unicamp.br/document/?code=vtls000051737.

Palau, Mercedes and Blanca Saiz. 1989. *Moxos: Descripciones exactas e historia fiel de los indios, animales y plantas de la provincia de Moxos en el virreinato del Perú por Lázaro de Ribera, 1786–1794*. Madrid: El Viso.

Payne, David L. 1981. Bosquejo fonológico del Proto-Shuar-Candoshi: evidencias para una relación genética. *Revista del Museo Nacional* 45: 323–377.

Payne, David L. 1989. On proposing deep genetic relationships in Amazonian languages: The case of Candoshi and Maipuran Arawakan languages. Society for the Study of Indigenous Languages of the Americas.

Peeke, Catherine. 1973. *Preliminary Grammar of Auca*. (Summer Institute of Linguistics: Publications in Linguistics 39). The Summer Institute of Linguistics and the University of Texas at Arlington.

Peeke, M. Catherine. 1968. *Preliminary grammar of Auca (Ecuador)*. Bloomington: Indiana University.

Perozo, Laura, Ana Liz Flores, Abel Perozo and Mercedes Aguinagalde. 2008. Escenario histórico y sociocultural del alto Paragua, Estado Bolívar, Venezuela. *Evaluación rápida de la biodiversidad de los ecosistemas acuáticos de la cuenca alta del río Paragua, estado Bolívar*, ed. by Josefa Celsa Señaris, Carlos A. Lasso and Ana Liz Flores, 169–180. (Boletín RAP de Evaluación 49). Arlington, VA: Conservation International.

Pike, Kenneth L. and Rachel Saint. 1962. Auca phonemics. *Studies in Ecuadorian Indian Languages*, vol. 1, ed. by Benjamin Elson, 2–30. Norman: Summer Institute of LInguistics.

Postigo, Adriana Viana. 2009. Alguns apontamentos bibliográficos sobre a língua guató (Macro-Jê). *LIAMES* 9: 99–106.

Proyecto de Documentación del Idioma Muniche. 2009. *Una Breve Descripción del Idioma Muniche*. Cabeceras Aid Project.

Quadros, Francisco R. Ewerton. 1892. Memoria sobre os trabalhos de exploração e observação efetuada pela secção da comissão militar encarregada da linha telegráfica de Uberaba a Cuiabá, de fevereiro a junho de 1889. *Revista do Instituto Histórico e Geográfico Brasileiro* 55, no. 1: 233–260.

Quatra, Miguel Marcello. 2008a. *Estructura básica del verbo jodï*. Caracas: Ediciones IVIC.

Quatra, Miguel Marcello. 2008b. *Bajkewa jkwïkïdëwa-jya jodï ine – Dodo ine. Diccionario básico Castellano – Jodï*. Caracas: Ediciones IVIC.

Querales, Ramón. 2008. *El Ayamán (Ensayo de reconstrucción de un idioma indígena venezolano)*. Barquisimeto: Concejo Municipal de Iribarren.

Ramos Cabredo, Josefina. 1950. Ensayo de un vocabulario de la lengua Tallán o Tallanca. *Cuadernos de Estudio del Instituto de Investigaciones Históricas* 3, no. 8. 11–55.

Rivet, Paul. 1924. La Langue Andakí. *Journal de la Société des Américanistes* XVI: 99–110.

Rivet, Paul. 1942. Un dialecte Hoka Colombien: Le Yurumangí. *Journal de la Société des Américanistes* 34: 1–59.

Rivet, Paul. 1949. Les langues de l'ancien diocèse de Trujillo. *Journal de la Société des Américanistes de Paris* 38: 1–51.

Rivet, Paul and Constant Tastevin. 1920. Affinités du Makú et du Puináve. *Journal de la Société des Américanistes* XII: 69–82.

Rivière, Peter G. 1966. Some ethnographic problems of Southern Guyana. *Folk* 8–9: 301–312.

Rojas Curieux, Tulio Enrique. 1998. *La lengua Paez*. Bogotá: Ministerio de Cultura.

Romero-Figeroa, Andrés. 1985. OSV as the basic order in Warao. *Lingua* 66(2–3). 115–134. doi:10.1016/S0024–3841(85)90281–90285.

Romero-Figeroa, Andrés. 1997. *A Reference Grammar of Warao*. (LINCOM Studies in Native American Linguistics 6). München: Lincom.

Rosenblat, Angel. 1936. Los Otomacos y Taparitas de los llanos de Venezuela. Estudio etnográfico y lingüístico. *Tierra Firme* 1, no. 4: 227–377.

Sakel, Jeanette. 2004. *A Grammar of Mosetén*. (Mouton Grammar Library 33). Berlin: Mouton de Gruyter.

Sakel, Jeanette. 2009. Mosetén and Chimane (Tsimane'). *Ambito Andino*, vol. 1, ed. by Mily Crevels and Pieter Muysken, 333–375. (Lenguas de Bolivia). La Paz: Plural Editores.

Schmidt, Max. 1905. *Indianerstudien in Zentralbrasilien: Erlebnisse und ethnologische Ergebnisse einer Reise in den Jahren 1900 bis 1901*. Berlin: Dietrich Reimer.

Seifart, Frank and Juan Alvaro Echeverri. 2014. Evidence for the Identification of Cara-bayo, the Language of an Uncontacted People of the Colombian Amazon, as Belong-ing to the Tikuna-Yurí Linguistic Family. *PLoS One* 9, no. 4e: 94814.

Seifart, Frank, Doris Fagua, Jürg Gasché and Juan Alvaro Echeverri (eds.). 2009. *A Multi-media Documentation of the Languages of the People of the Center. Online Publication of Transcribed and Translated Bora, Ocaina, Nonuya, Resígaro, and Witoto Audio and Video Recordings with Linguistic and Ethnographic Annotations and Descrip-tions.* Nijmegen: The Language Archive. https://hdl.handle.net/1839/00-0000-0000-001C-7D64-2@view.

Seler, Eduard. 1902. Die Sprache der Indianer von Esmeraldas. *Gesammelte Abhandlun-gen zur amerikanischen Sprach- und Alterthumskunde*, vol. I, 49–64. Berlin: A. Asher.

Slocum, Marianna C. 1986. *Gramática Páez.* Loma Linda: Editorial Townsend. www.sil.org/americas/colombia/pubs/abstract.asp?id=20108.

Sturtevant, William C. 2005. History of Research on the Native Languages of the South-east. *Native Languages of the Southeastern United States* (Studies in the anthropology of North American Indians), ed. by Heather Kay Hardy and Janine Scancarelli, 8–65. Lincoln: University of Nebraska Press.

Tadmor, Uri, Martin Haspelmath and Bradley Taylor. 2010. Borrowability and the notion of basic vocabulary. *Diachronica* 27, no. 2: 226–246. doi:10.1075/dia.27.2.04tad.

Tessmann, Günter. 1930. *Die Indianer Nordost-Perus: grundlegende Forschungen für eine systematische Kulturkunde.* Hamburg: Friederichsen, de Gruyter.

Teza, Emile. 1868. Saggi Inediti di lingue Americane. *Annali delle Università Toscane (parte prima): Scienze Neologiche* X. 117–143.

Thomason, Sarah G. and Daniel L. Everett. 2001. Pronoun borrowing. *Proceedings of the Berkeley Linguistic Society* 27: 301–315.

Tobar Gutiérrez, María Elena. 1995. *Modo, aspecto y tiempo en Cofán.* Bogotá: Univer-sidad de los Andes.

Tobar Ortiz, Nubia. 2000. La Lengua Tinigua: Anotaciones fonológicas y morfológicas. *Lenguas indígenas de Colombia: una visión descriptiva*, ed. by María Stella González de Pérez and María Luisa Rodríguez de Montes, 669–679. Santafé de Bogotá: Instituto Caro y Cuervo.

Torero, Alfredo. 2002. *Idiomas de los Andes: lingüística e historia.* Lima: IFEA, Instituto Francés de Estudios Andinos : Editorial Horizonte.

Trivero Ribera, Alberto. 2005. *Los primeros pobladores de Chiloé.* (Working Paper Series 25). Uppsala: Ñuke Mapuförlaget.

Tuggy, John C. 1966. *Vocabulario candoshi de Loreto.* (Serie Lingüística Peruana 2). Yarinacocha: Instituto Lingüístico de Verano. www.sil.org/americas/peru/html/pubs/show_work.asp?id=2444.

Vaquero, Antonio. 1965. *Idioma Warao: Morfología, Sintaxis, Literatura.* (Estudios Venezolanos Indígenas). Caracas: Editorial Sucre.

Vasconcelos, Ione P. 2004. *Aspectos da fonologia e morfologia da língua Aikanã.* Maceió: Universidade Federal de Alagoas.

Vergara y Vergara, Jose Maria and Evaristo Delgado. 1860. The Indians of Andaqui, New Grenada. *Bulletin American Ethnological Society* I: 53–72.

Viegas Barros, José Pedro. 1990. Dialectología Qawasqar. *Amerindia* 15: 43–73.

Viegas Barros, José Pedro. 2005. *Voces en el viento: Raíces lingüísticas de la Patagonia.* Buenos Aires: Ediciones Mondragon.

Viegas Barros, José Pedro. 2001. Evidencias de la relación genética lule-vilela. *LIAMES* 1: 107–126.

Viegas Barros, José Pedro. 2004. *Guaicurú no, macro-Guaicurú sí: Una hipótesis sobre la clasificación de la lengua Guachí (Mato Grosso do Sul, Brasil)*. Buenos Aires: CONICET – Instituto de Lingüística, Universidad de Buenos Aires. Manuscript.

Viegas Barros, José Pedro. 2006a. Reconstruyendo la morfosintaxis del proto-Chon. Paper presented at the "Avances en Lingüística Histórico-Comparativa Aborigen Sudamericana" en el 52° Congreso Internacional de Americanistas, Sevilla, 17–21 de julio de 2006.

Viegas Barros, José Pedro. 2006b. Proto-Chon Cultural Reconstructions from the Vocabulary. Paper presented at the Historical Linguistics and Hunter-Gatherer Populations in Global Perspective, Workshop at the Max Planck Institute for Evolutionary Anthropology, Leipzig 10–12/08/2006.

Vilera Díaz, Diana. 1985. *Introducción morfológica de la lengua Hödi*. Universidad Central de Venezuela.

Vilera Díaz, Diana. 1987. Introducción a morphosintaxis de la lengua Hoti: el lexema nominal. *Boletín de lingüística* 6: 79–99.

Villarejo, Avencio. 1959. Idiomas y dialectos antiguos y actuales. *La selva y el hombre*, 171–180. Lima: Editorial Ausonia.

Vilte Vilte, Julio. 2004. *Diccionario Kunza-Español: Español-Kunza*. Codelco Chile.

Voort, Hein van der. 2004. *A Grammar of Kwaza*. (Mouton Grammar Library 29). Berlin: Mouton de Gruyter.

Yost, James A. 1981. Twenty Years of Contact: The Mechanisms of Change in Wao ("Auca") Culture. *Cultural Transformations and Ethnicity in Modern Ecuador*, ed. by Norman E. Whitten Jr., 677–704. Chicago: University of Illinois Press.

Zamponi, Raoul. 2002. Notes on Betoi Verb Morphology. *International Journal of American Linguistics* 68, no. 2: 216–241.

Zamponi, Raoul. 2003. *Betoi*. (Languages of the World/Materials 428). München: Lincom.

Zamponi, Raoul. 2008. Sulla fonologia e la rappresentazione ortografica del lule. *Arte y vocabulario de la lengua Lule y Tonocoté*, ed. by Antonio Maccioni, xxi–lviii. Cagliari: Centro di Studi Filogici Sardi.

CHAPTER 11

LANGUAGE ISOLATES IN THE NEW GUINEA REGION

Harald Hammarström

1 INTRODUCTION

The Greater New Guinea area holds a large number of language isolates, belonging to the most diverse and isolate regions of the world (Table 11.1, using figures from Hammarström et al. 2015). In the present understanding, as many as 55 languages in this region are not demonstrably related to any other language. A much lower number of isolates for New Guinea emerges from the overviews of Foley (2000), Ross (2006), Wurm (1982) since these authors tend to give the benefit of the doubt in the opposite direction, or, in the case of Wurm (1982), have far more generous criteria for considering languages to be genealogically related (cf. Shafer 1965). Taking such, more 'lumping', views on the grouping of the languages of the New Guinea area is not without reason. New Guinea is the least studied region both in terms of documentation and genealogical relations (Hammarström and Nordhoff 2012), and there is therefore the expectation that languages which are not obviously related to their neighbours will prove to be so, once they are better documented and their potential relations are studied more intensively. However, empirical evidence from the Americas (Hammarström 2014) suggest that increased documentation and study does not necessarily lead to a drastically different understanding of genealogical relations than that of an initial assessment based on the comparison of basic vocabulary. For this reason we have chosen to adopt a rather strict criterion in the present survey, whereby a language has to have a bone-fide demonstration of relatedness (cf. Campbell and Poser 2008) with other language(s) for it not to be considered an isolate. Every entry, however, does have an individual explanation of why is it considered an isolate as well as a commentary on the possible genealogical links.

All the languages listed in the present survey have an attestation that exceeds at least a wordlist of basic vocabulary (Tadmor et al. 2010).[1] Usually a sociolinguistic survey or a vocabulary comparison underlies the language/dialect divisions adopted here (cf. Hammarström 2015) which determines whether a set of varieties count as an isolate or as a small family of more than one language and hence not included in the present paper.[2]

The number of isolates, and the linguistic diversity more generally, has bewildered every generation of Papuan language researchers. The classic view is that the diversity is due to some combination of ancient settlement (49,000 years ago) see Summerhayes et al. 2010 and geography (mountains, forests, swamps, etc.). This view is rarely articulated (but see Axelsen and Manrubia 2014, Gavin and Stepp 2014, Nettle 1999), and explanatory models have yet to be worked out. A different view, argued for the New Guinea area foremost by Laycock (1969, 1982a, b), who had considerable fieldwork and surveying experience from the Sepik region, is that the key to the diversity lies in a conscious ideology on the part of the speakers to keep and accentuate linguistic

TABLE 11.1 NUMBERS ON ISOLATES AND FAMILIES IN THE NEW GUINEA REGION COMPARED TO OTHER CONTINENTS

	# languages	# isolates	% families	% isolates	entropy	% lgs/lineage
New Guinea Area	2140	55	72	43%	2.89	16.85
Australia	343	9	23	28%	2.21	10.72
Eurasia	1654	12	23	34%	2.84	47.26
Africa	2207	17	33	34%	2.08	44.14
North America	619	31	40	44%	4.29	8.72
South America	574	64	43	60%	5.01	5.36

Source: All figures are computed from Hammarström et al. (2015).

Note: Entropy is a systematic measure of the diversity of a distribution (here, the division of languages into lineages), whereby a high entropy means high diversity, and vice versa.

identity. Impressionistically there is a concentration of isolates in different lowland areas, both south and north of the cordillera. This result, if it holds up under a more stringent formulation, would speak in favour of geographic determinism, rather than social factors.

For the sake of presentation, isolates are grouped into five geographic areas, moving roughly from West to East: East Nusantara, North Indonesian Papua (Mamberamo), Southern Fringe and Lowlands, Sepik, and, finally, East Papuan Islands. We provide the ISO 639–3[3] code, some sociolinguistic information, grammatical information when available, and a selection of references for each isolate. Fuller lists of bibliographical references can be found in Glottolog 2.6 (Hammarström et al. 2015). Unless otherwise noted, speaker numbers are from Lewis et al. (2015), the most comprehensive source available.

2 EAST NUSANTARA

2.1 Tambora [xxt] (extinct)

The speakers of the Tambora language of Central Sumbawa fell victim to a gigantic volcanic eruption in 1815, and the language must have gone extinct after the subsequent death of a few survivors. Of the language, only a wordlist of some 50 items remains, which is analyzed as far as possible in Donohue (2007). Save for a small number of loans, the lexical items are completely different from the surrounding Austronesian languages and non-Austronesian languages further east.

2.2 Maybrat

Maybrat is spoken by a sizeable population (~ 20,000) in the central area of the Bird's Head of Indonesian Papua. The language has a divergent dialect known as Karon Dori (Dol 2007:8), which is sometimes counted as a separate language. Maybrat is described in a modern grammar (Dol 2007). The language has long been hypothesized as belonging to a larger grouping in some constellation with other Bird's Head languages, but the lexical and grammatical evidence is insufficient for concluding a genealogical relation (see Klamer and Holton in press and references therein). Like many other Bird's Head languages, Maybrat is a very isolating SVO language, and is famous for lacking grammaticalized tense or aspect (Dahl 2001).

2.3 Abun [kgr]

Abun is spoken by some 3,000 speakers in the north-central area of the Bird's Head of Indonesian Papua, to the west of Mpur. Abun is described in a modern grammar (Berry and Berry 1999). The language has long been hypothesized as belonging to a larger grouping in some constellation with other Bird's Head languages, but the lexical and grammatical evidence is insufficient for concluding a genealogical relation (see Klamer and Holton in press and references therein). Like many other Bird's Head languages, Abun is a very isolating SVO language. Abun has a three-way tonal contrast (Berry and Berry 1999:20–22) but with low functional load, except for distinguishing the third person singular versus plural. Abun has adopted both maritime technology and terminology from Biak (Berry and Berry 1999:5–6), an Austronesian language in the vicinity.

2.4 Mpur [akc]

Mpur is spoken by some 7,000 speakers in the north-central area of the Bird's Head of Indonesian Papua, to east of Abun. Mpur is documented in a series of publications by Odé (2002a,b, 2004). The language has long been hypothesized as belonging to a larger grouping in some constellation with other Bird's Head languages, but the lexical and grammatical evidence is insufficient for concluding a genealogical relation (see Klamer and Holton in press and references therein). Like many other Bird's Head languages, Abun is a fairly isolating SVO language. Mpur uses tone for lexical contrast distinguishing four tonemes per syllable: high, midrising, mid/midfalling, and low (Odé 2002a).

2.5 Mor [moq]

Mor[4] is spoken by some 30 speakers (out of an ethnic group of 100 individuals) in the swampy lowlands along the Bomberai and Budidi Rivers on the Bomberai Peninsula. The only published data on Mor is the wordlists in Smits and Voorhoeve (1998), but on-going documentation is being conducted by Harald Hammarström. The language was swept into the Trans New Guinea family in spite of the lack of positive evidence in favour of this hypothesis (Voorhoeve 1975a:431), and subsequent examinations, *pace* obvious loans, find little evidence for this or any other relation with neighbouring languages. Mor is a SOV language with postpositions, alienability/inalienability distinction, reduplicated adjectives, and serial verbs (own field data).

2.6 Tanahmerah [tcm]

Tanahmerah,[5] also known as Sumeri, is the language of the area with the same name along the Gondu and Bapai Rivers of the northeast of the Bomberai Peninsula. The language was grouped together with the Mairasi languages to the southeast into the Trans New Guinea family on the basis of resemblant pronoun forms (Voorhoeve 1975a:424–431, Ross 2005:32), but this remains the only argument for this classification and, as such, insufficient. The language is typically listed as having around 500 speakers, but no researcher is recorded to have surveyed the speech community in situ. Essentially nothing is known of the grammar (Anceaux 1958), and documentation of the language is a high priority (Hammarström 2010b).

3 NORTH INDONESIAN PAPUA (MAMBERAMO)

3.1 Kehu [khh]

Kehu is spoken by some 200 people in the swampy lowland plain along the Poronai River to the east of the city of Nabire in Papua, Indonesia. Until recently, Kehu was one of Papua's most enigmatic languages with only two unpublished wordlists, but a longer published wordlist is now available thanks to the work of Kamholz (2012) with two ex-situ speakers. Kamholz (2012) shows that Kehu has tonal contrasts and is SOV, but not much more can be deduced about its grammar. The lexicon shows little resemblance to any of the surrounding languages (Kamholz 2012:252–254), but the unusually small sound inventory is reminiscent of the Lakes Plain languages.

3.2 Masep [mvs]

Masep is spoken in a single village just east of the mouth of the Mamberamo River on the north coast of Papua, Indonesia. Masep was first surveyed by van der Leeden (1954); next by the Summer Institute of Linguistics (SIL) in 1976 (Silzer and Heikkin-en-Clouse 1991:63, 94); and by Clouse, Donohue, and Ma in 1998 (Clouse et al. 2002). All three surveys found only 30–40 speakers but also found that the language was used by all ages and included spouses from the neighbouring village of Subu (Airoran speaking) who learned the language as adults (Clouse et al. 2002:4,11). Even though all Masep speakers are (at least) bilingual, this data makes Masep the smallest language on the planet attested in stable transmission across three generations. The only published information on the structure of Masep are the notes in Clouse et al. (2002:5–7) which show it to be a case-marking SOV language. The lexicon is completely different from neighbouring languages, and Masep is therefore considered an isolate (Clouse et al. 2002:9).

3.3 Burmeso [bzu]

Burmeso is spoken by some 250 people in and around the village of the same name along the eastern banks of middle and lower Mamberamo River in Indonesian Papua. Voorhoeve (1975b) classified Burmeso as a language isolate based on early wordlists available to him. Much more extensive materials collected by Donohue (2001) rein-force this position, as Burmeso, apart from being SOV, is typologically anomalous in the region. The only published data on Burmeso grammar is the description of the nom-inal class system by Donohue (2001). Six classes of nouns need to be distinguished to account for singular and plural agreement behaviour which also interacts with animacy marking.

3.4 Abinomn [bsa]

Abinomn is spoken by some 300 people in around the Baso tributary of the Idenburg branch of the Mamberamo River, not far from the Foya Mountains. Since it was first discovered by researchers to be a separate language, it has been listed as an isolate (Silzer and Heikkinen 1984:24) given the lack of similarity in vocabulary to all sur-rounding languages. The only published information regarding the linguistic features of Abinomn are the notes on the segmental inventory (Donohue 2007:529) and overt dual marking on nouns (Donohue and Musgrave 2007:365–366) extracted from Mark Donohue's field notes.

3.5 Dem [dem]

Spoken by some 1,000 individuals of Indonesian Papua near the headwaters of the Rouffaer branch of the Mamberamo River. The first publication with data on Dem was by Le Roux (1950) together with a careful analysis of the data. Le Roux (1950b:806–807) concluded that although Dem had words in common with the Dani and other highlands languages, it had so many unique words that "it merits being represented as separate on the map" (by which he may have meant language isolate in the sense of this paper). A lexicostatistical study involving the same highlands languages concluded Dem to be distantly related at least to the Dani languages (Larson 1977:14). But the cognation judgments involving Dem (Larson 1977:9–12, 39–40) look overly optimistic in that a match is judged if at least one segment matches, even as this procedure yields inconsistent sound correspondences. Remaining genuine matches are, however, better interpreted as borrowings into Dem than common inheritance (Larson 1977:16–17). Dem has a body-tally counting system (Le Roux 1950a:II:531) which seems to point to an areal connection with the Mek languages further east (Heeschen 1978). No new data on Dem grammar has surfaced since the phraselist in Le Roux (1950). This data allows Dem to be analyzed as an SOV language. Fieldwork on Dem is a high priority.

3.6 Damal [uhn]

Damal is spoken by some 14,000 people in the highlands of Indonesian Papua southeast of the source of the Kemandoga River. The language is featured in the careful analysis of Le Roux (1950b) who considered the language to have "its own vocabulary" and suspected that many Moni loans had crept into the list through a bilingual informant (Le Roux 1950b:806). A lexicostatistical study concluded Damal to be distantly related to surrounding highlands languages (Larson 1977:14). But the cognation judgments involving Damal (Larson 1977:9–12, 39–40) look overly optimistic in that a match is judged if at least one segment matches, even as this procedure yields inconsistent sound correspondences. Little exists in the way of published grammatical description of Damal. Voorhoeve (1975a:410–411) contains some notes compiled from missionary data available to him at the time[6] and various notes emanating from the fieldwork of Mark Donohue (Musgrave and Donohue 2007:5). From these, some basic typological features can be gleaned, such as the SOV word order of Damal.

3.7 Elseng [mrf]

Elseng is spoken by some 300 people in the swampy lowlands southwest of the Lake Sentani area. The language was first reported by Voorhoeve (1971:70–72) who saw a small amount of lexical overlap with the Border family of languages but preferred to interpret these as loans. The affiliation with the Border family still remains the most promising hypothesis for the genealogical affiliation of Elseng. Very little original data is available on Elseng, and that which exists emanates from ex-situ speakers (Voorhoeve

1971:70–72, Burung 2000, Laycock 1977). All these researchers had difficulties eliciting a full pronoun system for Elseng, leading Laycock (1977) to infer the lack of pronominal distinctions beyond 'me' versus 'the rest', and this made its way into some secondary literature as the smallest known pronoun inventory (e.g., Mühlhäusler 1990). However, Mark Donohue (personal communication, 2008) was able to elicit a minimal-augmented pronoun system for Elseng (cf. Harbour 2014:133–134). Only a modicum of data on Elseng grammar is available, but this is enough to gauge that Elseng is an SOV language (Voorhoeve 1971:72, Burung 2000).

3.8 Kapauri [khp]

Kapauri is spoken by some 200 people on the Idenburg (Taritatu) branch of the upper Mamberamo River. The first mention of Kapauri as a separate language along with language data (40 words) is Voorhoeve (1975b:45) based on a wordlist furnished by Myron Bromley. Voorhoeve (1975b) grouped Kapauri with the Kaure languages based on some lexical correspondences. However, a newer evaluation of the lexical relationships sheds considerable doubt on a genetic relation between the Kaure languages and Kapauri (Rumaropen 2006:13), since newer lexicostatistical figures are only in the range 5–6% (cf. Foley in press-a). A short wordlist (40 words) appears in Voorhoeve (1975b). There are 250 words and 15 sentences that will appear in an SIL Indonesia survey report (Rumaropen 2006), which also mentions translated Bible portions. The unpublished survey reports referred to in Silzer and Heikkinen (1984:31) may contain further wordlists. At present, Kapauri is being transmitted to the younger generation and is thus not an endangered language (Rumaropen 2006).

3.9 Kimki [sbt]

Kimki is spoken by some 500 people east of the Sobger tributary of the upper Mamberamo close to the Indonesia-PNG border. A tiny 11-word list of what is probably Kimki (Hammarström 2008b) was taken down as early as 1914 (Langeler 1915), but this wordlist has lingered in the unknown. Otherwise, references to Kimki go back no earlier than to 1978 in unpublished SIL Indonesia survey manuscripts (Silzer and Heikkinen 1984, Silzer and Heikkinen-Clouse 1991). The language is listed as "unclassified" (Silzer and Heikkinen 1984, Silzer and Heikkinen-Clouse 1991) until between 1996 and 2000 when Grimes (2000) groups it with neighbouring Yetfa-Biksi. However, the lexical evidence is not sufficient for concluding a genetic relation between the two (Hammarström 2008a). The only substantial data is an unpublished 250-word list and 15 sentences in an SIL survey report to appear (Rumaropen 2004).[7] The few sentences display SOV word order. At this time, Kimki is being transmitted to children and thus is not an endangered language (Rumaropen 2004).

3.10 Mawes [mgk]

Mawes is spoken by some 850 people in two villages Mawes Dai (West Mawes) and Mawes Wares[8] (East Mawes) in the north coast of Indonesian Papua, west of Jayapura. The language was first reported as a separate language as early as Robidé van der Aa (1879:112) but without accompanying data. Likewise, van der Leeden (1954) noted the separate identity of the language, but no actual language data surfaced until the 20 words of Galis (1955:118). Voorhoeve (1975b:40, 60) classified Mawes as a family-level isolate within his Tor-Lakes-Plain stock using unpublished lexical data (of which 40 words were later published). This classification has been retained in all later listings (e.g. Lewis et al. 2015) except that the Lakes Plain languages were later excised (Clouse 1997), leaving Mawes remaining in a subfamily with Tor and Orya. To be a family-level isolate (Voorhoeve 1975b:16) within the Tor-Lakes-Plain stock means that the language "shares 12%-27% cognates on a 100-word list" with at least one other Tor-Lakes-Plain language. However, the cognate identifications supporting this classification were never published and fail to reproduce using modern lexical data (Foley in press-a). Indeed, another independent count (Wambaliau 2006b) has Mawes cognate percentages never exceeding 6% with any Tor language (nor with any other language in the immediate region). Therefore, it seems best to consider Mawes an isolate until proven otherwise (Hammarström 2010a).

A substantial wordlist was finally published in Smits and Voorhoeve (1994) of which 20 words (Galis 1955) and 40 words (Voorhoeve 1975b) had appeared before. An SIL Indonesia survey report will include 250 words and 15 sentences (Wambaliau 2006b). The sentences show SOV word order.

Though the speaker number is not low (ca. 850), Mawes is under pressure from Indonesian and can be considered an endangered language (Wambaliau 2006b).

3.11 Kosare [kiq]

Kosare is spoken by some 250 people on the Idenburg (Taritatu) branch of the upper Mamberamo River. The Kosare may have been the same people that Oppermann met at Krau (Feuilleteau de Bruyn et al. 1915:664–666), but otherwise the first attestation is the wordlist in Heeschen (1978:41–44). This, along with the survey wordlist of Wambaliau (2006a) remains the only information about the language. Kosare was grouped with Kaure in Wurm (1982:197), presumably based on lexical matches. However, a newer look at the same languages reveal that there are relatively few resemblances to Kaure. Foley (in press-a) lists the matches and accepts the relationship, but in this chapter, we adopt a more cautious stance.

The 15 sentences of Kosare in Wambaliau (2006a) show SOV constituent order.

3.12 Afra [ulf]

Afra is spoken by 115 people in the remote area just east of Mount 6234 in Indonesian Papua. The colonial administration were aware of the Afra people as early as Hoogland (1940), but it is reported as a separate language (called Oeskoe), along with a wordlist, only in Galis (1956).

Voorhoeve (1971) has Afra (under the name Usku) as "unclassified", by which he means that no significant lexical relations are found with its neighbours, or, in other words, a language isolate. In Voorhoeve (1975a), however, it is classified as Trans New Guinea, but no evidence or arguments were ever adduced. Foley (in press-a) finds no significant resemblances to Trans New Guinea.

Published wordlists are collected in Smits and Voorhoeve (1994). There is also an SIL Indonesia survey report to appear which contains 250 words and 15 sentences (Im and Lebold 2006). There is also a brief anthropological report (Dumatubun and Wanane 1989).

At present, there are about 115 speakers, but the language is not immediately in danger. However, the younger generation is just as strong in Indonesian as in Afra (Im and Lebold 2006) which points to a weakening position of the vernacular.

3.13 Powle-Ma [msl]

Powle-Ma is spoken by 250 people principally in the village of Molof, located in the remote area northeast of Mount 6234 in Indonesian Papua. The Molof village was known to the colonial administration as early as Hoogland (1940) and a wordlist appears in Galis (1956).

Voorhoeve (1971) has Powle-Ma (under the name Molof) as "unclassified", by which he means that no significant lexical relations are found with its neighbours or, in other words, a language isolate. In Voorhoeve (1975a), however, it is classified as Trans New Guinea, but no evidence or arguments were ever adduced. Foley (in press-a) finds only flimsy resemblances to Trans New Guinea.

The only data on Powle-Ma available to the present author is the wordlists of Ruma-ropen (2005) and Smits and Voorhoeve (1994), but Foley (in press-a) gives a phoneme inventory for Powle-Ma emanating from the unpublished fieldwork of Mark Donohue. The phoneme inventory exhibits a nine-vowel system which is unusual for this region.

3.14 Sause [sao]

Sause is spoken by some 250 people in the area north of the Idenburg (Taritatu) River east of the Foau language (Lakes Plain family) and south of the Orya (Tor-Orya family) language. Sause is first mentioned as an ethnic group in early patrol reports, based on second-hand information (Hoogland 1939:7). Probably the first mention of Sause as a separate language along with language data (40 words) is Voorhoeve (1975b:45) based on Anceaux's collection of wordlists. Voorhoeve (1975b) grouped Sause with the Kapauri and Kaure languages based on some lexical correspondences. At some point, presumably on geographical grounds, the language started to be listed in the Tor-Lakes Plain stock (Silzer and Heikkinen-Clouse 1991:28–29), and when the Lakes Plain languages were excised (Clouse 1997), it remained as a Tor-related language (Lewis et al. 2015), but the lexical data available fails to support this (Foley in-press-a). The only published data is a wordlist in Smits and Voorhoeve (1994) of which 40 words appear in Voorhoeve (1975b). Mark Donohue has collected a short unpublished wordlist from a transient speaker (personal communication, August 2008). Unpublished survey reports referenced in (Silzer and Heikkinen-Clouse 1991:74) presumably contain wordlists too. Nothing further is known to the present author about the endangerment status of Sause.

4 SOUTHERN FRINGE AND LOWLANDS

4.1 Marori [mok]

Marori (Moraori) is spoken in a single village, located inland near the mouth of the Maro River, some 15 kilometres east of Merauke in Indonesian Papua. For as long as there have been figures available, the Marori has been a small nation: 50 speakers in 1917, 58 in 1925, 68 in 1927, 71 in 1934 (Nevermann 1939:34–37) and only 40 speakers were counted in Boelaars (1950:44). The latter figure led Foley (1986:24) to predict the demise of the language:

> In a shifting situation like this, small language groups may be gradually assimilated and disappear entirely. In the early 1950s Moraori (Boelaars 1950) of southern Irian Jaya was spoken by only about forty people, and the tribe was surrounded by the

numerically much larger and culturally aggressive Marind tribe. All Moraori were bilingual in Marind, and Marind influence on the language was extensive (Drabbe 1954). It is now likely that Moraori is extinct, or nearly so.

On the contrary, the language was not that quick to disappear. When Donohue (no date:10) visited a decade later, he reported that 150 out of the 200 inhabitants of the village knew the language and conjectured,

> It might be that the very history of being surrounded by numerically superior out-siders has made the Moraori more resistant to the sorts of cultural and linguistic decay that now face all the ethnolinguistic groups in the Wasur national park region: a long history of being in contact with a larger group has built in safeguards against rapid assimilation, and has given them a strong sense of local identity that was less essential in a large and culturally aggressive group with ties to many different areas.

Nevertheless, the language could ultimately not withstand the pressure, and by the time of Arka's (2012:151) fieldwork in 2008, the onset of broken transmission had finally come. Presently, the village has 119 inhabitants, and while there are older fully fluent speakers, young Maroris no longer actively speak their language, showing varying degrees of passive competence and shift to Indonesian/Malay and Marind (Arka 2012:151).

Wurm (1975a:327–335) classified Marori as part of his Trans-Fly stock, a subsection of Trans New Guinea including the neighbouring Kanum and Yei languages, on the basis of lexicostatistical figures. The underlying data and cognate judgements were never published, however, and newer independent assessments show much lower lexicostatistical figures with Kanum and Yei (Donohue no date:8). There is in fact a higher number of (near-identical) matches with Marind, which are presumably loans, given the sociolinguistic situation. There remains the possibility that Marori is remotely related to the Trans New Guinea languages (Evans et al. in press), at least that is suggested in its pronoun forms.

Fieldwork by I Wayan Arka has so far resulted in three publications with nuggets of Marori grammar. Arka (2013) shows that nominals in Marori can take a completive aspect clitic =on/=en to express a past property or relation. Marori shows a three-way number system (singular, dual, and plural) where dual is expressed by a combination of non-singular and non-plural morphology rather than by dedicated dual morphology (Arka 2011). The argument marking system of Marori has an unusual combination in that there is a clitic =i which marks patients, recipients as well as affected participants Arka (2012:153–154).

(1) Efi purfam na=i   kaswa=ri-ma-m.
     that person 1SG=U   hit=l-AUX-2/3NonPL.PST
     'The person hit me.'

(2) Robertus/Maria na=i   bosik i=mo-fi.
     Robert/Maria   1SG-U pig   1SG.give AUX-2/3.RPST
     'Robert or Maria gave me a pig.'

(3) Na=i   patar yu-nggo-f
     1SG=U cold 1SG-AUX.1/2-PST
     'I suffered from cold.'

4.2 Tabo [knv]

Tabo (also known as Waia) is spoken by some 3,000 speakers near the mouths of the Fly, Aramia, and Bamu Rivers in Western Province of Papua New Guinea. The first data on Tabo are patrol report wordlists of dubious quality (Austen 1921a,b,c). Later wordlists (Franklin 1973a, Reesink 1976) were also taken down in challenging circumstances. Wurm (1975a:325) classified Tabo as related to the Pahoturi languages but adduced no evidence for this claim, and there is certainly nothing obvious that links the two. Pronouns were not explicitly examined (and perhaps not implicitly either) by Ross (2005), but in any case, they do not match those of the Pahoturi languages. Lexical matches with the Kiwaian languages have been noted since (Reesink 1976:23–25, cf. Wichmann 2012:335–336) but are generally interpreted as loans. If this is correct, then Tabo is a language isolate. However, it is fair to say that there has been very little study of the genealogical relation(s) of Tabo, so the there is room for improvement in the search and comparison. An unpublished grammar of 354 pages was produced for Tabo in 2004 in combination with Bible translation (Schlatter 2003) but is only available in the archives of the Summer Institute of Linguistics at Ukarumpa, Papua New Guinea. This leaves the New Testament translations for the Aramia (No Author Stated 2006a) and Fly River dialects (No Author Stated 2006b) the only published materials available beyond wordlists. Tabo is an SOV language with adjective-noun order and requires a night/day distinction for all non-future tenses (Schlatter 2003).

4.3 Fasu [faa]

Fasu is spoken by a total of 1,200 people in three dialects to the west of Lake Kutubu near the border between the Southern Highlands and Western Provinces of Papua New Guinea. The first data to appear on Fasu is the sketch by Loeweke and May (1966) who subsequently produced a longer grammatical description (Loeweke and May 1980) and a dictionary of the principal dialect Namo Me (May and Loeweke 1981).

Similarities between Fasu and the East Kutubu language Foi were noted from the beginning (Franklin and Voorhoeve 1973), and Franklin (2001) argues that the languages are genealogically related. We take a more cautious interpretation because the most salient similarities adduced by Franklin (2001:311) are elements such as the counting system and the kinship terms which are easily diffused. The languages may be ultimately related (cf. Wichmann 2012:333–335), but resolving this question is difficult without published data on Fiwaga, the sister language of Foi.

Some highlights of Fasu grammar are a tonal distinction for 1PSG/2PSG independent pronouns (Loeweke and May 1980:24–25), verb stem suppletion for number of the subject (Loeweke and May 1980:44), and a well-developed evidentiality system (Loeweke and May 1980:54–66).

4.4 Dibiyaso [dby]

Dibiyaso is spoken by some 1,950 people in the vicinity of the Upper Bamu River in Western Province of Papua New Guinea. It was first made known through a short patrol report vocabulary (Rentoul 1924) which is superseded by the somewhat longer wordlists of Reesink (1976) and Z'graggen (1975).

Dibiyaso is often associated with its northern neighbour Bosavi through a small number of matching lexical items. Reesink (1976:12) gives a number of lexical lookalikes between Dibiyaso and Kaluli. These contain a few fairly convincing comparisons where Dibiyasu *p* corresponds to Kaluli *f*. The items in question are common to the entire Bosavi Watershed group (not just Kaluli), but none are found in the Etoro-Bedamini group. This suggests, that we are dealing with loans between Dibiyaso and the Bosavi watershed group. Similarly, Turumsa and Dibiyaso are said to share as much as 19% lexicostatistical similarity (Tupper 2007), but from a look at the items in question and the sociolinguistic situation, we find a loan scenario preferable to a genealogical one.

No information on the grammar of Dibiyaso is available, and documentation is thus imperative.

4.5 Pawaia [pwa]

Pawaia is spoken by some 4,000 people around the Purari and Pio Rivers in Karimui District, Simbu Province, lapping over into Gulf and Southern Highlands Provinces. The first data to appear on Pawaia is the patrol report vocabularies of Brown (1921) and Murray (1920), and the only substantial study of the language is Trefry's (1965) master's thesis, published as Trefry (1969). It was elaborated through 18 months of monolingual fieldwork by Trefry (1969:1).

Despite vocabulary cognacy of only 6%–8% to Kuman, Pawaia was included in Trans New Guinea family because of pronoun resemblances to Kuman and based on typological similarities. The typological similarities involve function only (Trefry 1969) and thus count for little in terms of genealogical relationship. The pronoun resemblances do not generalize to the Chimbu family (Foley 1986:69–71) and match only an *n* anyway, so they are better accounted for as accidental similarities than as deep relationship.

Pawaia has tone (Trefry 1969:13) and lacks medial clauses (Trefry 1969:26–28), i.e., clauses with a morphologically stripped down verb dependent on a final clause, but otherwise has a typical 'Papuan' typological profile.

4.6 Kibiri-Porome [prm]

The Kibiri-Porome language is spoken in two dialects totalling 1,180 people on some tributaries of the Kikori River in Gulf District, Papua New Guinea.

Franklin (1968, 1975b) counted Kibiri-Porome as one of the few isolates of Gulf District. Ross (2005) suggested an affiliation to the Kiwai languages, but this is based on pronoun resemblances only, and as such insufficient.

So far only a wordlist (Franklin 1973a, Z'graggen 1975) and one or two more notes on the language have been published (Franklin 1975b), so little can be said about its grammar.

4.7 Purari [iar]

Purari, formerly known as Namau, is spoken by some 7,000 people around the mouth of the Purari River in Gulf Province, Papua New Guinea. A wordlist of Purari appears as early as Bevan (1890) collected in the village Evorra.

The relative small number of lexical items shared by Purari and the Eleman languages are arguably loans, contra Brown (1973:286–290), leaving no convincing evidence for a genealogical relationship (Franklin 1995:198).

The first steps towards understanding Purari grammar was done by the missionary John Henry Holmes who also translated the New Testament (Holmes 1920). Ray (1907) is a rational analysis of early Purari scripture materials furnished to him by Holmes, while Holmes himself was struggling to fit Purari grammar into a Latinate frame. For example, Holmes (1913:130) marvels at the lack of comparative and superlative constructions of the kind he was used to seeing from European languages. Further documentation of Purari grammar can be found in Kairi and Kolia (1977) and Dutton (1979), but despite the long history of interaction, many aspects of Purari grammar remain to be described. Purari has a small consonant inventory of only eight stops/liquids and two glides featured in native words (Kairi and Kolia 1977:3, Dutton 1979:7–8). Like so many Papuan languages, Purari is SOV with postpositions and has a richer morphology for verbs than for nouns (Dutton 1979:6–7).

A pidgin language used by the Purari for trading with the seaborn Austronesian-speaking Motu is documented thanks to the efforts of Dutton (1979). The main lexifier for the pidgin is Motu.

4.8 Duna [duc]

Duna is spoken by some 25,000 people (San Roque 2008:1) at Lake Kopiago in the Southern Highlands province and adjacent territories of Papua New Guinea. While Europeans have passed through Duna territory since the mid-1930s, literature referencing the Duna as an ethnic group did not start to appear until the 1960s (e.g., Clancy 1962).

Duna is often grouped with the nearby minority language Bogaya (see Section 4.9) and then further into the Trans New Guinea family. Arguments for the relatedness for Duna and Bogaya are given in Voorhoeve (1975a:395–396), but pronouns do not match sufficiently well for an immediate Trans New Guinea affiliation, and apart from this, there are only capricious lexical similarities to other putative families (Shaw 1973). Voorhoeve (1975a:395–396) and Shaw (1973:53) give lexicostatistical figures above 20% between Duna and Bogaya, but the cognate judgments are never explicitly cited. When we look at the same data, we find such high figures difficult to reproduce, and in any case, loans would be expected from Duna to Bogaya given the sociolinguistic situation. If the proposed genealogical relation is real, it must be quite distant. Until a careful re-evaluation has taken place, also involving the nearby numerically dominant Huli language, we prefer to take a cautious stance and regard the relations of Duna and Bogaya as yet undemonstrated.

Duna is described in an extensive linguistically informed grammar (San Roque 2008). A conspicuous feature of Duna grammar is its elaborate evidentiality system with areal connections to adjacent highland languages. The following examples are from San Roque and Loughnane (2012:397):

(4)   Ita=na=ka   no   mbou   ali=tia.
      pig=SPEC=ERG   1SG garden dig.up=VISUAL
      'The pig dug up my garden.' (I saw it)

(5)   It=na=ka   no   mbou   ali=yaritia.
      pig=SPEC=ERG   1SG garden dig.up=SENSORY
      'The pig dug up my garden.' (I heard the sounds.)

(6)   It=na=ka   no   mbou   ali=rei
      Pig=SPEC=ERG   1SG garden dig.up=RESULT
      'The pig dug up my garden.' (I saw some dug-up earth and pig droppings.)

(7) It=na=ka   no mbou ali=noi.
     pig=SPEC= ERG 1SG garden dig.up=REASONING
     'The pig dug up my garden' (I saw some dug-up earth, and someone told me their
     pig had escaped.)

(8) It=na=ka   no mbou ali=norua.
     Pig=SPEC=ERG 1SG garden dig.up=REPORTED
     'The pig dug up my garden.' (I saw some dug-up earth and pig droppings.)

4.9 Bogaya [boq]

Bogaya is spoken by some 300 people living in the Strickland River valley and Muller
Ranges of the Southern Highlands of Papua New Guinea. It is not known exactly when
after 1930 the first contact between Europeans and the Bogaya occurred, but they are
mentioned in publication as 'Koi'iangi' or 'bush-Duna' from the early 1960s (Sillitoe
1993:3). The Bogaya share many cultural traits with their closest, larger neighbour Duna
(Sillitoe 1993:28).
    Bogaya is often grouped with its larger neighbour Duna (see Section 4.8) and then
further into the Trans New Guinea family. Arguments for the relatedness for Duna and
Bogaya are given in Voorhoeve (1975a:395–396), but pronouns do not match sufficiently well for an immediate Trans New Guinea affiliation, and apart from this, there
are only capricious lexical similarities to other putative families (Shaw 1973). Voorhoeve
(1975a:395–396) and Shaw (1973:53) give lexicostatistical figures above 20% between
Duna and Bogaya, but the cognate judgments are never explicitly cited. When we look
at the same data, we find such high figures difficult to reproduce, and in any case, loans
would be expected from Duna to Bogaya given the sociolinguistic situation. If the proposed genealogical relation is real, it must be quite distant. Until a careful re-evaluation
has taken place, also involving the nearby numerically dominant Huli language, we
prefer to take a cautious stance and regard the relations of Duna and Bogaya as yet
undemonstrated.
    Published information on the Bogaya language is limited to wordlists (Franklin 1973a,
Shaw 1973) so little can be said of Bogaya grammar.

4.10 Kaki Ae [tbd]

Kaki Ae is spoken in some six villages southeast of Kerema in Gulf Province, Papua New
Guinea. At the time of Clifton's (1994) fieldwork in 1993, the language was spoken by
essentially all members of the ethnic group of about 310 members and was still being
transmitted to children. Despite being squeezed in between larger Eleman and Angan languages and the presence of three linguae francae, the Kaki Ae were highly multilingual
but not shifting (Clifton 1994). However, the citation of 630 speakers out of an ethnic
population of 1,280 credited to SIL in 2004 in Lewis et al. (2015) suggests that this may
no longer be the case.
    The first data to appear is the wordlist of Strong (1911). Franklin (1975b:892–893)
initially considered the language an isolate but changed his mind after comparing Kaki
Ae and data from Eleman furnished to him. Franklin (1975b:892–893) found up to 21%
lexicostatistical similarity between Kaki Ae and Eleman and lists the proposed cognates.
However, as observed by Clifton (1995:33–34) the proportions of lexicon shared with
Kaki Ae, the semantic fields, metalinguistic awareness, and relevant sociolinguistic facts

strongly favour a borrowing scenario. The so-called sound shifts alluded to by Franklin (1995) are, in fact, perfectly predictable loan renderings given the phonemic systems of Eleman (which has no n/l/r-phonemic distinction) and Kaki Ae (which has no t/k distinction).

Clifton (1997) provides a sketch of Kaki Ae grammar. The verb agrees with the subject and object in person and number (for third person singular objects agreement is optional), and the subject may take ergative marking. The verb does not have dedicated tense marking, but a marker (labelled irrealis by Clifton 1997) is used under negation as well as for future reference. The relative clause precedes the noun.

4.11 Kamula [xla]

Kamula is spoken by some 800 people in the area around Wawoi Falls in Western Province, Papua New Guinea, south of the Bosavi family languages. The first data to appear on Kamula is the survey wordlist and notes by Reesink (1976).

Kamula is often grouped with the neighbouring Bosavi languages following Shaw (1973:53) who cites high lexicostatistical similarity (38% to 55%) with languages in the Bosavi Watershed group. However, the cognate judgments are not given explicitly, and we have failed to reproduce anything like these figures, nor have other comparisons such as Reesink (1976:15) who finds 5% similarity with Kaluli where Shaw (1973:53) has 44% and Routamaa (1994:7) with much improved knowledge of Kamula finds "very few similarities". In fact, Kamula, apart from a few obvious cultural *Wanderwörter*, appears to have a basic lexicon totally different from the Bosavi languages.

Routamaa (1994) furnishes a wealth of data on Kamula. In many ways, Kamula is a typical Papuan language with SOV order and postpositions. There is a morphologically marked switch-reference system for simultaneous clauses. Kamula has a causative construction where the verb *dema* 'do' appears sentence finally while the verb in the complement clause is in the imperative.

(9) Ye-ta   na:-ye   dlapa   ha-ne   de-wa
     3SG-SRCE 1SG-FOC   firewood   take-SG.IMPER   do-FPST
     'She told me to/made me fetch firewood.'

(10) Na:-ta   masemala-ye solo   uha-ne   de
     1SG-SRCE boy-FOC   salt   steal-SG.IMPER do
     'I made the boy steal some salt.'

4.12 Karami [xar]

Karami is an extinct language encountered by Flint (1918) on the left branch of the Turama River, northeast of the Mubami language area in Western Province, Papua New Guinea. The language has not been found in later surveys and is thus presumed extinct. Franklin (1973b:270–271) included Karami in his Inland Gulf family on the basis of a lexicostatistical comparison using the 94-item vocabulary of Flint (1918). The figure for Karami-Minanibai/Foia Foia is especially high (45%). However, the more careful scrutiny of the composition of the Inland Gulf (sub-)family by Usher and Suter (2015:125) attributes the Karami matches (which they revise to a 'modest' number) with the Inland Gulf to loans since the forms in question are nearly identical to Minanibai/Foia Foia. Nothing beyond the wordlist is known about the Karami people or language.

4.13 Wiru [wiu]

Wiru is spoken by some 15,300 people just south of Mount Ialibu in Ialibu District, Southern Highlands Province, at the southwestern edge of the central highlands of Papua New Guinea, between Kewa (Enga-Huli) to the west and Folopa (Teberan) to the south.

Wiru is often included in the Trans New Guinea family in some constellation including the languages of the putative East New Guinea highlands subfamily (Wurm 1982:120–128) with evidence that includes pronoun forms. The careful comparison by Kerr (1975) indeed shows that Wiru shares some cultural vocabulary and some typological features with the adjacent Engan languages, but is otherwise very different (Franklin 1975a).[9] We regard the genealogical relations of Wiru to (any) Trans New Guinea language(s) as yet undemonstrated.

Kerr (1967) is the only available study of the grammar of Wiru which provides a detailed description of medial clauses. The pronoun system of Wiru (corrected from Kerr 1967) is as follows (Harland Kerr, personal communication, 2011):

1P.SG	*no*	'I'
2P.SG	*ne*	'thou'
3P.SG	*one*	'he/she/him'
1P.DU	*tota*	'we two'
1P.PL	*toto*	'we all'
2/3P.DU	*kita*	'you two/they two'
2/3P.PL	*kiwi*	'you all/they all'

5 SEPIK

5.1 Pyu [pby]

Pyu is spoken by some 100 people in two villages, Biake 2 with its hamlets (north of the Sepik River and just east of the PNG-Indonesian border) and an unlocated village on the bend of the Sepik within Indonesian territory. According to a 1992 report by Arjen Lock, "people who are over 30 years and older are bilingual in Abau and [Pyu]. The children are claimed to lack fluency in both Abau and [Pyu]. They prefer to communicate in Tok Pisin". Although Lock's data did not come from observations in the language area, it seems very plausible that the language is highly endangered (Ian Tupper, personal communication, SIL-PNG September 2008).

Pyu was first reported in the literature by Laycock (1972) and was subsequently grouped in the Kwomtari-Baibai-Pyu phylum, but no actual evidence was actually presented (Laycock 1975b). There are no significant lexical links with neighbouring languages (Conrad and Dye 1975).

There are two short wordlists (Conrad and Dye 1975, Laycock 1972) and a sentence or two on grammar in Laycock (1975b:854). Further, there is an unpublished 200-word list collected by Arjen Lock compiled in 1992. Documentation of Pyu is of the highest priority.

5.2 Taiap [gpn]

Taiap is spoken by some 75 people in the village of Gapun, located on the north coast of Papua New Guinea (some 10 miles inland) near the border of East Sepik and Madang provinces. It was first reported with a wordlist by Höltker (1938) who made the arduous journey to the Gapun village. When Höltker (1938) visited, he counted only 33 village inhabitants. Laycock and Z'Graggen (1975:739) report 74 speakers. The detailed socio-linguistic fieldwork by Kulick and Stroud (1990) counted exactly 89 fluent Taiap speakers, all multilingual to various degrees, but already by then, no child under 10 had an active command of Taiap.

Laycock and Z'Graggen (1975:757) classified Taiap into Laycock's wide-ranging Sepik-Ramu family. The evidence adduced was essentially typological, clearly insufficient for concluding a genealogical relation.

The sketch by Kulick and Stroud (1992) is an excellent summary of Taiap grammatical features. Taiap is an ergative SOV language with postpositions. Relative clauses follow the head noun. Only animate nouns take obligatory morphological number marking (singular/dual/plural). Taiap nouns have a male/female gender distinction as revealed by agreement.

Taiap distinguishes male/female speech in some aspects of its lexicon and verb morphology (Kulick 1987:130).

5.3 Busa [bhf]

Busa or Odiai is spoken by some 240 people in the remote area north of the Upper Sepik River in Sandaun Province, Papua New Guinea. Busa was first reported by Loving and Bass (1964) in their survey of the Amanab sub-district of Sandaun Province. In 1980, Busa was spoken by 238 people, and though Tok Pisin usage was growing, Busa was not endangered (Graham 1981).

The Busa lexicon bears no significant relations to any other language in the region (Conrad and Dye 1975, Laycock 1975a).

There is a wordlist in Conrad and Dye (1975) and some very brief notes on grammar in Laycock (1975a). Documentation of the language would be of high value for our knowledge of Busa and the typology of the region more generally.

5.4 Asaba [seo]

Asaba is spoken by about 180 speakers (Little 2008:2) in the Kenu and Om Rivers in the Upper Sepik area of Sandaun Province, Papua New Guinea. Asaba was probably first reported (under the name Suarmin) by Healey (1964:108).

Laycock and Z'Graggen (1975) adduced typological arguments for a Leonard Schultze family together with Walio, but are insufficient as proof of a genealogical relationship. The lexical evidence does not show any conclusive genetic relationship either, be it inside or outside Leonard Schultze (Conrad and Dye 1975); with Sepik-Hill (as suggested in Lewis et al. 2015); or with Baiyamo (as Papi) (Conrad and Lewis 1988). However, a higher figure (29%) of Baiyamo-Asabo (as Papi-Duranmin) lexicostatistical relations was quoted by Laycock and Z'Graggen (1975:753), before the later superseding lower figure (10%) of Conrad and Lewis (1988:259), and some lexical data collected recently by anthropologists does contain matches between the two.

It remains to be worked out whether these are loans or indicative of a genetic relationship.

There are some very brief notes on grammar in Laycock and Z'Graggen (1975). There are extensive anthropological studies on the people (Little 2008, Lohmann 2000).

The Asaba language is still being transmitted to children (Roger Lohmann, personal communication, 2009).

5.5 Baiyamo [ppe]

Baiyamo is spoken by some 70 people on the Frieda River in Sandaun Province, Papua New Guinea. Baiyamo was first reported by Laycock (1973) as Papi (a village name).

Laycock and Z'Graggen (1975) adduced typological arguments for a Leonard Schultze family together with Walio, but these are insufficient as proof of a genealogical relationship. The lexical evidence does not show any conclusive genetic relationship either, be it inside or outside Leonard Schultze (Conrad and Dye 1975), with Sepik-Hill (as suggested in Lewis et al. 2015), or with Asaba (as Duranmin) (Conrad and Lewis 1988). However, a higher figure (29%) of Baiyamo-Asabo (as Papi-Duranmin) lexicostatistical relations was quoted by Laycock and Z'Graggen (1975:753), before the later superseding lower figure (10%) of Conrad and Lewis (1988:259), and some lexical data collected recently by anthropologists does contain matches between the two.

It remains to be worked out whether these are loans or indicative of a genetic relationship.

There is a wordlist in Conrad and Dye (1975) and some very brief notes in Laycock and Z'Graggen (1975:752–753).

The Baiyamo language is still being transmitted to children (Jack Kennedy, personal communication, 2009).

5.6 Guriaso [grx]

Guriaso is spoken by some 160 people in a few small villages east of the Kwomtari area east of Amanab in Sandaun Province, Papua New Guinea. Guriaso was reported as Menóu in the ethnography of Kwieftim and Abrau east of the Guriaso area (Kelm and Kelm 1980). There are scattered words of Menóu in Kelm and Kelm (1980) enough to confirm that it is the same language as that independently encountered on survey of the area previously assumed to be Kwomtari (Baron 1983:27). The latter survey named the language Guriaso after a central village of that name.

Guriaso was subsequently grouped with Kwomtari on very low cognate counts (3%–13%) and shared typological features (Baron 1983:27–29). In our judgment of the same data, these resemblances can just as well be explained by chance.

The only data (basic lexical and grammatical data) appears to be the 1983 unpublished SIL Survey (Baron 1983) and five numerals in Lean (1986). The notes on grammar in Baron (1983) show Guriaso to be an SOV language with postpositions, suffixal verb morphology, and adjective-noun order.

5.7 Yerakai [yra]

Yerakai is spoken by some 380 people in two villages west of Lake Chambri in East Sepik Province, Papua New Guinea. Yerakai was first reported in the literature by Dye et al. (1968:14) without any accompanying data.

According to the lexicostatistical figures in Conrad and Dye (1975:14), Yerakai shares no significant lexical relations with any Sepik language, except Ndu (Laycock 1973:23), but these could easily reflect loans from the adjacent Iatmul (from intermarriage)

(Conrad and Dye 1975:14, Aikhenvald 2008). No other argument for a Sepik affiliation in offered (Laycock and Z'Graggen 1975:738), and Yerakai is not mentioned in Foley's re-consideration of the Sepik family (Foley 2005).

There must be an (unpublished) SIL wordlist of Yerakai underlying Conrad and Dye (1975:14), and there are unpublished field notes by Laycock (no date). No data on Yerakai is published.

5.8 Yale [nee]

Yale is spoken by some 600 people in 6 villages south of the Kwomtari in the Upper Sepik area of Sandaun Province, Papua New Guinea. Yale was first reported by Loving and Bass (1964) in their survey of the Amanab sub-district of Sandaun Province. In 1980, Yale was spoken by 573 people and children were raised as monolingual in Yale (Graham 1981).

Yale has no significant lexical overlap with any of the languages in the vicinity (Loving and Bass 1964) and was one of the few languages Laycock (1975a) classified as an isolate.

There is an unpublished grammar sketch by SIL missionaries (Campbell and Campbell 1987) posted on the internet. Yale is an SOV language with postpositions and fairly rich (suffixal and prefixal) verb morphology. Adjectives can come before or after the modified noun. Reduplication of the verb stem signals plurality of the object (Campbell and Campbell 1987:35).

5.9 Banaro [byz]

Banaro is spoken by some 2,480 people on the Keram River in East Sepik Province, Papua New Guinea. The Banaro people were studied relatively early by the German ethnographer Thurnwald (1921).

Banaro [byz] shows some typological similarities to the neighbouring Grass, Ap Ma, and Ramu languages, but there is little lexical evidence for a possible genetic relationship (Z'graggen 1969:163–165, Foley in press-b). For this reason, contra Foley (in press-b), we find insufficient grounds to classify Banaro as genealogically related to any or all of the mentioned languages.

Published wordlists of Banaro are available in Davies and Comrie (1985), Z'graggen (1972) and Juillerat (1993:220) cites unpublished phonology, dictionary, and grammar manuscripts by William Butler of the Pioneer Bible Translators.

5.10 Yetfa-Biksi [yet]

Yetfa-Biksi is a language spoken by two ethnic groups totalling some 1,000 first language speakers in the border area east and north of the Sobger River. Despite only having some 1,000 native speakers, the language is spoken as an L2 by even smaller neighbouring ethnic groups.

Biksi was first reported in the literature by Laycock (1972), who had met with transients from Papua, Indonesia (then West Irian) while doing fieldwork on the Papuan (then Australian) side in 1970. Yetfa is mentioned for the first time in the 2nd edition of the *Index of Irian Jaya languages* (Silzer and Heikkinen-Clouse 1991) as an unclassified language – without any references to data – but the information presumably derives from

Doriot (1991) who trekked in parts of the Yetfa-speaking area in April-May 1991. Sometime between the 14th edition of the *Ethnologue* (Grimes 2000) and the 15th (Gordon 2005), it was realised that Yetfa and Biksi are so close as to be regarded as one language.

Biksi (by implication Biksi-Yetfa) was placed in the putative Sepik language family languages by Laycock and Z'Graggen (1975:740–741), and this has often been repeated since (Lewis 2009). Biksi-Yetfa was not considered by Foley in his re-assessment of the Sepik family for lack of data (Foley 2005:126–127). The lexical matches adduced by Laycock to various Sepik languages are sporadic and look more like loans or chance resemblances than the outcome of genetic inheritance (Hammarström 2008a). The lexical relations were also investigated independently by Conrad and Dye (1975:19) who found that Biksi shared no more than 4% probable cognates with any of the languages in the vicinity to the east, including Abelam.[10] (This lexical comparison includes numerals but no demonstratives or pronouns.) Yetfa-Biksi also shows similarly low figures with languages neighbouring to the west such as Kimki (Kim 2006).

Scanty notes on grammar can be found in Laycock and Z'Graggen (1975:740–741), and short wordlists are published in Conrad and Dye (1975), Laycock (1972). An unpublished SIL Indonesia survey contains 250 Yetfa words from 5 locations along with 15 sentences (Kim 2006). There are further unpublished wordlists from several locations collected by Doriot (1991). The sentences of Kim (2006) show that Yetfa-Biksi is an SOV language.

At this time, Yetfa is still being transmitted to children and so is not an endangered language (Kim 2006).

5.11 Ap Ma [kbx]

Ap Ma, also known as Botin, Kambot, or Kambrambo, is spoken by some 10,000 people in 15 villages scattered in the area south of the Sepik River between the Keram and Yuat Rivers in East Sepik Province, Papua New Guinea. The Ap Ma people have long been known to German missionaries operating in the Keram area (e.g., Speiser 1944).

Ap Ma shows some typological similarities to the Grass, Banaro, and Ramu languages, but there is little lexical evidence for any possible genealogical relationship (Z'graggen 1969:168–169, Foley in press-b). For this reason, contra Foley (in press-b), we find insufficient grounds to classify Ap Ma as genealogically related to any or all of the mentioned languages.

Published data on the Ap Ma language consists of a wordlist (Z'graggen 1972); two articles on specific grammatical topics (Pryor and Farr 1989, Pryor 1990); and a fairly long master's thesis grammatical description (Wade 1984). Like many Papuan languages, Ap Ma is an SOV language with medial verbs. The system of medial verbs is particularly extensive in Ap Ma, realizing nine different tense/aspect relationships with either same or different subject markers. Furthermore, different subject medial verbs in combination with various particles realize negation.

6 EAST PAPUAN

6.1 Kuot [kto]

Kuot is spoken by some 2,400 people in mid-northwest New Ireland, Papua New Guinea. Kuot was known by German colonial ethnographers early on to be a separate language (Walden 1911).

Though there are some typological parallels with other non-Austronesian languages of the East Papuan islands, there are insufficient grounds for concluding a genealogical relationship for Kuot with any or all of them (Dunn et al. 2002).

The grammar of Kuot is relatively well known thanks to the work of Chung and Chung (1996) and Lindström (2002). Kuot is famous for being the only non-Austronesian VSO language of the entire New Guinea Area. Kuot also has other word order feature typically associated with VSO languages such as prepositions, adjectives following the noun and postposed relative clauses. Kuot nouns have a covert male/female gender distinction and overt number marking distinguishing singular, dual, and plural.

6.2 Anem [anz]

Anem is spoken by approximately 843 people in 4 villages on the north coast approximately 45 kilometres east of Cape Gloucester in West New Britain, Papua New Guinea (Carter et al. 2012). A recent survey found the language "vital despite the highly multilingual nature of the Anem people and the addition of Tok Pisin to domains that used to be the sole territory of Anem" (Carter et al. 2012:3). The Anem language become known to linguists in 1969 (Thurston 1982:6).

Some hypotheses relate Anem to other languages of New Britain, especially with Pele-Ata, and the East Papuan islands based on typology or pronounes (see Dunn et al. 2005a,b, Ross 2001, Thurston 1992), but the resemblances are much too minor to conclude that they are genealogically related.

Anem is described in a comparative sketch by Thurston (1982). Anem has SVO word order and shares numerous grammatical features with the nearby Austronesian language Lusi.[11] Anem has a covert male/female gender distinction. A curiosity of Anem grammar is its verb stems. There are numerous stems which are suppletive, sometimes determined by the number of the subject and sometimes determined by the number of the object. One verb in Anem, to 'eat', must be analyzed as having a Ø-stem as it appears simply as the concatenation of subject prefix and object suffix (Thurston 1982:47–49).

6.3 Pele-Ata [ata]

Pele-Ata is spoken by some 2,000 people in 13 villages in the border area of West New Britain and East New Britain in Papua New Guinea. Pele-Ata is still being learned by children, but all speakers are (at least) bilingual in Tok Pisin, and younger speakers' Pele-Ate shows reduced morphology and lexical influences (Yanagida 2004:87–88).

Some hypotheses relate Pele-Ata to other languages of New Britain, especially with Anem, and the East Papuan islands based on typology or pronouns (see (Dunn et al. 2005a, 2002, 2005b, Ross 2001), but the resemblances are much too minor to conclude a genealogical relation.

As far as I have been able to tell, the first wordlist of Pele-Ata was collected by Grace (1956). Pele-Ata is documented in a dictionary (Hashimoto 1996, 2008), and an overview of typological features can be found in Dunn et al. (2002) drawing on an unpublished grammar manuscript. Pele-Ata is an SVO language with prepositions.

6.4 Bilua [blb]

Bilua is spoken by some 8,740 people on Vella Lavella Island in the Solomon Islands. A wordlist of Bilua appears as early as Schellong (1890), and Ray (1919) recognized its non-Austronesian isolate character.

Bilua is sometimes grouped with the other Central Solomons languages and beyond (Wurm 1975b), but closer inspection shows that a genealogical relation is not demonstrable (Dunn and Terrill 2012, Terrill 2011).

A grammar is available for Bilua (Obata 2003). Bilua is an SVO language with postpositions and adjective-noun order.

6.5 Kol [kol]

Kol is spoken by some 4,000 speakers in East New Britain, Papua New Guinea. As far as I have been able to tell, the first wordlist of Kol was collected by Grace (1956).

At present Kol has not been demonstrated to form a bona-fide family with any of the other languages of New Britain (Dunn et al. 2005a, 2002, 2005b, Stebbins 2009), but there are promising similarities between the noun class systems of Kol and the Baining languages that must be examined as soon as a more extensive description of Kol is published (cf. Stebbins 2009:229, 238).

Very little data on Kol has been published, and at present, the most extensive source of information is the article by Reesink (2005) which is mainly about Sulka, cf. also further tidbits in Stebbins (2009) and typological features in Dunn et al. (2002). Kol has SVO word order, prepositions, and noun-adjective word order (Dunn et al. 2002:39). Kol has a noun class system with three semantically based classes (masculine, feminine, neuter) and another six classes distinguishable on formal grounds (Stebbins 2009:238).

6.6 Sulka [sua]

Sulka is spoken by some 2,500 speakers along the Wide Bay coast of East New Britain, Papua New Guinea. The Sulka people and language were known early on to the German ethnographers (e.g., Rascher 1904), and Schmidt (1904) aptly recognized the non-Austronesian isolate character of the language.

At present Sulka has not been demonstrated to form a bona-fide family with any of the other languages of New Britain (Reesink 2005:145–146, Stebbins 2009, Dunn et al. 2005a, Dunn et al. 2005b).

Schneider (1962) produced a long description of Sulka. Tharp (1996) and Reesink (2005) are shorter but written in a more modern framework. Sulka has vowel morphophonemic vowel elision processes which result in long consonants/consonant clusters (Reesink 2005). Sulka is an SVO language with prepositions and noun-adjective order.

6.7 Lavukaleve [lvk]

Lavukaleve is spoken by some 1,780 speakers in the Russell Islands in the Solomon Islands. It was recognized by Ray (1927:124) to be a non-Austronesian language after inspecting vocabularies furnished to him.

Bilua is sometimes grouped with the other Central Solomons languages and beyond (Wurm 1975b); but closer inspection shows that a genealogical relation is not demonstrable (Dunn and Terrill 2012, Terrill 2011).

Lavukaleve is described in an extensive reference grammar (Terrill 2003). Lavukaleve is an SOV language with morphologically complex verbs, noun-adjective order, an NP-final definite article, and three covert genders. Number (singular, dual, plural) is overtly marked in a system with many irregularities. Demonstrative pronouns make a discourse-pragmatic distinction between 'last mentioned' and 'mentioned previously but not last'. Lavukaleve has clause chaining but no switch-reference marking.

6.8 Savosavo [svs]

Savosavo is spoken by some 2,420 speakers on Savo Island in the Solomon Islands. Data on Savosavo appeared as early as Codrington (1885), and Wilhelm Schmidt recognized the non-Austronesian character of the language after careful inspection of Codrington's data (Ray 1927:123).

Savosavo is sometimes grouped with the other Central Solomons languages and beyond (Wurm 1975b), but closer inspection shows that a genealogical relation is not demonstrable (Dunn and Terrill 2012, Terrill 2011).

Savosavo is described in an extensive reference grammar (Wegener 2012). Savosavo is a postpositional SOV language with relative clause and determiners preceding the noun. Enclitics are used for case-marking and number marking (dual and plural). Savosavo has a gender system with two classes, masculine and feminine. Savosavo has a 'marked nominative' case system, i.e. syntactic subject noun phrases are marked as nominative, while object noun phrases are unmarked. Clause chaining is a common phenomenon where, curiously, the unmarked form signals different subjects, and the marked form signals same subject. Tail-head linkage, i.e. the repetition of the last verbal predicate of the preceding clause as the initial predicate of a new clause chain, is also found in Savosavo.

6.9 Touo [tqu]

Touo (formerly known as Baniata) is spoken by 1,870 people on south Rendova Island in the Solomon Islands. Data on Touo first appeared in Waterhouse (1927).

Touo is sometimes grouped with the other Central Solomons languages and beyond (Wurm 1975b), but closer inspection shows that a genealogical relation is not demonstrable (Dunn and Terrill 2012, Terrill 2011).

Terrill and Dunn (2003) contains information on the linguistic background and orthography development for Touo, but the main source for data on Touo grammar remains the MA thesis by Frahm (1998). Touo is an SOV language with serial verb constructions (Frahm 1998).

6.10 Yele [yle]

Yele (locally Yélî Dnye) is spoken by all 6,000 natives of Rossell Island (2011 census) off the southeastern tip of Papua New Guinea. The first data on the Yele language to be published is the wordlist by Winter (1890).

Yele is sometimes grouped with the other languages of the East Papuan islands (Dunn et al. 2005a,b, Ross 2001, Wurm 1975b), but none of these groupings can be demonstrated with orthodox comparative methodology. Rossel Island is relatively isolated, being at a distance of 250 reef-ridden nautical miles from the Papua New Guinea mainland, and it is not clear a priori where one should look for its erstwhile relatives. Quite possibly its nearest relatives were spoken on islands which are now inhabited by Austronesian speakers, such as the nearby Sudest Island.

Published information on Yele grammar can be found thanks to the work of the missionaries Henderson and Henderson (Henderson 1995, 1975) who also produced a dictionary (Henderson and Henderson 1987, 1999). A longer draft grammar is in preparation by Stephen Levinson, drawing on the earlier work by the Hendersons as well as long-time fieldwork on the island. A number of papers on specialised topics have already appeared (e.g., Levinson 2006).

Like many Papuan languages, Yele is an ergative SOV language with postpositions, noun-adjective order, and postposed relative clauses. Beyond this, Yele has the reputation of being an extraordinarily complex language, on many levels. The phoneme inventory includes doubly articulated consonants and additionally distinguishes palatalized and labialized variants. If analyzed as single segments, the total number of distinctive segments for Yele is over 90 – the largest phonemic inventory of any non-click language in the world. The single-segment analysis is justified durationally, as the coarticulated segments are not different from simplex consonants, but they probably derive recently from consonant clusters, as Yele otherwise has no consonant clusters (Levinson ms). Grammatical categories such as tense, aspect, mood, and person/number of subject and object expressed in a huge inventory of portmanteau morphemes that are largely unsegmentable into constituent morphemes. Verbs come in a multitude of irregular paradigms and many verbs are suppletive across a range of categories (Levinson ms).

7 ACKNOWLEDGEMENTS

The underlying classification of Papuan languages has been elaborated during a long period of time during which it has benefited from comments and discussions with Tim Usher, Mark Donohue, Matthew Dryer, and Andrew Pawley. The usual disclaimers apply.

8 ABBREVIATIONS

U	undergoer
AUX	auxiliary
PST	past tense
SPEC	specific
ERG	ergative
VISUAL	visual evidential
SENSORY	sensory evidential
RESULT	resultative evidential
REASONING	inferred evidential
REPORTED	reported evidential
SRCE	source
FOC	focus
IMPER	imperative
FPST	far past

NOTES

1 Three unclear cases are worth noting. Fabritius (1855) encountered a tribe at the mouth of Mamberamo and noted down two words (the numerals 'one' and 'two') of their language. No language subsequently documented in that (or any other) area has matching forms, but we exclude it from the present listing since it is clearly insufficiently attested. Abom is a moribund language encountered on a survey of Tirio languages at the mouth of the Fly River. A 200-item wordlist was collected but it is

difficult to know if some crucial lexical items (and some tiny details of grammar) are inherited cognates with the Tirio languages or the reflection of language shift (Jore and Alemán 2002). The language of Kembra near the confluence of the Sobger and Nawa Rivers is attested with only a short wordlist taken down in challenging circumstances (Doriot 1991). From this it may be guessed that the language is related to Lepki and Murkim spoken further south.

2   The status of Kaure [nxu] and Narau [bpp] is worth noting. Indications from the field suggest that the two are in fact intelligible varieties of the same language (Dommel and Dommel 1991:1–3) but the region in question is poorly surveyed so we have refrained from asserting that this is the case for the purposes of the present chapter.

3   From the iso-639-3 code longer lists of alternative names can easily be retrieved.

4   Mor is not to be confused with the Austronesian language with the same name found on the islands northeast of the city of Nabire (Kamholz 2014). The two languages are too far away from each other to have had any direct interaction and the homophony of the names is a coincidence.

5   Not to be confused with several other places and languages in Indonesian Papua also called Tanahmerah (literally 'brown earth' in Malay).

6   There is now a full New Testament translation (Damal people and CMA 1988)

7   Doriot (1991) refers to an unpublished wordlist of Kimki from Mot, but Mot is listed in survey maps as Murkim speaking (Wambaliau 2004).

8   Mawes spoken in Mawes Wares is not to be confused with the Wares [wai], once a warlike tribe on the upper Biri River (Oosterwal 1961:26–27) that had to flee to the coast from their original territory in the 1950s (Koentjaraningrat 1965:135–136).

9   I am indebted to Tim Usher for bringing to my attention how different Wiru actually is from Engan.

10 The exact languages in question are Yerakai (0%), Chenapian (0%), Bahinemo (1%), Washkuk (1%), Yessan-Mayo (4%), Abelam (1%), Namie (0%), Abau (0%), May River Iwam (1%), Musan (0%), Amto (1%), Rocky Peak (0%), Ama (0%), Nimo (1%), Bo (0%), Iteri (0%), Owiniga (2%), Woswari (0%), Walio (0%), Paupe (0%), South Mianmin (0%), Nagatman (0%), Busan (1%), and Pyu (1%).

11 Thurston (1982) argues that this is probably the result of an originally Anem-like population adopting an Austronesian language because many of the Austronesian features in Lusi appear in a 'simplified' form.

REFERENCES

Aikhenvald, Alexandra Y. 2008. Language Contact along the Sepik River. *Anthropological Linguistics* 50: 1–66.

Anceaux, Johannes Cornelis. 1958. Languages of the Bomberai Peninsula: Outline of a Linguistic Map. *Nieuw-Guinea Studiën* 2: 109–121.

Arka, I. Wayan. 2011. Constructive Number Systems in Marori and Beyond. *The Proceedings of the International Lexical Functional Grammar (LFG2011) Conference, University of Hong Kong 19 July 2011*, ed. by Miriam Butt and Tracy Holloway King, 5–25. Stanford, CA: CSLI Publications.

Arka, I Wayan. 2012. Projecting Morphology and Agreement in Marori, an Isolate of Southern New Guinea. *Melanesian Languages on the Edge of Asia: Challenges for the 21st Century*, Nicholas Evans and Marian Klamer (Language Documentation and Conservation Special Publication 5), 150–173. Honolulu: University of Hawaii Press.

Arka, I Wayan. 2013. Nominal Aspect in Marori. *Proceedings of the LFG13 Conference*, ed. by Miriam Butt and Tracy Holloway King, 27–47. Stanford, CA: CSLI Publications.

Austen, Leo. 1921a. Vocabularies Daru Station, Western Division: Name of Tribe, Tapapi, Names of Villages, Ubaroniara, Bogabwi. *British New Guinea Annual Report* 1919–1920: 122–122.

Austen, Leo. 1921b. Vocabularies Daru Station, Western Division: Names of Villages, Hibaradai, Madawai, and Eriga. *British New Guinea Annual Report* 1919–1920: 122–122.

Austen, Leo. 1921c. Vocabularies Daru W.D. Station, Western Division: Name of Tribe, Hiwi, Name of Villages, Kaibenapi, Genapi, Wagumi, Bobonapi, Wariadai and Sarau. *British New Guinea Annual Report* 1919–1920: 123–123.

Axelsen, Jacob Bock and Susanna Manrubia. 2014. River Density and Landscape Roughness Are Universal Determinants of Linguistic Diversity. *Proceedings of the Royal Society of London B: Biological Sciences* 281(1784): 1–9.

Baron, Wietze. 1983. *Kwomtari Survey*. Unpublished manuscript, SIL Survey office, Ukarumpa, now posted at www.kwomtari.net/kwomtari_survey.pdf (15 December 2008).

Berry, Keith and Christine Berry. 1999. *A Description of Abun: A West Papuan Language of Irian Jaya* (Pacific Linguistics: Series B 115). Canberra: Research School of Pacific and Asian Studies, Australian National University.

Bevan, Theodore F. 1890. *Toil, Travel, and Discovery in British New Guinea*. London: Kegan Paul, Trench, Trubner.

Boelaars, J.H.M.C. 1950. *The Linguistic Position of South-Western New Guinea*. Leiden: E. J. Brill.

Brown, Herbert A. 1973. The Eleman Language Family. *The Linguistic Situation in the Gulf District and Adjacent Areas, Papua New Guinea* (Pacific Linguistics: Series C 26), ed. by Karl J. Franklin, 281–376. Canberra: Research School of Pacific and Asian Studies, Australian National University.

Brown, Loo N. 1921. Vocabularies Kikori Staion, Delta Division: Name of Tribe, Aurama, Name of Village, Uo-Ho. *British New Guinea Annual Report* 1919–1920: 124–124.

Burung, Wiem. 2000. *A Brief Note on Elseng*. SIL International, Dallas. SIL Electronic Survey Reports 2000–2001. www.sil.org/silesr/ abstract.asp?ref=2000-001.

Campbell, Carl and Jody Campbell. 1987. *Yade Grammar Essentials*. Ukarumpa: Unpublished Manuscript, Summer Institute of Linguistics.

Campbell, Lyle and William J. Poser. 2008. *Language Classification: History and Method*. Cambridge: Cambridge University Press.

Carter, John, Katie Carter, Bonnie MacKenzie, Janell Masters, Brian Paris, and Hannah Paris. 2012. *A Sociolinguistic Survey of Anem* (SIL Electronic Survey Reports 2012–2041). SIL International.

Chung, Kyung-Ja and Chul-Hwa Chung. 1996. Kuot Grammar Essentials. *Two Non-Austronesian Grammars from the Islands* (Data Papers on Papua New Guinea Languages 42), ed. by John M. Clifton, 1–75. Ukarumpa: Summer Institute of Linguistics.

Clancy, D.J. 1962. Through the Strickland Gorge. *Australian Territories* 2, no. 1, 12–19.

Clifton, John M. 1994. Stable Multilingualism in a Small Language Group: The Case of Kaki Ae. *Language and Linguistics in Melanesia* 25, no. 2: 107–24.

Clifton, John M. 1995. A Grammar Sketch of the Kaki Ae Language. *University of North Dakota Session* (Work Papers of the Summer Institute of Linguistics 39), 33–80. Grand Forks, North Dakota: Summer Institute of Linguistics.

Clifton, John M. 1997. The Kaki Ae Language. *Materials on Languages in Danger of Disappearing in the Asia-Pacific Region No 1: Some Endangered Languages of Papua New Guinea: Kaki Ae, Musom, and Aribwatsa* (Pacific Linguistics: Series D 89), ed. by Stephen A. Wurm, 3–66. Canberra: Research School of Pacific and Asian Studies, Australian National University.

Clouse, Duane A. 1997. Toward a Reconstruction and Reclassification of the Lakes Plain Languages of Irian Jaya. *Papers in Papuan Linguistics No. 2* (Pacific Linguistics: Series A 85), ed. by Karl J. Franklin, 133–236. Canberra: Research School of Pacific and Asian Studies, Australian National University.

Clouse, Duane, Mark Donohue, and Felix Ma. 2002. *Survey Report of the North Coast of Irian Jaya*. SIL International, Dallas. SIL Electronic Survey Reports 2002–2078. www.sil.org/silesr/abstract.asp?ref=2002-2078.

Codrington, Robert. 1885. *The Melanesian Languages*. Oxford: Clarendon Press.

Conrad, Robert J. and Ronald K. Lewis. 1988. Some Language and Sociolinguistic Relationships in the Upper Sepik Region of Papua New Guinea. *Papers in New Guinea Linguistics 26* (Pacific Linguistics: Series A 76), 243–273. Canberra: Research School of Pacific and Asian Studies, Australian National University.

Conrad, Robert J. and T. Wayne Dye. 1975. Some Language Relationships in the Upper Sepik Region of Papua New Guinea. *Papers in New Guinea Linguistics 18* (Pacific Linguistics: Series A 40), 1–35. Canberra: Research School of Pacific and Asian Studies, Australian National University.

Dahl, Östen. 2001. Languages without Tense and Aspect. *Aktionsart and Aspectotemporality in Non-European Languages*, ed. by Karen H. Ebert and Fernando Zúniga, 159–173. ASAS – Arbeiten des Seminars für Allgemeine Sprachwissenschaft, Universität Zürich.

Damal people & CMA. 1988. Haik-A Ongam Kal: Perjanjian baru dalam Bahasa Damal. Jakarta: Lembaga Alkitab Indonesia.

Davies, John and Bernard Comrie. 1985. A Linguistic Survey of the Upper Yuat. *Papers in New Guinea Linguistics 22* (Pacific Linguistics: Series A 63), 275–312. Canberra: Research School of Pacific and Asian Studies, Australian National University.

Dol, Philomena. 2007. *A Grammar of Maybrat: A Language of the Bird's Head Peninsula, Papua Province, Indonesia* (Pacific Linguistics 586). Canberra: Pacific Linguistics.

Dommel, Peter R. & Gudrun E. Dommel. 1991. Kaure phonology. *Workpapers in Indonesian Languages and Cultures* 9, 1–68.

Donohue, Mark. 2001. Animacy, Class and Gender in Burmeso. *The Boy from Bundaberg: Studies in Melanesian Linguistics in Honour of Tom Dutton* (Pacific Linguistics 514), ed. by Andrew Pawley, Malcolm Ross, and Darrell Tryon, 97–115. Canberra: Research School of Pacific and Asian Studies, Australian National University.

Donohue, Mark. 2007. The Papuan Language of Tambora. *Oceanic Linguistics* 46, no. 2: 520–537.

Donohue, Mark. no date. *The Languages of Wasur National Park, Irian Jaya*. Unpublished Manuscript, Sydney University, Australia.

Donohue, Mark and Simon Musgrave. 2007. Typology and the Linguistic Macrohistory of Island Melanesia. *Oceanic Linguistics* 46, no. 2: 348–387.

Doriot, Roger E. 1991. 6-2-3-4 Trek, April–May, 1991. Ms.

Drabbe, Peter. 1954. *Talen en dialecten van zuid-west Nieuw-Guinea* (Microbiblioteca Anthropos 11). Posieux/Fribourg: Institut Anthropos.

Dumatubun, A.E., and Teddy K. Wanane. ca 1989. *Orang Usku di daerah batas Timur, Senggi, Irian Jaya*. Jayapura: s.n.

Dunn, Michael and Angela Terrill. 2012. Assessing the evidence for a Central Solomons Papuan family using the Oswalt Monte Carlo Test. *Diachronica* 29, no. 1: 1–27.

Dunn, Michael, Ger Reesink, and Angela Terrill. 2002. The East Papuan Languages: A Preliminary Typological Appraisal. *Oceanic Linguistics* 41, no. 1: 28–62.

Dunn, Michael, Stephen C. Levinson, Eva Lindström, Ger Reesink and Angela Terrill. 2005a. Structural Phylogeny in Historical Linguistics: Methodological Explorations Applied in Island Melanesia. *Language* 84, no. 4: 710–759.

Dunn, Michael, Angela Terrill, Ger Reesink, Robert A. Foley and Stephen C. Levinson. 2005b. Structural Phylogenetics and the Reconstruction of Ancient Language History. *Science* 309: 2072–2075.

Dutton, Tom. 1979. Simplified Koriki: A second trade language used by the Motu in the Gulf of Papua. *Kivung* 12, no. 1: 3–73.

Dye, Wayne, Patricia Townsend and W. Townsend. 1968. The Sepik Hill Languages: A Preliminary Report. *Oceania* 39, 146–156.

Evans, Nicholas, Wayan Arka, Matthew Carroll, Yun Jung Choi, Christian Döhler, Volker Gast, Eri Kashima, Emil Mittag, Bruno Olsson, Kyla Quinn, Dineke Schokkin, Philip Tama, Charlotte van Tongeren, and Jeff Siegel. In press. The Languages of Southern New Guinea. Bill Palmer (ed.), *Papuan Languages and Linguistics*. Berlin: Mouton.

Fabritius, G. J. 1855. *Anteekeningen omtrent Nieuw-Guinea*. Tijdschrift voor Indische Taal-, Land- en Volkenkunde IV. 209–215.

Feuilleteau de Bruyn, W.K.H., J.V.L. Opperman, L. Doorman, and J. Th. Stroeve. 1915. Ethnographische gegevens betreffende de inboorlingen in het stroomgebied van de Mamberamo. *Tijdschrift van het Koninklijk Aardrijkskundig Genootschap* 32: 655–672.

Flint, L.A. 1917–1918. Vocabulary: Name of Tribe, Karami. People. Name of Village, Kikimairi and Aduahai. *Commonwealth of Australia. Papua: Annual Report for the Year* 1917–1918, 96–96.

Foley, William A. 1986. *The Papuan Languages of New Guinea* (Cambridge language surveys). Cambridge: Cambridge University Press.

Foley, William A. 2000. The Languages of New Guinea. *Annual Review of Anthropology* 29, no. 1: 357–404.

Foley, William A. 2005. Linguistic Prehistory in the Sepik-Ramu Basin. *Papuan Pasts: Studies in the Cultural, Linguistic and Biological History of the Papuan-Speaking Peoples* (Pacific Linguistics 572), ed. by Andrew Pawley, Robert Attenborough, Jack Golson, and Robin Hide, 109–144. Canberra: Research School of Pacific and Asian Studies, Australian National University.

Foley, William A. In press-a. The languages of Northwest New Guinea. *Papuan Languages and Linguistics*, ed. by Bill Palmer. Berlin: Mouton.

Foley, William A. In press-b. The Languages of the Sepik. *Papuan Languages and Linguistics*, ed. by Bill Palmer. Berlin: Mouton.

Frahm, Roxanne Margaret. 1998. *Baniata Serial Verb Constructions*. MA thesis, University of Auckland.

Franklin, Karl J. 1968. Languages of the Gulf District: A Preview. *Papers in New Guinea. Linguistics No. 8* (Pacific Linguistics: Series A 16), 19–44. Canberra: Research School of Pacific and Asian Studies, Australian National University.

Franklin, Karl J. 1973a. Appendices. *The Linguistic Situation in the Gulf District and Adjacent Areas, Papua New Guinea* (Pacific Linguistics: Series C 26), ed. by Karl J. Franklin, 539–592. Canberra: Research School of Pacific and Asian Studies, Australian National University.

Franklin, Karl J. 1973b. Other Language Groups in the Gulf District and Adjacent Areas. *The Linguistic Situation in the Gulf District and Adjacent Areas, Papua New Guinea* (Pacific Linguistics: Series C 26), ed. by Karl J. Franklin, 263–277. Canberra: Research School of Pacific and Asian Studies, Australian National University.

Franklin, Karl J. 1975a. Comments on Proto-Engan. *New Guinea Area Languages and Language Study Vol 1: Papuan Languages and the New Guinea Linguistic Scene* (Pacific Linguistics: Series C 38), ed. by Stephen A. Wurm, 263–276. Canberra: Research School of Pacific and Asian Studies, Australian National University.

Franklin, Karl J. 1975b. Isolates: Gulf District. *New Guinea Area Languages and Language Study Vol 1: Papuan Languages and the New Guinea linguistic scene* (Pacific Linguistics: Series C 38), ed. by Stephen A. Wurm, 891–896. Canberra: Research School of Pacific and Asian Studies, Australian National University.

Franklin, Karl J. 1995. Some further comments on Kaki Ae. *Language and Linguistics in Melanesia* 26: 195–198.

Franklin, Karl J. 2001. Kutubuan (Foe and Fasu) and Proto Engan. *The Boy from Bundaberg: Studies in Melanesian Linguistics in Honour of Tom Dutton* (Pacific Linguistics 514), ed. by Andrew Pawley, Malcolm Ross and Darrell Tryon, 143–154. Canberra: Research School of Pacific and Asian Studies, Australian National University.

Franklin, Karl J. and C.L. Voorhoeve. 1973. Languages Near the Intersection of the Gulf, Southern Highlands and Western Districts. *The Linguistic Situation in the Gulf District and Adjacent Areas, Papua New Guinea* (Pacific Linguistics: Series C 26), ed. by Karl J. Franklin, 149–186. Canberra: Research School of Pacific and Asian Studies, Australian National University.

Galis, Klaas Wilhelm. 1955. Talen en dialecten van Nederlands Nieuw-Guinea. *Tijdschrift Nieuw-Guinea* 16: 109–118, 134–145, 161–178.

Galis, Klaas Wilhelm. 1956. *Ethnologische Survey van het Jafi-district (Onderafdeling Hollandia)* volume 102. Hollandia (Jayapura): Gouvernement van Nederlands Nieuw-Guinea, Kantoor voor Bevolkingszaken.

Gavin, Michael C. and John Richard Stepp. 2014. Rapoport's Rule Revisited: Geographical Distributions of Human Languages. *PLoS One* 9, no. 9: e107623. 1–8.

Gordon, Raymond G. Jr. 2005. *Ethnologue: Languages of the World* (15th ed.). Dallas: SIL International.

Grace, George W. 1956. *1955–1956 Fieldnotes: Notebook 47*. Ms.

Graham, Glenn H. 1981. A Sociolinguistic Survey of Busa and Nagatman. *Sociolinguistic Surveys of Sepik Languages* (Workpapers in Papua New Guinea Languages 29), ed. by Richard Loving, 177–192. Ukarumpa: Summer Institute of Linguistics.

Grimes, Barbara F. (ed.). 2000. *Ethnologue: Languages of the World* (14th ed.). Dallas: SIL International.

Hammarström, Harald. 2008a. *A Reclassification of Some West Papua Languages*. Paper Presented at the International Workshop on Minority Languages in the Malay/Indonesian Speaking World, 28 June 2008 Leiden, The Netherlands.

Hammarström, Harald. 2008b. Two Hitherto Unnoticed Languages from Sobger River, West Papua, Indonesia. Submitted.

Hammarström, Harald. 2010a. *The Genetic Position of the Mawes Language*. Paper presented at the Workshop on the Languages of Papua 2, 8–12 February 2010, Manokwari, Indonesia.

Hammarström, Harald. 2010b. The Status of the Least Documented Language Families in the World. *Language Documentation and Conservation* 4: 177–212.

Hammarström, Harald. 2014. Basic Vocabulary Comparison in South American Languages. *The Native Languages of South America: Origins, Development, Typology*, ed. by Pieter Muysken and Loretta O'Connor, 56–70. Cambridge: Cambridge University Press.

Hammarström, Harald. 2015. Ethnologue 16/17/18th Editions: A Comprehensive Review. *Language* 91, no. 3: 723–737. Plus 188pp online appendix.

Hammarström, Harald, Robert Forkel, Martin Haspelmath, and Sebastian Bank. 2015. *Glottolog 2.6*. Jena: Max Planck Institute for the Science of Human History. http://glottolog.org (14 October 2015).

Hammarström, Harald and Sebastian Nordhoff. 2012. The Languages of Melanesia: Quantifying the Level of Coverage. *Melanesian Languages on the Edge of Asia: Challenges for the 21st Century* (Language Documentation and Conservation Special Publication 5), ed. by Nicholas Evans and Marian Klamer, 13–34. Honolulu: University of Hawaii Press.

Harbour, Daniel. 2014. Poor Pronoun Systems and What They Teach Us. *Nordlyd* 41, no. 1: 125–143.

Hashimoto, Kazuo. 1996. *Ata-English Dictionary*. Ukarumpa: Summer Institute of Linguistics.

Hashimoto, Kazuo. 2008. *Ata – English Dictionary with English – Ata Finderlist*. Ukarumpa: Summer Institute of Linguistics.

Healey, Alan. 1964. *The Ok Language Family in New Guinea*. Canberra: Australian National University doctoral dissertation. [Sometimes cited as *A Survey of the Ok Family of Languages* presumably because part of the thesis II-IV, which contains all linguistic data, carries this title.].

Heeschen, Volker. 1978. The Mek Languages of Irian Jaya with Special Reference to the Eipo Language. *Irian* VII, no. 2: 3–46.

Henderson, James. 1995. *Phonology and Grammar of Yele, Papua New Guinea* (Pacific Linguistics: Series B 112). Canberra: Research School of Pacific and Asian Studies, Australian National University.

Henderson, James E. 1975. Yeletnye, the Language of Rossel Island. *Studies in Languages of Central and South-East Papua* (Pacific Linguistics: Series C 29), ed. by Tom E. Dutton, 817–834. Canberra: Australian National University.

Henderson, James E. and Anne Henderson. 1987. *Rossel Language, Milne Bay Province: Rossel to English, English to Rossel* (Dictionaries of Papua New Guinea 9). Ukarumpa: Summer Institute of Linguistics.

Henderson, James E. and Anne Henderson. 1999. *Rossel Language, Milne Bay Province: Rossel to English, English to Rossel* (Dictionaries of Papua New Guinea 9). Ukarumpa: Summer Institute of Linguistics.

Holmes, John H. 1913. A Preliminary Study of the Namau Language, Purari Delta, Papua. *Journal of the Royal Anthropological Institute of Great Britain and Ireland* 43: 124–142.

Holmes, John H. 1920. *Ene amua Iesu Keriso onu kuruei voa: Nawawrea Eire*. London: British and Foreign Bible Society.

Höltker, Georg. 1938. Eine fragmentarische Worterliste der Gapun-sprache Neuguineas. *Anthropos* 33: 279–282.

Hoogland, J. 1939. Uittreksel uit het Dagboek van Hollandia over het tijdvak 16 Juni tot en met 13 Juli 1939. Nationaal Archief, Den Haag, Ministerie van Koloniën: Kantoor Bevolkingszaken Nieuw-Guinea te Hollandia: Rapportenarchief, 1950–1962, nummer toegang 2.10.25, inventarisnummer 24A.

Hoogland, J. 1940. Memorie van Overgave van de Onderafdeling Hollandia. Nationaal Archief, Den Haag, Ministerie van Kolonien: Kantoor Bevolkingszaken Nieuw-Guinea te Hollandia: Rapportenarchief, 1950–1962, nummer toegang 2.10.25, inventarisnummer 24.

Im, Youn-Shim and Randy Lebold. 2006. Draft Survey Report on the Usku Language of Papua. To appear in the SIL Electronic Survey Reports.

Jore, Tim & Laura Alemán. 2002. *Sociolinguistic survey of the Tirio language family.* SIL, Ukarumpa: Ms.

Juillerat, Bernard. 1993. *La révocation des Tambaran: les Banaro et Richard Thurnwald revisités* (CNRS Ethnologie). Paris: CNRS.

Kairi, T. and John Kolia. 1977. Purari language notes. *Oral History* V, no. 10: 1–90.

Kamholz, David. 2012. The Keuw Isolate: Preliminary Materials and Classification. *History, Contact and Classification of Papuan Languages* (LLM Special Issue 2012), ed. by Harald Hammarström and Wilco van den Heuvel, 243–268. Port Moresby: Linguistic Society of Papua New Guinea.

Kamholz, David. 2014. Austronesians in Papua: Diversi cation and change in South Halmahera-West New Guinea. University of California at Berkeley doctoral dissertation.

Kelm, Antje and Heinz Kelm. 1980. *Sago und Schwein: Ethnologie von Kwieftim und Abrau in Nordost-Neuguinea* (Studien zur Kulturkunde 51). Wiesbaden: Franz Steiner.

Kerr, Harland B. 1967. A Preliminary Statement of Witu Grammar: The Syntactic Role and Structure of the Verb. MA thesis, University of Hawaii.

Kerr, Harland B. 1975. The Relationship of Wiru in the Southern Highlands District to Languages of the East New Guinea Highlands Stock. *New Guinea Area Languages and Language Study Vol 1: Papuan Languages and the New Guinea Linguistic Scene* (Pacific Linguistics: Series C 38), ed. by Stephen A. Wurm, 277–296. Canberra: Research School of Pacific and Asian Studies, Australian National University.

Kim, So Hyun. 2006. Draft Survey Report on the Yetfa Language of Papua, Indonesia. To appear in the SIL Electronic Survey Reports.

Klamer, Marian and Gary Holton. In press. The Papuan Languages of East Nu santara. *Papuan Languages and Linguistics*, ed. by Bill Palmer. Berlin: Mouton.

Koentjaraningrat. 1965. Ichtisar Pola Kehidupan Masjarakat: Penduduk Pantai Utara Irian Barat Dan Potensinja Untuk Pembangunan. *Madjalah Ilmu-Ilmu Sastra Indonesia* 11. 129–194.

Kulick, Don. 1987. Language shift and language socialization in Gapun: A Report on Fieldwork in Progress. *Language and Linguistics in Melanesia* 15, no. 2: 125–151.

Kulick, Don and Christopher Stroud. 1990. Code-Switching in Gapun: Social and Linguistic Aspects of Language Used in a Language Shifting Community. *Melanesian Pidgin and Tok Pisin*, ed. by J.W.M. Verhaar, 205–234. Amsterdam: John Benjamins.

Kulick, Don and Christopher Stroud. 1992. The Structure of the Taiap (Ga-pun) Language. *The Language Game: Papers in Memory of Donald C. Laycock* (Pacific Linguistics: Series C 10), ed. by Tom Dutton, Malcolm Ross, and Darrell Tryon, 203–226. Canberra: Research School of Pacific and Asian Studies, Australian National University.

Langeler, J.W. 1915. Sobger-Rivier: 'Journaal loopende van 22 October 1914 t/m 7 Januari 1915. Betreffende eene patrouille te water tot exploratie van de twee groote linker zijrivieren der Idenburg-rivier op ongeveer 140 10/4 O.L. en tot aanpeiling van het hooggebergte'. KITLV Manuscripts and Archives, Leiden [D H 1163].

Larson, Gordon F. 1977. Reclassification of Some Irian Jaya Highlands Language Families: A Lexicostatical Cross-Family Subclassification with Historical Implications. *Irian* VI, no. 2: 3–40.

Laycock, Don. 1972. Looking Westward: Work of the Australian National University on Languages of West Irian. *Irian* 1(2): 68–77.

Laycock, Donald C. 1969. Melanesia Has a Fourth of the World's Linguistic Diversity. *Pacific Islands Monthly* 9: 71–76.

Laycock, Donald C. 1973. *Sepik Languages: Checklist and Preliminary Classification* (Pacific Linguistics: Series B 25). Canberra: Research School of Pacific and Asian Studies, Australian National University.

Laycock, Donald C. 1975a. Isolates: Sepik Region. *New Guinea Area Languages and Language Study Vol 1: Papuan Languages and the New Guinea Linguistic Scene* (Pacific Linguistics: Series C 38), ed. by Stephen A. Wurm, 879–886. Canberra: Research School of Pacific and Asian Studies, Australian National University.

Laycock, Donald C. 1975b. Sko, Kwomtari and Left May (Arai) Phyla. *New Guinea Area Languages and Language Study Vol 1: Papuan Languages and the New Guinea linguistic scene* (Pacific Linguistics: Series C 38), ed. by Stephen A. Wurm, 849–858. Canberra: Research School of Pacific and Asian Studies, Australian National University.

Laycock, Donald C. 1977. Me and You Versus the Rest: Abbreviated Pronoun Systems in Irianese/Papuan Language. *Irian* 7: 33–41.

Laycock, Donald C. 1982a. Linguistic Diversity in Melanesia: A Tentative Explanation. *GAVA': Studien zu austronesischen Sprachen und Kulturen Hans Kähler gewidmet*, ed. by Rainer Carle, 31–37. Berlin: Reimer.

Laycock, Donald C. 1982b. Melanesian Linguistic Diversity: A Melanesian Choice? *Melanesia: Beyond Diversity*, vol. I, R.J. May and Hank Nelson, 33–38. Canberra: Research School of Pacific Studies, Australian National University.

Laycock, Donald C. and John A. Z'Graggen. 1975. The Sepik-Ramu Phylum. *New Guinea Area Languages and Language Study Vol 1: Papuan Languages and the New Guinea Linguistic Scene* (Pacific Linguistics: Series C 38), ed. by Stephen A. Wurm, 731–764. Canberra: Research School of Pacific and Asian Studies, Australian National University.

Laycock, Donald C. (no date). Notebook D28. Ms.

Le Roux, C.C.F.M. 1950. Alphabetische woordenlijst: Dèm – Nederlands, Zinnen en uitdrukkingen: Nederlands – Dèm. *De Bergpapoea's van Nieuw-Guinea en hun Woongebied*, vol. II, 852–862, 892–895. Leiden: E. J. Brill.

Le Roux, C.C.F.M. 1950a. 15: Tellen en Rekenen – Maten – Tijdrekening – Windstreken – Kennis van Kleuren – Gebarentaal. *De Bergpapoea's van Nieuw-Guinea en hun Woongebied*, vol. II, 528–553. Leiden: E. J. Brill.

Le Roux, C.C.F.M. 1950b. 25: Taalkundige Gegevens. *De Bergpapoea's van Nieuw-Guinea en hun Woongebied*, vol. II, 776–900. Leiden: E. J. Brill.

Lean, Glendon A. 1986. *Sandaun Province* (Counting Systems of Papua New Guinea 7). Port Moresby: Papua New Guinea University of Technology. Draft Edition.

Levinson, Stephen C. 2006. The language of space in Yélî Dnye. *Grammars of Space: Explorations in Cognitive Diversity*, ed. by Stephen C. Levinson and David P. Wilkins, 157–203. Cambridge: Cambridge University Press.

Levinson, Stephen C. (ms) A grammar of Yele.

Lewis, Paul M. 2009. *Ethnologue: Languages of the World* (16th ed.). Dallas: SIL International.

Lewis, Paul M., Gary F. Simons, and Charles D. Fennig. 2015. *Ethnologue: Languages of the World* (18th ed.). Dallas: SIL International.

Lindström, Eva. 2002. *Topics in the Grammar of Kuot*. Doctoral dissertation, Stockholm University.

Little, Christopher A.J.L. 2008. *Becoming an Asabano: The Socialization of Asabano Children, Duranmin, West Sepik Province, Papua New Guinea*. MA thesis, Trent University, Canada.

Loeweke, Eunice and Jean May. 1966. Fasu grammar. *Anthropological Linguistics* 8, no. 6: 17–33.

Loeweke, Eunice and Jean May. 1980. General grammar of Fasu (Namo Me). *Grammatical Studies in Fasu and Mt. Koiali* (Workpapers in Papua New Guinea Languages 27), ed. by Don Hutchisson, 5–106. Ukarumpa: Summer Institute of Linguistics.

Lohmann, Roger Ivar. 2000. *Cultural Reception in the Contact and Conversion History of the Asabano of Papua New Guinea*. Doctoral dissertation, University of Wisconsin, Madison.

Loving, Richard and Jack Bass. 1964. *Languages of the Amanab Sub-District*. Port Moresby: Department of Information and Extension Services.

May, Jean and Eunice Loeweke. 1981. *Fasu (Námo Mē)-English dictionary*. Ukarumpa: Summer Institute of Linguistics.

Mühlhäusler, Peter. 1990. Towards an Implicational Analysis of Pronoun Development. *Development and Diversity: Language Variation across Space Time and Space: A festschrift for Charles-James N. Bailey* (Summer Institute of Linguistics: Publications in Linguistics 93), ed. by Jerold A. Edmondson, Crawford Feagin, and Peter Mühlhäusler, 351–370. Dallas: Summer Institute of Linguistics.

Murray, George H. 1920. Kerema Station, Gulf Division, Name of Tribe: Huaruha, Name of Village, Havoro. *Commonwealth of Australia. Papua: Annual Report for the Year 1918–1919*, 117–117.

Musgrave, Simon and Mark Donohue. 2007. Preposed Possessor Languages in a Wider Context. Handout from talk at Workshop on the Languages of Papua, Manokwari, August 2007.

Nettle, Daniel. 1999. *Linguistic Diversity*. Oxford: Oxford University Press.

Nevermann, Hans. 1939. Die Kanum-Irebe und ihre Nachbarn. *Zeitschrift für Ethnologie* 71: 1–70.

No Author Stated. 2006a. *Godokono Hido Tabo: Aramia River Tabo Testament*. Port Moresby: Bible Society of Papua New Guinea.

No Author Stated. 2006b. *Godokono Wade Tabo: Fly River Tabo New Testament*. Port Moresby: Bible Society of Papua New Guinea.

Obata, Kazuko. 2003. *A Grammar of Bilua: A Papuan Language of the Solomon Islands* (Pacific Linguistics 540). Canberra: Research School of Pacific and Asian Studies, Australian National University. Also as Obata, Kazuko. 2000. A grammar of Bilua, a Papuan language of the Solomon Islands. Ph.D. thesis, Australian National University.

Odé, Cecilia. 2002a. *Mpur Prosody: An Experimental-Phonetic Analysis with Examples from Two Versions of the Fentora Myth* (Endangered Languages of the Pacific Rim Publications Series A1-003). Osaka, Japan: Endangered Languages of the Pacific Rim.

Odé, Cecilia. 2002b. A Sketch of Mpur. *Languages of the Eastern Bird's Head* (Pacific Linguistics 524), ed. by Ger P. Reesink, 45–107. Canberra: Research School of Pacific and Asian Studies, Australian National University.

Odé, Cecilia. 2004. *Mpur Vocabulary = Daftar Kata Mpur*, vol. A1-009. Osaka, Japan: Endangered Languages of the Pacific Rim.

Oosterwal, Gottfried. 1961. People of the Tor: A cultural-anthropological study on the tribes of the Tor territory (Northern Netherlands New-Guinea). Rijksuniversiteit te Utrecht doctoral dissertation. Published by Van Gorcum, Assen.

Pryor, Bonita and Cynthia J. Farr. 1989. Botin deictics: Go and Come. *Language and Linguistics in Melanesia* 20: 115–145.

Pryor, John. 1990. Deixis and Participant Tracking in Botin. *Language and Linguistics in Melanesia* 21: 1–29.

Rascher, Matthias. 1903–1904. Die Sulka: Ein Beitrag zur Ethnographie von Neu-Pommern. *Archiv für Anthropologic, N. F.* 1: 209–235.

Ray, Sidney H. 1907. Grammar Notes on the Namau Language Spoken in the Purari Delta. *Linguistics* (Reports of the Cambridge Anthropological Expedition to Torres Straits III), ed. by Sidney H. Ray, 325–332. Cambridge: Cambridge University Press.

Ray, Sidney H. 1919. A New Linguistic Family. *The Bible in the World* 15: 149–150.

Ray, Sidney H. 1927. The Non-Melanesian Languages of the Solomon Islands. *Festschrift Publication d'hommage of ferte au P. W. Schmidt*, ed. by Wilhelm Koppers, 123–126. Vienna: Mechitharisten-Congregations- Buchdruckerei.

Reesink, Ger. 2005. Sulka of East New Britain: A Mixture of Oceanic and Papuan Traits. *Oceanic Linguistics* 44, no. 1: 145–193.

Reesink, Ger P. 1976. Languages of the Aramia River Area. *Papers in New Guinea Linguistics 19* (Pacific Linguistics: Series A 45), 1–37. Canberra: Research School of Pacific and Asian Studies, Australian National University.

Rentoul, Alex C. 1924. Vocabulary of Words Obtained from a Native of the Dibiasu Tribe Living in the Country in the Vicinity of the Upper Bamu (or Woi-Woi) Western Division. *Commonwealth of Australia. Papua: Annual Report for the Year 1924*, 74–74.

Robide van der Aa, Pieter Jan Baptist Carel. 1879. *Reizen naar Nederlandsch Nieuw-Guinea ondernomen op last der Regeering van Nederlandsche Indie in de jaren 1871, 1872, 1875–1876 door de Heeren P. van Crab en J.E. Teysmann, J.G. Coornengel, A.J. Langeveldt van Hemert en P. Swaan*. The Hague: Martinus Nijhoff.

Ross, Malcolm. 2001. Is There an East Papuan Phylum? Evidence from Pronouns. *The Boy from Bundaberg: Studies in Melanesian Linguistics in Honour of Tom Dutton* (Pacific Linguistics 514), ed. by Andrew Pawley, Malcolm Ross, and Darrell Tryon, 301–321. Canberra: Research School of Pacific and Asian Studies, Australian National University.

Ross, Malcolm. 2006. *Clues to the Linguistic Situation in Near Oceania before Agriculture*. Paper for presentation at the symposium Historical linguistics and hunter-gatherer populations in global perspective, MPI-EVA Leipzig, 10–12 August 2006.

Ross, Malcolm D. 2005. Pronouns as a Preliminary Diagnostic for Grouping Papuan Languages. *Papuan Pasts: Studies in the Cultural, Linguistic and Biological History of the Papuan-Speaking Peoples* (Pacific Linguistics 572), ed. by Andrew Pawley, Robert Attenborough, Jack Golson, and Robin Hide, 15–66. Canberra: Research School of Pacific and Asian Studies, Australian National University.

Routamaa, Judy. 1994. Kamula Grammar Essentials. Ms. www.sil.org/pacific/png/abstract.asp?id=50209 (1 August 2008).

Rumaropen, Benny. 2004. Draft Survei Sosiolinguistik pada ragam Bahasa Kimki di Bagian Tenggara Gunung Ji, Papua, Indonesia. To appear in the SIL Electronic Survey Reports.

Rumaropen, Benny. 2005. Laporan sosiolinguistik bahasa Poulle di Kampung Molof dan Waley, Kabupaten Keerom, Papua, Indonesia. To appear in the SIL Electronic Survey Reports.

Rumaropen, Benny. 2006. Draft Survey Report on the Kapauri Language of Papua. To appear in the SIL Electronic Survey Reports.

San Roque, Lila. 2008. *An Introduction to Duna Grammar*. Doctoral dissertation, Australian National University.

San Roque, Lila and Robyn Loughnane. 2012. Inheritance, Contact and Change in the New Guinea Highlands Evidentialitv Area. *History, contact and classification of Papuan languages* (LLM Special Issue 2012), ed. by Harald Hammarström and Wilco van den Heuvel, 387–427. Port Moresby: Linguistic Society of Papua New Guinea.

Schellong, Otto. 1890. *Weitere Wörterverzeichnisse* (Einzelbeiträge zur allgemeinen und vergleichenden Sprachwissenschaft 7). Leipzig: Wilhelm Friedrich.

Schlatter, Tim. 2003. Tabo Language Grammar Sketch (Aramia River). Ms.

Schmidt, Wilhelm. 1904. Eine Papuasprache auf Neupommern. *Globus* LXXXVI: 79–80.

Schneider, Joseph. 1962. *Grammatik der Sulka-Sprache (Neubritannien)* (Micro-Biblioteca Anthropos 36). Posieux: Anthropos Institut.

Shafer, Robert. 1965. Was New Guinea the Graveyard of 100 South Asian and Pacific Cultures? *Orbis* 14, no. 2: 312–385.

Shaw, Daniel R. 1973. A Tentative Classification of the Languages of the Mt. Bosavi Region. *The Linguistic Situation in the Gulf District and Adjacent Areas, Papua New Guinea* (Pacific Linguistics: Series C 26), ed. by Karl J. Franklin, 189–215. Canberra: Research School of Pacific and Asian Studies, Australian National University.

Sillitoe, Paul. 1993. *The Bogaia of the Muller Ranges, Papua New Guinea.* Sydney: University of Sydney.

Silzer, Peter J. and Heljä Heikkinen. 1984. Index of Irian Jaya Languages. *Irian* XII: 1–124.

Silzer, Peter J. and Heljä Heikkinen-Clouse. 1991. *Index of Irian Jaya Languages* (Special Issue of Irian: Bulletin of Irian Jaya) (2nd ed.). Jayapura: Program Kerjasama Universitas Cenderawasih and SIL.

Smits, Leo and C.L. Voorhoeve. 1994. *The J. C. Anceaux Collection of Wordlists of Irian Jaya Languages B: Non-Austronesian (Papuan) Languages (Part I)* (Irian Jaya Source Material No. 9 Series B 3). Leiden-Jakarta: DSAL-CUL/IRIS.

Smits, Leo and C.L. Voorhoeve. 1998. *The J. C. Anceaux Collection of Wordlists of Irian Jaya Languages B: Non-Austronesian (Papuan) Languages (Part II)* (Irian Jaya Source Material No. 10 Series B 4). Leiden-Jakarta: DSAL-CUL/IRIS.

Speiser, Felix. 1944. Eine Initiationszeremonie in Kambrambo am Sepik Neuguinea. *Ethnologischer Anzeiger* 4: 153–157.

Stebbins, Tonya N. 2009. The Papuan Languages of the Eastern Bismarcks: Migration, Origins and Connections. *Discovering History Through Language: Papers in Honour of Malcolm Ross* (Pacific Linguistics 605), ed. by Bethwvn Evans, 223–243. Canberra: Research School of Pacific and Asian Studies, Australian National University.

Strong, Marsh W. 1911. Note on the Tate Language of British New Guinea. *Man* 11, no. 101: 178–181.

Summerhayes, Glenn R., Andrew Fairbairn, Matthew Leavesley, Herman Mandui, Judith Field, Anne Ford, and Richard Fullagar. 2010. Human Adaptation and Plant Use in Highland New Guinea 49,000 to 44,000 Years Ago. *Science* 330, no. 6000: 78–81.

Tadmor, Uri, Martin Haspelmath, and Bradley Taylor. 2010. Borrowability and the Notion of Basic Vocabulary. *Diachronica* 27, no. 2: 226–246.

Terrill, Angela. 2003. *A Grammar of Lavukaleve* (Mouton Grammar Library 30). Berlin: Mouton de Gruyter.

Terrill, Angela. 2011. Languages in Contact: An Exploration of Stability and Change in the Solomon Islands. *Oceanic Linguistics* 50, no. 2: 312–337.

Terrill, Angela and Michael Dunn. 2003. Orthographic Design in the Solomon Islands: The Social, Historical, and Linguistic Situation of Touo (Baniata). *Written Language and Literacy* 6, no. 2: 177–192.

Tharp, Douglas. 1996. Sulka Grammar Essentials. *Two Non-Austronesian Grammars from the Islands* (Data Papers on Papua New Guinea Languages 42), ed. by John M. Clifton, 77–179. Ukarumpa: Summer Institute of Linguistics.

Thurnwald, Richard. 1921. *Die Gemeinde der Banáro.* Stuttgart: Ferdinand Enke.

Thurston, William. 1982. *A Comparative Study of Anem and Lusi* (Pacific Linguistics: Series B 83). Canberra: Research School of Pacific and Asian Studies, Australian National University.

Thurston, William R. 1992. Sociolinguistic Typology and Other Factors Effecting Change in North-Western New Britain, Papua New Guinea. *Culture Change, Language Change: Case Studies from Melanesia* (Pacific Linguistics: Series C 120), ed. by Tom Dutton, 123–139. Canberra: Research School of Pacific and Asian Studies, Australian National University.

Trefry, David. 1965. *A Comparative Study of Kuman and Pawaian: Non-Austronesian Languages of New Guinea.* Sydney: University of Sydney MA thesis.

Trefry, David. 1969. *A Comparative Study of Kuman and Pawaian* (Pacific Linguistics: Series B 13). Canberra: Research School of Pacific and Asian Studies, Australian National University.

Tupper, Ian. 2007. *Endangered Languages Listing: TURUMSA* [tqm]. Document posted at www.pnglanguages.org/pacific/png/show_lang_entry.asp?id=tqm (1 May 2007).

Usher, Timothy and Edgar Suter. 2015. The Anim Languages of Southern New Guinea. *Oceanic Linguistics* 54, no. 1: 110–142.

van der Leeden, Alexander Cornelis. 1954. *Verslag over taalgebieden in het Sarmische van de Ambtenaar van het Kantoor voor Bevolkingszaken* volume 35. Hollandia: Gouvernement van Nederlands-Nieuw-Guinea, Dienst van Binnenlandse Zaken, Kantoor voor Bevolkingszaken.

Voorhoeve, C.L. 1971. Miscellaneous Notes on Languages in West Irian, New Guinea. *Papers in New Guinea Linguistics 14* (Pacific Linguistics: Series A 28), 47–114. Canberra: Research School of Pacific and Asian Studies, Australian National University.

Voorhoeve, C.L. 1975a. Central and Western Trans-New Guinea Phylum Languages. *New Guinea Area Languages and Language Study Vol 1: Papuan Languages and the New Guinea linguistic Scene* (Pacific Linguistics: Series C 38), ed. by Stephen A. Wurm, 345–460. Canberra: Research School of Pacific and Asian Studies, Australian National University.

Voorhoeve, C.L. 1975b. *Languages of Irian Jaya, Checklist: Preliminary Classification, Language Maps, Wordlists* (Pacific Linguistics: Series B 31). Canberra: Research School of Pacific and Asian Studies, Australian National University.

Wade, Martha L. 1984. *Some Stratificational Insights Concerning Botin (Kambot), a Papuan Language.* MA thesis, University of Texas, Arlington.

Walden, Edgar. 1911. Die ethnographischen und sprachlichen Verhältnisse im nördlichen Teile Neu-Mecklenburgs und auf den umliegenden Inseln. *Korrespondenz-Blatt der Deutschen Gesellschaft für Anthropologie, Ethnologie und Urgeschichte* 42: 28–31.

Wambaliau, Theresia. 2004. *Draft Laporan Survei pada Bahasa Murkim di Papua, Indonesia.* To appear in the SIL Electronic Survey Reports.

Wambaliau, Theresia. 2006a. Draft Laporan Survei pada Bahasa Kosare di Papua, Indonesia. To appear in the SIL Electronic Survey Reports.

Wambaliau, Theresia. 2006b. Draft Laporan Survei pada Bahasa Mawes di Papua, Indonesia. To appear in the SIL Electronic Survey Reports.

Waterhouse, Ray. 1927. The Baniata Language of Rendova Island. *Man* 27, no. 45, 64–67.

Wegener, Claudia U. 2012. *A Grammar of Savosavo* (Mouton Grammar Library 61). Berlin: Mouton de Gruyter.

Wichmann, Søren. 2012. A Classification of Papuan Languages. *History, Contact and Classification of Papuan Languages* (LLM Special Issue 2012), ed. by Harald Hammarström and Wilco van den Heuvel, 313–386. Port Moresby: Linguistic Society of Papua New Guinea.

Winter, F.P. 1890. Collection of Words of Rossel Island Dialect (Compiled by the Hon. F.P. Winter.). *Annual Report of British New Guinea 1889–1890:* 157–157.

Wurm, Stephen. 1982. *Papuan Languages of Oceania* (Ars Linguistica 7). Tübingen: Gunther Narr.

Wurm, Stephen A. 1975a. The Central and Western Areas of the Trans-New Guinea Phylum: The Trans-Fly (Sub-Phylum-Level) Stock. *New Guinea Area Languages and Language Study Vol 1: Papuan Languages and the New Guinea Linguistic Scene* (Pacific Linguistics: Series C 38), ed. by Stephen A. Wurm, 323–344. Canberra: Research School of Pacific and Asian Studies, Australian National University.

Wurm, Stephen A. 1975b. The East Papuan Phylum in General. *New Guinea Area Languages and Language Study Vol 1: Papuan Languages and the New Guinea Linguistic Scene* (Pacific Linguistics: Series C 38), ed. by Stephen A. Wurm, 783–804. Canberra: Research School of Pacific and Asian Studies, Australian National University.

Yanagida, Tatsuya. 2004. Socio-Historic Overview of the Ata Language, an Endangered Papuan Language in New Britain, Papua New Guinea. *Kan minami Taiheiyoo no gengo 3 [Languages of the South Pacific Rim 3]* (ELPR Publications Series A1–008), ed. by Shibata Norio and Toru Shionoya, 61–94. Suita: Faculty of Informatics, Osaka Gakuin University.

Z'graggen, John. 1975. Comparative Wordlists of the Gulf District and Adjacent Areas. *Comparative Wordlists I* (Workpapers in Papua New Guinea Languages 14), ed. by Richard Loving, 5–116. Ukarumpa: Summer Institute of Linguistics. Rearranged version of Franklin ed. (1973): 541–592, with typographical errors.

Z'graggen, John A. 1969. *Classificatory and Typological Studies in Languages of the Madang District New Guinea*. Canberra: Australian National University doctoral dissertation.

Z'graggen, John A. 1972. *Comparative Wordlist of the Ramu Language Group, New Guinea*. Alexishafen: Anthropos Institute.

CHAPTER 12

LANGUAGE ISOLATES OF AUSTRALIA

Claire Bowern

1 INTRODUCTION

Language isolates are languages with no *demonstrable* relationship to other languages (Campbell, this volume), in effect, language families with a single member. Under this definition, strictly applied, there are six language isolates in Australia. However, the languages of Australia have long been assumed to be all ultimately related to one another (Wurm 1972; Dixon 1980) at some level of remoteness. Indeed, one might argue that one of the recurrent "tropes" of work on Australian Aboriginal languages is not their diversity but the insistence on their similarity, either through shared inheritance or through longstanding language contact. It is not difficult to find statements that a particular language is "typical" of the languages in the region or continent. Compare, for example, Goddard (1985:167), Dixon (1977:1), Butcher (2006:187), and Tsunoda (2012:1), amongst others.

Despite these assumptions of large-scale similarity, it has not always been the case that all the languages of Australia were assumed to be related, even within the Pama-Nyungan family. Statements of this type are not hard to find in the literature. Dixon (1976:2) writes "It has long been believed (although, of course, it has not yet been proved) that all or most Australian languages are genetically related." Here, Dixon mentions two languages that were treated as possible exceptions: Mbabaram and Anewan (also known as Nganyaaywana). Harvey's (2001) discussion of relations in the Darwin region, discussed in Section 2.5, also explicitly presupposes a single family of Australian languages. Australian languages are thus a good illustration of Campbell's point in the introduction to this volume that there is nothing *linguistically* special about language isolates, since their status as isolates may change as our knowledge of language history changes. Overview and discussion of those languages, particularly Mbabaram, Anewan (Nganyaaywana), Tiwi, and Anindilyakwa, are provided in Section 2. I also discuss the languages of Tasmania in Section 3, since they have sometimes been treated as a single language isolate.

Another striking feature of the Australian continent is the number of primary subgroups in the major family of the area (Pama-Nyungan; Bowern and Atkinson 2012; Bowern and Koch 2004), including languages, such as Warumungu, Anewan, and the Torres Strait language, where the most recent common ancestor is Proto-Pama-Nyungan. That is, they do not seem to share innovations with any intermediate proto-language. They might be considered "subgroup-level isolates". I review a few of these cases in Section 4.

The degree of language attrition and extinction is such in Australia that there are far fewer languages currently spoken than at the time of European settlement (beginning in the late 18th century). This has produced quite a few modern isolates; that is, languages where all known relatives have ceased to be spoken.

Some background on Australian languages overall is in order. The Australian mainland is home to 27 phylic families, ranging in size from 1 to almost 200 languages. The largest of these is Pama-Nyungan, covering 90% of the Australian mainland land mass, while the Non-Pama-Nyungan families are clustered in a small area in the North, in the Northern Territory and the Kimberley region of Western Australia. The languages of Tasmania constitute another group. There is also a Papuan language, Meryam Mir, spoken in the Eastern Torres Strait. This much is agreed on. More remote relations between Australian languages are less clear. Three major proposals exist at present. Heath (1990) suggests that there is a primary split between Proto-Pama-Nyungan and Proto-Non-Pama-Nyungan, the two constituting primary branches of a putative Proto-Australian family. Dixon (1997) does not provide explicit discussion of relationships between Pama-Nyungan and Non-Pama-Nyungan languages, but his (untenable) assumption that Pama-Nyungan reflects the initial peopling of Australia implies that Pama-Nyungan languages are no more closely related to one another than they are to the rest of Australia's Aboriginal languages (for further discussion, see Bowern 2006). The third proposal is due to Evans and McConvell (1997) (see also Evans 2003) and argues that the Tangkic, Garrwan, and Gunwinyguan families are the Non-Pama-Nyungan families most closely related to Pama-Nyungan. The evidence for this is, however, slight: it is based on a few pronominal forms and the presence of a putative sound change of *n > η word-initially in Pama-Nyungan languages.

The linguistic evidence for Proto-Australian is very small. Even amongst Pama-Nyungan languages, there are sufficiently high rates of lexical replacement across the family that lexical reconstruction is difficult. For example, Alpher (2004) finds only about a hundred well-attested Pama-Nyungan etyma. On the 200-item list of basic vocabulary used in Bowern and Atkinson (2012), Tangkic and Garrwan share only 18 and 12 items, respectively, with any Pama-Nyungan subgroups (Bowern 2015). Nonetheless, the matches are amongst the most stable items in basic vocabulary, implying that they are probably retentions from a shared common ancestor, rather than loans.

The primary evidence for common ancestry of Australian languages has been a) similar sound inventories; b) a small set of recurring monosyllabic verb roots such as *ma 'put' and *wa 'give' (Merlan 1979; Dixon 1980; McGregor 2002); and c) widespread pronominal forms such as the first person singular *ŋayu (Blake 1990a; Blake 1990b). For example, Harvey (2001:3–5) gives two pieces of evidence that Limilngan is related to other languages in Australia (though at a remote level). The first is that seven of the verbs reconstructed for Proto-Australian by Dixon (1980:Ch.12) appear to have reflexes in the language. The second is the presence of reflexes of widespread pronominal forms such as first person singular *ŋay and second plural *gu-rV.

2 PUTATIVE ISOLATES OF AUSTRALIA

All classifications of Australian languages, from Schmidt (1919) onwards, include language isolates within the Australian continent. That is, setting aside the putative (but unproven) status of descent from a common Proto-Australian, all authors recognize a series of single languages with no close relatives. However, the composition of this list varies among authors. Isolates in some of the early sources simply reflect a lack of knowledge of languages at the time; many descriptions of Australian languages were created after 1960, for example, and the classifications of the 1970s were still digesting those results. (See Bowern 2016: 7 (Figure 1) for an approximation of publication rates over the 20th century.) In the interests of space, I concentrate here primarily on the languages repeatedly identified as isolates across classifications and on the languages that have featured in discussions about the universal relatedness of Australian languages.

Several languages of off-shore islands, particularly Tiwi (Bathurst and Melville Islands) and Anindilyakwa (Groote Eylandt), are very divergent from their nearest geographic neighbors on the mainland. It is often assumed that long periods of diversification in isolation have led to languages that share very few features with their neighbors.

Just as some putative isolates elsewhere in the world have been shown to be members of small families (compare the case of Japanese ~ Japonic discussed in Campbell, this volume), so too in Australia, the "isolate" status of some languages depends on the analysis of them as being either a single language with internal dialect diversity, or a cluster of closely related languages. In all too many cases, there is only one well-documented language in the family. For example, Wardaman forms a cluster with Yangman and Dagoman (Merlan 1994), but the materials for the latter two varieties are so sparse that we cannot tell how distinct they are from each other, or from Wardaman. An example of a case where an isolate has been shown to be, in fact, a cluster of related languages is Giimbiyu. Treated as a single language in Dixon (2002), a recent description (Birch 2006) shows that there are three languages – Urninangk, Erre, and Mengerre(dji) – that make up the subgroup. Harvey (2002) treats these as dialects of a single language but on the basis of admittedly small amounts of material. At no point in the language descriptions do the authors consider relationships outside this family.

There are also cases of languages which are too poorly described to be classified with certainty at this point, and some known by name only. These include the Minkin language of Bourketown (discussed by Evans (1990)), where evidence points to some relationship with Tangkic, but a remote one at best.

I review below the classifications of each of the languages that Campbell (2013:168) lists as isolates in Australia. All the languages except for Tiwi and Anindilyakwa are now extinct. All are found in the Top End region of Australia's Northern Territory. Map 12.1 gives the region and languages found there; isolates are highlighted.

2.1 Anindilyakwa/Enindhilyakwa

Anindilyakwa (also spelled Enindhilyakwa) is spoken on Groote Eylandt. It has approximately 1300 speakers, according to the Australian national census from 2006. This number is supported by estimates in van Egmond (2012). The ISO-639 code is AOI; the Glottolog identification number is anin1240, and the AIATSIS code is N151.

Anindilyakwa is claimed to be an isolate by Rademaker (2014), following O'Grady et al. (1966). Evans (2005:250) argues that, although there are some similarities between the language and Wubuy (Heath 1984), there is sufficiently little shared vocabulary that the language should be considered an isolate, at least at the language family level (that is, a language family comprising a single language, but perhaps related to other Australian languages at a more remote level).

Van Egmond (2012) reviews the evidence and suggests, contra previous claims, that Anindilyakwa is fairly closely related to other Gunwinyguan languages of the area, including Wubuy. The linguistic evidence includes partly typological information, including the presence of lamino-dentals (van Egmond 2012:21, 318). Lexical cognates include – *m+aḏaŋkwa* 'flesh' (< Proto-Gunwinyguan *ḏaŋku* 'meat' (Harvey 2003a)), – *m+akuẚa* 'skin' < *kuḻak, and *ẚang* 'head' (incorporated element, not the free form) < *Long ~ rong (L is a lateral unspecified for retroflection). Van Egmond (2012:313) suggests that

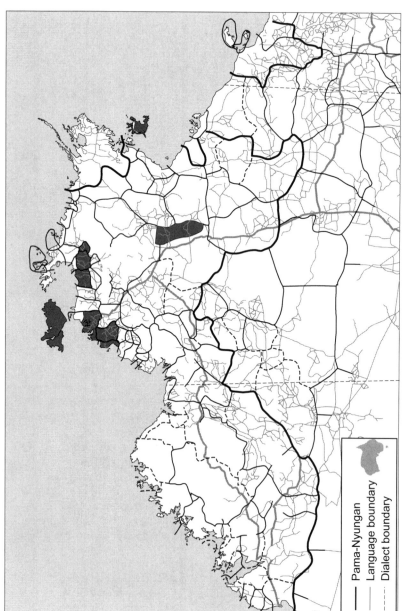

Pama-Nyungan

MAP 12.1 NON-PAMA-NYUNGAN LANGUAGES OF NORTHERN AUSTRALIA; ISOLATES ARE SHADED

Source: Base map from Harvey (nd).

about 40% of Anindilyakwa's basic vocabulary is cognate with items in Wubuy. The sound correspondences presented by van Egmond (2012) are regular and are attested in lexical items from a variety of semantic fields (though concentrated in basic vocabulary). Moreover, Wubuy and Anindilyakwa show a few shared innovations in sound change, including Proto-Gunwinyguan *ḏ > ḻ. Wubuy and Anindilyakwa share a number of complex predicates, as presented in Table 12.1 (from van Egmond 2012:315ff).

Van Egmond (2012:348ff) also presents evidence that shows that Wubuy, Ngandi (another Gunwinyguan language), and Anindilyakwa have matches in verb conjugation membership; that is, the putatively cognate verb roots belong to parallel conjugation classes, further indicative of genetic relationships.

The linguistic evidence for genetic relationships is corroborated by the archaeological evidence, which implies that settlement on Groote Eylandt was sporadic after 4000 BP and increased only about 1300 years ago. This would imply that there was relatively little time for linguistic diversity between Groote Eylandt and the mainland to accrue and that it is plausible that Anindilyakwa's closest linguistic relatives may still be represented in the region. Note that the composition of the Gunwinyguan family itself is controversial, with Alpher, Evans, and Harvey's (2003) and Harvey's (2003a) proposals being incompatible with Green's (2003) proposal for a macro-family of the Non-Pama-Nyungan languages of Arnhem Land. Green's proposal, however, includes only some of the languages traditionally classed as Gunwinyguan.

Whether or not one treats Anindilyakwa as an isolate or member of the Gunwinyguan family, the language has a number of interesting typological features and puzzles for linguistic analysis. Anindilyakwa's phoneme inventory is given in Table 12.2. The different treatments of the language vary extensively in the contrastive segments they recognize;

TABLE 12.1 COMPLEX PREDICATES SHARED BY WUBUY AND ANINDILYAKWA

Anindilyakwa		Wubuy	
-ḻawur+ka-	'taste, try, test'	-ḻawi+wa-	'ask, inquire'
-wal+ka-	'sneak up on'	-wa:l+ka-	'sneak up on'
-ḻar+ka-	'send'	-ḻar+ka-	'send'
-yeŋ+bi-	'speak'	-yam+bi-	'speak'

TABLE 12.2 PHONEME INVENTORY OF ANINDILYAKWA

		Place of Articulation						
		Labial	Alveolar	Retroflex	Dental	Palatal	Velar	Velar rounded
Manner of articulation	Stop	p	t	ṭ	t̪	c	k	kʷ
	Nasal	m	n	ṇ	n̪	ɲ	ŋ	ŋʷ
	Lateral		l	ḷ	ḻ	ʎ		
	Vibrant		r					
	Glide			ɻ		j		w
	Nasal + stop	mp	nt	ṇṭ	n̪t̪	ɲc	ŋk	ŋkʷ
	Complex	kp						
	segments	ŋp						
		ŋm						

Source: After van Egmond (2012:15).

a thorough summary is given in van Egmond (2012). Previous treatments recognize one, two, or four vowels; in the last case, the qualities of the vowels also vary. Van Egmond argues for an asymmetric, four-way vowel distinction between i, ɛ, ə, and a (that is, with no phonemic rounded vowels in the language). Stokes (1981:154) also finds four phonemes (i, u, ɛ, and a); Leeding (1989) argues for just i and a as contrastive vowels. The crux of the difficulty lies in the extent to which vowels and consonants are coarticulated and thus the degree to which one analyzes distinctive features on the consonant, when they are also (or even primarily) realized on the following vowel.

Anindilyakwa, like other Non-Pama-Nyungan languages of the region (including languages of the Gunwinyguan family), is morphologically complex. It shows both noun-class prefixation and multiple agreement morphology on verbs. The voice system is also complex, including an applicative prefix *mən-* and reflexive, reciprocal, and causative morphology. The language exhibits noun incorporation and prefixation for quantification. In summary, it is clear from van Egmond's evidence that Anindilyakwa is a member of the Gunwinyguan family.

2.2 Kungarakany

In some cases, the classification of languages shifts depending on the catalogue but in no case is evidence presented in favor or against a particular classification. We are thus left to rely on the word of the linguists themselves for the claims of relationship. An example of the problem is given here for Kungarakany (ISO-639 GGK, Glottolog KUNG1259, AIATSIS N14), a now-extinct language of the region south of Darwin. Kungarakany is treated as an isolate in Wurm (1972), but in the Gungaraganyan subgroup of Gunwinyguan in *Ethnologue* (Lewis, Simons, and Fennig 2013), and a member of the "Arnhem" group in Dixon (2002). None of these sources provides evidence for their classifications. Evans (1988:92) quotes Harvey (1986) as identifying a discontinuous Non-Pama-Nyungan family comprising Kungarakany and Warray but does not give evidence for this. Harvey's (1990: 14–15) grammar of Warray summarizes Harvey (1986) and says the following:

> In brief Warray is a member of the large Kunwinjkuan language family. Within that family it was probably most closely related to the extinct Wulwulam language. The most closely related living language is Jawoyn. From the little information available on Uwiynmil it is clear that it and Warray are reasonably closely connected. Gungarakayn is also a member of the Kunwinjkuan language family, but the connection between it and Warray is much more distant than those between Warray and its eastern neighbours. Warray is not related to the other neighbouring languages, except in so far as these languages are members of the Australian language family.

Harvey (1986:12) states the following:

> Linguistically Waray is a member of the Kunwinjkuan language family. Within this family Waray appears to be closest to Jawoyn. Jawoyn was original spoken on the east of Uwinjmir and as such is not contiguous with Waray. The next closest language would appear to [be] Waray's eastern neighbor Uwinjmir, followed by its western neighbor Kungarak:anj. Larrajia, Wulna, Limilngan and Wakiman may also be members of the family, but they are certainly not close sisters of Waray if they are.

Parish (1983:1) quotes Tryon (1968:23) as grouping Kungarakany with Larakia and War-ray in a 'Northern' branch of Daly languages; none of these languages is included in the later publication of the Daly survey (Tryon 1981). Tryon's (1968:24) putative cognate percentages between Kungarakany and other languages are in single digits, except for Warrai [= Warray] (12.8%), Matngala [= Matngele] (11.2%), and Kamor (15.3%). Data for Larrakia is not presented, and no discussion is given for why Kungarakany should be grouped with Warrai here, rather than Kamor [=Kamu].

Kungarakany is poorly described. The only available descriptive materials to my knowledge are in Parish (1983), though Parish mentions that several other lin-guists have collected materials on the language. The pronouns are structured in a minimal-augment (Ilocano) system (Greenberg 1988; McGregor and Greenberg 1989). Both subject and object markers are prefixes on the verb; there is some variation in person marking depending on tense. The ordering of agreement markers depends on the person hierarchy, with first person preceding second or third. This is illustrated in example (1):

(1)   a   **ar-in-*kiɲfin***
          1min.S-2aug.O.nf-leave
          'I left you [pl].'

      b   **kan-i-*kiɲfin***
          1min.O-2aug.S.nf-leave
          'You [pl] left me.'   (Parish 1983:17, bold emphasis added)

The language has extensive morpho-phonological alternations, like many of the lan-guages of the region. Kungarakany has phonemic /f/, relatively rare for Australian lan-guages but well represented in the Daly region (about 25% of the languages in Gasser and Bowern's 2014 survey of phonological patterns in Australian languages have phone-mic fricatives). Kungarakany has other features that are shared across many Australian languages, such as the verb roots *bu-* 'hit' and *ni-* 'sit'. Kungarakany also has features which are found in other Australian languages, but which are not meaningful for estab-lishing genetic relatedness. For example, verbal negation involves marking the verb with potential mood and using a preverbal clausal negator *moloŋ* (Parish 1983:38). The same negation strategy is used in Bardi and other Nyulnyulan languages, as well as a number of other Non-Pama-Nyungan languages. But irrealis/potential and negation marking is also common outside Australia, and so its presence in several different areas of the country should not be seen to signal a particularly close genetic affiliation. We must therefore treat Kungarakany's affiliation as "uncertain" at this point.

2.3 Tiwi

Perhaps the prototypical linguistic isolate within the Australian continent is Tiwi (ISO-639 TIW, Glottolog code tiwi1244, AIATSIS code N20), spoken by about 3000 people on Bathurst and Melville Islands and in the neighboring city of Darwin. Evans (2005) says explicitly that no one would doubt that it should be classified as a primary branch of Proto-Australian (assuming that one believes in the unity of Australian languages). Dixon (1980:225) includes Tiwi and Djingili as the two languages whose genetic affili-ation with the rest of Australia remains unresolved. He says that "Australian" under this definition should be taken as excluding Tiwi and Djingili, but he does, in fact, use data

TABLE 12.3 HARVEY'S NON-PAMA-NYUNGAN BOUND PRONOMINAL RECONSTRUCTIONS COMPARED WITH TIWI

		Non-Pama-Nyungan	Tiwi
MIN	1	*ŋa-	ŋi-
	1/2	*mV-	mu-
	2	*cV-	ɲi- (NP), ci-
	3	*ka (NP), ø-	a- (NP), yi-, ci-
AUG	1	*ɲV-rV-	ŋi-
	1/2	*ŋV-rV-	ŋa-
	2	*nV-rV-, *ku-rV-	ɲi-
	3	*pV-rV-	wu- (NP), pi-

from Tiwi in adducing support for certain Proto-Australian reconstructions, such as *ŋin '2sg' (Tiwi ɲinhtha) and *ŋayu '1sg' (Tiwi ŋiya). He also states that "Tiwi has a normal Australian phonemic system" (Dixon 1980:487). Wilson (2013:17) compares Tiwi bound pronoun markers with those reconstruction for a number of Northern families by Harvey (2003b:500). That evidence is summarized in Table 12.3. Harvey's Non-Pama-Nyungan pronominal reconstructions are presented along with the Tiwi forms that are assumed to be cognate.

While the resemblances are striking, they are also only a single segment in most cases. Tiwi has a morpheme rri- which occurs in the same position as the non-singular marker reconstructed by Harvey (2003b) for Proto-Non-Pama-Nyungan, but it denotes past tense rather than subject number. While the semantic connections between tense and number are difficult, there are examples elsewhere in Australia of changes in paradigm structures where sequences of morphemes have been reanalyzed, such that morphemes formerly associated with one category come to be analyzed as denoting something else. For example, Bowern (2012a) describes a case in the Nyulnyulan family where transitivity marking is reanalyzed as the exponent of tense. However, in that case, the languages are sufficiently close that one can easily find matches across other paradigms, as well as in the lexicon. The reconstructions presented as evidence for Tiwi's connections to other Non-Pama-Nyungan languages are much sparser.

Tiwi is perhaps most famous within the literature on linguistics for its 'young people's variety' (Lee 1987). That is, there is a sharp division between the 'traditional' language and the contact variety that emerged in the 1960s as familiarity with English increased. Differences between the traditional language and modern Tiwi center on the verb morphology. Traditional Tiwi morphology is considerably more complex than the Modern variety, where the number of distinctions marked on the verb, as well as their nature, is much reduced. For example, the minimal-augment system of Traditional Tiwi, which includes, by nature, distinctions in clusivity, has been lost, and the Modern Tiwi system includes only singular and plural. The first person inclusive and exclusive markers have been refunctionalized (Smith 2008) as tense markers. Traditional Tiwi exhibits noun incorporation, but the modern language does not allow this. Tiwi has thus been important in Australian languages as a case study for the types of "simplifying" changes that morphologically complex languages can undergo and how morphological distinctions may be refunctionalised or obliterated. There is no evidence at this point that Tiwi is closely related to other Australian languages.

2.4 Mangarrayi

Mangarrayi is another Non-Pama-Nyungan language. It is now extinct but was formerly spoken inland along the Roper River in the Northern Territory. The ISO-639 code is MPC; the Glottolog code is man1381, and the AIATSIS code is N78. There is conflicting classification. Alpher, Evans, and Harvey (2003) include it in the Gunwinyguan family, but Merlan (1982:x) suggests that it is a member of the same family as Mara, Alawa, and Warndarrang. Dixon (2002) includes Mangarrayi as the sole member of one of thirteen primary divisions in his 'Arnhem Land Group [NB]'. This group includes the members of both Gunwinyguan and Maran families, but Dixon does not recognize these families *per se*. Merlan's primary evidence for including Mangarrayi within Maran is shared archaisms in derivational verbal morphology. Further evidence from shared noun-class morphology is discussed in Merlan (2003).

Conversely, Alpher, Evans, and Harvey (2003) suggest that Mangarrayi's verb paradigms are sufficiently similar to other Gunwinyguan languages that it should be treated as a branch of Gunwinyguan. Harvey (2012), moreover, casts doubt on the status of Maran, by suggesting that most of the features shared between Mara and Warndarrang (two of the four languages of the Maran family) have been borrowed, rather than inherited from a recent common proto-language. It should be noted that Gunwinyguan itself has been the subject of some debate. Evans (2003:13) succinctly summarizes the competing positions. One of the most contentious issues is the inclusion] of Mangarrayi (as discussed above), Anindilyakwa (for which see van Egmond 2012 and Section 2.1 above), Wardaman and its close relatives, and Wagiman. The issue for Mangarrayi, then, as Merlan (2003) notes, is whether all these similarities point to a remote relationship between *both* Maran and Gunwinyguan (including Mangarrayi), or whether some of the shared features are better explained through language contact. Certainly, Mangarrayi has been in fairly intensive contact with its Gunwinyguan and Maran neighbors for a considerable period of time. These questions are at this point unresolvable without further systematic study and reconstruction of the relevant languages.

2.5 Gaagudju

Gaagudju, a language of the Darwin hinterland, is also extinct. Harvey (2002:15–16) summarizes his position on relationships between Gaagudju and its neighbors as follows:

> Gaagudju is a member of the Australian language family. As such it is related to its neighbours, all of which appear to be members of the Australian language family. However, there is nothing to suggest a closer genetic relationship to any of its neighbours. In areal terms, Gaagudju appears to be the westernmost member of a sprachbund which extends eastward along the coast to Darwin. The other members of this sprachbund are Larrikiya, Limilngan, Umbugarla and Wuna. The members of this sprachbund share the following characteristics which distinguish them from other neighbouring languages:
>
> 1-2   a   A tendency to reduce unstressed vowels. . . .
>   b   Complex, lexically controlled noun class systems.
>   c   Extensive Absolutive-Ergative pronominal prefixing
>   including prefixing for noun class.

Note that Harvey appears to have reversed 'east' and 'west' in this description, since Gaagudju was spoken to the east of Darwin, not west, and the other languages Harvey mentions as being part of the Darwin region Sprachbund are all coastal between Darwin and Jabiru, but to the east of Darwin.

Just as in the case of Mangarrayi discussed in the previous section, longstanding language contact potentially obscures remote relations. Note also that the features that Harvey mentions in the quote above are all typological features, and unlikely to be diagnostic of genetic relationships in the absence of systematic similarities in phonological form. However, these types of features are similar to what some have used to argue for *genetic* relationships (though not Harvey, whose claims for classification are usually based on shared morphology and structures in complex verbal paradigms). Thus we should probably treat Gaagudju as another isolate within Australia.

2.6 Bachamal and Wadjiginy

Bachamal (also spelled Patjtjamalh or Batyamal) is another language of the Daly region. The main source is Ford (1991). Tryon (1981:228) classifies the language as Western Daly with close relatives Pungu-Pungu and (especially) Wadjiginy. Ford (1998:33–34), however, says that "they [Bachamal and other Daly languages-CB] do not appear to be in any way related, except as Australian languages. . . . There are grammatical and conceptual similarities between the two languages, which may well be the result of long-term contact, but close examination reveals important differences in phonology, morphology, syntax and semantics." Ford does, however, accept the relationship of other Daly River languages to one another. Tryon (1981) notes that Wadjiginy has also been called Wogait in the literature, but Wogait is a group term that refers to coastal people anywhere between the mouth of the Daly River and Delissaville (near Darwin); thus it could potentially refer to speakers of languages other than Wadjiginy. He also says that while Pungu-Pungu and Bachamal are lexically close, there is sufficient morphological differentiation to treat them as distinct languages.

2.7 Other small families or single languages

In addition to the languages discussed above, there are several small Non-Pama-Nyungan families whose degree of internal diversity and wider affiliation is still a matter of discussion. To take just one example, Wardaman, Yangman, and Dagoman are a small group of closely related varieties (Merlan 1994), either a single language with three dialects or three closely related languages. Their Australian affiliation has been presumed but never demonstrated, nor is there evidence of the families within Australia with which they are most closely associated.

As discussed briefly in Section 2.5 above, Limilngan shows pronominal and verbal forms that are similar to other Australian languages. Harvey (2001:3–9) reviews the evidence for Limilngan's closest relatives and concludes that there is enough evidence to relate Limilngan to Wuna, its neighbor immediately to the West. He finds a number of presumed lexical cognates and a morphological one. The locative is *lakgaṇi* in Limilngan and *-kgaṇi* in Wuna. Beyond that, however, there are few similarities (though the documentation for Wuna is not extensive), and it could be that these forms are borrowings. Certainly, it is suspicious that the lexical and morphological matches are so close, when the languages otherwise show few (if any) similarities.

The final set of languages to discuss in this region are Umbugarla and Ngombur. Umbugarla is poorly attested; the only description to my knowledge is Davies (1989), a synthesis of brief field notes from Gavan Breen, Mark Harvey, Nicholas Evans, and Frances Morphy. Harvey (2001:9) suggests that Umbugarla and Ngombur formed their own family; Davies (1989) contains no information about classification. They remain as isolates given the lack of further information (and none is likely to be forthcoming in the future).

2.8 Languages now shown to be clearly related to other Australian languages

As discussed briefly in Section 1, there are some languages which were earlier thought to be unrelated to the rest of the languages of the Australian continent. For example, Crowley (1976:23) summarizes Wurm's position on non-Australian languages in Australia. He gives Tasmanian, Mbabaram, and Anewan as the three languages that as of 1972 were unclassifiable (or only very remotely related to other Australian languages).

Early works (Tindale and Birdsell 1941, O'Grady, Voegelin, and Voegelin 1966) list Mbabaram as a language that is possibly not related to other Australian languages. Dixon (1966) emphasizes the difference between Mbabaram and the Paman languages further north that Hale (1964) discussed; however, he (Dixon 1966: 103) also notes strong similarities between Mbabaram and the languages most closely related to Dyirbal, along with Dyirbal itself. Work by Dixon (1991) showed that Mbabaram is fairly clearly Pama-Nyungan, and Barrett (2005:170ff) suggests that it is a sister to Maric, either within, or as a coordinate branch within, Pama-Maric.

Another Pama-Nyungan language in this situation is Anewan (or Nganyaaywana; not to be confused with the adjacent language Enneewin, about which nothing is known). Crowley (1976) thoroughly reviews the evidence for language relatedness and concludes that several sound changes obscured the relationship between Anewan and other Pama-Nyungan languages. In particular, he provides cognates between Gumbayngirr (Eades 1979) (or other languages of the New South Wales North Coast) and Anewan which are indicative of shared inheritance. Representative terms are given below, with the Gumbayngirr term (as given by Crowley) preceding the Anewan.

(2)   *wi:gan* 'snow'; cf. *ikana*
       ma:ni 'take'; cf. *ani*
       di:rra 'tooth'; cf. *ira*
       ganay 'yamstick'; cf. *naya*
       dimin 'lice'; cf. *mina*
       mi:l 'eye'; cf. *ila*
       ŋu:ra 'camp'; cf. *urala*

Anewan shows reflexes of sufficiently many terms that are securely reconstructed within Pama-Nyungan, that there should be no doubt that it is a Pama-Nyungan language. Its position within Pama-Nyungan is uncertain, however. Bowern and Atkinson (2012) did not include Anewan in their sample due to lack of data; subsequent expansions of Pama-Nyungan phylogenetic work have included data from Anewan, but results are inconclusive. Most frequently, it appears in the tree as a sister to Gumbayngirric (Gumbayngirr and Yaygirr), but with fairly low posterior probability (0.7). This is because most of the cognate items are retentions from Proto-Pama-Nyungan, rather than indicative of a closer relationship with other languages in the family. All but one of the items listed above in (3), for example, are reconstructible to Proto-Pama-Nyungan (the exception is *ikana* 'snow').

Back in the Non-Pama-Nyungan region, Djingulu (Jingulu, Jingili) was also treated as an isolate in some early work. Harvey (2008) provides the clearest evidence that Jingulu is a primary branch of Mirndi and thus related (though fairly distantly) to Jaminjungan and Ngurlun languages (including Wambaya). This follows earlier work by Chadwick (1984; 1997).

3 TASMANIAN LANGUAGES

The third 'language' discussed by Wurm (1971; 1972) as potentially not related to other Australian languages was Tasmanian. From the earliest descriptions of the languages of Tasmania, there have been doubts about the number of languages represented by the sources. Tasmanian languages are attested by about 10,000 words of vocabulary and a few short sentences (from a *lingua franca* used on the Flinders Island Mission). The materials were recorded between 1770 and the early 1900s. Tasmanian languages were not historically named, though local bands were; this has exacerbated the confusion about the number of distinct languages represented in the sources.

The extant records for Tasmania were published in Plomley (1976). Earlier works on the languages, including Schmidt (1952), Roth (1899), and Jones (1974), came to different conclusions about the number of languages represented in the sources, and their relationships to the languages of the Australian mainland. Some early work suggested that Tasmanian languages were related to those of the Australian mainland, because of certain lexical resemblances. However, those resemblances stem from a single source – a Ben Lomond vocabulary recorded by Charles Robinson (son of George Augustus Robinson). Amery (1996) has shown conclusively that the words in that list are Kaurna, a Pama-Nyungan (Thura-Yura) language of the Adelaide Plains in South Australia, and were most likely recorded from a sealer. Moreover, those words are all on a single manuscript page and in a different handwriting from the rest of the Ben Lomond vocabulary. Once those words are removed from the Tasmanian dataset, there is no resemblance between the languages of Tasmania and those of the Australian mainland.

In Bowern (2012b), I discuss previous family divisions within Tasmania, including the number of languages represented in the data. I found evidence that the extant materials for Tasmania cover at least 12 distinct languages, from 4 or 5 different families. Only 26 'cognates' are attested across each of the families, and these words are either clearly introduced items, such as cattle, flora/fauna terms, such as *boobyalla* 'native willow' (*Acacia longiflora*) – which is probably a loan – or mythological terms which might also be expected to be subject to diffusion. While there was some evidence that the Southeast and Eastern families were related more distantly, there was no evidence of a single Tasmanian language family, let alone a single Tasmanian language.

4 FAMILY-LEVEL ISOLATES IN PAMA-NYUNGAN

A striking feature of many classifications of Pama-Nyungan before Bowern and Atkinson (2012) is their rake-like nature: that is, the lack of internal structure and intermediate subgroups between Proto-Pama-Nyungan and the approximately 30 subgroups identified by classifications such as O'Grady, Voegelin, and Voegelin (1966); Wurm (1972); and

Dixon (1980; 2002). Just like the Non-Pama-Nyungan families with multiple one- or two-language families, so too in Pama-Nyungan there are numerous subgroups with one or two languages and little evidence of where they appear in the family.

Work by Bowern and Atkinson (2012) and subsequent work on further language relationships by Bowern has resolved many (but not all) of these family-level isolates within Pama-Nyungan. Bowern and Atkinson (2012) found four coordinate branches of Pama-Nyungan but did not have sufficient evidence to reduce the number of primary branches further. Subsequent work (cf. Bowern 2015) suggests that there are two main branches of Pama-Nyungan: a Western branch (also found by Bowern and Atkinson 2012) that includes the Yolngu, Warluwaric, Pilbara, Ngumpin-Yapa, Wati, and Nyungic subgroups and an Eastern branch with further divisions. A tree based on the Stochastic Dollo model of cognate evolution for 104 representative languages is given in Figure 12.1.

Subsequent work on the internal structure of Pama-Nyungan has clarified the classification of a number of these "isolates" within the family. I here briefly discuss some illustrative languages: Warumungu, Bigambal, Anewan, and the Western Torres Strait language (Kala Lagaw Ya and related dialects).

4.1 Anewan and Bigambal

Anewan (Nganyaaywana; see Section 2.8 above) and Bigambal are two languages of the New South Wales north coast. Neither is used as main languages of communication anymore, though both have group of peoples with heritage knowledge. Classification of both languages has been unclear in previous literature and both languages are known primarily from 19th century materials. Bigambal has been variously classified as belonging to the Central New South Wales group (O'Grady, Voegelin, and Voegelin 1966; Oates and Oates 1970) or Bandjalangic (Dixon 2002). Wafer and Lissarrague (2008) group Bigambal with Yugambal in a separate subgroup (which they term "East Queensland Board"); Yugambal itself has been the subject of uncertain classification, including both Bandjalangic (Sharpe 1994) and Yuin-Kuri.

The problem in classifying these languages arises from their patterns of lexical and morphological retention and innovation. The languages have enough retentions that they are clearly Pama-Nyungan. But their innovations are extensive and unique; that is, while they show both innovations and retentions, their innovations are mostly confined to the single language itself and are not shared with their neighbors, while the retentions are mostly of Pama-Nyungan antiquity, and so are of no use in determining relationships *within* the family. For example, Bigambal's word for 'earth' is *ṯaku*, shared with Arandic, Central NSW, Karnic, Bandjalangic, Paman, Waka-Kabi, and Yuin-Kuri. The word is not found in Western Pama-Nyungan languages but is well attested in all Eastern Pama-Nyungan branches. 'Mouth' is *yiṟa*, which is very widespread and found in all parts of the family (both Western and Eastern) in the meaning 'lips', 'mouth', or 'teeth'.

The same is true for Nganyaaywana, where the problem is, if anything, even more acute. Most of the language's basic vocabulary is untraceable at this stage, except for some items which are of Proto-Pama-Nyungan antiquity, such as *ṉina* 'sit'. Thus rates of change have been fast enough that the evidence for intermediate classification has been obliterated.

4.2 Western Torres Strait Language

The Western Torres Strait language (Haddon 1935; Ray and Haddon 1891; Alpher, O'Grady and Bowern 2008; Bani 1976; Bani and Klokeid 1972) is a cluster of fairly

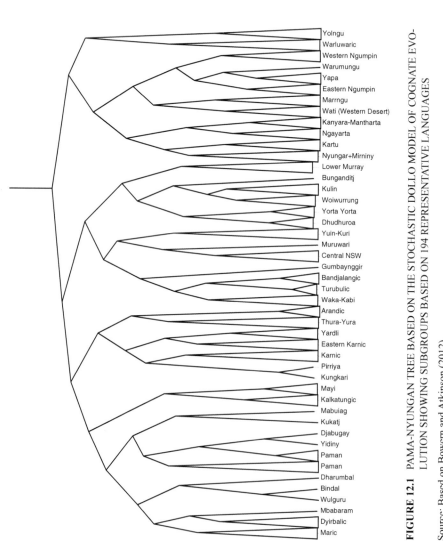

Yolngu
Warluwaric
Western Ngumpin
Warumungu
Yapa
Eastern Ngumpin
Marrngu
Wati (Western Desert)
Kanyara-Mantharta
Ngayarta
Kartu
Nyungar+Mirniny
Lower Murray
Bunganditj
Kulin
Woiwurrung
Yorta Yorta
Dhudhuroa
Yuin-Kuri
Muruwari
Central NSW
Gumbaynggir
Bandjalangic
Turubulic
Waka-Kabi
Arandic
Thura-Yura
Yardli
Eastern Karnic
Karnic
Pirriya
Kungkari
Mayi
Kalkatungic
Mabuiag
Kukatj
Djabugay
Yidiny
Paman
Paman
Dharumbal
Bindal
Wulguru
Mbabaram
Dyirbalic
Maric

FIGURE 12.1 PAMA-NYUNGAN TREE BASED ON THE STOCHASTIC DOLLO MODEL OF COGNATE EVO-LUTION SHOWING SUBGROUPS BASED ON 194 REPRESENTATIVE LANGUAGES

Source: Based on Bowern and Atkinson (2012).

closely related varieties spoken on the western islands of the Torres Strait (between Cape York Peninsula and the Papua New Guinea mainland). Surrounding languages are 'Papuan' to the east and north, and the Northern Paman group of Paman languages to the south. Though the Western Torres Strait language is clearly Pama-Nyungan, it is not closely related to its nearest neighbors. It shares none of the sound changes that characterize Paman languages, for example, especially the complicated stratigraphies of Northern Paman (Hale 1964). Lexically, it suffers in classification from the same problems as Bigambal and Nganyaaywana: viz., that its shared features are shared retentions from a high level in the family. In Bowern and Atkinson (2012), its nearest relative is Kukatj. Kukatj is usually classified as Paman but without further discussion or with contradictory statements. Breen (1992:2), for example, says both that Kukatj is the sole member of a Flinders Paman subgroup, which is most closely related to Norman Paman and that there are no higher level subgroups that include Norman Paman, Kukatj, and no further languages (which implies by definition that Norman Paman is therefore *not* the most closely related subgroup to Kukatj). It is consistent with previous cursory classifications that Kukatj is a sister to Paman (along with Western Torres) rather than a subgroup within Paman. The relative closeness of Kukatj and Western Torres in Bowern and Atkinson (2012) is interesting, since the two languages are spoken on opposite sides of the Paman subgroup. This possibly implies that the Paman group was an expansion in Cape York Peninsula that replaced earlier linguistic communities.

Davis (2004:234) suggests that the Western Torres Strait Islands have been continuously settled and fished for the last 3,000 years (see also Carter 2001), implying that Western Torres is probably not a recently introduced language to the region.

4.3 Warumungu

Warumungu is still spoken; speakers live in the Northern Territory, in the area of Tennant Creek. There is a Warumungu sketch grammar (Simpson and Heath 1982) and learner's guide (Simpson 2002) but little other available materials. Simpson (2008) treats the classification of Warumungu as uncertain, since the language is bordered by several subgroups of Pama-Nyungan, as well as Non-Pama-Nyungan languages. As in the case of other family-level isolates discussed above, Warumungu has features that set it apart from its neighbors. For example, phonologically, Warumungu has a fortis-lenis stop contrast, which is absent from other Pama-Nyungan languages in the region.

5 FURTHER DISCUSSION AND CONCLUSIONS

In summary, the family-level isolates discussed in the previous section provide clues to the formation of isolates more generally. We see two processes that isolate languages in Pama-Nuyngan from their nearest relatives. The first is geographical isolation, where population movement elsewhere in the region leads to a language being cut off from its nearest phylogenetic relatives; this obscures relationships. The second is where there is sufficient change that the only traces of language relationship are stable features that are shared by many languages of the family. That is, they are diagnostic of family-level relationships but not of subgroup-level relationships.

We must remember, however, that there is still much to be known about the history of Australian languages and that further work would likely elucidate both the family-internal Pama-Nyungan relationships described here, as well as the relationships among Non-Pama-Nyungan languages.

Thus in conclusion, Australia has 'family-level' isolates: phylic families comprising a single language. Even if one assumes that all Australian languages are ultimately related, those relationships are sufficiently remote that we should consider the relationships to be hypothesized (rather than demonstrated), and we should treat these languages as 'isolates' for purposes such as typological sampling.

Furthermore, the time is right for a new evaluation of Proto-Australian and potential subfamilies. Previous proposals all have problems. The biggest problem is that each proposal involves different evidence. Many of the claims are difficult to evaluate in the absence of other information about overall levels of diffusion (for example). Others would appear to make claims about diffusion when independent, parallel innovation is just as plausible. Moreover, it is difficult to know what to do with claims about relationships based on very small amounts of phonological material. And typological claims alone are not good evidence for shared relationship, since they could equally well be the result of independent development, diffusion, or simply universal (or common) features of particular typological profiles. In some cases, the languages are no longer spoken, and we will probably never be able to solve the problem.

REFERENCES

Alpher, Barry. 2004. Pama-Nyungan: Phonological Reconstruction and Status as a Phylogenetic Group. *Australian Languages: Classification and the Comparative Method*, ed. by Claire Bowern and Harold Koch, 93–126. Amsterdam: John Benjamins.

Alpher, Barry, Geoffrey N. O'Grady, and Claire Bowern. 2008. Western Torres Strait Language Classification and Development. *Morphology and Language History: In Honour of Harold Koch*, ed. by Claire Bowern, Bethwyn Evans, and Luisa Miceli, 1–15. Amsterdam: John Benjamins.

Alpher, Barry, Nicholas Evans, and Mark Harvey. 2003. Proto Gunwinyguan Verb Suffixes. *The Non-Pama-Nyungan Languages of Northern Australia: Comparative Studies of the Continent's Most Linguistically Complex Region*, ed. by Nicholas Evans. Canberra: Pacific Linguistics, 305-352

Amery, R. 1996. Kaurna in Tasmania: A Case of Mistaken Identity. *Aboriginal History* 20: 24–50.

Bani, Ephraim. 1976. The Language Situation in Western Torres Strait. *Languages of Cape York Peninsula, Queensland*, ed. by Peter Sutton, 3–6. Canberra: Australian Institute of Aboriginal Studies.

Bani, Ephraim and Terry Jack Klokeid. 1972. *Kala Lagau Langgus-Yagar Yagar: The Western Torres Strait Language*. Manuscript. Canberra, ms.

Barrett, Bevan. 2005. *Historical Reconstruction of the Maric Languages of Central Queensland*. Canberra: Australian National University MA Thesis.

Birch, Bruce. 2006. *Erre, Mengerrdji, Urningangk: Three Languages from the Alligator Rivers Region of North Western Arnhem Land, Northern Territory, Australia*. Jabiru: Gundjeihmi Aboriginal Corporation.

Blake, Barry J. 1990a. Languages of the Queensland/Northern Territory border: Updating the Classification. *Language and History: Essays in Honour of Luise A. Hercus*, ed. by Peter Austin, R.M.W. Dixon, Tom Dutton, and Isobel White, 49–66. (Pacific Linguistics C-116). Canberra: Dept. of Linguistics, Research School of Pacific Studies, Australian National University.

Blake, Barry J. 1990b. The Significance of Pronouns in the History of Australian Languages. *Linguistic Change and Reconstruction Methodology*, ed. by Philip Baldi,

435–450. (Trends in Linguistics: Studies and Monographs 45). Berlin/New York: Mouton de Gruyter.

Bowern, Claire. 2006. Another Look at Australia as a Linguistic Area. *Linguistic Areas*, ed. by Yaron Matras, April McMahon, and Nigel Vincent, 244–265. London: Palgrave Macmillan.

Bowern, Claire. 2012a. Nyikina Paradigms and Refunctionalization: A Cautionary Tale in Morphological Reconstruction. *Journal of Historical Linguistics* 2, no. 1: 7–24.

Bowern, Claire. 2012b. The Riddle of Tasmanian Languages. *Proceedings of the Royal Society B: Biological Sciences.* doi:10.1098/rspb.2012.1842. http://rspb.royalsociety publishing.org/content/early/2012/09/22/rspb.2012.1842 (21 December 2012).

Bowern, Claire. 2015. Pama-Nyungan Phylogenetics and Beyond. Plenary Address. Leiden Lorentz Center Workshop on Phylogenetic Methods in Linguistics.

Bowern, Claire. 2016. Chirila: Contemporary and Historical Resources for the Indigenous Languages of Australia. *Language Documentation and Conservation, 10*: 1–40. http://scholarspace.manoa.hawaii.edu/handle/10125/24685 (11 July 2016).

Bowern, Claire and Harold Koch. 2004. *Australian Languages: Classification and the Comparative Method.* Amsterdam: John Benjamins.

Bowern, Claire and Quentin Atkinson. 2012. Computational Phylogenetics and the Internal Structure of Pama-Nyungan. *Language* 88, 4: 817–845.

Breen, Gavan. 1992. Some Problems in Kukatj Phonology. *Australian Journal of Linguistics* 12, no. 1: 1–43. doi:10.1080/07268609208599470.

Butcher, A.R. (2006). Australian Aboriginal Languages: Consonant-Salient Phonologies and the 'Place-of-Articulation Imperative'. *Speech Production: Models, Phonetic Processes, and Techniques*, ed. by Jonathan Harrington and Marija Tabain, 187–210. New York: Psychology Press.

Campbell, Lyle. 2013. *Language Isolates and Their History.* Unpublished ms.

Carter, Melissa. 2001. New Evidence for the Earliest Human Occupation in Torres Strait, Northeastern Australia. *Australian Archaeology* 52: 50–52.

Chadwick, Neil. 1984. The Relationship of Jingulu and Jaminjungan. Manuscript. Canberra, ms.

Chadwick, Neil. 1997. The Barkly and Jaminjungan Languages: A Non-Contiguous Genetic Grouping in North Australia. *Boundary Rider: Essays in Honour of Geoffrey O'Grady*, ed. by Darrell Tryon and Michael Walsh, 95–106. (Pacific Linguistics C-136). Canberra: Pacific Linguistics, Research School of Pacific and Asian Studies, Australian National University.

Crowley, Terry. 1976. Phonological Change in New England. *Grammatical Categories in Australian Languages*, ed. by R.M.W. Dixon, 19–50. (Linguistic Series 22). Canberra/ Atlantic Highlands, NJ: Australian Institute of Aboriginal Studies.

Davies, Jennifer. 1989. *Umbugarla: A Sketch Grammar.* Honours thesis: University of Melbourne.

Davis, Richard. 2004. *Woven Histories, Dancing Lives: Torres Strait Islander Identity, Culture and History.* Canberra: Aboriginal Studies Press.

Dixon, R.M.W. 1966. Mbabaram: A Dying Australian Language. *Bulletin of the School of Oriental and African Studies* 29.1: 97–121.

Dixon, R.M.W. 1976. *Grammatical Categories in Australian Languages.* Canberra: Australian Institute of Aboriginal Studies.

Dixon, R.M.W. 1977. *A Grammar of Yidiny.* Cambridge: Cambridge University Press.

Dixon, R.M.W. 1980. *The Languages of Australia.* Cambridge: Cambridge University Press.

Dixon, R.M.W. 1991. Mbabaram. *The Handbook of Australian Languages*, vol. 4, ed. by R.M.W. Dixon and Barry J. Blake, 349–402. Melbourne: Oxford University Press.

Dixon, R.M.W. 1997. *The Rise and Fall of Languages*. Cambridge: Cambridge University Press.

Dixon, R.M.W. 2002. *Australian Languages: Their Nature and Development*. [[Cambridge University Press]]. www.cambridge.org/catalogue/catalogue.asp?isbn=0521473780 (11 September 2009).

Eades, Diana. 1979. *Gumbaynggir*, ed. R.M.W. Dixon and Barry Blake, 244–361. Canberra: Australian National University Press.

Egmond, Marie-Elaine van. 2012. *Enindhilyakwa Phonology, Morphosyntax and Genetic Position*. Ph.D. thesis, University of Sydney, Sydney. http://ses.library.usyd.edu.au:80/handle/2123/8747 (15 February 2016).

Evans, Nicholas. 1988. Arguments for Pama-Nyungan as a Genetic Subgroup, with Particular Reference to Initial Laminalization. *Aboriginal Linguistics* 1: 91–110.

Evans, Nicholas. 1990. The Minkin Language of the Bourketown Region. *Studies in Comparative Pama-Nyungan*, ed. by Geoffrey N. O'Grady and Darrell Tryon, 173–207. Canberra: Pacific Linguistics.

Evans, Nicholas (ed.). 2003. *The Non-Pama-Nyungan Languages of Northern Australia: Comparative Studies of the Continent's Most Linguistically Complex Region*. (Pacific Linguistics 552). Canberra: Pacific Linguistics.

Evans, Nicholas. 2005. Australian Languages Reconsidered: A Review of Dixon (2002). *Oceanic Linguistics* 44, no. 1: 242–286.

Evans, Nicholas and Patrick McConvell. 1997. The Enigma of Pama-Nyungan Expansion in Australia. *Archaeology and Language I*, 174–191. London: Routledge.

Ford, Lysbeth. 1991. *The Phonology and Morphology of Bachamal (Wogait)*. ANU Canberra MA Thesis. http://pubman.mpdl.mpg.de/pubman/faces/viewItemOverviewPage.jsp?itemId=escidoc:400944 (14 April 2016).

Ford, Lysbeth. 1998. *A Description of the Emmi Language of Northern Territory of Australia*. PhD thesis, Australian National University, Canberra.

Gasser, Emily and Claire Bowern. 2014. Revisiting Phonological Generalizations in Australian Languages. *Proceedings of the Annual Meetings on Phonology*.

Goddard, Cliff. 1985. *Yankunytjatjara Grammar*. Alice Springs: Institute for Aboriginal Development.

Green, Rebecca. 2003. Proto Maningrida within Proto Arnhem: Evidence from Verbal Inflectional Suffixes. *The Non-Pama-Nyungan Languages of Northern Australia: Comparative Studies of the Continent's Most Linguistically Complex Region*, ed. by Nicholas Evans, 369-421. Canberra: Pacific Linguistics.

Greenberg, Joseph H. 1988. The First Person Inclusive Dual as an Ambiguous Category. *Studies in Language* 12, no. 1: 1–18.

Haddon, Alfred Cort. 1935. *Reports of the Cambridge Anthropological Expedition to Torres Straits*. CUP Archive.

Hale, Kenneth. 1964. Classification of Northern Paman Languages, Cape York Peninsula, Australia: A Research Report. *Oceanic Linguistics* 3, no. 2: 248–265. doi:10.2307/3622881.

Harvey, Mark. 1986. *Ngoni Waray Amungal-yang: The Waray Language from Adelaide River*. Canberra: ANU MA Thesis.

Harvey, Mark. 1990. *Warray Grammar and Dictionary*. Unpublished manuscript. University of Sydney.

Harvey, Mark. 2001. *A Grammar of Limilngan: A Language of the Mary River Region, Northern Territory, Australia.* Pacific Linguistics, Research School of Pacific and Asian Studies, the Australian National University.

Harvey, Mark. 2002. *A Grammar of Gaagudju.* Berlin: Walter De Gruyter.

Harvey, Mark. 2003a. An Initial Reconstruction of Proto Gunwinyguan Phonology. *The Non-Pama-Nyungan Languages of Northern Australia: Comparative Studies in the Continent's Most Linguistically Complex Region*, ed. by Nicholas Evans, 205–268. Canberra: Pacific Linguistics.

Harvey, Mark. 2003b. Reconstruction of Pronominals Among the Non-Pama-Nyungan Languages. *The Non-Pama-Nyungan Languages of Northern Australia: Comparative Studies of the Continent's Most Linguistically Complex Region.* Canberra: Pacific Linguistics.

Harvey, Mark. 2008. *Proto Mirndi: A Discontinuous Language Family in Northern Australia.* Canberra: Pacific Linguistics.

Harvey, Mark. 2012. Warndarrang and Marra: A Diffusional or Genetic Relationship? *Australian Journal of Linguistics* 32, no. 3: 327–360. doi:10.1080/07268602.2012.705578.

Harvey, Mark. nd. Northern Australian Aboriginal Languages. Unpublished map.

Heath, Jeffrey. 1984. *Functional Grammar of Nunggubuyu.* Canberra: Australian Institute of Aboriginal Studies.

Heath, Jeffrey. 1990. Verbal Inflection and Macro-Subgroupings of Australian Languages: The Search for Conjugation Markers in Non-Pama-Nyungan, *Linguistic Change and Reconstruction Methodology*, ed. by Phillip Baldi, 403–417. The Hague: Mouton.

Jones, R. 1974. Tasmanian tribes. *Aboriginal Tribes of Australia*, ed. by Norman Tindale, 319–354. Berkeley, CA: University of California Press

Lee, J. 1987. *Tiwi Today: A Study of Language Change in a Contact Situation.* Canberra: Pacific Linguistics.

Leeding, Velma. 1989. *Anindilyakwa Phonology and Morphology.* PhD thesis, Department of Anthropology, University of Sydney.

Lewis, M. Paul, Gary F. Simons, and Charles D. Fennig. 2013. *Ethnologue: Languages of the World* (17th ed.). Dallas, TX: SIL International.

Ling Roth, H. 1899. *The Aborigines of Tasmania.* Halifax: F King and Sons.

McGregor, W.B. 2002. *Verb Classification in Australian Languages.* Berlin: Walter de Gruyter.

McGregor, William B. and J.H. Greenberg. 1989. Greenberg on the First Person Inclusive Dual: Evidence from Some Australian Languages. *Studies in Language*, 13, no. 2: 437–458.

Merlan, Francesca. 1979. On the Prehistory of Some Australian Verbs. *Oceanic Linguistics* 18, no. 1: 33–112.

Merlan, Francesca. 1982. *Mangarrayi.* Amsterdam: North Holland Publishing Company.

Merlan, Francesca. 1994. *A Grammar of Wardaman: Language of the Northern Territory of Australia [Wardaman/English].* Berlin: Mouton de Gruyter.

Merlan, Francesca. 2003. The Genetic Position of Mangarrayi: Evidence from Pronominal Prefixation. *The Non-Pama-Nyungan Languages of Northern Australia: Comparative Studies of the Continent's Most Linguistically Complex Region*, ed. by Nicholas Evans, 353–367. Canberra: Pacific Linguistics. www.jstor.org/stable/24046742 (10 March 2016).

O'Grady, Geoffrey N., C.F. Voegelin, and F.M. Voegelin. 1966. Languages of the World: Indo-Pacific Fascicle Six. *Anthropological Linguistics* 8, no. 2: 1–197.

Oates, W.J. and Lynette F. Oates. 1970. *A Revised Linguistic Survey of Australia.* (Australian Aboriginal Studies/Linguistic Series 33/12). Canberra: Australian Institute of Aboriginal Studies.

Parish, Lucy. 1983. *Some Aspects of Kungarakany Verb Morphology.* MA Thesis, Australian National University, Canberra.

Plomley, N.J.B. 1976. *A Word-List of the Tasmanian Aboriginal Languages.* N. Plomley in association with the Government of Tasmania. Hobart.

Rademaker, Laura. 2014. Language and Australian Aboriginal History: Anindilyakwa and English on Groote Eylandt. *History Australia* 11, no. 2: 222.

Ray, Sidney H. and Alfred C. Haddon. 1891. A Study of the Languages of Torres Straits, with Vocabularies and Grammatical Notes (part I). *Proceedings of the Royal Irish Academy (1889–1901)* 2: 463–616.

Schmidt, W. 1952. *Die Tasmanischen Sprachen.* Utrecht: Spectrum.

Schmidt, Wilhelm. 1919. *Die Gliederung der australischen Sprachen: Geographische, bibliographische, linguistische Grundzüge der Erforschung der australischen Sprachen.* Vienna: Mechitharisten-Buchdruckerei.

Sharpe, Margaret C. 1994. An All-Dialect Dictionary of Banjalang, an Australian Language No Longer in General Use. *First Asia International Lexicography Conference, Manila, Philippines-1992*, ed. by Bonifacio Sibayan and Leonard Newell, 35–48. Manila. http://www-01.sil.org/asia/Philippines/ling/Margaret_C._Sharpe._An_all-dialect_dictionary_of_Banjalang,_an_Australian. . . . pdf (18 February 2014).

Simpson, Jane. 2002. *A Learner's Guide to Warumungu: Mirlamirlajinjjiki Warumunguku apparrka.* Alice Springs, Australia: IAD Press.

Simpson, Jane. 2008. Reconstructing pre-Warumungu pronominals. *Morphology and Language History: In Honour of Harold Koch*, ed. by Claire Bowern, Bethwyn Evans, and Luisa Miceli, 71–87. (Current Issues in Linguistic Theory 298). Philadelphia: John Benjamins.

Simpson, Jane and Jeffrey Heath. 1982. *Warumungu Sketch Grammar.* Cambridge, MA: MIT and Harvard University. Australian Institute of Aboriginal and Torres Islander Studies MS 1860, ms.

Smith, John Charles. 2008. The Refunctionalisation of First Person Plural Inflection in Tiwi. *Morphology and Language History*, 341–348. Amsterdam: John Benjamins.

Stokes, Judith. 1981. Anindilyakwa Phonology from Phoneme to Syllable. *Australian Phonologies: Work Papers of Summer Institute of Linguistics–Australian Aborigines Branch, Series A* 5. 139–181.

Tindale, Norman Barnett and Joseph Benjamin Birdsell. 1941. *Tasmanoid Tribes in North Queensland.* Hassell Press.

Tryon, Darrell T. 1968. The Daly River Languages: A Survey. *Pacific Linguistics. Series A. Occasional Papers* (14): 21–46.

Tryon, Darrell T. 1981. *Daly Family Languages, Australia.* repr. of 1974. Vol. 32. (Pacific Linguistics : Series C, Books). Canberra: Department of Linguistics, Research School of Pacific Studies, The Australian National University.

Tsunoda, Tasaku. 2012. *A Grammar of Warrongo.* Berlin: Walter de Gruyter.

Wafer, Jim and Amanda Lissarrague. 2008. *A Handbook of Aboriginal Languages of New South Wales and the Australian Capital Territory.* Nambucca Heads, NSW: Muurrbay Aboriginal Language and Culture Co-operative.

Wilson, Aidan. 2013. *Tiwi Revisited: A Reanalysis of Traditional Tiwi Verb Morphology*. MA Thesis, University of Melbourne, Melbourne.

Wurm, S.A. 1971. *Classifications of Australian Languages, Including Tasmanian*. Part 1, 721–778. (Current Trends in Linguistics 8). The Hague: Mouton.

Wurm, S.A. 1972. *Languages of Australia and Tasmania*. The Hague: Mouton.

CHAPTER 13

ENDANGERMENT OF LANGUAGE ISOLATES

Eve Okura

1 INTRODUCTION

The death of a language is great loss to humanity on scientific, personal, social, and cultural levels. In Michael Krauss' words:

> In this circumstance, there is a certain tragedy for the human purpose. The loss of local languages, and of the cultural systems that they express, has meant irretrievable loss of diverse and interesting intellectual wealth, the priceless products of human mental industry.
>
> (Krauss 1992:36)

When that dying language is an isolate, the loss is even more dramatic. An entire system for coding human knowledge disappears from the earth with no way of retrieving that information. Although the loss of any language is a tragedy, in some cases, there are at least genetically related languages – surviving sister languages – that may share and thus preserve in a sense some of the features and richness lost in the extinct language. In the case of isolates, there are no surviving relatives.

How many of the world's language isolates are in danger of disappearing? What is the urgency of the situation? This chapter defines language endangerment and how it relates to language isolates. It reports on the current endangerment status of the world's language isolates and discusses factors contributing to language loss and why we should care, and it considers what is being done in attempts to reverse language loss with regard to isolates, with suggestions for what can be done. It also reviews language isolates that have recently become dormant.

While there are differences in opinion regarding whether some languages are isolates or not, making compilation of a definitive comprehensive list of the world's language isolates very difficult, there is general agreement about the majority of language isolates of the world and their total approximate number. This paper relies on the list of language isolates in Campbell (this volume). That list contains 159 language isolates. Of the 159 language isolates in the world, 4 are regarded as "safe" (2.5%) – meaning that approximately 97.5% of the world's language isolates are either extinct or endangered.

2 WHAT IS "LANGUAGE ENDANGERMENT"?

As Rogers and Campbell (2015) clarify, "more precisely, it is not a language itself that is endangered, but rather it is the continued use of the language that is under threat." They explain that language endangerment is not a matter of a clear "yes-or-no" but rather a matter of degree (*how* endangered a language is). Language endangerment is a complex issue involving a variety of factors. Those factors determine how the degree of endangerment is measured.

2.1 How is language endangerment measured?

Just as a person's vital signs (e.g. pulse, blood pressure, etc.) are taken to determine their overall physical condition, languages similarly have "vital signs" which serve as clues to the critical nature of their use – and ultimately their continued existence. Linguists have developed various scales in attempts to measure these "vital signs," to determine how endangered a language is. Some of these endangerment scales include the Graded Intergenerational Disruption Scale (GIDS) (Fishman 1991), the Expanded Graded Intergenerational Disruption Scale (EGIDS) (Lewis and Simons 2010), and the Language Endangerment Index (LEI) (Lee and Van Way 2016). This current study uses the Language Endangerment Index (LEI), produced with the *Catalogue of Endangered Languages* (at www.endangeredlanguages.com). There are several factors that determine how much a language is "under threat" of being lost. The LEI relies primarily on four factors that determine whether a language is falling into disuse (see also Rogers and Campbell 2015):

1   The absolute number of speakers
2   Lack of intergenerational transmission (whether or not children are learning it as their first language in the home)
3   A decrease in the number of speakers over time
4   Decrease in the domains of use (where and in which contexts the language is used)

The LEI gives a rating for each of these four factors for a language and combines the scores to determine an overall level of endangerment. In addition to an endangerment level, each language's endangerment status is also given a percent of certainty, based on for how many of the four factors information was available. If data is not available for all four factors for a given language, then the endangerment level is assigned based on the information that is available, but with a lower percent of certainty.

Each of the four factors is ranked 0–5 ("Safe" to "Critically endangered"). Lee and Van Way emphasize that the LEI measures endangerment as opposed to vitality, so the higher the score, the greater the language's risk.

The level of endangerment is calculated using the four factors in the following way:

Level of endangerment = {[(intergenerational transmission score × 2) + absolute number of speakers score + speaker number trends score + domains of use score]/ total possible score based on number of factors used} × 100.

(Lee and Van Way 2016:25)

Intergenerational transmission is given twice as much weight as the other factors, since it is the most significant factor in determining whether or not a language remains in use. The LEI categories are:

Safe: 0%
Vulnerable: 1–20%

TABLE 13.1 LANGUAGE ENDANGERMENT INDEX (LEI)

	Critically endangered (+5)	Severely endangered (+4)	Endangered (+3)	Threatened (+2)	Vulnerable (+1)	Safe (0)
Absolute no. of native speakers	1–9 speakers	10–99 speakers	100–999 speakers	1,000–9,999 speakers	10,000–99,999 speakers	>100,000 speakers
Intergenerational transmission	"There are only a few elderly speakers."	"Many of the grandparent generation speak the language, but the younger people generally do not."	"Some adults in the community are speakers, but the language is not spoken by children."	"Most adults in the community are speakers, but children generally not."	"Most adults and some children are speakers."	"All members of the community, including children, speak the language."
Speaker number trends	"A small percentage of the community speaks the language, and speaker numbers are decreasing very rapidly"	"Less than half of the community speaks the language, and speaker numbers are decreasing at an accelerated rate."	"About half of community members speak the language." Speaker numbers "decreasing steadily, but not at an accelerated rate"	"A majority of community members speak the language. Speaker numbers are gradually decreasing."	Most community members "speak the language. Speaker numbers may be decreasing, but very slowly."	"Almost all community members speak the language, and speaker numbers are stable or increasing."
Domains of use	"Used only if a few very specific domains" (e.g. "ceremonies songs, prayer. . . limited domestic activities")	"Used mainly just in the home and/or with family"; "may not be the primary language even in these domains for many"	"Used mainly just in the home and/or family, but remains the primary language of these domains for many"	"Used in some non-official domains along with other languages, and remains the primary language used in the home for many"	"Used in most domains except for official ones" (e.g. "government, mass media, education, etc.")	"Used in most domains, including official ones" ("e.g. government, mass media, education, etc.")

Source: Lee and Van Way 2016.

Threatened: 21–40%
Endangered: 41–60%
Severely endangered: 61–80%
Critically endangered: 81–100%

If a language has 100,000 native speakers or more, but no information was available for the other three factors, it is labeled "at risk" in ELCat, as even a language with 100,000 speakers will disappear from use within a couple of generations if it is not being passed on to children (the "intergenerational transmission" factor). The LEI category "dormant" is for languages that have no known native speakers, that are sometimes referred to as "extinct." Many prefer to avoid the term "extinct" because it may discourage language group members who otherwise might attempt to revive their heritage languages. Many find the term "extinct" offensive because, though attributed to a people's language, it can get misconstrued to mean that the people and their identity are also extinct. So the term "dormant" is used in the *Catalogue of Endangered Languages*. Some communities actually prefer the term "extinct" for their language because it elevates awareness of their plight. Both terms are used in this chapter, reflecting both views.

3 HOW "IN DANGER" OF DISAPPEARING ARE THE WORLD'S LANGUAGE ISOLATES?

The relationship between language endangerment and language isolates has strong implications for language classification and language history. To attempt to answer the question of whether a language is an isolate, it is necessary to look at all accumulated past and present information on the language, but it is not possible to predict whether or not a language will continue to be an isolate in the future. If a language isolate has dialects, with enough subsequent change, the dialects can become mutually unintelligible and thus become independent, separate languages. When this happen, the language ceases to be an isolate and becomes a language family of multiple members. However, if the language isolate is endangered (as the vast majority of them are), it may become extinct, cancelling the potential for its dialects to diverge into independent languages.

Table 13.2 provides an overview of language isolates, their endangerment statuses, and the number of native speakers for the languages for which speaker numbers are available. As mentioned, this list follows that of Campbell (this volume). The endangerment status of each language isolate is derived from the language's assigned LEI status in the *Catalogue of Endangered Languages* (ELCat). There are two types of languages in Table 13.2 that are frequently not in ELCat: (1) safe languages and (2) language isolates that have been extinct for quite some time. Because ELCat is a catalogue of languages that are at risk, languages that are "vigorous" or "safe" are not included in the Catalogue. The dormant languages in ELCat are typically those that have been reported as having no known speakers only recently. Languages that have long been extinct (e.g. isolates Elamite, Hattic, Meroitic, etc.) are not listed in the Catalogue. Language isolates that are either safe or long extinct, not listed in ELCat, do not have an LEI status; for these, the *Ethnologue* EGIDS was used. *Ethnologue* uses the term "developing" to refer to a language in which 100% of the ethnic population speaks the language, but for which there is a relatively small ethnic population (Lewis, Simons, and Fennig 2016). For the purposes of this chapter, *Ethnologue*'s "developing" category has been grouped with LEI's "safe," for languages that were not considered endangered enough to be entered into ELCat. The column "*Native speakers worldwide*" contains a note with the source of the endangerment

TABLE 13.2 LANGUAGE ISOLATES AND ENDANGERMENT STATUSES

Africa (6)

	Isolate	ISO 639–3	Endangerment status	# of L1 speakers	Source and notes
1	Bangi Me	dba	threatened	2000	Blench 2005, ELCat 2015
2	Hadza	hts	threatened	~800	Blench, this volume
3	Jalaa* (=Cun Tuum)	cet	dormant	0?	Blench, this volume; 10–99. A small number of elderly people among the Dijim speak this language (ELCat 2015, Blench 2011)
4	Laal	gdm	endangered	300	Mous 2003
5	Ongota	bxe	critically endangered	8	Graziano 2003, ELCat 2016
6	Sandawe	sad	vulnerable	60,000	Brenzinger 2011, ELCat 2016

Australia (7)

	Isolate	ISO 639–3	Endangerment status	# of L1 speakers	Source and notes
7	Bachamal*	wdj	dormant	0	Campbell, this volume
8	Gaagudju*	gbu	dormant	0	Bowern, this volume
9	Kungarakany*	ggk	dormant	0	Bowern, this volume; Evans 2001
10	Mangarrayi*	mpc	dormant	0	Bowern, this volume
11	Tiwi	tiw	threatened (ELCat)	3000	Bowern, this volume
12	Umbugarla* (Ngurmbur)	umr	dormant	0	Bowern, this volume; Evans 2001
13	Wagiman* (Wageman)	waq	dormant	0	Campbell, this volume

Central America and Mexico (4)

	Isolate	ISO 639–3	Endangerment status	# of L1 speakers	Source and notes
14	Cuitlatec*	–	dormant	0	Heaton, this volume
15	Huave	hue, huv, hvv, hve	endangered	15,993	Heaton, this volume, citing INALI (2008–2012)
16	Purépecha (Tarascan)	tsz, pua	threatened	117,221	Capistrán 2015, ELCat 2016
17	Seri	sei	endangered	760? 800–900	Heaton, this volume

Eurasia (11)					
18	Ainu*	ain	dormant	0	Campbell, this volume
19	Basque	eus	safe	714,136	Gobierno Vasco 2012, ELCat 2015
20	Burushaski	bsk	threatened	100,300	Munshi 2014, ELCat 2016
21	Elamite*	elx	dormant	0	Campbell 2013
22	Hattic*	xht	dormant	0	Campbell 2013
23	Hruso-Aka	hru	threatened	<3,000	Van Driem 2011, ELCat 2016
24	Kassite*	–	dormant	0	Michawolski, this volume
25	Kusunda	kgg	critically endangered	2	Gautam 2012, ELCat 2016; some competent speakers in year 2004; Georg, this volume
26	Nihali	nll	threatened	1,000–2,000	Hammarström 2010, ELCat 2016
27	Nivkh (Gilyak)	niv	severely endangered	700	14% of ethnic population Georg, this volume; 200 in 2010 census
28	Sumerian*	sux	dormant	0	Campbell 2013
North America (23)					
29	Adai*	xad	dormant	0	Mithun in this volume
30	Alsea*	aes	dormant	0	Mithun in this volume
31	Atakapa*	aqp	dormant	0	Mithun in this volume
32	Beothuk*	bue	dormant	0	Mithun in this volume
33	Cayuse*	xcy	dormant	0	Mithun, this volume
34	Chimariko*	cid	dormant	0	1950s Martha Zigler
35	Chitimacha*	ctm	awakening	0	Galla 2009: 176
36	Coahuilteco*	xcw	dormant	0	Mithun, this volume
37	Cotoname*	xcn	dormant	0	Mithun, this volume
38	Esselen*	esq	awakening	0	Shaul 2014:56 1st CA lang ext?

(*Continued*)

TABLE 13.2 (CONTINUED)

39	Haida (Xaad Kil)	hai	critically endangered	30	Ignace 2006, ELCat 2016
40	Karankawa*	zkk	dormant	0	Campbell 2013
41	Karuk	kyh	critically endangered	<12	Golla 2011, ELCat 2016
42	Kootenai (Kutenai)	kut	severely endangered	26	FPCC; ELCat 2016
43	Natchez*	ncz	awakening	0	K.T. Fields 2016, personal communication
44	Siuslaw*	sis	dormant	0	Mithun, this volume
45	Takelma*	tkm	dormant	0	Mithun, this volume
46	Tonkawa*	tqw	dormant	0	Campbell 2013
47	Tunica*	tun	awakening	0	Tunica Tulane Language Project 2012; ELCat 2016
48	Washo	was	severely endangered	~20	Golla 2011, ELCat 2016
49	Yana*	ynn	dormant	0	Mithun, this volume
50	Yuchi (Euchee)	yuc	critically endangered	5	Austin 2008, ELCat 2016
51	Zuni	zun	threatened	~9,000	ELCat 2016
Pacific (54)					
52	Abinomn	bsa	critically endangered	~300	Hammarström, this volume
53	Abun	kgr	threatened	~3,000	Hammarström, this volume
54	Afra	ulf	threatened	115	Hammarström, this volume
55	Anêm	anz	safe	~843	Hammarström, this volume
56	Ap Ma	kbx	vulnerable	~10,000	Hammarström, this volume; ELCat 2016, Lewis, Simons, and Fennig 2016 "developing"
57	Asaba	seo	threatened	180	Hammarström, this volume, citing Little 2008:2
58	Baiyamo	ppe	threatened	70	Hammarström, this volume
59	Banaro	byz	threatened	2,569	Laycock 1973, ELCat 2016

#	Language	Code	Status	Population	Source
60	Bilua	blb	threatened	8,740	Hammarström, this volume
61	Bogaya	boq	endangered	300	Hammarström, this volume
62	Burmeso	bzu	endangered	250	Lewis, Simons, and Fennig 2016
63	Busa (Odiai)	bhf	endangered	240	Hammarström, this volume; citing Graham 1981
64	Damal (Uhunduni, Amung)	uhn	threatened	4,000–5,000	ELCat 2016 citing Wurm 2007
65	Dem	dem	threatened	1,000	Hammarström 2010, ELCat 2016
66	Dibiyaso	dby	threatened	1,950	Hammarström, this volume
67	Duna	duc	safe	25,000	San Roque 2008; "developing"; Lewis, Simons, and Fennig 2016
68	Elseng (Morwap)	mrf	endangered	300	Laycock 1973, ELCat 2016
69	Fasu	faa	threatened	1,200	Hammarström, this volume
70	Guriaso	grx	endangered	160	Hammarström, this volume
71	Kaki Ae	tbd	endangered	266	Wurm 2007, ELCat 2016
72	Kamula	xla	endangered	800	Hammarström, this volume
73	Kapauri	khp	vulnerable	~200	Hammarström 2010, ELCat 2015
74	Karami*	xar	dormant	0	Hammarström, this volume; Campbell, this volume
75	Kehu	khh	severely endangered	25	Lewis, Simons, and Fennig 2016
76	Kibiri-Porom	prm	threatened	1,180	Hammarström, this volume
77	Kimki	sbt	at risk		Hammarström 2010
78	Kol	kol	threatened	4,000	Hammarström, this volume
79	Kosare	kiq	endangered	~250	Hammarström, this volume; Lewis, Simons, and Fennig 2016

(Continued)

TABLE 13.2 (CONTINUED)

80	Kuot	kto	threatened	2,400	Hammarström, this volume; Lewis, Simons, and Fennig 2016
81	Lavukaleve	lvk	threatened	1,700	ELCat 2016 citing Terrill 2003
82	Masep	mvs	severely endangered	25	Lewis, Simons, and Fennig 2016
83	Mawes	mgk	endangered	~850	ELCat 2016 citing Hammarström 2010
84	Maybrat	ayz	safe	~20,000	Hammarström, this volume; Ethnologue status: "developing"
85	Mor (of Bomberai)	moq	severely endangered	60	Wurm 2007 (data from 1977)
86	Moraori (Marori)	mok	endangered	413	Arka 2012 ELCat 2016; according to UNESCO (2010) there are 50 speakers (which would make it severely endangered)
87	Mpur	akc	threatened	7,000	Odé 2002, ELCat 2016
88	Pawaia	pwa	threatened	4,000	Hammarström, this volume
89	Pele-Ata	ata	threatened	~2,000	Hammarström, this volume
90	Powle-Ma (Molof)	msl	endangered	200	Lewis, Simons, and Fennig 2016
91	Purari	iar	threatened	7,000	Hammarström, this volume
92	Pyu	pby	endangered	~100	Hammarström, this volume
93	Sause	sao	endangered	300	Wurm 2007, ELCat 2016
94	Savosavo	svs	threatened	2,500	Wegener 2008, ELCat 2016
95	Sulka	sua	threatened	2,500	Hammarström, this volume
96	Tabo (Waia)	knv	threatened	3,000	Hammarström, this volume
97	Taiap	gpn	severely endangered	75	Hammarström, this volume
98	Tambora*	xxt	dormant	0	Hammarström, this volume
99	Tanahmerah	tcm	endangered	500	Hammarström, this volume
100	Touo	tqu	threatened	1,870	Hammarström, this volume

101	Wiru	wiu	vulnerable	15,300	Hammarström, this volume; Lewis, Simons, and Fennig 2016
102	Yale (Yalë, Nagatman)	nce	endangered	~600	Hammarström, this volume; Lewis, Simons, and Fennig 2016
103	Yele (Yélî Dnye)	yle	threatened	6,000	Hammarström, this volume
104	Yerakai	yra	endangered	380	Lewis, Simons, and Fennig 2016
105	Yetfa-Biksi	yet	threatened	1,000	Hammarström, this volume
South America (54)					
106	Aikanã	tba	vulnerable	175–200	van der Voort 2013
107	Andaquí*	ana	dormant	0	Siefart and Hammarström, this volume
108	Andoque	ano	endangered	597	Crevels 2012
109	Arára do Rio Branco* (Arára do Beiradão, Mato Grosso)	axg	dormant	0	Crevels 2012, ELCat 2016
110	Awaké* (Uruak, Arutani)	atx	dormant	0	Campbell; ELCat 2016
111	Betoi-Jirara*		dormant	0	Siefart and Hammarström, this volume
112	Camsá (Kamsá)	kbh	threatened	4,773	Crevels 2012
113	Candoshi-Shapra	cbu	vulnerable	1,586	Crevels 2012
114	Canichana*		dormant	0	3 rememberers in year 2000
115	Cayubaba* (Cayuvava)	cyb	dormant	<10	Siefart and Hammarström, this volume
116	Chiquitano	cax	threatened	~4,665	Crevels 2012
117	Chono*	–	dormant	0	Siefart and Hammarström, this volume
118	Cofán (A'ingaé)	con	threatened	1,017	Crevels 2012, ELCat 2016

(*Continued*)

TABLE 13.2 (CONTINUED)

119	Culli* (Culle)	–	dormant	0	Siefart and Hammarström, this volume
120	Esmeralda* (Esmeraldeño, Atacame)	–	dormant	0	Siefart and Hammarström, this volume
121	Fulniô	fun	threatened	1,000	Crevels 2012, ELCat 2016
122	Guachí*	–	dormant	0	Siefart and Hammarström, this volume
123	Guamo*	–	dormant	0	Siefart and Hammarström, this volume
124	Guató*	gta	dormant	0	Campbell, this volume
125	Iréntxe	im	severely endangered	40	Siefart and Hammarström, this volume
126	Itonama	ito	critically endangered	1	Crevels 2012
127	Jeikó* (Geico)	–	dormant	0	Campbell 1997
128	Jotí (Yuwana)	yau	endangered	767	Crevels et al. 2012
129	Kapixaná (Kanoê) [APEXTAB]	kxo	critically endangered	3	Crevels et al. 2012
130	Kunza* (Atacameño)	kuz	dormant	0	Siefart and Hammarström, this volume
131	Kwaza (Koayá)	xwa	severely endangered	25	ELCat; 7 speakers (Siefart and Hammarström, this volume)
132	Leco* (Leko)	lec	dormant	0	Siefart and Hammarström, this volume
133	Máko* (Maku)	wpc	dormant (2002)	0	Siefart and Hammarström, this volume
134	Matanawí*	–	dormant	0	Siefart and Hammarström, this volume
135	Mochica*	omc	dormant	0	Siefart and Hammarström, this volume
136	Moseten-Chimane	cas	vulnerable	~4,800	Sakel 2009, ELCat 2016
137	Movima	mzp	threatened	1,400	Siefart and Hammarström, this volume
138	Munichi* (Muniche)	myr	dormant	0	Siefart and Hammarström, this volume
139	Ofáyé (Opaye)	opy	severely endangered	12	Crevels 2012
140	Omurano*	omu	dormant	0	Siefart and Hammarström, this volume

141	Páez	pbb	vulnerable	60,000	Crevels 2012
142	Payagua*	–	dormant	0	Campbell in press
143	Pirahã (Muran)	myp	vulnerable	389	Crevels 2012, ELCat 2016
144	Puinave	pui	threatened	7,154	Crevels 2012
145	Puquina*	puq	dormant	0	Siefart and Hammarström, this volume
146	Puri-Coroado*	prr	dormant	0	Campbell in press; Zamponi, this volume
147	Rikbaktsá	rkb	threatened	1,085	Silva 2010, ELCat 2016
148	Sapé* (Kaliana)	spc	dormant	0	Campbell et al. 2013
149	Taruma*	tdm	dormant	0 (1 semi-speaker)	Campbell in press
150	Taushiro	trr	critically endangered	1	Crevels 2012 (data from 2008)
151	Tequiraca* (Tekiraka, Aewa, Aiwa)	ash	dormant	0	Siefart and Hammarström, this volume
152	Trumai	tpy	critically endangered	50	Guirardello-Damian 2014
153	Urarina	ura	threatened	<3,000	Siefart and Hammarström, this volume; Olawsky 2006, ELCat 2016
154	Waorani	auc	threatened	1,616	Crevels 2012, ELCat 2016
155	Warao	wba	vulnerable	~28,000	Seifart and Hammarström, this volume
156	Yagan (Yámana)	yag	critically endangered	1	Crevels 2012, ELCat 2016
157	Yaruro (Pumé)	yae	threatened	7,400	Crevels 2012 (data from 2001)
158	Yuracaré	yuz	threatened	1,809	Crevels 2012
159	Yurumanguí*	–	dormant	0	Campbell, this volume

level for these "safe" or "dormant" language isolates that were not in ELCat. Where more recent data was available (e.g. from the chapters in this volume), I used the more recent source for numbers of native speakers.

As the other chapters in this volume detail the geography, the histories, and the unique typological features of individual isolates, in this chapter, I concentrate only on endangerment statuses and numbers of speakers. Languages are presented in alphabetical order by region (also in alphabetical order). The content of this chapter concerns endangerment of language isolates rather than the nuances of which languages are in fact isolates, which are unclassified, and which are perhaps small families. For these distinctions and discussions of the status of particular languages, I defer to the other chapters in this volume.

Dormant:	55
Critically endangered:	11
Severely endangered:	10
Endangered:	21
Threatened:	43
Vulnerable:	10
Safe:	4
At risk:	1
Awakening:	4
Total:	159 language isolates

One of the challenges in keeping up with a language's endangerment level is that its status changes: it is a moving target. In some cases, even the most recent published speaker number data for a language is already several years old. When there are only a few speakers left or when the only speakers are very elderly, in those few years the numbers of speakers may have changed significantly. Unfortunately, unless active efforts are made to turn the tides of language loss, those changes usually result in an even more precarious situation for the language. Even when there appear to be recent sources, sometimes the data cited in these publications is from a much earlier source. There is a constant need for more up-to-date information on the situation of these languages.

The following section provides a brief analysis of the endangerment status of the language isolates for each of nine categories, the five LEI endangerment levels and the four additional statuses, that is: dormant, awakening, critically endangered, severely endangered, endangered, threatened, vulnerable, safe, and "at risk." Each of the sections discusses specific examples of language isolates from Table 13.2 and explains them in greater detail. This breakdown shows concrete examples of ratings of the four factors and how these were used to calculate the overall endangerment status of the language isolates.

3.1 Dormant isolates

Of the 159 language isolates in this list, 59 are dormant or awakening ("extinct" in traditional terms) – there is no known person left in the world who speaks any of these languages natively. More than half – approximately 58% – of all known extinct language families are isolates; this figure includes language isolates, which are language families of only a single member – 55 isolates from out of 95 language families. However, this figure may be due in part to the fact that we know so little about ancient extinct languages.

It may be that there are many more extinct language families than the 95 of which we are certain but that we only have clear information about these. It is also possible that some of those 55 dormant language isolates were actually related to other now-extinct languages about which no information has survived, and so based on the information available to us today, they remain dormant language isolates.

In any event, this amount of extinction reveals a huge loss of the linguistic knowledge. With 55 out of the 159 isolates already dormant, only 104 language isolates (65%) remain in use today in any form, and as seen in Figure 13.1 and in Table 13.2, many of the still surviving language isolates are highly endangered.

It may be instructive to examine a relatively recent case of language extinction in order to understand the process from language endangerment to extinction and the rate at which this process can occur. The dormant isolate Munichi was spoken in Peruvian Amazonia, in the "southwestern part of the *departamento* of Loreto" (Michael et al. 2013). The language is categorized as dormant, as there are no known fluent speakers. However, ELCat does cite "3 rememberers" – those who are not currently fluent in the language, but who do remember aspects of the language (ELCat 2015, Michael et al. 2013). In 2008 and 2009 linguists conducted fieldwork on the language. At that time, there were ten rememberers, none of whom self-identified as fluent in the language, and only three of whom remembered any significant amounts of the language. These three last rememberers who worked with field linguists were Alejandrina Chanchari Icahuate (approximately 90 years old at the time), Melchor Sinti Saita (approximately 70 years old at the time), and Donalia Icahuate Baneo (57 years old at the time of the fieldwork, born in 1951). However, of even these three strongest rememberers, all of them "either had not used the language for most of their adult life or were never fully fluent in the language" and were more comfortable speaking in either Spanish or Quechua (Michael et al. 2013: 311). The eldest, Alejandrina, had not used the language in decades. Melchor had never been fully fluent. According to oral histories, the last fluent speakers were born from 1915–1925. Around 1930 the language had already become moribund.[1]

There are other similar examples of language isolates that have gone from having a couple of rememberers to no speakers very rapidly. Some of these other dormant isolates

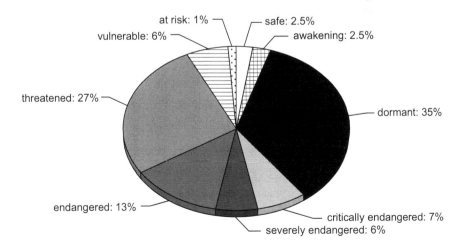

FIGURE 13.1 THE ENDANGERMENT STATUS OF THE WORLD'S LANGUAGE ISOLATES

are recognized as having had no known L1 speakers for some decades. Takelma, of Oregon, was extinct by the 1940s, and at least one speaker of Alsea, also of Oregon, survived into the 1940s. Chief Benjamin Paul and Delphine Decloux Stouff were the last two speakers of Chitimacha, in Louisiana; Mrs. Stouff died last, in 1940. Sesostrie Youchigant was the last speaker of Tunica, in Louisiana; died after 1950. Madeline England, the last speaker of Kungarakany (Australia), listed as dormant, passed away in 1989 (Frawley 1997: 119). Although not included in the list of 159 isolates in this chapter due to purposes of consistency, Tuxá of Brazil (Seifart and Hammarström, this volume) had two rememberers in 1961 (Moseley 2010). By the 1970s the language was found to have no known native speakers (Meader 1978). (Because of the very limited attestation of this language, many consider it not an isolate, but unclassified.)

3.2   Critically endangered isolates

What is the difference between a dormant language and a critically endangered one? The distinction can be surprisingly fuzzy. According to Crystal (2000: 2) "If you are the last speaker of a language, your language – viewed as a tool of communication – is already dead. For a language is really alive only as long as there is someone to speak it to." In this interpretation, even a language that is still known by one person is as good as dormant, since the language is not actually in use, nor could it be. There is also another kind of complication. In *The Last Speaker Is Dead – Long Live the Last Speaker!*, Evans (2001) discusses the difficulties of determining who the last speaker of a language is. Evans mentions cases in which for cultural reasons some competent speakers of a language hang back and do not claim to speak it. At times it may be to respect an elder who is recognized as the last speaker of the language; in other cases it may be that they do not have cultural rights to claim "ownership" of the language. Once the last culturally recognized speaker has passed away, these speakers may come forth and are more willing to share their language knowledge. The reverse also occurs. For example, Butcher Knight was the last fluent speaker of the isolate Umbugarla. While Evans did fieldwork with Knight, Knight's speech was sometimes quiet or unclear, making it difficult to document. Another member of the community, Talking Billy, assisted Evans by repeating Knight's utterances more clearly. This led Evans to assume that Talking Billy "was at least a partial speaker of Umbugarla" (Evans 2001: 273). Evans reports that, after the death of Butcher Knight, "Without having Butcher Knight there to make the initial utterance, however, he was totally unable to recall any Umbugarla" (Evans 2001: 273). Both Butcher Knight and Talking Billy are now deceased. A similar situation occurred with the now-dormant language Kungarakany (Evans 2001: 273). With the difficulty of determining who the last speaker is, comes the difficulty of determining how many speakers of a language there are. Even defining "speaker" is problematic.

Out of the 104 living language isolates, more than one-tenth (11) are considered "critically endangered." Only 4 out of the 11 critically endangered isolates are spoken by more than 10 people – there are 7 critically endangered isolates that are spoken by 10 or fewer people. Three of the critically endangered isolates – Itonama, Taushiro, and Yagan – are reported to have only one speaker left, with some sources for some of these reporting differently that there are zero speakers left; others have no recent reports, meaning the sole survivor may well have died since the last report. For example, the report of a single surviving Taushiro speaker is from 2008 (see Catalogue of Endangered Languages, www.endangeredlanguages.com; Crevels 2012).

3.3 Severely endangered isolates

Severely endangered is the second highest level of urgency for endangered languages. At first glance it might appear that severely endangered languages are not as in dire of a situation when compared with critically endangered languages, yet even severely endangered languages are likely to go dormant within a single generation. Of the 10 severely endangered language isolates, only one, Nivkh (Gilyak), has more than 100 living native speakers. While Nivkh in Asia has approximately 300 speakers, the other severely endangered languages are much closer to critical in their status. In the Pacific, Masep has only 25 speakers. While the source for Mor (of Bomberai) is a 2007 publication, the data is from 1977. This is the case for speaker number data for many languages – many sources recite the only published data available. Recent publication dates may inadvertently give the appearance of recent data. However, often the recent publication is citing an older publication, which cites an older publication, which cites data that is even older. While accurate metadata is available for the number of speakers of some endangered languages, more current speaker number counts are needed for others to have a more accurate understanding of the situation. Mor had 60 living speakers in 1977 (Wurm 2007, ELCat 2015); Hammarström (this volume) reports 30. Taiap has 75 speakers. In North America, Kootenai (Ktunaxa) has 26 speakers, and Washo has about 20. In South America, according to Crevels 2012 Irantxe had approximately 90 speakers. Only 4 years later, that count has dropped to less than half of that, with a current estimate of 40 speakers (Seifart and Hammarström, this volume).

As with other severely endangered languages, Kwaza (Koaya) is in a complex linguistic situation. Van der Voort (2005) explained this as follows:

> Today, the remaining 25 speakers of Kwaza no longer constitute a unified community. There are basically two ethnically mixed families in which the Kwaza language is spoken on a daily basis. They live to the south of their original habitat on the indigenous reserve Tubarão-Latundê, among a majority of about 150 speakers of Aikanã and as neighbors of the remaining 19 speakers of Latundê. There are also some elderly individuals who remember fragments of Kanoê, Sabanê (Nambikwara), and Salamãi from their childhood. Some young Rikbaktsa (Macro-Jê) people married Aikanã, as did some Terena (Arawak) missionaries, but none of their languages are used on the reserve. Some speakers of Kwaza live in the towns of Vilhena, Pimenta Bueno, and Chupinguaia. Another family of mixed Aikanã and Kwaza ethnicity lives on the indigenous reserve Kwaza do Rio São Pedro, on traditional Kwaza lands, but here the language is no longer used. Most Kwaza speakers are trilingual in the sense that they also speak Aikanã and Portuguese.
>
> (van der Voort 2005:367)

"Today" in the quotation refers to 2005. In sources 11 years later, the numbers have dropped. According to the most recent count, Kwaza has lost 72% of its speakers since 2005. As of the year 2016, there are 7 people living who speak the Kwaza language (Seifart and Hammarström, this volume). This more recent number actually changes Kwaza's status from severely endangered to critically endangered. Ofayé (Opayé) has 12 speakers. The count for Trumai was 51 speakers in 2007. There may be even fewer now.

3.4 Endangered isolates

The term "endangered" can refer generally to all of the language isolates of any degree of vitality other than "safe," "dormant," or "awakening." However, "endangered" is also the label for the specific LEI status between "threatened" and "severely endangered." In Section 3.4 the term "endangered" refers to the specific LEI status. Laal is the only endangered isolate (in the LEI sense of the word), spoken in Africa.

The majority of language isolates categorized as "endangered" (in LEI's technical sense) – 16 out of 21 – are spoken in the Pacific. They are: Bogaya (300 speakers), Burmeso (250 speakers), Busa (Odiai) with 238 speakers, Guriaso with 160 speakers, Kaki Ae (266 speakers), Kamula (800 speakers), Kosare (about 250 speakers), Mawes with about 850 speakers, Moraori with 50 speakers, Morwap (Elseng) with 300 speakers, Powle-Ma (Molof) with 200 speakers, Pyu (about 100 speakers), Sause (300 speakers), Tanahmerah (500 speakers), Yale with about 600 speakers, and Yerakai (380 speakers). (See Hammarström, this volume.)

Two of the 21 "endangered" isolates are spoken in South America. Andoque is spoken by about 597 speakers in southern Colombia. According to data from 2001, Jotí was spoken by 767 speakers in central Venezuela, 100% of the ethnic population.

Huave and Seri are the two isolates spoken in the Mexico with the LEI level "endangered." Huave is spoken in the state of Oaxaca along the Pacific by about 15,993 according to the 2010 census. Seri is spoken by about 760 people in Sonora, Mexico, near the Gulf of California and just west of Hermosillo.

3.5 Threatened isolates

There are 43 threatened language isolates, outnumbering those in any other endangerment category except dormant. Languages categorized as threatened have a very large range of numbers of speakers. For example, on the lower end are Hadza (northern Tanzania, Africa) with about 800 speakers, Yatê (Fulniô) (eastern Brazil) with 1,000 speakers, the Tiwi language in Australia, with about 3,000 speakers, and Kuot in the Pacific with approximately 2,400 speakers. While the source for the number of Kuot speakers was published in 2016, the data is actually from 2002. This is not a deficiency on the part of the publication – it is simply the most recent published data available. In 15 years, a speaker number population of 2,400 may have changed. It is also possible that numbers may have remained stable. Until more current speaker number data is gathered, Kuot – and those languages like it – will continue to be known by an endangerment status that may or may not reflect the reality of their current situation.

On the other end of the spectrum are threatened isolates with high speaker numbers relative to other endangered languages. These include Burushaski (northern Pakistan, Asia) with 100,300 speakers and Tarascan (Purépecha) (central Mexico) with 117,221 speakers.

3.6 Vulnerable

There are ten vulnerable isolates: one in Africa, Sandawe; there are three in the Pacific: Ap Ma, Kapauri, and Wiru. The majority of vulnerable isolates – six – are in South America: Aikanã, Candoshi-Shapra, Moseten-Chimane, Páez, Pirahã, and Warao in northeastern Venezuela. The geographic distribution of vulnerable isolates reveals that there are no vulnerable isolates in North America, Central America, Mexico, Australia, or Eurasia. While vulnerable is still a level of endangerment, it is the most vital below "safe." It may be that those isolates that are located in more geographically remote areas are more "protected" from outside influence, enabling them to maintain a higher level of vitality. Although there may still be pressure from dominant and neighboring languages to shift, the pressure has not been as pronounced.

Aikanã, a vulnerable isolate of Brazil, is spoken by roughly 150 people. It is spoken in a mixed community in the state of Rondônia, together with Kwaza (Koaya, isolate) and Latundê (Nambikwaran).

3.7 Awakening

Currently several language isolates are "awakening," including Chitimacha in Southern Louisiana, Esselen in California, Natchez in Oklahoma (originally from Louisiana), and Tunica in Louisiana. Natchez, usually reported as dormant in some of the literature, is currently being awakened (Kent T. Fields, personal communication, October 27, 2016). Kent Fields, who has some knowledge of the language, has developed the Natchez Nation's online dictionary, and he is adding to it daily.

As a recently awakening isolate, Tunica has no native speakers. All who have some degree of proficiency in it are learning it as a second language. Heaton (in press) has analyzed and described some of the unique grammatical features of Tunica, including its interaction between gender, "animacy, definiteness, and number" (Heaton in press). One such feature is that Tunica is "one of the few languages of the world that shows evidence of an unmarked feminine gender," as opposed to the masculine gender being the unmarked one (Heaton in press). This is one example of the significant contributions to language typology that isolates can offer. When a language isolate is endangered, in addition to the personal human and cultural losses, we are at risk of losing a greater than normal piece of the puzzle in the field of linguistics as a whole.

3.8 "Safe," "vigorous," and "developing" isolates

Out of the 104 language isolates in use today, only 4 are rated as "safe" (in LEI; or "developing" or "vigorous" in *Ethnologue*). Of these 4 safe languages, only one – Basque – has more than 100,000 speakers. Each of the other 3 safe languages ("vigorous" or "developing" in *Ethnologue*) have fewer speakers: Anêm with 843; Duna with 25,000; and Maybrat with 20,000 speakers. It is perhaps more than mere coincidence that all three of the safe/vigorous/developing languages with smaller populations are in the same geographic region. This leads us to the question – is there any significant correlation between the geographic region of an isolate and its vitality? For example, Burushaski, of Pakistan and Kashmir, with about 100,300 speakers, is considered "threatened."

4 WHERE ARE LANGUAGE ISOLATES BECOMING ENDANGERED?

In this chapter the endangered isolates of the world are divided into seven major geographic regions: (1) Africa, (2) Australia, (3) Central America/Mexico, (4) Eurasia, (5) North America, (6) Pacific, and (7) South America. ELCat divides language entries into ten geographic regions: (1) Africa, (2) Asia, (3) Australia, (4) Caucasus, (5) Central America and Mexico, (6) Europe, (7) Near East, (8) North America, (9) Pacific, and (10) South America. The languages in Asia, Europe, the Caucasus, and the Middle East were combined for the Eurasia region in this chapter. The other regions were kept the same.

The number of endangered language isolates per region was derived by taking the total number of isolates in the region and subtracting the number of dormant isolates and the number of "safe" isolates.

TABLE 13.3 LANGUAGE ISOLATES BY REGION AND ENDANGERMENT STATUS

	Dormant	Awakening	Critically endangered	Severely endangered	Endangered	Threatened	Vulnerable	Safe	At risk	Total number of isolates	Total number endangered
Africa	1	0	1	0	1	2	1	0	0	6	5
Australia	6	0	0	0	0	1	0	0	0	7	1
Central America/ Mexico	1	0	0	0	2	1	0	0	0	4	3
Eurasia	5	0	1	1	0	3	0	1	0	11	5
North America	13	4	3	2	0	1	0	0	0	23	10
Pacific	2	0	1	4	16	24	3	3	1	54	49
South America	27	0	5	3	2	11	6	0	0	54	27
Totals:	55	4	11	10	21	43	10	4	1	159	100

TABLE 13.4 ENDANGERED ISOLATES VS. NON-ISOLATE ENDANGERED LANGUAGES BY REGION

Africa (5)	534	North America (10)	199
Australia (1)	326	Pacific (49)	322
Central America & Mexico (3)	119	South America (27)	376
Eurasia (5)	1,002		

Total: 2,878 languages in ELCat (2015)

While South America and the Pacific have the same number of language isolates, there are 27 extinct isolates in South America and only 2 extinct isolates in the Pacific. There are many variables, so the reason for this extreme difference in vitality rates of isolates in these two regions cannot be known with certainty. However, as mentioned previously, the relative geographic isolation of islands in the Pacific may be a factor in preserving the vitality of language isolates, especially in New Guinea, where there are many languages and where contact with the outside world has been more recent and less intense.

How does the distribution of endangered isolates compare with endangered languages in general? Table 13.4 shows the count of endangered languages in each region according to the *Catalogue of Endangered Languages*.[2] The number in parentheses next to the region name is the number of endangered language isolates in the region to show a comparison.

5 WHY ARE LANGUAGES DISAPPEARING?

Both physical and cultural factors are involved in language isolates falling into disuse. This section outlines the various physical dangers and cultural factors leading to the endangerment of language isolates. Specific examples of real language isolate situations are given for some of the factors.

5.1 Physical dangers

One type of factor contributing to language loss is physical danger. If an entire community of people is killed, their language dies with them. Crystal (2000) lists some of the physical factors that have caused language death:

1   Natural disasters
2   Disease
4   Famine
5   Economic (e.g. environmental changes, deforestation)
6   Political (war, genocide)

(Crystal 2000:70–76)

The following section provides examples of language isolates that have gone extinct due to natural disasters and disease. Cases involving natural disasters are particularly tragic because of loss of human life and language all at once. Their unpredictable nature and devastating effects can cause a vibrant community and language to disappear almost instantaneously. One historical example of this is Tambora, a language isolate that was spoken on Sumbawa Island in Indonesia. It was spoken by roughly 11,000 people. In 1815 Mount Tambora erupted, killing virtually every person in the area, including all speakers of Tambora (Raffles 1817, Donohue 2007).

Although located in Indonesia, Tambora was clearly not an Austronesian language (Donohue 2007). All is known of the Tambora language are a few lexical items.

Taushiro is a critically endangered language isolate spoken in Peru. One of the primary factors causing it to become critically endangered was disease, in combination with cultural factors:

> Due to an epidemic disease in the same decade and to the fact that most survivors have intermarried with non-Taushiro speakers and have adopted Spanish or a variety of Quechua, the language is now on the brink of extinction with 1 speaker out of an ethnic group of 20.
>
> (Crevels 2012: 213; ELCat 2015)

Taushiro has only one speaker and an ethnic population of only 20 individuals. As can be seen in this case, disease and other physical dangers not only reduce language use, but they put the entire ethnic population of a group at risk. This can be contrasted with metadata for languages at risk due to cultural dangers.

6 WHAT IS BEING DONE AND WHAT REMAINS TO BE DONE?

What can be done about the critical situation of the world's endangered language isolates? What efforts are being made to revitalize and document these languages? What policies are relevant to the vitality/endangerment of language isolates? And what still needs to be done? Some of the factors leading towards language loss are out of human control – e.g. natural disasters. However, some of the cultural and political factors can be influenced by human choice and action. The three routes of action focused on here are: (1) policy versus intergenerational transmission in the home, (2) revitalization, and (3) documentation.

6.1 Policy and intergenerational transmission

Political policies have played a role in the demise of languages; they have also played a role in their revitalization. This section does not delve into the details of particular nations' policies. Rather, it provides an overview of some international policies that have already been proposed. The next step in improving the situation for endangered language isolates (and endangered languages generally) is to implement these policies and to enact the ideals they state.

On June 9, 1996, the World Conference on Linguistics Rights was held in Barcelona, Spain. The conference – run by the Translations and Linguistics Rights Commission of the International PEN Club and the Escarre International Center for Ethnic Minorities and the Nations – drafted the Universal Declaration on Linguistic Rights, as an extension of the Universal Declaration of Human Rights from 1948 (see United Nations 1998). The declaration summarizes various causes of language loss (e.g. genocide, colonialism, economic policies, etc.), establishes rights of speakers of all languages and promotes linguistic diversity.

6.1.1 Official use

Section I, Article 15, of the declaration declares that: "All language communities are entitled to the official use of their language within their territory." This policy has not been adopted by the governments of many nations. If speakers of endangered languages were allowed to use their languages in official settings, this could potentially greatly increase the prestige of the language. Article 16 adds that:

> All members of a language community have the right to interrelate with and receive attention from the public authorities in their own language. This right also applies to central, territorial, local and supraterritorial divisions which include the territory to which the language is specific.
>
> (UNESCO 1996:7)

If the Universal Declaration of Linguistic Rights were implemented, speakers of endangered language isolates would be able interact with public authorities in their languages. In addition, since many public officials might not speak endangered languages, this enactment would probably create jobs in interpretation and translation for speakers of endangered languages. One of the reasons minority language speakers give for not passing the language on to children is that it is more economically advantageous for their children to speak a majority language. While the value of a language exceeds economics, if minority languages were given official status, it could create some economic benefits for speaking those languages.

6.1.2 Education

Appropriate policies regarding minority language use in education could also help curb the loss of language isolates and languages generally. Section II, Article 23, of the Universal Declaration on Linguistic Rights states that:

> (2) Education must help to maintain and develop the language spoken by the language community of the territory where it is provided; (3) Education must always

be at the service of linguistic and cultural diversity and of the harmonious relations between different language communities throughout the world.

(UNESCO 1996:9)

Currently, the opposite of this is happening in many locations – where official policies favor compulsory education in the majority language, further pushing out endangered languages.

However, Romaine (2002) points out that the creation of language policy alone is not enough to ensure the maintenance of a language. Many language policies (including the Universal Declaration on Language Rights) sought ideals, but the policies are not implemented or enforced. The number one factor resulting in language death is a lack of inter-generational transmission – i.e., parents do not teach the language to their children in the home or children do not attempt to learn their parents' language, so the next generation does not speak the language.

The solution may not be to abandon efforts to create effective language policies (e.g. granting minority languages official status, providing for multilingual education). Rather, efforts could be supplemented with a focus on implementing policies. In the past, government and institutional policies have often played a major role in the demise of languages (e.g. the well-known cases of boarding schools in the US, Canada, and Australia, where indigenous children were forbidden to speak their native language or were punished for doing so).

Nonetheless, changes in official policies have also opened up the way for language revitalization programs in some contexts. For example, in 1978, an amendment to the state of Hawai'i constitution designated Hawaiian as an official language on par with English (Lucas 2000, Romaine 2002).[3] This opened the way for the Hawaiian language revitalization movement. The next three decades saw the development of Hawaiian immersion schools, Hawaiian immersion programs at the university level, students writing masters theses completely in Hawaiian, and Hawaiian language announcements at local airports, among other breakthroughs. Official status for and education in the language can assist the revitalization of a language. However, while official status and formal education can assist language maintenance, these do not guarantee intergenerational transmission. They do, however, provide the possibility of expansion of domains where the language can be spoken, increasing the likelihood of use.

Hinton's (2013) *Bringing Our Languages Home* emphasizes the importance of inter-generational transmission within the home. There have been examples of successful efforts of intergenerational transmission within the home, without assistance from official status or formal education policies, e.g. the Baldwin family's successful revitalization of the Miami language (Baldwin et al. 2013, Hinton 2013).

6.2 Revitalizing language isolates

Examples of language isolates that are currently being revitalized or awakened include Karuk (Karok), Natchez, and Tunica. Tunica currently has no native speakers, but it does have several heritage language learners.

6.2.1 Karuk

Karuk, spoken in northern California, is another isolate that is being revitalized. There are fewer than a dozen native speakers of Karuk; however, many members of the Karuk tribe are studying and learning the language. However, in contrast to Tunica, Karuk revitalization efforts began before its last fully fluent native speakers passed away, so although it is critically endangered, it has never gone through a period of being completely dormant (i.e. of having no living speakers).

This desire for the upcoming generation to have access to the Karuk language has motivated development of Karuk language programs for children. There is currently a curriculum for kindergarten to third grade (approximately 5 year olds to 8 year olds) focused primarily on language revitalization, but instruction also includes traditional cultural knowledge, values, and practices. The tribe is working on a curriculum for kindergarten to 12th grade (for those 5 years old to 18 years old) for any schools that are interested in incorporating it. The community is working with a linguist. In addition, from 2008 to 2011 the Karuk tribe received an ANA (Administration for Native Americans) grant for a Master-Apprentice program. There are also online resources, including a Karuk-English online dictionary and Karuk texts[4] (Beck, personal communication, August 20, 2015; Cramblit 2011).

6.2.2 Natchez

The Natchez Nation is working to awaken the Natchez language. Kent T. "Hutke" Fields is heading the effort with the compilation of an online English-Natchez dictionary.[5] The language is considered dormant, now awakening, and has had no known native speakers since at least 1965. Fields has some knowledge of the language. The Natchez Nation also participates in the Breath of Life workshop held at the Smithsonian Institution as part of their efforts to recover as much of the language as possible.

6.2.3 Tunica

The Tunica community and linguists are collaborating to revitalize the Tunica language, one of five awakening isolates. The Tunica-Biloxi Tribe of Louisiana and Tulane University work together to develop the Tunica Language Project. Efforts began in 2010. Since then, the partnership has developed summer language camps since 2012, a practical orthography, children's books, and audio recordings in Tunica[6] (Maxwell 2014).

6.3 Documenting language isolates

There is sometimes assumed to be tension between whether to focus limited time, resources, and personnel on revitalizing or on documenting an language that is at risk. There is no single answer for all situations. It ultimately depends on the wishes of language speakers. It is clear, however, that revitalization needs language documentation materials to base its learning materials and exercises on. It is also clear that documentation and revitalization are not necessarily separate activities – often revitalization and documentation efforts take place simultaneously – as, for example, when younger community members are involved in creating a talking dictionary and to do so consult native speaking elders, thus learning aspects of the language as they create the dictionary and involve other community members in the documentation process.

In addition to being highly endangered, many of the world's language isolates have little to no documentation. In Hammarström's (2010) *The Status of the Least Documented Language Families in the World*, about 23 of the 27 least documented language families

TABLE 13.5 LEAST DOCUMENTED ISOLATES AND SPEAKER NUMBERS

	Language isolate	Amount of documentation (Hammarström 2010)	Endangerment status (ELCat 2016)	Number of speakers
1	Awaké	worldists, some phrases	dormant	0
2	Tekiráka (Tequiraca)	wordlists	critically endangered/dormant?	0 native speakers
3	Nihali	long wordlists, a little text, possibly more	threatened	1,000
4	Lepki	ca 200 words	endangered	328
5	Busa	short wordlist	endangered	238
6	Dem	wordlist and some sentences	threatened	1,000
7	Guriaso	short wordlist and short grammar notes	endangered	160
8	Kapauri	"ca 250 words and 15 sentences"	vulnerable	~200
9	Kimki	"ca 250 words and 15 sentences"	at risk/vulnerable?	500
10	Mawes	"ca 250 words and 15 sentences"	endangered	~850
11	Mor (?) (of Bomberai)	short wordlist, possibly sentences	severely endangered	60 (in 1977, fewer now)
12	Sause	ca 200 words	endangered	300

he cites are language isolates or possible language isolates.[7] Table 13.4 reports levels of documentation for the least documented isolates according to Hammarström (2010).

The reality is, if the language has not been recorded and becomes extinct, there is no extant scientific/linguistic method to retrieve that lost knowledge. If there has been linguistic documentation prior to the death of the last fluent speaker (video and audio recordings with transcriptions and morpheme-by-morpheme glosses, dictionaries, and grammars are best; scant wordlists and grammar sketches are better than nothing), then it may be possible to attempt to "wake" the language up.

Dem, Kapauri, Kimki, and Nihali are categorized as less at risk than some of the others. However, even though Kapauri (Kapori) is categorized as "vigorous" by *Ethnologue* (due to high intergenerational transmission), its total number of speakers is only about 200. (The *Catalogue of Endangered Languages* considers it "vulnerable.") As was seen in the case of Tambora, even a language that has several thousand speakers could disappear in an instant if catastrophe were to strike.

7 CONCLUSION

The vast majority of the world's living language isolates – 100 out of 104 (96%) – are in danger of disappearing. Approximately 35% of all known language isolates have already become extinct. Of the living language isolates, even within the handful of "safe" or "vigorous" languages (of which there are only four), Anêm, Duna, and Maybrat may be considered to have relatively small numbers of speakers.

Intergenerational transmission in the home is the primary way for a language to be perpetuated. While official policies can be helpful, even without such policies, individuals, families, and communities can collaborate to revitalize a language on their own. However, official policies – including guaranteeing language rights and formal education – when implemented, can provide external reinforcement of efforts from within the home and the community.

For linguists (including linguistic students) looking for a language to document, some of the languages that most urgently need to be documented are isolates that are both endangered and among the least documented language families of the world. The most urgent ones include: Busa, Guriaso, Kapauri, Kimki, Mawes, Mor of Bomberai, and Sause. Their situation is dire because: (1) there is little to no linguistic description of these languages; (2) they are on the verge of disappearing, which would eliminate any chance of ever learning about these languages; and (3) they are one-member language families. Once these isolates disappear, not only do we lose all chance at learning about them directly, but there are no other languages related to them to give us any idea of the genetic or typological uniqueness of the language or of the richness of information they might have contained and provided.

NOTES

1 Campbell defines "moribund" as having fewer than ten speakers (1997: 107). Generally, those few speakers are very elderly, and no children speak the language anymore (Crystal 2000: 21).
2 Data is from the August 2015 version of ELCat. There may have been minor changes to the catalogue since then.
3 www.unesco.org/most/vl4n2romaine.pdf.
4 http://linguistics.berkeley.edu/~karuk/; see also: http://linguistics.berkeley.edu/~karuk/links.php.
5 www.natcheznation.com/Language.html, accessed 11/1/16.
6 http://tunica.wp.tulane.edu/about/about-the-tunica-language-project/ (see also: http://tulane.edu/liberal-arts/newsletter/tunica-jan-2014.cfm).
7 Hammarström (2010) lists 5 of the 23 least documented language families as possibly isolates: (1) Shom Pen, (2) Asaba, (3) Baiyomo, (4) Mor, and (5) Tanahmerah. Lepki in Hammarström's (2010) list may be considered unclassified (cf. Campbell, this volume).

REFERENCES

Arka, Wayan. 2012. Projecting morphology and agreement in Marori, an isolate of southern New Guinea. Language Documentation & Conservation Special Publication No. 5 (December 2012) Melanesian Languages on the Edge of Asia: Challenges for the 21st Century, ed. by Nicholas Evans and Marian Klamer, 150–173. https://scholarspace.manoa.hawaii.edu/bitstream/10125/4563/1/arka.pdf
Austin, Peter, ed. 2008. 1000 languages: The worldwide history of living and lost tongues. London: Thames & Hudson.

Blench, Roger. 2005. *Baŋgi me, a language of unknown affiliation in Northern Mali.* Cambridge: Cambridge University Press.

Blench, Roger. 2011. *An Atlas of Nigerian Languages.* [Available at http://www. rogerblench.info/Language/Africa/Nigeria/Atlas%20of%20Nigerian%20 Languages-%20ed%20III.pdf] [accessed 12–26–2016.]

Blench, Roger. 2016. Language isolates in Africa. *Language Isolates*, ed. by Lyle Campbell, Alex Smith, and Thomas Doughtery. London: Routledge.

Baldwin, Daryl, Karen Baldwin, Jessie Baldwin, and Jarrid Baldwin. 2013. Starting from Zero. *Bringing Our Languages Home*, ed. by L. Hinton. California: Heyday.

Brenzinger, Matthias. 2011. The twelve modern Khoisan languages. *Khoisan Languages and Linguistics*, ed. by Alina Witzlack-Makarevich and Martina Ernszt. Proceedings of the 3rd International Symposium, July 6-10, 2008, Riezlern/Kleinwalsertal.

Campbell, Lyle. 1997. *American Indian Languages: The Historical Linguistics of Native America.* Oxford: Oxford University Press.

Campbell, Lyle. 2013. *Historical Linguistics* (3rd ed.). Cambridge: MIT Press.

Campbell, Lyle. In press. *Languages of South America.* Atlas of the World's Languages, ed. by Christopher J. Moseley and Ronald E. Asher. London: Routledge.

Capistrán, Alejandra. 2015. Multiple Object Constructions in P'orhépecha. Leiden & Boston: BRILL. http://csh.izt.uam.mx/sistemadivisional/SDIP/proyectos/archivos_rpi/ dea_25585_39_467_1_2_1.%20Galera%20_Capistran%20Garza_text_proof-02.pdf.

Cramblit, André. 2011. Karuk Language Restoration Committee. *Native News Network.* http://nativenewsnetwork.posthaven.com/karuk-language-restoration-committee (20 August 2015).

Crevels, Mily. 2012. Language Endangerment in South America: The Clock Is Ticking. *The Indigenous Languages of South America: A Comprehensive Guide*, ed. by Lyle Campbell and Verónica Grondona, 167–234. Berlin: Mouton de Gruyter.

Crystal, David. 2000. *Language Death.* Cambridge: Cambridge University Press.

Donohue, Mark. 2007. The Papuan Language of Tambora. *Oceanic Linguistics* 46, no. 2: 520–537.

Evans, Nicholas. 2001. The Last Speaker Is Dead-Long Live the Last Speaker! *Linguistic Fieldwork*, ed. by Paul Newman and Martha Ratliff, 250–281. Cambridge: Cambridge University Press.

Fishman, Joshua. 1991. *Reversing Language Shift.* Clevendon: Multilingual Matters.

Frawley, William J. 1997. *International Encyclopedia of Linguistics.* Oxford University Press.

Galla, Candace K. 2009. Indigenous language revitalization and technology from traditional to contemporary domains. *Indigenous Language Revitalization. Encouragement, Guidance & Lessons Learned*, ed. by Jon Reyhner and Louise Lockard. Flagstaff, AZ: Northern Arizona University.

Gautam, Bimal. 2012. *Nepal's mystery language on the verge of extinction.* British Broadcasting Corporation (BBC). 13 May 2012. http://www.bbc.com/news/world-asia-17537845.

Gobierno Vasco (Basque Government). 2012. V. Inkesta Soziolinguistikoa. Servicio Central de Publicaciones del Gobierno Vasco. http://www.euskara.euskadi.eus/contenidos/ noticia/inkesta_soziol_2012/es_berria/adjuntos/Euskal_Herria_Inkesta_Soziolinguistikoa11_es.pdf.

Golla, Victor. 2011. *California Indian Languages.* Berkeley: University of California Press.

Graham, Glenn H. 1981. A Sociolinguistic Survey of Busa and Nagatman. Sociolinguistic Surveys of Sepik Languages (Workpapers in Papua New Guinea Languages 29), ed. by Richard Loving, 177–192. Ukarumpa: Summer Institute of Linguistics.

Graziano, Savá. 2003. Ongota (Birale), a moribund language of Southwest Ethiopia. *Language Death and Language Maintenance: Theoretical, Practical and Descriptive Approaches*. eds Mark Janse and Sijmen Tol. Amsterdam: John Benjamins Publishing Company.

Guirardello-Damian, Raquel. 2014. Reduplication and Ideophones in Trumai. In Gale Goodwin Gómez and Hein Voort (eds.) *Reduplication and Ideophones in Trumai*. 217–246. Leiden: Brill.

Hammarström, Harald. 2010. The Status of the Least Documented Language Families in the World. *Language Documentation and Conservation* 4: 183–212.

Heaton, Raina. In press. *When Animals Become Human: Grammatical Gender in Tunica*.

Hinton, Leanne. 2013. *Bringing Our Languages Home*. California: Heyday.

Ignace, Marianne. 2006. Northern (Massett) Haida Toponymy and Geographic Knowledge. *HRELP Abstract*. London: SOAS.

Krauss, Michael. 1992. The World's Languages in Crisis. *Language* 68: 4–10.

Laycock, Donald C. 1973. Sepik languages: checklist and preliminary classification. *Pacific Linguistics* (series) Edited by Wurm, Stephen A. Canberra: The Australian National University.

Lee, Nala Huiying and John Van Way. 2016. Assessing Levels of Endangerment in the Catalogue of Endangered Languages (ELCat) Using the Language Endangerment Index (LEI). *Language in Society* 45: 271–292. [Available on CJO2016. doi:10.1017/S0047404515000962.]

Lewis, M. Paul and Gary F. Simons. 2010. Assessing Endangerment: Expanding Fishman's GIDS. *Revue Roumaine de Linguistique* 55: 103–120.

Lewis, M. Paul, Gary F. Simons, and Charles D. Fennig, eds. 2016. *Ethnologue: Languages of the World* (19th ed.). Dallas, TX: SIL International. [Online version: www.ethnologue.com (31 January 2016.]

Little, Christopher A. J. L. 2008. *Becoming an Asabano: The socialization of Asabano children, Duranmin, West Sepik Province, Papua New Guinea*. Canada: Trent University. Master's thesis.

Lucas, Paul F. Naoho. 2000. E ola mau kākou i ika ʻōlelo makuahine: Hawaiian Language Policy and the Courts. *Hawaiian Journal of History* 32: 1–28.

Maxwell, Judith. 2014. *Language Revitalization: The Case of Tunica, Louisiana's Sleeping Language*. http://tulane.edu/liberal-arts/newsletter/tunica-jan-2014.cfm (24 February 2016).

Meader, Robert E.1978. *Indios do nordeste: Levantamento sobre os remanescentes tribais do nordeste brasileiro*. Translated by Yonne Leite. Cuiabá: SIL Internacional.

Michael, Lev., Stephanie Farmer, Gregory Finley, Christine Beier, and Karina Sullón Acosta. 2013. A Sketch of Muniche Segmental and Prosodic Phonology. *International Journal of American Linguistics* 79: 307–347.

Mous, Maarten. 2003. *Loss of Linguistic Diversity in Africa*. Language Death and Language Maintenance: Theoretical, practical and descriptive approaches. Amsterdam: John Benjamins.

Munshi, Sadaf. 2014. *The Burushaski Language Documentation Project (website)*. University of North Texas. http://ltc.unt.edu/~sadafmunshi/Burushaski/language.html

Moseley, Christopher (ed.). 2010. *Atlas of the World's Languages in Danger*. Paris: The United Nations Educational, Scientific and Cultural Organization. [Online version: www.unesco.org/culture/languages-atlas/en/atlasmap.html. 28 April 2016.

Odé, Cecilia. 2002. A Sketch of Mpur. In Ger P. Reesink (ed.) Languages of the Eastern Bird's Head, 45–107. Canberra: Australian National University.

Olawsky, Knut. 2006. A Grammar of Urarina. (Mouton Grammar Library, 37.) Berlin, New York: Mouton de Gruyter.

Raffles, Stamford. 1817 [1830]. *History of Java*, Vol. 2, appendix F, 198–199. London: Black, Parbury and Allen (1817); London: J. Murray (1830).

Rogers, Christopher and Lyle Campbell. 2015. Endangered Languages. *Oxford Research Encyclopedia of Linguistics*, ed. by Mark Aronoff. http://linguistics.oxfordre.com/.

Romaine, Suzanne. 2002. The Impact of Language Policy on Endangered Languages. *International Journal on Multicultural Societies*. 4(2). www.unesco.org/most/vl4n 2romaine.pdf.

San Roque, Lila. 2008. *An introduction to Duna grammar*. Ph.D. Dissertation. Australian National University. [Available at www.academia.edu/10281818/An_introduction_to_ Duna_grammar [accessed 3–14–2016.]

Shaul, David L. 2014. *Linguistic Ideologies of Native American Language Revitalization: Doing the Lost Language Ghost Dance*. New York: Springer.

Silva, Léia de Jesus. 2010. *Diagnóstico sociolinguístico do povo rikbaktsa*. Levantamento realizado no quadro do Projeto de Documentação da Língua Rikbaktsa. Setembro/ outubro de 2010. Museu do Indio/UNESCO. http://prodoclin.museudoindio.gov.br/ images/conteudo/rikbaktsa/produtos_pesquisadores/Diagnóstico_sociolin gu%C3%ADstico-fim_recebido_lea.pdf

UNESCO (United Nations Educational, Scientific, and Cultural Organization). 1996. *Universal Declaration on Linguistic Rights*. Barcelona: United Nations. Available online: http://unesdoc.unesco.org/images/0010/001042/104267e.pdf [accessed 4-12-2016.]

van der Voort, Hein. 2005. Kwaza in a Comparative Perspective. *International Journal of American Linguistics*. October 2005, 71(4): 365–412.

van der Voort, Hein. 2013. Fossilised fictive quotation: Future tense in Aikan~a. Boletim do Museu Paraense Em'ilio Goeldi. Ciências Humanas. 8(2). May/Aug 2013. 359–377 http://www.scielo.br/scielo.php?script=sci_arttext&pid=S1981-81222013000200009.

van Driem, George. 2011. Tibeto-Burman subgroups and historical grammar. *Himalayan Linguistics*, 10 (1) [Special Issue in Memory of Michael Noonan and David Watters]: 31–39. http://www.himalayanlanguages.org/files/driem/pdfs/2011TBsubgroups.pdf.

Wegener, Claudia U. 2008. *A grammar of Savosavo: A Papuan language of the Solomon Islands*. Radboud Universiteit Nijmegen: Ph.D. thesis. http://pubman.mpdl.mpg.de/ pubman/item/escidoc:102834:4/component/escidoc:2300986/Wegener_2008_A%20 grammar%20of%20Savosavo.pdf.

Wurm, Stephen. 2007. Australasia and the Pacific. *Encyclopedia of the World's Endangered Languages*, ed. by Christopher Moseley, 425–577. London: Routledge.

INDEX